Elder Law Answer Book
Second Edition

by Robert B. Fleming

The world is aging, and the legal problems faced by elders grow more numerous and more complex every day. With practice issues ranging from age discrimination and nursing home rights, to Medicaid and other public benefits programs, to traditional estate planning and administration, to the rights of grandparents in visitation and custody disputes, the scope of many elder law practices is broad and diverse. *Elder Law Answer Book* includes detailed information about each of those disparate, but frequently related, aspects of elder law practice. Seasoned elder law practitioners looking for answers to questions outside their practice area, non-lawyers dealing with elder law issues, new elder law practitioners looking for a solid introduction to their new practice area, all will find *Elder Law Answer Book* to be an invaluable resource. The easily accessible question-and-answer format is supplemented by examples drawn from real world experiences intended to consolidate and focus the information in each chapter into one or more scenarios of the sort that practitioners of all experience levels have encountered, or will encounter, in actual practice.

Highlights of the 2009 Cumulative Supplement

Supplement prepared by Robert B. Fleming and Lisa Nachmias Davis

The 2009 Cumulative Supplement brings you up to date on the latest cases, statutes, and developments including:

- A revised Chapter 4, Non-Tax Aspects of Estate Planning: Wills, Trusts, and Other Transfers of Property Upon Death, with expanded discussions, including those on the following topics:
  - What are "special" and "general" powers of appointment? (Q 4:20)

Wolters Kluwer
Law & Business

— What is a "self-proving affidavit"? (Q. 4:26)

— Are there other ways to change a will besides a codicil? (Q 4:35)

— Is probate always required if a decedent owns assets? (Q 4:38)

— What are the drawbacks of probate? (Q: 4:40)

- An expanded Chapter 5, Estate Planning, with new and updated information on:

— Which states impose an estate tax? (Q 5:13)

— Which states now impose some kind of estate or inheritance tax and/or gift tax? (Q 5:14)

— Can states impose estate or inheritance taxes on nonresident decedents? (Q 5:15)

— Who typically prepares estate, inheritance, and gift tax returns? (Q 5:16)

— What is a 5 & 5 Power, and is anything included in the estate of a decedent who holds such a power? (Q 5:44)

— Which clients must be concerned about the tax aspects of estate planning? (Q 5:54)

— If there is a disparity between the assets of the respective spouses, how can the estates be equalized in order to utilize the marital deduction? (Q 5:64)

— What is qualified terminable interest property? (Q 5:71)

- An updated Chapter 8, Will and Trust Contests, including revised questions on:

— What is an "*in terrorem*" provision and is it an effective protection against will contests? (Q 8:19)

— What is the process for contesting the validity of wills? (Q 8:20)

— Who pays for a will contest? (Q 8:22)

- An updated Chapter 16, Other Benefit Programs, including additional information concerning:

— How does the Department of Veteran's Affairs determine eligibility for benefits? (Q 16:23)

— How is eligibility and the amount of the Improved Pension determined? (Q 16:31)

— Can attorneys charge for assisting with applications for veterans benefits? (Q 16:41.1)

The Index has been updated to reflect these changes.

11/08

For questions concerning this shipment, billing, or other customer service matters, call our Customer Service Department at 1-800-234-1660.

For toll-free ordering, please call 1-800-638-8437.

Elder Law
Answer Book

2009 Cumulative Supplement

This supplement supersedes all previous supplements.

ASPEN PUBLISHERS

Elder Law Answer Book

Second Edition

2009 Cumulative Supplement

Robert B. Fleming
Lisa Nachmias Davis

Wolters Kluwer
Law & Business

AUSTIN   BOSTON   CHICAGO   NEW YORK   THE NETHERLANDS

This publication is designed to provide accurate and authoritative information in regard to the subject matter covered. It is sold with the understanding that the publisher is not engaged in rendering legal, accounting, or other professional services. If legal advice or other professional assistance is required, the services of a competent professional should be sought.

—From a *Declaration of Principles* jointly adopted by
a Committee of the American Bar Association and
a Committee of Publishers and Associations

Printed in the United States of America

ISBN 978-0-7355-7464-9

1 2 3 4 5 6 7 8 9 0

About Wolters Kluwer Law & Business

Wolters Kluwer Law & Business is a leading provider of research information and workflow solutions in key specialty areas. The strengths of the individual brands of Aspen Publishers, CCH, Kluwer Law International and Loislaw are aligned within Wolters Kluwer Law & Business to provide comprehensive, in-depth solutions and expert-authored content for the legal, professional and education markets.

CCH was founded in 1913 and has served more than four generations of business professionals and their clients. The CCH products in the Wolters Kluwer Law & Business group are highly regarded electronic and print resources for legal, securities, antitrust and trade regulation, government contracting, banking, pension, payroll, employment and labor, and healthcare reimbursement and compliance professionals.

Aspen Publishers is a leading information provider for attorneys, business professionals and law students. Written by preeminent authorities, Aspen products offer analytical and practical information in a range of specialty practice areas from securities law and intellectual property to mergers and acquisitions and pension/benefits. Aspen's trusted legal education resources provide professors and students with high-quality, up-to-date and effective resources for successful instruction and study in all areas of the law.

Kluwer Law International supplies the global business community with comprehensive English-language international legal information. Legal practitioners, corporate counsel and business executives around the world rely on the Kluwer Law International journals, loose-leafs, books and electronic products for authoritative information in many areas of international legal practice.

Loislaw is a premier provider of digitized legal content to small law firm practitioners of various specializations. Loislaw provides attorneys with the ability to quickly and efficiently find the necessary legal information they need, when and where they need it, by facilitating access to primary law as well as state-specific law, records, forms and treatises.

Wolters Kluwer Law & Business, a unit of Wolters Kluwer, is headquartered in New York and Riverwoods, Illinois. Wolters Kluwer is a leading multinational publisher and information services company.

ASPEN PUBLISHERS SUBSCRIPTION NOTICE

This Aspen Publishers product is updated on a periodic basis with supplements to reflect important changes in the subject matter. If you purchased this product directly from Aspen Publishers, we have already recorded your subscription for the update service.

If, however, you purchased this product from a bookstore and wish to receive future updates and revised or related volumes billed separately with a 30-day examination review, please contact our Customer Service Department at 1-800-234-1660 or send your name, company name (if applicable), address, and the title of the product to:

ASPEN PUBLISHERS
7201 McKinney Circle
Frederick, MD 21704

Important Aspen Publishers Contact Information

- To order any Aspen Publishers title, go to *www .aspenpublishers.com* or call 1-800-638-8437.
- To reinstate your manual update service, call 1-800-638-8437.
- To contact Customer Care, e-mail *customer.care@ aspenpublishers.com,* call 1-800-234-1660, fax 1-800-901-9075, or mail correspondence to Order Department, Aspen Publishers, PO Box 990, Frederick, MD 21705.
- To review your account history or pay an invoice online, visit *www.aspenpublishers.com/payinvoices.*

Preface

The very nature of elder law makes production of *Elder Law Answer Book* a challenge and, ultimately, a rewarding experience. With practice areas ranging from age discrimination and nursing home rights to Medicaid and other public benefits programs and to traditional estate planning and administration, the scope of many elder law practices is very broad indeed. This single volume includes detailed information about each of those disparate, but frequently related, aspects of elder law practice. The question-and-answer format of this book makes it possible to cover the broad field of practice in an intelligible manner, providing precise guidance on the most common concerns of practitioners.

Reflecting the diversity of elder law, this book is divided into separate parts for each of the broad practice areas included in many practices. Each part is further divided into chapters covering individual practice topics. Topics covered include:

- *Medicaid and long-term care planning.* The federal/state Medicaid program is bewilderingly complex, and even seasoned practitioners are likely to get lost in its rules. Although ostensibly subject to federal guidelines, the program is administered quite differently in each state, and the state variability increases over time. This volume summarizes the rules, pointing out significant state variations in the context of the individual principles. The usefulness of long-term care insurance is also discussed, including specific suggestions both for review of insurance contracts and for consideration of the value of insurance for individual clients.

- *Estate planning.* Many elder law practitioners are uncomfortable with tax-driven estate planning concepts and approaches. The principal techniques are explained in plain language, together with the appropriate situation for implementation of each approach. Even as the significance of tax-driven estate planning diminishes with the increase in the size of estates avoiding any federal taxation, the complexity of planning for larger estates is compounded by the certainty of change. Nontax planning considerations are also explored, as are the usefulness, design, and administration of powers of attorney.

- *Guardianship and conservatorship.* Although state variations in this area of the law are profound, there are a number of common themes, and procedures are often similar. Residency requirements for surrogates, court processes, inventory and accounting requirements, and limitations on the powers of guardians and conservators are all described.

- *Probate and trust administration.* An explanation of the need for probate proceedings and demystification of the process itself will help in explanations to clients. Different administration requirements for trusts and probate proceedings are described, as well as methods of avoiding the probate process entirely.

- *"Special needs" trusts.* Though a growing portion of many elder law practices, special needs trust planning and administration remain unfamiliar territory for many elder law attorneys. Questions about the propriety of special needs trusts for particular clients, language necessary to effect special needs provisions, tax treatment of trusts, and other administrative concerns are covered in depth.

- *Medicare.* Although nearly all seniors rely on Medicare for most of their medical care, few practitioners are sufficiently familiar with the operation, limitations, and entitlements of that program. A thorough discussion of the program will help guide the practitioner through clients' problems and needs.

- *Patient autonomy and the right to die.* Constitutional and statutory provisions governing the right of a client to direct the withholding or withdrawal of medical care are described, and suggestions made for particular documents and approaches.

- *Ethical issues.* Elder law practitioners daily navigate an ethical minefield. Questions about conflicts of interest, multiple representation, duties to report client misconduct, and other ethical issues are analyzed and suggestions offered for resolution of the ethical problems that do arise.

- *Practice management.* Technology (including computers and software) has revolutionized the practice of law, especially in elder law and estate planning. Business development, once anathema to lawyers, is now a requirement for survival. Questions and answers about practice development and management, including uses of technology, are offered, with particular emphasis on the characteristics that make an elder law practice unique.

Age discrimination, veteran's and Railroad Retirement benefits, nursing home rights, and other topics encountered by elder law attorneys (albeit less frequently) are also explained. A growing area of practice for many elder law attorneys—the rights of grandparents and other family members to visitation with and/or custody of minor children—is also addressed and discussed.

Elder Law Answer Book is intended for several audiences. Lawyers looking for answers to frequent questions about elder law issues somewhat outside their usual area of practice should be able to find those answers here. Sometimes lawyers with another practice focus have no desire to practice elder law, but they find that elder law issues persist among their clients; this book should help those lawyers answer clients' questions (and direct those clients to appropriate resources) without requiring that they become elder law practitioners. Many non-lawyers deal with elder law issues, including accountants, brokers, financial planners, geriatric case managers, guardians and conservators, medical personnel, social workers, discharge planners, and others. They will find that this volume explains concepts clearly and concisely. Elder law constantly attracts new practitioners who come to the practice from such disciplines as estate planning, benefits law, and family law, and from public practices and legal aid organizations. For these attorneys, *Elder Law Answer Book* will serve as a solid introduction to their new practice area. Even seasoned elder law practitioners should find help with aspects of the practice they do not regularly encounter.

One principal goal throughout this book has been to make explanations comprehensible. In other words, every effort has been made to retain the use of the English language and to avoid legalese, circumlocution, and jargon. That approach, coupled with the question-and-answer format, should make the material understandable to the clients of elder law practitioners as well.

Another main purpose has been to give real-world relevance to the questions and answers. To that end each chapter concludes with a set of examples drawn from personal practice experience and discussions with practitioners. These are intended to consolidate and focus the information in each chapter into one or more scenarios of the sort that practitioners of all experience levels have encountered (or will encounter) in actual practice. While individual questions can often be answered in a few sentences, those reality-based scenarios should help place many answers in better context.

The question-and-answer format of *Elder Law Answer Book* is uniquely helpful to an understanding of elder law issues. Although other reference books are invaluable resources for analyzing the law, it is often difficult to understand the interrelationship of legal principles and to integrate concepts from a recitation, albeit orderly, of the relevant points. Our personal attraction to this format is entirely practical; from our own real-world experience with other volumes in the Answer Book series we can report that it is truly wonderful to find our precise question asked and answered in a few sentences. We hope to provide other readers with that same satisfaction.

Elder law is rapidly evolving, both in terms of styles of practice and in the substantive law. The Deficit Reduction Act of 2005 radically altered the approach many practitioners must take when helping clients who desire to protect their assets against the costs of long-term care. The Foster Care Independence Act of 1999 reinstated transfer penalties for Supplemental Security Income (SSI) and subtly altered the landscape of special needs trusts, but despite that change, the use of special needs trusts has grown tremendously in recent years, with an accompanying growth in interest among elder law practitioners. On the practical side, technology and other practice management issues have also seen dramatic changes in past years.

While the national legal community initiates a discussion of "multi-disciplinary practices," elder law attorneys across the country have pioneered the use of staff social workers and accountants and important and valuable linkages with medical, case management, insurance, and other professionals. Litigation-based ethical rules about governing representation of multiple clients are strained by both traditional estate planning and newer elder law client scenarios.

It has been a challenge to try to address the volume of material and pace of change inherent in a modern elder law practice. The future of elder law is uncertain, and the practice may appear very different in a few short years. In addition to the certainty of change, however, there is another certainty: the world is aging, and the legal problems faced by elders grow more numerous and more complex every day. Along with tremendous new demands on an already overburdened long-term care system, the future holds new medical technology that may extend life while challenging individual concepts of quality of that life. New family dynamics, already a hallmark of the past half-century, will further change the needs and care options of the next generation of seniors. Government benefit programs, which are strained financially and administratively, must be adapted in coming decades; increased emphasis on in-home care may reduce the strain on those programs or, paradoxically, may increase that strain. Abolition of the federal estate tax, often suggested as a popular measure, may lead to reintroduction of the concept of "carry-over basis" for capital gains tax purposes. In other words, the tools described in this volume, though the best available today, will have to be adapted for future elders.

Robert B. Fleming
Lisa Nachmias Davis
August 2006

About the Authors

Robert B. Fleming is a partner in the Tucson law firm of Fleming & Curti, P.L.C., with a practice limited to guardianship, conservatorship, estate planning, and probate. His interest in this area was developed while serving as the Pima County Public Fiduciary for five years prior to starting his current practice. Mr. Fleming has been selected as a fellow of both the American College of Trust and Estate Counsel and the National Academy of Elder Law Attorneys, and he regularly writes and lectures on elder law issues. He is a past Chair of the State Bar of Arizona's Mental Health and Elder Law Section and Probate and Trust Section; he has also served as a Member of the Board of Directors of the National Academy of Elder Law Attorneys. At different times he served as President of both the Pima County Bar Association (he is now a member of the Board of Directors of that association) and the Young Lawyers Section of the State Bar of Arizona (he no longer qualifies to be a member). He was named as a delegate to the 1995 White House Conference on Aging and was a member of the Arizona State Legislature Committee on Health Care Powers of Attorney, Living Wills and Advance Directives in 1991. Mr. Fleming is the webmaster for his firm's extensive website at *www.elder-law.com* and writes a weekly newsletter distributed by e-mail from that website. He is a member of the Pima County Bar Association, the State Bar of Arizona, and the State Bar of Montana. Mr. Fleming received his J.D. at University of Arizona College of Law and his B.S. at Utah State University. He is a co-author of *Alive and Kicking: Legal Advice for Boomers*, Carolina Academic Press (2007).

Lisa Nachmias Davis established a solo practice in New Haven, Connecticut in 2006 after years working in larger firms, most recently as a partner in the firm of Tyler Cooper & Alcorn. She is certified as an Elder Law Attorney (CELA) by the National Elder Law Foundation. She practices primarily in the areas of elder law and special needs, estate planning, estate administration, and the law of nonprofit organizations. She is a frequent speaker on topics in these areas. She maintains a website, *www.sharinglaw.net*, that has become a widely used resource for elder law attorneys in Connecticut and elsewhere. With Edward Dale (now of AARP) she developed the website *http://www.CTElderLaw.org* that is now maintained by Connecticut Legal Services, and the site includes her contributions on the topics of Living Wills, Powers of Attorney, and Funeral Planning. She has also created the website for the Agency on Aging of South Central Connecticut, where she serves as a member of the Board of Directors and on its Executive Committee, and she operates a private e-mail discussion group for Connecticut elder law attorneys. She serves on the Executive Committee of the Connecticut Bar Association Elder Law Section and is a member of the American Bar Association Real Property Probate and Trust Law Section, the New Haven County Bar Association, and the National Academy of Elder Law Attorneys, as well as its Connecticut chapter. She is a member of the Special Needs Alliance and is a professional member of the National Alliance for the Mentally Ill and PLAN (Planned Lifetime Assistance Network) of Connecticut. Since 1998, Ms. Davis has also been a co-director of the Yale Law School Nonprofit Organization Law Clinic, teaching students how to represent nonprofit organizations. Ms. Davis received her B.A. in history, magna cum laude, from Yale College in 1982 and her J.D. from The Yale Law School in 1990, after which she served as law clerk to the late Justice David M. Shea of the Connecticut Supreme Court.

How to Use This Book

Elder Law Answer Book integrates the most current information regarding the various areas of elder law including estate planning, retirement planning, medical and long-term care planning, and fiduciary administration into a single-volume reference. It is designed for attorneys and other professionals who need quick and authoritative answers to help them work within the complex programs and to comply with the multitude of legal, tax, and regulatory provisions.

The authors write in straightforward language, avoiding technical jargon as much as possible. Citations of authority are provided throughout the volume and will serve as research aids for those who wish to pursue particular items in greater detail.

The question-and-answer format helps clarify for the reader the important issues in this complex area and offers a clear and useful guide to understanding the many areas of law that comprise elder law. This format enables the reader to focus rapidly on particular problems.

Numbering System: This cumulative supplement uses a point system of numbering items that augment material from the Second Edition. For example, Q 1:1 would be followed by Qs 1:1.1 and 1:1.2. Whenever a question from the Second Edition is updated, it is repeated in its entirety.

List of Questions: The detailed List of Questions that follows the Table of Contents in the front of this book helps the reader locate areas of immediate interest. This list serves as a detailed table of contents that provides both the question number and the page on which it appears.

Index: The index is a further aid to locating specific information. All references in the index are to cumulative supplement question numbers rather than page numbers.

Contents

Part II Estate and Retirement Planning

CHAPTER **3**

Retirement Planning

Contents

CHAPTER **6**

Post-Mortem Estate Planning

Part III Fiduciary Administration

CHAPTER 10
Powers of Attorney

Part IV Paying for Medical and Long-Term Care

CHAPTER 11
Long-Term Care Options

Contents

CHAPTER 12

Paying Privately for Long-Term Care:
Long-Term Care Insurance

CHAPTER 13

Medicare Benefits

CHAPTER **14**

Medicaid Benefits

Contents

Part V Health Care Decision-Making and Protection of the Elderly

Contents

List of Questions

Chapter 2 Ethical Issues in Client Representation

Overview

Representing Married Couples and Families

Dealing with the Incompetent Client

Part II Estate and Retirement Planning

Chapter 3 Retirement Planning

Information Gathering

ERISA

Participation and Nondiscrimination Requirements

Types of Qualified Retirement Plans

Simplified Employee Pension Plan (SEP)

Savings Incentive Match Plan for Employees (SIMPLE Plan)

Individual Retirement Accounts

Spousal Rights

Chapter 4 Non-Tax Aspects of Estate Planning: Wills, Trusts, and Other Transfers of Property Upon Death

Requirements for a Valid Trust

Using Trusts to Protect Assets

Trustees

Chapter 5 Estate Planning

Overview

Estate and Gift Tax Basics

Education IRAs or "Coverdell Accounts"

529 Plans

Estate Tax

Overview of Estate Planning Techniques

Marital Deduction Planning

Chapter 6 Post-Mortem Estate Planning

Part III Fiduciary Administration

Chapter 7 Probate and Trust Administration

Chapter 8 Will and Trust Contests

Chapter 9 Guardianship and Protective Proceedings

The Appointment Process

Powers and Duties

Health Care Decisions

Practice-Related Issues

Chapter 10 Powers of Attorney

Overview

Durable Power of Attorney

Health Care Power of Attorney

Continuing Care Retirement Communities

Assisted Living

Skilled Nursing Facilities and Nursing Homes

Chapter 12 Paying Privately for Long-Term Care: Long-Term Care Insurance

Overview

Purchase of Long-Term Care Insurance

Long-Term Insurance Policy Provisions

Tax Issues

Practice-Related Issues

Chapter 13 Medicare Benefits

Overview

Medicare Advantage Program

Medigap Insurance

Medicare Appeals Process

Health Insurance Other than Medicare

Chapter 14 Medicaid Benefits

Dependent's Benefits

Application for Benefits

Chapter 16 Other Benefit Programs

Supplemental Security Income

Part V Health Care Decision-Making and Protection of the Elderly

Chapter 17 Special Needs Trusts

Chapter 19 Elder Abuse, Neglect, and Exploitation

Chapter 20 Age Discrimination

Chapter 21 Grandparents' Rights

Grandparent Caretakers

Grandparents Raising Grandchildren

Part I

Establishing and Managing an Elder Law Practice

Chapter 1

Practice Considerations

Elder law is a growing practice area—some might say specialty—nationally. The growth of elder law has primarily been fueled by a rapid growth in the older segment of our population, coupled with the increasingly complex tax, medical, and social issues they face. Elder law attorneys tend to be solo practitioners, members of smaller or boutique specialty practice members. The type of practice, and the lawyers drawn to it, lends itself to a more casual and friendly (and less adversarial) office structure. Both new lawyers assaying their practice choices and existing lawyers who are unhappy with their current practices are considering changing to the elder law field, and many are taking the steps to make the transition. This chapter discusses what an elder law practice is, and distinguishes it from other practice areas; how to develop an elder law practice; and law practice issues including office design, attorney fees and billing, law practice management, and computer software and technology for the elder law office. It is intended to provide insight into these issues, and suggestions for both new and existing elder law practitioners as they develop their practices.

Characteristics of the Elder Law Practice

Q 1:1 What is elder law?

Elder law began to develop as a practice focus in the early 1980s. Recognizing that their practices focused on similar topics, most of which did not fit well into existing specialty areas, a number of individuals from different states began to meet regularly to discuss the emerging practice area.

A common observation among these practitioners was that their clients were predominantly older, or were the children of older parents seeking assistance with the elders' legal problems. From this observation grew the use of the term "elder law," even though innovators realized that the term was imprecise. Many of the common legal problems of the elderly are shared by younger clients who may be disabled, or poor enough to qualify for government assistance, or terminally ill, or wealthy enough to require tax planning assistance despite their age. Still, most elder law clients tend to be older, and many elders tend to share similar legal problems.

Today, elder law is a much better recognized area of practice. Usually, elder law attorneys focus their practices in a handful of areas. Those focus areas typically include long-term care planning, guardianship and conservatorship, advance medical directives, and the more traditional trust and estate planning. Other elder law attorneys spend considerable time dealing with Medicare and other government benefits, abuse, neglect, and exploitation issues, age discrimination, charitable giving, probate administration, and a host of other practice areas.

Although not necessarily an "elder" issue, one other topic has become important in many elder law practices in recent years. Planning for children or others with disabilities has opened up a related practice area in special needs planning. Even as special needs trusts established by parents, grandparents or spouses have become more important to many elder law practitioners, similar planning by and for the person with disabilities himself or herself has also become more commonplace. The entire area of special needs trust planning has developed into a significant focus of many elder law practitioners.

Of course, elderly individuals can have any sort of legal problem, and a practice devoted to serving the elderly is likely to be quite diverse; however, most elder law attorneys will find that they concentrate their practices in a few substantive areas, or even in one area alone.

Q 1:4 What sorts of legal issues regularly arise in an elder law practice?

Legal problems faced by the elderly and by persons with disabilities are wide-ranging; however, most practitioners who consider themselves elder law attorneys focus much of their professional energy in a handful of areas. A few practice in most or all of those areas, while others may limit themselves to only one, or even to a subset of one. The most common practice areas for elder law attorneys include, in no particular order:

1. Long-term care planning, including advice regarding long-term care insurance and the availability of Medicaid;

2. Guardianship of the person and conservatorship of the estate;

3. Estate planning, including more advanced tax planning issues;

4. Probate (or other procedures required on a person's death), including will contests, and questions relating to the administration of trusts;

5. Planning and implementation of "living wills" and other advance directives and health care rights;

6. Caring (and providing) for children—or clients—with disabilities, including planning, drafting and administering special needs trusts;

7. Access to Social Security, Medicare, and health benefits or insurance; and

8. Nursing home rights and procedures, including discharges from nursing home care, quality of care, patient's rights to privacy and association, and similar problems.

Less frequently, but often enough to require familiarity with the legal issues, an elder law attorney might be asked for advice regarding:

1. Access to veteran's benefits, railroad retirement benefits, public housing benefits, and other benefit programs less widely available than Social Security and Medicare;

2. Age discrimination;

3. Dissolution of marriage (or separation) where one spouse is physically or mentally disabled;

4. Guardianship of grandchildren or even great-grandchildren, and visitation rights of grandparents, as family life tends to become more fragmented and nontraditional domestic arrangements proliferate;

5. Elder abuse, not infrequently at the hands of spouses or caretaker children; and

6. Exploitation of elderly clients and efforts to recover lost assets.

Even as the practice of law becomes more specialized, the issues commonly seen in an elder law practice seem to multiply over time. As a result many elder law practitioners choose to "specialize" in only one or two of the individual areas described here.

Q 1:5 Is it possible to specialize in elder law, and does it make sense to do so?

Although the legal profession is primarily regulated by state bar associations, state supreme courts and other state-level organizations, the national tendency has been to recognize elder law as a distinct specialty practice. In fact, the National Elder Law Foundation (6336 N. Oracle Rd., Suite 326, Box #136, Tucson, AZ 85704, (520)-881-1076, *www.nelf.org*) conducts a certification process and conveys the designation of Certified Elder Law Attorney (CELA). The program has been accredited by the American Bar Association, and permits identification of the CELA designation in a majority of the states. CELA certification requires a minimum of five years of practice and 16 hours per week devoted to elder law practice handling at least 60 elder law matters during the three years preceding the application, and successful completion of a certification examination. In addition, a CELA must pass a peer review process and have completed 45 hours of continuing legal education in elder law in the three years before certification.

Q 1:5.1 Which states permit lawyers to publicly hold themselves out as holding the CELA designation?

State regulatory organizations (mostly state bar associations) take different approaches to the certification process. Some states prohibit any mention of certification or specialization altogether. Other states have no restriction against identifying certification, as long as the communication listing the CELA designation is true and not misleading. In most of the remaining states, communications with clients and the public may include the CELA designation, either because the American Bar Association has accredited the National Elder Law Foundation's program or because the individual state has separately approved the CELA designation. The status of certification in each state is available online at the ABA website: *http://www.abanet.org/legalservices/specialization/directory/*

The states permitting identification of the CELA designation include Alabama, Alaska, Arizona, Arkansas, California, Delaware, Florida, Hawaii (requires a petition by the CELA to secure individual approval by the state Supreme Court), Idaho, Indiana, Maine, Minnesota, Mississippi, Montana, Nebraska, Nevada, New Hampshire, New Jersey, North Carolina, South Dakota, Tennessee, Texas, Utah, Vermont, and Wisconsin. Some of these states may require any communication to identify the NELF as the certifying agency.

States permitting identification of the CELA designation but requiring a disclaimer with any communication include Colorado, Illinois, Massachusetts, Missouri, New Mexico, New York, Ohio, Oklahoma, Rhode Island, Virginia, Washington, and Wyoming.

States currently prohibiting any communication of certification include Connecticut (beginning 1/2009), Iowa, Louisiana, Maryland, and West Virginia.

States imposing no restrictions on communication of certification (other than accuracy) include Georgia, Kansas, Kentucky (requires identification of the certifying agency), Michigan, North Dakota, Oregon, and Washington, DC.

States which have not yet dealt with CELA designation, but for which the mechanism exists for future approval, include Connecticut, Iowa, and Louisiana.

Five states, Florida, Pennsylvania, South Carolina, Tennessee, and Vermont, have created their own elder law certification program. Florida, Tennessee, and Vermont also recognize the CELA designation, while South Carolina only recognizes out-of-state certification programs if it does not have one of its own.

Q 1:13 Where is specialized training in elder law provided?

At the law school level, the University of Kansas School of Law offers an L.L.M. in Elder Law (*www.law.ku.edu/elder_law/*). Western New England College of Law offers an L.L.M. in "Estate Planning and Elder Law" (*www.law.wnec.edu/llm*), and Stetson University College of Law has announced a new L.L.M. program to be offered through "distance learning" beginning in 2007 (*www.law.stetson.edu/excellence/elderlaw*). Stetson University College of Law already offers a "certificate of concentration" program in elder law. Most other law schools offer at least one elder law course (for a summary of available classes at many law schools, see the details maintained by the Stetson University College of Law Center for Excellence in Elder Law (*www.law.stetson.edu/excellence/elderlaw/surveyview.asp*). The University of Illinois College of Law publishes the Elder Law Journal twice a year, reflecting at least some academic focus on elder law issues.

For practitioners, the National Academy of Elder Law Attorneys (NAELA) (*www.naela.com*) offers what is probably the most reliably comprehensive and useful elder law programming for a national audience. Each year NAELA produces a Symposium (in Spring) and an Institute (in Fall), typically with three or four days of seminars and workshops dealing with elder law subjects. In addition, NAELA typically offers an introductory course on the day before one or both programs.

The National Elder Law Foundation (*www.nelf.org*) offers a review program for candidates for the Certified Elder Law Attorney designation in conjunction with the Institute each year. This program is more advanced, since it is intended as preparation for the certification exam, but an examination application is not required for attendance at the program. The NELF program includes a home-study component.

One annual program deserves special mention. For the past several years, NAELA has conducted an unusual program in Dallas, Called "The Unprogram." This three-day session brings practitioners of different levels of sophistication together in a relatively unstructured format. Rather than lectures by recognized experts, the Unprogram relies on the experiences and expertise of the participants themselves. Sessions are conducted in small groups of six to fifteen, with topics selected by participants at the time of the program. Vigorous (and enlightening) discussions might focus on computer software, cutting-edge techniques for obtaining Medicaid eligibility, real-world problems with administering guardianships and conservatorships, or whatever topic is of interest or concern to a particular attendee. Such seminars often provide an extraordinary opportunity to resolve actual practice dilemmas and share trade secrets with other participants. The Unprogram is currently open only to NAELA members and, in most states, will not qualify for mandatory continuing legal education credits (since it does not have traditional presenters or written materials).

Finally, NAELA offers a separate program for advanced elder law practitioners. The dates, structure, and qualifications may change from year to year, but qualified practitioners may find this programming more intense and productive than other national elder law programming.

Q 1:13.1 Is elder law programming available on a state level?

Many state bar associations offer annual elder law programs, some one-day and others multi-day seminars. Notable among the state bar offerings are those of North Carolina (*www.ncbar.org*), New Jersey (*www.njsba.com*) and Minnesota (*www.mnbar.org*), all of which have been offered annually for several years.

Commercial CLE providers like PESI (*www.pesi.com*) and the National Business Institute (*www.nbi-sems.com*) regularly offer state-specific elder law programming. As the practice of elder law has become more widespread it is increasingly common to see specific elder law CLE programming offered by most providers.

Q 1:15 What is the National Academy of Elder Law Attorneys, and how is it important to the elder law practitioner?

NAELA was formed in 1986 with a core of about three dozen members from around the country. The organization was first envisioned as a result of several meetings of the principals at American Bar Association meetings over a few years, and the surprise most of them felt at finding lawyers with similar practices from other states. Since that time, the organization has grown to about 5,000 lawyers, with representatives in every state.

Membership in NAELA confers a number of important benefits:

1. Information about (and reduced rates to attend) three national seminars each year, which are consistently among the best continuing legal education programs available to elder law attorneys.

2. Subscription to a weekly e-mail update with case law reports, news, and developments relevant to elders and elder law attorneys, periodic essays analyzing a topical area in more detail, and news reports about other NAELA members.

3. Newsletters and "special interest group" (SIG) participation which help keep the lawyer current in the area, and within sub-specialties of elder law. Current SIGs in NAELA include Guardianship/Capacity, Health Care, Practice Development/ Management, Tax, Trusts, and Advocacy/Litigation.

4. Participation in an extraordinary e-mail list, where hundreds of lawyer-participants share information, practical experiences, and tips, and answer questions for one another with an exceptional openness and spirit of cooperation. If this list were the only benefit of NAELA membership, it would be worth the membership dues.

5. Access to other members, both as resources and as referral sources.

Q 1:16.1 What other resources are available online for elder law practitioners?

With a minimum of computer literacy, the interested elder law practitioner can locate a wealth of information online. Websites with a focus on elder law include those of the authors of this volume—Robert Fleming's *www.elder-law.com* and Lisa Davis' *www.sharinglaw.net*—as well as those of other practitioners. A list of the more useful and interesting sites include:

1. *www.elder-law.com*. The website of Tucson, Arizona based Fleming & Curti, PLC includes access to the archives of the firm's weekly e-mail newsletter and details on how to subscribe, plus answers to frequently asked questions about elder law issues.

2. *www.sharinglaw.net*. Lisa Davis' private labor of love includes articles on issues of concern to elders and elder law practitioners, plus links to a wealth of additional resources on elder law.

3. *www.tn-elderlaw.com*. Tennessee elder law attorney Tim Takacs maintains this site with his weekly newsletter and a collection of articles and information of interest to elder law practitioners.

4. *www.elderlawanswers.com*. This commercial website, which has no affiliation with this Elder Law Answer Book, is constructed to provide referrals to member attorneys from browsers who reach the site, but it contains a useful collection of information for the practitioner (and an opportunity to join the member attorneys if it seems like it might be a useful source of referrals).

5. *www.seniorlaw.com*. The website of New York lawyers Goldfarb Abrandt Salzman & Kutzin LLP contains a collection of articles, links, and resources useful to practitioners and seniors alike.

Developing a Practice

Q 1:23 What referral sources are particularly likely to be useful to an elder law attorney?

Although referral sources will vary tremendously from attorney to attorney, some generalizations can be made about the possible sources of new elder law clients. Referral sources include:

1. *Other attorneys.* Many attorneys are loath to get involved in elder law issues. As a consequence, other lawyers often make the best referral sources for the elder law practitioner. This is particularly true of attorneys who practice in fields that do not deal with issues of aging, such as personal injury, domestic relations, bankruptcy, and real estate law. Even many estate planning attorneys choose not to get involved in long-term care issues, and can be an excellent referral source for an elder law attorney eager to work on long-term care planning but unlikely to take estate planning work from the referrer.

2. *Social workers, hospital discharge planners, nursing home administrators, assisted living facility directors, geriatric care managers, and other social service/medical workers.* Elder law issues frequently arise in the context of family medical and social emergencies. Hospital staff, doctor's offices, and nursing home administrators can be among the most regular referral sources.

3. *Organizations.* Local support groups, organizations focusing on specific diseases, government agencies, and quasi-government groups all maintain contact with attorneys familiar with elder law issues. Most such organizations prefer to give clients a choice of three or more names, so even a new elder law attorney should be able to get some referrals from organizations. Of course, it helps if the local branch of the Alzheimer's Association, the state adult protective services (or similar agency), the local area agency on aging, and other groups are familiar with the lawyer's philosophy and practice; an appropriate comfort level is most easily achieved if the lawyer volunteers time and energy working with the organizations, speaking to member and support groups, and cheerfully answering the occasional legal question from staff members.

4. *Individuals.* Not only clients and former clients, but neighborhood activists, senior volunteers, and other individuals can be valuable sources of referrals in the senior community, and often turn into clients in their individual capacities.

Although elder law has been a widely recognized practice area for over a decade, there is still plenty of room for growth in this area of the law. Many options are open for someone just beginning an elder law practice or trying to build on an existing practice. Before developing a marketing strategy, or setting up an outreach program, the elder law attorney might be well-advised to consider which of the many prospective referral sources is being targeted, whether other attorneys, social service and medical providers, individuals, or other professional groups.

Q 1:24 What are some good ways to generate referrals from other attorneys?

To reach other attorneys who might make referrals, offer to present continuing legal education programs for related legal professionals. A presentation to personal injury lawyers on Medicaid eligibility and how personal injury settlements can affect future eligibility, or on the use of special needs trusts in settling personal injury actions, can simultaneously improve the level of practice among the personal injury bar and spread the presenter's name as one familiar with this area of law. Some suggested CLE topics are:

1. Concerns about how parents or other family members manage and use personal injury settlement proceeds won for minors or incapacitated adults. Too often, personal injury lawyers believe that their responsibility (and liability) ends with the settlement, and that they have no continuing liability for the possible misdeeds of the parent/conservator.

2. Dealing with the aging spouse, possibly with diminished capacity, in divorce proceedings. Determining what effect the division of marital property may have in future long-term care financing considerations is not familiar territory for most domestic relations lawyers.

3. Hospital and medical staff liability for failure to comply with advance directives. Most hospital lawyers are familiar with the issues and concerns, but may not have considered the value or importance of outreach efforts, ethics committees, careful documentation, and family mediation.

4. The interface of probate and bankruptcy courts. Bankruptcy practitioners may not be familiar with the creditor's claims procedures in probate, or the effect of one spouse's death on the debts of the

other spouse. The ability to discharge liability for breaches of fiduciary duty is of obvious importance to both kinds of lawyers.

5. A general overview of government benefit programs, and particularly long-term care. The confusing nature of government programs discourages not only clients and prospective applicants, but also fellow lawyers who might start with the notion that a poverty-based program should not be too difficult to understand.

Q 1:26 What are some good ways to generate individual prospects?

Individual prospective clients can be the most difficult to reach. Experienced elder law practitioners disagree widely on the effectiveness of outreach efforts, but tend to agree that clients and prospective clients appreciate candid, useful advice and answers to at least occasional real-world questions. Some ways to reach individual clients include:

1. *Traditional advertising programs, ranging from telephone listings to newspaper and radio advertising.* Some practitioners insist that telephone listings are too easily lost in the crowd of advertisements, while others maintain that the telephone book remains the most steady and reliable source of new clients. Some elder law practitioners have experimented with regular weekly radio shows devoted to elder law issues, while others have reported success with shared radio shows (perhaps rotating through six or seven legal specialty areas on a set schedule).

2. *Newsletters.* Like health professionals, individuals tend to be starved for reliable legal information. The glut of information currently available in some ways only tends to exacerbate the problem—whereas it was once difficult to get any information, it is now difficult to assess the quality of the information pouring into the client's mailbox, computer, and through other sources. It may take time to develop a reputation for accurate and reliable newsletters, but the reputation will be increasingly valuable over that time.

3. *Websites.* Recent years have seen steady growth in the use of computers among the elderly. Perhaps more importantly, the children of the elderly are often the motivating factor in seeking legal advice, and they tend to be quite computer-savvy. While opinions differ on the profitability of internet websites, the fact remains that it is a relatively inexpensive way for the new elder law practitioner

to establish a niche and simultaneously build some public credibility—and failure to maintain at least some internet presence may be a deterrent for potential clients.

4. *Public seminars.* Entire national organizations have been built on the simple premise that the public is starved for reliable information. Offer a public seminar on estate planning, long-term care planning, or medical decision-making, and expect a substantial crowd to attend. Often, these work best if they are co-sponsored by a charitable community organization or an institution; do not be shy about contacting various organizations to see if they are interested in promoting such a presentation. Be prepared to provide useful information and hand out explanations. Many of the attendees will have gone to several competing presentations, and will be looking for the one presenter who seems to speak to them most directly. Do not be surprised if a client shows up months or even years after such a presentation; it is an easy way for the timid prospective client to seek general legal information without having to make an early commitment to one professional. Most seminar presenters indicate that the current "hot" topic is living trusts, with nursing home expenses closing in rapidly. If this is true in your area, you may wish to advertise the presentation with references to either or both of these topics, and then be sure to provide accurate, timely, and informative advice on the advertised topics. To reach an elderly audience, schedule the presentation for late morning or late afternoon, offer refreshments, and hold the seminar in an attractive (but easily accessible) location. To reach an audience of professionals or the working children of the elderly, schedule the presentation for an evening or weekend, unless the presentation is being held at a place of business.

Q 1:51 What computer hardware should an elder law attorney expect to purchase?

Every lawyer, and particularly every elder law attorney, should expect to use and be proficient with computers. This means that a computer should sit on every desktop in the office, and staff should be expected to prepare documents, maintain calendars, update and manage cases, take and receive telephone messages, and complete all sorts of other tasks on those computers.

In order for computerization to be maximally effective, an office network is essential. Any office with two computers should expect to have them hooked together and communicating. This will require not only a machine on each desk, but also the equipment (e.g., computer cards and cables or wireless router) necessary to create a network with shared resources and information.

Recent rapid increases in the pace of hardware development have resulted in a dramatic reduction in the cost of hardware and the failure of most software packages to take full advantage of hardware capabilities. This, in turn, simplifies the process of purchasing new office computers; there is little gain in productivity by purchasing the fastest, most powerful system currently on the market, and substantial savings to be realized by purchasing the second (or third) most powerful offering.

Even as the lawyer chooses to save costs by purchasing less-powerful computers, there are several areas in which the rules are reversed. In general, more money should be spent on these items:

1. *Monitors*. Larger monitors are easier to work with, and make staff and lawyers happier with their worklife. CRTs (Cathode Ray Tubes—the old-fashioned monitors that resemble televisions) have been all but replaced by LCD (Liquid Crystal Display) panels in recent years. An LCD panel typically will have a usable area about the same size as a CRT (cathode ray tube) described as two inches larger (i.e., a 17 LCD panel is roughly comparable to a 19 CRT monitor). In addition to space savings, LCD panels generate less heat and, for most people, less eyestrain. For most new computer purchases, include the largest affordable LCD monitor. Experiment with multiple monitors so that, for instance, you can maintain a website open on one screen while composing a letter or memorandum on the other, or keep your case management program available for addresses, dates, and case information while working in a document without having to switch between programs on the same screen.

2. *Storage devices*. Not too long ago, hard disks with 20 megabytes (MB) of storage and floppy disks with 360 kilobytes maximum were industry standards. Few people could imagine a world in which those numbers were inadequate. Today, even a simple word processing program might require 50 MB of space on the hard drive, and individual files can easily exceed the capacity of even high-density floppy drives. Eighty and one hundred gigabyte hard disks are standard. Rewritable CD and DVD drives allow the user to "burn" up to 700 MB or nearly 5 GB (respectively) of data to a single disk. CD and DVD burners are available in built-in or

portable configurations, and the plug-in capability of the latter make them particularly attractive as a data backup instrument. "Flash" drives—tiny USB connections with built-in storage capability—may hold a gigabyte of data or more. All of these options have nearly spelled the end of floppy disk drives—today there is little point in even including a floppy drive in most new computer purchases.

3. *Memory.* Random access memory (RAM) prices have been low for an extended period. Just as memory storage requirements have grown, so too have RAM requirements; any new machine should have a minimum of a gigabyte of RAM, and more RAM should be considered in most cases.

4. *Connectivity.* Handheld organizers (like the Palm™ or Windows Mobile™ machines), network printers, and multi-purpose machines (fax, photocopier, scanner, and printer all in one) are extremely useful. Bluetooth and wireless technology make it easier than ever for the peripherals to communicate with the computer network, and with cell phones, headsets, and the like. Make current purchases with this technology in mind; one or all of the mentioned peripherals are likely to be added shortly after the initial hardware investment.

Q 1:52   How should a lawyer work with computers?

Any modern law practice requires the active use of computers by lawyers as well as support staff. The complexities of practice, competition from other lawyers and nonlawyers, the increasing sophistication of clients, and the ubiquitous nature of the internet compel not only the active use of computers, but also a broad understanding of the possibilities and capabilities of technology generally and computers in particular. Because of the usual case loads involved in an elder law practice and the arcane nature of statutory and regulatory provisions, that basic principle is even more apparent in the elder law practice than in many other legal fields.

The lawyer who proudly proclaims unfamiliarity with technology is doomed to professional extinction. Every lawyer should have a computer on his or her own desktop, and should be proficient at word processing and legal research. Office calendars and to-do lists should be maintained on the computer, even if old habits require that the calendar be printed out periodically. The lawyer should be capable of checking the calendar and updating appointments and projects. Time and billing should be completed on the computer, rather than on paper sheets or slips to be entered later by a clerical staff member.

In the mid-1980s, the fax machine became an office essential. E-mail has established itself as the fax machine of the current decade. Clients, family members, and colleagues will increasingly expect lawyers to have ready access to e-mail, and to communicate quickly and effectively through this new medium. In fact, commercial providers now offer a fax number that will automatically forward received documents to an e-mail address, making it possible to merge fax and e-mail into a single technology without the necessity of maintaining a separate fax machine.

During the past decade, legal research has moved out of books and onto CD-ROM disks. Indeed, many legal research sources have taken the next step and are now more easily available on the internet. Both CD-ROM and internet research ultimately require the lawyer to be personally familiar with computers and able to work through their particular logic. Lawyers who were trained on proprietary paper "digests" (such as the Decennial Digest used by an earlier generation of lawyers) learned not only how to use the available research systems but also their limitations. Similarly, a modern lawyer must not only be proficient at computerized research, but also recognize the limitations of the medium. All of these proficiencies require regular hands-on use by the lawyer, working at the lawyer's own desktop.

Q 1:54 What types of software are important for an elder law practice?

Any elder law attorney should have, install, and use the following kinds of software:

1. *Word processing.* Once a software field filled with programs and innovators, the word processing market has been reduced to Corel's WordPerfect and Microsoft Word. Word's market share is steadily gaining, but WordPerfect's last market niche is the legal business. Ideally, be familiar with both—WordPerfect because it is a better program, Word because clients will have Word and will only be able to view Word attachments. More recent versions of WordPerfect have improved—but not perfected—the ability to open Word documents and save in a Word format. Word, on the other hand, has made no effort to provide compatibility with WordPerfect files.

2. *Presentation software.* Obliquely related to word processing is presentation software such as Microsoft PowerPoint. This program allows you to develop slides for viewing onscreen or to be projected using a connected projector. Presentation software can be very helpful in explaining complicated planning options to clients and, of course, for outlining and simplifying public presentation material.

3. *Time and billing.* Sage's Timeslips remains the most commonly used entry in this legal-niche software category, while Billing Matters from LexisNexis and PCLaw, Jr. from Alumni Computer Group have partisans and substantial market share. Other programs in this category include Client Project from Micro Billing Systems, Inc.; RTG Bills from RTG Data Systems; and TimePro from TimePro Legal Software, Inc. For the more computer-literate elder law attorney, one choice might be to utilize Microsoft's Access database and customize a time-and-billing system. From its initial introduction in mid-2003, Billing Matters has rapidly grown to become the primary challenger in this category.

4. *Case management.* Capable case management programs merge the ability to keep track of clients and other contacts, cases, word processing and other computer files, calendars and to-do lists, and telephone and e-mail messages all in one place. Case management has become the front-end software through which most other software packages are accessed. At the same time, the word processing, billing, and other software entries are indexed and linked on the basis of dates (date of creation, due date, review date, etc.), contacts (clients, vendors, opposing attorneys, etc.), cases, and tasks. Most case management programs were designed for litigators, and the paradigm of adversary relationships make them less useful for the elder law practitioner. Two programs that stand out for their ease of use and ability to adapt to a consultative practice are LexisNexis' Time Matters and Gavel and Gown's Amicus Attorney. Although not specifically designed for the legal field, and much less for elder law attorneys, Microsoft's Outlook is worth consideration, if for no other reason than its ubiquity.

5. *E-mail.* Software choices include Microsoft's Outlook (or Outlook Express), free programs from Mozilla (Thunderbird), and Pegasus Mail, and Eudora from Qualcomm Inc. Modern case management programs (like Time Matters and Amicus Attorney, described above) include e-mail clients as part of the program; this permits incoming and outgoing e-mails to be automatically connected to

the appropriate contact or case, improving the ability to find all the documents and activities related to a particular case or client in one place. One notable downside of Outlook is its susceptibility to viruses, not due to any inherent flaw in the program, but because its use is so widespread that virus- or worm-generators will look for the Outlook mailbox when spreading their infections.

6. *Internet browsers.* Despite an abundance of early program choices, the field has been left almost entirely to Microsoft's Internet Explorer, though Mozilla's Firefox browser has recently made some inroads into Internet Explorer's market share. Some sites are better viewed using Explorer, though even that distinction has faded in significance.

7. *Document assembly.* Lawyers generally, and elder law attorneys particularly, recycle phrases, clauses, and whole documents endlessly. Automating that process is both time-consuming and labor-intensive (it almost requires active involvement by one or more lawyers), but is nonetheless immensely rewarding, both personally and financially. Both WordPerfect and Word have tremendous document assembly abilities built into their word processing software. More usable (but still difficult to master) stand-alone programs are available, but the market leader by far is HotDocs from LexisNexis.

8. *Number processing.* Lawyers who will be managing assets in a fiduciary capacity, planning for Medicaid eligibility, or preparing tax returns will need, at a minimum, a spreadsheet program such as Microsoft Excel or Corel QuattroPro, and probably a financial management/check-writing program such as Quicken or Quickbooks (or PCLaw for legal-specific use). zCalc, now a product of Thomson Fast-Tax, is an Excel add-on that includes estate planning computations, such as annuity or income factors, and PowerPoint slides explaining the planning choices and decisions. An attorney whose practice is weighted towards estate administration may decide to explore the handful of remaining estate tax preparation packages, such as Fast-Tax or Gillett Estate Management Suite (GEMS) software. All attorneys should also be able to utilize the computational features built into the table functions of Word and WordPerfect.

9. *Publishing in print and on the internet.* Most attorneys may prefer to keep it simple and produce newsletters and handouts using ordinary word processing programs. If one is up to the challenge, however, desktop publishing software such as Microsoft

Publisher can create a much more polished and professional product. Similarly, attorneys who want to try their hands at a website may be able to get by with FrontPage or FrontPage Express (bundled with various iterations of Microsoft Office products) or Netscape Page Composer (bundled with the Netscape browser), but the ambitious may want to explore Dream-weaver MX or other web design programs.

Q 1:56.1   How much should an elder law attorney expect to do himself or herself with software?

Although it may have once made sense for a computer-savvy attorney to figure out how to implement software programs in his or her office, the day for that kind of do-it-yourself mentality has largely passed. Two important suggestions about implementation of any computer-based change or addition in your practice:

1. Get professional help. Unless you are uncommonly familiar with computers and software, and willing to invest a tremendous amount of your (billable) time in poking around under the computer's hood, you will benefit from having someone who actually knows what they are doing setting up your system. Just as you counsel clients that they should not try to figure out how to draft their own estate planning documents, even though there is a significant chance they will do just fine, you should not try to figure out how to do computer work that you are not trained for or qualified to do.

2. Don't wait for the system to be completed before rolling it out. Perfection will never be attained, and being able to use just the calendaring function of your case management program, or prepare only simple powers of attorney with your document assembly program, will generate real dollar savings AND encourage you and your staff to think about how the system might be made even more useful. Too many offices wait for that mythical moment of perfection to implement computer changes, only to find that the target has shifted, the cost has become exorbitant, and the jarring change for staff is too much to process and absorb. Start small.

Chapter 2

Ethical Issues in Client Representation

Two ethical considerations generally arise in any elder law practice. First, elderly (and disabled younger) clients can be mentally impaired, or so physically impaired as to be vulnerable even if not incompetent;[1] even fully competent clients may be statistically more likely to become incompetent in the not-too-distant future. Second, elder law attorneys are frequently consulted by family members (or friends) "on behalf of" an elderly person. Both of these circumstances lead to possible confusion about the identity of the lawyer's client, and what duties the lawyer owes to that client, or to other third persons. This chapter will discuss common ethical problems that arise in elder law practice including conflict of interest, confidentiality, client competency, and fiduciary representation. These situations are as difficult to resolve, as they are frequent of occurrence. This chapter should be seen as no more than a starting point in analyzing these issues.

---

[1]In many states, the traditional term "incompetent" has been replaced by "incapacitated" or "incapable," or more specifically, "incapable of" followed by a statutory listing of activities for which a person is not capable of acting without a surrogate. The shorthand "incompetent" may not be a legal term, but is used here to describe a person who has been adjudicated incapable of making decisions regarding his or her care and assets.

Overview

Q 2:2 Are there special ethical problems for attorneys who work in larger firms?

In addition to conflict of interest rules applying to the individual lawyer, most states (and the Model Rules of Professional Conduct) prohibit other firm members from undertaking representation that would be impermissible for any one member of a firm. This rule is no different for larger firms or elder law attorneys. The high volume of clients in most elder law practices, coupled with the larger number of clients in larger firms, places a practical premium on computerized conflict checking in those larger firms. Of course, even a smaller firm must have and utilize some regular form of conflict checking, and this task is especially suited to computerization. One qualification: The Model Rules, at least, prohibit a firm member from "knowingly" representing a client when another firm member would be prohibited from doing so. This safe haven should not be seen as encouragement to avoid efficient conflict checking systems. For an illustration of the kind of problem that can flow from an ineffective conflict check—even though the mechanism is in place and the problem turns on a misspelling of a client's name—consider *A. v. B. v. Hill Wallack* [158 N.J. 51, 726 A.2d 924 (1999)], in which the law firm's conflict check failed to reveal that the defendant in a paternity action it filed was also a client of the firm.

The finer points of the rules of professional conduct do permit representation in some situations that may cause concern. Model Rule 1.9 prohibits representation that is adverse to a *former* client only in a "substantially similar" matter. The large firm's prior representation of a nursing home in a real estate matter may not preclude the firm's attorneys from representing a resident alleging mistreatment, assuming any information received in the real estate matter remains confidential. This being said, as a practical matter the larger firm will not welcome representation of one of many smaller, poorer clients against corporations that are likely to be more potentially remunerative clients over the long haul. To practice elder law in the larger firm, the elder law attorney must be sensitive to these dynamics and willing to turn some matters over to colleagues elsewhere.

Q 2:7 What other resources and commentaries address ethics in the context of an elder law practice?

The American College of Trust and Estate Counsel (ACTEC) Commentaries on the Model Rules of Professional Responsibility [American College of Trust and Estate Counsel, 4th Edition, 2006] were written with regard to the traditional role of trust and estate lawyers as family counselors and the generally nonadversarial nature of this area of practice. Because a trust and estate practice is similar to an elder law practice in many ways, the ACTEC Commentaries provide excellent guidance to the elder law attorney, including proper explanation of fiduciary duties to the client(s), representation of co-fiduciaries, communications with nonclient beneficiaries, notice of acts or omissions of the fiduciary client, fee arrangements with nonclient entities (such as third-party fiduciaries or family members), and issues surrounding gifts to the attorney (such as bequests in a will). The Commentaries can be found online at *http://www.actec.org/pubInfoArk/comm/toc.html.*

The ACTEC Foundation is currently working on a Fourth Edition addressing the revised Rules.

Another important reference is the recommendations of the Second National Guardianship Conference known as "Wingspan." This Conference, which took place in December 2001, brought together judges, attorneys, and other experts to make recommendations regarding the practice of guardianship law nationwide. The Conference recommendations include the following:

> 62. A lawyer petitioning for guardianship of his or her client *not* (a) be appointed as the respondent's counsel, (b) be appointed as the respondent's guardian ad litem for the guardianship proceeding, and (c) seek to be appointed guardian except in exigent or extraordinary circumstances, or in cases where the client made an informed nomination while having decisional capacity.

> 63. The lawyer for a client with diminished capacity not attempt to represent a third party petitioning for guardianship over the lawyer's client.

The Wingspan recommendations may be found online at *http://www.law.stetson.edu/lawrev/abstracts/PDF/31-3Recommendations.pdf*

Representing Married Couples and Families

Q 2:13   What problems arise when representing multiple generations of the same family, and how can these be resolved?

One of the best indications that representation is successful is when clients refer family and friends to the lawyer for legal representation.

When the family members so referred are also named as fiduciaries and beneficiaries of the initial client's estate plan, however, the possibilities for conflicts of interest should be apparent.

Sometimes multi-generational conflicts will be relatively benign. If the lawyer has represented parents in estate planning and long-term care planning, later preparation of the children's wills and trusts should not be too problematic. Where the lawyer first represents the children, and parents then consult the same lawyer about the possibility of transferring property into the children's names, the conflict possibilities are more apparent. If the suggestion to transfer assets to the children's names comes from the lawyer (even though appropriate because of the parent's tax or long-term care situations), the conflict becomes even more problematic.

For instance, an attorney may find herself in an untenable position if she represents both the principal and the agent in a "half a loaf" gifting program established to qualify the principal for Medicaid benefits. (See chapter 14 for a discussion of Medicaid.) Under this scenario, a portion of the principal's assets is set aside for the principal's care and the rest is gifted to beneficiaries (usually the children). The attorney who represents the principal only would advocate for a greater sum to be set aside for the principal so that all eventualities and emergencies would be covered. The attorney for the children would push for larger gifts, and try to eliminate any risk that at the end of the three-year Medicaid lookback period there would be a sum left over that would have to be spent. Thus the attorney representing both generations has an inherent conflict, even when ending up with the same figures that opposing counsel would have reached through negotiation.

In the Medicaid scenario, the solution is to make clear from the outset whose interests are represented in the engagement. As a matter of policy, most elder law attorneys will state that they represent the elder principal in any matter that involves planning or recommendations concerning the elder's assets. If someone from the younger generation seeks advice, he or she can seek independent advice on what the plan entails, but not assistance in "inducing" the older family member to change plans. The second part of the solution is to phrase all recommendations with reference to the risks and benefits to the older person. For example, larger gifts may leave the older person at risk if the children die, divorce, or are subject to claims of creditors. The elder may still choose to take that risk, but it should be quite clear who the attorney represents.

The same problems can arise when the context is not Medicaid, but federal estate tax planning. Estate tax savings benefit the family, not the client. Annual gifts may make tax sense if the goal is estate tax savings, but the attorney must be certain that this is the client's goal, not the goal of the younger family members.

Dealing with the Incompetent Client

Q 2:23 Can the lawyer who believes the client cannot manage his or her own affairs seek the appointment of a guardian *ad litem*?

Yes. Model Rule 1.14(b) provides: "When the lawyer reasonably believes that the client has diminished capacity, is at risk of substantial physical, financial or other harm unless action is taken and cannot adequately act in the client's own interest, the lawyer may take reasonably necessary protective action, including consulting with individuals or entities that have the ability to take action to protect the client and, in appropriate cases, seeking the appointment of a guardian ad litem, conservator or guardian." As the Rule implicitly indicates, the decision to initiate a formal protective proceeding—including appointment of a guardian *ad litem*—should be a last resort, after all attempts to resolve the problem in a less invasive manner have been attempted. The lawyer's determination that his or her client is so impaired as to require initiation of a guardianship or conservatorship inevitably leads to ethical conflicts. Except in those rare cases where the client acknowledges a need for protective proceedings, this conflict is irresolvable.

Even though ethically permitted to initiate proceedings, a lawyer may attempt to find alternate ways to resolve the dilemma, and should decline any further involvement in the proceedings (except to be available as a witness, at least as to those matters not covered by the attorney-client privilege). While the attorney may act on his or her own volition, it is good practice to seek medical advice before seeking the appointment of a guardian. The lawyer should not attempt to be appointed as the guardian, unless there are exigent circumstances, and should not represent a third party seeking such appointment over the client's expressed objections regardless of what the lawyer thinks of the client's capacity at the time the objections are made.

Although this problem arises infrequently, it is a relatively more common occurrence for elder law attorneys, who deal with marginally competent clients on a regular basis.

Q 2:25 What is the lawyer's obligation when appointed as a guardian *ad litem*?

In many states, lawyers are still appointed as a guardian *ad litem* in guardianship and conservatorship proceedings. (See chapter 9.) The original language of the Uniform Probate Code (UPC), for example, provided that if an attorney were to be appointed to represent any unrepresented person against whom a guardianship was sought, the attorney would "have all the powers and duties of a guardian *ad litem*." [UPC 1990, § 5-303(C)] The current draft revisions to that section delete the reference to the powers and duties of a guardian *ad litem*. [UPC 1998 (Draft), § 5-303(b)] Note that in both versions of the UPC, appointment of an attorney is included in alternative provisions, that is, the National Conference of Commissioners on Uniform State Laws has taken no position on whether appointment of counsel should be mandatory in every guardianship proceeding. Regardless of the statutory scheme in any state, the client with diminished capacity is entitled to meaningful legal representation, especially in a proceeding as formal as guardianship or conservatorship. [In re Lee, 132 Md. App. 696 (2000)]

One problem is that no one seems to be clear what powers and duties a guardian *ad litem* has or should have. The growing consensus is that the guardian *ad litem* is something other than the alleged incompetent's advocate or advisor, and may have a duty to advocate for the client/ward's "best interests" instead of his or her wishes. Where the lawyer attempts to act as both guardian *ad litem* and advocate for the client, there may be an insuperable conflict between the roles.

As a constitutional matter, persons alleged to be incompetent should have a right to counsel, and that right should be meaningful. The nature of the attorney-client confidential relationship is to encourage the full discussion of legal options and strategies, without fear that the client's opinions or statements will one day be used as part of the legal proceedings themselves, to show the client's inability to manage personal affairs, his or her delusions, or other limitations. The lawyer should consider the attorney-client relationship paramount and reject the "powers and duties of a guardian *ad litem*" where necessary to effect the attorney-client relationship. It may even be necessary to seek the appointment (by the court) of a separate guardian *ad litem* in some cases, although modern commentators question the need for a formal advocate for the potential ward's best interests, because that is the province of the court itself.

Part II

Estate and Retirement Planning

Chapter 3

Retirement Planning

Clients frequently are unfamiliar with pension rights, and private retirement programs are generally misunderstood or poorly understood by beneficiaries of the programs. Even the ubiquitous individual retirement account (IRA) is the source of much client and public confusion as to the rights of the plan. As a result of the boom in retirement planning in the last two decades, it is increasingly common to see retirees with substantial portions or even the majority of their wealth tied up in retirement plans. Most elderly clients may be past the age when active contributions to retirement plans are an issue, but many will still be employed (or self-employed) and covered by IRAs, Keogh plans, 401(k) and 403(b) plans, and other private pension plans.

Once retirement benefits are in place, particularly when those benefits are in any of the self-directed defined contribution plans, the rules for administration, distribution, and rollover are myriad. This chapter discusses the different types of pension plans and retirement accounts, who can make contributions, how much can be contributed on a tax-deferred basis, and the rules and tax consequences of distributions from these plans.

Inevitably, a situation will present itself that seems to fall outside the basic information included in this chapter. Other resources that may be useful include:

- S. Lockwood, D. Levy & M. Fleisher, *Individual Retirement Account Answer Book* (13th Ed.) (Aspen Publishers 2006)

- Natalie Choate, *Life and Death Planning for Retirement Benefits* (6th Ed.) (Ataxplan Publications 2006)
- IRS Publication 590
- Final regulations under Code Section 401. [Treas. Reg. § 1.401A-9] An amusingly annotated version is available on the website of attorney Noel Ice *(http://trustsandestates.net)*, who can be relied upon to provide copious notes on anything new that is tax-related.

Information Gathering

Q 3:7 In what types of retirement plans might a client have accumulated benefits?

Many different types of retirement plans might be available to individual workers. Among the common plans (and types of plans) the elder law practitioner will frequently encounter are:

- Profit sharing plan (see Q 3:30)
- Money purchase pension plan (see Q 3:31)
- Defined benefit pension plan including 412(i) plans (see Q 3:32)
- Target benefit plan (see Q 3:33)

- Thrift or savings plan (see Q 3:37)
- Section 401(k) plan (see Q 3:38)
- Section 403(b) plan (see Q 3:39)
- Stock bonus plan (see Q 3:34)
- Leveraged employee stock ownership plan (ESOP) (see Q 3:35)
- Keogh plan (see Q 3:40)
- Cash balance plan (see Q 3:41)
- Simplified employee pension IRA (SEP-IRA) (see Q 3:42)
- Savings incentive match plan for employees (SIMPLE) plan (see Q 3:47)

Less frequently, the client may have benefits in any of several other retirement accounts (most nonqualified for income tax purposes, and therefore taxed to the beneficiary at the time of contribution):

- Rabbi trusts (see Q 3:110)
- Secular trusts (see Q 3:111)
- Supplemental executive retirement plans (SERPs) (see Q 3:112)

In addition to the above, all of which require some form of employment or employer sponsorship, there are retirement accounts established completely by individuals:

- Individual retirement account (IRA) (see Q 3:50)
- Roth IRA (see Q 3:95)

ERISA

Q 3:10 What is ERISA preemption?

ERISA expressly provides that its Title I and Title IV (governing retirement accounts generally and certain types of defined benefit plans specifically) preempt any contrary state laws. This has had a tremendous impact on state laws in a number of contexts, from abrogation of state community property laws [Boggs v. Boggs, 520 U.S. 833, 117 S. Ct. 1954 (1997)] to claims under state law for tortious breach of contract arising from handling of insurance claims [Pilot Life Insurance Co. v. Dedeaux, 481 U.S. 41, 107 S. Ct. 1549 (1987), but see Kentucky Ass'n of Health Plans, Inc. v. Miller, 538 U.S. 329, 123 S. Ct. 1471 (2003), invoking ERISA's provision allowing laws "which regulate insurance" to avoid ERISA preemption] to invalidation of state laws of succession after divorce. [Egelhoff v. Egelhoff, 532 U.S. 141, 121 S. Ct. 1322 (2001)]

Q 3:12 What is the ERISA preemption in the health care context?

Because ERISA preempts any state laws that "relate to any employee benefit plan" [29 U.S.C. § 1144(a)], the scope of preemption has been extended to include even employer-provided health plans, such as insurance coverage or health maintenance organization (HMO) membership. However, despite this broad sweep, ERISA states that preemption does not apply to generally applicable state laws that regulate insurance. [29 U.S.C. § 1144(b)(2)(A)] This "insurance" exception has recently gained ground. The broad sweep of ERISA preemption eroded significantly in 1999 when the U.S. Supreme Court decided *UNUM Life Insurance Company of America v. Ward* [526 U.S. 358 (1999)], applying a much looser test to determine whether a law merely regulates insurance. Result: fewer state laws and regulations affecting insured pension plans fall under the axe of ERISA preemption, and many laws (such as anti-subrogation laws) may now be upheld against "fully insured" plans. [See, e.g., Singh v. Prudential Health Care Plan, 335 F.3d 278 (4th Cir. 2003), *cert. denied*, 124 S. Ct. 924 (2003)] That is not to say that ERISA preemption is dead—definitely not. Generally, if a complaint alleges a denial of benefits by an employer it will be preempted by ERISA. Benefit claims against a "fully insured" employer-sponsored plan may not be preempted. Claims not involving denial of benefits, such as medical malpractice, fraud, or unfair insurance practices, are not preempted.

Participation and Nondiscrimination Requirements

Q 3:18 What nondiscrimination rules apply to qualified retirement plans?

Qualified retirement plans cannot discriminate in favor of highly compensated employees. [I.R.C. § 401(a)(4)]"Highly compensated employees" include those employees who either (1) own a 5 percent or greater interest in the employer, or (2) received a salary of $105,000 in the preceding year (2008 figure) and are among the top-paid group in the organization. Regulations contain "safe harbors" in plan design, so that plans constructed in accordance with regulations will clearly pass the nondiscrimination tests. [Treas. Reg. § 1-401(a)(4)-2]

Types of Qualified Retirement Plans

Q 3:31 What is a money purchase pension plan?

A money purchase pension plan is a qualified, defined contribution plan. In a money purchase pension plan, the employer is required to make annual contributions to the account of each participant/owner at a fixed percentage of compensation. Annual contributions are limited to 100 percent of compensation or $46,000 (2008 figures), whichever is less. [I.R.C. § 415(c)(1)]

Q 3:32 What is a defined benefit pension plan?

A defined benefit pension plan is a qualified plan that promises a specific benefit on retirement usually based on the number of years of service and the compensation received by the employee. The benefit is normally an annuity. The employer is required to make annual contributions regardless of profits and bears the risk of bad investment returns on pension plan funds. An advantage of a defined benefit plan is that it does not limit the amount of employer contributions; the contribution can be whatever is necessary to fund the projected benefit. Because there is no limit on employer contributions, defined benefit plans are attractive to small employers whose key employees are older and have limited time to save for retirement.

There are three general types of defined benefit pension plans: the fixed benefit plan, flat benefit plan, and unit benefit plan. In a fixed benefit plan, the participant/owner's retirement benefit is calculated according to a formula, usually based on the average (or, in some cases, maximum) salary earned over a period of time, usually the last several years (sometimes the highest-paid years) of employment. Usually, this salary figure is divided by the years of service to determine the average salary figure on which the retirement benefit is based. The figure so calculated is multiplied by a constant to determine the fixed benefit; subsequent cost-of-living adjustments may raise that figure over time.

A flat benefit plan is one in which the retirement benefit is calculated solely based on the participant/owner's salary. Typically, benefits under such a plan are computed by multiplying the employee's average monthly compensation by a fixed percentage, without regard to either length of service or increases in salary level late in the employment cycle.

A unit benefit plan rewards length of service by calculating the retirement benefits based on the average salary multiplied by the years of service. This figure is then multiplied by a constant percentage to determine the monthly retirement benefit.

One kind of defined benefit plan for a very small business is the 412(i) plan which is funded by insurance and annuity products and is exempt from the minimum funding requirements of other defined benefit plans. Plans must be funded with level contributions, but may be funded annually; the assets inside the plan are protected from creditors by virtue of being in a qualified plan. Two downsides: (a) no loans are permitted; and (b) plans have been used abusively by certain insurance companies.

Q 3:39   What is a Section 403(b) plan?

A Section 403(b) plan is a tax-deferred annuity plan that is only available to employees of public schools and tax-exempt educational, charitable, and religious organizations. Although some of the distribution rules vary slightly from those for 401(k) plans, the two types of retirement plans are quite similar. Section 403(b) plans are usually arranged with one or a few private investment organizations (mutual funds, etc.) by each employer, and the participant/owners contribute pre-tax dollars (by salary reduction) to purchase an annuity. A 403(b) plan, depending upon its terms, may permit a retiree to make post-retirement contributions for five years, since contribution rights are tied to "includible compensation," defined in I.R.C. § 403(b)(3) as excluding deferred compensation received more than five years after termination from employment. Such annuities typically include optional distribution provisions such as payouts with cost-of-living adjustments. Regulations promulgated June 15, 2004, now permit those who have already purchased such annuities to change the payout options prior to retirement, or upon marriage.

For 2008, the basic amount employees can contribute to a 403(b) is $15,500 (unchanged from 2007). In addition, those who meet certain criteria may contribute up to an additional $5,000, or for those 50+, can contribute $6,000. The total 2008 contribution limit on combined employee/employer contributions is 100% of includible compensation or $46,000, whichever is less.

Simplified Employee Pension Plan (SEP)

Q 3:43 What contributions can be made to a SEP?

The employer may make an annual contribution to each employee's SEP-IRA up to the lesser of 25 percent of the employee's compensation or $46,000 (in 2008). [I.R.C. § 402(h)(2)] The employer is not required to make any contribution in any year.

Q 3:45 What effect does a SEP have on the employee's other retirement planning choices?

Employees who participate in a SEP may contribute up to $5,000 to a regular IRA ($6,000 if 50 or older). The deductible amount is phased out as adjusted gross income (AGI) exceeds $53,000 for single individuals and $85,000 for married couples filing jointly. [I.R.C. §§ 219(g)(1), 219(g)(5)(A)(v)] Contributions in excess of the yearly limitation may be withdrawn without penalty by the due date for filing the tax return and are includible in the employee's gross income.

Savings Incentive Match Plan for Employees (SIMPLE Plan)

Q 3:48 What contributions can be made to a SIMPLE plan?

Annual employee contributions are capped at $10,500 for 2008 [I.R.C. § 408(p) (2)(A)(ii)], with catch-up contributions of $2,500 for those age 50 and older (both unchanged since 2007), and need not comply with the nondiscrimination and top-heavy rules that apply to SEPs and most other retirement plans. Generally speaking, employers are required to match employee contributions up to 3 percent of the employee's compensation; alternatively, the employer may choose to make mandatory contributions of 2 percent of the employee's compensation (with a maximum compensation figure of $230,000 for 2008). For employers wishing to make larger contributions to their own retirement funds, a SEP or conventional retirement account may be more attractive.

Individual Retirement Accounts

Q 3:51   Who can establish an IRA?

Anyone who receives compensation at some point during the year and who is under age 70½ at the end of the year may establish an IRA. [I.R.C. § 219(d)(1)] Compensation includes wages, salaries, professional fees, commissions, alimony, and earnings from self-employment. [I.R.C. § 219(f)(1)] An IRA can be established even if the individual is covered by another retirement plan; however, if the individual is covered by another retirement plan, deductibility of the IRA contribution may be reduced or eliminated (see SQ 3:56).

Q 3:53   What types of IRAs can be established?

Traditionally, there are two different types of IRAs: contributory and rollover. These IRAs differ only in the source of funding for the account. The SEP-IRA discussed above is an employer-sponsored plan that includes use of an IRA.

In addition, Congress created two specialized types of IRAs, the Roth IRA and the Education IRA, in 1997. The Roth IRA (see Q 3:95) and the Education IRA have different tax rules and effects. The Education IRA, not really a retirement device but rather a mechanism for paying for future educational expenses (usually of children or grandchildren) with tax-favorable treatment, has much less significance in most elder law practices but is discussed in Chapter 5.

A contributory IRA is established by the annual contributions of the plan beneficiary augmented by the growth and income generated by the plan assets. Various rules govern the maximum amount of annual contributions, but contributions may not exceed $5,000 even if those rules are met. [I.R.C. § 219(b)(1)] Contributory IRAs are important, and can grow to significant size over a number of years, but are not usually the central focus of retirement planning and elder law issues.

Rollover IRAs are created by the distribution of qualified pension plan benefits at the time of retirement, termination of employment, plan termination, or death of a participant/owner. In order to avoid the immediate income taxation of qualified plan benefits, a beneficiary spouse may elect to roll over the plan assets into an IRA and be governed thereafter by his or her own IRA accumulation and distribution rules. Such conversions to an IRA are permissible only upon retirement or termination from employment, or by a spouse upon the death of the participant/owner. A similar—but different—rollover opportunity is given to non-spouse beneficiaries, though the inherited rollover in such a case will continue to be subject to the participant/owner's minimum withdrawal requirements.

Q 3:54 How much can an individual contribute to an IRA?

The maximum annual contribution to a traditional IRA is the lesser of $5,000 (in 2008) or 100 percent of the individual's annual compensation. [I.R.C. § 408(A)(1)] The taxpayer can have more than one IRA (including a Roth IRA), but the overall maximum annual contribution for all the IRAs, regular and Roth combined, is still $5,000. Married couples may contribute a maximum of $10,000, which can be allocated between the spouses as long as neither spouse is credited with more than $5,000. [I.R.C. § 219(c)(2); Prop. Treas. Reg. § 1.219(a)-3(c)] Replace "$5,000" with "$6,000" for each spouse who is 50 or over. [SQ 3:54.1]. In addition, the "Enron" provision included in section 831 of the Pension Protection Act of 2006 permits "applicable individuals" (in general, those who had participated in 401(k) plans in which there was a 50% or more employer match of employer stock, which ended with the employer's bankruptcy *and* in which the employer or others had criminal convictions for transactions related to the plan) to contribute an additional $3,000. This provision applies only during 2007-2009. For 401(k) and 457 defined contribution plans the limit on employee pre-tax contributions (or elective deferrals) is $15,500 for 2008.

Q 3:54.1 What are "catch-up" contributions?

The Job Creation and Worker Assistance Act of 2002 (JCWAA), H.R. 3090, contains several provisions relating to pensions and technical corrections of EGTRRA. Under EGTRRA, an individual age 50 or over may make additional catch-up contributions to certain retirement plans, up to a specified limit ($5,000 is the upper limit in 2008). The JCWAA clarifies that the catch-up limit applies to all qualified retirement plans, tax-sheltered annuity plans, SEPs, and SIMPLE plans maintained by the same employer on an aggregated basis, as if all plans were a single plan;

however, if there is only a SIMPLE plan, the catch-up contribution limit for 2008 is $2,500.

Q 3:55   What is a spousal IRA?

Each spouse, including a homemaker who does not work outside the home, can make a deductible IRA contribution. Prior to 1997, spouses who did not work outside the home could not make deductible IRA contributions in the same manner as their spouses who worked outside the home. Married taxpayers who file a joint return can now contribute up to $5,000 for each spouse (2008 figure), including a nonworking spouse who has no earned income, if the combined compensation of both spouses is at least equal to the contributed amount. [I.R.C. § 219(c)] The spousal IRA is the IRA for the nonworking spouse or the spouse with less than $5,000 of income. For each spouse over 50, replace "$5,000" with "$6,000."[SQ 3:54] The contribution may be a deductible contribution to a regular IRA or a nondeductible contribution to a Roth IRA.

Q 3:56   Are contributions to the IRA always deductible?

Not all contributions to an IRA are deductible. Whether an individual's contributions are deductible depends on whether the individual or spouse is an active participant/owner in an employer-sponsored retirement plan, the modified adjusted gross income of the individual and spouse, and the individual's filing status.

Individuals who are not active participant/owners in qualified retirement plans (and whose spouse is not an active participant/owner) are not subject to any income limits and can deduct the entire contribution to the IRA.

An individual covered by an employer's retirement plan may have the IRA deduction reduced or eliminated depending upon income and filing status. The deduction is phased out for active participant/owners in a qualified employer retirement plan whose adjusted gross income exceeds certain levels. [I.R.C. § 219(g)(2)] Separate rules apply to determine if an employee is an active participant/owner in an employer-sponsored retirement plan. Note that a person will not be considered an active participant/owner in an employer-sponsored retirement plan merely because the spouse is considered one. [I.R.C. § 219(g)(1)]

Beginning in 2006, the deduction for employees covered by another retirement plan decreases based on income. In 2008, the deduction for joint filers with an income of $85,000 begins to decrease and will be unavailable if income exceeds $105,000. Single filers are subject to a similar phase-out of the deduction for adjusted gross income over $53,000 with no deductibility for income in excess of $63,000. [I.R.C. § 219(g)(2)(A)] For spouses filing jointly where one spouse is an active participant/owner in a plan and the other spouse is not an active participant/owner, the spouse who is not the active participant/owner can make a deductible IRA contribution up to $5,000 ($6,000 if over age 50). The phase-out range for deductibility is between $159,000 and $169,000 of total income. [I.R.C. § 219(g)(7)]

If the individual's adjusted gross income falls within the phaseout range, the maximum contribution will be the greater of $200 or 20 percent of the amount by which income is less than the higher phase-out figure applicable in each case.

Example 3-1. John and Martha file a joint return for the year 2008. John reports $70,000 of employee income, and Martha reports $18,000 of employee income, for a total of $88,000. John is covered by a retirement plan at his employment, but Martha is not. Each contributes $5,000 to an IRA for 2006. Martha's entire contribution is deductible, because their income is below the $85,000 threshold for married couples and she is not covered by an employer's plan. John, on the other hand, is covered by an employer's plan, and so his income must be compared to the phase-out tables. Because their combined income exceeds $85,000, he is limited to the greater of $200 or 20 percent of the difference between their total income and the maximum phase-out figure ($105,000 in John and Martha's case, for a difference of $17,000). In other words, John may deduct only $340 of his IRA contribution. He may elect to have the balance returned to him by April 15, 2009, or he may treat it as a nondeductible contribution.

Spousal Rights

Q 3:58 What rights does a surviving spouse have in retirement benefits?

ERISA requires qualified plans to provide benefits payable in the form of a qualified joint and survivor annuity (QJSA). [I.R.C. § 401(a)(11)] Under such an arrangement, the participant/owner receives a benefit for life; after the participant/owner's death, the participant/owner's surviving spouse is entitled to receive a lifetime benefit of at least 50 percent of the participant/owner's own benefit. [I.R.C. § 417(b)] The participant/owner may elect to receive benefits under a different structure, but the participant/owner's spouse must sign any waiver of the QJSA. [I.R.C. § 417] Such a waiver must be completed within 90 days of the annuity's starting date. [Treas. Reg. § 1.417(e)-1(b)(3)]

When a plan participant/owner dies before the annuity starting date (one month after retirement), the participant/owner's surviving spouse will be entitled to a qualified preretirement survivor annuity (QPSA). [I.R.C. § 401(a)(11)(A)(ii)] This protection becomes available immediately upon vesting of the participant/owner's interest in the plan. The QPSA must provide a benefit of at least 50 percent of the amount the participant/owner would have received if he or she had retired the day before the date of death, without regard to the participant/owner's age. In other words, the amount is calculated as if the participant/owner was retired, even though he or she could not have qualified for retirement.

Final regulations promulgated June 15, 2004, provide that when a single annuity has been purchased by an employee with the employee's balance in a defined contribution plan, the annuity may be converted to a joint and survivor annuity upon the employee's subsequent remarriage. [26 C.F.R. § 1.409(a)(1)-6 (69 Fed. Reg. 33293)]

IRAs are not subject to ERISA and therefore a surviving spouse may have no right to amounts held in an IRA. Further, many states do not include IRA funds as part of the decedent's estate as to which a spouse may make an election to take a share even if omitted as a beneficiary by the deceased spouse.

Distributions

Q 3:62 May a participant in a qualified plan take early retirement payments?

Whether or not the participant may take payments from a plan (or, for that matter, loans) will depend on the terms of the plan. Even if the Code permits early distributions, the plan may not permit them.

Assuming the plan does permit early payments, the participant must still pay a 10 percent penalty on distributions taken prior to age 59½.

The 10 percent penalty on early distributions does not apply to the following types of distributions, however:

1. Rollovers from a qualified plan or IRA into an IRA within 60 days after the date of distribution [I.R.C. § 72(t)(1)];

2. Trustee-to-trustee rollovers from a qualified plan to a Roth IRA provided income is recognized at time of rollover, or from a traditional IRA to a Roth IRA if the taxpayer's income is under $100,000 [Pension Protection Act of 2006 § 826];

3. Distributions from a qualified plan or IRA to a beneficiary because of the participant/owner's death [I.R.C. § 72(t)(2)(A)(ii)];

4. Distributions from a qualified plan or IRA taken by a military reservist called to active duty for a period of 179 or more days [Pension Protection Act of 2006 § 827];

5. Distributions from a qualified plan to a plan participant who separates from service after the year in which he or she reaches age 55 [I.R.C. § 72(t)(2)(A)(v)];

6. Payments from a plan or IRA as part of a series of "substantially equal periodic payments" spread over the participant/owner's life expectancy [I.R.C. § 72(t)(2)(A)(iv)];

7. Distributions based on the participant/owner's total or partial disability [I.R.C. § 72(t)(2)(A)(iii)];

8. Distributions to pay medical expenses in excess of 7.5 percent of adjusted gross income (AGI). [I.R.C. § 72(t)(2)(B)]; or

9. "Hardship" distributions, defined by regulation to include a hardship or unforeseeable emergency of a participant's spouse or dependent, or, pursuant to section 826 of the Pension Protection Act of 2006, of a designated beneficiary.

Q 3:63 Is there a penalty for early withdrawals from an IRA?

Yes. The penalty rules for IRA early withdrawals are similar to the early withdrawal rules that apply to qualified employer retirement plans (see Q 3:62). There is a 10 percent additional tax on distributions prior to age 59½. [I.R.C. § 72(t)(2)(A)(I)] The 10 percent penalty on early withdrawals does not apply to the following distributions in addition to those described in 3:62 as applying to distributions from IRAs:

1. Made after the taxpayer attains age 59 ½ [I.R.C. § 72(t)(2)(A)(i)];

2. Made to a beneficiary or the taxpayer's estate because the taxpayer has died [I.R.C. § 72(t)(2)(A)(ii)];

3. Part of a series of substantially equal annual payments over the participant/owner's lifetime or life expectancy or the joint lives or life expectancies of the participant/owner and a designated beneficiary [I.R.C. § 72(t)(2)(A)(iv)];

4. Made on account of disability [I.R.C. § 72(t)(2)(A)(ii)];

5. To pay for medical expenses in excess of 7.5 percent of AGI [I.R.C. § 72(t)(2)(B)];

6. To pay health insurance premiums for individuals who are unemployed for more than 12 months [I.R.C. § 72(t)(2)(D)];

7. To pay for qualified higher education expenses for the taxpayer, the taxpayer's spouse, child, grandchild, or spouse's child or grandchild [I.R.C. § 72(t)(7)(A)];

8. For first-time home purchases up to $10,000 [I.R.C. § 72(t)(2)(F)];

9. Transfers to a spouse's IRA incident to divorce [I.R.C. § 408(d)(6)];

10. Made after December 13, 1999, for IRS levies on IRAs. [I.R.C. § 72(t)(2)(A)(vii)]

Minimum Required Distributions

Q 3:64 Do the same rules for minimum required distributions apply to qualified plans and IRAs?

Most defined contribution plans are covered by the same minimum distribution rules. Separate rules apply to distributions from ESOPs (see SQ 3:94) and no such rules apply to nonqualified plans. The same minimum distribution rules also apply to IRAs, SEPs, Keoghs, and 401(k) plans. [I.R.C. § 4974(b)] Separate rules apply to distributions from defined benefit plans and section 403(b) annuities. In particular, Final Regulations promulgated June 14, 2004 address common provisions in annuities purchased by employees with their defined contribution plan accounts, such as employer-sponsored plans through TIAA-CREF, which typically permit cost of living increases or variable distribution provisions.

While there are some important distinctions between qualified plans and IRAs when it comes to beneficiaries and distributions, there are far more similarities. The key distinctions to remember are:

1. The ERISA rules on spousal rights to post-death distributions do not apply to IRAs;

2. Recent laws permitting longer deferral of distributions for participants/owners do not apply to IRAs; and

3. Qualified plan accounts and IRAs cannot be combined to meet the various minimum distribution requirements.

Beneficiaries

Q 3:85 What is the consequence of naming a nonspouse as the designated beneficiary?

Upon the death of the participant/owner, the nonspouse beneficiary will simply receive the remainder of the plan's assets. The beneficiary may elect, however, to withdraw the plan assets according to the minimum distribution rules (see Q 3:65), and thereby minimize the tax effect of each year's withdrawals. [I.R.C. § 401(a)(9)(B)(iii); Treas. Reg. § 1.401(a)(9)-3] The required minimum distribution amount for the beneficiary will be computed using the beneficiary's life expectancy according to the IRS table for beneficiaries, not owners. [See IRS Pub. 590]See Table 3-1 for further explanation. Beginning January 1, 2007, the beneficiary may also "roll over" the plan's assets to an individual retirement account (IRA) which will be treated as an inherited IRA—that is, distribution must begin by December 31st of the year following the year of the original owner's death, rather than upon the beneficiary's retirement or reaching age 70½. Pension Protection Act of 2006, sec. 829. This is a major improvement, as many IRAs were willing to accommodate a beneficiary's desire to "stretch" distributions over the beneficiary's lifetime.

Q 3:86 What is the consequence of naming a trust as the designated beneficiary?

A trust can be named as beneficiary of a qualified plan or IRA, but there may be serious adverse consequences. Unless the trust meets special rules, the participant/owner will be said to have had no designated beneficiary, with all that this implies (see Qs 3:74 and 3:75.)

In order for the IRS to "look through" to the trust's beneficiaries, who are then treated as the designated beneficiaries, a trust must meet the following tests *by September 30 of the year following the participant/owner's death:*

1. The trust must be irrevocable (originally, or by its terms becoming irrevocable upon the death of the IRA owner);

2. The trust beneficiaries must all be individuals;

3. The beneficiaries must be identifiable from the trust instrument; and

4. The trust must be valid under state law.

[Treas. Reg. § 1.401(A)(9)-4]

Further, by October 31 of the year following the year of death, the trustee must either provide a final list of all beneficiaries as of September 30 of the year following the year of death, certified as correct and complete, or provide the custodian or plan administrator a copy of the trust instrument. [Treas. Reg. § 1.401(A)(9)-4, 4.6(b)]

Peculiarly, for purposes of the new rule permitting nonspouse beneficiaries to "roll over" to an IRA, a trust may itself be treated as the designated beneficiary "to the extent provided in rules prescribed by the Secretary." Pension Protection Act of 2006, section 829. It is not yet clear as of this writing (August 2006) what this can mean, as presumably a trust cannot own an IRA.

Q 3:86.1 For purposes of the rules that "look through" a trust to the trust beneficiaries, what is a "beneficiary"?

It depends. If a trust is a "conduit" trust, passing IRA or qualified plan distributions to the trust directly to the beneficiaries, only the primary trust beneficiaries are considered when computing distributions over beneficiaries' life expectancies—contingent beneficiaries and remainderpersons are disregarded. If the trust is anything other than a conduit trust, remainder beneficiaries may well be counted. [Treas. Regs. § 1.401(a)(9)-5] The disposition: in trust for my son John for his lifetime, on his death to UNICEF, with no conduit provisions, would cause a severe problem because UNICEF would be counted as beneficiary for such purposes and because it is not an individual, would cause the entire amount to be distributed as if there were *no* designated beneficiary. Reg. Section 1.401(a)(9)-5, A-7(c) goes on to say that "a person will not be considered a beneficiary for purposes of determining who is the beneficiary with the shortest life expectancy ... or whether a person who is not an individual is a beneficiary, merely because the person *could* become the successor to the interest of one of the employee's beneficiaries after that beneficiary's death. However, the preceding sentence does not apply to a person who has any *right* (including a contingent right) to an employee's benefit beyond being a mere potential successor to the interest of one of the employee's beneficiaries upon that beneficiary's death." It was thought that this caused no problem if the contingent beneficiaries of a non-conduit trust took only in the event of the premature death of a primary beneficiary, since the premature death was not reasonably likely to happen and did not give the contingent remainderman a "right" to succeed the beneficiary's interest. For example: in trust for my son John until he reaches the age of 35, then outright to John; but if he dies before age 35 then to his older brother Samuel—or to my church. (This would compare with: To my son John until he reaches the age of 75, but if he dies before age 75, then to UNICEF, which would remain problematic.) Unfortunately, one Private Letter Ruling (applying the Proposed Regs. and not the Final Regs., it should be noted) shed doubt on this conclusion. PLR 2002-28025 involved an accumulation trust that terminated when the child beneficiary was 30, and the Service did count the remainderperson as a beneficiary for life expectancy purposes. By contrast, in PLR 2002-35038 the Service disregarded the remainder beneficiaries because at death the trust would pass to younger individual beneficiaries appointed by the child. No mention is made of the age of a default taker if the power is not exercised, but presumably that person was merely a "potential" successor. The reasoning follows arcane distinctions in trust law about interests that are vested subject to divestment versus those that are not vested. Combined, these rulings suggest that any non-conduit trust that may be the beneficiary of an IRA should give the beneficiary whose life expectancy should be counted, the power to appoint the trust to younger beneficiaries. In other words, language such as "if the beneficiary dies before 35, to such younger persons as the beneficiary may appoint, but in default of appointment, to the beneficiary's 90-year-old aunt" may just work. Since this area of the law is still unsettled, one drafting such a trust with a significantly older, or charitable, remainderperson would do well to check Natalie Choate's website, *http://www.ataxplan.com*, and current letter rulings, which may be found on the tax research website, *http://www.legalbitstream.com*.

Q 3:86.2 Can the separate beneficiaries of a trust create separate accounts and take distribution over their separate life expectancies?

Apparently the Service now says "no." Rulings issued since the final regulations were adopted [Priv. Ltr. Ruls. 2003-17041, 2003-17043, and 2003-17044] state that *only* if an IRA itself sets up separate accounts for separate beneficiaries, may their separate life expectancies be used to compute distributions. This means that even if a trust divides at death into three sub-trusts, one for each beneficiary, and even if each subtrust is a pass-through with respect to retirement assets distributed to the trust, they will have to use the life expectancy of the oldest beneficiary to compute distributions. A solution might be to have the beneficiary designation name each separate subtrust specifically as the beneficiary of a separate share, rather than naming the initial trust agreement and allowing the Trustee to make the division as to the trust terms. Note that amendments to the regulations issued June 15, 2004 purportedly included "changes" to Reg. Section 1.401(a)(9)-8(a), the "separate accounts" provision, but the text shows no changes since the 2002 Final Regulations, and certainly no change to affect the holding of the rulings.

Q 3:88 Why would a client want to name a trust as beneficiary of a qualified plan or IRA?

There are two reasons to mix trust planning and retirement beneficiary designations. The client who has established a revocable living trust as a means of avoiding probate, and perhaps controlling the use of funds for the benefit of children, may want to save the costs and possible conflicts inherent in establishing separate trusts for the retirement benefits and nonretirement assets. In other cases, a married client may want to use trust planning to attempt to maximize the credit shelter amount, especially where the retirement accounts are the major part of the estate. For clients who merely wish to prevent beneficiaries from withdrawing account funds in a lump sum, and don't see the need for a conduit trust, an alternative may be a "trusteed" retirement account described in I.R.C. § 408(a), rather than the custodial accounts used most commonly, which is described in I.R.C. § 408(h), if a bank will agree to serve as Trustee. IRS Form 5305, a standardized trust form used for this purpose, includes an "additional provision" section that may be used to restrict the beneficiary's withdrawal rights. (This form can also be a handy way to create a simple QDOT IRA for a non-citizen spouse.)

Roth IRAs

Q 3:97 Who may establish a Roth IRA?

After-tax contributions of up to $5,000 per year ($6,000 if age 50 or older) in 2008 may be made to a Roth IRA by taxpayers with AGIs of less than $99,000 for a single person, or $156,000 for a married couple filing jointly. [I.R.C. §§ 408A(c)(3)(A), 408A(c)(3)(C)] For slightly higher income levels the maximum contribution is reduced, so that no contribution can be made for individuals with AGIs of $116,000 or married couples with AGIs of $169,000. Beginning December 1, 2007, contribution limits are indexed for inflation using 2005 as a base year. [Pension Protection Act of 2006, section 833(c)].

> **Example 3-7.** Robert, a single man, has an AGI for 2007 of $102,000. He makes no other IRA contribution, and he wishes to establish a Roth IRA. His Roth IRA contribution is limited to $1,000. This is calculated by deducting the phase-out threshold ($99,000) from his AGI, dividing that figure by $15,000 and multiplying the maximum Roth IRA contribution ($5,000 in Robert's case, because he is single and has made no IRA contribution) by the resulting fraction. The maximum contribution amount is then reduced by this figure.

There are no age limits for Roth IRA contributions. Individuals over age 70½, even though they may have begun to receive benefits from other retirement accounts, may contribute to a Roth IRA. [I.R.C. § 408A(c)(4)] Compensation income (generally, wages and salary) must be at least as much as the Roth IRA contribution, so those who are completely retired and have no earned income will be unable to contribute to a new Roth IRA.

Q 3:105   What is a conversion or rollover Roth IRA?

Money accumulated in a regular IRA can be converted into a Roth IRA. [I.R.C. § 408A(d)(3)] Although the conversion will trigger income taxation of the accumulated IRA, money transferred into the Roth IRA will begin to grow tax-free. In 1998, Congress permitted special treatment for Roth IRA conversions: Taxation of the IRA benefits could be spread over a five-year period (four years plus the year of distribution). Conversions after 1998 will cause full income inclusion in the year of the conversion. [I.R.C. § 408A(d)(3)(F)] Under section 824 of the Pension Protection Act of 2006, taxpayers with AGI of $100,000 or less may "roll over" traditional IRAs or other retirement accounts to Roth IRAs, provided the income is recognized for tax purposes at the time of the rollover—but the 10% early distribution penalty does not apply. One Roth may also be rolled over to a new Roth.

Q 3:107   When planning for retirement, should an individual establish a traditional IRA or a Roth IRA?

Assuming that a given individual is able to make a regular or Roth IRA contribution, the latter will be preferable in most cases. This is true because the Roth IRA permits tax avoidance, rather than simply tax deferral.

Q 3:107.1   Can "Roth" treatment apply to retirement contributions outside of IRAs?

Yes. "Roth Contributions," which were added to the Internal Revenue Code by the Economic Growth and Tax Relief Reconciliation Act of 2001 (EGTRRA), to be effective beginning January 1, 2006, permit employees to designate all or a portion of their section 401(k) employee deferrals as Roth contributions. As such these contributions will be treated as if they were contributions to a Roth IRA, i.e., no deductibility upon contribution but distributions plus earnings would be tax free. Final regulations on Roth contributions were adopted January 3, 2006. 71 Fed. Reg. 6-11. Supplementary regulations were also proposed by the IRS at the same time. 71 Federal Register 4320-4331 (January 23, 2006).

Nonqualified Plans

Q 3:112   What is a supplemental executive retirement plan?

A supplemental executive retirement plan or top-hat plan is a non-qualified deferred compensation plan. It may be established in addition to a qualified retirement plan, to increase the retirement benefits available to the executive beyond the level permitted by qualified plans. They are frequently used when the executive earns well in excess of the maximum compensation ($230,000 in 2008) for which most retirement benefits may be calculated, or to permit the total plan to discriminate in favor of highly compensated individuals.

Practice-Related Issues

Q 3:125   What are some of the practical problems that might arise in counseling clients about retirement planning?

Retirement planning is not always carefully considered by lawyers, accountants, financial planners, and clients. It may be necessary to ask probing questions about retirement accounts. Clients are often unaware that there are options to consider, much less that those options may have a significant effect on the beneficiaries of their retirement funds. The designation of beneficiaries on retirement accounts can also dramatically change the minimum distribution rules during the client's life. Few clients appreciate the importance of careful beneficiary designations during their lifetime. The kinds of problems that arise in retirement planning are illustrated in the following examples, one covering beneficiary grandchildren inheriting an estate with a large rollover IRA as half its assets, and another covering a client trying to determine the type of retirement program to establish for her small retail business.

Example 3-9. Clint has a relatively modest estate of $800,000, but half of that is in a rollover IRA. He is single (his wife died several years ago) and 68 years old. His two children are both professionals and have accumulated substantial wealth. Clint is interested in using his estate to provide for the education of his four grandchildren, who range in age from 2 to 22.

Clint could simply leave his entire estate to his grandchildren, and even name them as beneficiaries of his IRA; however, he is likely to have concerns about the ability of at least his younger grandchildren to handle the proceeds. In order to ensure that the money is used for educational purposes, and to distribute it to the grandchildren only after they are able to handle the proceeds, he will probably prefer to establish a trust for their benefit or even separate trusts for each grandchild's benefit.

The IRA presents a special challenge (and two opportunities). Although Clint could name all four grandchildren as beneficiaries, this would cause two problems: an inability to control the use or accumulation of the proceeds (the same problem for the non-IRA benefits described previously) and the necessity of using the oldest grandchild's life expectancy for all distributions. During Clint's life, the second problem would not be of much concern (even the youngest grandchild will be treated as if he were only 10 years younger than Clint); however, upon Clint's death, the oldest grandchild's life expectancy will dictate the withdrawal schedule unless the account is physically divided into separate accounts for each grandchild.

Given Clint's goals and the size of his IRA, he should probably consider establishing four separate trusts, one for each grandchild. His own will (or trust) could divide his assets into those separate trusts upon his death. Finally, he should divide his IRA and name each trust as beneficiary of one of the four divided IRA accounts. He may also be able to name each trust as a beneficiary of a fractional share of a single IRA, but should be sure to verify with the IRA custodian that the appropriate life expectancies may be used.

Given his age and the size of his estate, Clint has only two estate tax concerns to consider: He might die before the credit shelter amount has risen to the level necessary to exempt his estate, or his estate might grow to a taxable size. If he is concerned about either of those possibilities, he might look into lifetime gifts to his grandchildren (or to Crummey trusts for their benefit), a charitable remainder trust (perhaps with a life insurance component for the benefit of his grandchildren) or a family limited partnership or limited liability company to reduce the value of his non-IRA assets.

Example 3-10. Olivia is the owner of a small retail business with four full-time employees and several part-time and seasonal employees. She is beginning to show a profit in her business, and wants to consider establishing some sort of retirement plan for herself and her employees. She seeks advice about which of her various choices she should adopt.

Establishing a retirement plan can be a daunting task. The complexity of plan documents and administration has generated a significant industry of plan salespersons and administrators. Olivia may want to avoid some of those complications by opting for a SIMPLE plan. The chief attractions of the SIMPLE plan are its simplicity and the ability to benefit some individuals disproportionately. The principal drawback is that annual contributions are limited to $8,000 per participant/owner (2003).

Olivia might prefer a SEP. Like SIMPLE plans, SEPs are easy to adopt; the employer need only sign the specimen plan form provided by a mutual fund company, brokerage house, or bank. Contributions are made into individual accounts for each employee, and the continuing administration of those plans is undertaken by the mutual fund company, brokerage firm, or bank, with no continuing reporting requirements for the employer. The maximum contribution Olivia can make for any employee is 25 percent of their salary. Whatever contribution level she sets must be the same for all qualified employees. Qualified employees are those who are in at least their third year of service. She can make the same 25 percent contribution to her own account, but again she must contribute the same percentage to all qualified employees as she does to her own account. Incidentally, she need not fund her own SEP-IRA at all, if the purpose of the retirement plan is to benefit the employees more than her. Next year, if the business is not as profitable, she can make a smaller percentage contribution to the SEP-IRAs or no contribution at all.

Olivia might choose to establish a Keogh plan for herself and her employees. Permitted contributions will be higher, and the ability to disproportionately benefit herself and highly paid employees will be increased somewhat. The reporting requirements and administration of the plan will create significant additional work for Olivia, however.

Chapter 4

Non-Tax Aspects of Estate Planning: Wills, Trusts, and Other Transfers of Property Upon Death

A key aspect of any estate plan is determining the disposition of an individual's assets after death either by drafting a will and having the property go through the probate process or by relying on alternative means of transferring property through either a trust or joint tenancies. Increasingly, a client's assets are held in a manner that can avoid the probate process, simplify estate planning, or defeat creditors' claims. This chapter covers basic will and trust requirements and discusses the advantages and disadvantages of going through the probate process versus avoiding probate using joint tenancies.

Overview

Q 4:1 What non-tax considerations are important in preparing an estate plan?

In addition to minimization of estate and gift taxes (see Chapter 5) and avoidance of probate proceedings, a number of other considerations require attention in preparing and reviewing estate plans for clients. Concern about the possibility of future incapacity, dealing with presently incapacitated spouses, children, and other beneficiaries, and the need to prepare for possible long-term care costs all play an important role in estate planning. The effect of gifts or bequests on the beneficiary should be considered, especially where the beneficiary is disabled or receiving government or other benefits.

Taxes, probate avoidance, and planning for future incapacity have become the three pillars of modern estate planning. Oddly, the original purpose of estate planning—to provide for the orderly transfer of wealth to succeeding generations and to impose such limits or restrictions as the property owner wishes to use to encourage or prevent certain behavior—is often nearly overlooked. To clients, the lawyer's fixation on taxes, probate avoidance, and incapacity may seem somewhat misplaced.

Wills

Who Should Make a Will

Q 4:5 Are there any other documents that should be prepared when making a will?

Although circumstances may differ and should control which documents will be provided in individual cases, most clients planning their estates will also want to consider making arrangements for their possible future incapacity. Durable powers of attorney are tremendously powerful (and dangerous) instruments, but with appropriate safeguards they will be a part of most clients' estate plans. (See chapter 10 on durable powers of attorney.) Health care directives (whether denominated as living wills, health care proxies, health care powers of attorney, or other names by local law and practice) will also be a part of most clients' estate plans. (See chapter 18 on advance directives and patients' rights to control medical treatment in advance.) In many cases, particularly where tax planning is involved, or disposition complicated, the client will need to execute a "pour-over" trust agreement (see SQ 4:36), into which the estate will "pour" by way of a direction in the will itself.

Will Clauses and Distribution Provisions

Q 4:11   What is an "in terrorem" clause?

As previously noted, many laypersons believe that will contests are much more common than they actually are. In order to prevent a will contest, or to encourage family harmony generally, many clients are interested in providing a penalty for any family member or devisee who seeks to challenge the validity or effect of the client's will. A clause that provides for the disinheritance of anyone contesting the will is usually referred to as an "in terrorem" clause. "In terrorem" or "no contest" clauses may also be included in trust agreements.

Q 4:12   Is an "in terrorem" clause effective to prevent will contests?

Although "in terrorem" clauses are popular (and widely used), their effectiveness is limited by two factors. First, state laws (in some but not all states) disfavor such clauses, at least where there may have been a reasonable basis to challenge the validity of the will. Second, disinheritance may not be much of a deterrent to a family member who has already been substantially or completely disinherited by the terms of the will itself.

In many states a provision purporting to disinherit a will contestant partially or completely will be unenforceable if there is "probable cause" (or some other level of evidence) to support the challenge. The Uniform Probate Code (UPC), for example, provides that a will provision "purporting to penalize an interested person for contesting the will or instituting other proceedings relating to the estate" will be unenforceable "if probable cause exists for that action." [U.P.C. § 2-517] The UPC has been adopted in 19 states, and as of this writing, has been proposed for adoption in Massachusetts as well. The following 19 states are UPC states: Alaska, Arizona, Colorado, Hawaii, Idaho, Maine, Massachusetts, Michigan, Minnesota, Montana, Nebraska, New Jersey, New Mexico, North Dakota, Pennsylvania, South Carolina, South Dakota, Utah, and Wisconsin. Of course, that leaves 31 non-UPC states with their own idiosyncratic laws. The UPC and other uniform laws can be viewed online at *http://www.nccusl.org/*. In some states, a separate proceeding may be initiated to determine whether there is a sufficient basis for the challenge. The purpose of such a proceeding is not to determine the validity of the will but to determine whether the potential objector may be permitted to even bring a contest.

On a more practical level, a disinherited child cannot effectively be further penalized for challenging the document that purports to disinherit him or her. In order effectively to prevent will contests, a will should provide for at least a meaningful inheritance for any person who might be expected to initiate a contest and then provide for the loss of that inheritance if that person commences filing any such contest. For the *in terrorem* clause to be effective, the potential challenger must have something worthwhile to lose. Even if the client successfully avoids probate, there may still be challenges to anticipatory gifts, court orders to freeze assets held in trust or otherwise disposed of, and frozen bank accounts.

Q 4:13   What provisions should a will make for simultaneous death?

One problem that can arise is the possibility that a testator and his or her devisee might die in a common accident, or close together in time. If this happens, the cost of administering the will may increase because the first decedent's estate must be probated in order to confirm title in the second decedent, and the second decedent's estate must also be probated. Simultaneous death can also frustrate the first decedent's testamentary plans. He or she might wish property to pass to another person if the second decedent happens not to live long enough to enjoy the property, and if no provisions exist to deal with simultaneous death the second decedent's heirs or devisees will acquire the first decedent's property. Determining the order of death can be difficult, particularly in a common accident, and an inability to decide which decedent died first may make the disposition of either or both decedents' property problematic. Finally, although federal estate tax credits are provided for property passing through two estates in quick succession, simultaneous death can result in increased estate tax liability.

In order to protect against the problems inherent in simultaneous death, the will drafter can include a provision requiring the devisees to survive for a specific period of time before inheriting. This requirement might be short enough to prevent problems arising from a common accident (e.g., five, seven, or ten days, "or under such circumstances that it is impracticable to determine the order of our deaths"), or long enough to ensure that no property will pass to a decedent's estate (e.g., until the distribution of the property in probate or for a fixed period approximating the length of probate). For large estates, a provision requiring devisees to survive by 90 days (but no more) permits a gift to "skip" a generation without the imposition of a death tax in the devisee's estate and without imposition of a generation-skipping transfer tax (imposed when gifts of $2 million or more skip generations, under Code Section 2601) on the testator's estate.

Many state probate codes provide for a default provision upon simultaneous death. Under that approach, unless the decedent's will provides otherwise, every devisee must survive the decedent by at least a specified short period, frequently five days. That, for example, is the approach of the UPC, which provides for a 120-hour (five-day) default survivorship requirement in UPC Section 2–702. The portion of the UPC dealing with simultaneous death has also been promulgated as the Uniform Simultaneous Death Act and has been adopted in at least six non-UPC jurisdictions (Arkansa, District of Columbia, Kansas, Kentucky, Ohio, and Virginia), and is being considered for adoption in Oklahoma. States that have not adopted this rule may provide that the property of each passes as if the devisee had predeceased the testator. [See, e.g., Connecticut General Statutes § 45a-440 ("When the title to property or the devolution thereof depends upon priority of death and there is no sufficient evidence that the persons have died otherwise than simultaneously, the property of each person shall be disposed of as if he had survived, except as provided otherwise in this section.")]

Q 4:14 What is the difference between "per capita" and "per stirpes" distribution?

When the recipient of property under a will (or by intestate succession) dies before the death of the person leaving the property, a determination must be made as to who will receive the property. If the will provides that the deceased devisee's share should lapse, or should be given instead to a substitute devisee, then those instructions will apply; however, where the will or the law of intestate succession direct that the deceased devisee's share should go to his or her descendants, a determination must be made about how to divide the property. The two most common methods of dividing property among descendants are referred to by the shorthand designations per capita and per stirpes. Per stirpes is Latin for "by way of the stocks" or "stems," and per capita is Latin for "by way of the heads." The difference between the two methods is best illustrated with an example:

> **Example 4-1.** Assume that the testator is survived by a child and two grandchildren who are the children of a predeceased child of the testator. If the will provided for per stirpes distribution, the surviving child would take one half, and each of the grandchildren would take one quarter (i.e., divide the total by the number of "stems" or "stocks," and thus the grandchildren split the share that would have gone to their parent if he or she had survived). If, on the other hand, the will provided for per capita distribution, then each of the surviving child and the two grandchildren would take one-third (i.e., divide the total by the number of heads).

Q 4:15 What is meant by "right of representation"?

Some wills, rather than using the shorthand per capita or per stirpes designations, provide for distribution by "right of representation." In most states, this structure is defined to mean the same thing as per stirpes distribution. The UPC, in its most recent version, provides otherwise. In UPC Section 2–709, the UPC defines "right of representation" to mean "per capita at each generation." This is a reversal of prior UPC law, which made per stirpes and right of representation synonymous. Rather than risk the possibility of unintentionally changing the client's desired distribution scheme, it is probably advisable either to use the more precise per capita or per stirpes language or to spell out the succession provisions in the document itself.

Q 4:16 How is property distributed if there is no will, or if the will does not specify whether per capita or per stirpes distribution is to be used?

Most states also provide for a default choice to be applied in the absence of specific language. Thus, per stirpes distribution will be the distribution mechanism in most states unless the decedent has specifically provided otherwise. Once again, however, the most recent version of the UPC provides for the opposite default provision; UPC Section 2–706 establishes "representation" (synonymous with "per capita at each generation") as the methodology to be used unless the decedent has provided otherwise.

It is important to note that the rules applicable to "intestate succession" (how property is distributed if there is no will) do not necessarily match those applicable in the event of a "lapse" (where no provision is made as to disposition in the event of a deceased beneficiary). Some states may even impose a default where the document appears to specify in favor of a lapse. The recent Connecticut case of *Ruotolo v. Tietjen*, 93 Conn. App. 432 (2006), *aff'd per curiam*, _ Conn. _ (2007), held that a bequest to the beneficiary "if he survives me" did not escape the state "anti-lapse" law. Although the facts of the case involved the lapse of a share of the residuary, the higher court's affirmation appeared to say that only explicit rejection of the anti-lapse statute as such or the express addition of a clause providing for an alternate disposition would defeat the statutory default. A typical clause that might have caused the lapse to hold would have been, "Any bequest to a person who does not survive me shall lapse and the property disposed of as a part of my residuary estate."

Q 4:17   What are specific, pecuniary, and residuary devises?

A will may provide for the distribution of a specific piece of property, an amount of money, or a portion (or the whole) of the rest of the estate. The first of these ("I hereby devise my 1969 Mustang Convertible to my daughter June") is a specific devise. The second ("I hereby give the sum of $10,000 to my son David") is a pecuniary devise, sometimes referred to as a "pecuniary legacy." After specific and pecuniary devises have been provided for, the will should (but does not always) direct distribution of the remaining property ("I hereby give, devise, and bequeath all the rest and residue of my estate in equal shares to my three children, *per stirpes*") in a residuary devise. The residue might be distributed to a single person or multiple persons, in equal shares or fractional shares. Failure to include a residuary devise will not invalidate a will, but may result in a "partial intestacy." In that situation, the other provisions will be given effect, and the residue of the estate will pass as if there was no will. Three problems can arise when making specific devises or bequests:

1. The will disposes of all the property item by item and then makes a residuary bequest—but there is nothing left for the residue. The result may be (a) unintended consequences when the testator

actually meant to benefit the residuary beneficiary and (b) problems in getting the taxes and expenses paid when there is no residue left to pay them (requiring "abatement" or reduction of the other bequests).

2. The will makes specific dispositions that are very large and generate taxes that then consume the entire residue. This means the "tax clause" will require attention, as discussed in chapter 5.

3. The will disposes of specific property that cannot be found, or is no longer owned, when the testator dies (see Q 7:38).

Q 4:20 What are "special" and "general" powers of appointment?

The distinction between a "special" (also known as "limited") power of appointment and a "general" power of appointment can have critical importance for tax purposes, as discussed in chapter 5. A general power of appointment is defined for federal estate tax purposes as a power to appoint property to any one or more of the powerholder, his or her estate, his or her creditors, and the creditors of his or her estate. Any one of these powers will cause the power of appointment to be a general power for federal estate tax purposes. [Treas. Reg. § 20.2041-1(b)] Such a power might be created intentionally (e.g., "Beneficiary shall have the power to appoint the remaining property upon beneficiary's death to the creditors of his estate") or unintentionally ("to A and B for life, upon the death of the survivor of A and B, to C's revocable trust," because C could direct that C's trust pay to C's creditors, etc.). The general power may be included intentionally to prevent a "generation-skipping transfer" from occurring on a trust's termination; instead, the property subject to the general power held by a child is includible in the child's estate on the child's death, rather than being subject to the very high GST tax when the trust terminates and is paid to grandchildren.

A special (or limited) power is any other power of appointment. Some practitioners feel it is sufficient to specify a class of beneficiaries that does not include the prohibited categories, such as "my children" or "my issue." Others, fearful of having the power treated as a general power, and pointing out that a child might be the powerholder's creditor, will specifically exclude the powerholder, his or her estate, his or her creditors, and the creditors of his or her estate.

Beyond the more obvious personal power to "appoint" to one's estate, creditors, or creditors of one's estate, a general power will also be found to exist if the person—even if acting as a Trustee, in a fiduciary capacity—whether acting alone, or in conjunction with any third party who is not "adverse," has the discretion to direct that property be paid to himself or herself without binding limitations on that discretion known as an "ascertainable standard,"—the idea being that this is tantamount to being able to appoint to oneself without limitation. An "ascertainable" standard is one sufficiently definite that a beneficiary would be able to bring legal action if the standard were violated. "Health, education, maintenance, and support" is one such standard. Another is "health, education, maintenance in reasonable comfort, and support." Although the distinction appears slight, the power to direct property to be paid to oneself for one's "welfare" or "comfort" (not maintenance in comfort, just comfort) or similar phrases, will be treated as holding a power of appointment. [Treas. Reg. § 20.2041-1(c)(2)] Many states have adopted statutes prohibiting distribution by a Trustee to himself or herself in amounts that would exceed an "ascertainable" standard, in order to prevent trust property being included in a Trustee's estate because the drafting attorney failed to use the U.S. Treasury-approved language limiting the Trustee's discretion.

A beneficiary will also be found to hold a general power of appointment if he or she has the power to "remove and replace" another party (usually, the trustee) who has the right to exercise the power in favor of the beneficiary. However, the IRS has conceded that provided the replacement is a truly "independent" person (obviously, other than the beneficiary), defined as one who is neither "related" nor "subordinate" to the removing party as those terms are defined in Code Section 672, the power will not be imputed to the beneficiary with the removal power. [Rev. Rul. 95–58, 1995–2 C.B. 191]

What is the significance of holding a general power of appointment? Property subject to a general power of appointment is included in the estate of the decedent powerholder for estate tax purposes; exercise of the power is a taxable gift by the powerholder for gift tax purposes; a "release" of the power may be a gift and, if rights are retained by the powerholder, may also be ineffective to remove the property subject to the power from the powerholder's estate at death. However, there are some exceptions: property subject to a general power of appointment that was "irrevocable" on or before October 22, 1942 (i.e., the power was included in a trust that was irrevocable by that date or a decedent's will executed before that date and who died before July 1, 1949), will not be taxed as part of the powerholder's estate unless the powerholder exercises the power. [Treas. Reg. § 20.2041-1(e)] It may be very important that the holder of a pre-1942 general power of appointment not exercise the power, and an attorney could commit malpractice by failing to draw this to the testator's attention when preparing a will that exercises the power. Similar to a general power of appointment is a right to take out, withdraw, or appoint property of a trust to such a degree that one is treated as the owner of the trust. Conversely, the IRS has decided that this power will be considered de minimis, and disregarded, when the power extends to property that does not exceed the greater of 5 percent of the trust property or $5,000. This is known as a "5 & 5 power" and is commonly included in trusts to give the surviving spouse better access to trust funds than if he or she had to depend upon the judgment of the trustee. It is used as a limiting provision whenever a surviving spouse or beneficiary might otherwise be treated as the trust owner, such as a credit shelter trust. However, if the owner dies with such a power still exercisable, that 5 percent will still be included in his or her estate for tax purposes.

Finally, while general powers of appointment are often problematic, special or limited powers of appointment can be very useful. The broadest kind of "limited" power gives unlimited power to designate beneficiaries excluding only the powerholder himself or herself, creditors, estate, or creditors of the estate. A more typical limited power specifies a class of beneficiaries such as "descendants." Either way, retention of the power is sufficient to prevent the occurrence of a completed gift for tax purposes only and is often used in Medicaid planning to permit some continued control to the donor while making a gift that will be final and complete for Medicaid purposes.

Requirements for a Valid Will

Q 4:22 Who is competent to make a will?

Any competent adult may sign a will. State law will define competence, but the classic formulation under the English common law has been adopted (with some variations) in every state. In order to be adjudged competent to sign a will, the signer (referred to in the law as the "testator") must:

1. Know the natural objects of his or her bounty (i.e., know of and understand the existence of spouse, children, and, where appropriate, grandchildren);

2. Be aware of the nature and extent of his or her estate (although detailed knowledge is not usually required); and

3. Be able to form a donative intent (this requirement is sometimes described as being able to understand the nature of the act of signing a will).

In most states a person will be assumed to have testamentary capacity even though he or she has a guardian. [See, for example, the recent case of Toler v. Murray, 886 So. 2d 76 (Ala. 2004)] In some states, the appointment of a guardian of the person or estate may create a presumption of incapacity to sign a will, though that presumption may be overcome by an affirmative showing of capacity. A mere diagnosis of a disabling condition, even if the condition demonstrates a diminution of capacity, will not be a disqualifying factor. In other words, even a dementia patient may demonstrate the ability to execute a will, depending on the ability to meet the classic three-part test of testamentary capacity.

Fortunately for attorneys who may not feel capable themselves of making capacity determinations, at least one court has held that an attorney has no duty to make such a determination, and that heirs cannot charge the attorney with malpractice for failure to do so. [Moore v. Anderson Zeigler Disharoon Gallagher & Gray, 109 Cal. App. 4th 1287, 135 Cal. Rptr. 2d 888 (2003)]

Q 4:23 What are the formal requirements for a will to be valid?

Unless the state recognizes oral or holographic (handwritten) wills, a valid will must be signed by the testator as his or her will and witnessed by two people (or in Vermont, three). "Signature" may include the mark of someone incapable of forming an entire signature. It is important that the testator state, whether in writing or orally to the witnesses, that the document is the testator's will. Usually this is obvious, but not always. There must be an indication that the testator intended the document to act as a will (i.e., to actually provide for the disposition of property at death), not only to indicate a wish for such a disposition. Some states permit the testator to direct another person to sign on his or her behalf. The "two witness" requirement is not universal. Vermont still requires three witnesses [14 Vt. Stat. Ann. § 5], as many states did in past years. Louisiana's statute on "mystic" or "sealed" wills requires three witnesses to the testator's having placed the document in a sealed envelope. [La. Civ. Code art. 1584] The witnesses may be required actually to witness the testator's signature, but may be permitted by state law simply to witness the testator's acknowledgment that he or she signed the will. Typically, the witnesses must also sign in the testator's presence and in the presence of each other. In general, any competent adult can act as a witness. However, only individuals who have no interest whatsoever under the will should act as witnesses. Where an "interested" individual (or his or her spouse) acts as a witness, most states provide that any will provision for the individual's benefit is void unless there are two other witnesses. Depending on the state, this may also apply to provisions appointing an executor, because an executor is entitled to a fee. Notarization is not required, although some states propose a notarized "self-proving affidavit" that is included with, and follows at the end of, the will (see Q 4:26). Special issues may arise when the testator is blind or visually impaired, illiterate, or does not speak the language in which the will is drafted. Whether and how the will can be validly executed will vary depending on state law. Many practitioners require the testator and the witnesses to initial at the bottom of each page as a guard against forgery. Some also require dating of each page, although this can be problematic when someone makes a mistake. Some require that the paragraphs break across page endings, for the same reason. These are not usually legal requirements, but attorney preference, just as some attorneys may require that all parties use the same pen, or a certain type of pen. Similarly, as a guard against claims of "undue influence," some practitioners require that the testator execute out of the presence of any interested party, or insist that the witnesses know the testator personally. It may be useful, in the event of a future will contest, to follow the same ritual every time. On the other hand, it may be necessary to adjust any ritual to accommodate the client's own need and feelings.

Q 4:25   Should any special arrangements be made if the client owns property in a foreign country?

International estate planning is not just for rich playboys. Even an elder law attorney whose client base is mostly middle class or those of yet more modest means can expect in his or her lifetime to come across the client with property, usually real estate, in a foreign country. While international estate planning can be a complex topic, involving tax treaties and special U.S. tax rules for nonresident aliens, there are few general points to keep in mind when a client owns real estate in a foreign country:

1. It may be desirable to encourage the client to execute two wills, one disposing of the U.S. estate, and the other, disposing exclusively of the foreign property, prepared by a local attorney in the foreign jurisdiction. In this situation, typically the "exordium" or introductory portion of the will should state that it does not

dispose of the property in the other jurisdiction. At the very least, if the clients are elderly, encourage them to develop a legal contact in the foreign jurisdiction with whom there is some ability to communicate in English or another language in which you have fluency. E-mail is also helpful if there are time zone issues that make telephone contact a problem.

2. If executing only one will, determine whether the other country is a signatory to the Convention of October 26, 1973, Providing a Uniform Law on the Form of an International Will, and if so, follow its requirements. In general, the execution requirements are very similar to the most common U.S. procedures; however, the statute requires that each page of the will be numbered and signed by the testator; that an "authorized person" (typically, an attorney licensed to practice in the jurisdiction or a U.S. consul) also sign the will; and that in order to provide "conclusive evidence" of due execution, a certificate must be executed by the authorized person, at the time of execution, attesting to the circumstances of the execution. A will that does not qualify in all respects may also be admitted to probate, but for a signatory nation a will that follows the Convention *must* be admitted. See Table 4-1 for a list of countries that have signed the convention.

3. Be wary of unforeseen tax consequences in other jurisdictions. Many have an "inheritance tax" structure and will require proof of payment before allowing transfer of title.

4. Consider how the two documents relate when it comes to a source of funds for payment of taxes and expenses. For example, if probate in Germany of a German will is required, and the U.S. will requires the U.S. residue to pay "all" expenses of administration and "all" taxes, do these also cover the German property passing under the German will? Or are there two estates, each with its own residue, each responsible for the expenses and taxes relating to the property in the jurisdiction? This is particularly problematic with large estates.

5. Avoid trusts. Most jurisdictions do not recognize or understand trusts, although they may have arrangements that mimic the benefits of trusts (the usufruct interest in France, for example). When it comes to real estate, keep it simple, name the surviving spouse if at all possible, and see if you can have the client dispose of the property *inter vivos* to children (if allowed—it is not always possible to divest property during lifetime) to avoid the probate issue entirely.

Table 4-1. Countries that Accept International Wills According to the Convention of October 26, 1973, Providing a Uniform Law on the Form of an International Will

States that Signed the Convention	States that have Acceded to the Convention
Iran	Niger
Sierra Leone	Portugal
United States of America	Canada
Laos	Libyan Arab Jamahiriya
Holy See	Yugoslavia
Belgium	Cyprus
Ecuador	Italy
United Kingdom	Slovenia
France	Bosnia-Herzegovina
Russian Federation	
Czechoslovakia	

Source: Official Web Site of the International Institute for the Unification of Private Law (UNIDROIT), *http://www.unidroit.org.*

Table 4-2. Estate and Gift Tax Treaties with Other Nations

Estate tax treaties exist with the following countries:

Australia*	France*	Italy	South Africa
Austria*	Germany*	Japan*	Switzerland
(No estate tax treaty with Canada, but income tax protocols address certain problems created by death-triggered "capital gains" tax in Canada)	Greece	Netherlands	United Kingdom*
Denmark*			(Estate tax treaty with Sweden terminated in 2007)
Finland	Ireland	Norway	

*Indicates that a gift treaty also exists.

Q 4:26 What is a "self-proving affidavit"?

Most states permit the use of a special provision that avoids the necessity of producing witnesses at the time the will is admitted to probate. Typically, the provisions require testimony that the testator and witnesses all sign in one another's presence and the presence of a notary public. Although most states will, by principles of comity, permit probate of a will validly executed in another state according to that state's laws, even when the procedures would not have been valid in the state of probate, it is important that the self-proving affidavit follow the formalities required in the state in which the will is to be probated. Even if such an affidavit is traditionally executed at the same time as the will and is appended to the will, it does not necessarily need to be executed at the same time as the will. That is, while one may typically want two witnesses as well as the attorney or notary (who will take the oath of the witnesses signing the affidavit), if that is not possible, the two witnesses may later execute the affidavit before a notary who was not present when the will was actually signed. This will, of course, depend upon the statutory requirements in that state for a "self-proving" affidavit. In states which also require that the testator sign the affidavit as well as the will, separate execution of an affidavit will not be possible. It cannot be overemphasized—anyone preparing a will must check the specific requirements of the jurisdiction, and not rely on generalities!

Types of Wills

Q 4:35 Are there other ways to change a will besides a codicil?

Some clients believe they can change the will by crossing out one provision and inserting something different. This may either be ineffective or at worst may constitute a revocation of the entire will. It is important to advise clients that to change a will, they should execute a codicil or a new will. In dire emergency, where intestacy is preferable to the will and there is no time to make a change, the testator could revoke the will. Methods of revocation are usually specified by statute but typically include burning, tearing in half, or "canceling," but only if actually done by the testator's own hand. A will may also be revoked when specified events occur such as divorce or remarriage; this too varies state to state. If an original will may not be found, in many states a presumption arises that it has been revoked; this is sometimes a reason to store the will with an attorney (see Q 4:4). It may be possible to "restore" the provisions of a prior will that has been superseded, merely by revoking the intervening will. This is called the "doctrine of relative revocation" and does not apply in every state. The principle behind this doctrine is that any will is preferable to intestacy.

Probate

Q 4:38   Is probate always required if a decedent owns assets?

No. Most states have a simple procedure for disposing of a person's assets, even though held in sole name, without involving the full probate process. The procedure usually involves filing an "affidavit" that lists assets briefly and states that funeral expenses and creditors have been paid (or asking that they be paid from the funds remaining). The affidavit then either states that there is nothing left, or in some states, requests approval to distribute what remains to the persons named in the will, or who take by interstate succession. This affidavit is filed in the probate court in lieu of administration, and it is the probate court that issues the order for any distribution of funds to pay claims or to distribute to heirs. One way to put this is to say that so long as a decedent owns one dime, there will be some probate involvement, a kind of "mini-probate," but that it will be very simple. While the 50 states each have additional requirements for making this "mini-probate" available—a common one being that there is no real property held in the decedent's sole name—Table 4-3 provides a quick look at the maximum value permitted for the "affidavit in lieu" process for small estates. The table is current through March 1, 2002, and attorneys should be aware that states vary on the use of an affidavit or other abbreviated process in lieu of full probate, and those variations may not be adequately captured in this table.

Table 4-3. When is Probate Required?

State	Probate Required if Gross Probate Exceeds:	Probate Required, Without Regard to Column 2, If:	Probate Not Required, Without Regard to Column 2 or 3, If:
Alabama	$3,000		
Alaska	$15,000		
Arizona	$50,000 (there is a separate single-filing proceeding available for real property with a value up to $75,000)	Estate includes over $5,000 in compensation	

Table 4-3. (Cont'd)

State	Probate Required if Gross Probate Exceeds:	Probate Required, Without Regard to Column 2, If:	Probate Not Required, Without Regard to Column 2 or 3, If:
Arkansas	$50,000		
California	$20,000 real property, $100,000 personality	$20,000 or more net of liens, encumbrances, expenses	Less than $20,000 net of liens, encumbrances, expenses
Colorado	$27,000		
Connecticut	$40,000	Any real estate	
Delaware	$20,000		
District of Columbia	$40,000		
Florida	$25,000 for Summary Administration (but Family Administration may be available if under $60,000)		No administration if nonexempt personal property does not exceed funeral expenses and expenses of last illness; Summary if decedent dead for two years
Georgia	No provision	Always unless (1) interstate and (2) mutual distribution agreed	
Hawaii	$100,000		
Idaho	$25,000		
Illinois	$50,000		
Indiana	$25,000		
Iowa	$10,000, $15,000 or $50,000 depending on who requests		
Kansas	$10,000		

Table 4-3. (Cont'd)

State	Probate Required if Gross Probate Exceeds:	Probate Required, Without Regard to Column 2, If:	Probate Not Required, Without Regard to Column 2 or 3, If:
Kentucky	No provision	Always, unless mutual distribution	
Louisiana	$50,000		
Maine	$10,000		
Maryland	$30,000 net of secured debts		Personal representative must post bond if $10,000 or more after expenses
Massachusetts	Car + $15,000		
Michigan		$15,000 net	
Minnesota	$20,000		
Mississippi	$20,000		
Missouri	$40,000		
Montana	$20,000		
Nebraska	$25,000 less liens		
Nevada	$50,000		
New Hampshire	$10,000		
New Jersey	$10,000 to spouse, $5,000 to heirs		
New Mexico	$30,000		
New York	$20,000	Any real property	
North Carolina	$10,000; $20,000 if passing to surviving spouse only	Any real property	
North Dakota	$15,000		
Ohio	$35,000	(In some circumstances may be up to $100,000)	
Oklahoma	$60,000		

Table 4-3. (Cont'd)

State	Probate Required if Gross Probate Exceeds:	Probate Required, Without Regard to Column 2, If:	Probate Not Required, Without Regard to Column 2 or 3, If:
Oregon	$50,000 personality, $90,000 real property		
Pennsylvania	$25,000		
Rhode Island	$15,000	Any real property	
South Carolina	$10,000		
South Dakota	$25,000		
Tennessee	$25,000		
Texas	$50,000	Any real property	
Utah	$25,000		
Vermont	$10,000	Any real property	
Virginia	$10,000		
Washington	$60,000		
West Virginia	No provision	No provision	
Wisconsin	$20,000		
Wyoming	$70,000		

Many states also have a procedure for an abbreviated administration. The will is offered for probate, a representative (or if no will, an administrator) is appointed, notice is provided to creditors, and many of the other requirements apply, but formal accounting procedures are not required.

Q 4:40 What are the drawbacks of probate?

Much is sometimes made of the delay and loss of privacy when an estate must be probated. Another issue can be the expense of court fees, accounting fees, and attorneys' fees. Last, and sometimes most important, is the forum it provides to disgruntled family members. In most cases, these considerations will not be of great importance, but in some cases, probate avoidance can be critical to achieving the client's goals. Delay: As noted, the delays required by the probate deadlines are not very long and not unreasonable given the issues involved, such as creditors' claims and tax computations. More pertinent is the supposed delay in getting money out to the family that may require access to the estate assets in order to live. There are two responses to this concern. First, probate and non-probate assets are not mutually exclusive; keep a joint bank account and/or small life insurance policy to provide liquidity. Second, most states permit the surviving spouse to request a "spousal allowance" paid from the estate as an expense of administration during the pendency of probate. Loss of privacy: Probate records are public records. An inventory of the decedent's property and the dispositive provisions of the will may be pored over by curious eyes for years. Some websites specialize in the wills of celebrities. Presumably a celebrity's affairs will always be public, but for the rest of the world, a pour-over will and trust will take care of most of these concerns. This concern is ameliorated somewhat in many states by provisions permitting inventories and accountings to be sent to interested parties (heirs and devisees) but not filed with the court, but the fact remains that the probate process is more open to public scrutiny than alternatives such as living trusts or beneficiary designations. Expense: Probate courts charge fees in connection with the probate proceeding, usually some fraction of the estate. If proceedings are complex and require an attorney, the attorney will also charge. What this all means will vary considerably from state to state. In Connecticut, for example, the maximum probate fee, no matter how large the estate, is $12,000. A fee is assessed based on the larger of the inventory, the Connecticut taxable estate, or the federally taxable estate, and is imposed whenever there is any probate filing, including the abbreviated "non-probate" filing, to obtain authorization for transfer of a bank account. By contrast, the attorney's fee must be "reasonable" and there is no statutory minimum. In other states, there may be a much higher court fee, the fee may only apply to the probate estate, and the attorney involved in probate may be entitled to a minimum statutory fee no matter how simple the probate process. Probate will also probably require preparation of a "probate accounting," showing changes that have occurred between date of death and distribution of the assets; this expense might be mitigated by funding a pourover trust with actively traded securities (so that no accounting is required for those assets) while leaving other assets in the decedent's name; moreover, some state requirements for a "probate accounting" will not be significantly more onerous than the work otherwise required to prepare an income tax return. In short, probate in some states may be an expensive proposition, but not in other states. This is an area that must be examined on a state-by-state basis. Problems with heirs and creditors: In almost every state a will must be "admitted" after a hearing or the right to request a hearing is made available. The disgruntled, disinherited heir can seize this occasion to bring a will contest. If there is no probate, and the plan is implemented by way of a trust, the disgruntled heir, if not a beneficiary, (1) may have no right to information about the plan in the first place, and (2) if the plan is discovered, will have to bring a suit in a court of general jurisdiction in order to "break" the trust. When it comes to creditors, the probate process provides a convenient forum in which creditors may present claims, and a fiduciary who owes the creditors a duty. By contrast, although the trust is also subject to the claims of creditors, the trustee, who owes creditors no duty, may freely distribute trust assets before claims are presented, and the creditors (like the disgruntled heir) may have more trouble discerning what was in the trust and presenting a claim. Without probate, disgruntled heirs and creditors are put to more effort in challenging the decedent's goals.

Q 4:41   What assets are not subject to probate?

As a general rule, assets that pass by beneficiary designation or by operation of law pass "outside" of probate. Assets held in trust or in joint tenancy with right of survivorship bypass probate proceedings, as do pay-on-death (or transfer-on-death) benefits payable to third parties, as well as life insurance, annuity, or other contractual rights that name beneficiaries on the death of the insured or annuitant. Real estate can "pass" to another person on the death of one owner in the case of joint tenancy or a life estate. In addition, some states authorize the use of beneficiary deeds or transfer on death deeds for real estate (including at least Arizona, Arkansas, Colorado, Kansas, Missouri, Nevada, New Mexico, Ohio, and Wisconsin), which effects the same result as pay-on-death titling does for bank accounts. The Arizona beneficiary deed, for example, is fully revocable during the grantor's life, and the beneficiaries gain no interest in the property until the death of the grantor. [Ariz. Rev. Stat. § 33–405(G)] Language to create a "beneficiary deed" can be included in any deed form, and is both straightforward and simple: "I (WE) HEREBY CONVEY TO (GRANTEE) EFFECTIVE ON MY (OUR) DEATH THE FOLLOWING DESCRIBED REAL PROPERTY (property description)." Other states (e.g., California) reach a similar result with "revocable" deeds.

Joint Tenancy

Q 4:43 What is joint tenancy?

Joint tenancy is commonly used to refer to titles held as "joint tenants with the right of survivorship" (JTWROS). JTWROS is a form of multiple ownership of real or personal property, by which full title passes intact to the survivor(s) on the death of a tenant. The distinguishing characteristic of JTWROS titling is that, upon the death of any joint tenant, the deceased joint tenant's interest in the property automatically passes to the remaining joint tenants. Thus, if three individuals own a piece of real property as joint tenants, they each own an undivided one-third interest and have equal rights to use and possession of the property. Upon the death of one of the three joint tenants, the remaining two automatically own a one-half undivided interest in the property, with each retaining the right to use and possession of that property. JTWROS deeds can usually be detected either by use of the language "jointly with rights of survivorship," or by a conveyance to A and B "and the survivor of them." Joint tenancy is not to be confused with "tenancy in common," in which multiple parties may own a share of the property but without the right of survivorship. The share owned by a tenant in common will pass not to the other tenants, but to the decedent's heirs or devisees. Indeed, some deeds indicate that a deed is JTWROS by expressly stating that the property passes "to A and B as joint tenants and not as tenants-in-common." But beware: If the language is not clear, whether the law presumes that a deed to more than one party creates rights of survivorship or not will vary from state to state.

Almost any property can be held in JTWROS form. Real estate, bank accounts, stocks and bonds, and most other properties are routinely titled in joint tenancy, particularly as between spouses. When it comes to the owners' rights during their lifetimes, however, these assets are treated differently. Most states give joint bank account holders the right to use 100 percent of the account assets. The same may or may not be true of securities accounts, and few brokerage accounts allow each joint owner unlimited access to account securities. With JTWROS real estate, the consent of all title-holders is required to convey; however, one joint owner can convey his or her proportionate share to a third party, thereby "breaking" the JTWROS status or "unity of title" and converting the title to a tenancy in common. (In one instance known to the author, when a couple cohabiting for 20 years purchased a house as JTWROS, one member of the couple conveyed to a straw party who reconveyed back, in order to sever the joint tenancy and permit the party to leave one share to the couple's child rather than the survivor.)

Q 4:46 What are the drawbacks to holding property in joint tenancy?

While holding property in joint tenancy can be an effective tool for allowing property to pass unimpeded to a spouse or child and bypasses probate, there are the following drawbacks:

1. Heirs of the decedent tenant lose out completely. For instance, if a husband with children from a former marriage and his second wife own a home in JTWROS, and the husband dies first, the second wife gets full title to the home and the children of the first marriage get no share of the home.

2. Joint tenancy can be cumbersome if the tenants divorce or a need to sell the property arises—the consent of all joint tenants is needed to sell the property, even if one formerly owned the property as his or her separate property and put the name of the other joint tenant(s) on the deed for convenience or as a gift. (A deed signed by only one party will "sever" the joint tenancy, creating a tenancy in common, and result in a conveyance of only the signatory's interest—not likely to be of interest to a buyer.)

3. Property held in joint tenancy cannot be transferred to a trust and maintain its character. The trust grantor who wishes to better control the distribution of that property must persuade the other tenant(s) to change the ownership of the property.

4. There is no income tax benefit to joint tenancy—in fact, the IRS will deem the property wholly owned by the decedent tenant unless and until the other tenant(s) can prove that *both* the joint tenants acquired the property by gift, devise, or inheritance, or that the survivor financially contributed to the ownership or maintenance of the property. [I.R.C. § 2040]

5. In some states, should one of the joint owners require Medicaid, the state may be able to seek recovery against, or place a lien upon, that owner's share, depending on who the other owners are and whether they live in the property as their "home." Even though the property will pass automatically to the survivors, the lien may survive; even if the lien is supposed to be extinguished, there may be trouble getting the Medicaid agency to remove the lien from the land records.

6. Creating a joint tenancy may subject the property to the claims of the second party's creditors (and self-interested intentions). Although the Uniform Multi-Party Accounts Statute states that joint tenants own jointly held accounts in proportion to their actual contributions (and thus an account ought not to be subject to the claims of a non-contributory tenant), it is not clear whether this will apply to brokerage accounts; at the very least, litigation may be required to prevent the claim. [See, e.g., Deutsch, Larrimore Farnish, P.C. v. Johnson, 2002 Pa. Super. 13 (2001)]

7. In community property states, holding property in joint tenancy destroys the 100 percent "step-up" in basis that otherwise would apply at the death of the first of the husband and wife pursuant to a glitch in the tax code. (see Q 4:48)

Q 4:48.1   What are the community property states?

The following states have some form of community property scheme: Arizona, California, Idaho, Louisiana, Nevada, New Mexico, Texas, Washington, and Wisconsin.

Joint-Name Bank Accounts

Q 4:50   What are the differences between "POD," "ITF," and "TOD" accounts?

Funds held in a "Payable on Death," or POD, account (usually a bank checking account), are owned solely by the decedent during his or her lifetime, and then payable at his or her death to a third party or parties designated by him or her. Most state laws now permit POD accounts at banks, savings associations, and credit unions. An alternative designation is "In Trust For," usually abbreviated as ITF. ITF accounts are sometimes also referred to as Totten trusts, after the famous New York case. [Matter of Totten, 179 N.Y. 112, 71 N.E. 748 (1904)] This form of ownership of a bank account as "A in trust for B" is essentially an implied revocable trust.

Thus, a bank account may be held in the name of "John Jones, POD Dennis Jones" or even "John and Mary Jones, POD Dennis and Diane Jones." In each case, the POD beneficiary has no ownership interest in (or ability to control the use of) the account until the death of the primary account holder, but the account can be transferred automatically on the death of the primary owner(s) without the necessity of probate administration in those states in which it is recognized.

The Uniform Multiple-Person Accounts Act [§ 12, 1, 8B U.L.A. 178 (1993)] permits POD or ITF designations as described here. The 1989 version of the act has been adopted by nine states or jurisdictions (Alaska, Arizona, Colorado, District of Columbia, Montana, Nebraska, New Mexico, North Dakota, and South Dakota). An earlier version of the act, the 1969 version (included in the Uniform Probate Code), was adopted by 18 other states (California, Florida, Georgia, Hawaii, Idaho, Indiana, Kentucky, Maine, Maryland, Minnesota, New Jersey, Oregon, South Carolina, Texas, Utah, Virginia, Washington, and Wisconsin). Although the remaining states have not expressly adopted the Uniform Multiple-Person Account Act, most states have specifically authorized POD or ITF accounts by statute. States recently adopting POD accounts (generally, in 1997) include Massachusetts, Nevada, New Hampshire, and North Carolina. As of 2002, New York and Pennsylvania still do not appear to recognize POD or ITF designations.

"Transfer on Death" (TOD) designations are now permitted by forty-nine states and the District of Columbia for stocks, bonds, mutual funds, and brokerage accounts. The lone holdout, Louisiana has not adopted any version of the Uniform TOD Security Registration Act promulgated by the National Conference of Commissioners on Uniform State Laws (NCCUSL). Neither has Texas, though that state has adopted its own statutory TOD registration provision (see SQ 4:52). As discussed earlier, some states permit the functional equivalent of TOD/POD titling for real estate (see SQ 4:41).

Q 4:52 Are "payable on death" and "in trust for" accounts permitted for stocks, bonds, and brokerage accounts?

Although ITF designations are not available for stocks, bonds, or brokerage accounts, most states permit either POD ("payable on death") or TOD ("transfer on death") accounts. The Uniform TOD Security Registration Act, finalized in 1989, has been adopted by 48 states and the District of Columbia. Only Louisiana and Texas have not yet adopted the Act, and only Louisiana does not recognize the TOD designation at all. The TOD title designation is functionally equivalent to the POD bank account title (see SQ 4:50).

It is important to note that the TOD beneficiary remains liable to the estate administrator for expenses, and (depending on which version the state has adopted) may also be liable to creditors to the extent of the property value.

The Uniform TOD Security Registration Act permits various account titles:

1. "John S. Brown TOD John S. Brown, Jr." (On John S. Brown's death, the securities are automatically transferred to his son, John S. Brown, Jr.)

2. "John S. Brown and Mary B. Brown, JTWROS, TOD John S. Brown, Jr." (John and Mary Brown own the securities jointly, and the survivor will take the entire interest by right of survivorship. On the second death, the securities will automatically transfer to their son, John S. Brown, Jr.)

3. John S. Brown and Mary B. Brown, JTWROS, TOD John S. Brown, Jr. SUB BENE Peter Q. Brown. (Same as item 2, except that if John S. Brown, Jr., is not living at the time of the death of the surviving spouse the securities will automatically go to the "substituted beneficiary" Peter Q. Brown.)

4. John S. Brown and Mary B. Brown, JTWROS, TOD John S. Brown, Jr., LDPS. ("LDPS" stands for "lineal descendants per stirpes"—this titling automatically transfers the securities to John S. Brown, Jr., on the second death but to his descendants if he is not then living.)

Trust

Types of Trusts

Q 4:60 What is an irrevocable trust?

An irrevocable trust is a trust that cannot be revoked (or significantly amended) once the trust instrument is signed; thus, the transfer of assets into the trust may qualify as a completed gift of a present interest in property, and the grantor theoretically gives up control of the assets once the transfer is made. By using the trust vehicle rather than making an outright gift, the grantor can dictate in advance, even from the grave, how assets are managed and distributed. Although the trust itself is irrevocable, the terms of the trust may be drafted with enough flexibility to cope with changes in circumstances. Such provisions include: power to remove and replace trustees; powers held by the trustee only, to amend or reform the trust to deal with changes in circumstances; powers held by the trustee to distribute to a new trust; powers held by the trustee to confer or take away distribution rights of beneficiaries; and the like. "Irrevocable" trusts may also be crafted as intentionally "incomplete" gifts if the grantor retains a power of appointment, creating a "step-up" in basis at the grantor's death.

An irrevocable trust may also be an effective vehicle when the grantor wishes to protect assets from his or her own creditors. Great care must be taken, however, to avoid what could be construed as a fraudulent transfer. Most states have statutes either criminalizing fraudulent conveyances or permitting creditors to avoid such conveyances, or both. The Uniform Fraudulent Transfer Act, for example, makes transfers voidable if they were made "with actual intent to hinder, delay, or defraud any creditor of the debtor." Recently, asset protection devices using a combination of irrevocable trusts and trustees beyond U.S. jurisdiction ("offshore trusts") have begun to fail, in some cases subjecting the settlor to criminal penalties. Moreover, many states consider a "self-funded" trust to be against public policy to the extent that it could be used to defeat the claims of creditors while at the same time allowing the settlor to benefit fully from the trust property. For example, in *Greenwich Trust Co. v. Tyson* [129 Conn. 211 (1942)], Connecticut's Supreme Court held that such a trust is subject to the claims of the settlor's creditors without regard to the terms of the trust instrument. (Ten states have now statutorily conferred creditor protection on self-settled "discretionary asset protection trusts"; these states are Alaska, Delaware, Missouri, Nevada, Oklahoma, South Dakota, Rhode Island, Tennessee, Utah, and Wyoming. Some of these "DAPTs" are subject to claims for alimony and child support, and most require that the trustee be a banking institution doing business in the jurisdiction.) Federal Medicaid law treats property held in a trust as fully available to the settlor (or spouse) to the extent that the trustee might, under any circumstances, be able to distribute that property to the settlor (or spouse). [42 U.S.C. § 1396p(d)(3)(B). This statute replaces the earlier "Medicaid qualifying trust statute," (former) 42 U.S.C. § 1396a(k)(2), repealed Aug. 10, 1993, but which applies to trusts established prior to that date. See further discussion in chapter 14.]

Q 4:62 What are the advantages of executing a revocable living trust agreement?

Living trusts are often (and not completely incorrectly) marketed as estate tax savings devices. However, living trusts do not, in and of themselves, effect any estate or income tax savings. While married couples with combined assets in excess of $2 million usually need a trust to avoid losing certain tax advantages further discussed in chapter 5, they do not necessarily need an *inter vivos* trust agreement, whether funded (a "living trust"), or unfunded. Income taxes will usually be unaffected by living trusts, even most irrevocable living trusts. One exception is that some capital gains tax savings can be accomplished in community property states by treating trust assets as community property (and thereby receiving a full step-up in tax basis on the death of the first spouse), even though the assets might have been one spouse's separate property, or held by the spouses as joint tenants, prior to establishment of the trust. However, a living trust agreement (funded or unfunded) does have some important advantages. Clients with real estate in more than one state should seriously consider establishing a revocable living trust. Because the cost of probate will be compounded by the necessity of initiating proceedings in each state where real property is located, the benefit of bypassing probate is more apparent for such individuals. The client with a trust agreement, even a simple one, can avoid the ancillary probate by the simple expedient of executing a deed transferring the real estate to the trustee and recording the deed on the land records. Funding a living trust with actively traded securities can also eliminate the expense of a probate accounting at death. The funded living trust is appropriate whenever there is a need for management and distribution by a party other than the grantor him- or herself. The advantage of private management may also be useful to those who are not incapacitated, but want to enact a wall of privacy and control between their assets and those who would make demands upon them, such as an abusive or demanding spouse or children. The trustee is the person who can say no to those that prey upon the grantor/beneficiary's good will. The trust is particularly important, however, when the grantor becomes incapacitated. The trust agreement will permit trust assets to be managed and distributed in accordance with the grantor's wishes even when the grantor becomes incapacitated, without the need for a court-appointed and supervised fiduciary or court proceedings that will be matters of public record. Those who value privacy as a general matter especially favor this aspect. This advantage is available so long as the trust is set up, even if no assets have yet been transferred to the trustee's custody, provided a power of attorney can be used to transfer property to the trust when the time comes. Thus, the most important advantage to living trusts will often be neither probate avoidance nor tax savings, but the avoidance of court supervision of property at a later date if the grantor should become incapacitated. Even as probate rules have been liberalized in most states, the guardianship and conservatorship process (or guardianship of the person and property, as it is called in some states) has remained procedurally mired in 18th century common law. While this helps provide wonderful protection for incapacitated wards, the cost is extremely high in both financial and emotional terms. For many laypersons, the prospect of submitting their personal and financial affairs to close court supervision is anathema, and a living trust may seem like a fair investment to avoid that possibility. Durable powers of attorney will accomplish much the same result, but suffer from the drawback that many third parties will resist accepting instructions from an attorney-in-fact. Trustees do not encounter such problems and therefore more effectively avoid the necessity of court proceedings. Living trusts are also often touted as a means of avoiding controversies among the intended beneficiaries of an estate plan. While most states have statutes or case law making trust contests essentially similar to will contests, the practical reality is that the lack of court supervision inherent in trust administration makes it less likely that any beneficiary (or disinherited family member) will institute a legal proceeding to contest the terms or administration of a trust. For those reasons and others, funded living trusts represent a substantial and growing portion of the estate planning marketplace. In many jurisdictions, lawyers routinely discourage the use of living trusts, particularly for clients of modest assets, but the growth of living trusts continues nonetheless. To a considerable extent, that growth is fueled by financial planners, insurance salespersons, accountants, bankers, and others who may have their own vested interest in marketing ancillary services (e.g., life insurance, investment, accounting, or banking services), but the strong public interest in avoiding the probate process is undoubtedly the principal motivating force behind the living trust phenomenon.

Q4:71　What are the disadvantages of having a joint revocable trust?

If a couple's total combined assets are more than the federal estate tax-exempt amount, $2 million in 2006, and set to increase to $3.5 million in 2009, and those assets are not roughly equally divided between the spouses, there may be some tax consequences to the estate. First, the entire trust could possibly be included in the estate of the first spouse to die (though proper drafting can easily overcome this concern). This may occur even if that spouse did not contribute all or any of the assets to the trust. Second, the entire trust may be included in the estate of the second spouse to die. This is so even if part of the trust was intended to qualify as a unified credit or bypass trust that was not supposed to be included in the estate of the second spouse (again, proper drafting should address this concern in every instance).

Q 4:72   Is it considered a "gift" for gift tax purposes when assets are transferred into the joint trust?

Yes, but a gift in any amount to a spouse is exempt from gift taxation. More importantly, the gift may be uncompleted (and the asset transferred to the trust remains in the transferor spouse's estate) if the transferor spouse retains a reversionary interest in the asset.

Q 4:73.1   What happens if the beneficiaries want to change or terminate a trust that is irrevocable?

The answer is "it depends," and it depends significantly upon what state law applies. In many states, a trust can be terminated or changed if the trustee and the beneficiaries all agree, period. In other states, the rule will be that this can be accomplished provided termination does not defeat a specified purpose or goal of the grantor. These results are usually achieved in Uniform Trust Code states. In other states, however, termination is not possible simply because trustee and beneficiaries agree. The court must find that continuation will frustrate a purpose of the settlor, perhaps even that this is the result of a change in circumstances; similarly, any change in the trust may require either reformation or application of the doctrine of "deviation," also based on the concept that change must be made to prevent frustration of the grantor's or settlor's intent. In states which do not permit "virtual representation," a court proceeding may be necessary with a guardian *ad litem* to represent the interests of unborn beneficiaries, usually the issue of the living generation.

Faced with these difficulties, practitioners may try alternate routes. Close examination of spray provisions, or provisions that permit distribution "for the benefit of" beneficiaries, may provide authority for a trustee to make distribution of virtually all assets to a modified trust. The prudent trustee may wish to obtain consent of the living generation to bind future generations through "virtual representation," and/or ensure that the recipient fund still preserves the beneficial interests of the beneficiaries of the existing trust. Drafters may also want to write into trusts provisions giving trustees broad latitude to establish other trusts and distribute to them, to terminate, etc.

Q 4:74 What kinds of trusts might an elder law attorney encounter or prepare in practice?

Although the revocable living trust currently enjoys tremendous popularity for estate planning, there are any number of variations on the basic theme. Irrevocable trusts are used less frequently, but are an important part of many estate plans. For example, an irrevocable trust may have been established to own or purchase life insurance in order to keep the insurance policy's value out of the taxable estate, or an irrevocable trust (a charitable remainder trust or charitable lead trust) may have been established to take advantage of charitable deductions while avoiding capital gains tax on substantially appreciated property. Some clients will have more than one kind of trust. The commonly used names for types of trusts are frequently nondescriptive, but among the more common trust types are the following:

- Revocable living (*inter vivos*) trusts
- Credit shelter (or exemption equivalent or "A/B") trusts (see SQ 5:65)
- Qualified terminable interest property (QTIP) trusts (see Q 5:71)
- Qualified domestic trusts (QDTs) (see SQ 5:63)
- "Crummey" trusts (see Q 5:28)
- Irrevocable life insurance trusts (ILITs) (see Q 5:88)
- Special needs (or supplemental benefits) trusts (see chapter 17)
- Charitable remainder trusts (see Q 5:77)
- Charitable lead trusts (see Q 5:83)
- Grantor retained annuity trusts (GRATs) (see Q 5:101)
- Qualified personal residence trusts (QPRTs) (see Q 5:101)
- "Grantor" trusts (not really a type of trust, but a category for determining the income tax treatment of some trusts) (see Q 4:64)

Although they may have special importance in Medicaid benefit planning (see chapter 14 for a discussion of Medicaid Trusts) rather than general estate planning, the following trust types are also frequently seen:

- "Miller" (or, sometimes, "qualified income") trusts
- "d(4)(A)" trusts (or, sometimes, "payback" trusts)
- Pooled trusts
- Income-only trusts (not to be confused with "qualified income" trusts)

Requirements for a Valid Trust

Q 4:77   What capacity is required to sign a living trust?

The standard for competency to create and sign a trust agreement may be higher than the standard applying to execution of a will (see SQ 4:22). In addition to knowing what he or she has and to whom he or she wishes his or her assets distributed, the grantor must be able to comprehend and express a desire that the assets be entrusted to another for a period of time, ultimately to be distributed to a third party. The Uniform Trust Code provides that the capacity to create and sign a revocable trust is the same as that to execute a valid will. [U.T.C. § 601] As of this writing (2007), 20 states and the District of Columbia have adopted the Uniform Trust Code in some form: Alabama, Arizona, Arkansas, District of Columbia, Florida, Kansas, Maine, Missouri, Nebraska, New Hampshire, New Mexico, North Carolina, North Dakota, Ohio, Oregon, Pennsylvania, South Carolina, Tennessee, Utah, Virginia, and Wyoming have adopted the Uniform Trust Code. Proposals for adoption of the UTC have been introduced (and may be re-introduced) in Connecticut, Oklahoma, and Massachusetts. However, many jurisdictions have made significant amendments to the UTC, so its value as a "uniform" statute is somewhat questionable.

The attorney should take particular care with married couples that both trustors are fully competent and fully involved, even to the extent of interviewing them separately. There must be a clear delineation of community and separate property, and each spouse must understand exactly where his or her trust assets will go. While intestate laws of succession protect the rights of children of former marriages, the complexities of a trust may lead to the inadvertent bypassing of these persons. As with any matter involving a couple, if the attorney senses that one spouse is dictating the terms of the trust and the other seems a little too willing to defer, a separate interview would probably be in order.

Q 4:78   What steps might an individual consider to protect against his or her own future incapacity?

Every trust document should contain some provision for the grantor's incapacity, so that if the grantor lacks the capacity to manage the trust assets or to modify or revoke the trust, the co-trustees or successor trustees can take over some or all of those responsibilities. The tests for determining incapacity may vary; typical language requires written confirmation from two doctors, one of whom is the grantor's treating physician, that the grantor lacks the capacity to continue to manage the trust. Third parties dealing with the successor trustees may (and should) require such documentation before entering into agreements with the successor. Powers of attorney may be established during the individual's lifetime, in which he or she designates others to take over health care and financial decision-making when he or she is no longer able to do so. A health care power of attorney names an agent who can act for the incapacitated person with regard to housing and health care decisions; usually this person does not have the power or authorization to handle money matters (although a health care power of attorney standing alone may be a sufficient indication of trust for the Social Security Administration to grant the agent payee status). A general durable power of attorney gives the agent the power to handle all the assets of the incapacitated person, including the ability to buy and sell real estate. It is usually effective upon execution; those who do not wish to grant such broad powers right away may opt instead for a *springing* power of attorney, which would take effect upon the incapacity of the principal. As with a trust, language should be incorporated in the *springing* power of attorney that would set the requirements for determining incapacity. If an individual has established an "unfunded" trust, or if any assets remain outside the individual's partially funded trust, a power of attorney should expressly authorize the transfer of the individual's assets to the trustee. (See chapter 10 for a discussion of powers of attorney.)

Using Trusts to Protect Assets

Q 4:79 What standards should a trust set for distributions by the trustee?

Although not technically required for a trust to be valid, a key provision in every trust is the kinds of distributions that must or may be made by the trustee. Options include one or more of the following:

- Required distribution of "income" only (the meaning of "income" then determined by the instrument itself and state law, which may include one or more versions of the Uniform Principal and Income Act; in general, "income" does not include realized capital gains)—this is a mandatory provision that does not require exercise of discretion

- The same, but with discretion to "spray" income among beneficiaries pursuant to a standard

- Discretionary distribution of principal for one beneficiary pursuant to a standard (known as a "principal invasion power")
- Discretionary distributions of principal (the power to "spray" principal) among a class of beneficiaries pursuant to a standard
- Discretionary distribution of income among one or a class of beneficiaries

Where there is no discretion on the trustee's part, limits on who may serve as trustee are fewer, but opportunities for asset protection are also fewer. Standards to be used for discretionary distributions fall into one or more of the following categories:

- For "support" (making the trust a "support" trust and thus not immune from demands by Medicaid agencies that the trust principal be spent on the beneficiaries' needs)
- Pursuant to an "ascertainable standard" that may, but need not, include the term "support" (see Qs 4:20, 5:66)—this standard is typically used so that a beneficiary may serve as trustee without the trust property being included in the beneficiary's estate for tax purposes
- "Absolute" discretion, with no objective standard (making the trust a fully "discretionary" trust and likely to be immune from the demands of creditors as a spendthrift trust and possibly, but not necessarily, protected from demands of Medicaid agencies)
- "Absolute" discretion tempered by an instruction not to make distributions that would reduce or replace government benefits (a "special needs trust," as discussed in chapter 17)

Q 4:80   Can trust assets be protected from creditors?

To the extent that a grantor has control over the trust assets, those assets will be considered available to him or her and will thus be vulnerable to creditors. This is true of assets transferred into the standard revocable living trust, as long as one or both grantors is alive (but separate property of one spouse may not be subject to the debt obligations of the other spouse, depending on state law regarding spousal obligations). A beneficiary of a trust, on the other hand, does not have control over the assets until those assets are actually distributed to him or her. Depending on the terms of the trust and state law, the beneficiary may not have the power to compel distributions provided the trustee has acted in good faith. If the grantor wishes to make sure of this, the grantor will include in the trust instrument language that confirms this, usually called the "spendthrift provision." The language typically states that neither principal nor income from the trust can be anticipated by or assigned to the beneficiary, nor can any creditor of the beneficiary attach it. The creditor cannot in effect "garnish" the trust funds or demand that the trustee pay a judgment to the creditor rather than the beneficiary. A possible exception is the IRS; a case on point holds that the Treasury may be able to levy upon even a spendthrift trust. [Internal Revenue Service v. Orr, 180 F.3d 656 (5th Cir. 1999)] Of course, once the distribution is made, the trust offers no protection to the beneficiary against his or her creditors. In many—perhaps most—states, the trust will *not* protect the assets from the grantor's own creditors if the grantor is also the beneficiary, if there are any circumstances under which the trustee could make distributions to the beneficiary. Thus, if the trust states that "only income" is payable to the grantor-beneficiary, but not principal, the principal may be immunized. By contrast, if the principal can be paid to the grantor-beneficiary "in the trustee's discretion," principal may be protected in some states, but not in others. [See, e.g., Greenwich Trust Co. v. Tyson, 129 Conn. 211 (1942)] See, however, Q 4:60 listing states that confer creditor protection on self-settled discretionary asset-protection trusts.

Q 4:82   Are gifts to an irrevocable trust subject to gift tax?

In order for a donor to be able to treat a gift to a trust as excluded from gift tax by virtue of the $12,000 (in 2006–2008) per donor, per donee "annual exclusion," the trust must be designed to satisfy the requirement that the gift be a gift of a "present interest." This usually means including provisions giving the beneficiary certain rights to withdraw the gift. These are discussed at SQ 5:28. While it is possible to limit these rights in order to safeguard some beneficiaries against imprudent withdrawal, it may not be possible to include these rights and at the same time ensure that the beneficiary will be eligible for public or medical assistance benefits. Since in most states no gift tax will actually be payable until the grantor's gifts have reached a total of anywhere from $675,000 to $2 million, it may be preferable to risk the eventual gift tax than to include the withdrawal rights.

Note also that a trust in which the grantor retains some dispositive powers, such as a power to appoint among issue, will be considered an "incomplete" gift not subject to gift tax. See further examples in Treasury Regulations Section 25.2511.

Trustees

Q 4:88 What is the "prudent investor" rule, and how does it differ from the "prudent person" rule?

Criticism of the "prudent person" rule has focused on a number of concerns. Although the prudent person rule does not expressly condone review of individual investment decisions without reference to the larger investment strategy of the trustee, in application the effect has often been to isolate individual investments that perform poorly and charge the trustee for mistakes with the benefit of perfect hindsight. The result of that tendency (or perception, at least) has historically been conservative investment strategies and resultant low rates of return. In order to permit a more balanced investment approach, the Restatement of the Law of Trusts (Third Edition, currently under revision and partially published) has adopted a "prudent investor" approach to analyzing the trustee's investment decisions. A number of states have followed suit by explicitly adopting the prudent investor principle. The Uniform Prudent Investor Act incorporates the Restatement approach, and despite having only been released in 1994, by 2008 it had already been adopted in 45 states plus the District of Columbia, excepting only Delaware, Florida, Georgia, Kentucky, Louisiana, and New York. [See *http://www.nccusl.org*]

Q 4:92 Is a corporate trustee the best choice?

Not necessarily. Corporate trustees may refuse to become trustees of trusts with assets deemed too minimal, and grantors may wish to do some research on typical corporate trustee fees before designating them in their trust instruments. There is an argument that corporate trustees have a built-in conflict, because their employers benefit to the extent that they can hang on to the assets of the trust. Some trustors prefer that level of conservatism, especially when the trust beneficiaries tend to be irresponsible, but a family member or friend will probably have a much better understanding of the needs of the beneficiaries. Corporate trustees may also be limited by their parent firms as to how the trust assets are to be invested. Banks often have a single national pooled fund for assets of all trusts (or all trusts under a certain figure, such as $2 million), which may or may not be sufficiently diversified or well-suited for certain assets. The trustees may be unable to take advantage of investment opportunities in their own communities. Again, the trustor may prefer this level of conservatism rather than risk having a family member invest all the assets frivolously. Finally, the corporate trustee's mechanism for making decisions on discretionary distributions may be too slow and cumbersome for some clients, particularly those establishing trusts for "special needs" beneficiaries. If this is an issue, it is important to investigate how such decisions will be handled, and to explore such options as a non-corporate "committee" to make (or "recommend") distribution decisions.

Chapter 5

Estate Planning

Estate and gift tax considerations have been the major factor shaping estate planning decisions in the past several decades. However, in fact most Americans now have little reason for concern about the prospect of owing taxes at death. With the federal tax exemption equivalent amount now $2,000,000 (in 2008), and scheduled to increase progressively to $3,500,000 in 2009, with ultimate repeal in 2010, few decedents' estates face any federal tax liability. Even if the full repeal never is effected, current political discussions focus on an exemption in the range of $3,500,000 to $5,000,000. Prior to 2004, under federal law the exemption applied to asset transfers made during one's lifetime as well as those made at death using a "unified system." This has meant that those not expecting to pay estate taxes at death did not have to be concerned about gift taxes during lifetime. The estate and gift tax exemptions parted company in 2004, when the estate tax exemption equivalent reached $1,500,000 and the gift tax exemption remained fixed at $1,000,000, but either number is larger than the total value of 98% of Americans' estates (according to the Internal Revenue Service).

Why make the effort to understand these tax regimes, then? Leaving aside the possibility that one may encounter wealthy clients with obviously taxable estates and would prefer not to refer them to others, there are also those times when clients who seem to live modestly find themselves unexpected millionaires. In the late 1990s, before the steep stock market declines, many professionals saw their humble retirement funds zoom into the millions; localized real estate booms can cause the vacation cottage to be valued as if it were a palace; and an old family business or farm with hard assets like land or machinery could turn out to be an "estate" incurring more tax than cash on hand with which to pay.

This chapter discusses the exclusions, exemptions, and deductions available to ease the tax burden including the unified credit exemption equivalent, referred to above, and the marital deduction, which allows assets to pass tax-free to the donor's or decedent's spouse. For those whose estates are valued at (or might reach) taxability, there are a number of estate planning choices to consider. Estate and gift tax basics are also discussed, as are the most commonly used estate planning approaches, including lifetime gifts, marital deduction planning, charitable giving, life insurance, and valuation discounts. It is important for the beginner or general practitioner to recognize that some of the techniques described in this chapter are considered "complex" estate planning and it is advisable to do further study or obtain an expert's review before undertaking such techniques alone. Helpful resources include:

- William D. Mitchell, *Estate & Retirement Planning Answer Book* (2006 Ed.) (Aspen Publishers).
- BNA Tax Management Portfolio Series (available on disk or in multiple spiral volumes)—although expensive, if one were to choose a single resource for tax information, this would be the one; it may be available in a law library near you.
- Jeffrey N. Pennell, A. James Casner, *Estate Planning* (6th Ed.) (Aspen Publishers).
- Howard M. Zaritsky, *Tax Planning for Family Wealth Transfers: Analysis with Forms* (RIA) (other titles also useful).
- For charitable planning: Conrad Teitell, *Deferred Giving*; also *Portable Planned Giving Manual* (and many

other titles), published on Mr. Teitell's own label, Tax-wise Giving (*http ://www.taxwisegiving.com*).

- Archives of the discussion groups ABA-TAX and ABA-PTL (*see http://www.abanet.org*).

Overview

Q 5:1 What are the major estate planning approaches during phase-in of the federal estate tax repeal?

The major estate planning approaches include:

1. *"Bypass" planning.* Gifts or bequests to spouses are tax-free regardless of value, so it is simple (from a tax perspective) to leave a decedent's entire estate to the surviving spouse. By this method, any tax liability will be due only at the second death. But there are good reasons to "bypass" some of the marital deduction and incur at least some tax liability on the first spouse's death, if for no other reason than to utilize the full exemption equivalent amount for each spouse. Thus, a couple worth $4 million, both dying in 2008, can effectively pass their entire joint estate to devisees without incurring any tax liability, so long as they have planned appropriately to take advantage of the $2 million exemption equivalent amount on each death; the first spouse's exemption

is "lost" if everything passes to the survivor and is only taxed at his/her death. Credit shelter trusts, QTIP (qualified terminable interest property) trusts, and QDOTs (qualified domestic trusts) fare typically used in marital deduction planning. Estate tax repeal as adopted in 2001 will accelerate the increase in the exemption equivalent amount, but will retain federal estate taxes until 2010. Meanwhile, state estate tax systems, long relegated to near-irrelevance by the use of the federal credit for state estate taxes paid, will gradually increase in importance as individual states decide whether to abandon, maintain, or even increase their estate tax collections.

2. *Lifetime gifts.* Gifts completed during the decedent's lifetime can reduce the taxable estate on death. The fact that the federal tax system is unified—that is, gift and estate taxes are calculated on the basis of the total amount given during life and at death— reduces the effectiveness of lifetime gifts, and the lower exemption amount for lifetime gifts as compared with transfers at death (since 2004) further complicates lifetime giving. Still, gifts of $12,000 per year or less ($10,000 plus an inflation factor that by 2006 had increased the amount to $12,000, with an almost certain increase to $13,000 likely in 2009) avoid gift taxation altogether, so annual gifts can be structured to reduce the final estate size without incurring any current tax liability. A common method of making gifts is to transfer life insurance (or give cash to be used to pay life insurance premiums) to maximize the value of the property received by the beneficiary. Gifting techniques to make transfers without incurring tax frequently involve irrevocable life insurance trusts (ILITs) and so-called "Crummey" trusts (see Q 5:28). Under some circumstances, it may even be advisable to make gifts early and incur gift tax liability, if tax liability is certain to occur later on. The reason for this is that the amounts used to pay the gift tax will not be subject to the gift tax themselves, whereas the entire estate is taxed even though some must go to pay taxes. Phase-out and ultimate repeal of the federal estate and generation-skipping taxes will not necessarily affect the gift tax, which is also subject to a cap.

3. *Charitable giving.* Lifetime gifts and bequests (at death) to charitable organizations avoid taxation altogether. They do not usually increase family wealth; the estate tax saved is usually offset or exceeded by the "loss" of the gifted property. (One way of putting this to a client is that the client can choose to leave something to

charity or to have the IRS take it instead.) Some of the more complicated charitable instruments can at least theoretically actually reduce taxes while maintaining (or even possibly increasing) total estate size, but these should be viewed with some skepticism. If it looks too good to be true, it probably is. In addition to outright gifts or bequests to charity, charitable planning techniques include charitable remainder trusts (CRTs) and charitable lead trusts (CLTs). The financial value of these devices will decrease as the estate tax repeal is phased in, though income tax benefits will continue to be realizable using charitable planning.

4. *Irrevocable trusts.* Technically not a separate planning device at all, irrevocable trusts are usually used as a means of effecting one tax planning technique (lifetime giving) without giving up the ability to impose restrictions on the use of the gift by its recipients. An irrevocable trust can be designed to receive (or purchase) life insurance on the grantor's life, in which case it will often be referred to as an irrevocable life insurance trust. With the increase in federal exemption equivalent amounts and the ultimate elimination of federal estate taxes, irrevocable trusts will become less important as an estate planning tool. This is especially true because gift taxes will remain in effect, although the elimination of basis step-up may actually make some gifts easier to make during life.

5. *Valuation discounts.* Several of the more popular modern estate planning techniques are effected by discounting the value of assets. This can be accomplished by limiting the transferability or majority control of property, for example. Because of the relationship of capital gains taxes and estate taxes, such valuation discounts do not avoid taxes altogether: What is saved in estate taxes will later incur capital gains taxes, although the capital gains tax rates will be far less. Because of the wide difference in the maximum tax rates between those two systems, coupled with the desire to delay tax liability to later dates, valuation discounts can still significantly increase the total amount distributed to heirs. Some of the more common examples of valuation discount techniques include family limited partnerships (FLPs), limited liability companies (LLCs), and qualified personal residence trusts (QPRTs). Valuation discounts often are accompanied by a gifting regimen: The value of the gift can be reduced, permitting larger portions of discounted assets to be transferred and, in turn, further increasing the valuation discount. If estate taxes continue

to be phased out, and "carryover basis" is reinstated as scheduled for 2010 (that is, no more "step up" in basis at death for assets over a certain amount), valuation discounts will become unattractive in most circumstances.

Q 5:2 What tax considerations affect estate planning choices?

The estate and gift tax system was established by the federal government to prevent individuals from accumulating great wealth and passing it intact to succeeding generations. Avoidance of these taxes, or minimizing their impact, was the impetus behind the creation of most current estate planning techniques. Transfers of property during lifetime and at death are subject to federal taxes. The system of transfers taxes has been "unified," with a total exemption for both kinds of transfers. Estate planning took this into account and aggressive planners could reduce estate taxes by making transfers early, so that growth on the transferred assets would escape estate taxes. The Tax Reform Act of 1001 (also known as EGTRRA) changed this. While the system is still "unified," with both kinds of transfers "counted" at death when computing estate tax, gifts have a lower threshold for tax and gifts that might not incur tax at death will incur tax if made during lifetime. The reason? As the tax thresholds increase, the concern was that taxpayers would decide to make gifts for income tax avoidance—shifting income-producing property to children with lower income-tax brackets.

In addition to a unified system for lifetime transfers and transfers on death, the federal tax system had for many years included a "credit" for state death taxes paid, whether estate taxes (imposed on the total assets of the decedent) or an inheritance tax (imposed on the recipient, and often varying with the type of recipient). Accordingly, over the years states had gradually abandoned their separate tax systems in favor of a "pick-up" tax that was tied directly to the federal tax credit. (see Table 5-3 in Q 5:14) With the Tax Reform Act of 2001, the "credit" changed to a mere "deduction," and by 2004, no further deduction was available. Since 2001, therefore, as the federal estate taxes have been disappearing, the states have been forced to recreate their separate death tax schemes to recoup the revenue lost by the disappearance of the old "pick-up" tax. The result is a much more complicated tax situation facing the estate planner. No longer can planning address primarily the federal tax consequences but must take into account multiple tax thresholds depending upon the decedent's domicile and the location of the property (if real estate).

Against this background of confusion, however, is the overall increase in the amount most taxpayers may pass free of tax, whether gift tax or estate tax. Presently, the vast majority of American taxpayers are not affected by estate or gift tax planning concerns, because federal law imposes estate tax only on those estates that exceed $2,000,000 (in 2006) (increasing to $3.5 million in 2009). (The estate tax is scheduled to be completely eliminated in 2010 and replaced by a capital gains tax based approach (see Table 5-1 in SQ 5:7), but Congress has again declined to make this change permanent and most practitioners believe it likely that some form of estate tax will remain.) The estate tax system includes various exclusions, exemptions, and deductions that are still relevant to estate planning for those clients whose assets exceed the threshold amounts. The most important of these are the unified credit exemption equivalent, which exempts (for estate tax purposes) combined gift and estate transfers up to $2,000,000 in 2006 [I.R.C. § 2010(c)] and the unlimited marital deduction, which allows assets to pass tax-free to the donor's or decedent's spouse. [I.R.C. §§ 2056, 2523] (Note, however, that the unlimited marital deduction is not available to a noncitizen spouse (see SQ 5:62).) Prior to 2004, the federal estate and gift tax systems had lock-step identical exemptions, but they have now parted company. (See Table 5-1 in SQ 5:7.) This means that a gift during lifetime might incur tax even though if made at death it would not do so.

Other tax concerns that affect estate planning include the "generation-skipping tax" (GST, see SQ 5:102), the capital gains tax (because at death an asset's basis is "stepped up" so that holding an asset until death may save capital gains tax for the ultimate recipient), and the "kiddie tax" (by which the net unearned income of a child under age 14 at the end of the taxable year is generally taxed at the parent's marginal rate if it is greater than the child's rate). Finally, income tax rules will affect estate planning, including steeper income tax brackets for trust income than for individuals and income tax imposed on accelerated distributions from retirement plans and annuities that may be imposed when trusts are named as beneficiaries.

Q 5:3   What is the general relationship of estate planning to long-term care planning?

Although estate and inheritance tax considerations and long-term care concerns may be incorporated into the same client's estate plan, the direct connection will appear relatively infrequently, and sometimes, the planning involved may be directly contradictory. Still, a client with tax planning issues may also have a child, spouse, or other beneficiary with long-term care concerns, so an elder law attorney must be conversant with both tax and long-term care issues in order to adequately assess clients' needs (see chapters 14 through 18 for a discussion of long-term care).

Even though most clients concerned about paying for long-term care expenses need not also fear paying estate tax, they must nonetheless be advised of the importance of estate planning as part of the long-term care plan. It may be desirable, or even necessary, to disinherit a disabled spouse or child, for example, or to provide for a spouse's share to be held in a testamentary trust, in order to qualify for public assistance (see chapter 14 for a discussion of Medicaid trusts and chapter 17 for a discussion of special needs trusts).

Other taxes may be more important in planning for long-term care expenses, particularly if the gift is large and the possibility of requiring long-term care uncertain. These will include gift taxes, particularly in states which impose gift taxes on transfers far below federal thresholds; capital gains tax payable by transferees; loss of the capital gains tax exclusion on sale of a principal residence when the home is transferred; potential loss of property tax exemptions for the elderly (or gain of such exemptions by transfer to a disabled person); and income tax payable when retirement assets are cashed in. Finally, the standard estate planning techniques appropriate to save estate taxes may have disastrous consequences when long-term care planning is involved. A typical problem is the "bypass" trust for a surviving spouse created within an *inter vivos* trust instrument, which permits invasion of principal for the surviving spouse's needs but does not permit trust termination. Under Medicaid laws, this trust must be entirely consumed before the surviving spouse can be eligible for benefits.

Estate and Gift Tax Basics

Q 5:4   Where are the relevant tax statutes and regulations found?

The Internal Revenue Code of 1986 is a comprehensive code, covering income, estate and gift taxes, as well as administrative matters. Chapter 11B, Estate Tax [26 U.S.C. §§ 2001 et seq.], and chapter 12B, Gift Tax [26 U.S.C. §§ 2501 et seq.], are the principal sources of law on estate and gift taxes.

A large body of regulations interprets the federal tax code. Private letter rulings, tax court, and other court decisions add to the extraordinary abundance of law on tax and tax planning issues. Add innumerable commentaries and treatises, and the interpretation of the tax laws can be seen as a major national industry. It is important for the practitioner to remember that private letter rulings may not be cited or used as precedent by anyone except the private party that requested the ruling; the IRS is not bound by decisions of state courts interpreting state law except those of the highest state court; and the IRS is not bound by decisions of federal courts, except by decisions of federal appeals courts in the circuit with jurisdiction over the taxpayer.

There are many useful online sources for the tax code and other tax research materials, provided the practitioner is attentive in checking how current the available copies. Leaving aside the commercial sites (such as CCH) that may be helpful but expensive, the following are some useful free web sites:

- Internal Revenue Code (FINDLAW site): http://caselaw.lp. findlaw.com/casecode/uscodes/toc.html
- Code of Federal Regulations (Check Title 26 for the Treasury Regulations): http://www.access.gpo.gov/nara/cfr/index.html
- IRS Forms (this site has changed its URL often, and you may have to return to the IRS main page): http://www.irs.ustreas.gov/ formspubs/index.html
- Revenue Rulings (and more): http://www.taxlinks.com/
- Letter Rulings and IRS materials: http://www.legalbitstream.com
- Chief Counsel Notices: http://www.irs.gov/foia/lists/0, id=97652,00. html; Chief Counsel Bulletins: http://www.irs.gov/foia/lists/0, id=97720,00.html

Q 5:6   What is the interplay between federal estate taxes and gift taxes, and how may "annual exclusion" gifts escape both?

Through 2004, the federal estate and gift tax structure provided for a unified estate and gift tax structure. (See Table 5-1 in SQ 5:7.) The federal estate and gift tax system at death exempts total combined transfers up to an "exemption equivalent amount," set at $1 million in the year 2002 and scheduled to increase incrementally thereafter until 2009, reaching $2 million by 2006. [I.R.C. § 2010(c)] (Starting in 2004, the threshold at which tax is imposed diverged, with $1 million set as the threshold for gift tax and the estate tax increasing progressively.) Both taxes are graduated, so that larger gifts (and estates) incur a higher percentage tax. Because the federal estate tax and gift tax are "unified,"

with earlier gifts included when computing tax at each gift and ultimately, at death, the rate will be based on the entire value of gifts and
estate transferred during life and at death. In other words, if a taxpayer
with $2.5 million made a lifetime gift of $2 million in 2006, and died with
only the $500,000 retained, the only tax *at death* would be imposed on the
$500,000 by which total assets passing during lifetime and at death
exceeded the $2 million threshold. (When making the $2 million gift,
she would have had to pay gift tax on the $1 million by which the gift
exceeded the $1 million gift tax threshold, since the gift was made after
2004.) However, "annual exclusion" lifetime gifts escape both gift and
estate taxes entirely. The "annual exclusion" was $10,000 per year but
has been given inflation adjustments since 1999, and is now is available
for each $12,000 gift per donor, per donee, in each year, provided the gift
is of a "present interest" (see Q 5:19). The amount doubles if the donor's
spouse agrees that both partners' annual exclusions may be used even if
the gift is actually made by just one partner, provided the other spouse
agrees to have all gifts taxed the same way as if made half by each. Thus, a
couple with five children and five unusually lovable sons- or daughters-
in-law might give $240,000 per year, if they so chose, without any gift or
estate tax consequences whatsoever.

> **Example 5-1.** Mrs. Jones has an estate valued at $2 million. In 1999,
> she made a gift of $500,000 to her daughter, and in 2000 another gift
> of $250,000 each to her daughter and granddaughter. Mrs. Jones dies
> in 2002. The 1999 gift reduced her lifetime exemption equivalent
> amount by $490,000 (the first $10,000 of that gift bore no gift tax
> consequences—the annual exclusion then was $10,000 and had not
> yet increased to $12,000), leaving her with a total available credit
> exemption amount in that year of $160,000 ($650,000, the applicable
> exemption equivalent amount in 1999, minus the $490,000 used by
> the gift). Because she did not die in 1999, the remaining exemption
> equivalent amount in that year became irrelevant.
>
> Mrs. Jones's 2000 gifts would have reduced her exemption
> equivalent amount by an additional $480,000 (because $10,000 of
> the gift to each recipient bore no tax consequences), except for the
> fact that in 2000 she had only $185,000 remaining of her exemption
> equivalent amount ($675,000—the 2000 equivalent amount—minus
> the $490,000 used by the 1999 gift). Consequently, she had to pay a
> gift tax on $295,000 of the gift (the $480,000 taxable gift minus the
> remaining $185,000 exemption equivalent amount).
>
> In the year of her death, the exemption equivalent amount rose to
> $1 million. She used only $675,000 of that, so the next $325,000 of

her estate will pass tax-free. The result: even though she paid gift taxes at the time of her 2000 gift, the increasing estate tax exemption equivalent amount operated to relieve her estate of some of the additional estate taxes in subsequent years. Of course, if her total estate had been just enough to incur gift taxes with her 2000 gifts and not enough to reach the exemption equivalent amount upon her death in 2002, she would have paid transfer taxes that she could have avoided by simply retaining her assets until death.

This interplay between federal estate and gift taxes ended in 2004. In that year the estate tax exemption amount rose to $1.5 million but the gift tax exemption amount remained at $1 million. The gift tax exemption amount does not change, though the exemption amount increases for estate taxes and the estate tax is, ultimately, scheduled for repeal. After the estate and gift taxes are "decoupled" but before repeal of the estate tax, use of the gift tax exemption amount will continue to reduce the remaining available estate tax exemption equivalent amount, but taxable gifts over $1,000,000 during the donor's lifetime will be subject to gift taxation even though there might not have been an estate tax if the donor held the same property until death. But if Mrs. Jones' second round of gifts had occurred in 2004, with a $1 million gift tax exclusion, and her death in 2005, with a $1,500,000 estate tax exclusion, the only transfer tax paid by her or her estate would have been on the amount remaining in her estate over $500,000 at the time of her death.

Q 5:7 How exactly does the unified estate and gift tax system work?

The Internal Revenue Code imposes a tax on gift transfers [I.R.C. § 2501] and estate transfers [I.R.C. § 2001], but allows U.S. citizens a substantial credit, or exemption, on all transfers under both categories. [I.R.C. §§ 2505, 2010, respectively] Gift tax is cumulative over the lifetime of the donor, that is, even if no tax is owed yet, it must be recalculated every time a taxable gift is made. At the death of the donor, any amount of the gift tax credit not used during the donor's lifetime can be applied to his or her estate tax liability. If gift transfers have used up the unified credit, no exemption is available for death transfers on the same individual's estate. However, even if the gift tax credit is used up, the now greater estate tax credit (or exemption) will be available.

From 1987 through 1997 the unified credit was $192,800, which was the tax imposed on an estate valued at $600,000. In other words,

$600,000 of one's estate would not be subject to estate or gift tax, thus constituting a tax savings of $192,800. The Taxpayer Relief Act of 1997 (TRA '97) increased the exemption amounts gradually, and were expected to increase the amount to $1 million in the year 2006. [Former I.R.C. § 2010(c)] The Economic Growth and Tax Relief Reconciliation Act of 2001 further modified the schedule for incremental increases in the exemption amount (and ultimate repeal of the estate tax). At the same time the maximum estate and gift tax rate decreases from the pre-2001 55 percent (including a 5 percent surcharge immediately repealed beginning in 2002) to a high of 45 percent in 2007 (with a 1 percent decrease each year in the top tax rate beginning in 2003). Under the 2001 Act, exemption equivalent amounts for the two taxes will increase (though not identically) and maximum tax rates decrease as shown in Table 5-1.

Table 5-1. Estate and Gift Tax Exemptions and Rates

Year	Federal Estate Tax Exemption Equivalent	Maximum Rate	Gift Tax Exemption	GST Exemption
2002	$1 million	50% (+5% surcharge)	$1 million	$1.1 million
2003	$1 million	49%	$1 million	$1.1 million
2004	$1.5 million	48%	$1 million	$1.5 million
2005	$1.5 million	47%	$1 million	$1.5 million
2006	$2 million	46%	$1 million	$2 million
2007	$2 million	45%	$1 million	$2 million
2008	$2 million	45%	$1 million	$2 million
2009	$3.5 million	45%	$1 million	$3.5 million
2010	Tax Repeal	0%	$1 million	Tax Repeal
2011	$1 million	50%	$1 million	$1.1 million

Until 2004 the tax burden was the same whether the decedent's property was transferred during his or her lifetime, after death, or both. Moreover, gift tax is "tax-exclusive," meaning that the tax is imposed only on the amount actually transferred to the donee, and the amount used to pay the gift tax is not subject to tax. Estate tax is "tax-inclusive," because the tax is imposed on the value of the property transferred and on funds used to pay the tax. At least at face value, making a lifetime gift looked preferable, although it had to be kept in mind that the donor and donee would lose the value of the tax money paid for the period between the time of the gift and the time of the donor's death. The total amount of tax paid (assuming no significant diminution in the donor's estate size) would always be lower with substantial gifts, and so wealthy clients were well advised to make gifts even though the credit amount may be fully utilized and the tax paid. This good planning technique largely evaporated after the decoupling of estate and gift taxes in 2004—gifting early would result in tax that would never have to be paid if the assets were held until death, and the only benefit of early gifts would be to remove from one's estate any growth that would incur after the gift, and provided that the gift did not exceed $1 million.

Further thoughts on planning in light of these tax changes may be found in Q 5:55.

Q 5:8   What is the "step-up" in basis, and what is "carryover basis"?

Capital gains tax is imposed on the difference between the proceeds of a sale or other disposition of an asset (other than a gift), and the owner's "basis" in the property. "Basis," in the hands of the original owner, is what he or she paid for the property.

Under existing law, when one person gives property to a second person, the second person "takes" the first person's "basis" in the property. That is carryover basis. If A buys Black acre for $100, and gives it to B (at which time it is worth $200), when B sells it for $300, B pays capital gains tax on the difference between B's sales price ($300) and A's original basis ($100). Capital gains tax is due on $200.

Under existing law, when one person dies owning property, and as a result the property passes to a second person, the property's basis is "stepped up" to its value on the date of death. This is the "step-up" in basis. If A buys Blackacre for $100, and dies leaving the property to B, at which time it is worth $200, when B sells it for $300, B pays capital gains tax on the difference between B's sales price ($300) and the date of death value ($200). Capital gains tax is due on $100. Also under current law, if the property were worth $50 when A died, B would pay capital gains tax on the difference between $300 and $50—this is a step *down*, something not seen in many years, but now commonplace with the steep stock market declines following the year 2000.

The Economic Growth and Tax Relief Reconciliation Act of 2001 [H.R. 3, 107th Cong. (2001)], if not repealed or amended, calls for the imposition of a modified carryover basis structure beginning in 2010 (after full repeal of the estate tax). Property received as a result of the death of the original owner will maintain the same income tax basis as it had in the original owner's estate (unless the fair market value on the date of the decedent's death is lower than the decedent's basis), resulting in the imposition of capital gains taxes upon sale by the recipient. This is the same rule that now applies to property received by gift.

This significant change in the income tax treatment of inheritances would be tempered by a substantial exemption. The recipient(s) of a decedent's property will be permitted to claim a basis "stepped-up" to the date of death values totaling $1.3 million, and surviving spouses will receive an additional $3 million of "stepped-up" basis. In other words, the appreciation in value (not the total value at death but the increase in value) during the decedent's life will remain untaxed up to as much as $4.3 million. Any increase in value over that exempt amount will be taxed to the recipients at sale.

Q 5:9   If the "step up" is eventually lost under EGTRRA, how will values be determined so that carryover basis exemptions can be determined?

Under the Economic Growth and Tax Relief Reconciliation Act of 2001 the carryover basis exemptions will be established by the decedent's personal representative based on fair market values as of the date of death. Final regulations for determining carryover basis in individual situations will need to be adopted before the effective date of the carryover basis regime. Unfortunately, there is no relief for taxpayers who did not receive the exemption and who cannot establish the original basis. Many practitioners feel that a "carryover basis" regime will be a nightmare of administrative complexity. In many cases, clients seem quite unable to track their own basis in property, and it is inconceivable that a family will be able to track basis for centuries as it is "carried over" from generation to generation.

Q 5:10   What assets are subject to estate and gift taxes?

For purposes of federal tax computation and payment, the "gross estate" includes all property, real or personal, tangible or intangible, under the control of the decedent immediately prior to death (or gift), including revocable living trusts, most life insurance, and innumerable other categories of assets, but excluding annual exclusion gifts and other excluded gifts. [I.R.C. § 2033] Most states follow the same approach to defining "estate" for tax purposes, although "inheritance tax" states may exclude certain types of property, such as life insurance, or the employer-provided portion of retirement benefits. The definition of "estate" for probate purposes has almost no relevance to estate or gift tax considerations.

Q 5:12 How do the states' estate and gift tax systems figure into estate planning decisions?

Most states have estate and gift taxation systems modeled on the federal tax structure. Although a handful (about 15) impose an inheritance tax, and states are free to set their estate tax at whatever level they choose, until 2001 the trend was to track the federal exemption equivalent amount.

Moreover, until 2005 federal estate and gift tax included a tax credit (not a deduction but rather a dollar-for-dollar reduction of federal tax liability generated by payment of state taxes) for state estate and gift taxes paid. The federal tax credit was limited by a formula set out in the federal Tax Code. As a result, if a state chooses to set its estate and gift tax in accordance with the federal credit formula, the state tax was effectively paid through the federal tax liability. [I.R.C. § 2011(b)] Thus, a state could choose to impose such a tax without increasing the tax liability of its decedents' estates, and most states had followed the federal invitation.

This federal credit system was phased out under the Economic Growth and Tax Relief Reconciliation Act of 2001, which became effective in 2002. For 2002 the value of the state estate tax credit was reduced by 25 percent, and shrank by 25 percent each year until complete repeal of the credit in 2005, and is now obsolete. Instead, beginning in 2005, state estate taxes actually paid will be a deduction (but not a credit) against federal estate taxes. States that tied their own estate tax to the amount of the federal *credit* saw their estate tax revenues shrink and disappear altogether in 2005.

States have responded to this change either by leaving their statutes in place (resulting in an automatic reduction and eventual elimination of tax), by changing their laws to leave the current rates unchanged (usually by revising the law so that the tax is computed based on the credit available in 2000 or 2001 and thereby effectively increasing the total estate tax liability), or by increasing their estate taxes in some other way in order to take advantage of the savings in taxes by estates. Individual states may respond differently, depending on local politics, budget considerations, and history of state transfer taxes.

States have taken essentially two tacks: (1) ignore or scale back the increases in the exemptions; and (2) tie the tax to the state death tax credit prior to EGTRRA, such as December 31, 2001. The result is a hodgepodge of tax computations often requiring the filing of an obsolete 706 in order to compute the then-effective credit. For those that change the exemption, it is common to set back the exemption to $850,000 in 2004, $950,000 in 2005, and $1,000,000 in 2006 through 2009. For those that use a different state death tax credit, in most cases the option chosen is to tie the state's tax to the credit in effect in 2001, computed as follows:

Table 5-2. State Death Tax Credit 12/31/2001

Adjusted Taxable Estate	*Maximum Tax Credit*
Not over $90,000	$8/10$ of 1% of the amount by which the adjusted taxable estate exceeds $40,000
Over $90,000 but not over	$400 plus 1.6% of the $140,000 excess over $90,000
Over $140,000 but not	$1,200 plus 2.4% of the over $240,000 excess over $140,000
Over $240,000 but not	$3,600 plus 3.2% of the over $440,000 excess over $240,000
Over $440,000 but not	$10,000 plus 4% of the over $640,000 excess over $440,000
Over $640,000 but not	$18,000 plus 4.8% of the over $840,000 excess over $640,000
Over $840,000 but not	$27,600 plus 5.6% of the over $1,040,000 excess over $840,000
Over $1,040,000 but not	$38,000 plus 6.4% of the over $1,540,000 excess over $1,040,000
Over $1,540,000 but not	$70,800 plus 7.2% of the over $2,040,000 excess over $1,540,000
Over $2,040,000 but not	$106,800 plus 8% of the over $2,540,000 excess over $2,040,000

Table 5-2. (Cont'd)

Adjusted Taxable Estate	_Maximum Tax Credit_
Over $2,540,000 but not	$146,800 plus 8.8% of the over $3,040,000 excess over $2,540,000
Over $3,040,000 but not	$190,800 plus 9.6% of the over $3,540,000 excess over $3,040,000
Over $3,540,000 but not	$238,800 plus 10.4% of over $4,040,000 the excess over $3,540,000
Over $4,040,000 but not	$290,800 plus 11.2% of over $5,040,000 the excess over $4,040,000
Over $5,040,000 but not	$402,800 plus 12% of the over $6,040,000 excess over $5,040,000
Over $6,040,000 but not	$522,800 plus 12.8% of over $7,040,000 the excess over $6,040,000
Over $7,040,000 but not	$650,800 plus 13.6% of over $8,040,000 the excess over $7,040,000
Over $8,040,000 but not	$786,800 plus 14.4% of over $9,040,000 the excess over $8,040,000
Over $9,040,000 but not	$930,800 plus 15.2% of over $10,040,000 the excess over $9,040,000
Over $10,040,000	$1,082,800 plus 16% of the excess over $10,040,000

Q 5:13 Which states impose an estate tax?

In 2001, every state imposed an estate and gift tax of at least the federal credit amount, and most relied solely on the credit amount, at least for estates taxed solely within the state. Reduction in the state death tax credit, and increases in the federal unified credit exemption equivalent, followed ultimately by complete elimination of the state death tax credit, has meant massive loss of tax revenues to those states. These "pick-up" taxes remain on the books—presumably in case the tax repeal statute does, in fact, "sunset," and the _status quo ante_ returns in 2011.

In the meantime, the solution for many states has been to "decouple" their statutes from federal law—to impose taxes notwithstanding federal repeal. Some states chose to follow the old approach, but to apply the rules as if it were still 2001; others have created their own estate tax system; yet others have simply retained their existing "inheritance" taxes imposed on those who inherit (usually, at rates differing depending upon who inherits). All in all, as of April 2008, twenty-one states imposed some kind of "death tax." For those with pre-existing inheritance taxes, tax may be due on relatively small estates; for those with estate taxes, the threshold for tax ranges from $675,000 at the low end to $2 million at the higher end.

While for many states, the trend has been to enact new legislation preserving some estate tax revenues despite the repeal of the federal death tax credit for state death taxes, other states have followed the national Republican push for death tax repeal by repealing their own death taxes. Numerous states repealed their own inheritance tax schemes in the period preceding the federal estate tax changes of 2001 and the trend continued even after loss of the estate tax credit (for example, South Dakota repealing its tax in 2002), with eight states having repealed inheritance tax since 2003. Moreover, states like Florida, with a constitutional prohibition against any "death tax," are effectively unable to address the loss of revenue from the repeal of the state death tax credit.

This variation among the states can be particularly problematic for those who own property in multiple states. New York's approach is to pick up the difference between the total decoupled state death tax credit (for ALL property in the estate, whether or not the other property is in a state that has decoupled) and the share of the state death tax credit allocated to property in those other states. Result: there may be significant New York death tax even if the rest of the property is in a state that has not decoupled. One solution has been to, in effect, change the situs of the property OUTSIDE of New York State by contributing it to a limited liability company or partnership—a trust will no longer do the trick.

Q 5:14 Which states now impose some kind of estate or inheritance tax and/or gift tax?

As of April, 2008, twenty-one states impose either an inheritance tax, a "stand-alone" estate tax, or a "frozen" pick-up tax, (meaning that the tax equals what the federal "state death tax credit" *would* have been were the federal estate tax of a prior year, e.g. 2001 or 2002, still in effect) (see Table 5-3). Only two, Connecticut and Tennessee, imposed their own separate gift taxes; Louisiana and North Carolina both having repealed their gift tax statutes in the last five years. However, most of the schemes provide an unlimited marital deduction. Where states have retained an inheritance tax, the rate is usually far less—in the single digits—for transfers to lineal descendants.

Table 5-3. States Imposing "Death Taxes" and/or Gift Taxes

State	Imposes Estate or Inheritance Tax/ (Threshold)	Imposes Separate Gift Tax (Threshold)
Connecticut	Separate Estate Tax ($2 million; tax imposed on all assets, not only those over threshold) CGS § 12-391(e)	Gift tax ($2 million)
District of Columbia	"Pick-up" type ($1 million) DC 47-3702, 47-3701	
Illinois	"Pick-up" type ($2 million) 35 ILCS 405/3.	
Indiana	Inheritance tax (exempts proceeds of life insurance; transfers to descendants exempt up to $100,000; rates start at 1% for descendants up to 20% maximum rate for unrelated parties) IC 6-4-1.2 et seq.	
Iowa	Inheritance tax (100% exemption for spouses and lineals) Iowa Code sec. 450.1; 450.9 (exemption)	
Kansas	(1) Succession tax repealed eff. 1/1/2007 (2) Separate estate tax ($1 million) K.S. 79-15,203	
Kentucky	Inheritance Tax (rate depends on class; tax on amounts from $20,000 up at 2%–10%) KRS 140.010	

Table 5-3. (Cont'd)

State	Imposes Estate or Inheritance Tax/ (Threshold)	Imposes Separate Gift Tax (Threshold)
Louisiana	Inheritance tax was repealed eff. July 1, 2005. (Acts 2004, No. 884, § 2)	Repealed eff. July 1, 2008. (Acts 2007, No. 371, § 3) For prior years: RS 47:1201 ($30,000 exemption)
Maine	"Pick-up" ($1 million) Maine Rev. Statutes Title 36, sec. 4062	
Maryland	"Pick-up" ($1 million) MD TAX GENERAL §§ 7-304; 7-309.	
Massachusetts	"Pick-up" ($1 million) MA ST 65C §§ 2A(a).	
Minnesota	"Pick-up" ($1 million) MN ST §§ 291.005; 291.03;	
Nebraska	Inheritance tax (1% of amount over exemption—40,000 for close relatives, 15,000 exemption for others) NEB REV ST. § 77-2001, et seq.	
New Jersey	"Pick-up" ($675,000) 54:38-1; Inheritance tax (transfers OUTRIGHT to spouses and lineals excluded—54:34-1	
New York	"Pick-up" ($1 million) NY TAX §§ 952; 951;	
North Carolina	"Pick-up" ($2 million) NC ST §§ 105-32.2; 105-32.1; 105-228.90.	Repealed eff. 1/1/09. HB 2436, SESSION LAW 2008-107, sec. 28.18(a). 105-188

Table 5-3. (Cont'd)

State	Imposes Estate or Inheritance Tax/ (Threshold)	Imposes Separate Gift Tax (Threshold)
Oklahoma	Separate estate tax (until 1/1/2010) ($2 million) 68-802 et seq.	
Oregon	"Pick-up" ($1 million) Title 12, chapter 118.	
Pennsylvania	Inheritance Tax (4.5% for descendants, 12% siblings, 15% for unrelated) 72 Pa. Code § 0116	
Rhode Island	"Pick-up" ($675,000) RI ST § 44-22-1.1.	
Tennessee	Inheritance Tax ($1 million); starts at 5.5%, up to 9.5% for estates over $440,000 in excess of exemption 67-8-303; 67-8-316 (exemption)	67-8-101
Vermont	"Pick-up" ($2 million) VT Title 32, sec. 7442a	
Washington	Separate estate tax ($2 million; tax on excess over $1 million starts at 14%, increases to 19%) RCW 83.100.040 (threshold at RCW 83.100.050)	

Q 5:15 Can states impose estate or inheritance taxes on nonresident decedents?

Every state has a mechanism for capturing estate or inheritance taxes on property located in the state, even where the owner-decedent is a nonresident of the state. Most states adopt one of two mechanisms for calculating the tax: Either the tax is levied on all property with an actual situs in the state (thereby avoiding taxation of resident decedents' out-of-state property) or the estate tax is computed as a fractional share of the total amount, based on the proportion of the taxable estate located in the taxing state, or there is simply a credit, if any, for taxes paid to another state. These two calculation methods can lead to different results; consequently, even though two or more states limit their estate tax, a decedent's estate with assets in two states could end up paying far more state estate taxes than if all property had been owned in one state each computation, the situs of a decedent's intangible personal property is usually deemed to be the state of the decedent's domicile, while tangible personal property and real property is deemed to have a situs in the actual state in which it is located. Personal effects, however, are usually considered to be located in the state of domicile, and if actually situated elsewhere, treated as if they are only "temporarily" outside the state of domicile. Problems can arise when valuable items are actually located out-of-state, such as jewelry.

Q 5:16　Who typically prepares estate, inheritance, and gift tax returns?

Some lawyers routinely prepare tax returns. Indeed, some tax practitioners insist that the only way truly to understand estate and gift tax planning issues is regularly to prepare the tax returns. They are uncommonly complicated, and require a great deal of specialized knowledge. Some choices made on an initial estate tax return are final, even if the return is later amended, so there is tremendous opportunity for unrecoverable mistakes if an attorney unfamiliar with the mechanics of estate tax calculation and payment prepares the returns. By the same token, few accountants are familiar with estate and gift tax return preparation. Before retaining an accountant to prepare the returns, the attorney should determine whether he or she has any prior experience with their specialized preparation. Most lawyers and accountants who prepare estate and gift tax returns rely on one of a handful of tax return preparation software packages. Although software properly formats the returns, makes calculations easily and reliably, and forces the user to prepare the appropriate supporting schedules, such software does not substitute for familiarity with the actual returns and the method of preparation. On the other hand, any lawyer or accountant who regularly prepares estate or gift tax returns should unquestionably invest in tax preparation software. For states with their own inheritance or estate tax systems, particularly those that require tax returns for estates far below the federal threshold, the attorney rather than an accountant usually prepares the state tax returns. Many software programs will not even include a component that permits preparation of the state tax return.

The inexperienced attorney should keep in mind that new rules imposed by the Treasury Department on practitioners of "tax law" ("Circular 230") as well as new "preparer penalties" imposed by Congress, may create liability if certain procedures are not followed when or if aggressive positions are taken, and choose to defer questions on these issues to accountants.

Gift Tax

Q 5:17   What transfers are subject to the federal gift tax?

With some exceptions, property transferred for less than "an adequate and full consideration in money or money's worth" will be subject to gift tax [I.R.C. § 2512]; the tax applies to the amount by which the property value exceeds the value of the consideration. There are the obvious gift transfers of cash, cars, real estate, and jewelry; however, the Code also characterizes as gift transfers the forgiveness of loans and the transfer of ownership of a life insurance policy. [Rev. Rul. 77-299, 1977-2 C.B. 343]

Services provided are usually not characterized as gifts, nor is the refusal to accept a gift or bequest (as, for example, by a properly executed disclaimer; see chapters 6 and 7 for a discussion of disclaimers). There is no tax imposed on any gifts made to one's spouse, to a government unit, to a veterans' organization, or to any qualifying entity organized for religious, charitable, scientific, or educational purposes. (Note, however, that a gift to a foreign charitable organization may be exempt for gift tax purposes but not give rise to an income tax deduction, which requires a gift to a "domestic" charitable organization.) Finally, a gift is taxed only when "complete"—certain powers, if retained, render the gift "incomplete" and prevent imposition of gift tax until the donor dies (at which point the gift will likely be included in the donor's estate anyway). An example is a gift in trust while retaining the power to "appoint" the property among a class of beneficiaries. The "retained limited power" will prevent the imposition of gift tax at the time the gift is made. This retained power is most often combined with a gift in trust, but some practitioners have also attempted to include the concept in conveyances of real estate.

Q 5:18   What is the annual gift tax exclusion?

Under Code Section 2503, taxpayers may make gifts of $10,000 annually to each of an unlimited number of persons, with no gift tax consequences. Beginning in 1999, under the Taxpayer Relief Act of 1997, the $10,000 gift exclusion is indexed annually for inflation, rounded to the nearest $1,000 increment. [I.R.C. § 2503(b)] In 2002, the number rose to $11,000, and in 2006 to $12,000. In 2008, it remained at $12,000.

The amount doubles if the donor files a federal gift tax return on which the donor's spouse agrees that *all* gifts made that year will be treated as having been made by both partners, so that both partners' annual exclusions may be used. [Treas. Reg. § 25.2513-1(b)] Thus, a couple with five children and five unusually lovable sons- or daughters-in-law might give $240,000 per year, if they so chose, without any gift or estate tax consequences whatsoever. [I.R.C. § 2513] It is important to remember that the election applies to all gifts, not only annual exclusion gifts. [Treas. Reg. § 25.2513-1(b)(5)] This can be an issue if both spouses wish to make a $24,000 gift to their child, but only one spouse wishes to make taxable gifts (in excess of the exclusion) to children of a first marriage. Of course, if the gift is made from jointly-owned assets, or from non-separate property in a community property state, the gift will simply be treated as made one-half by each spouse, without the need for the election.

Q 5:19   What is the present interest requirement for annual exclusion gifts?

The $12,000 annual exclusion applies only to gifts of a so-called "present interest." [I.R.C. § 2503(b)(1)] A "present interest" means the right to immediate use and enjoyment of the property. A gift made in trust will usually not meet the present interest test. Exceptions: the gift of a present right to all the income or principal from a trust, or a percentage of trust income or principal, for a defined period of time, constitutes a present interest. [Treas. Reg. § 25.2503-3(b)] Thus, a "Crummey Trust" will typically allow the beneficiary the right to withdraw the amount of any gift to the trust for a "reasonable" period of time, in order that the gift will qualify as a present interest. Gifts in trust (or other gifts of interests while retaining an interest such as a life estate) can, however, present other problems (see Q 5:100).

Q 5:20   When does an individual have to file a gift tax return?

Any gift greater than $12,000 (2007/2008 figures) made by a single donor to a single donee in any given year must be reported. Married couples can make gifts from jointly held or community property totaling

$24,000 to a single recipient without having to file a return. In a non-community property state, if the gift were made from solely owned property, that spouse would have to file a return on which the non-giving spouse would consent to have the gift treated as made equally by each spouse, but he or she would not have to file a separate return as well. [Treas. Reg. § 25.2513-1(c)]

Although gifts in excess of the annual exclusion amount must be reported, no tax liability is incurred unless the donor exceeds the exemption equivalent amount in effect in the year of the gift. In other words, a donor who makes a $50,000 gift to a single donee in 2008 must file a return, but will not pay any federal tax. The donor will, however, have used $38,000 (the amount of the gift reduced by the annual exclusion amount) of his or her exemption equivalent, and will therefore have an estate tax liability if he or she dies in 2008 owning more than $1,962,000 (the 2008 $2,000,000 exemption equivalent amount minus the $38,000 used by the 2007 gift). Note that because the maximum lifetime gift tax exemption is no longer identical to the estate tax exemption amount, it is possible to incur a gift tax liability on lifetime transfers that would have escaped taxation if made at death instead.

If a state imposes its own gift tax regime, however, a gift that exceeds the annual exclusion amount for that state (usually tied to the federal exclusion) may require the payment of tax even if the donor has not exhausted the federal exemption equivalent.

Q 5:21 Are there any lifetime transfers that can be made with no gift tax consequences?

Yes. The federal estate and gift tax system allows certain *inter vivos* and testamentary transfers to be made with no tax consequences. For instance, an unlimited amount of wealth may be transferred to a spouse or to charity, and, as previously discussed, gifts of up to $12,000 (in 2008) each (indexed; $121,000 in 2006) to an unlimited number of individuals may be made annually. [I.R.C. § 2503(b)]

In addition, the grantor can make unlimited payments to medical providers and educational institutions for health and tuition, respectively. [I.R.C. § 2503(e)] These gifts are not subject to the gift tax and do not use up any exclusions or deductions. For example, a grandparent may pay the college tuition of a grandchild without gift tax consequences. The payments must be made directly to the educational institution or medical provider. But the medical expense exclusion does not apply to amounts that are later reimbursed by an insurance company. [Treas. Reg. § 25.2503-6(b)(3)] An important point: the exemption is for "medical care (as defined in section 213(d))," and that covers payment of health insurance premiums. [I.R.C. § 213(d)(1)(D); 26 Code of Federal Regulations § 1.213-1]. With the rise in health costs, this can be a major additional way to benefit family members without transfer tax consequences.

Finally, investments in tuition savings accounts defined in Code Section 529 are not only treated as "present interest" gifts despite the intended beneficiary's lack of direct access to the funds, but the five years' worth of annual exclusion may be "bunched" into the first year. [I.R.C. § 529(c)(2)] Provided the donor survives the five years, the donor will have been able to exclude $60,000 in 2007 made in the first year. This gives the account, which grows tax-free, an extra four years of growth on the funds. (See Q 5:38.)

Gift Tax Planning

Q 5:24   What disadvantages are there to making substantial gifts during a lifetime?

One never knows what life holds in store: Will one live another 3 years or 30 years? What about chronic illness? Remarriage? Will the value of remaining assets increase or decrease? Will future acts of family members cause one to regret making gifts to them now? Will there be more descendants in the future, and will one of them have a medical emergency? Thoughtful planners should advise clients of all the ways the assets they are considering gifting now could come in handy down the road. Moreover, since the diversion of the gift tax exclusion amount from the estate tax exclusion, making a gift that exceeds the exclusion will result in a tax that would have been avoided had the asset been retained until death.

Q 5:25   What advantages are there to making substantial gifts during the donor's life?

Assuming the donor has determined that he or she can afford to (or simply wishes to) make gifts in excess of the annual exclusion amount, there are several estate tax benefits. Any gifts will not only reduce the estate by the amount of the gift, but also by the income that would have been generated by the gift for the rest of the donor's life. In addition, if the wealthy donor's income tax bracket is higher than that of the donee, there will be some net income tax savings from the transfer.

Most important, a large gift directly reduces the total estate and gift tax liability. This is true because the gift tax due on a large gift does not count as an additional gift. By contrast, the tax due on an estate remains part of the estate for tax calculation purposes. The effect of this difference in estate and gift tax calculations is that the total savings on taxable gifts made during life will equal at least the amount of the (estate) tax that would have been paid on the amount of (gift) tax actually paid.

This benefit calculation changed somewhat in 2004, when estate tax exclusion amounts began to exceed gift tax exclusion amounts. The calculation should change even more radically in 2010 if the eventual repeal of federal estate taxes remains on the books. After that time, substantial gifts (in excess of the exemption amount) will incur a tax that could have been avoided altogether by holding the property until death. In the meantime, gift planning remains a viable and important part of general estate planning.

Q 5:27 What steps must be taken to obtain the $12,000 exclusion when making gifts to a trust?

To qualify for the annual exclusion, a gift must be of a present interest (see Q 5:19). A gift directly to a trust will therefore usually not qualify for the exclusion, unless the recipient has the power to revoke the trust or withdraw the trust property. Typical examples of these powers may be found in the "Crummey" trust (see Q 5:28); the "minor's trust" under IRC § 2503(c) (see Q 5:31).

It is important to understand that the exclusion availability is not the same as removing the asset from the grantor's taxable estate. It is possible to make a completed gift (and thereby remove the gifted amount from the grantor's estate) without qualifying for the gift tax exclusion (as, for example, in the case of a gift to an irrevocable trust for the sole benefit of the recipient). With some exceptions (QPRTs; see Q 5:101), the usual purpose of the gifting process is to both remove the asset from the grantor's estate and simultaneously qualify for the exclusion.

Q 5:28 What is a "Crummey" trust?

One of the most popular and pervasive of the gift planning techniques is the so-called "Crummey" trust, named after the case *Crummey v.*

Commissioner. [397 F.2d 82 (9th Cir. 1968)] In order for a gift to be deemed completed by the Internal Revenue Service, the donee must receive a present interest in the gift—in other words, the donee must have an unrestricted right to the possession or use of the property transferred. This creates a problem when the grantor wants to delay distribution of a gift to a beneficiary, especially a minor beneficiary. Grantors can reap substantial tax benefits by giving $12,000 per year to a child, but making an immediate and outright gift is unwieldy and usually undesirable. Gifts subject to state laws following the Uniform Transfers to Minors Act must be released to the beneficiary when he or she reaches the age of 21 (see Q 5:31); gifts to "minor's trusts" must permit the beneficiary to withdraw the entire trust property within a reasonable time after reaching age 21. [I.R.C. § 2503(c)]

To address this problem, the grantor can establish an irrevocable trust with "Crummey" powers that gives to one or more of the beneficiaries the power to withdraw from the trust either all or a portion of the amount given to the trust. If this provision is included, the trust language can delay the distribution of the trust assets to the beneficiary to any age. However, if the person holding the Crummey power does not hold a significant interest in the trust, the power may be considered only a sham. Usually, the Crummey power holder will have the right to unqualified distribution at some future point, but this is not necessarily required. The point is that one must be able to show that the non-exercise of the power was not as the result of a pre-arranged scheme, but was actually in the power-holder's interest.

How does the Crummey power work? The beneficiary is given a short window (typically 30 days, but maybe even shorter) to withdraw the gift from the trust; if no withdrawal is made, that window closes and the gift becomes part of the irrevocable trust. For tax purposes, the donor has made a gift to the beneficiary, and the beneficiary (by allowing the power to lapse) has in turn made a gift to the ultimate trust beneficiaries. The second gift ordinarily has no gift tax consequences, because the recipient of most of that gift is the beneficiary himself or herself, but two separate gifts have been completed. To further prevent any gift tax liability on the second gift, the beneficiary can be given a special testamentary power of appointment (a power to name the trust's remainder beneficiaries in his or her own will, from among a group of candidates; see also Q 4:20); this will result in the second gift having no tax consequences at all.

It is important to recognize that a gift into a trust is still "completed" in the sense that the gifted property is removed from the estate of the donor. The failure to provide a Crummey power in a gift-recipient trust will simply cause the annual gift tax exclusion to be unavailable for that gift, and therefore result in reduction of the unified credit exemption amount for the donor (and the imposition of gift tax in a state that does not follow the same "unified" approach). If, on the other hand, the annual gift exclusion amount has already been utilized for that recipient in the year of gift into a trust for the same beneficiary, there is no need to add Crummey withdrawal powers to the gift. For that reason, as well as out of concern for future changes in the tax law governing Crummey-type transfers, some practitioners provide that the Crummey withdrawal terms appear in the gift deed or other transferring document itself, rather than in the text of the trust.

Why does the Crummey power work? First, because there is no statutory requirement that the beneficiary be notified of this power or of the time frame for its exercise, many practitioners feel that the power alone, without more, should be sufficient to withstand IRS objections. Second, even though the Internal Revenue Service insists that reasonable notice and a reasonable time frame be offered in order for the arrangement not be treated as a sham, the relatively short period of thirty days has been found acceptable to the IRS. (An advance waiver of notice of gifts made in future years has not passed IRS scrutiny, however.) Third, the grantor can tactfully suggest that gifts to the trust might be discontinued if the beneficiary insists on exercising the power. Particularly if the trust property consists of life insurance, so that future gifts are essential to preserving the death benefit, this is a persuasive argument. However, the donor must be careful not to set any actual conditions on the gifts, or the IRS will consider them incomplete transfers. Finally, the right to withdraw is generally noncumulative, so the beneficiary cannot withdraw an amount greater than what was contributed to the trust in any given year. The only exception would be when a "hanging power" is included. The "hanging" power states that the withdrawal right continues to the extent that the value of the amount subject to the right exceeds the greater of $5,000 or 5 percent of the value of the trust property. This is to prevent a gift by the holder of the power, which might otherwise be deemed to "own" the trust. As a practical matter, this means that it is preferable that each beneficiary's withdrawal right not exceed $5,000. If it does, the attorney must choose between a hanging power and a power of appointment retained by the beneficiary holding the power to avoid the deeming of any inadvertent gifts.

Q 5:30 What are "Christofani" powers?

Some tax practitioners have taken Crummey powers to the next level by giving withdrawal rights to several individuals who may not otherwise be beneficiaries of the trust. Assuming the withdrawal powers lapse unexercised, a larger gift can thus be made to the trust (and, ultimately, the beneficiary or beneficiaries) without exceeding the annual exclusion amount for any of the individual holders of the withdrawal powers. This technique is sometimes referred to as using "Christofani" powers after the Tax Court case of *Christofani v. Commissioner.* [97 T.C. 74 (1991)] Typically, several family members are given withdrawal rights as to the annual exclusion amount (in 2006, $12,000) gifts for each, and upon lapse of the unexercised rights the combined gifts become part of the irrevocable trust for the primary intended beneficiary. Of course, if any individual actually exercises the withdrawal right, the donor's intention is frustrated, at least as to the amount of the withdrawn gift.

The Internal Revenue Service persists in its disapproval of Christofani-type powers, despite having a perfect record of losses in courts considering the validity of the gifting technique. The IRS has nonetheless served notice that it will continue to challenge such trusts where it determines that the particular arrangement is abusive, although it is not clear what specifics offend the IRS more in some cases than in others. [See IRS *Action on Decision,* 1996-010, 1996-29 I.R.B. 4] A compromise technique may be used by giving some members a small interest in the trust, sufficient to satisfy the IRS concern that there has been a pre-arranged agreement not to withdraw, but small enough to satisfy the donor's wish to benefit primarily other parties. Thus, a trust intended to provide the benefit of insurance proceeds to one child with special needs might give smaller interests, perhaps 5 percent, to other children who could hold Crummey powers.

Q 5:31 How else might one make gifts to a minor?

Gifts to minors can be made directly to the child, although for obvious reasons this is not advisable if the gift exceeds several thousand dollars, or to their parents, who may or may not follow the donor's wish that the gift be held for the direct benefit of the child. If the minor is under the supervision of a court-appointed guardian/conservator, the court will monitor management of the gift. The money will be distributed as soon as the child reaches majority and the conservatorship terminates. In many states, a gift that exceeds a certain amount may require the appointment of a guardian, who will also be required to post a bond, file accountings, and meet other burdensome requirements.

Most states have adopted some form of the Uniform Transfers to Minors Act (UTMA) or its predecessor, the Uniform Gifts to Minors Act (UGMA). Instead of requiring a court-appointed conservator or guardian, the UTMA allows the gift assets to be managed by a custodian, who may be the donor, the child's parent or other adult, or a professional fiduciary. The bank account, real estate, or other asset is titled in the name of the custodian, who is designated by the title as custodian of the assets under the state's version of the UTMA. Transfers into UTMA accounts in amounts greater than $12,000 (2006 number) will be subject to gift tax or generation-skipping tax as if they were made directly to the minor. [Rev. Ruls. 56-86, 1956-1 C.B. 449; 59-357, 1959-2 C.B. 212]

As long as the assets are managed prudently, the custodian has the power to invest the money as he or she wishes for the benefit of the minor, without regard to the minor's other assets, including the resources or support obligations of the parents. Under the UTMA and most court-appointed conservatorships, the presence of the transferred assets does not release the parents from their support obligations, but if in the best interests of the child some assets are used to provide for his or her support, those transfers may be considered income to the parents and taxed accordingly. Some states forbid a parent acting as custodian to use the UTMA funds for the child's support or have found a parent liable for breach of fiduciary duty by so doing. [See, e.g., Hall v. Hall, (Conn. Super. Ct. April 11, 2002) (unreported decision)]

Although state versions of the UTMA may differ, some types of UTMA accounts may be continued in the account until the beneficiary reaches 21, even though the age of majority may be 18. UTMA usually does require the assets to be turned over to the child at the age of 21 (up to 25 in California), so some donors may prefer a more formal trust device to exercise greater control over the distribution.

Another option, similar to the Crummey trust, is the "minor's trust" under Code Section 2503(c). Instead of giving an annual notice, the trust simply provides that once the minor reaches age 21, (s)he either receives the funds entirely (similar to an UTMA account), or, more likely, has the right to withdraw all of the trust assets at age 21, for a specified, usually brief, period of time. In effect, there is a single massive Crummey power. For the client that prefers greater control, and deferral of distribution, the risk of a minor's trust is that at age 21 the child will have sufficient assertiveness to exercise the power, but not the judgment to deal with the assets prudently. On the other hand, the point can still be driven home that exercise of the power may have repercussions the child would not appreciate. Certainly this approach may be easier to cope with than the UTMA account.

What to do if the UTMA account has already been used, or a minor's trust requires distribution? There are two options donor parents may choose:

1. Practically speaking, possession is 9/10 of the law. That is, although the child may have the right to the funds, as a practical matter the parent may simply delay in affording the child his or her rights, and the child is unlikely to force the issue. The same is true for the minor's trust.

2. The parent may "encourage" the child to fund a trust for the child's benefit with the parent as trustee. This will not insulate the funds from the child's future creditors, but will put a level of bureaucracy and control between the child and the money.

Q 5:32 What options are available to a donor who wishes to provide specifically for the education of a child, grandchild, or other individual?

Donors may make gifts for the benefit of individuals without using their $12,000 annual exemptions, permitting larger gifts (and therefore greater reductions of the donor's estate) in some circumstances. Tax-free gifts that do not utilize the annual exemption amount include:

1. Direct payment of educational expenses for the beneficiary;
2. Contributions to state prepaid tuition plans;
3. Education IRAs; and
4. Education gifts to "Section 529" plans.

Education IRAs or "Coverdell Accounts"

Q 5:34 Who may establish an Education IRA?

An Education IRA may be established for any individual under the age of 18. Contributions must be in cash, but may come from the beneficiary or any other person. The total amount of contributions in any one year may not, however, exceed $2,000. [I.R.C. § 530(c)] Any contributions to a qualified state tuition program on behalf of the beneficiary will preclude any Education IRA contributions.

529 Plans

Q 5:38 What is a 529 plan and what are its advantages and disadvantages?

A Section 529 account works as follows: A contributor sets up the account in a state's 529 plan and names a beneficiary. Provided the contribution is no more than $12,000 (or even $60,000, in which case the gift is treated as if spread over five years, using five years' worth of annual exclusion), the gift is treated as a "present interest" and does not incur gift tax, even though the beneficiary does not have full access to the funds. No income tax is paid as the account funds grow or generate income. When the beneficiary needs the funds to finance higher education, the account owner authorizes their release. No tax is paid on distributions for tuition, room, board, and certain other expenses. The account owner can elect to name a new beneficiary for any remaining funds, or instead, can elect to have the funds revert, subject to a 10 percent penalty and payment of tax on deferred income. The funds are not included in the account owner's estate at death.

The disadvantage, from the donor's standpoint, is that the right to take back the funds (subject to penalty) might leave the funds vulnerable to claims against the donor. A few states have chosen to include creditor protection features in their 529 plans, but these are in the minority (as of 2002, only Ohio, Pennsylvania, Alaska, Colorado, Kentucky, Louisiana, Maine, Nebraska, Tennessee, Virginia and Wisconsin). And the Federal Bankruptcy statutes were amended to exclude from the bankrupt's estate contributions to 529 accounts made two years prior to filing. ($5,000 is protected if contributed between 1 and 2 years prior to filing.) However, no state appears to exclude 529 plan accounts from consideration as "available assets" for purposes of Medicaid eligibility. [For a discussion of this potential drawback, see L. Davis, "Keeping the Promise of Section 529 a Reality," Elder Law e-Bulletin (April 30, 2002), available only online at *www.tn-elderlaw.com/telb/ 020430.html#e1*]

For a comprehensive and constantly updated survey of individual state plans and their benefits and drawbacks, see *www.savingforcollege. com.* The site author, Joseph Hurley, also sells a book that provides yet more details about different state plans. It is particularly important to determine what happens to a 529 account when the "owner" dies. If the plan passes by will, it may be that the new "owner" with power to withdraw funds, change beneficiaries, etc., will be someone quite different from the beneficiary or relative. Imagine the catastrophe if a donor fails to name a successor "owner" of a 529 account for a grand-child and leaves his or her estate to charity. On death, the charity owns the 529 plan account and may be obligated to withdraw the funds unless some kind of legal action is taken (e.g., claiming a constructive trust).

Estate Tax

Q 5:44   What is a 5 & 5 Power, and is anything included in the estate of a decedent who holds such a power?

Yes. Similar to a general power of appointment (property subject to such a power being included under Section 2041) is a right to take out, or withdraw, or appoint property of a trust to such a degree that one is treated as the owner of the trust. Conversely, the IRS has decided that this power will be considered *de minimis*, and disregarded, when the power extends to property that does not include the greater of 5 percent of the trust property, or $5,000. This is known as a "5 & 5 power" and is commonly included in trusts to give the surviving spouse better access to trust funds than if he or she had to depend upon the judgment of the trustee. It is used as a limiting provision whenever a surviving spouse or beneficiary might otherwise be treated as the trust owner, such as a credit shelter trust. However, if the owner dies with such a power still exercisable, that 5 percent will still be included in his or her estate for tax purposes. One method of minimizing this risk is to permit the power to be exercised only during the last month of the year—leaving eleven months available for the power-holder to die without having the amount includible in his or her estate.

Q 5:46   What is meant by the "alternate valuation date"?

Estate assets are normally valued at their fair market value on the date of death. The valuation can instead be made on the six-month anniversary of the date of death, but only if the total estate size and total estate tax liability are both reduced by the use of the alternate valuation date. (In other words, it is not possible to use an alternate valuation date in a non-taxable estate in order to increase the basis and thus reduce future capital gains taxes.) Where an alternative valuation date is used, *all* assets must be valued on the alternate date—one cannot pick and choose the assets that will use that date. In those cases where the alternate valuation date is to be used, assets that have been disposed of between the date of death and the alternate valuation date will be valued at the sale price (or fair market value on the date of distribution). [I.R.C. § 2032(a)(2)] The alternate valuation election must be made on the federal estate tax return, IRS Form 706. The election is irrevocable and must be made on a timely filed return or the first late return within one year of the due date. [I.R.C. § 2032(d)]

> **Example 5-2.** George, a single man, died September 1, 1999, with an estate valued at $1 million and consisting primarily of marketable securities. His will leaves his entire estate to his children in equal shares. On March 1, 2001, the remaining securities were worth $650,000 and another $200,000 of securities had been liquidated to pay claims against the estate. His executor may elect to use the alternate date of death valuation for the remaining securities, and value the liquidated securities at the $200,000 sales price, because both his estate size and the amount of tax due will be reduced by using the alternate valuation date.

If, on the other hand, George's estate had been valued at $600,000 on the date of his death and $450,000 (including the actual sales price of liquidated securities) on the alternate valuation date, the election would not be available. In the latter case, while George's estate would be reduced by use of the alternate valuation date his estate tax would remain $0 using either valuation date. Of course, using the alternate valuation date would not benefit the estate or heirs anyway, as the only practical effect would be to reduce the heirs' basis in the inherited property. Unfortunately, it is not possible to use the special valuate date to *increase* basis when the assets appreciate during the six months following date of death.

Q 5:49   Are there any credits against the estate tax?

After the taxable estate has been determined (by subtracting deductions from the gross estate) and the tax due has been calculated, a handful of credits are available to be applied against that tax. Those credits include:

1. The unified credit available to every decedent's estate (to the extent that it has not been utilized as a credit on gift taxes due

during life). Under the Economic Growth and Tax Relief Reconciliation Act of 2001 the 2006 credit is $2 million and will increase to $3.5 million in 2009 before repeal of the estate tax.

2. The credit for state death taxes paid. The Code permits a credit on federal estate taxes for all state inheritance, estate, or death taxes paid by the estate or on property passing as a result of the death of the decedent. This credit is limited to a percentage of the estate, which increases as the estate grows larger. [I.R.C. § 2011] Under the Economic Growth and Tax Relief Reconciliation Act of 2001 the state death tax credit was reduced by 25 percent in 2002, and continued to be reduced by 25 percent each year until it was eliminated altogether in 2005.

3. Gift taxes previously paid on property includible in the decedent's gross estate. [I.R.C. § 2012]

4. Estate taxes previously paid on the same property when received by the decedent from another decedent's estate. [I.R.C. § 2013] This credit is allowed only for property passing (and taxed) in the 10 years before the current decedent's death, and is reduced by 20 percent every two years (in other words, 100 percent for prior estate taxes is available for the first two years after the first decedent's death, but is reduced to 80 percent for the next two years and so on, until the credit is limited to 20 percent of the tax previously paid in the 9th and 10th years after the death of the first decedent).

5. Death taxes paid to a foreign country, to the extent that such taxes were imposed on property located in the foreign country but still included in the decedent's estate for U.S. tax purposes. [I.R.C. § 2014] (Tax treaties may provide an alternative method for applying a credit for foreign death taxes.)

Overview of Estate Planning Techniques

Q 5:53 What common techniques are available to reduce or eliminate federal estate taxes?

The taxpayer can simply maintain the estate at or below the unified credit amount by gifting excess assets to individuals, through the $12,000 annual exclusion ($24,000 for couples if an election is made) or payment of educational and medical expenses, and gifting to charities, all with no tax consequence. To escape any tax fully the gift must be complete—that is, the donor cannot retain indicia of ownership or a reversionary interest. The donor does have the option of making the gift through an irrevocable trust, and thereby exercising some control over the method and timing of distribution of the gift assets. An elderly parent who spends down his or her estate through gifts to his or her children may hope that the children use part of that money to care for him or her in the future, but there cannot be any such legal commitment attached to the gift. Estate planners should carefully weigh the benefits of saving taxes against the security that a sizeable estate can provide an aging individual, especially in an age when individuals may live 20, 30, or 40 years after they stop earning income.

For larger estates (that is, when a structured use of exclusion gifts is insufficient to reduce the estate below taxable levels), several types of planning devices are available. Principal techniques in the estate planner's toolbox include marital deduction planning, charitable giving, and valuation reductions (see ensuing discussion).

Q 5:54 Which clients must be concerned about the tax aspects of estate planning?

Individuals and married couples whose accumulated wealth is approaching the exemption equivalent amount in any given year, and those who stand to benefit from *inter vivos* and death transfers of that wealth, have the most to gain from the tax avoidance aspects of estate planning. Many clients do not realize their estate (or their parents' estate) is large enough to trigger estate and gift tax consequences, and the estate planner must interview them thoroughly to determine all potential sources of wealth. A client with assets less than the unified credit amount may see his or her personal value skyrocket as a result of an inheritance or a bull market, or may not be aware of all the different kinds of assets that are counted when computing the value of the estate at death (e.g., the face value of life insurance policies).

Clients frequently undervalue their assets, for whatever reason. In evaluating the relevance of tax considerations, always assume that assets exceed stated values, that significant assets have been overlooked, and that growth will be greater (and expenditures less) than clients estimate. Consequently, any client with identified assets over $100,000 in value should be a candidate for at least rudimentary tax planning analysis.

Q 5:55   How can one plan for the possible repeal of the estate tax?

Rapid reduction, ultimate repeal, and possible subsequent restoration of the federal estate tax poses significant challenges to the estate planner. Among the challenges: the lack of federal regulations interpreting the new provisions, and the prevailing notion that estate tax repeal may not ever be fully implemented despite adoption of the Economic Growth and Tax Relief Reconciliation Act of 2001. Nonetheless, a few planning points are clear:

1. Smaller estates (less than the 2006 exemption amount of $2 million and those of healthy individuals slightly above that figure) can safely be planned without consideration of federal estate tax liability unless and until estate taxes are reimposed in the near future. State estate tax changes triggered by the federal action must be considered, and clients with property in (and ties to) more than one state may require more careful planning, especially in the near term.

2. Larger estates, especially for young and healthy individuals and couples, may benefit from disclaimer trusts which will permit the surviving spouse or heirs to elect whether estate tax planning is necessary after the death of the property holder. An alternative approach is a "Q-Tippable" trust (one that may qualify as a Q-TIP marital trust, but need not) that leaves it up to the executor to decide how much will be included in the estate of the first to die, and how much in the estate of the second.

3. Very large estates will, at least in the short term, continue to benefit from the same estate tax planning devices in widespread use for the past two decades, so long as (a) the client understands that the funds that are held in the bypass trust (and thus not entirely available to the survivor) will increase and may result in a "lopsided" arrangement; and (b) the formula clauses already in place will work in the current scheme.

4. Carryover basis will not seriously begin to affect estate planning choices for the next several years, allowing some time for regulations (and possible legislative adjustments) to clarify the rules and permitting practitioners to develop appropriate strategies.

5. It appears ever more likely that some estate tax may be retained, and carryover basis not imposed, due to budgetary constraints—but this will remain to be seen.

Q 5:59   Other than using the marital and charitable deductions and the unified exemption amount, what techniques are available to reduce federal estate taxes?

Valuation discounts can reduce the tax liability by the simple device of lowering the value of the client's assets. Ideally, the technique for lowering the value will be temporary, and the value can be restored to the pre-planning level some time after the client's death. More sophisticated planners may opt to use family limited partnerships, limited liability companies, or other business organizations to reduce the open-market value of the underlying assets. The client-donor can make the partnership the recipient of gifts pursuant to the annual exclusion (in other words, instead of writing $12,000 checks to four children, the client can place the $48,000 in the partnership and continue to exercise control over the funds and protect them from the children's creditors).

While insurance planning is not actually a means of reducing federal estate taxes, it may be useful to guarantee that the decedent's heirs will have sufficient liquid resources to pay the estate tax when it comes due. Insurance planning typically involves the transfer of an existing life insurance policy directly to the heirs or devisees, or to a trust for their benefit (utilizing "Crummey" powers effectively to remove the insurance from the grantor's estate). Alternatively, the grantor may choose to gift an amount sufficient to permit the heirs or devisees to pay annual premiums on a life insurance policy; those gifts might be made to a trust as a means of providing for continuity and control while still removing the premium amounts (and the policy itself) from the grantor's taxable estate.

Marital Deduction Planning

Q 5:60   What property interests qualify for the marital deduction?

As previously mentioned (see Q 5:57), the marital deduction is the unlimited estate and gift tax deduction for transfers made to a spouse either during life or at death. [I.R.C. § 2523] All assets that qualify for inclusion in the donor's or decedent's gross estate are potentially eligible for the marital deduction, including probate assets, joint tenancy, any property in which the surviving spouse has a general power of appointment, and, in some instances, transfers made within three years of death. Where a credit shelter trust (see SQ 5:65) has been established or a devise made to someone other than the surviving spouse, the remainder of the estate distributed to the spouse will qualify for the deduction. The importance of the unlimited marital deduction continues under the phased-in elimination of the estate tax, at least until full elimination in 2010. Thereafter the much larger carryover basis exemption will continue to emphasize transfers to spouses.

Transfers that qualify for the marital deduction (at death, or even during lifetime) include:

- Outright gifts and bequests; payments of life insurance or annuity proceeds;
- Gifts in trusts in which (1) the spouse has the right to withdraw all of the assets, (2) all income is distributable to the spouse, and (3) no property may be distributed to any other party during the spouse's lifetime ("general power of appointment" trust) [IRC § 2056(b)(5)];
- Life insurance or annuity payments with power of appointment in surviving spouse [IRC § 2056(b)(6)]; and
- "Terminable interests" that qualify under § 2056(b)(7).

Terminable interest property can qualify for the marital deduction (and therefore be "qualified terminable interest property" or a QTIP election) if it passes from the decedent, the surviving spouse has an income interest for life (and a right to demand that the property be made income-producing), no other person has the power to appoint any portion of the property away from the spouse, and a proper election has been made on the decedent's estate tax return. [I.R.C. § 2056(b)(7)(B)(i)] A "legal life estate" is also eligible for QTIP treatment. [I.R.C. § 2056(b)]

The "decoupling" of federal and state estate taxes has led to some particular problems surrounding the QTIP. A key feature of the QTIP marital deduction is that a "QTIP election" is made on the federal estate tax return. With decoupling, an estate valued at $800,000 might have to pay state estate tax in the home state (say, New Jersey), but never file a 706 Return. Suppose further that the credit equivalent in New Jersey were only $675,000. The remaining $125,000 in the estate, if a terminable interest, might never receive QTIP treatment in New Jersey because there would be no federal estate tax return upon which to make an election. Recognizing this problem, the "decoupling" states are beginning to recognize the need for a state QTIP election, provided the election made does not conflict with any federal return that actually is filed.

Q 5:61 What requirements must be met for a transfer to qualify for the federal estate tax marital deduction?

The following requirements must be met for the transfer to qualify for the federal estate tax marital deduction:

1. The decedent must be a U.S. citizen or resident at the time of death;

2. The property must pass to a surviving spouse who is a U.S. citizen (but see SQ 5:62);

3. The interest in property must be included in the decedent's gross estate; and

4. The surviving spouse must not receive a nondeductible terminable interest in the property.

A fifth, but obvious requirement: the spouse must survive the decedent. In a recent case, the Tax Court held that a spouse could not be "deemed" to survive by virtue of a will provision. *Estate of Kwang Lee v. Commissioner*, T.C. Memo 2007-371 (December 20, 2007).

Q 5:62 Can a transfer qualify for the marital deduction if the surviving spouse is not a U.S. citizen?

Yes. If the surviving spouse is not a U.S. citizen the marital deduction is allowed if the property passes to the surviving spouse in a qualified domestic trust, *or* if the spouse becomes a citizen within nine months of the decedent's death. [I.R.C. §§ 2056(b)(7)(B)(i), 2056(b)(7) (B)(ii)(II)]

Q 5:63 What is a qualified domestic trust?

The unlimited marital deduction is not available for gifts or bequests to noncitizen spouses. Consequently, where the spouse is not a citizen the exemption equivalent amount will be used for any transfer of the decedent's assets to the spouse. For larger estates, that may lead to tax liability even where the spouse is the primary beneficiary. The loss of marital deduction availability is not absolute.

A qualified domestic trust is a QTIP trust (see Q 5:71) created by a grantor whose surviving spouse is not a U.S. citizen. Assets passing to a U.S. citizen ordinarily do not qualify for the marital deduction, but QTIP trust language adhering to Sections 2056 and 2056A of the Internal Revenue Code (clarified in the Taxpayer Relief Act of 1997) can make the assets of the trust eligible.

For the trust to qualify (and therefore be a qualified domestic trust), four criteria must be met, either at date of death, or pursuant to a reformation commenced within nine months of death:

1. At least one trustee must be a U.S. citizen or domestic corporation, and that trustee must consent before any distribution of principal can be made;

2. The executor of the decedent's estate must make a QDOT election on the estate tax return by its due date (including extensions);

3. Treasury regulations intended to ensure the collectibility of estate taxes imposed on the trust must be met—in general terms, every distribution of principal from the trust is hit with the estate tax that *would* have been imposed on the decedent's estate had no trust existed; and

4. The surviving alien spouse must be entitled to all income from the trust (on at least an annual basis), as in any other marital deduction qualifying trust.

Q 5:64   If there is a disparity between the assets of the respective spouses, how can the estates be equalized in order to utilize the marital deduction?

One common problem is that the first spouse to die may not have sufficient assets to utilize fully the exemption equivalent amount. If there is a great disparity between the assets of the respective spouses (often the case in second marriages, where one or both spouses have substantial separate property), the richer spouse may wish to make gifts to the poorer spouse during his or her lifetime to permit full use of the exemption regardless of which spouse is the first to die. The wealthier spouse may even determine that the gift should be large enough to equalize the estates completely, in order to lower the marginal tax bracket for the wealthier spouse.

One method to equalize estates is through a gift of life insurance or through an irrevocable life insurance trust (see Q 5:87), whereby proceeds of the policy pass to the surviving spouse at death. The donor-decedent cannot retain any rights of ownership in the policy or the tax benefit is lost, so generally a gift is made of the policy itself, even if the donor continues to pay the premiums personally.

Another method of equalizing estates is for the wealthier spouse to establish an *inter vivos* QTIP trust. The QTIP trust is more frequently established after the wealthier spouse's death, but the rules and effect are essentially similar (see Q 5:71). This technique can also be used to get a quicker "step-up" in basis on the death of a sicker spouse so that the portfolio can be diversified without incurring capital gains tax.

Q 5:65 What is a "credit shelter trust"?

The primary purpose of the classic credit shelter trust, also called an A/B trust or bypass trust, is to protect the unified credit exemption of both spouses. A (unified) credit shelter trust is a joint living trust created by both spouses who have sufficient assets to trigger estate tax consequences. It protects the unified credit exemption of both spouses, so that a maximum amount equal to double the current unified credit (which in 2006 stands at $2,000,000) can be protected. No estate tax is usually owed at the death of the first spouse because the unlimited marital deduction protects the transfer. But without a trust, the estate value exceeding the unified credit will be vulnerable to estate tax at the death of the second spouse. A properly constructed credit shelter trust protects the unified credit of the first spouse to die by placing certain restrictions on the surviving spouse's access to the assets that shield the assets from being taxed in the surviving spouse's estate.

At least in community property states, a credit shelter trust may be a joint revocable trust created by the agreement of both spouses during their lifetimes. At the death of the first spouse, such a trust separates into two subtrusts: the decedent's trust (also sometimes referred to as the B trust, bypass trust, exemption trust, or credit shelter trust), which is irrevocable, and the survivors trust (or A trust), which is revocable and whose assets may be distributed outright. At the first death, the assets of the deceased spouse held as part of the parent trust are segregated into the decedent's trust. The maximum amount so segregated will usually, but not always, be limited to the exemption equivalent amount, so that no estate tax is incurred on the first death. In common law jurisdictions, a joint approach is frowned upon out of concern that the surviving spouse will be considered to have funded the decedent's trust, so it is more common to use mirror, but separate, revocable trust agreements, and to divide assets between the spouses.

The decedent's trust is usually maintained for the benefit of the surviving spouse, although he or she cannot be a remainder beneficiary of the subtrust. The survivor may collect all income from the decedent's trust. The decedent's trust may also pay for all expenses related to the survivor's health, education, maintenance, or support, such as mortgage payments, dentist bills, tuition toward a graduate degree, or clothing. The trust may even give the surviving spouse the right to demand an annual distribution of up to $5,000 or 5 percent of the trust principal, whichever is greater, without causing the decedent's trust to be treated as part of the surviving spouse's estate.

In other words, the surviving spouse—who often is the trustee of the decedent's trust as well—has broad access to the trust assets, but there is at least the possibility of some protection of those assets for remainder beneficiaries. As with any trust, the remainder beneficiaries may take the trustee to court if they have evidence of mismanagement or misapplication of trust benefits. This may not be a likely option when the trustee is a parent, and the grantors may want to take this into consideration when creating the revocable trust and appointing trustees.

Credit shelter planning, formerly the cornerstone of an estate planning practice, has been thrown into disarray with the "decoupling" of state estate taxes from federal estate taxes. If a state has decoupled, the simple scheme of putting up to the federal credit shelter amount in a credit shelter trust, with the balance to the spouse, may now result in significant state tax.

Q 5:67　What is the difference between a "fractional share" and "pecuniary" clause?

Trust or will language pertaining to the distribution of assets typically directs that the distribution be made in "pecuniary," or straight monetary amounts, or in "fractional shares," by which each beneficiary is assigned a percentage of the assets. For instance, the testator or grantor may provide for "My daughter Annie, $20,000," or "My daughter Annie, 30 percent (30%) of the residuary estate." A fraction can be applied creatively, however: for example, "My daughter, Annie, a fraction of my estate of which the numerator is $20,000 and the denominator is the total value of my residuary estate."

Q 5:71 What is qualified terminable interest property?

Despite the general rule that terminable interests do not qualify for the marital deduction, some such interests do qualify. Property that meets the test for such qualification goes by the unromantic description of qualified terminable interest property or QTIP. QTIP interests are usually conveyed by trusts, whether testamentary or *inter vivos*. An *inter vivos* QTIP trust may be irrevocable at the time of establishment or a subtrust of a previously revocable trust that becomes irrevocable upon the death of the grantor. The QTIP election allows an interest in trust property to qualify for the marital deduction. A QTIP trust must provide that the surviving spouse is entitled to receive all of the income for life, and may compel the trustee to invest any unproductive trust assets productively.

In order to qualify for the marital deduction, the QTIP trust's provisions must state that all income from the property will be distributed to the surviving spouse during his or her lifetime, and that neither the trustee nor anyone else (including the spouse) may not appoint the QTIP trust property to someone other than the spouse. [I.R.C. § 2056(b)(7)(B)] As with the credit shelter trust, the trustee is allowed to distribute to the surviving spouse such principal of the QTIP trust corpus as is needed for the health, education, maintenance, and support of the survivor, or may use a broader standard since the property will be included in the survivor's estate in any event. The spouse's income interest must continue for his or her lifetime; a provision terminating the income interest on death would be fatal to the marital deduction. A jealous testator might, however, restrict other interests (such as the possibility of discretionary principal invasion) in the event of remarriage.

Q 5:72 What is a reverse QTIP election?

Until recently, the estate tax exemption equivalent amount and the generation-skipping tax exclusion were different (for example, $1,000,000 and $1,100,000, respectively, in 2002), a possibility existed that making a QTIP election would result in no estate tax on the first spouse's death but increased GST on the death of the second spouse. In such a case, the surviving spouse might have made a "reverse" QTIP election, permitting the QTIP interest to escape estate taxation on the first death, but still utilize the first decedent's GST exemption in excess of the estate tax's exemption equivalent amount. Now that the GST exemption is tied to the estate tax credit equivalent (see Table 5-1 in SQ 5:7), the reverse QTIP election may be less important.

Q 5:73   How is the QTIP election handled?

QTIP interests will actually receive the marital deduction only if an election is made on the grantor-decedent's initial estate tax return (the failure to make a QTIP election cannot be rectified by filing an amended return). Because the surviving spouse is likely to be the person filing the estate tax return, he or she will frequently have discretion as to whether to treat an otherwise qualified interest as QTIP. The QTIP election is irrevocable. [I.R.C. § 2056(b)(7)(B)] The executor for the decedent spouse must elect to take the marital deduction (see Q 6:11).

The QTIP election must be made at the time of the filing of the estate tax return at the death of the first spouse, with a six-month extension possible. The post-mortem planner can elect or fail to elect a marital deduction with respect to a portion or all of the QTIP trust. If only a portion of the trust is covered under the election, then any appreciation or depreciation of the trust assets must be allocated pro rata, under Code Section 2056(b)(10). If a reverse QTIP election is made, it must cover all the property in the trust. Some planners prefer to provide in the trust the authority for the trustee to split the QTIP into two trusts, in case the survivor makes a partial election.

With decoupling of the federal and state estate taxes, the QTIP election has become even more complicated. Some states will recognize a QTIP trust arrangement and permit a QTIP election to be made for purposes of the state estate taxes (which frequently has a lower exemption amount) while not making the election for federal tax purposes. This may require severing the QTIP trust or the trust instrument might itself set up different trusts to permit the different elections.

Q 5:74   When is a QTIP trust most likely to be useful?

When spouses have unequal assets, it may be difficult to ensure that the maximum exemption equivalent amount ($2,000,000 in 2006) is utilized in each estate. If the wealthier spouse dies first, there may be plenty of assets fully to fund a credit shelter trust, but the wealthier spouse may be reluctant to give the surviving spouse control over the assets by leaving them outright. If the poorer spouse dies first, there may not be sufficient assets to fund the credit shelter trust at all, and the wealthier spouse may be reluctant to make a lifetime gift of assets large enough to ensure that the poorer spouse can fully utilize the exemption. QTIP trusts give the wealthier spouse a chance to reduce the total estate tax (by fully using the exemptions for both spouses) regardless of which spouse dies first, and without giving the poorer spouse control over the final disposition of the property. Consequently, QTIP trusts are especially useful in second marriage situations.

When the wealthier spouse dies first, he or she can fund a QTIP trust that will qualify for the marital deduction. The surviving spouse cannot encumber or distribute the principal, so the wealthy spouse can ensure that the property ultimately goes to his or her choice of beneficiaries. In addition, the total estate tax liability of the couple can be reduced by the consequent full use of the exemption equivalent.

To protect against the tax consequence of the poorer spouse dying first, the wealthy spouse may choose to fund a lifetime QTIP trust. Such a trust will be treated as part of the poorer spouse's estate upon his or her death, and still flow to the wealthy spouse's chosen beneficiaries.

In addition, unlike the credit shelter trust that places few restrictions on the surviving spouse (although they are important restrictions, and must be adhered to for the tax benefits to apply), the grantor can place additional restrictions on the assets through the use of QTIP trust language. For example, grantors who have children from a former marriage, or who do not want to risk their assets passing to the surviving spouse's new family if he or she remarries, could place additional restrictions on the assets by using a QTIP trust.

With the progressive reduction in estate taxes, the QTIP has become important for its flexibility. The trust that qualifies for QTIP treatment, but only if the election is made on the 706, may be divided to suit the best tax wisdom at the time of the first death, simply by making the election as to one portion of the trust, and not making it for the balance.

Charitable Gift Planning

Q 5:78 What is the difference between a charitable remainder unitrust and a charitable remainder annuity trust?

The income beneficiary of a charitable remainder unitrust is paid at a fixed percentage rate of the corpus of the trust, while the income beneficiary of a charitable remainder annuity trust is paid a fixed amount. With both trusts, income must be paid at least annually, and the income interest can be distributed during the life of the beneficiary or for a fixed number of years.

With a unitrust, the amount of the payment will vary as the trust value varies. In other words, the actual investment and earnings experience of the trust will benefit (or harm) both the income beneficiary and the charitable beneficiary; higher investment return will simultaneously increase the unitrust calculation in future years and increase the value of the trust corpus ultimately distributed to the charitable beneficiary. On the other hand, both beneficiaries will share negative investment experience as well, so the income beneficiary will be unable to rely on the future stream of income.

The grantor of an annuity trust must fix the amount of the annuity at the creation of the trust. Even if investment experience changes, the annuity amount will not vary. If investments underperform the annuity amount, the trust will slowly (or rapidly) diminish in value. Meanwhile, the income beneficiary will have a predictable and reliable stream of income.

An important benefit of a unitrust is its ability to allow a "zero-out" of the generation-skipping transfer tax. Property can be left in a charitable remainder unitrust for a long period of time, remainder to grandchildren. If the property is worth more than $2,000,000 (the GST exemption amount in 2006), there may be significant tax if the value cannot be reduced through the application of a discounting formula. However, this is only permitted if a unitrust, not an annuity trust, is the vehicle chosen.

Life Insurance as an Estate Planning Tool

Q 5:84   Can life insurance be used as an estate planning tool?

Planning an estate using insurance proceeds is sensible but often risky. Making a probate or trust estate the beneficiary of life insurance proceeds is desirable when the rest of the estate assets are not sufficiently liquid to take care of taxes and administrative expenses; however, if the insured retains any ownership rights in the policy, the entire policy proceeds will be included in the insured's estate and thus subject to estate tax. [I.R.C. § 2042] If the policy is gifted to another, the value of the policy will be subject to gift tax, and if the gift is made within three years of the insured's death, it will still be deemed includible in the insured's estate. [I.R.C. § 2035]

For most people, estate taxation of life insurance is not an issue because the value of their assets is far less than the $2,000,000 unified credit exemption (in 2006); neither the insured's estate nor the beneficiaries are required to pay taxes on the proceeds. For those who have substantial assets, adding a $100,000 life insurance policy can translate into quite a tax risk, because the initial taxable rate is usually 37 percent. In other words, it is easy to overlook the value of life insurance in calculating the likely estate tax liability while estate planning, particularly for younger clients who may have smaller estates but large life insurance policies.

Q 5:89   What are some of the problems with using life insurance trusts?

An ILIT (or an STDLIT—second-to-die life insurance trust) is not without its administrative costs and problems. In addition to the expense of establishing the trust, the arrangement requires (like all nongrantor irrevocable trusts, and unlike revocable grantor trusts) that a separate tax identification number be assigned to the trust at its creation. If the trust has any income over $100 (the standard deduction for trusts) the trustee must file annual returns. (During the grantor's lifetime the trust is a "grantor trust" and the trustee need only provide a statement to the grantor for inclusion in the grantor's tax return, while providing information about to whom the statement was delivered when filing the trust's own 1041 income tax return; after the grantor's death, Crummey power-holders may have to be treated as partial "grantors" of the trust, with the rest treated as a complex trust subject to the steep income tax brackets imposed on trusts.) As discussed in Q 5:28, any life insurance trust will likely be designed as a "Crummey" trust, requiring annual notices to beneficiaries of their Crummey withdrawal rights—a requirement that clients tend to forget but are unwilling to pay their attorneys to remember.

There are additional problems, related to the very nature of life insurance. First, some clients may intend to access the cash value of the policy for future needs, and will be unpleasantly surprised to find that the cash value is no longer available, and they can no longer borrow against the policy, since trust assets may not be used for the client's own benefit. Second, the life insurance itself, not the trust, may cause anguish. Examples of problems: the agent sells a policy with an "increasing premium"—here the problem is obvious. Or the agent touts the policy as able to "pay for itself" in 5 years, 10 years, or 15 years, but uses overly optimistic forecasts of dividend performance. When the anniversary rolls around, the client finds that further premiums are still required, perhaps indefinitely. Or the agent sells a blended policy of term and whole life, expecting to buy additional paid-up whole life with any dividends and ultimately phase out the term component, and the client does not understand the complexity of the arrangement and is unhappy with the risk of paying premiums into infinity. The attorney must at all costs avoid being associated in the client's mind with an insurance agent who the client believes has over-promised or who is unwilling to respond clearly and in detail to the client's fears.

Q 5:91   How are the premiums paid during the life of the insured?

The trust may be funded or unfunded. A funded life insurance trust has both the insurance policy (or policies) and other assets that produce enough income to pay the premiums. Policy premiums in an unfounded trust are paid through gifts to the trust from the insured. These gift transfers are covered by the annual gift exclusion, which allows up to $12,000 per year to be transferred with no tax or reporting consequences. Planners usually advise against funded trusts, because the settlor may have to pay the gift tax upon the transfer of income-producing assets into the trust, and income tax on the trust's income. Furthermore, if community property rather than the separate property of the insured is used either to fund the trust or pay premiums, the IRS will consider the noninsured spouse a settlor of the trust and its tax advantages are lost. [Treas. Reg. § 20.2042-1(c)(5)] Sometimes, however, the insurance policy itself may generate income that is then the property of the trust, such as a dividend from a policy that does not permit dividends to be applied to reduce premium, or a stock dividend if an insurance company de-mutualizes.

Q 5:92   What is the difference between a "Crummey" trust and an irrevocable life insurance trust?

As discussed in Q 5:28, a "Crummey" power written into a trust enables the settlor of the trust to make annual gifts to the trust and still maintain some control over how the transferred assets are managed and distributed. As long as the beneficiary is allowed a brief window period each year (usually two to four weeks) during which he or she can withdraw the assets, the IRS will consider transfers into the trust to be completed present-interest gifts rather than a gift of a future interest and the $12,000 annual gift tax exclusion will apply.

One of the most common uses of Crummey provisions is in the purchase of life insurance. In order to prevent the value of life insurance from being counted as part of a decedent's estate, the decedent must not have been the owner of the policy within the three years prior to his or her death. This requirement can often be met by having other individuals (usually the children) purchase the policy, even if the purchase is made with funds given to the individuals each year. An irrevocable life insurance trust may, however, be more attractive, because it permits the grantor some assurance that the insurance will remain in force, and that the proceeds will be available to ensure liquidity of the estate after the grantor's death.

Some practitioners believe that a Crummey trust must have liquid funds available for the beneficiary during the withdrawal window. This would mean that the settlor of the trust must transfer enough money into the trust not only to cover the insurance policy premiums, but also to provide available funds for the beneficiary if he or she exercises the withdrawal right. There are additional problems if the sole asset of the trust is a single insurance policy and multiple beneficiaries are given Crummey powers in the trust: If one beneficiary wishes to exercise his or her right of withdrawal, the insurance company might demand that the beneficiaries agree to this before the policy can be invaded. However, other practitioners believe there is authority that a Crummey ILIT is effective even if the only asset that may be used to meet the beneficiaries' withdrawal rights is life insurance, even, the IRS has held, group term life insurance. The reasoning is that the Trustee can always borrow to meet the withdrawal obligation. Another, more conservative approach is to require that the contribution to the trust be made sufficiently in advance of the premium due date that for the period of time subject to the withdrawal power, the trust does in fact hold liquid assets. Once the period (for example, 30 days) has expired, the trustee can make the wise investment choice to pay the policy premium. Those who elect this approach are still uncomfortable with trusts funded only with group term life insurance, but there have been several IRS letter rulings approving such arrangements.

The settlor must take care that the language of the trust document allows for the withdrawal of an amount no greater than the annual exclusion amount, or the entire trust corpus may be deemed includible in the beneficiary's estate at his or her death. In addition, as discussed in Q 5:28, a trust that expects to hold insurance with high premiums, but have few beneficiaries to share the withdrawal rights over contributions, may need a "hanging power" to prevent beneficiaries from being deemed owners of the policy, and for some attorneys, this provision is boilerplate.

Q 5:93   Can the generation-skipping tax exemption language be incorporated into a life insurance trust?

Yes. Settlors who wish to name grandchildren or other "skip persons" as beneficiaries of their estates should consider generation-skipping insurance trusts. A great deal of money can be leveraged through such an insurance vehicle because for generation-skipping tax purposes, the premium constitutes the transfer, not the face value of the policy. Because up to $2 million in gift or death transfers is exempt if made to skip persons, both the settlor and the trust can benefit from that exemption. Transfers either of assets or of premium payments into the trust are exempt up to $1 million; thus the settlor can ensure the beneficiaries a substantial "return" on the premiums paid.

However, the final generation-skipping tax regulations have now made it clear that the "leveraging" made possible by an insurance trust funded by "annual exclusion" gifts used to pay premiums, will not work unless the "skip" generation, the grandchildren, each have separate shares of the trust as to which the exclusion gifts apply. It is no longer possible, therefore, to set up a trust that benefits children and grandchildren, fund it with gifts that qualify for the annual exclusion, have the trust continue for the lifetimes of children and grandchildren with benefits for both, and then pass GST tax-free to the grandchildren. Instead, the trust would have to be set up from the beginning with separate sub-trusts for each grandchild only. [Treas. Reg. § 26.2642-1(c)(3)]

Valuation Discounts as an Estate Planning Tool

Q 5:94   What are valuation discounts?

Where one individual controls all of the rights with regard to a given asset, it will be valued at its fair market value—what a willing buyer and willing seller would agree upon as a price to exchange the asset. Where the owner's ability to transfer or control the property has been reduced, the property's value to a willing buyer will be lower.

Example 5-3. Kathleen owns The Widget Factory and all its machinery, receivables, and inventory. It has been valued at $5,000,000. Kathleen creates TWF, Inc., and transfers all of the assets to the new corporation in return for all of the shares of stock of TWF. Her resulting 500,000 shares are worth $10 each, and her investment retains its original total value. When Kathleen sells (or gives away) 100 shares of TWF, Inc., her remaining stock is no longer worth $10 each; even though she has disposed of only $1,000 worth of stock, an appraiser determines that her remaining stock is now worth only $3,500,000. Her principal asset has thereby been reduced in value, and on her death her estate will pay tax only on the lower value.

Q 5:95 How can discounting be utilized in estate planning?

Valuation discounting usually comes into play when assets of the donor-decedent are held in a family limited partnership, limited liability company, or other non-individual capacity. A share in such a partnership may be worth much less on the open market than its fractional value of the underlying assets would indicate, especially where the share is a minority share with only limited control over the total assets. Discounting can substantially reduce the tax liability, although it will almost always require the services of a professional appraiser, an audit, and an argument.

For the client with nondiscounted assets and a desire to minimize estate taxes, establishment of an appropriate ownership vehicle may permit a substantial reduction in the assets' value. Although most of the early use of discounting occurred with family limited partnerships, the concept of a limited liability company (LLC) recently developed in many states has made the LLC the instrument of choice for most practitioners.

A family limited partnership (FLP) usually provides that the parents act as general partners, with other family members holding limited partnership interests. The structure of the FLP will permit the general partners to determine when and whether to distribute income, but problems may arise with any structure that permits distribution to be allocated on anything other than a non-pro rata basis, either because the parents will be deemed to have so much control that the FLP is includible in their estate, or because the possibility of never receiving a distribution will make the gift to children ineligible for the annual exclusion by failing the "present interest" test. (See Q 5:19.) Because the limited partners have some rights with regard to the partnership's assets, even though limited, the value of the general partner's ownership interest is thus reduced, resulting in a lower value for estate tax purposes. Depending on the structure of the FLP (e.g., whether the limited partners share in current profits), the reduction in value may be more or less.

In general terms, the LLC combines the tax advantages of partner-ships with the inherent advantages of corporations (primarily reduc-tions in personal liability for LLC "members"), permitting the separation of ownership and voting rights, simplifying the reporting requirements, and minimizing the income tax effect, while still permit-ting the individuals to shield themselves from the prospect of personal liability for the LLC's actions. The valuation reduction for assets trans-ferred to an LLC will be similar to those for an FLP's property, and for the same reasons of reduced control and marketability.

Typically, an LLC (or FLP) will be established by the owner of the assets to be included, and the assets transferred to the entity. Other family members will either purchase shares in the entity, or receive their shares as gifts (subject to the annual gift exclusion amount). Immediately upon the transfer of a small minority interest, the value of the entity's remaining shares will be substantially reduced. Over time, as more shares are transferred, the remaining value may become a minority interest, with even larger valuation discounts. If the entity is funded with real estate, it is important to consider whether the transfer of control from the original owner (as majority stakeholder) to the other parties, will be considered a transfer of a controlling interest subject to a special conveyance tax known in some states as the "controlling interest transfer tax." In cases likely subject to dispute, where the stakes are high, it may be worthwhile to make such annual transfers large enough to require filing of a gift tax return, in order to start the state of limita-tions running on the valuation used in determining the gift value. Only if a gift tax return has been filed advising the Service that a valuation discount has been used, is the Service precluded from revisiting the valuation issue upon the donor's death.

In many cases, the death of the original owner will vest the remain-ing interests in the other owners (usually the decedent's children). The value of the remaining interests at the time of the decedent's death will be reduced as a result of the partial ownership, thereby substantially reducing the taxable estate. [Rev. Rul. 93-12, 1993-1 C.B. 202]

Q 5:96   Are there negative tax effects of using valuation discounts?

Upon the subsequent liquidation of the LLC/FLP and distribution of the proceeds, the recipients will recognize a substantial capital gain for income tax purposes, because they will "carry over" the original owner's basis. Nonetheless, the result is favorable: The capital gains tax may be incurred many years later, and will (at least under current tax law) be no more than 20 percent of the gain, while estate tax liability is incurred immediately upon the death of the original owner, and may be as high as 50 percent (reduced in 2003 to 49 percent) of the value of the assets. Of course, after the scheduled elimination of the federal estate tax and imposition of carryover basis rules in 2011, the calculus of valuation discounts will change radically.

Three other practical considerations complicate the use of LLC/FLP to "reduce" the value of assets. First, because the Internal Revenue Service has a long-running hostility to the use of the technique, despite repeated losses in the courts, it is likely that the technique will result in an audit, an assessment of an underpayment penalty, and the need for a negotiated settlement, all of which will increase the attorneys' fees involved in settling the estate. The IRS has repeatedly tried to argue that the grantor or founder of the LLC/FLP has somehow retained a taxable interest in the assets transferred. Second, where the technique plays out over time and a grantor first funds the LLC/FLP and then transfers interests, it will be necessary to file gift tax returns that fully disclose the discount taken in order to start the statute of limitations running. And third, new, strict "preparer penalties" set by Congress, together with the new rules for tax practitioners set out in "Circular 230," create the possibility of financial liability for the attorney who counsels a taxpayer to use the technique aggressively.

Generation-Skipping Tax Planning

Q 5:102   What is the "generation-skipping tax"?

The generation-skipping tax is a tax imposed under Code Section 2601 on any transfer of assets to a skip person (e.g., grandchildren or more distant issue), whether the transfer is a bequest or gift outright to a "direct skip" or is channeled through a taxable distribution or taxable termination. The intent of the generation-skipping tax is to prevent families from accumulating wealth by establishing multigenerational "dynasty trusts" in order to escape repeat taxation.

The GST is a flat tax, equal to the highest federal transfer tax rate in existence at the time of the transfer, 50 percent in 2002. Originally, each transferor had a $1 million exemption, indexed for inflation, increasing annually; starting in 2004, the exemption tracks the estate tax exemption, beginning at $1,500,00 in 2004 (although gift tax will still be imposed on gifts in excess of $1,000,000)

The generation-skipping tax is imposed in addition to any gift tax or estate tax payable by the transferor and is based on the amount received by the transferee. [I.R.C. § 2623]

Q 5:103 What changes are planned for the generation-skipping tax in the future?

Individuals. As with the estate tax itself, the generation-skipping tax is slated for complete repeal in 2010. In the meantime, starting in 2004 the GST exemption amount tracks the estate tax amount.

Table 5-4.   **Changes in Generation-Skipping Tax Exemption Amounts and Rates Made By EGTRRA**

Year	Exemption	Maximum Rate
2002	$ 1,100,000	50%
2003	$ 1,100,000 (plus inflation adjustment)	49%
2004	$ 1,500,000	48%
2005	$ 1,500,000	47%
2006	$ 2,000,000	46%
2007	$ 2,000,000	45%
2008	$ 2,000,000	45%
2009	$ 3,500,000	45%
2010	N/A repealed	Repealed

Business Owners. Current estate tax law allows some owners of family businesses to pass a larger amount to their heirs without incurring state taxes. Prior to 2004, at least some small business owners could take advantage of the so-called QFOBI (Qualified Family Owned

Business Interests) rules to pass a total of up to $1.35 million without estate taxes. Since these special deductions ended in 2003, however, they are not discussed here.

Q 5:105 Are there any exceptions to the GST?

Yes. There are two important "exceptions." There is a "predeceased ancestor" exception to the skip rule: a bequest from a grandparent to a grandchild whose parent is deceased will not be subject to the GST. [I.R.C. § 2651(e)] This also applies to great-nieces and great-nephews. Whether or not the ancestor is "predeceased" is determined 90 days after the transfer occurs. This makes it desirable to include in documents dealing with sums over the GST exemption that a person is deemed to have predeceased if (s)he does not survive 90 days after the testator's death. Very important: the timely disclaimer by a child is *not* treated as if the child had predeceased the testator. The child who disclaims $2.2 million so that it passes instead to a grandchild will have caused a direct skip of $2.2 million, resulting in a significant tax. Secondly, trusts that were irrevocable when the GST tax was created, October 22, 1986, are "grandfathered" and distributions from or terminations of such trusts are *exempt* from the GST. However, if the trust is substantially reformed or amended, the exemption disappears. There are innumerable letter rulings in which beneficiaries sought IRS approval for changes to GST-grandfathered trusts that would not affect the exemption, usually when multiple beneficiaries wish to sever the trust into separate trusts. Usually it is inadvisable to exercise any power of appointment over a grandfathered trust, as well.

[I.R.C. § 2515] When a direct skip is made from a trust, the trustee is liable for the tax. [I.R.C. §§ 2603(a)(3), (2)]

Q 5:109.1 What is an ETIP?

An "ETIP" is an "estate tax inclusion period" during which time the generation skip has not occurred, and upon termination of the ETIP, the skip is deemed to occur and the generation-skipping tax exclusion must be elected or the tax paid, if appropriate. An example of an ETIP is the term of a qualified personal residence trust or QPRT if upon termination the QPRT will pass to "skip" persons, grandchildren. Not until the term of the QPRT terminations can the generation skipping tax exemption be allocated to the gift.

Q 5:111   How should an attorney draft to avoid the imposition of the generation-skipping transfer tax?

In this area as in many others, flexibility is the key. Some attorneys are inclined to assume the "worst" (or in another sense, the best) case: that the client will die with more assets than the GST exemption amount, or that the amount held in trust for a long period of time, such as the lifetime of the client's children, will ultimately exceed the GST exemption amount. Taken to its extreme, this can result in a client with relatively modest assets carrying home a 50-page trust document complete with GST-exempt and non-GST-exempt shares. Why? If the GST exemption is not "allocated," at the client's death, entirely to one share and not at all to the other share, a proportion of each distribution to a skip person will be subject to the GST. This is annoying, to say the least, and thorough drafters will wish to put everything in place to avoid such an eventuality entirely.

However, an alternative is simply to be sure that the Trustee has the power to divide any trust into two shares. If "worst" comes to worst and the client dies with over $2,000,000, the trustee can carve up the shares, allocate the exemption to the biggest shares, and try to make distributions to non-skip persons from the non-exempt shares. Of course, this may result in "wasted" GST exemption if the trusts to which the exemption is allocated wind up being consumed for the benefit of children rather than lasting to the next generation. But the attorney should remember that the ultimate goal of estate planning is to meet the client's dispositive wishes, not to take advantage of every tax strategy in the book in order to extend tax exemptions into perpetuity if possible.

This approach can also be used for the division between bypass and marital shares of a trust, but the disadvantage is that the entire trust property must be set up so as to qualify for QTIP treatment in order to give the trustee the option to make such a choice. With the trust-splitting for GST exemption purposes, there need not be any change to the trusts.

Q 5:112   What is an intentionally defective irrevocable trust?

When a living grantor has determined that it is appropriate to incur the GST during life, usually in order to transfer highly appreciating property to future generations before the value increases exponentially, it is possible to improve the tax effect of such a transfer even further. Because the rules for estate, gift, and generation-skipping tax treatment differ from those for income tax treatment of trusts, it is possible to retain a power in the grantor that has the effect of causing the future income of the trust to be taxed to the grantor even as the trust's assets are moved out of the grantor's estate for transfer tax purposes. In other words, assets with a value of up to the GST exemption amount can be transferred into a GST trust even as the grantor is treated as the owner for income tax purposes, and pays the income tax incurred by trust earnings for the rest of the grantor's life. This effectively increases the amount transferred to "skip" generations, because any outright gift to skip persons would result in the recipients' paying income taxes on subsequent earnings. The value of this type of planning will be limited to high-income assets (whether because of yield or recognition of capital gains) owned by extremely wealthy individuals so that they would prefer to bear the income tax themselves, thereby further reducing the taxable estate while concomitantly *benefiting* future generations.

> **Example 5-4.** Diane has an estate of $10,000,000. She establishes an intentionally defective (grantor) lifetime GST trust for her grandchildren, and transfers $2,000,000 in growth stock to the trust. During her life, she will pay tax on the trust's income (including any capital gains generated by sale and reinvestment); upon her death, the trust will have grown by the full amount of capital growth and accumulations without any reduction for tax paid, while Diane's estate will have been reduced not only by the initial gift but also by the income taxes paid on the trust's income.

Practice-Related Issues

Q 5:114 How should the elder law attorney advise clients with over $2 million in assets who wish to leave everything ultimately to their only child?

A married couple consults an attorney about establishing tax-wise estate planning. The couple's assets consist of just under $2 million in total nonretirement assets, but the husband has a $500,000 rollover IRA. Absent tax restrictions, the couple would prefer to leave everything to one another and, upon the second death, to their only son. Knowing how little their son has set aside for his own retirement, they hope to allow him to use the IRA as his own retirement account, extending the tax deferral as far as possible into his life expectancy. What planning might the attorney undertake to meet this couple's goals?

The clients have several choices, and each choice can be constructed to meet two of their three goals. It will be impossible to meet all three.

In order to provide sufficient funds for the wife (assuming she survives the husband), the husband might choose to name her as beneficiary of his IRA. The couple could then establish credit shelter trusts for one another (whether by a joint revocable trust that divides into two trusts on the first death or by two separate trusts, each holding half the couple's assets). This approach maximizes the benefit for the surviving spouse (particularly assuming that the wife survives), and also permits a slight reduction in the minimum required distribution (because joint lives can be utilized). If, however, the wife dies before the husband and after his required beginning date, the IRA must pay out over his remaining life expectancy, which may be much shorter than the son's. If the husband dies first, the wife will either be forced to disclaim a portion of the IRA, or his credit shelter trust will be insufficiently funded; if the wife dies first, her credit shelter trust will always be underfunded. Although scheduled increases in the exemption equivalent amount may alleviate any estate tax problems, likely growth in both the IRA and nonretirement assets will increase the probability that the estate of the second spouse to die will bear at least some estate tax liability.

The husband could, instead, name the son as beneficiary of the IRA (but only with the wife's consent). This would permit easy funding of the credit shelter trust if the husband died first (a portion of his assets would still need to go into the trust, but there should be sufficient assets to fund it fully). If the wife died first, her credit shelter trust might be inadequately funded. On the plus side, the son would be able to use his life expectancy to slow the withdrawals from (and maximize the income tax benefit of) the IRA after the husband's death. Unfortunately, this approach completely misses the couple's primary planning goal by not giving the wife access to the IRA benefits if she survives her husband.

A third approach would be to name a credit shelter trust as beneficiary of the IRA. Of course, the precise rules governing the use of trusts as beneficiaries of retirement assets must be complied with, but this approach permits the minimization of estate tax (at least if the husband dies first) while keeping the IRA assets out of the wife's estate. The goal of extending the payout period is only minimally met: The IRA would have to make distributions based only on the wife's life expectancy after the husband's death. This approach may be an improvement over simply naming the wife as beneficiary (because it gets money out of her estate for estate tax purposes), but it has one significant drawback over that approach: All distributions of IRA "principal" (for accounting purposes) will be taxed as "income" to the trust at the highest marginal rate. This will reduce the security afforded to the wife by the IRA.

Q 5:115 How should the elder law attorney advise a conservator of a living parent's estate regarding the estate tax consequences of the parent's death?

An adult child has been appointed conservator of the assets of his mother, a widow, which total more than $2 million. He is concerned about estate tax consequences when she dies. What questions should the attorney ask, and what advice can he give?

Possibilities for tax planning do not necessarily end with the loss of the principal's capacity. Depending on state law, it may be possible for the conservator to secure authority to make gifts of his mother's assets or even to engage in more complicated tax planning approaches such as establishment of a family limited partnership or limited liability company.

Under most state statutes governing gifts or transfers by conservators, a key question will be whether the ward has previously engaged in gifting or other tax planning. A full history of gifts should be obtained from the conservator-client, along with any indications of his mother's feelings regarding taxes in general and estate taxes in particular. In addition, even an incapacitated ward may have some ability to understand and participate in tax planning decisions; every effort should be made to explain the value and importance of tax planning to the ward and secure her approval (even if it is limited by her ability to comprehend the nuances of the proposed plan) for presentation to the court. To that end, it may be advisable to secure independent counsel for the ward; if a court-appointed attorney was involved in the initial proceedings, he or she may be in a position to participate in the subsequent petition for approval of the tax plan.

Once information about the ward's history and wishes has been accumulated, a proposal might be made to the court for permission to make appropriate tax plans. In most cases, the obvious choice will be to request authority to make gifts from the ward's estate. That may require showing that there has been a history of gift-giving in the past, that the ward's welfare will not suffer as a result of the gifts, or that the ward's personal value system would support making gifts to reduce taxes paid by her heirs. If approval for a program of gift-giving is sought, it might make sense to request that the authority continue for future years, to permit the annual exclusion amount to be gifted to each of the ward's heirs or devisees on a repeating basis.

Q 5:116 What are some important estate planning considerations for a married couple with a large estate whose eventual beneficiaries may include their children and various charitable interests?

This question may be best answered with an example:

Example 5-5. Homer and Fern are 63 and 60. They have been married for 40 years and raised three children. They have a combined estate of over $5 million, which includes a significant amount of highly appreciated stock and investment real estate, both of which categories produce little income but great potential for growth. Their children are all successful professionals, and have children of their own. None of Homer and Fern's children will depend on an inheritance from their parents to make their own ways in life. Homer and Fern have long been interested in the arts and their local university; they are both actively working, and with their investment income they are in the highest income tax bracket.

Homer and Fern might want to consider a charitable remainder unitrust. They could transfer some portion (or all) of their appreciated stock and investment real estate to the trust, and the trust could immediately sell the property so transferred. The proceeds would not be subjected to capital gains taxes and could be invested in less risky holdings (with more modest growth) more suitable for Homer and Fern's future needs. The unitrust payment would be recalculated each year based on the current value of the trusts assets, so they could expect the payments to grow over time.

Importantly, Homer and Fern would have thereby converted non-income-producing property into a reliable annual yield of, say, an 8 percent return on their investment. Although their actual payout might go down over time (if market growth fails to keep up with the 8 percent payout requirement), it will never be eliminated entirely, so they will continue to enjoy a high level of security. Meanwhile, they will receive a current charitable income tax deduction of about 20 percent to 25 percent of their contribution (depending on the payout structure, their precise ages, and the then-current interest rate presumed by the IRS regulations). They may elect to make a series of contributions over a period of years, each one calculated to have maximum effect based on their taxable income for that year.

Because the remaining trust assets will pass to charities on the death of both Homer and Fern, there is no property to be included in their taxable estate. They may even retain the power to change the ultimate charitable beneficiary without compromising the integrity or effectiveness of the trust, so that the final distribution can reflect their wishes as of the latest possible opportunity.

The principal problem with this plan is that Homer and Fern's children will not receive any of the property given to the charitable remainder trust after Homer and Fern die. If this concerns them, Homer and Fern may choose to use a portion of their 8 percent income to purchase life insurance with a value approximating that of the gifted assets; such an arrangement, of course, would need to be accomplished through either an irrevocable life insurance trust or by gifts of the premium amounts to their children each year. But if they have been actively making gifts to their children as a means of reducing their estates, they will not be able to increase the amount of the gifts to cover the life insurance premiums without eating into their lifetime exemption equivalent amount.

A secondary problem may be that the trust return cannot keep up with the 8 percent requirement. Recent stock market events have caused interest rates to fluctuate, and the "adjusted federal rate," used to compute the tax deduction upon funding the trust, is as of this writing (April 2006) at 5.6 percent. Homer and Fern may wish to wait until there is some recovery in the market before undertaking this plan.

Chapter 6

Post-Mortem Estate Planning

Qualified disclaimers and other post-mortem planning techniques have become more important in recent years. With more estates at taxable levels, and with retirement accounts and the value of real estate both rising rapidly in many estates, the circumstances when the estate was originally planned are often no longer operative at the time of death. This chapter is intended to provide an understanding of disclaimers and post-death elections and their use in post-mortem estate planning.

Post-Mortem Tax Reporting

Q 6:2 What tax liabilities will a decedent's estate incur?

The death of the decedent may require the personal representative, executor, trustee, or even heirs to deal with at least three different types of tax liability at the state and/or federal level:

1. Estate (and possibly inheritance) tax;

2. Decedent's final income tax; and

3. Fiduciary income tax.

Usually, each type of tax will require both federal and state (and sometimes local) filings.

Q 6:8 When must the estate fiduciary tax return be filed?

The personal representative or executor of the decedent's estate must file an income tax return—Form 1041 (U.S. Income Tax Return for Estates and Trusts)—for any taxable period during which the estate's gross income is $600 or more or if any beneficiary is a nonresident alien. [I.R.C. § 6012(a)(3); Treas. Reg. § 1.6012-3(a)] The estate's taxable income is income that the estate receives during the period of administration or settlement. [Treas. Reg. § 1.641(b)-3(a)] The fiduciary must also file a separate Schedule K-1 for each beneficiary. This schedule must show the beneficiary's share of income, deductions, and credits. The estate fiduciary tax return is due on the fifteenth day of the fourth month following the close of the tax year of the estate. The executor can choose either a calendar or fiscal year. The personal representative chooses the estate's accounting period when the first Form 1041 is filed. (Form SS-4, which is used to apply for an estate tax identification number, requests a fiscal year, but it is not required to be completed, and can be changed.) Estates must pay estimated taxes in the same manner as individuals and use the same estimated tax payment. Form 1041-ES is used to pay estimated taxes. New estates for their first two years do not have to report and pay estimated taxes. [I.R.C. § 6654(1)]

Q 6:8.1 What planning considerations exist in connection with the estate's fiduciary income tax return?

There are two particular areas of concern in filing fiduciary income tax returns for a decedent. First, there are questions about which kinds of administrative deductions should be taken on the income tax return and which are only estate tax deductions. Second, questions might be raised about what qualifies as an "administrative expense" on the fiduciary income tax return.

Timing of deductions may also be important. The estate may "pass through" to the beneficiaries any excess estate administration expenses not claimed on the estate tax return, but *only* on the final tax return. [I.R.C. § 642(h)(2) and Treas. Reg. § 1.642(h)-2] It is therefore advisable if possible to incur the expenses during what will probably be the estate's final tax year so that the beneficiaries can take advantage of the deductions distributed to them.

Not all expenses related to administration of the estate are clearly deductible on the fiduciary income tax return, however. The IRS has adopted a distinction between "transmission expenses" and "management expenses" in an attempt to clarify confusion occasioned by the Supreme Court holding in *Commissioner of Internal Revenue v. Estate of Hubert*, 520 U.S. 93 (1997). The former, expenses related to the actual transfer of property to the successors, are chargeable to the estate tax return. The latter, expenses related to investment, preservation and maintenance of the estate's property during administration, would be deductible on the fiduciary income tax return. The problem, of course, then becomes one of determining whether a given expense is "transmission" or "maintenance" in nature. As Justice O'Connor wrote in the plurality opinion in *Hubert*, "logic and taxation are not always the best of friends." (Justice O'Connor was actually quoting Justice McReynolds from a 1922 dissenting opinion.)

Another, more recent Supreme Court decision has stilled discussions and concerns about a related issue: whether some estate (or trust) administrative expenses are fully deductible. At issue in *Knight v. Commissioner of Internal Revenue*, 128 S. Ct 782 (2008) was whether a trust's investment advisory fees were deductible as administrative expenses, and therefore not subject to the "2% floor" imposed on most deductions. The trustee argued that although individuals might choose to incur investment advisory fees, a fiduciary was required to do so in order to discharge his fiduciary obligations. Therefore, according to the argument, the fees were administrative in nature, and not subject to the 2% floor. The Supreme Court disagreed, and accepted the IRS definition, which essentially held that "administrative expenses" are limited to those items which only a trust or estate will incur.

Q 6:9   What is income in respect of a decedent?

While not a tax return filed by the estate or a trustee, income in respect of a decedent (IRD) filings require some special mention. Income in respect of a decedent is any item of gross income that cannot properly be included on the decedent's final return, but to which the decedent had a right and which the decedent would have received if he or she had not died. [I.R.C. § 691(a)(1)] When the income is instead paid out to the beneficiary (for example, by a distribution from an inherited IRA), the beneficiary must pay income tax on the distribution just as the decedent would have done. In those cases where the decedent's estate was taxable and included income items (such as individual retirement account or pension benefits payable directly to a beneficiary), the beneficiary's income tax will be affected by the amount of estate tax paid; that is, the beneficiary will be able to deduct a portion of the estate tax paid that was attributable to the IRD items. This does not require a special filing by the estate or trustee but is important to keep in mind in post-mortem planning. Most beneficiaries will be unaware of the concept of IRD and will not realize that they will have to make complicated tax calculations on income received from the decedent in the future in order to take advantage of the deduction. It is vitally important that beneficiaries of IRD be made aware that what they receive will be subject to income tax payable by them, to avoid unpleasant surprises.

Estate Tax Elections and Valuations

Q 6:11 How is the qualifying terminable interest property election handled?

The qualified terminable interest property (QTIP) election allows a property interest to qualify for the marital deduction (see Q 5:71) even though the surviving spouse receives an income interest rather than outright ownership of the property. The QTIP election is irrevocable. [I.R.C. § 2056(b)] The election is usually made as to a trust for the benefit of the surviving spouse, and has the effect of causing the property subject to the election to be taxable in the surviving spouse's estate rather than the decedent spouse's estate.

In order to qualify for the QTIP election, the surviving spouse must have an income interest in the trust for life, payable at least annually, and the income interest cannot be appointed to anyone other than the spouse. The QTIP election must be made at the time the estate tax return is filed at the death of the first spouse. A QTIP election may also be made with respect to an inter vivos gift in trust to a spouse, in which case the election would be made on the gift tax return. An extension to make a QTIP election may be allowed at the discretion of the IRS if the taxpayer demonstrates that he or she acted reasonably and in good faith and granting the relief will not prejudice the government. [Treas. Reg. § 301.9100-1(c)] The executor can make the QTIP election by listing the QTIP on Schedule M on the estate tax return and deducting its value. The current procedure requires the action on the part of the executor to elect out of the QTIP marital deduction. The post-mortem planner can elect or fail to elect a marital deduction with respect to a portion or all of the QTIP trust. If only a portion of the trust is covered under the election, then any appreciation or depreciation of the trust assets must be allocated pro rata, under Internal Revenue Code Section 2056(b)(10).

Sometimes it may be beneficial to the entire community estate to choose not to make the QTIP election, even as to a trust that was expressly established to meet QTIP rules. When such a "reverse QTIP election" is made, it must cover all the property in the trust. Some planners prefer to provide in the trust the authority for the trustee to split the trust, in case the survivor makes a partial election. Such a reverse election might, for example, be made to maximize the credit exemption equivalent amount in the first spouse's estate or intentionally to incur estate taxes on the first death in order to prevent later taxation at higher bracket rates (though of course this latter approach is much less common in the current environment of uncertain increases in exemption amounts).

More commonly, the term "reverse QTIP election" is used to describe the election made when the executor of the first spouse to die elects to treat estate property for which the QTIP election has been made as if it had not been made, in order that the decedent's (GST) exemption can be allocated to that property. [Treas. Reg. § 26.2652-1(a)(3)] Otherwise, the surviving spouse would be treated as the transferor because the property will be includible in his or her estate by virtue of the QTIP election made by the first spouse to die. The easiest way to plan for this possibility (when it is not a certainty) is to be sure that the executor or trustee has the power to split any QTIP trust into shares, one of which can receive the reverse QTIP election, and one will not. This used to be standard practice when planning for couples with large estates, because the marital share was likely to exceed the amount of the GST exemption less the credit shelter amount. Soon, for all except those with significant taxable gifts or bequests, the credit shelter amount will probably meet or exceed the GST exemption, and this technique may become an anachronism. Instead, the trustee will need to have the power to split the credit shelter trust into shares—but no QTIP issue will be involved. If the fiduciary makes a QTIP election on an early federal income tax return, and the spouse subsequently disclaims the property, the disclaimer is deemed valid and the QTIP election is ignored. [Rev. Rul. 83-26, 1983-1 C.B. 234]

Q 6:12 Are there times when it makes sense to pay estate tax at the death of the first spouse?

Fiduciaries can administer the marital deduction and QTIP election either to equalize the tax burdens of both the decedent's and the survivor's trust, or defer the tax burden until the death of the second spouse. Equalization is possible through the use of the marital deduction when the spouse with the larger estate dies first; although taxes may therefore become due on the death of the first spouse, this may reduce the tax risk at the death of the survivor. The fiduciary should first determine the amount likely to be needed by the survivor for his or her remaining years; if the survivor is young, a deferral may make more sense. Then the choice between equalization and deferral should be based on a comparison of the income earnings likely on the deferred tax and the tax liability itself. This sort of calculation, however, is made incalculably more difficult by the combination of a changing estate tax exemption equivalent amount and uncertainty about the near-term future of the estate tax itself. Savings from earlier payment of estate taxes are likely to be small, and the possibility that tax paid on the first spouse's death might turn out to have been altogether avoidable is large.

Example 6-1. John dies in 2008 with an estate of $10,000,000. His surviving (and second) wife, Mary, has a $1,000,000 estate of her own. John's will names his oldest son as executor and establishes a trust for Mary's benefit that will be funded with the maximum exemption equivalent amount ($2,000,000 in the year of his death); the rest of his estate passes to a QTIP trust for Mary's benefit and, upon her death, to his children from his first marriage. Assuming a full QTIP election, no estate tax will be due on John's death. On Mary's death, the entire remaining QTIP trust balance will be subject to estate tax as part of her estate, which might cause taxation (assuming no growth or reduction in value of the trust or her estate and no change in the current tax structure—all of which assumptions are, of course, flawed) at 45 percent. Instead, John's executor (his son) might choose not to elect QTIP treatment for the entire trust and (assuming he has authority to make a partial reverse QTIP election by dividing the trust into two separate trusts) instead incur and pay the tax on some portion or all of the QTIP trust. By doing so, he causes an immediate estate tax liability. Although the calculation requires guesses about future earnings and losses, expenditures by the surviving spouse, an estimate of the likely date of death for the surviving spouse, and predictions about the status of the estate tax in that future year, it may sometimes be appropriate to voluntarily incur some estate tax liability on the earlier death. Note that any net savings will inure to the benefit of the remainder beneficiaries, and at the expense of possibly lowering income distributions to the surviving spouse for his or her remaining life.

Q 6:13   How can taking the elective share ("electing against the will") benefit the surviving spouse?

State statutes often allow the surviving spouse to take an election that would allow the elective share to pass to him or her from the decedent under Code Section 2056 and thus qualify for the marital deduction. For instance, in some states the surviving spouse could elect to take his or her intestate share if it qualifies for the marital deduction, then make a gift of that share to the children. The post-mortem planner should examine the state laws closely to see which strategies are possible.

Example 6-2. Mary died in 2008, leaving an estate of $4,000,000. She is survived by her husband John and their children. Her will provides for establishment of a bypass trust for the benefit of John, with the balance of the estate being transferred to a QTIP trust. Upon John's death, both trusts devolve to a combination of the couple's children, other individuals, and several named charities. John has substantial assets already and does not wish to accumulate additional income for the remainder of his life; he also wishes primarily to benefit the children and not the other beneficiaries of Mary's estate (thereby making disclaimer a less-attractive option). He might elect under state law to receive his intestate share rather than the benefits provided by Mary's will, and then to gift all or a portion of that share to the children. By doing so, he might use up his lifetime exemption amount but reduce the total tax paid by the combined estates and effectively alter the dispositive provisions of Mary's will.

Q 6:14   How might taking the elective share not benefit the surviving spouse?

For purposes of eligibility for long-term care benefits under Medicaid, the spouse is usually required to elect to take the statutory or spousal share by virtue of the requirement that a Medicaid applicant try to access all available resources. Failure to make the election most likely will be treated as a disqualifying transfer, even if the spouse is incapable. However, making the election will not benefit the spouse but rather the Medicaid authority, which will cease providing benefits to the spouse who is now over assets (if the election results in a distribution of principal to the spouse) or, if the "elective share" results only in income payable to the spouse, the Medicaid authority will benefit by requiring the income to be paid to the nursing facility. Of course, if the spouse has needs not covered by Medicaid and that can be met from the spousal share, making the election can be to the spouse's advantage.

Q 6:15   How can the alternate valuation date election be used to save taxes?

An estate's assets are valued based on their fair market value of the assets. The fiduciary can, however, be inventive in his or her approach to valuation. First, for estate tax purposes the estate assets can be valued as of the date of death or as of six months after the decedent's death. [I.R.C.§ 2032] If the latter is selected, then assets sold or distributed during that six months can be valued as of the date of sale or distribution of the property. The alternative valuation methods can be elected only if by doing so the estate tax (and generation-skipping tax) due is decreased, under Code Section 2032, and the election must be made on the federal estate tax return, IRS Form 706. In other words, the alternate valuation date cannot be selected solely to increase basis to reduce capital gains tax upon a subsequent sale, and is not available at all if the estate is not taxable with either valuation method. The election is irrevocable and must be made on a timely filed return or the first late return within one year of the due date. [I.R.C. § 2032(d)] If the election is made, all property in the estate must be valued the same way, with property liquidated or distributed before the alternate valuation date valued as of the date of its disposition.

> **Example 6-3.** Mary's estate consists of real estate and various stock holdings. Since her death four months ago, market forces have resulted in a substantial reduction in the value of her largest single stock holding; if by the alternate valuation date (two months from today), the stock has not recovered its value, the estate tax savings on that stock could be substantial. Unfortunately, both the real estate and the remaining stock have increased in value beyond the substantial loss, and the total estate value has increased. Mary's executor might elect to sell the real estate and the appreciating stocks before the alternate valuation date, and thereby gamble that the poorly performing stock will not recover. Complicating the

calculation, of course, is the dilemma of capital gains incurred by the estate; by sale of the appreciating assets, capital gains tax costs will be passed along to the devisees. If, however, Mary's estate is not subject to estate tax, the alternative valuation election will not be available.

Q6:16   How does the valuation date election affect the income tax basis?

Under Code Section 1014, the valuation of estate property serves as the income tax basis of the property. The fiduciary of a small estate may wish to select the valuation date that shows a higher value for property likely to be sold in the reasonably near future in order to achieve a higher stepped-up basis for the beneficiaries to whom the property is to be transferred. However, the "alternate valuation date" must be used for all assets, not only those for which one is desirous of getting a higher basis. Also, the requirement that the alternative valuation date be used only when it will reduce *estate* taxes means that when the estate is not "taxable" in any event (whether or not Form 706 is required), the executor cannot choose to elect to report *higher* values occurring six months after death in an attempt to increase the "stepped-up" basis.

Q6:17   How does the lack of marketability discount and minority interest discount affect valuation of estate assets?

Substantial valuation discounts (often as high as 35 percent or even 45 percent) may reduce the estate (and/or gift) tax liability when assets are difficult to value or market. This discount can be effected for partnership and limited liability corporation (LLC) interests, corporate stock, real estate, and mortgages. The management of a closely held corporation holding estate assets may consist of family members, which may also affect the desirability of the corporate stock. Although the value of a closely held business may be uncertain, IRS rules require the valuation to be made by reference to similar but publicly traded corporate interests. [I.R.C. § 2031(b)] Minority interests get an even greater discount because there are fewer buyers interested in holding anything but a controlling interest. This is particularly true in the case of minority interests in family or closely held businesses, as it exacerbates the already difficult task of valuation. Even a majority interest will usually be subject to some valuation discount if there are other, minority interest holders who must be contended with. When planning for valuation discounts, careful drafting and qualified appraisals are important. The IRS frequently takes an adversary position with regard to discounts for assets that would otherwise be easily divided (such as passive investment holdings in an LLC or limited partnership), and careful documentation of the validity of the claimed reduction in value is critical (see Qs 5:95–5:97). The IRS will typically allow only a modest discount for jointly held real estate (such as 15 percent) to reflect the costs of partition. It can be cost effective to pay a significant fee for a professional appraisal of the discounted interest if the savings to be achieved justify the cost.

Q 6:18   How can the special use valuation be used to save taxes?

Under Code Section 2032A, the executor may elect for estate tax purposes to value qualified real property according to the use under which it is qualified, rather than using fair market value. The property must have been acquired by a qualified heir from the decedent and used for a "qualified use" by the decedent or the decedent's family at the time of the decedent's death. The fiduciary must go by the "highest and best use" of the property. The special use valuation rules apply only to real property located in the United States and used for farming purposes or in a closely held business. The special use valuation must be elected on a timely filed estate tax return (Form 706) or on the first return filed after the due date if no timely return was filed. [I.R.C. § 2032A(d)(1)] It can only be used to reduce the value of the property by $750,000 (adjusted annually for inflation; in 2007, $940,000). It must be signed, and the election is irrevocable. The IRS can recapture the lost taxes if within 10 years the property is no longer being used for farming, closely held business purposes, or is transferred to someone other than a family member or qualified heir. [I.R.C. § 2032A(c)]

Q 6:19   What elections can the executor make to defer payment of the estate tax?

While the estate tax is generally due nine months after the decedent's death, the executor may make the following elections:

1. *Code Section 6161.* To defer paying estate taxes for 12 months from the date the tax is due. The IRS may extend the time for payment of the estate tax for up to 10 years. The executor must show reasonable cause for the extension, and the election must be

approved by the IRS. Form 4768 is used to request the extension and must include a written statement explaining why it is impossible or impractical to pay the estate tax on time.

2. *Code Section 6166.* To pay the part of the estate tax bill in up to 10 annual installments and defer paying estate taxes if a substantial portion of the estate consists of interests in closely held businesses or farm property. The interest rate on the first $1,000,000 (adjusted annually for inflation in multiples of $10,000; 2008 value: $1,280,000) in value of the closely held business is 2 percent, and the remainder of the federal estate tax bears interest at 45% of the interest rate charged for late payments (see IRC § 6601(j). For this election to apply, the decedent's closely held business must equal at least 35 percent of the gross estate. This election allows a small business to keep operating after the owner dies. The election is made by attaching a Notice of Election to the estate tax return on IRS Form 706. For further IRS insight into what closely held business interests might apply for installment payments, consider Revenue Ruling 2006-34. Prior to the holding in *Estate of Roski v. Commissioner,* 128 T.C. 10 (2007), the IRS routinely required a bond to ensure payment of the tax; that requirement is now individually considered (see IRS Notice 2007-90).

3. *Code Section 6163.* To postpone paying the estate tax attributable to reversions or remainder interests that are includible in the decedent's gross estate. Payment of the applicable amount of the estate tax can be deferred until six months after the reversion or remainder interest is in the hands of the decedent's estate or heirs. The IRS has the discretion to defer the payment for up to three years if it determines that there is reasonable cause for the additional extension. The executor should note on IRS Form 706 that a Code Section 6163 election was made.

Income Tax Elections

Q 6:20 What is the election to treat a revocable trust as part of the probate estate?

The executor of an estate can make an irrevocable election to treat revocable trusts as part of the deceased person's probate estate for income tax purposes. [I.R.C. § 645(a)] Unless the election is made, the trust is treated as a separate taxpayer (and must have a tax identification number different from that of the decedent's Social Security number). The election must be made by the due date, including extensions, of the first income tax return. The election, which is irrevocable, is in effect for two years from the date of the decedent's death if no estate tax return is filed, or, if an estate tax return is required, until six months after getting the IRS "closing letter" finally determining the liability for estate tax. [I.R.C. § 645(b)(2)] To qualify for the election, the trust must be a qualified revocable trust. A trust is a qualified revocable trust if the decedent retained a power of the trust such as the power to affect beneficial enjoyment of the income for a period commencing after the occurrence of some stated event. [I.R.C. § 676]

Q 6:21   How can the revocable trust election be used to save taxes?

By electing to have a revocable trust included in the probate estate for income tax purposes, the trustee and personal representative may realize significant tax savings. This is not the case for the majority of trusts, of course, because trusts are usually distributed quickly and little income is earned during their administration. The tax savings can be accomplished in several ways:

1. Trusts as separate entities must adopt calendar years, while probate estates can choose a noncalendar tax year, but no later than the year ending in the same month as the month preceding death. The Taxpayer Relief Act of 1997 has made it possible for fiduciaries to elect to include the trust in the probate estate and choose a noncalendar tax year [I.R.C. § 645], which can be particularly advantageous when, for instance, a significant amount of income is expected within a limited period of time.

2. Estates are permitted a charitable deduction for amounts permanently set aside for charitable purposes, while post-death revocable trusts are allowed a charitable deduction only for amounts paid to charity.

3. With the passage of the Taxpayer Relief Act of 1997, trusts created after August 5 of that year no longer have to follow the "throwback rule." Under the law as it existed before the 1997 Act, beneficiaries whose trust bequests earned income during one year but were not distributed until the following year were required to file amended income tax returns for the years in which they earned income. The throwback rule did not apply to income distributions from probate estates. Code Section 645 (adopted as part of the

Taxpayer Relief Act) permits the executor and trustee jointly to elect to treat the trust as part of the estate for income taxation purposes, effectively eliminating the throwback rule when the election is made.

4. Whereas a probate estate can realize a loss when funding a pecuniary bequest with depreciated property, a trust cannot take a similar loss deduction, under Code Sections 267(a), 267(b)(5), 267(6). (The trust administrator can still recognize a loss by selling property to an unrelated party.) Both probate estates and trusts realize gain on appreciated property used to fund a pecuniary bequest.

5. Under Code Section 642(b), a probate estate can take a $600 personal exemption, while trusts are entitled only to a $300 personal exemption, if all the assets are to be distributed immediately, or a $100 personal exemption if the trust will be in existence long enough to draw income.

6. A trust administrator may wish to take advantage of certain probate estate rules regarding passive losses on real estate rentals. Whereas either trusts or probate estates can deduct up to $25,000 per year in such losses, estates have the advantage of being able to extend this over a two-year period. [I.R.C. §§ 469(g), 469(i)(4)] The post-mortem planner can take advantage of this extension by electing to bring the trust into the probate estate, but should first investigate whether this benefit will outweigh the disadvantage of having the rental property pass through probate.

Deduction of Administrative Expenses

Q 6:22 Does the post-mortem planner have any flexibility with regard to administration expenses of the estate?

The fiduciary and his or her advisers will have numerous expenses, both deductible and nondeductible, incurred as a result of administration of the estate. Nondeductible expenses (for estate or income tax purposes) include federal income taxes and those expenses not allowable under Code Section 2053(a). Expenses deductible for income tax but not estate tax purposes include foreign, state, and city income taxes, as well as property taxes and other obligations accruing after the decedent's death. Expenses deductible for estate tax purposes but not income tax purposes include funeral expenses, certain claims against the estate, and federal gift and income taxes. Some expenses can be deducted as either estate or income tax items, and here the fiduciary's creativity comes into play. These items include:

- Medical expenses paid within one year of the decedent's death;
- Casualty and theft losses;
- Fees and commissions of the attorney, fiduciary, and accountant;
- Court costs for probate;
- Expenses "necessary" in the administration of the estate;
- Interest on deferred estate taxes; and
- Broker's commissions and closing costs if property was sold to pay estate taxes.

The fiduciary should select the expenses to characterize as income or estate tax deductions (or both, for certain expenses) by comparing the marginal estate tax bracket with the marginal income tax bracket of the estate and of the beneficiaries of distributions from the estate. Often the decision means shifting the tax burden from one class of beneficiaries to another, and the fiduciary must weigh the consequences. Where a choice is allowed, the fiduciary should characterize expenses as income tax deductions in estates where estate tax is not an issue (e.g., insolvent estates or those whose transfers would be protected by the marital deduction).

What expenses are "necessary" to administering the estate may or may not include the executor's fee if the probate estate is small. In *Estate of Grant v. Commissioner* [294 F.3d 352, 353 (2d Cir. 2002), *aff'g* T.C. Memo. 1999-396], the Second Circuit Court of Appeals upheld the Service's position that there can be no estate tax deduction for the portion of an executor's fee attributable to non-probate property where state law expressly links the fee to the size of the probate estate. Mrs. Grant had a very small estate and a very large revocable trust and deductions were sought for both executor and trustee commissions.

Q 6:23 If deductions are made on the estate's income tax return, must the estate tax deduction be waived?

Double deductions are generally prohibited. Deductions may be taken on the estate's income tax return if the executor waives the right to take the deduction for estate tax purposes. [I.R.C. § 642(g)] A waiver of the estate deduction is filed with the IRS for the district in which the return was filed. The waiver may be filed at any time before the expiration of the statutory period of limitations applicable to the taxpayer for which the deduction is sought. Prior to filing the waiver, the executor can tentatively claim the deductions against the estate tax because the deductions may not be allowed by the IRS; the estate can preserve the opportunity to take the deductions against the income tax. Once the waiver is filed, the option to use the deduction against the estate tax return is lost.

If, however, the executor deducts certain "transmission"-type administrative expenses attributable to assets for which a marital deduction is taken, the result may be to *reduce* the marital deduction without the ability to take an offsetting administrative expenses deduction. Reg. § 20.2056(b)-4 (revised following the case of *Estate of Hubert*, 520 U.S. 93 (1997)) By the same token, these "transmission" type expenses are not deductible against the estate tax.

Practice-Related Issues

Q 6:46 When is disclaimer planning utilized in actual practice?

Post-mortem planning, particularly the use of disclaimers, is usually encountered when planning before death was inadequate; however, post-mortem planning can be anticipated and even encouraged by the decedent. Two typical scenarios illustrate the use of disclaimers in practice:

1. *Curing a defective plan.* Steven's wife Wynette has just died. She had property worth over $3 million, and Steven himself is worth another $3 million. The couple had two children, both attending high school. Although they had meant to come in for more elaborate trust planning, they had not gotten around to it. Wynette's will, drafted when the couple was first starting out in their now-successful business, leaves everything to Steven and, if he is deceased, to a trust for the benefit of their two children, to be distributed to them when they are 21. Her assets consist of her interest in the business, a stock portfolio (in joint tenancy with Steven), a small retirement account, and her half of the family home. Steven wants to know what he can do to minimize estate taxes.

   Of course, if Steven does not disclaim any property there will be no estate tax as a result of Wynette's death; however, Steven will now be worth over $6 million. If he dies within the next few years his estate may pay a substantial estate tax. He might choose to disclaim some of Wynette's property in order to reduce the ultimate tax liability.

Selecting which assets to disclaim will involve consideration of a number of factors. If Wynette's interest in the family business is held by a trustee for the benefit of Steven's children, it might cause some difficulties in the future if he decides to sell out, expand, or change the business's direction. On the other hand, if Steve owns only a portion of the business it will be valued at a lower amount on his later death, and he will have not only helped fund Wynette's credit shelter trust but reduced the tax on his own estate at the same time. Depending on the business organization (stock, Subchapter S, partnership, LLC), there may be other advantages or problems with disclaiming the business interest.

The joint tenancy stock portfolio can also be disclaimed, although there is some concern that Steven might have accepted the benefits of Wynette's interest in the portfolio prior to contacting the lawyer. Depending on the state and the broker, the mechanics of disclaiming joint tenancy property may be more or less problematic. From a tax standpoint, the stock account may be the most attractive candidate for disclaimer. It is easily divisible, and the administration of the trust will not likely adversely affect Steven's use or administration of his own assets.

Wynette's half interest in the home could be disclaimed, despite the fact that Steven has resided there continuously since her death (as a joint tenant or tenant in common, he has the right to possession—he has not received any "benefit" from the use of her interest). The mechanics of disclaiming may once again be problematic depending on state law and title insurance practices. If any of these three assets (business, stock, or home) is disclaimed, a probate proceeding will almost assuredly be required, increasing the cost of the disclaimer decision.

Steven can easily disclaim his rights to receive Wynette's retirement account; however, doing so will result in immediate income taxation of the benefits, and the account may then flow to the children outside the trust (depending on the beneficiary designation on the account).

In balancing all these considerations, Steven will have to consider whether the size of his estate is sufficient to provide him adequate security, whether the ability to make gifts and other tax planning choices during the rest of his life will sufficiently protect his estate from taxes, whether the trust established for his children is adequately protective of their interests, and the mechanical and tax considerations involved in each kind of proposed disclaimer.

2. *The rapidly growing estate during a period of uncertainty about the estate tax.* Harvey and Sandra are in their mid-40s, both professionals, and have two children. Their estate now is valued at approximately $1.6 million (including retirement benefits), plus some life insurance. They anticipate that their combined earning potential is increasing, but that expenses of college and launching their children will consume most of their income for the next few years. They understand that the exemption equivalent amount is scheduled to increase sharply in the next few years, and the estate tax may be completely repealed before either is likely to die. Both are in good health. Harvey and Sandra are co-owners of a start-up business with a significant upside potential, though the future of their business presently is anything but certain.

Harvey and Sandra are not particularly good candidates for credit shelter trusts. Although their combined estate is nearly at the taxable level, that level will likely increase faster than their net worth at least for the next 5 to 10 years. In fact, there is a considerable likelihood that the federal estate tax will have been completely repealed before the death of either spouse. In a post-estate tax world, the state estate tax may have become an important planning issue, or may have also been repealed. They are relatively young, and it is not too likely that both will die within the 5-to-10-year period during which their estate plan will remain fixed, and during which the future of the estate tax will become clearer.

If they should have a slight increase in their estate in the near future and then die in rapid succession, the estate tax consequence could be serious. Similarly, if their children do not go to college, or accept scholarships, or if Harvey and Sandra do not get around to revising their estate plans for a decade or more, or if their business flourishes and they fail to revise their plans regularly, they may be seriously adversely affected by estate taxes.

On the other hand again, a credit shelter trust could be unnecessarily restrictive in their current situation. If Harvey were to die this year, Sandra might chafe under the restrictions imposed by dividing the estate into two shares and placing one in an irrevocable trust for the rest of her life, which is likely to be fairly long. The same reaction might be expected of Harvey if Sandra were to die in the near future.

A disclaimer trust might be exactly what this couple needs. By placing all their assets into a joint trust, or funding two separate trusts, or transferring assets into a tenancy in common, coupled with a bequest to each other and an alternate bequest to a credit shelter trust, they can proceed secure in the knowledge that the survivor can assess the circumstances at the time of the first death and make an appropriate election to either receive the deceased spouse's property outright or partially or fully fund a credit shelter trust for estate tax minimization.

Part III

Fiduciary Administration

Chapter 7

Probate and Trust Administration

Upon the death of someone close, one of the first questions faced by the survivor (or survivors) is whether it will be necessary to probate the estate of the decedent. The circumstances requiring probate proceedings can be confusing, as can the probate process itself. This chapter will address the necessity for probate proceedings, administration of the probate estate, the duties and responsibilities of the personal representative, the principles of estate distribution, the rights of the surviving spouse, and the closing of the estate. It will also briefly discuss the administration of trusts upon the death of the settlor (or settlors) and how the administration rules differ for trusts and probate estates. More detailed discussion of the tax planning involved may be found in other chapters.

Overview

Q 7:2 What is the Uniform Probate Code and what has been its effect on probate?

Until a few decades ago, laws governing the management and transfer of assets at death varied significantly from state to state, and many states still had vestiges of old English common law. Probate costs increased disproportionately when decedents' estates included property in several different states. The laws also varied greatly from state to state with regard to the guardianship of minors and incapacitated individuals and the protection of their assets. A joint effort between the Probate Section of the American Bar Association and the National Conference of Commissioners on Uniform State Laws produced a Model Probate Code that was revised and ultimately approved in 1969, and was subsequently revised periodically with a thorough rewrite in 1991.

The Uniform Probate Code (UPC) includes a comprehensive approach to interstate succession, wills, trusts, probate, guardianship and conservatorship, nonprobate transfers and fiduciary relationships in general, and is an attempt to make those proceedings more consistent from state to state. More fundamentally, the UPC has promoted a less formal and more independent structure for the probate process, rather than requiring direct court supervision for every aspect of administration. In UPC states, the personal representative of an estate is usually given broad latitude to liquidate probate assets, pay debts, negotiate claims, and even make distributions without prior court approval; in fact, accountings and inventories can be avoided altogether in most cases. Unless a beneficiary or creditor objects to the administration of an estate, the UPC approach is to assume that the personal representative is acting appropriately.

While only 18 states have adopted the Uniform Probate Code in its near-entirety (and many of these still adhere to the original 1969 version), portions of the Code have been adopted by approximately 20 other states. Even some states that have not expressly adopted the probate administration provisions of the UPC have either changed their procedures to conform to some of the UPC concepts and principles, or already used a less formal approach and chose not to make the further changes required by the UPC.

Table 7-1. Uniform Probate Code States

Alaska	Michigan	North Dakota
Arizona	Minnesota	Pennsylvania
Colorado	Montana	South Carolina
Hawaii	Nebraska	South Dakota
Idaho	New Jersey	Utah
Maine	New Mexico	Wisconsin

Q 7:4   What property is subject to the probate process?

Generally, only property in the sole name of the decedent at the time of death is subjected to the probate process. This includes the decedent's interest in property held as a "tenant in common," because the decedent retained the right to dispose of the interest. Property held in trust or "joint tenancy," in tenancy by the entireties or community property with right of survivorship, accounts bearing "Payable on Death" (POD), "In Trust For" (ITF) or "Transfer on Death" (TOD) designations, and assets passing "by contract," through the designation of beneficiaries will usually not be subjected to probate unless (1) the beneficiary named was the decedent's own estate, or (2) the named beneficiary (or joint tenant) has predeceased the decedent, is deemed to predecease because of a disclaimer, or has been disinherited by operation of law (see chapter 4). Assets held in a "529 Plan" for the education of a beneficiary may pass as part of the probate process when no contingent owner is specified by the original account owner. "Choses in action," that is, pending lawsuits or legal claims, will also be included in the probate estate.

Q 7:10   What property is subject to probate in community property states?

Under community property laws, each spouse has the power to bequeath only his or her one-half share of the marital estate and his or her separate property. The survivor keeps his or her one-half share (that is, it is not transferred to him or her) and dower and curtesy interests do not apply. The decedent's share, to the extent that it has not been assigned to bypass vehicles such as living trusts or POD designations, will be subject to probate. Because at the death of one spouse the marital community is terminated, and because the debts of the decedent are presumed to be the debts of both spouses (the community), the entire community property may be subject to probate administration until all obligations are satisfied. Community property may be used to satisfy community debts, but only the deceased spouse's half of community property may be used to satisfy separate debts (and then usually only after separate property has been exhausted) (see Q 7:28). In some community property states (including Arizona, California, Nevada, Texas, and Wisconsin) community property may be held "with right of survivorship." The effect of this titling is to overlay the survivorship principles of joint tenancy on community property assets.

Q 7:12   How can the probate process be avoided?

When planning for the distribution of property to be made after death, an individual who wishes to avoid probate has many vehicles through which he or she can direct assets to beneficiaries. Assets transferred to revocable and irrevocable trusts set up before the decedent's death will bypass probate (unless, of course, the trust directs payment to the settlor's estate upon death or includes a power of appointment exercised in favor of the estate). Life insurance policies, IRAs, deferred compensation, qualified plans, and annuities all commonly provide for beneficiaries to be paid on death without the necessity of court involvement. Joint tenancy property and community property specified as "with right of survivorship" pass outside the probate process. "Payable on death" (or "in trust for") designations on bank accounts, and the similar "transfer on death" designation on stocks, bonds, and brokerage accounts, are available in most states to bypass the probate process. A small but growing handful of states even permit a "transfer on death" or "beneficiary deed" designation for real estate. States with beneficiary/TOD deed provisions include Arizona, Arkansas, Colorado, Kansas, Missouri, Nevada, New Mexico, Ohio, and Wisconsin.

Q 7:19   How is the reasonableness of a personal representative's fee determined?

In those states that have adopted a "reasonable fee" standard it may be difficult to determine what constitutes a reasonable fee. Some guidance can be had by reference to lawyers' ethical rules on reasonable attorney's fees. Rule 1.5(a) of the American Bar Association's Model Rules of Professional Conduct sets out the elements to consider when assessing the reasonableness of an attorney's fee, and most of those elements are equally applicable in determining a reasonable fee for a personal representative. Those elements, with modest adjustments made to accommodate their use in probate estates, include:

1. The time and labor required, the novelty and difficulty of the question involved, and the skill requisite to perform the service properly;
2. The likelihood that acceptance of the particular employment will preclude other employment by the personal representative;
3. The fee customarily charged in the locality for similar services;
4. The size of the estate and any especially favorable results obtained in the course of the estate's administration;
5. The time limitations, if any, imposed by the need to complete the estate quickly;
6. The experience, reputation, and ability of the personal representative; and
7. The use, where appropriate, of a percentage fee calculation.

Similarly, the following formulation, specifically directed towards fiduciaries and to be tailored when addressing an attorney's fee, has long been the rule in Connecticut:

> " '[R]easonable' means what is fair in view of the size of the estate, the responsibilities involved, the character of the work required, the special problems and difficulties met in doing the work, the results achieved, the knowledge, skill and judgment required of and used by the executors, the manner and promptitude in which the estate has been settled and the time and service required, and any other circumstances which may appear in the case and are relevant and material to this determination."

[Hayward v. Plant, 98 Conn. 374, 384-385 (1923)]

The Michigan courts have adopted a similar standard for judging the reasonableness of fiduciary fees, including:

> "(1) the size of the trust; (2) the responsibility involved; (3) the character of the work involved; (4) the results achieved; (5) the knowledge, skill and judgment required and used; (6) the time and services required; (7) the manner and promptness in

performing its duties; (8) any unusual skill or experience of the trustee; (9) the fidelity of the trustee; (10) the amount of risk; (11) the custom in the community for allowances to trustees and (12) any estimate of the trustee of the value of its services." Quoting *Matter of McDonald*, 140 Misc.2d 49, 530 N.Y.S.2d 453 (1988)]

[Comerica Bank v. Adrian, 179 Mich. App. 712 (1989)]

Issues have arisen recently regarding the deductibility for income tax purposes of an investment manager's fee when the personal representative chooses to delegate the duty of managing funds as is permitted by such statutes as the Uniform Prudent Investor Act. Notwithstanding that the fiduciary would have been compensated for his or her own time in fulfilling the duty to manage and invest assets, and that the fiduciary's fee would have been fully deductible, the U.S. Supreme Court has held that the broker or other manager's fee should only be deductible as a "miscellaneous" expense, that is, to the extent it exceeds 2 percent of adjusted gross income. *Knight v. Commissioner of Internal Revenue*, 128 S.Ct. 782 (2008)

Q 7:22 What controls the distribution of the decedent's assets?

The distribution of a decedent's estate will be controlled either by the terms of the decedent's will or (if there is no valid will, or if a portion of the decedent's estate is not disposed of by the will) by the rules of intestate succession; however, even if there is a will, the probate process may include protections for some classes of beneficiaries, particularly spouses and minor children. A number of the principles governing estate distribution may be default rules, provided only in the event the decedent's will is silent on a particular point. Thus, for example, a given state statute may provide that a bequest to a child presumptively passes *per stirpes*, or by "right of representation." In that case, if the child predeceases the parent the child's issue will take the deceased child's share. This is known as an "anti-lapse" statute. The same state might provide that bequests to unrelated individuals do not flow by right of representation (that is, they lapse if the devisee predeceases the testator) unless expressly provided for in the will. Another state might provide that all bequests presumably lapse, or that all bequests presumably pass by right of representation. Regardless of which state the decedent lived (or died) in, the decedent's will might provide for any of the distribution choices, and the default rule of each state would be unimportant. A statement that property passes "to my son if he survives me" imposes a survival requirement that should trump the "anti-lapse" statute—but not always. A recent Connecticut case held that addition of the words "if she survives me" to a residuary bequest did not sufficiently indicate an intent to negate the anti-lapse statute where the testator failed to specify an alternate disposition. [Ruotolo v. Tietjen, 890 A.2d 168 (Conn. App. 2006), aff'd, 916 A.2d 1 (Conn. 2007)]. Whether the court would have so held if the situation did not involve a residuary bequest is open to debate.

Principles of Estate Distribution

Q 7:27 What right does a surviving spouse have in community property states?

A handful of states have adopted the French and Spanish concept of "community property" to deal with the property acquired by married couples during the marriage. The community property states are Arizona, California, Idaho, Louisiana, Nevada, New Mexico, Texas, Washington, and Wisconsin. In addition, Alaska permits property held in Alaskan trusts to be treated as community property. Under community property laws, each spouse has the power to bequeath only his or her one-half share of the marital estate and his or her separate property. The survivor already owns a one-half share (that is, it is not transferred from the deceased spouse's estate), and dower and curtesy interests (see Q 7:29) do not apply. The essential characteristic of community property is often seen as a substitute for the elective share approach, because the surviving spouse is the presumptive owner of half of all property acquired during the marriage.

In community property states, all income and assets obtained during the marriage are considered community property except those acquired through gift, inheritance, or devise. There is a presumption that all property in either spouse's name is community property, although the presumption can be overcome by showing that the property was brought into the marriage, or received as a gift or inheritance. Spouses can agree to hold assets in a form other than community property, although it may be difficult to prove the couple's intentions after the death of one spouse. Typically, a written agreement will be used to "convert" community property to separate property.

Keep in mind that in most cases, only spouses actually domiciled in a community property state, or which were domiciled in such a state at the time property was acquired, will have community property. This will depend upon the individual state's laws, however. Property that might be community property if owned by spouses domiciled in the community property state, may be only a tenancy-in-common when owned by non-domiciliary spouses.

Q 7:29 What are "dower," "curtesy," and "election against the will"?

At common law a widow was entitled to receive a minimum distribution from her deceased husband's estate (dower), and a widower was entitled to a similar allowance (curtesy). Most states have abandoned the concepts of dower and curtesy, and have employed the "election against the will" strategy (or community property) instead. Those states retaining an explicit dower and/or curtesy provision include Arkansas, Massachusetts, New Jersey, New York (as to dower only, and then only as to couples married before 1930), Ohio (dower only), and Virginia (as to interests "vested" before 1991). The right of election entitles the surviving spouse to take a statutory share rather than be governed by the terms of the will. Typically, elective-share law entitles the surviving spouse to one-third of the decedent's estate. Whereas community property states promulgate the "partnership" theory of marriage, that is, a spouse is deemed to have contributed equally to the marriage even if a higher proportion of the assets were in the decedent's name, elective-share statutes relegate the spouse to a lower status. In effect, spouses may end up with more assets through divorce proceedings, which typically entail an equitable division of assets, than through right of election. Moreover, in some states it is still possible to entirely disinherit a surviving spouse simply by taking the necessary steps to avoid probate. For example, in Connecticut the elective share is a life interest in one-third of the decedent's *probate* estate, with no rights whatsoever to other assets, and without the share taking into account other assets including those held in revocable living trusts. Other states will "gross up" the estate to include assets held in revocable trusts or otherwise not passing through probate, for purposes of computing the spouse's statutory share, which is often 50%. The Uniform Probate Code has redesigned the right of election to better reflect the more modern "partnership theory" of marriage, by using a schedule correlating years of marriage with entitlement to assets. Although proceedings for elective share claims vary from state to state, the UPC suggests that the election must be made by filing the petition in court and delivering it to the personal representative within nine months after the date of the decedent's death, or within six months after initiation of probate proceedings, whichever limitation expires later. State statutes often allow the surviving spouse to elect to have the statutory share pass to him or her from the decedent under Internal Revenue Code (I.R.C. or Code) Section 2056 and thus to qualify for the marital deduction.

Q 7:32 What happens when an heir or beneficiary has died before the decedent?

An heir or beneficiary may die before the decedent, or may be treated as having died before the decedent. The latter can happen in any of several circumstances, including when the heir or beneficiary disclaims any interest, when the heir or beneficiary fails to survive for a certain period of time (set either by the will or by state statute), or when the heir or beneficiary is responsible for the death of the decedent (as defined by the state's "slayer statute" or equivalent law; see Q 7:33). When the heir or beneficiary predeceases or is treated as predeceasing the decedent, the applicable state law or the provisions of any will may direct that the interest:

1. Lapses (e.g., returns to the estate to be divided among remaining distributees or to be distributed to the residuary devisee);
2. Is distributed to a named substitute beneficiary or beneficiaries; or
3. Is distributed to the heir's (or beneficiary's) issue, usually by right of representation or *per stirpe* (see Q 7:26).

Q 7:33 What happens when an heir or beneficiary murders the decedent?

At common law a person criminally responsible for the death of another could not inherit from that person's estate; the killer is usually treated as if he or she predeceased the victim. That commonsense provision has been incorporated into the law in every state, although the precise approach varies somewhat. These provisions are frequently referred to as "slayer statutes," and the formulation of the Uniform Probate Code is typical:

"[Forfeiture of Statutory Benefits.] An individual who feloniously and intentionally kills the decedent forfeits all benefits under this Article with respect to the decedent's estate, including an intestate share, an elective share, an omitted spouse's or child's share, a homestead allowance, exempt property, and a family allowance. If the decedent died intestate, the decedent's intestate estate passes as if the killer disclaimed his [or her] intestate share.

"[Revocation of Benefits Under Governing Instruments.] The felonious and intentional killing of the decedent:

(1) revokes any revocable (i) disposition or appointment of property made by the decedent to the killer in a governing instrument, (ii) provision in a governing instrument conferring a general or nongeneral power of appointment on the killer, and (iii) nomination of the killer in a governing instrument, nominating or appointing the killer to serve in any fiduciary or representative capacity, including a personal representative, executor, trustee, or agent; and

(2) severs the interests of the decedent and killer in property held by them at the time of the killing as joint tenants with the right of survivorship transforming the interests of the decedent and killer into equal tenancies in common." UPC section 2-803(b) and 2-803(c)

Actual applications in individual states may vary. In a community property state, for example, the fact that the victim and killer were married will not cause the killer to lose his or her interest in community property, though it will prevent inheritance of any of the victim/spouse's community interest. Similarly, the fact that the killer's heirs benefit from the slaying will not necessarily prevent them from inheriting. [In re Estates of Covert, 97 N.Y.2d 68 (2001)] A guilty or "no contest" plea may be treated differently from a conviction after a criminal trial. [In Matter of the Estates of Swanson, 2008 MT 224 (2008)] Finally, some states may only disinherit the killer in the event of a criminal conviction; a failed conviction, even if followed by a successful suit for wrongful death, will not cause disinheritance.

Q 7:34   What is meant by "right of representation"?

At common law, "right of representation" referred to a distributive scheme under which the deceased beneficiary's share would be distributed to his or her children in equal shares, with any deceased child's share to be further divided among his or her children in equal shares.

Example 7-1. Martha died leaving an estate of $150,000. Martha had three children, a son Sam (who predeceased her) and daughters

Diane and Deborah. Sam had two children, Diane has four children, and Deborah three children. Under the right of representation, Sam's children will split his share equally (i.e., they will receive $25,000 each). Diane and Deborah each inherit $50,000, and their children get nothing.

Example 7-2. With the same family relationships described in Example 7-1, Diane also predeceased Martha. Sam's two children will still receive $25,000 each (i.e., one-sixth of the estate). Deborah will receive one-third, as before. The remaining third will be divided equally among Diane's children, so that they will each receive $12,500 (i.e., one-twelfth of the estate).

The calculation becomes more convoluted if all representatives of a given generation have died. "Right of representation" requires that the shares be calculated at the first generation with surviving members.

Example 7-3. In the preceding example, all three of Martha's children have predeceased her. Her nine grandchildren will share the estate equally, without regard to how many of the grandchildren have common parents.

At common law and expressly in most states, right of representation is synonymous with *per stirpes* distribution (see Q 7:35). Inexplicably, the latest revision of the Uniform Probate Code redefines the phrase "right of representation" to be synonymous instead with *per capita* distribution (see Q 7:36). In order to prevent a reversal of a client's intentions when he or she moves into states having adopted the latest version of the Uniform Probate Code, it is probably preferable to utilize the terms *per stirpes* and *per capita* even though they may be less understandable to clients.

Q 7:35 What is *per stirpes* distribution?

Per stirpes (Latin: "by roots" or "by stocks") refers to a distributive scheme under which the deceased beneficiary's share would be distributed to his or her children in equal shares, with any deceased child's share to be further divided among his or her children in equal shares. It is synonymous with the "right of representation" concept described above (see Q 7:34) before the changes introduced by the UPC. It is to be distinguished from the other common (though less common) distributive scheme, *per capita* distribution.

Q 7:36 What is *per capita* distribution?

Per capita (Latin: "by head") distribution describes a mechanism whereby each member of the surviving family shares equally in the estate. *Per capita* distribution tends to "reward" grandchildren from larger families, while *per stirpes* distribution "rewards" grandchildren from smaller families. The difference between *per capita* and *per stirpes* is best illustrated with an example. Assume that a child, and two grandchildren who are the children of a predeceased child of the testator survive the testator. If the will were to provide that the issue take *per stirpes*, then the surviving child would take one half, and each of the grandchildren would take one quarter (i.e., divide the total by the number of "stems" or "stocks," and thus the grandchildren split the share that would have gone to their parent if he or she had survived). If, on the other hand, the will were to provide that the issue take *per capita*, then each of the surviving children and the two grandchildren would take one third (i.e., divide the total by the number of heads).

The Probate Process

Q 7:43 What notice must be given of a pending probate proceeding?

Depending on the nature of the proceeding, all interested parties, including known and as-yet-unidentified creditors, beneficiaries named in the will, and all family members who could conceivably be deemed heirs of the decedent should be given notice. For instance, creditors do not necessarily need to be notified of a hearing set to determine intestate succession and appointment of the personal representative, but they should be given notice immediately upon initiation of the estate and appointment of the personal representative. Adequate notice must be given of the hearing date and the nature of the proceedings, and generally those entitled to notice must receive it no less than two weeks prior to the proceeding.

Most states will have specific notice requirements that must be closely followed. Typically, notice must also be published one or more times in a newspaper of general circulation in the community where the proceedings have been initiated; at least in theory, this gives unknown heirs an opportunity to appear and make their claims. Some states will impose the notice requirement on the probate court itself, while other states impose that responsibility upon the personal representative.

Estate Administration

Q 7:61   What other tax returns must be filed for a decedent?

If the decedent left an estate worth more than the amount of the unified credit for that year ($2 million in 2008 and scheduled to rise to $3.5 million in 2009; see SQ 5:7 and Table 5-1), taking into consideration lifetime gifts that would have eaten up some or all of the unified credit, then a Form 706 estate tax return is required. [I.R.C. § 2001 et seq.] There is significant variation among the states with regard to estate taxation, and it is the personal representative's responsibility to become familiar with state requirements (or hire someone well versed in this area). The Form 706 estate tax return is due nine months after the date of the decedent's death, and must be filed by the personal representative or, if there is no personal representative, the individual or officer with information about the decedent's taxable estate (e.g., the trustee, surviving spouse, surviving joint tenant, or beneficiary). [I.R.C. § 2203] While a six-month extension can be granted, the tax must still be paid within the original nine-month period.

In addition, a gift tax return (Form 709) is due by April 15 following the year in which any taxable gift was made. [I.R.C. § 6075] In the event of a gift in the last year of the decedent's life, a gift tax return may also be required.

Claims Against the Estate

Q 7:64   Do different claims have different priorities?

Some claims will be preferred over others. The priority of payments will be determined by state law, usually, state statute. Typically, costs of administration have the highest priority, and are paid first. Funeral expenses and the expenses of the last illness may follow in priority order. Secured claims come next. General, unsecured claims (and the unsecured portion of secured claims) will usually have the lowest priority. Although not a claim against the estate, statutory family allowances and the election, dower, or curtesy rights of surviving spouses may be considered "expenses of administration" or otherwise be entitled to payment before even priority claims, or may be given priority over other expenses. In effect, this can provide a way to get funds to the surviving family rather than the creditors. Secured creditors do not actually receive priority status, but usually are permitted to exercise their security interests even though the effect may be to remove assets from the estate and thereby defeat even family allowances and priority claims.

Trust Administration

Q 7:71 What rules control trustees administering the trust estate?

The common law of trust administration is one of the best-developed areas of the law. Most of the general principles governing trust administration are relatively well-settled, and an abundance of case law exists to guide the trustee and his or her counsel. The Restatement (Third) of Trusts [Volume 3, covering trustee powers and duties and a reincorporated prudent investor volume, was published in 2007; Volumes 1 and 2 were published in 2003 by the American Law Institute, *www.ali.org*] extensively details the existing law and aspirations for the developing law. The Uniform Trust Code (formerly the Uniform Trust Act) currently being prepared by the National Conference of Commissioners on Uniform State Laws generally codifies the preexisting common-law principles governing trust administration in its Chapter 8, although it makes many other significant changes. [NCCUSL, Uniform Trust Code, §§ 801–817] The Uniform Trust Code has been adopted in 20 states as of 2008 (Alabama, Arizona, Arkansas, Florida, Kansas, Maine, Missouri, Nebraska, New Hampshire, New Mexico, North Carolina, North Dakota, Ohio, Oregon, Pennsylvania, South Carolina, Tennessee, Utah, Virginia, and Wyoming) and the District of Columbia. The UTC was initially adopted, and then repealed before its effective date, in Arizona. Of course, individual states may have more- or less-developed case law or statutory requirements relating to trust administration.

Q 7:72 How do default distribution rules apply to trusts?

As has been previously discussed, probate statutes usually provide for default rules of interpretation, so that *per stirpes* or *per capita* distribution is presumed, or distributions do not lapse as a result of the death of a devisee who is a family member, for example. Those default rules do not usually apply to trusts, with the result that the distribution must be provided for in the trust document. Without well-developed default rules, a failure to specify distribution provisions may result in unanticipated distributions or even the failure (or partial failure) of the trust itself.

Q 7:73 Must a trust be established by a writing?

At common law a trust could be established without any written memorandum, and so an oral trust may be enforceable absent any statute requiring a writing. [Restatement (Third) of Trusts § 10] The same principle is codified in the Uniform Trust Code. [NCCUSL, Uniform Trust Code, 2000 draft, § 401] Trusts involving real estate may, by individual state interpretations of the statute of frauds, require a written and signed transfer of the property into trust executed according to requirements for the conveyance of real estate in that jurisdiction. [Restatement (Third) of Trusts § 16]

Q 7:74 How may a trust be amended or revoked?

The law of wills usually provides that revocation can be accomplished by destruction of the original will [see U.P.C. § 2-507], and that a missing will gives rise to a presumption of revocation [see U.P.C. § 3-415]. Trusts are usually revoked in accordance with the terms of the trust itself, and destruction of the original trust document will ordinarily not be sufficient to revoke the trust. Consequently, a missing trust does not give rise to a presumption of revocation. [Restatement (Third) of Trusts § 63, which does not expressly discuss a presumption of revocation rising from a missing original document, but notes that the evidence of any intent to revoke must be shown by "clear and convincing evidence of the settlor's intention to do so."] At common law, a trust was presumed to be irrevocable unless the settlor expressly reserved the right to revoke or amend the trust, although the accidental failure to include a power to revoke might not preclude revocation if it could be shown that the omission was a mistake. [Restatement (Second) of Trusts §§ 330, 332] The Restatement (Third) of Trusts, has abandoned the common law rule and instead opted for a presumption that the trust is revocable, at least when the settlor retains any interest in the trust. [Restatement (Third) of Trusts, § 63 comment (c)] The same approach is adopted in the Uniform Trust Code as currently proposed. [NCCUSL, Uniform Trust Code, 2000 draft, § 602(a)] Assuming that the trust is revocable and amendable, the validity of an amendment or revocation will be tested by the terms of the trust instrument. The trust may, for example, require that any revocation or amendment be delivered to the trustee before it becomes effective. Such a requirement will usually be strictly enforced.

Chapter 8

Will and Trust Contests

Disgruntled heirs or devisees may contest the validity of a testator's will. Elder law attorneys may represent the contestants or may have represented the decedent and prepared the contested will. In either event it is important to understand how will contests proceed, how likely they are to succeed, and how to minimize the likelihood of will contests while conducting estate planning. In addition, it is becoming increasingly common for contests to be filed by disgruntled trust beneficiaries; what once would have been a will contest may now manifest itself as a trust contest because of the testamentary effect of the living trust. This chapter discusses the bases and procedures for contesting a will or a trust and possible challengers of wills and trusts.

Wills: Validity and Challenges

Q 8:3 What is required to establish due execution of a will?

To help guard against challenges based on the mental state of the testator and undue influence, all states have set minimum requirements for will execution. While oral ("nuncupative") wills may be valid in some states for limited amounts of property, the general rule is that the will must be signed; state statutes vary as to whether the testator can sign by proxy and how many witnesses are required. (See chapter 4 for a detailed discussion of wills executions.) Some states require that the will be signed in the actual presence of the witnesses; others allow the testator to sign the will in private and then acknowledge the signing to the attesting witnesses. While the precise rules vary by state, they are almost all based on the English common-law statute of wills, which required three witnesses (now reduced to two in all states but Vermont) to be present at the time of the testator's signing, and the testator to be present when the witnesses signed. Although usually the witnesses are not required to be disinterested parties, there are sound practical reasons to utilize only disinterested witnesses; in the event of a later contest, the honesty of a witness who benefits from his or her own testimony is subject to an obvious challenge. (In most states, a witness who is named in the will may not take the legacy the will contains.)

The exception to statute of wills principles is the holographic will, which is not witnessed but is signed by the testator and is entirely in the testator's handwriting. A minority of states permit holographic wills, though some will recognize a holographic will that was valid in the place and at the time it was executed (see Q 4:32). Section 3.3 of the *Restatement (Third) of Property: Wills and Other Donative Transfers*, and 1990 amendments to the Uniform Probate Code (at section 2-503) both adopt a more liberal approach to the formalities of will execution. According to this modern view, a "harmless error" in the execution of a will does not invalidate the document if its proponent can show, by clear and convincing evidence, that the decedent intended the document to be his will.

Q 8:4   What is required to establish due execution of an amendment of a will?

Usually the will may be amended only by a codicil signed with the same formality as is the will itself. A codicil is an amendment to a will, changing only some of the provisions of the original document. Notes in the margins and corrections in the text could be interpreted as a revocation of the instrument rather than an amendment, and even clearly worded marginal notes will not satisfy the formalities of a will or codicil. Arguably, in states permitting holographic wills, marginal notes signed by the testator may have been "duly executed." As with wills themselves (see Q 8:3), the modern view adopted by the Restatement (Third) and the Uniform Probate Code is to permit amendments to be proved by clear and convincing evidence even though they may not comply with formal requirements. This shift in emphasis is perhaps most important in the analysis of amendments when unrepresented testators make handwritten changes directly on the will itself, or even on a copy of the will.

Q 8:9 What happens when the testator's will cannot be found?

A missing will usually gives rise to a presumption that the testator destroyed the original with the intent to revoke it; however, the presumption is not absolute, and the proponent must be able to establish that the will was still in existence at the time of the testator's death, or that the original will was not in the testator's possession (and therefore could not have been destroyed by the testator personally), or that the testator was incapacitated at the time the will was destroyed. In such cases, a copy of the will may be admitted to probate; in unusual cases, it may even be possible to "prove" the contents of a missing will by testimony from witnesses who saw the document and remember its contents. In some states, if wills are executed in duplicate, loss of only one will not give rise to the presumption of revocation. California Probate Code 6124 (although proof of an intentional revocation of either revokes both, Section 6121). This is fairly unique to California, however. When each will says that it "revokes" all earlier wills, a duplicate will could give rise to its own confusion.

Q 8:11.1 Can a person diagnosed with dementia have sufficient capacity to execute a will?

Yes. To be sure, a diagnosis of dementia, or the appearance of symptoms, may well provide the basis for a will contest [Cf. Estate of Halbert, 172 S.W.3d 194 (Tex. App. 2005)]. But courts have repeatedly held that even those with diminished capacity may either retain sufficient overall capacity to execute a will, or may have "windows of lucidity" during which a will may be executed. [See, e.g., Estate of Williams, 787 N.Y.S.2d 444 (Sup. Ct. 2004); Baun v. Estate of Kramlich, 667 N.W.2d 672 (S.D. 2003)] Courts have held the same with challenges to the exercise of a power of appointment. [Estate of Scott, 119 P.3d 511 (Colo. App. 2004)]

Q 8:19   What is an *in terrorem* provision, and is it an effective protection against will contests?

A will may include language that purports to disinherit any person who challenges the validity of the will itself. Such a provision is often referred to as an *in terrorem* or "no contest" clause. Of course, if the testator was incompetent to execute a will in the first place he or she was also incompetent to disinherit an heir or prior devisee. Given the strong presumption in favor of the validity of testamentary documents, and the law's desire to effect the wishes of the decedent, the general trend is to permit such provisions to be effective. However, concern about the possibility that legitimate heirs who contest invalid documents could be disinherited, many states permit contests despite the language of *in terrorem* provisions. In some states, the contestants must first establish that there is a reasonable basis for the contest before initiating it. In some other states the reasonableness of the challenge is determined after the fact when the challenge fails; in others, as an alternative to enforcement of *in terrorem* clauses, the loser in a will contest is required to pay the attorneys' fees of the prevailing party. For a summary of the law on no-contest clauses, see D. Bashaw, "Are In Terrorem Clauses No Longer Terrifying?," 2 NAELA Journal 349 (2006). As a strategic and drafting matter, an *in terrorem* provision should always be accompanied by a significant bequest to the otherwise disinherited individual. Outright disinheritance creates no disincentive to trigger the *in terrorem* clause. It is only when the disgruntled heir has something to lose by a challenge that the provision has any effectiveness.

Q 8:20   What is the process for contesting the validity of wills?

Although a handful of states permit a court proceeding to determine the validity of a will before the death of the testator, the common rule is that a will contest must be filed in response to the probate (or proposed probate) of a decedent's will (see chapter 7 for a discussion of probate). Procedures for filing a will contest will vary by state, not only as to the process but even as to the terms. For example, a will contest may be referred to as a "caveat" in some jurisdictions, as an "appeal" in others.

Q 8:22   Who pays for a will contest?

Ordinarily the costs of a will contest are borne by the contestants, whether successful or unsuccessful. In the case of a challenge to a will where a personal representative or executor has already been appointed, the estate may bear the cost of even an unsuccessful defense of the will by the personal representative, provided that the personal representative has acted reasonably. In the case of a successful will contest by one of several beneficiaries the costs of litigation may in some circumstances be charged to the estate on the theory that the successful challenger(s) acted for the common good of the true beneficiaries of the estate. Some states have statutorily declared that "no contest" clauses are unenforceable while simultaneously requiring the loser to pay the attorneys' fees of a prevailing party.

Trust Challenges

Q 8:29 Is reformation of a trust allowed?

Reformation of trusts is allowed under the Restatement of Trusts and the common law of most states, and courts are usually willing to allow reformation if there is some evidence of the original intent of the trustor. In states that follow the Uniform Trust Code, reformation may be simple if all interested parties agree and the court can find that the change will not violate a "primary" purpose of the trustor. In common law states, it is often necessary to allege that a change in circumstances makes reformation necessary in order to prevent frustration of the intent of the trustor. In some states, extrinsic or parol evidence may be admissible if it sheds light on the intent of the trustor; in more traditional states, such evidence is only admissible in the event of ambiguity, but may be admissible to show a "change in circumstances." An increasing number of courts are adopting the doctrine of "probable intent" in order to construct an instrument that may be contrary to the express language of the document, and will bring in parol evidence to assist them with this construction. Some construction is necessary anyway when there is ambiguous language addressing substantive issues. Trusts may also be reformed (or construed in a manner that effectively requires reformation of the text) on the basis of "scrivener's error," a situation most attorneys would really rather avoid. When the reformation of a trust creates a tax advantage, it may be subject to challenge by the Internal Revenue Service. Generally speaking, the IRS will not be bound by the agreements of trust (or will) beneficiaries in interpreting the documents, and may effectively require relitigation (in the tax court or other tax forum) to determine whether the beneficiaries could have obtained the same result in a contested proceeding. Even if the court rules in favor of the reformation, and the IRS does not oppose that conclusion, it still may not be bound by the court's decision unless it is the decision of the highest state court. [Commissioner v. Estate of Bosch, 387 U.S. 456 (1967)] This can be a real problem for parties seeking certainty when reforming a trust.

Chapter 9

Guardianship and Protective Proceedings

Guardianship and conservatorship are among the most state-specific (some might even say idiosyncratic) areas of practice encompassed by elder law. Although the Uniform Probate Code and the Uniform Guardianship and Protective Proceedings Act have brought some consistency to state statutes, even those states adopting the "uniform" acts have tended to modify them extensively. This area of elder law practice varies widely by state, and the entire body of guardianship and conservatorship law is usually contained in state statutes even though common law on guardianship and conservatorship developed early. This chapter discusses guardianship and conservatorship proceedings including when a guardian or conservator can be appointed, who can petition for guardianship or conservatorship, the rights of the ward, the appointment process, powers and duties of the guardian or conservator, the role of the guardian in health care decision-making, conflicts of interest, and termination of the guardianship or conservatorship.

Overview

Q 9:3   What is a "guardian of the estate" or "conservator of the estate"?

The conservator, or guardian of the estate, is appointed by the court to manage the assets of a person determined to be in need of protection. Some evidence is usually required that the assets would otherwise be "wasted," or improperly spent, by the ward. A disorderly payment history such as an occasionally missed utility bill is probably not enough. Such evidence must be something substantial; examples include, for instance, the vulnerable elder, absolutely convinced that he is about to win, whose entire monthly Social Security check is spent on sweepstakes entries and "Special Gifts Just for You" orders; the absent-minded widow with $1,000 credit on her account with one utility while simultaneously receiving final shut-off notices for nonpayment on another, or the confused elder who falls for the high pressure door-to-door salesman every month when he comes to remind her that it is time to reseal her driveway again. The guardian of the estate and the guardian of the person are often the same individual, but the court may scrutinize more closely the appropriateness of the petitioner when there are substantial assets at stake. A court-appointed conservator is usually, but not always, given the full authority to make all financial decisions for the protected person, including decisions regarding the purchase and sale of real estate and investment of estate assets.

For purposes of this chapter, unless the context indicates otherwise the language of the Uniform Guardianship and Protective Proceedings Act (UGPPA) and the Uniform Probate Code (UPC) is used: "guardianship" of the person, "conservatorship" of the estate.

A general durable or springing power of attorney executed by a competent individual provides the designated agent with nearly the same degree of authority as that of a conservator (see chapter 10); however, because of the potential for abuse the cautious planner may decide against signing such a power of attorney, opting instead to compel family members to go through the more burdensome process of court appointment so that there is proper notice to all interested parties, bonding of the estate assets, and monitoring of the conservatorship by the court.

Q 9:4 What is the Uniform Guardianship and Protective Proceedings Act?

The Uniform Guardianship and Protective Proceedings Act (UGPPA) began as a stand-alone version of Article 5 of the Uniform Probate Code (relating to guardianship and conservatorship proceedings).

An updated version of the UGPPA was finalized in 1997; it has been adopted in Alabama, Colorado, Hawaii, Minnesota, and Montana. In addition, a number of states have adopted the essentially similar provisions of the Uniform Probate Code governing guardianship and conservatorship proceedings.

The drafters of the UGPPA sought input from a task force that included, among others, the ABA Commissions on Legal Problems of the Elderly and Mental and Physical Disability Law, as well as a variety of other groups interested in guardianship, such as AARP and the National Senior Citizens Law Center. In describing the new Act, the Commission on Uniform Laws states:

> The 1982 Act, with its emphasis on limited guardianship and conservatorship, was groundbreaking in its support of autonomy. This revised Act builds on this and the revisions occurring in the states, by providing that guardianship and conservatorship should be viewed as a last resort, that limited guardianships or conservatorships should be used whenever possible, and that the guardian or conservator should always consult with the ward or protected person, to the extent feasible, when making decisions.

Q 9:10.1 Is there another standard for determining an individual's need for a conservator?

At least one court applied a "management competency test" in determining the need for a conservator of the estate. In *In re Conservator for Demoville* [856 So. 2d 607 (Miss. App. 2003)], the court considered "ability to manage, or improvident disposition, or dissipation of property, or susceptibility to influence or deception by others, or similar factors." [*Id.* at 610]

Selection or Appointment of a Guardian or Conservator

Q 9:21 Must the guardian or conservator live in the same state as the ward?

Once again, state rules differ. In many states, the fiduciary must either be a resident of the same state as the ward, or must at least designate a state resident who will serve as agent for the service of process. There may be logistical problems with serving as guardian or conservator of a person residing in another state, but there are fewer legal barriers today than in previous decades. Most states (with the exception of Illinois, Oklahoma, and Virginia) will allow a nonresident individual to act as conservator for both minors and adults. Arkansas will appoint a nonresident conservator for a minor, but not for an adult. [ACTEC Studies, Oct. 1998, The American College of Trust and Estate Counsel, Study 3: Rights of Nonresident Individuals to Act as Fiduciaries in Various States]

Practically speaking, it may be perfectly acceptable to have an out-of-state guardian or conservator of the estate, but counterproductive to have a guardian or conservator of the person who lives out of state. The job of guardian or conservator of the person may require frequent personal visits, review of medications, discussions with physicians, emergency medical decisions, arrangements for transportation, and attending to personal needs. Unless it is clear that the guardian or conservator of the person is able to appropriately delegate these duties, it may not be possible for someone at a distance to fulfill these duties.

At least in one case, the court even allowed an out of state individual to file a guardianship/conservatorship action over a foreign national who was neither a resident nor owner of property in the jurisdiction. The court held that physical presence is the only requirement for a guardianship order. [In re Uwazih, 822 A.2d 1074 (D.C. 2003)]

Q 9:22 Can an individual select his or her own guardian or conservator?

Fully competent individuals can sign powers of attorney designating health care and financial agents to manage their affairs when they are no longer able to do so. If the powers of attorney prove to be insufficient for some reason, and guardianship/conservatorship proceedings are necessary, powers of attorney may be presented as evidence of the proposed ward's preferences. Wingspan recommends that "[s]tatutes give preference to the person nominated in the advance directive, power of attorney, or other writing in appointing the guardian." [Wingspan No. 18]

Some states specifically authorize a person to make an advance selection of conservator "for future incapacity," using formalities similar to those used for power of attorney or other health care directive. If there are no such documents, the proposed ward will have the opportunity to communicate his or her preferences with his or her lawyer, guardian *ad litem*, or other persons appointed by the court. If the ward is able to attend the hearing, the judge will usually make every effort to elicit testimony from the ward.

Most state statutes (and particularly more modern ones) give at least some priority to the person nominated as guardian or conservator by the proposed ward. Usually, that priority exists even if the nomination is made when the ward is already incapacitated. To help ensure that the individual's choice of surrogate is honored wherever possible, elder law attorneys should consider adding language to powers of attorney nominating an appropriate person (usually the agent named in the power of attorney) as guardian or conservator in the event a later appointment is made and, in those states that specifically provide a form for advance designation, should consider routinely suggesting that clients may wish to do so. Clients should be advised that the most likely scenario in which a guardian or conservator is to be appointed for someone who has executed appropriate powers of attorney is where the agent has misbehaved in some fashion. In such cases, the court hearing the request for appointment of a fiduciary is unlikely to honor the client's earlier nomination.

In *Conservatorship of Ramirez* [90 Cal. App. 4th 390 (2001)], the ward had named her son as fiduciary in her living trust and durable power of attorney. The ward's daughter, however, sought appointment of an independent, professional fiduciary. The court permitted the son to serve as conservator. The court reasoned that there was no evidence that the son had done anything but take excellent care of his mother, the ward possessed at least sufficient capacity to nominate the son as conservator, and her wishes were consistent with those in her living trust and durable powers of attorney. In another case, a ward had previously executed a power of attorney naming her son as conservator if one was ever required. Later, during proceedings to appoint a conservator, she again expressed preference for his appointment. The court found, however, that statutory preference for the ward's nominee can be overcome if the court determines appointment of another person would be in the ward's best interests. [In re Iwen, 2003 WL 21007240 (Minn. App. May 6, 2003)]

The Appointment Process

Q 9:28   Who, other than the proposed ward, might object to the guardianship or conservatorship proceeding?

As with initial petitions, any interested person may object to the appointment of a guardian or conservator (or simply intervene in the proceedings) in most states. Few guardianship or conservatorship proceedings are contested by either the proposed ward or any other interested person; experience suggests that the most likely contest is raised by a family member who feels that the "wrong" person is seeking appointment. Contested proceedings may involve two (or three, or more) different positions taken by various parties, and can and do often resemble custody proceedings, with the twist that the children are usually battling over custody of a parent. Those who are permitted to object to the proceeding may or may not have "standing" to appeal. A recent case held that a son, who was already acting as an agent under durable power of attorney by the proposed ward, had standing to appeal. [Marchentine v. Brittany Farms Health Center, Inc., 84 Conn. App. 486, 854 A.2d 40 (2004)]

Powers and Duties

Q 9:41   What resources are available for guardians and conservators in fulfilling their responsibilities?

Wingspan recommends that lawyers turn to the National Guardianship Association Standards of Practice [National Guardianship Association, "Standards of Practice," reprinted in 31 Stetson L. Rev. 941, 996–1026 (2002)] and "A Model Code of Ethics for Guardians"[Michael D. Casasanto, Mitchell Simian & Judith Roman, (Natl. Guardianship Assn. 1991). A copy of this work in PDF format is available through the National Guardianship Association's Web site at *www.guardianship.org/associations/2543/files/CODEOFET2.pdf*], in absence of mandatory minimum standards. [Wingspan No. 65] A conservator or guardian whose ward suffers from mental impairment, whether lifelong (such as schizophrenia), the result of a dementing illness, or a temporary symptom of illness or treatment (such as dementia resulting from an infection) should have at least a passing acquaintance with the symptoms and treatments of these conditions. A valuable resource on psychotropic medication is the website of the National Alliance for the Mentally Ill; the local Alzheimers Association chapters or other on-line resources may also provide valuable information. When the ward's placement or care plans are at issue, the lawyer serving as conservator may also wish to consult other professionals not yet in place, such as care managers and social workers, both private and those available through a state agency on aging.

Q 9:45 What limitations should be considered on a guardian's or conservator's authority?

Guardians and conservators are encouraged to allow the ward to make as many decisions as possible concerning his or her care, comfort, and finances. The court will usually make every effort to restrict the fiduciary if plenary powers would be too burdensome, and these restrictions will be reflected in the letters of appointment.

Certain rights are considered so inviolable that guardians may be precluded from substitute decision-making, at least without approval from the court. Incapacitated people fall in love and sometimes wish to marry. The guardian may support the idea of marriage and be willing to provide whatever assistance is necessary, but guardians generally do not have the power to prohibit a ward from marrying. A petition to the court and appointment or reappointment of counsel for the ward may be necessary. At least one court disallowed a guardian/conservator to file for divorce on behalf of the ward. The court reasoned that the relationship between spouses is highly personal and to allow the action would permit a guardian to "interfere in his or her ward's personal relationships."[In re Marriage of Denowh and Denowh, 78 P.3d 63 (Mont. 2003)] The guardian should not be allowed to vote for the ward, but may be able to assist the ward at the voting booth. Wingspan recommends that the guardian not have the power to consent to civil commitment, electric shock treatment, or dissolution of marriage without obtaining specific judicial authority.

When it comes to executing substituted judgment regarding estate planning matters, guardians or conservators are usually limited in their ability to make substantive changes. The old rule was clear. In *Sanford v. Hayes* [19 Conn. 591 (1849)], the court held: "The parties [the conservator and a contracting party] attempted to settle her estate, before she was dead. This they could not do."[*Id.* at 596] The court's concern was dilution of the Statute of Wills, and courts still share this concern. [In re Falucco, 2002 Pa. Super. 3, 791 A.2d 1177 (2002)] Exceptions may arguably be made where the change is in the ward's best interests rather than the interests of third parties. In one recent case a guardian/conservator was denied authority to amend the ward's living trust because the guardian/conservator failed to produce clear and convincing evidence that the proposed amendment was in the ward's best interests. [Guardianship and Conservatorship of Garcia, 631 N.W.2d 464 (Neb. 2001)] By contrast, when it comes to funding an OBRA '93 Trust, courts have held that the authority arises from the fact that the trust's establishment is in the ward's interest. [Department of Social Services v. Saunders, Conservatrix, 247 Conn. 686, 709 (1999)]

The trend may be changing, however. In the recent case of *In re Keri* [181 N.J. 50, 853 A.2d 909 (2004)], the court adhered to a "substituted judgment" standard to allow the guardian to execute half-a-loaf Medicaid planning, holding that "[w]hen a Medicaid spend-down plan does not interrupt or diminish an incompetent person's care, involves transfers to the natural objects of the person's bounty, and does not contravene an expressed prior intent or interest, the plan clearly provides for the best interests of the incompetent person and satisfies the law's goal to effectuate decisions an incompetent would make if he or she were able to act." In so doing, the court expressly followed the reasoning in *Shah v. DeBuono* [694 N.Y.S.2d 88, 257 A.D.2d 256 (N.Y. App. Div. 2d Dep't, July 6, 1999)], holding that a community spouse acting as guardian may exercise substituted judgment to transfer all assets to herself and subsequently exercise the right of "spousal refusal."[See SQ 14:83.] These cases are simply extensions of a series of earlier cases permitting guardians to make "exempt transfers" of a home to a spouse or in some cases, a child. [E.g., In the Matter of the Guardianship of FEH, 154 Wis. 2d 576, 453 N.W. 2d 882 (1989); Matter of Labis, 314 N.J. Super. 140, 714 A.2d 335 (1998)].

For that matter, the ward may still be capable of making his or her estate plan. Many incapacitated persons are capable of making a will; as long as a person knows what his or her assets are and to whom he or she wishes to bequeath them, the standard of competency for a will is met. The guardian or conservator who suspects that the will might be challenged may wish to better document the execution. Some attorneys bring in a mental health professional and videotape the proceeding, including an interview of the incapacitated person by the mental health professional about his or her wishes prior to the signing. Statutes regarding the rights of wards vary widely from state to state and should be scrutinized by petitioners or their attorneys.

Health Care Decisions

Q 9:52 May a guardian of the person authorize or direct the withholding of life-sustaining medical treatment?

State statutes may be unclear about whether the guardian has the authority to make this decision. If the ward signed a health care power of attorney and living will during his or her competency, the treating physicians may accept this as sufficient authorization under certain circumstances (see chapter 18). In Connecticut, recent legislation requires a conservator to implement the ward's advance directives and provides that the healthcare representative's authority to make these decisions survives the appointment of a guardian [Conn. Public Acts 07-116]. If there is some concern on the part of the doctors, family members, or any other interested parties that there is insufficient evidence of the wishes of the ward, then the guardian may wish to seek permission for termination of life-sustaining treatment from the court. The court may require appointment or reappointment of counsel for the ward so that all constitutional protections are met.

In some jurisdictions, the question for the guardian (or the judge, if the matter is submitted to the court) is whether there is clear and convincing evidence of the ward's prior expressed wishes regarding continued treatment. In most states the guardian and the court will be concerned first about those expressed wishes and then, if there is no clear prior expression of intent, about the "best interest" of the ward—with the realization that "best interest" can sometimes be served by termination of treatment. This may be particularly true when the burden of the treatment is substantial (e.g., it is painful or invasive) or the possibility of recovery is slight.

Recent cases reflect a trend toward permitting guardians to make the decision to withhold or withdraw life-sustaining treatment. [But see Conservatorship of Wendland, 26 Cal. 4th 519, 28 P.3d 151 (2001)]

Practice-Related Issues

Q 9:63   What are some of the practical problems that arise in the guardianship and conservatorship arena?

A guardianship and conservatorship practice can be as diverse as the whole range of human experience. The elder law attorney with a substantial practice in guardianship and conservatorship may appear before tribunals and agencies as diverse as the Federal Elections Commission (marginally competent wards frequently are caught up in political developments, and may spontaneously send large donations to favored candidates) and state adult protective services. Some common themes do tend to repeat themselves in guardianship and conservatorship law, however. The practice-related problems discussed below include: (1) representing an uncommunicative fiduciary, (2) determining whether guardianship or conservatorship are needed, (3) justifying immediate withdrawal after representing a client in a guardianship or conservatorship proceeding.

1. *The uncommunicative fiduciary.* Some months ago the attorney represented a client in her petition for guardianship and conservatorship of her mother. At the time, there was no objection from the only other sibling, a brother. He now calls the attorney and complains that his sister has moved his mother into a nursing home, but will not tell him where she is, and that he has no idea what the daughter has done with the contents of the apartment his mother used to occupy. Should the attorney continue to communicate with the brother? If the brother's complaints turn out to have some validity, can the attorney continue to represent the daughter? As long as the attorney communicates early in the conversation that her client is the sister, and determines that the brother is not represented by separate counsel, she may continue to gather information. A subsequent conversation with the daughter may reveal that there are in fact some excellent reasons for the daughter's actions—the brother may have been abusing or otherwise upsetting the mother, and the daughter may have felt it was in her mother's best interests to keep the brother

away from both his mother and the personal property. If in fact the daughter is acting arbitrarily, the attorney may be faced with a practice dilemma. There is no conflict, of course, and she may continue to represent the daughter if she believes that she can help resolve the problem. Such family disputes can, however, be time-consuming and expensive, and the attorney must advise the daughter that her fees related to the dispute probably could not be charged against the conservatorship estate. If the guardian refuses to come to terms with her brother or refuses to pay the attorney's fees out of her own pocket, the attorney may withdraw.

2. *The need for guardianship and conservatorship.* The attorney has been appointed by the court to represent the interests of a proposed ward in a petition for guardianship and conservatorship. She visits her client at his home, which is littered with uneaten food and dog feces. The client appears to be malnourished and his teeth are rotting, and he appears to be oblivious to his surroundings. However, as soon as the attorney identifies herself, the client explodes, "I know what this is about! My kids are trying to run my life again! There's nothing wrong with me and I'll be happy to go to that hearing next month and tell the judge myself!" The attorney is now confronted with the classic "substituted judgment versus best interest" dilemma. What should she do?

3. *Immediate withdrawal following the hearing.* An attorney has represented a pleasant but none-too-bright client in his petition for guardianship and conservatorship of his aged mother. There are considerable assets in the estate, and the attorney helps the client set up a fiduciary account and advises him to keep track of all records. The attorney fears that the client, although honest, will not do a competent job of managing the records and check register and that the annual accounting will be a nightmare. Is he justified in withdrawing from representation as soon as the hearing is over and the letters of appointment issued? Attorneys routinely and with impunity withdraw from representation immediately after the hearing. The withdrawing attorney in this case would, however, be doing his client a disservice if he does not advise the client, in writing, of the client's obligations with regard to the annual accounting. The client should be encouraged to hire a bookkeeper or paralegal soon after the hearing to assist him with the books, and the attorney should provide forms and sample accountings for guidance. The attorney should advise the client about the kinds of issues he might face as guardian, including

placement or health care decisions, and any reporting requirements or other obligations, such as an annual report to update the court about the ward's circumstances.

4. *The impoverished ward.* In some states, attorneys or other third parties are recruited to serve as conservators or guardians of individuals who are impoverished and typically wind up as Medicaid beneficiaries in nursing homes. The problem is that the system may provide no or inadequate payment to those conservators, creating a disincentive for a conservator to enforce the resident's rights. The state of Massachsuetts has ruled that conservators may be paid out of the beneficiary's income as, in effect, a medical expense, under the "remedial cost" category. [Rudow v. Commissioner of Div. of Medical Assistance, 707 N.E.2d 339, 429 Mass. 3218 (Mass. 1999)] Thus far, however, Massachusetts is apparently unique in officially permitting such a diversion of income, although one NAELA member succeeded in having expert and legal fees paid by the state and/or out of the ward's income in a case involving restoration to capacity of a ward. [Weismann v. Maram, Case No. 03 C 4047 (N.D. Ill. 2004), *NAELA News* October 2004]

Chapter 10

Powers of Attorney

The power of attorney enables a designated individual to take over the affairs of another person in the event of incapacity or absence. It is really an agency agreement by which the person who signs (the "principal") grants powers and authority to a designee (the "agent" or "attorney-in-fact"). The durable power of attorney, which allows a competent adult to appoint individuals to manage his or her own affairs even after he or she becomes disabled, ill, or otherwise unable to manage his or her own affairs, has become a key element in long-term care and estate planning. This chapter discusses the different kinds of powers of attorneys, the duties and powers of the attorney-in-fact, and termination and revocation of the power of attorney.

Overview

Q 10:5 Can a power of attorney avoid the necessity of conservatorship (or guardianship of the estate)?

Powers of attorney are usually executed for the express purpose of avoiding court proceedings. A health care power of attorney can anticipate and preclude the need for guardianship of the person, and a general durable or springing power of attorney is usually sufficient authority for third parties so that conservatorship of the estate is not necessary. In many cases, the mere existence of a valid power of attorney will be found to be the less-restrictive alternative, obviating the need for a guardianship or conservatorship. The power of attorney may also give rise to a presumption that the agent has priority for appointment as guardian or conservator, even if the court decides to appoint a fiduciary in the face of the power of attorney. In fact, a power of attorney might include a specific nomination of the agent as guardian or conservator in the event that a court later determines such appointment is in the principal's best interest; most state guardianship/conservatorship laws give priority for appointment to the ward's nominee. The principal should be advised beforehand of the drawbacks and benefits of powers of attorney, on the one hand, and guardianship and conservatorship on the other: While a power of attorney is convenient and allows the principal to choose the agent, guardianship and conservatorship proceedings ensure notice to all interested parties and at least some degree of monitoring by the court.

Q 10:6   Can a power of attorney ever survive the death of the principal?

No American jurisdiction recognizes power of attorney after the death of the principal, although some state provisions may give agents authority to consent to autopsy or burial arrangements. Even a durable power of attorney ends as soon as the agent has received notice of the death of the principal.

Durable Power of Attorney

Q 10:9   What distinguishes a durable power of attorney from a nondurable power?

At common law, all powers of attorney ceased upon the death or disability of the principal (except for those circumstances where the agent was unaware of the principal's death or disability). Legislatures traditionally avoided giving greater powers to agents both because of centuries of legal tradition and because the potential for abuse was so great, but eventually American jurisdictions began to acknowledge the need for an alternative to court proceedings. Pursuant to the widespread enactment in the 1970s of the Uniform Probate Code (UPC) and the Uniform Durable Power of Attorney Act, all states now have statutes that allow competent adults to appoint individuals of their own choosing to manage their affairs even after they become disabled, ill, or otherwise unable to manage their own affairs.

In most states, durable powers of attorney must contain language stating that the power will not be affected by the subsequent disability of the principal or will become effective upon the principal's disability. In a handful of states, any power of attorney is presumed to be durable unless expressly made non-durable (see, for instance, Pennsylvania C.S.A. § 5601.1). In addition, a state may include other requirements. For example, North Carolina law provides that in order for the agent to continue to have authority after the disability of the principal, the durable power of attorney must be recorded. [NCGA 32A-9]

Q 10:15 Which is better in most cases, a "springing" power of attorney or a "surviving" power of attorney?

Once again, the answer will depend on many factors. Principal among these factors, of course, is the client's wish; common local practice and the routine acceptance of durable powers of attorney may also play a part in the choice.

For the client who is uncomfortable with establishing a currently effective (surviving) power of attorney, several points should be made. First, if the client is in any way reluctant to entrust the power to his or her chosen agent during capacity, the client should seriously reconsider whether the agent should be given such broad powers after the principal is unable to monitor the agent's behavior. Second, to the extent that the purpose of a durable power of attorney is to avoid the necessity of any formal declaration or finding of incapacity, a springing power of attorney will defeat that purpose. Third, the client should be reminded that establishment of a power of attorney does not limit the principal's authority; the agent is an additional person able to handle the principal's personal and financial affairs, and does not usurp the principal's own authority over those same affairs. Finally, the administration of a "springing" power of attorney may be more problematic: Banks and other third parties may be more reluctant to accept the authority of an agent under a springing power of attorney, and may require periodic demonstrations of the principal's continued incapacity.

All of those considerations notwithstanding, many clients will simply be uncomfortable with giving current authority to the agent. In such a case, the client's peace of mind should not be overburdened, and some sort of mechanism must be utilized to prevent current use of the power of attorney.

Florida, notably, does not expressly permit the creation of a "springing" power of attorney. Fla. Stat. Ann. § 709.08(1) provides that all durable powers of attorney are immediately effective, though the statute mentions powers that are "conditioned upon the principal's lack of capacity" and provides that such powers are "exercisable" only on presentation of appropriate affidavits. In the absence of clear statutory authority, it may be inadvisable to utilize springing powers of attorney.

Health Care Power of Attorney

Q 10:19   What is a "health care power of attorney"?

Powers of attorney at common law terminated with the disability of the principal, so their use was limited to commercial transactions. With the advent of durable powers of attorney in the last three decades, the classical conception of powers of attorney has shifted. Concurrent with the development of durable powers of attorney, the science of medicine developed to the point where the lives of at least some permanently unconscious individuals could be maintained for extended periods of time. Eventually, lawyers and health care advocates began to recognize the utility of durable powers of attorney for health care decision-making.

Every state and the District of Columbia recognize some form of health care power of attorney. Although the concept has been modeled on the commercial durable power of attorney, the specific state statute authorizing a health care power of attorney may refer to the instruments as an "advance directive" (the generic term for health care powers of attorney, "living wills" and, in some states, "do not resuscitate" orders), a "health care proxy," or another similar term. Some states may have a different term for the document that grants authority regarding end-of-life decisions than is used for more routine health care decisions. Regardless of the state's choice of terminology, the documents have the same effect as any other durable power of attorney, except that the purpose is to provide for medical and personal, rather than commercial or financial, decision-making. (See chapter 18 for a discussion of health care decision-making.)

Q 10:20.1   What is the relationship between HIPAA and powers of attorney?

The Health Insurance Portability and Accountability Act of 1996 (HIPAA) established, for the first time, national standards for protection of health information. Although HIPAA was enacted on August 21, 1996, privacy rules were not promulgated until 2002. Because the HIPAA privacy rules (Title 45, CFR, Parts 160 and 164, available online at http://www.dhhs.gov/ocr/combinedregtext.pdf) operate to protect an individual's medical and other personal health information, today health care powers of attorney play a more vital role in allowing significant others to participate in the health care decisions of their loved ones. See Chapter 18 for more details on HIPAA.

Q 10:20.2   Should health care powers of attorney contain language in reference to HIPAA?

Yes. A power of attorney should include language specifically dealing with HIPAA provisions so that the intent to release information (and, in the case of health care powers, to give authority to the agent) is clear. This is particularly important with "springing" powers of attorney, since the ability to secure medical information to trigger the effectiveness of the power of attorney may be compromised in the absence of express authority in the document itself. The following is an example of one HIPAA provision for a power of attorney:

Example. My agent is authorized to review my medical records, reports and charts and to consult with and secure information from treating physicians, dentists, health plan providers, hospitals, clinics, laboratories, pharmacies, or any other health care provider, as to as any insurance company or medical information bureau, and to sign consents and acknowledgments on my behalf pursuant to the Health Insurance Portability and Accountability Act of 1996 (HIPAA) as amended.

Duties and Powers

Q 10:28.1 Does the attorney-in-fact have any duties or liabilities to third parties?

Unlike a personal representative, an attorney-in-fact does not owe a duty to third parties or creditors of the principal. Depending on the circumstances, however, the agent may have a duty to pay the principal's bills. Although the law is not settled in this area, the Restatement (Second) of Agency suggests that affirmative duties of this nature may arise from (1) the terms of the instrument if the agent named has in fact "accepted" the agency, especially for compensation, and/or (2) if the agent creates a situation where one would rely upon the agency, e.g., the principal names an agent and believes that the agent is paying the bills and the agent does not tell the principal that the agent has decided not to accept the agency. [Restatement Sec. 378] Whether or not the agent might be liable to a third party would depend on either a third party beneficiary theory or the principal's having assigned its claims to the third party (such as the state Medicaid agency). For example, a claim that the agent has misappropriated the principal's funds so as to defeat the principal's testamentary intentions has been brought successfully by a beneficiary under the will, and Medicaid agencies can and do seek recovery from an agent who has made gifts of the principal's assets without authority.

The courts so far have appeared reluctant to impose upon the agent the same liability that would have been imposed upon the principal. In one case, a nursing home with a judgment against a resident brought proceedings against the resident's attorneys-in-fact, alleging that they had a fiduciary duty to account to the principal and that the creditor could assert the right to such accounting. The creditor then deemed the accounting inadequate and argued that the agent had the burden of proving the accuracy of its accounting and the validity of expenditures. The Indiana appellate court affirmed the trial court's denial, holding that the burden of proof of showing the breach of fiduciary duty lay with the creditor. [WW Extended Care, Inc., v. Swinkunas (Ind. App. March 19, 2002)] On the other hand, in the case of *Sunrise Healthcare Corp. v. Azarigian* [176 Conn. App. 800 (2003)], a court held an agent under durable power of attorney liable to a nursing home for charges during the months in which the principal was not eligible for Medicaid on the theory that the agent had signed the admissions contract as "responsible party." See further discussion at SQ 11:35.1. This case did not turn on the agent's status as agent under a durable power of attorney, but it common for an agent to find himself or herself in such a role.

Q 10:37 What should a gift-giving power include?

As with all estate planning issues, the primary concern is to determine the actual wishes of the client; however, a gift-giving power might typically be limited in any of several ways:

1. The power to make gifts might be limited to the annual exclusion amount ($12,000 per donee per year in 2006). If this approach is to be used, consider wording the gift-giving authority in such a way as to permit larger gifts as the exclusion amount increases. Such a power might be effected by, for example, including the following language: "I specifically authorize my agent to make gifts to or among my issue and the spouses of my issue in an annual amount not to exceed the applicable federal gift tax exclusion amount in each year such gifts are made." It might be advisable in individual circumstances to either compel equal gifts among all issue (or all issue at the same level of descent), or to require that resulting gifts to the agent himself or herself be consented to by another person, preferably not one of those entitled to consideration for gifts (in order to avoid any concerns about either self-dealing or inclusion of a power of appointment in the agent's estate).

2. If the intent is to permit the agent to make gifts in order to qualify the principal for Medicaid coverage of long-term care costs, the gift-giving power should expressly permit unlimited gifts, or gifts in the pure discretion of the agent. Because of the tremendous opportunity for abuse, this type of unlimited authority should not be used routinely, and really requires separate discussion with clients before signing. To effect this authority, the power of attorney might include language like: "I authorize my agent to make gifts in an unlimited amount to or among my issue in such proportions as my agent determines appropriate, including specifically the power to gift all or substantially all of my assets if my agent determines such transfer would be in my best interests to allow me to qualify for future government benefits or otherwise." Some attorneys assist clients in providing a more detailed letter to supplement the power of attorney and explaining thoroughly the client's wishes in the event that long-term care is required—not because they fear abuse, but in order to protect the agent from liability for carrying out the principal's wishes.

Q 10:38 Should gift-giving powers be included in every durable power of attorney?

No—with one possible exception.

The gift-giving power is obviously riskier than any other power included in most financial powers of attorney. Particularly where the power of attorney includes an unlimited power to make gifts, including gifts to the agent and his or her family, the effect can be a literal license to steal.

Even where the agent is completely trustworthy, and can be absolutely relied upon to exercise the gift-giving power only in accordance with the wishes and plans of the principal, there are good reasons to limit the authority or exclude it altogether. If, for example, the agent has an unrestricted power to make gifts and dies before the principal does, the argument is occasionally made that the agent died holding a general power of appointment over the principal's estate. Theoretically, this could lead to the result that the principal's entire estate must be included in the deceased agent's estate for purposes of calculating estate tax liability. This would be true even though the agent never exercised the power to make gifts, or exercised it only in accordance with the prior, limited gifting patterns of the principal.

The concern about inclusion of the principal's estate in the deceased agent's estate for tax purposes may be an entirely theoretical concern. No reported cases invoke such a doctrine, and there is certainly no widespread effort by the IRS to force such a result. Still, the possibility of that result should alarm any agent who happens to have a taxable estate, if the principal's estate is also significant.

The possible exception is the power to make gifts to the principal's spouse. For many practical purposes it may become necessary to be able to move assets from one spouse to the other, and in community property states, it may be vital to convert community property to separate property. A better solution may be multiple or alternate agents, each with the authority to make or approve gifts to persons not including himself or herself, so that, for example, a spouse may have power to make gifts to children and one child the power to make gifts to the principal's spouse. Even if the only attorney-in-fact is the spouse, it is still advisable to include ample power to make gifts to that spouse, unless (1) there is serious concern about the tax implications for a taxable estate, or (2) there is mistrust between spouses—in the latter case, of course, the spouse should probably not be named as agent at all.

Termination and Revocation of Power of Attorney

Q 10:46 Can an incompetent principal revoke a durable power of attorney?

An incompetent individual can revoke the power of attorney, but the revocation can be proven to be invalid by the agent (of course if the principal destroys the only copy of the document, the argument may be moot). Rather than raising the incapacity issue in litigation, the attorney-in-fact may instead choose to petition for guardianship and conservatorship, an arena specifically designed for determining incapacity and appointment of an agent (see chapter 10 for a discussion of guardianship). Alternatively, the attorney-in-fact may simply seek to utilize the power of attorney, armed with appropriate evidence (an affidavit from the principal's attending physician, for example) of the ineffectiveness of the revocation in the event that any third party challenges the validity or currency of the power of attorney.

Paradoxically, these problems can be more pronounced when dealing with a health care power of attorney. Despite the fact that the agent may be dealing with the principal's health care providers, and that those same providers are clearly aware of the principal's incapacity, they may be less willing to accept instructions from the agent in the face of the incompetent principal's revocation. This may be because the level of capacity required to make health care decisions is generally conceded to be lower than that required for financial decisions, or because of the inherent conservatism of medical professionals when dealing with legal issues, or a mixture of both. In any event, the health care agent may find that the only remaining avenue after revocation by an incompetent principal is to pursue guardianship of the person, despite the intention of the principal to avoid such proceedings by the initial execution of the health care power of attorney.

Part IV

Paying for Medical and Long-Term Care

Chapter 11

Long-Term Care Options

The aging of the American population has become a matter of much public discussion in recent years. As the "baby boomer" generation begins to turn fifty, the prospect of medical and long-term care for a rapidly increasing segment of the population becomes even more important, both on a public policy level and as it affects more and more individual families. Aging need not be (and is not) automatically associated with high medical costs, debilitating conditions, and the need for protective housing. In fact, recent studies indicate that the American population is aging comparatively well—that the incidence of nursing home placement and debilitating medical treatments may actually decrease as longevity grows over the next few decades. The sheer size of the aging population does make the availability of medical and long-term care critically important for many individuals and families. This chapter discusses the continuum of care and the long-term care options available including home care, congregate living, assisted living, adult care facilities, continuing care retirement communities, nursing homes, and hospice care.

Overview

Q 11:1 What are some settings in which medical care might be provided?

The aging of the population, the popular perception of breakdown of the nuclear family, longer lifespans, increased government benefits, and the relative prosperity of many senior citizens have brought about profound changes in the long-term care marketplace in the past 20 years. Although most people still have a visceral fear of ending up in a nursing home, there have never been more choices available for everyone from the healthy or frail elderly to the chronically ill. Nursing home stays can be quite short or extended. According to Census Bureau statistics, the need for assistance increases dramatically with age: Although only about 8 percent of non-institutionalized individuals aged 65 to 69 suffer from limitations in the ability to care for themselves, 28 percent of those over age 85 require assistance. [Census Bureau: "Selected Characteristics of Civilian Noninstitutionalized Persons 65 and Over"—see *http://www.census.gov/hhes/www/disable/census/tables/tab2us.html*]. The 2000 Census shows that nearly 42 percent of the population 65 and over have a disability of some kind. [Census Bureau: "Table DP-2. Profile of Selected Social Characteristics: 2000"—see *http://factfinder.census.gov*] Similarly, while 1 percent of those aged 65 to 74 lived in nursing homes in 1990, nearly one-quarter of those aged 85 or older did. [Census Bureau: "Sixty-Five Plus in the United States" Statistical Brief, 1995] While diagnosis and projections of dementia (one of the most frequent causes of need for assistance) have proven to be particularly difficult, medical research indicates that between one-third and one-half of all those aged 85 or older suffer from some form of dementia. [Cf. Skoog, *A Population-Based Study of Dementia in 85-Year-Olds*, N. Engl. J. Med. 328(3): 153–158 (Jan. 21, 1993)] The average stay in a nursing home of those who remain is 2.5 years (897 days); for short-stay patients, who are discharged rather than dying in the institution, the average stay is only 272 days, for a combined average of 1.6 years. The National Nursing Home Survey: 1999 Summary (see report on National Center for Health Statistics website *http://www.cdc.gov/nchs*).

Increasingly sophisticated home health care services allow many individuals to continue to live at home and, if they choose, to die at home. Hospitals now focus their care on short-term, acute illnesses, and injuries, and discharge patients as quickly as possible to rehabilitation facilities, nursing homes, assisted living facilities, board and care homes, or, if possible, the patients' own residences. As Alzheimer's disease and other dementias claim an increasing number of victims, in part because of increased longevity, day care and respite care programs provide relief for exhausted family caretakers. Many nursing homes now have locked Alzheimer's units.

Of course much medical care is still provided in hospitals. Government pressure to reduce the cost of medical care, coupled with individual preferences, have driven much medical care out of those hospitals and into rehabilitation facilities and outpatient care. The former may look like a hybrid between a traditional hospital and a nursing home; the latter may require one or a few short visits to a hospital-based or community clinic, but rely heavily on family care and support during the recovery process.

Q 11:4   What choices are available for long-term care?

Those who can afford to pay for their own long-term care have almost unlimited choices, including total care in the home. Those dependent on Medicaid benefits are limited to facilities that meet Medicare and Medicaid requirements, and may not be allowed to live at home if it is not cost-effective for the provider. Medicaid will not pay for mere custodial care—the applicant must have mental or physical conditions that require medical care—but room and board are covered if the applicant is medically eligible (see chapter 14 for a discussion of Medicaid). In most communities, those needing long-term care and their families can choose among a number of long-term care facilities, including nursing homes, board and care homes, and assisted living facilities. Case management services can be especially useful in helping families choose the best care for the money, and monitoring that care after the patient has moved into the facility.

The government's participation varies tremendously by the type of care. Government money is particularly important in the nursing home industry, and in recent years government support for home care services has grown substantially. Among the choices for long-term placement are (ranging, roughly, from less to more restrictive):

1. *Home care.* Home care encompasses a wide variety of services and levels of care. Home care is provided by both nonprofit agencies and for-profit franchises. Some seniors can be cared for at home by one caretaker who visits a few times a week, or every day.

Others may require live-in assistance, perhaps from family members (or a combination of family and paid caregivers). At the other extreme, home care can duplicate the highest level of care provided by skilled nursing facilities (or even hospital care), but usually at a tremendous cost. While home care is the stated preference of most seniors, the practical realities of providing medical care at home may make it prohibitively expensive, particularly if the resident requires round-the-clock nursing care. The cost of that level of care will probably be four or five times the cost of comparable nursing home care. By contrast, the cost of occasional home visits, housework, and assistance with meal preparation (a typical combination for the largely independent senior) may be a fraction of any of the other care alternatives. This financial divide may change, however. Medicaid home care waiver programs are now being developed that would permit State-paid "personal care assistants" chosen by the patient individually, thereby expanding the pool of care providers to include friends and other independent caregivers who might not have had the financial incentives to devote sufficient time to the individual's needs. Other incentives for home care will be developed to prevent institutionalization or even return institutionalized individuals to the community.

2. *Continuing care retirement communities (CCRCs).* CCRCs have now been around for some time. They usually combine several levels of care in a single campus or facility. In theory, a resident can move into an "independent living" apartment with the knowledge that, if he or she should fail, assisted living and even nursing home placement will be available (or at least nearby) without having to move to another facility. CCRCs frequently require a substantial down-payment, which may or may not be refundable when the resident moves out of the complex or dies. Many CCRCs are marketed as luxury complexes, and so (while costs may vary tremendously) they tend to be extremely expensive care alternatives in the short run while the resident is able to manage independently. If, however, the contract requires a large down payment or "loan," and also guarantees lifetime skilled nursing care at no extra charge, and the resident later requires the care, the gamble can pay off. The contract and payment provisions also tend to be quite complex, often requiring legal assistance and advice in negotiation before entering the facility, and making it very difficult to shop around.

3. *Board and care facilities.* More commonly referred to today as adult care homes or residential care homes, these facilities usually provide room and board for four or five to twenty or more elderly residents. While private rooms are usually available, most adult care home residents will share a room with at least one other resident. All meals and social activities are provided at the home, which frequently will be owned and run by a resident manager or an owner who lives nearby and spends most days working at the home. Most elderly residents find adult care homes to be quieter, more home-like, and more pleasant than nursing homes, although adult care homes usually are unable to deal with serious medical conditions. As a result, incontinence, the need for breathing assistance or tube feedings, or any other serious medical condition will probably result in the transfer of the resident to a nursing home. The costs of adult care homes also vary widely, but may typically be between half and two-thirds of the cost of a nursing home in the same locale. A related class of facility is a residential care facility that may be as large as a nursing home (and to many residents, indistinguishable from such a facility). However, because it is not a skilled nursing facility it will not accept Medicaid payments. Instead, the state supplemental security income payment may be tailored to meet the facility cost for those that qualify.

4. *Congregate living.* Large apartment-like complexes may house many elderly residents who have access to a common dining room and activities but also have individual apartments with kitchens (and perhaps with spare bedrooms). Although there may be nursing staff on site, the primary focus of congregate living facilities is to provide a comfortable, supportive apartment setting where residents may, but need not, participate in services. Typically, congregate living arrangements provide two meals a day (perhaps a single meal on Sunday), programs, excursions, and social events. The residents may be expected to provide their own third meal. Independence is encouraged, but limited support is available when needed. Congregate living costs may vary from as little as the cost of a nice apartment complex in the area to as much as a nursing facility.

5. *Assisted living facilities.* Assisted living facilities provide an apartment-like setting, accompanied by on-staff nursing assistants and oversight. Meals are usually provided in a central dining facility, and staff regularly check on residents every day. Group activities

may help maintain mobility, orientation, and socialization. Costs for assisted living facilities vary widely, though they will generally be less expensive than comparable nursing facilities. Much of the higher cost of some such facilities comes from additional amenities: better food, private apartments, nicer common areas, and more activities, for example. Many facilities "unbundle" their charges so that those with more needs pay an additional fee on top of the standard fee. Others include partial endowment or large "entrance fee" requirements and then try to keep the monthly charges lower.

6. *Skilled nursing facilities.* With prices ranging from $3,500 (Louisiana) to $15,000 (Alaska) per month, depending on geography and level of care, nursing homes are today the most familiar long-term care settings. Although they are now commonplace, the phenomenon is largely a recent development; nursing homes have their organizational roots in the "poor houses" and old-age homes of earlier centuries. Modern nursing homes are based on a strong medical model of care: Even though the primary problem of the resident may be social (no place to live, or no family to help provide care), the care provided will be medical, and will be at the hands of nurses, nurses' aides, therapists, and other medical professionals.

7. *Hospice care.* Although the hospice movement is relatively new (the first hospice organization in this country was established in Branford, Connecticut, in 1974), it has grown quickly. One of the key reasons for that growth has been the increasing coverage for hospice benefits through the federal Medicare program. The Medicare hospice benefit was first provided in 1990 and in the 10 years since then, expenditures quintupled, at a time when total Medicare expenditures increased by about 60 percent. Hospice care is based on the premise that death is itself a natural event, and that care for a participating terminally ill patient should focus on comfort, reassurance, and support rather than curative measures. Hospice care can be provided in a separate facility or in the home; in fact, hospice care at home (or in whatever facility the patient is in at the time of initiation of hospice services) has become the norm in most communities.

8. *Green Houses?* Coming soon to a theater near you—the "Green House" is a prototype of a kind of supportive living arrangement group home for elders that would permit "aging in place" in a non-institutional, "human-scale" environment. Residents share

living and dining areas that resemble those of a large home and continue to live in private bedrooms. Those involved with hands-on care, known as "shahbazim" (a Persian word) are given a greater role and responsibility as compared to "management." Staffing levels are also higher than in traditional nursing homes. In the words of *ncbcapital.org*, which provides information and funding resources: "Developed by Dr. William Thomas and rooted in the tradition of the Eden Alternative, a model for cultural change within nursing facilities, The Green House is intended to de-institutionalize long-term care by eliminating large nursing facilities and creating habilitative, social settings." According to a January 2008 report by National Public Radio, there are now thirty-five "green houses" nationwide on thirteen campuses. The Robert Wood Johnson Foundation, in partnership with NCB Capital Impact, is reportedly spending $10 million to assist in the nationwide expansion of this model. As the "baby boomers" age, one can expect other "outside the box" alternatives to traditional institutional settings.

Home Care

Q 11:10.1 Can an individual pay family members to provide home care?

The answer to this question depends on the context of the question. Contracts may be entered into among family members. Such contracts should be enforceable. On the other hand, Medicaid agencies look with suspicion upon transfers of assets between related parties and agreements for personal services may be subject to challenge if payment for services is not made on an ongoing basis (which will probably create taxable income to the family member and raise issues about employment taxes and liability) but are instead transferred shortly before application is made for Medicaid benefits. In a 2006 case, a contract to pay $1,000 per month was upheld against an "arbitrary" rejection by the state Medicaid agency when payment was only made over two years later prior to application. The amount involved was approximately $28,000. Although the agreement was ultimately upheld and Medicaid approved, the legal expenses may have significantly reduced the value of the agreement. On the other hand, without the agreement, it might not have been possible to provide any compensation, no matter how deserved, without jeopardizing Medicaid eligibility. [See Carpenter v. State of Louisiana, Department of Health and Hospitals, La. Ct. App., 1st Cir., Sept. 20, 2006]

Q 11:10.2   Who can get a reverse mortgage?

First, to get a reverse mortgage, you must own a home. For the federally-insured "Home Equity Conversion Mortgage" (HECM), the home must be a single-family, two-four family, or approved condominium or planned unit development (PUD). For Fannie Mae's "Home-Keeper" mortgage, the home must be a single-family home, PUD, or condominium. Reverse mortgages are not presently available for co-ops or mobile homes. All commercially available mortgages require that all borrowers be 62 or older. The common wisdom was that all parties with a name on the deed had to be 62 or older, and that a life use/remainder to a child arrangement would preclude a reverse mortgage. Nowadays, the industry has adapted to life use/remainders by permitting reverse mortgages provided all parties consent. In other words, if Mom has a life use and Son a remainder, Mom can get a reverse mortgage if Son consents, but on Mom's death, the mortgage must be repaid, which will likely mean selling the home. This can be a problem when the remainderman lives in the home, is under 62 and disabled, and thus would be entitled to the home outright if the parent simply went off to a nursing home on Medicaid. In theory, private lenders might permit a reverse mortgage for a person under 62, and at least one company is offering a reverse mortgage product for those aged 60+, marketed as the "Simply 60" mortgage.

Q 11:10.3   When should a client be discouraged from entering into a reverse mortgage?

Questions to ask a client considering a reverse mortgage include: (1) Are there any liens? Liens must be paid off at closing and a surprise lien such as a lien for state assistance can wipe out the benefit of the mortgage. (2) Do you plan to live there for the rest of your life—or if there are two borrowers—if one person dies, will the other want to stay on, or move? The high financing charges will cut steeply into what may be realized upon a sale and reduce funds available to relocate to an assisted living or retirement community. (3) Does someone under 62 live with you who would not want to move after your death? And (4) Will the money be enough? If the money is not enough, sale will be inevitable and at a much higher cost.

Q 11:10.4 Where can a client get a reverse mortgage?

Many lending institutions offer reverse mortgages, from banks to mortgage companies, but virtually all reverse mortgages are issued by or sold to a single entity, Financial Freedom Lending Corp. Thus, the product will be essentially the same. Home Equity Conversion Mortgages (HECMs) are the only federally insured reverse mortgages. "Home-keeper" mortgages are offered through Fannie Mae. In many cases the HECM will yield more than the Homekeeper. In addition, "jumbo" mortgages ($417,000 or more as of 2008) known as "proprietary" because not resold may be issued by Financial Freedom Corp. There is also the possibility of an uninsured private reverse mortgage, unless prohibited by local law. Creative use of a reverse mortgage can protect the financial contributions of family members who can no longer be "reimbursed" or "thanked" by the elder person without risk of transfer penalties under the Deficit Reduction Act. If the mortgage secures the repayment and the contributions made are contemporaneously documented, presumably the family "lender" is assured of repayment which then protects assets from being spent on long-term care in an institution. For those concerned about imputed interest on no-interest loans, it is useful to remember that for loans of $100,000 or less, the imputed interest cannot exceed the actual investment income of the borrower.

Q 11:10.5 Where can one find out more about reverse mortgages?

There is considerable consumer information available on reverse mortgages, especially the following websites: http://www.aarp.org/revmort (AARP, including a handy calculator) and http://www.reverse.org. In 2005, the National Council on Aging published two new pamphlets bringing together the latest information on reverse mortgages; these are also available online at http://www.ncoa.org/content.cfm?sectionID = 250.

Q 11:11 What programs may benefit caregivers of those elders at home?

Caregivers may find some measure of relief from The Family Caregiver Initiative of the Older Americans Act, The Family and Medical Leave Act, and any state caregiver respite programs. In addition, the Alzheimer's associations or similar groups may have a private program to pay for "respite" for caregivers.

The Family Caregiver Initiative, establishing the National Family Caregiver Support Program administered by the Agency on Aging, is intended to provide help to those caring for individuals who require assistance with two or more ADLs, or who have a "cognitive impairment that requires supervision because of health or safety risks." There are two major components of the program: Respite Services and Supplemental Services. Respite Services can provide services such as adult day care, home health aide support, homemaker, companion, skilled nursing visits, and/or short-term stays in a nursing or assisted living facility. Supplemental Services can include payment for one-time, health-related items or services such as durable medical equipment, medically necessary items, minor home modifications, transportation, seasonal clothing, or emergency items or services. The program is not means-tested, but local programs may ask for a contribution or co-pay. The program is administered locally by a state's local agency on aging office, which should be contacted for more information. In 2003, funding for the program was $155.2 million.

The Family and Medical Leave Act of 1993 (FMLA) does not provide any additional government resources to help care for homebound elders, but it does mandate some relief for family caregivers. Under the FMLA, an employer is required to permit up to 12 weeks per year of unpaid leave for employees who must provide care for parents, spouses, or children as a result of serious health conditions. [29 U.S.C. § 2612(a)(1)(C)] The affected employee must be permitted to return to his or her prior position after the leave is completed. [29 U.S.C. § 2614(a)]

In 2003, Congress failed to pass legislation (to be known as the "Family Caregiver Relief Act of 2003") that would have given family caregivers a $5,000 income tax credit; similar legislation may be proposed in the future.

Q 11:12.1 When will Medicaid pay for home care services?

Medicaid includes a "home and community based services" benefit that is supposed to permit coverage for services wherever they can prevent institutionalization, but strict income limits will apply. Many states have applied for Medicaid waivers to permit long-term care to be provided as home care rather than in a skilled facility, or have created their own home care programs. A significant issue for a senior planning a move may be what kind of Medicaid home care program is available in his or her state! In Connecticut, for example, the Connecticut Home Care Program for elders offers a host of options to cover care at home in an effort to prevent premature institutionalization, including a "Personal Care Assistant" benefit that permits the individual to hire almost anyone (except a spouse) to provide care at state expense. It is important to remember that the prohibition on liens of the home during the Medicaid beneficiary's lifetime do not apply where the beneficiary is receiving long-term care at home under a Medicaid waiver (unless other lien prohibitions are applicable). And in that situation, the "home care" lien must be paid when the senior relocates to a nursing home.

Q 11:15 What is adult day care?

Some programs provide care for seniors from one to eight hours each day, usually at a separate facility or as an adjunct to a nursing home, assisted living, or other facility. An adult day care program may be certified by Medicare or Medicaid, and will ordinarily provide nursing supervision, meals, and activities intended not only to provide care for but also to engage participants. Assistance with activities of daily living should also be provided in an adult day care program. Such a program may help the participant maintain a higher level of functioning by regular interaction and engagement with others, while simultaneously providing respite for home caregivers. Caregivers may obtain assistance with adult day care expenses through the Family Caregiver Support Program administered by area agencies on aging. (See SQ 11:11)

Continuing Care Retirement Communities

Q 11:17 What is a continuing care retirement community?

Continuing care retirement communities (CCRCs) are a recent trend in retirement living and have become controversial because of the contractual arrangements they require. CCRCs provide a continuum of care in one complex. As the individual's needs change, he or she moves to a facility that provides more care. An individual can, for example, start in an independent living facility and move to assisted living and then into a nursing home if necessary. A characteristic of the CCRC is payment of a high admission fee, sometimes referred to as a "deposit" or styled as a "loan."

Before deciding on a CCRC, healthy seniors must first try to predict their futures: Will they enjoy continued health and mercifully quick death, or will they succumb to dementia or chronic illness and need skilled nursing care for many years? Those who fear the latter can contract with a CCRC which typically requires a large admission fee or purchase of real property such as a cooperative, plus monthly payments in return for lifetime accommodations and nursing home care if needed. When the resident dies, some or all of the admission fee remains with the community regardless of whether the resident needed nursing care. The advantage is that nursing home costs are at least theoretically fixed at an affordable rate; the disadvantage is that the resident may turn over a significant portion of his or her estate to a facility without ever having used the services. Critics warn that once the admission fee is paid, the facility has little incentive to maintain high-quality assisted living and nursing services. Because the financial stability of the community is based on actuarial expectations, a greater-than-average number of residents needing nursing care could endanger the assets of all the residents. The unhappy resident may not be able to leave the facility without losing equity in the cooperative and, of course, the admission fee.

CCRCs usually accept Medicare and Medicaid payments (and may be required by state regulations to accept such payments); however, because government benefits are available only for skilled nursing care, most CCRC residents will receive few benefits from Medicare or Medicaid, at least until they enter the facility's skilled nursing facility. Because of the substantial financial commitments required by most CCRCs and the potential exposure to additional financial risk, they tend to cater to wealthier seniors.

Many CCRCs are nonprofit facilities. Because church-sponsored groups providing lifetime care for members with no family spurred the initial growth of the industry, the industry continues to be dominated by religious organizations.

Q 11:18.1 Are CCRC deposits and fees tax-deductible?

As with assisted living facilities, at least a portion of the monthly charge for staying in a CCRC will be tax-deductible. (See SQ 11:29) Recently, the U.S. Tax Court held that even a couple in an "independent living" unit of a CCRC could use a percentage method to deduct a portion of their monthly charges, but could not deduct additional amounts spent on medical use of pool, spa, and exercise facilities. [Delbert L. v. Commissioner of Internal Revenue (T.C., No. 448-02, Feb. 19, 2004)] In addition, the portion of the advance payment that is allocable to medical care will also be deductible. [See Rev. Rul. 75-302; Rev. Rul. 67-185]

Q 11:18.2 Are CCRC entrance fees countable resources for Medicaid eligibility purposes?

Yes. Pursuant to the Deficit Reduction Act of 2005 [at 42 U.S.C. § 1396p(g)(2)], entrance fees are countable resources to the extent that the resident has the right to use the fee for payment of care costs, the resident is entitled to a refund on death or departure, and the fee did not purchase an ownership interest in the CCRC.

Q 11:19 Are CCRC life-care contracts enforceable?

As with any contract claim, residents must show a breach of the contract and ensuing damages for a valid action against the facility. Arguments that the contract is unconscionable, voidable for lack of consideration, or lacking mutuality have generally not succeeded. Most life-care contracts have a probationary period, during which time the resident can leave and obtain a full refund of money and property minus the cost of care. If the resident dies during the probationary period, the estate can collect. State insurance law will regulate life-care contracts, and the National Association of Insurance Commissioners has drafted stringent requirements for liquid reserves for CCRCs.

Certain provisions in a CCRC, however, may violate nursing home residents' rights law. A recent case invalidated a CCRC contract provision requiring a couple to maintain their assets so as not to qualify for Medicaid, at least when one member of the couple enters the facility's nursing home directly. [Oak Crest Village Inc. v. Murphy, 379 Md. 229 (2004)]

Q 11:21 Who regulates CCRCs?

The only federal regulation of CCRCs occurs when Medicare or Medicaid provides reimbursement for nursing or home health services provided by the CCRC. Because the lifetime CCRC contract resembles an insurance arrangement, most states regulate the industry through state insurance commissioners; some also regulate through the social services department. Regulation may be no more than a rule requiring full disclosure and certain warnings; or it may be more extensive. In addition, the state may regulate the operation of the nursing or other health care facility that is part of the CCRC. Although CCRCs are located across the country, nearly half are concentrated in five states: Pennsylvania, California, Florida, Illinois, and Ohio. [American Association of

Homes and Services for the Aging (AAHSA), Continuing Care Retirement Communities (1999)]

Many CCRCs are members of the AAHSA, which provides consumer information and suggestions. [AAHSA, 901 E St. NW, Suite 500, Washington, DC 20004-2011, (202) 783-2242, *http://www.aahsa.org*] A national accreditation organization, Continuing Care Accreditation Commission (CCAC), shares office space with and is sponsored by AAHSA and also provides some assistance and oversight, albeit voluntary. [CCAC, 901 E. St. NW, Suite 500, Washington, DC 20004, (202) 783-7286, *http://www.ccaconline.org*]

Q 11:22 What should the elder law attorney consider in reviewing a CCRC contract?

A CCRC contract can be daunting, not only for the client-resident but also for the elder law practitioner. Among the myriad of concerns raised by consideration of a CCRC contract are the following:

1. *Fees.* What is the entry fee and monthly fee, and how are they calculated? Are they based on actuarial assumptions, or designed to ensure that the CCRC is able to sustain itself? Is any portion of the entry fee refundable, and under what conditions? Is some portion of the entry fee tax deductible as a medical expense? What are the due dates and penalties for monthly fees? Is there a provision limiting the amount of future increases on monthly fees?

2. *Facility and services.* Does the agreement clearly specify which unit the resident will occupy, and under what circumstances the resident may choose to change locations? Is the resident's unit easily accessible, both now and if the resident loses mobility? Are meals, housekeeping, recreational activities, transportation services, and guest provisions clearly delineated?

3. *Health and nursing services.* Does the agreement provide for the availability and cost of home health care and possible future nursing care? Will the CCRC's onsite nursing facility be able to handle the care of the resident for any likely future medical condition? Are there limitations for preexisting conditions? Who will determine what level of care the resident requires, and what appeal rights will the resident have if forced to move to a higher level of care? What will happen to the resident's unit if there is a

temporary placement in the assisted living or skilled nursing facilities? What provisions are made for the relocation of the resident's spouse in the event the resident is institutionalized?

4. *Financial disclosure requirements.* CCRCs commonly require new residents to disclose their assets and income, and sometimes demand an agreement that the resident will use those resources for care rather than make transfers or other arrangements to secure eligibility for public assistance earlier before they might be anticipated to do so. Although such provisions may have been of questionable enforceability before, the Deficit Reduction Act of 2005 clearly authorizes the practice [42 U.S.C. § 1396r(c)(5)(v)].

5. *Future care.* Because most CCRCs carefully guard their tax-exempt status, they probably have some internal provisions for the continuing care of residents after financial resources are exhausted. Does the contract make any reference to such a policy? If not, what are the terms of the CCRC's policy, and what has been its practice to date?

6. *Residence councils and governance.* What provisions are made for self-determination for the CCRC's residents? Is there a council or advisory group established for residents to voice their concerns and desires for change or improvement? Are residents' rights spelled out in a policy manual or handbook, and if so who has the power to change those provisions and under what circumstances?

7. *Financial stability.* One of the most pressing problems for CCRCs has been financial failures in the industry. What arrangements has the CCRC made for a fund to cover future expenses, especially medical care? Is any such fund based on a calculation of the present value of future expenses, including assumptions about resident mortality and morbidity? What organization sponsors the CCRC, and is its financial backing sufficient to help ensure success? Has the CCRC operated for a period of time already? Are the CCRC's finances currently sound?

8. *Quality of care.* Is the CCRC accredited by the Continuing Care Accreditation Commission? How does the nursing facility rate in reviews of such institutions? (Check, among other sources, the Centers for Medicare and Medicaid Services' "Nursing Home Compare" page at *http://www.medicare.gov/NHCompare/home.asp.*))

Assisted Living

Q 11:29 How much should a resident of an assisted living facility deduct as an itemized medical expense for income tax purposes?

An important feature for many elderly individuals is the ability to deduct the high cost of care from income for tax purposes. While deductibility is obvious for such expenses as nursing homes, it is less clear for the costs of an assisted living facility when the resident may initially require only a modest amount of assistance and is really moving as a form of insurance against increasing needs.

IRS Notice 97-31 explains that "qualified long-term care services" are deductible, defined as: "Necessary diagnostic, preventative, therapeutic, curing, treating, mitigating, and rehabilitative services, and maintenance or personal care services that are required by a chronically ill individual and provided pursuant to a plan of care prescribed by a licensed health care practitioner," defined as someone who cannot, without substantial assistance from another individual, perform at least two out of six ADLs (eating, toileting, transferring, bathing, dressing, and continence), or requires substantial supervision to protect from threats to health and safety due to severe cognitive impairment.

While there is no bright-line test, a common wisdom is that (1) residents who live in the assisted living facility independently and require no assistance cannot deduct; (2) those who receive some assistance, but that is not the primary reason for residing in the facility (e.g., a spouse), can deduct only the medical care portion, and should ask the facility to provide a percentage figure unless those charges are tabulated separately; and (3) those whose primary reason for staying in assisted living can deduct 100 percent. [Treas. Reg. § 1.213-1(e)(1)(v)(a). See also Rev. Rul. 67-185, 1967-1 C.B. 70; Rev. Rul. 75-302, 1975-2 C.B. 86; Rev. Rul. 76-481, 1976-2 C.B. 82; Levine v. Commissioner, 695 F.2d 57, 59-60 (2d Cir. 1982), *aff'g*, T.C. Memo. 1981-437, Estate of Smith v. Commissioner, 79 T.C. 313, 319 (1982)]

Q 11:30 How should one choose an assisted living facility?

A key issue for anyone considering moving to an assisted living facility will be the cost, both the "daily rate" and the hidden expenses: extra charges for medical expenses; extra charges for supplies the facility encourages the resident to purchase through the facility; $35 per trip for escort to a doctor's appointment or elsewhere. Especially if the client will be spending down principal to meet the monthly costs, and hoping to live longer than the money, financial planning is a must. For cost calculation, one approach is to demand to see the "evaluation" form the facility uses, not for the preliminary intake needs assessment, but for follow-up, and "check off" what you think the resident might need, then ask for a quote at that price. Needless to say, it is absolutely essential to review the entire assisted living contract before making the decision.

A good summary of these and other issues, a checklist, and a cost-calculator may be found in an article published by Consumer Reports, "Is Assisted Living the Right Choice?" [Consumer Reports Jan. 2001, p. 26] Other resources are the industry-sponsored National Center for Assisted Living, *http://www.ncal.org*, which offers a consumer guide and list of questions to ask, and the Consumer Consortium on Assisted Living, *http://www.ccal.org*.

Skilled Nursing Facilities and Nursing Homes

Q 11:34 Who pays for nursing home care?

Depending on geography and the level of care needed, nursing home residency can cost between $3,500 and $15,000 per month. The 2007 "MetLife Market Survey of Nursing Home and Home Care Costs" reported a 3.4 percent increase in nursing home costs over 2006, while a 2003 GE Financial study showed average increases of 7 percent annually. According to the 2007 MetLife survey, the national average was $189/day, with the most expensive (Alaska) averaging $183,960/ year for a semi-private room, and Hartford, Connecticut following not far behind at $124,465/year. [See *http://www.metlife.com/FileAssets/ MMI/MMIStudies2007NHAL.pdf*.] The survey also revealed that costs varied widely, from a low of $99 per day at one nursing home in Arkansas to a high of $641 per day at a facility in Alaska. Few patients can afford to foot the total bill for more than a few months, so Medicaid benefits often make up the difference. An increasing number of individuals purchase long-term care insurance, which is expensive if purchased at 70 or older, but can generally enable residents to choose a high-quality nursing facility.

Q 11:35   How are Medicare and Medicaid benefits apportioned?

Medicare Part A benefits pay for skilled nursing facility care for medical, nursing, and rehabilitation services (see chapter 13 for a discussion of Medicare). Once the patient has been hospitalized for three successive days (not counting the day of discharge), a total of 100 days of SNF care is covered by Medicare; the first 20 days are totally covered, while the remaining 80 days requires a co-pay of $128 per day (2008 figure; $133.50 in 2009) from the patient. [42 C.F.R. § 409.85] SNF services include room and board, nursing care, therapy, and drugs.

Medicaid benefits vary by state, but they are generally need-based and require that the patient be impoverished and pay almost all of his or her income for his or her share of the cost of care (see chapter 14 for a discussion of Medicaid). Medicaid pays for both skilled nursing and long-term care costs, and because federal law requires that a nursing facility provide services that would attain or maintain the highest practicable physical and mental well-being of the resident, the nursing home cannot deny services such as therapy or psychiatric assessments as not being covered by Medicaid.

Other than copayments, deductibles, and mandated contributions to the cost of care, Medicare and Medicaid patients cannot be charged for any medically related services, social activities, or personal hygiene items. [42 C.F.R. § 483.10(c)(8)] The patient must foot the bill for telephone and television use, cosmetic items, clothing, and books. Under Medicaid, patients are allowed anywhere from $20 or so to as high as $75 (some states use fixed amounts, which may or may not change each year, others tie the figure to the maximum SSI benefit) per month, which may be applied toward such personal use. Nursing homes are forbidden from requiring waivers of Medicare or Medicaid benefits from patients. [42 C.F.R. § 483.12(d)(1)] And finally, Medicaid patients must be informed if their assets grow to a point where their need-based benefits may be threatened. [42 U.S.C. § 1396r(c)(6)(B)]

Q 11:35.1   What is a "responsible party," and what is it responsible for?

Most nursing home admissions contracts will include provisions that apply to a "responsible party." This person is sometimes identified as being the person who has access to the resident's funds for the purpose of paying the facility's bills. The law does not prohibit a facility from "requiring an individual, who has legal access to a resident's income or resources available to pay for care in the facility, to sign a contract (without incurring personal financial liability) to provide payment from the resident's income or resources for such care." [42 U.S.C. 1396r(c)(5)(B)(ii)] Often, the contract will also use the "responsible party" as a person entitled to required notices, and who will consult with the nursing home about the resident's plan of care.

Lately, nursing home have begun to include ever more promises that the responsible party makes to the nursing home if he or she signs the admissions agreement. These may include: promises to pay; promises to use the resident's funds solely to pay the nursing home; promises not to engage in Medicaid planning; promises to accept custody of the resident if there is no longer a source of payment; and the list goes on.

Although the standard advice has been that such clauses are unenforceable, at least one court has flatly rejected the argument and ruled that the "contract of adhesion" objection won't work. [Briarcliff Nursing Home, Inc. v. Turcotte, 2004 Ala. LEXIS 20 (Feb. 6, 2004) (arbitration clause could be enforced against resident when attorney-in-fact signed the contract agreeing to the clause); compare, however, Bedford Care Center—Monroe Hall, LLC v. Lewis (No. 2005-CA-00382-SCT, Mississippi, January 25, 2005) (refusal to sign clause followed by nursing home providing services meant that clause did not apply)]

A terrible case that imposed liability upon a "responsible party" to the full amount of the resident's funds even though the party, an attorney-in-fact, had indeed used the resident's funds for the resident's welfare in part in addition to making gifts, is the Connecticut case of *Sunrise Healthcare Corp. v. Azarigian* [76 Conn. App. 800 (2003)]. The case concluded that the requirement that the responsible party use the resident's funds for the resident's "welfare" did not permit the responsible party to pay for anything (in this case, a personal companion) not typically covered by the Medicaid program! The facts suggest that this was a case of "Medicaid planning gone wrong," because the resident's husband had tried to establish a discretionary trust using a revocable trust agreement rather than a testamentary trust, resulting in a penalty period not anticipated when the responsible party also made gifts. Had Medicaid been approved, there would not have been a liability issue. More recently, however, a "responsible party" has been held liable for misapplied income, i.e., failure to pay income to the nursing home, and could even be liable for the costs of collection if the nursing home were able to prove "bad faith." Northfield Care Center, Inc. v. Anderson (Minn. App. January 1, 2005).

In the face of cases like *Azarigian* and *Northfield Care Center*, what advice can we give to the client who may be asked to sign as "responsible party"? The best advice may be "don't." Courts are increasingly inclined to enforce these promises on the theory that they were entered into voluntarily by the third party. Since failure to sign as responsible party would not appear to be grounds for discharge under the nursing home residents' rights rules, once the resident is physically present (such as through hospital discharge when the resident is still on Medicare), a client should be able to refuse to sign without negative implications, provided there is a realistic source of payment. A tougher case is an admission from the community. In that situation, the initial application must be completed in order to get a spot on the waiting list, or to enter. The application may require a responsible party to be identified; the eventual admissions contract may incorporate the information on the application without reminding the signatory of the implications of being named a responsible party. Other options, in order of preference: (1) negotiate removal of the offending provisions; (2) cancel and initial offending provisions *before* the agreement is signed by nursing home personnel; or (3) sign as "Resident X by John Doe, X's attorney-in-fact." When possible, procrastinate and avoid signing the agreement. A practice development note: Potential liability for the responsible party if Medicaid is denied can provide an added incentive for seeking professional help with Medicaid planning and application for benefits.

Q 11:36   Can nursing homes require third parties to pay the bill?

Technically, No. Nursing homes are prohibited under federal law from requiring a third party—for instance, an adult child—to assume responsibility for nursing home costs as a condition of admission. [42 U.S.C. § 1396r(c)(5)(A); 42 C.F.R. § 483.12(d)(2)] Although it is settled law that one person is not responsible for the debts of another, nursing homes often manage to lure third parties into signing contracts that ensure payments. In at least one case, a court held that although a guarantee could not be *required* as a condition to admission, it could be enforced if it was agreed to voluntarily. [SWA, Inc., v. Straka, 2003 Ohio 3259 (Ohio App. 2003)] The *Azarigian* case discussed in SQ 11:35.1 created a situation tantamount to a guarantee.

Note that a few states may still carry on their books statutes imposing on children the duty to support a parent. Normally, where Medicaid eligibility exists, these laws have no effect, because a nursing home may not collect from two sources of payment. However, in at least one case a court has cited the state law statute imposing such a duty of support in a situation in which a transfer (to the child) rendered the parent ineligible for Medicaid. [Presbyterian Medical Center v. Budd, 832 A.2d 1066 (Pa. Sup. 2003)]

Q 11:36.1 Can a nursing home require an applicant to put down a deposit as a condition for admission?

Deposits and required prepayments are prohibited when care is covered under Medicare, or when the applicant is already a Medicaid recipient. [42 C.F.R. § 483.12(d)(3)] There are no restrictions on deposits for *private pay* patients or those covered under other forms of insurance unless state law provides otherwise, but the facility is required to make its deposit policy public. Some states, like Connecticut, have more stringent requirements. In addition, a recent memorandum issued by the Centers for Medicare and Medicaid states that the rules protecting resident funds require that "[I]n instances where the deposit fee is refundable and remains funds of the resident, the facility must have a surety bond that covers the deposit amount." [Center for Medicaid and State Operations/Survey and Certification Group Memorandum 04-17 (January 8, 2004)]

When the deposit policy begins to read more like a guarantee of indefinite payment, however, one must begin to question its validity under the nursing home residents' rights law. That law states that a skilled nursing facility must not require individuals to waive their rights to benefits. [42 U.S.C. § 1395i-3(c)(5)(A)(i) (Medicare rules); 42 U.S.C. § 1396r(c)(5)(A)(i) (Medicaid rules)] Isn't requiring that two years' worth of assets be *maintained* the same as requiring an individual to waive Medicaid for two years? This issue is not addressed in the CMS Memorandum, which is being challenged by practitioners.

There is some question, however, whether a nursing home, as a creditor, has standing to bring suit against a resident's fiduciary—conservator, guardian, attorney-in-fact, trustee of a revocable trust—for supposed "negligence" that results in a denial of Medicaid benefits and accordingly, causes a loss to the nursing facility. In a Connecticut case, the state supreme court recently allowed a nursing home to claim on a conservator's bond for failures in handling the patient's finances, so that the funds were neither paid for care, nor dealt with in a timely fashion to ensure quick Medicaid eligibility. [The Jewish Home for the Elderly of Fairfield Cty., Inc. v. Cantore, 257 Conn. 531 (2001)]

As discussed in SQ 11:35.1, however, nursing homes may find other arguments that result in the "responsible party" being found liable for the bill.

Q 11:36.2 Can the nursing home bill the resident while a Medicaid application is pending?

In many states, the answer is "no." As a practical matter, a facility may not do so because it would be fruitless: Once the application is granted, the facility would have to refund the amounts paid. Unfortunately, however, a recent CMS Memorandum seems to approve the practice of billing the "Medicaid-pending" resident. The memorandum states: "When a nursing home resident or applicant applies for Medicaid, the facility often requires the resident to pay for NF services (usually at private pay rates) during the period it takes to determine Medicaid eligibility. A NF is permitted to charge an applicant or resident whose Medicaid eligibility is pending, typically in the form of a deposit prior to admission and/or payment for services after admission." [Center for Medicaid and State Operations/Survey and Certification Group Memorandum 04-17 (January 8, 2004)]. Even if the resident recieves a bill, however, it may be understood that the resident would only be expected to pay should Medicaid be denied.

Q 11:36.3 Once Medicaid is granted, if the resident has paid privately while the application was pending, does the resident receive a refund?

Yes. Medicaid can be granted retroactive to three months prior to the month of application. At all times that the resident is eligible for Medicaid, the facility cannot accept any other payment from the resident besides Medicaid. [42 U.S.C. § 1396r(c)(5)(D)] Therefore, the facility is required to refund to the resident. [Center for Medicaid and State Operations/Survey and Certification Group Memorandum 04-17 (January 8, 2004)]

Q 11:36.4 What can a family do to best ensure the patient's safety and good care in the nursing home?

Probably the single most important thing an attorney can tell clients to do in order to ensure a loved one is well cared for in the nursing home, is to make frequent visits. Visits provide an opportunity to ask questions and to make demands, but just as importantly, to let the facility know that someone is watching. The difference between care and neglect may be the number of visits the family makes. NCCNR's publication, Nursing Homes, Getting Good Care There, is essential, and some practitioners purchase copies to loan to clients. (See SQ 19:20.)

There are still concerns about the safety standards states impose on nursing homes. The International Association of Fire Chiefs released its 2005 "Healthcare Fire Safety Roundtable Report" recommending improvements, inspired at least in part by a deadly 2002 fire in a Connecticut nursing home. Funding constraints have limited the "feasibility" of retrofitting nursing homes with advancements such as sprinkler systems. Family members may find a role in taking action with state legislatures to ensure such improvements in safety.

A new concern for families of nursing home residents is disaster preparedness. Few will forget the story of St. Rita's Nursing Home in Chalmette, Louisiana, in which forty residents, many of them strapped to their beds, were found drowned by rising waters after Hurricane Katrina struck in September, 2005. (The nursing home owners were charged with their death but acquitted, following a trial, in 2007). Yet evacuation also carries risk, as was demonstrated by a fatal fire that engulfed a bus evacuating nursing home residents from Hurricane Rita in Texas, fueled in part by the passengers' oxygen tanks. Protecting frail elderly from natural disasters will remain a difficult problem and a cause for concern for residents' families.

Q 11:37 What should the lawyer for a patient or patient's family look for in an admission contract?

The agreement to be signed by the patient or responsible party at the time of admission should clearly state the costs of care, services covered by those costs (including meals and social activities), legal responsibilities of the patient, the patient's rights under federal and state laws, and grievance procedures. The agreement should *not* name a third party as a responsible party, should *not* require a deposit for Medicare patients or more than two months' advance payment for Medicaid patients, and should *not* require a "donation" to the facility.

Patients and their families should also be wary of any waivers of liability, particularly contractual provisions that release a nursing home from responsibility if the patient is injured after restraints are removed. Experts suggest that such provisions are against public policy and may violate state consumer protection statutes. If a patient challenges the admission contract and is not admitted as a result, the state long-term care ombudsman should be notified.

Other contract provisions to watch for include any requirement that the resident have or sign an advance medical directive or consent to particular medical procedures, any restriction on visiting hours or contact by family members, and any requirement that the resident's income be automatically turned over to the facility. Sadly, many contracts do not live up to the requirements. Then the family must choose:

- reject the nursing home out of hand, despite the fact that the care and facilities are the best available;

- annotate the document to delete offensive positions and hope this will be a sufficient defense should problems arise (unilateral modifications, one hopes, may at worst nullify the contract entirely);

- sign, but only in a capacity as agent; or

- sign what and how the nursing home wants, and hope that all such provisions are against public policy or preempted, and therefore unenforceable.

Q 11:37.1 When is an arbitration clause in a nursing home contract enforceable?

It is more and more common to see provisions in nursing home contracts by which the parties agree that any dispute will be submitted to binding arbitration. This will not seem particularly important until the resident is injured and the family seeks compensation, which may be awarded with more generosity by an outraged jury than by an arbitrator. As with the clauses described above, it may be possible to annotate the contract and "opt out" of such provisions. In several cases, arbitration clauses in contracts signed by an agent under durable power of attorney were invalidated on the basis that the durable power of attorney did not specifically confer on the agent the power to waive important legal rights, such as the right of access to the courts. The cases are divided on this issue. A 2008 Florida court refused to apply an arbitration clause where a nursing home contract was signed by an agent under power of attorney where there was no express authority to agree to arbitration. [Estate of McKibbin v. Alterra Health Care Corp., Case No. 2D06-5452, 2008 Fla. App. LEXIS 500 (Jan. 18, 2008); see the text of the case in *http://www.flprobatelitigation.com/2D06-5452.pdf*].

However, in 2007 another Florida court upheld an arbitration clause in an assisted living facility contract. [See, e.g., Alterra Healthcare Corporation v. Bryant, Fla. Ct. App., 4th Dist., Sept. 13, 2006 (assisted living facility), *http://www.4dca.org/Sept%202006/09-13-06/4D05-4409.op.pdf*]; Some practitioners advocate drafting powers of attorney that specifically exclude the power to waive the right to trial; the concern is that if the agent signs without authority, does he take personal responsibility, as not acting pursuant to the power of attorney? An alternative approach has been to object to the clause after the fact on a theory of "unconscionability" and although case law is also divided on this point, there is some slight indication that at least where the facility's clause is expansive, the courts may side with the resident. Compare Woebse v. Health Care & Retirement Corp. of America et al., Case No. 2D06-720, 2008 Fla. App. LEXIS 1446 (Feb. 6, 2008) (full case online *at http://www.2dca.org/opinion/February%2006%202008/2D06-720.pdf*) finding a clause unconscionable with Cynthia Manley, as the Pers. Rep. of the Estate of Patricia Manley v. Personalcare of Ohio d.b.a. Lake Med. Nursing and Rehabilitation Center, et al. (Ohio Ct. App. Jan. 29, 2007), upholding the clause against a claim of unconscionability. Two articles by Brian G. Brooks published in the November 7, 2006 and December 5, 2006 editions of the NAELA e-bulletin address various legal theories that may be used to defend against the assertion of arbitration clauses in nursing home contracts.

Q 11:44 What are the staffing requirements for nursing homes?

Nursing home staff are regulated. Licensed nursing staff must be on duty 24 hours per day, a registered nurse must be on site at least 8 hours a day, and all patients must be seen by a physician or, in some states, an alternative professional such as a nurse practitioner or physician's assistant. [42 U.S.C. § 1395r(b)(4)(C)(i)] Nursing homes with more than 120 patients must have at least one full-time social worker on staff. [42 C.F.R. § 483.15(g)] Staff must be checked against a state registry listing persons convicted of abuse or theft (see Q 11:45). Minimum requirements are also set by the NHRA for training and in-service education.

Unfortunately, no federal national minimum patient/staff ratio has been established by law or regulation. The absence of such a requirement has been criticized, and is the subject of continuing legislative discussions. See, for example, the Department of Health and Human Services' 2000 study which suggests that a reasonable minimum staff ratio might be one full-time nurse's aide for every four residents, and about one RN/LPN for every eight residents. The federal study also determined that about half of nursing homes studied fell below those minimum standards. Phase II of the study, published in 2002, presents "thresholds" below which there are more likely to be quality of care deficits but above which there may be little improvement, coming to essentially the same conclusions, and concluding that few U.S. nursing homes meet this level. [Report to Congress: Appropriateness of Minimum Nurse Staffing Ratios In Nursing Homes Phase II Final Report] Both reports are available at *http://www.cms.hhs.gov.*

Q 11:48   What notice must be provided by a nursing home before discharging a resident?

The nursing home patient must be given at least 30 days' notice prior to transfer or discharge unless an emergency situation exists or if the patient can be upgraded immediately to a less restricted environment. The notice must include the reasons for the transfer, the patient's rights with regard to appeals, and the name, address, and telephone number of the local long-term care ombudsman or similar advocate. [42 U.S.C. § 1396r(c)(1)(B)]

Nursing homes are no longer allowed to refuse to readmit a Medicaid patient who has been transferred for hospital care. If the patient's bed is filled during his or her absence, another must be made available when he is ready for discharge from the hospital. [42 U.S.C. § 1396r(c)(2)(D); 42 C.F.R. § 483.12(b)(3)] Some nursing homes set a "limited bed" policy, whereby only a certain number of beds are available for Medicaid patients. A federal court has held that such a practice violates Medicaid and civil rights laws. [Linton v. Commissioner of Health and Environment, 65 F.3d 508 (6th Cir. 1995), upholding the district court determination in Linton v. Carney, 779 F. Supp. 925 (M.D. Tenn. 1990)] Moreover, a facility is prohibited from moving a resident from a non-Medicaid bed to a Medicaid-bed if that is "a" reason for the move. (See SQ 11:49.1.)

Q 11:49.1   What rights does a resident have when a nursing home wants to move the resident to another room?

Federal regulations require that a nursing home provide proper notice before it changes the resident's room. [42 U.S.C. 1396r(c)(1)(A)(v)(II), "accommodation of needs"; 42 C.F.R. § 483.15(e)(2)] Residents have the right to refuse a transfer to another room if "a" purpose is to relocate the resident from a portion that is not a "skilled nursing facility" under Title XVIII to a portion that is, i.e., from a non-Medicaid-participating wing to a Medicaid wing. [42 U.S.C. § 1396r(c)(1)(A)(x)] (The resident is still entitled to Medicaid coverage, however.) Because a facility is not required to provide a private room, this does permit the transfer to a semiprivate room if the person was private pay and becomes a Medicaid covered individual. [42 U.S.C. § 1396r(c)(1)(A)]

However, if the resident can argue that a private room is medically necessary, he or she can protest the change in room on those grounds. An example might be a patient whose emphysema requires a room temperature below what can be tolerated by most residents (i.e., air conditioning), unless another resident can be found with the same condition; more difficult would be a resident with a mental disorder such as paranoia where the presence of another person would be medically dangerous.

Q 11:49.2 Can a family pay the nursing home extra in order for the resident to keep a private room?

Whether or not a nursing home is allowed to receive an additional payment as consideration for keeping a resident in a private room is a matter of interpretation of federal law, and may also be affected by state law. Under 42 U.S.C. § 1395i-3(c)(6)(D) a "The facility may not impose a charge against the personal funds of a resident for any item or service for which payment is made under this subchapter or subchapter XIX of this chapter," and under 42 U.S.C. § 1396r(c)(5)(A)(iii), cannot "charge, solicit, accept, or receive, in addition to any amount otherwise required to be paid under the State plan under this title, any gift, money, donation, or other consideration as a ... requirement for the individual's continued stay in the facility." Arguably if the facility is already being paid for room and board under Title XIX, it cannot impose a separate charge for a private room.

Likewise, 42 U.S.C. §§ 1395i-3(a)(5)(A)(ii) and 1396r(c)(5)(A)(ii) provide that a nursing home cannot "require a third party guarantee of payment to the facility as a condition of admission (or expedited admission) to, *or continued stay in*, the facility." Arguably, negotiating a contract with the family requiring payment as a condition of continued stay in the same room, might violate this provision. However, there is a caveat: 42 U.S.C. § 1396r(c)(5)(B)(iii) permitting facilities to "charge a resident who is eligible for Medicaid for items and services" the resident has requested and received, and that are not specified in the State plan as included in the term "nursing facility services." Thus, different states have taken markedly different positions on this issue. An informal survey generated the following results (March, 2004):

State	Side Payment Permitted or Prohibited	Amount of Extra Payment
Alabama	Permitted	
Connecticut	Prohibited (Based in part on state law "sole source of payment" law)	
District of Columbia	Prohibited	
Florida	Permitted, by explicit regulation	
Illinois	Permitted	
Kentucky	Permitted	
Maine	Permitted	
Maryland	Prohibited	
Michigan	Permitted	
Missouri	Permitted	
New Jersey	Permitted	Family can be required to pay the difference between private-pay private-room rate and the Medicaid rate for a semi-private room.
New York	Prohibited	
Ohio	Permitted	
Texas	Permitted	
Virginia	Permitted	Family can be required to pay the difference between private-pay private room rate and private-pay semi-private room rate.

Chapter 12

Paying Privately for Long-Term Care: Long-Term Care Insurance

A 2002 study found that 44 percent of those turning 65 years of age will spend some time in a nursing facility, and that of those who enter, 53 percent will stay for at least one year and 19 percent will stay for over five years. [B. Spillman and J. Lubitz, *New Estimates of Lifetime Nursing Home Use: Have Patterns of Use Changed?*, Medical Care, Vol. 40, No. 10 (March 2002)] Those significant numbers do not even include the vast majority of aging persons who receive long-term care at home.

Nearly half of all formal long-term care costs are paid for by private wealth—the savings and income of the patients or their families. Informal care arrangements also abound, from spouses caring for one another to children and grandchildren who quit outside employment and stay at home to care for ill elders. Although the value (and the lost-opportunity costs) of such informal care arrangements is not well documented, it is clear that considerably less than half of long-term care is provided in institutions or other formal arrangements.

With costs averaging between $30,000 and $150,000 or more per year (depending on the area of the country and the level of care required), long-term care costs can easily bankrupt most families. Protecting against the cost of long-term care can take the form of planning for government (usually Medicaid) benefits, accumulation of substantial wealth, or advance purchase of

long-term care insurance to cover the risk. This chapter discusses purchasing long-term care insurance;
costs; policy provisions including the benefit period,
elimination period, inflation protection, preexisting
condition coverage, and guaranteed renewability;
deductibility of long-term care insurance premiums;
and taxation of long-term care insurance benefits.

Overview

Q 12:1   Who actually pays for long-term care?

Payments for nursing home and home care costs can come from
several sources. As reported by the Congressional Budget Office in a
2004 study, over 60 percent of nursing home costs have been paid
either by the federal-state Medicaid program (35 percent) or Medicare
(25 percent). Veteran's benefits pay for a small portion, as do other
government programs—other than Medicaid and Medicare, government or charity payments amount to barely 3 percent of the total cost
of nursing home care.

What does this mean in dollars? According to the Congressional
Budget Office's statistics, in 2006 Medicaid paid $54.7 billion on long-
term care costs, with increases projected at 9 percent annually for the
foreseeable future, while Medicare paid out $19.5 billion, with increases
projected at 5 percent to 7 percent annually in the future. [For these and
other projections about the governmental spending, see the Congressional Budget Office March 2007 report, "Detailed Projections for Medicare, Medicaid, and State Children's Health Insurance Program" at
http://www.cbo.gov/ftpdoc.cfm?index = 7861&type = 1]

The same study reported that private insurance in 2000 paid a mere
4 percent of the total cost of nursing home care nationwide. That figure

includes both long-term care insurance and the small portion of long-term care costs paid by Medicare supplemental insurance policies. A study by the American Association or Long-Term Care Insurance reported that the industry paid out $3.3 billion in 2006 on long-term care insurance claims, but this includes a disproportionately high percentage of home care spending.

The balance (27 percent in 2000 of the entire cost of nursing home care) is paid by private savings and income. This does not count the costs of "informal" care that is provided without financial compensation. That figure has steadily decreased since the inception of Medicare and Medicaid; in 1980, for example, 40 percent of nursing home expenses was paid by private wealth. These statistics are from the Centers for Medicare and Medicaid Services' Office of the Actuary, National Health Statistics Group. At the time of publication, 2000 statistics were the most current available. Statistical updates can be reviewed at the CMS/HCFA website.

According to the Congressional Budget Office's statistics, in 1995 Medicare and Medicaid together paid about 56 percent of long-term care costs for the elderly. Medicare's share of all long-term care costs (including in-home services) is projected to remain in the range of 24 percent through 2020. Medicaid's share is expected to rise from its present 35 percent level to 41 percent in 2010 before dropping back to 37 percent in 2020. The CBO also projects that long-term care insurance will increase from about 5 percent of total long-term care costs to approximately 20 percent by 2020; the total dollars contributed by long-term care insurance are expected to increase from $5 billion annually in 2000 to $36.2 billion in 2020. [For these and other projections about the payment of long-term care costs, see the CBO's Projections of Expenditures for Long-Term Care Services for the Elderly, March, 1999, at *http://www.cbo.gov/showdoc.cfm?index = 1123*]

Q 12:2   How much does nursing home care cost the country?

In 2006, total national nursing home and home health care costs amounted to $177.6 billion. That figure represented an increase of almost $10 billion over the previous year, and an increase of more than $100 billion over the 1990 figure. By comparison, hospital care cost Americans $648.2 billion, physician's services cost $447.6 billion, and drugs and other nondurable medical supplies cost $276 billion. Incidentally, "other personal care" (including, but not limited to, a portion of the cost of home care) cost about $62.2 billion; that figure does not include the informal care arrangements and lost opportunity involved in family caregiving. [Centers for Medicare & Medicaid Services, National Health Expenditure Data at *http://www.cms.hhs.gov/ NationalHealthExpendData/downloads/tables.pdf*]

Q 12:3　How much does nursing home care cost individuals?

Individual nursing home costs vary tremendously by state, and sometimes by city within a given state. Generally, urban nursing homes cost substantially more than their rural counterparts. "Extra" care costs can inflate costs in individual circumstances even further, and make it much more difficult to predict the real cost of nursing care in any given case. In the more rural parts of smaller states, the cost of nursing home care may be as low as $2,000 to $2,500 per month. In urban New York, the base cost may range above $9,000 per month. In most areas of the country, nursing home residents should expect to pay between $3,500 and $4,500 per month for the lowest level of nursing home care, and more for higher levels of care. In 1998, the average actual nursing home cost per day was about $130, or $4,000 per month (source: Kiplinger's Retirement Report, February 1999), and a MetLife Mature Market Institute study of 2007 costs found an average daily charge of $189 for a semi-private room (or $68,985 annually) and $213 for a private room (or $77,745 annually). The MetLife study revealed an increase of 3.4 percent in the private-room rate over 2005 figures, and a 3.3 percent increase for semi-private rates. That rapid increase is consistent with recent history, which has shown an annual rate of increase in nursing home costs significantly greater than the general inflation rate. The MetLife study is available online at *http://www.metlife.com/ FileAssets/MMI/MMIStudies2007NHAL.pdf.*

Q 12:7　Is long-term care covered under federal veteran's benefits?

Nursing home care and some home health benefits are provided through the Department of Veterans Affairs, but usually such services are limited to veterans who are deemed 50 percent or more disabled. Until recently, services were also limited because of the shortage of bed space at VA facilities. There has been a movement to provide all veterans with long-term care benefits, using other non-VA facilities in the community (see chapter 16 for a discussion of veteran's benefits). Retired servicemen and women who participate in TRICARE receive an extended period of coverage for skilled nursing care of the type that Medicare would cover but for the 100-day facility care limit. The "aid and attendance" benefit does provide a source of funds to help veterans and their survivors pay for home care.

Q 12:8 What role does long-term care insurance play in financing care?

Although long-term care insurance has historically paid an almost insignificant portion of total long-term care costs, that small share is growing. Despite limited market penetration, in individual cases the availability of long-term care insurance can and does provide financial security and promote autonomy and independence. Recent government initiatives have further emphasized the utility of long-term care insurance, at least for some seniors (and younger persons concerned about the future cost of care). Three additional facts will inexorably lead to a greater role for long-term care: (1) individuals recognize that long-term care insurance may be essential to preserve the option of staying at home; (2) insurers are recognizing that assisted living is cheaper than nursing home care and adding an assisted living facility benefit; and (3) employers are starting to include long-term care insurance in the stable of options presented to employees. In other words, the idea of long-term care insurance is no longer for the anxious few, but is becoming the norm. In a recent survey by the Connecticut insurance department, 94 percent of respondents said that coverage for home and community-based services was very important in their decision to purchase long-term care insurance. [*Executive Summary of the Connecticut Partnership For Long-Term Care Evaluation, July 1, 2003–June 30, 2004 (http://www.opm.state.ct.us/pdpd4/ltc/researcher/evalrept.htm)*]

Purchase of Long-Term Care Insurance

Q 12:10 Which clients should purchase long-term care insurance?

Generally, there are at least three kinds of clients who should consider purchasing long-term care insurance:

1. Those with assets well in excess of Medicaid eligibility minimums, but insufficient to provide their preferred mode of long-term care (including home care) solely from their income (or, if the client is willing to experience diminution of principal, from

their income and assets amortized over a period of time at least as long as their life expectancy),

2. Those clients who are completely risk-averse, and who wish to leave the maximum possible amount to their heirs or devisees regardless of the current cost, and

3. Those clients concerned that the "spousal improvishment" rules will be inadequate to prevent premature improvishment of the healthier spouse should the other spouse's needs wipe out the couple's combined retirement savings.

Although probable costs of long-term care vary tremendously by region of the country, the first and third groups can safely be described as the middle class. Most individuals with lower levels of assets (and income) are likely to find it difficult to afford long-term care insurance; however, if a person with a smaller estate strongly feels that the quality of Medicaid-subsidized care might be inferior to that of privately paid care, he or she might choose to purchase long-term care insurance to minimize the likelihood of ever requiring government assistance with such care. Conversely, wealthier individuals will find that they can afford to pay for long-term care from income.

In a recent survey by the Connecticut Partnership for Long-Term Care, more than one-half (54 percent) of respondents who had purchased long-term care insurance reported assets over $350,000, while 12 percent indicated their assets were less than $100,000. Thirty-four percent fell into the $100,000–$350,000 range. (In Connecticut, a three-year nursing home stay in a semi-private room would cost approximately $311,000 in 2005.) Clearly, those with something to lose by waiting until Medicaid would be available to pay for care purchased most long-term care insurance.

Q 12:11 At what age should a client consider long-term care insurance?

In 2007 the average age of initial long-term care insurance purchasers was 61, down from 68 in 1990, according to a study sponsored by America's Health Insurance Plans, a national insurance trade association (*http://www.ahipresearch.org/PDFs/LTC_Buyers_Guide.pdf*). That reflects not only a decrease in the average age at purchase, but also a significant increase in younger policyholders.

Age at the time of purchase is one of the most important factors in determining the price of long-term care insurance, so potential purchasers should consider buying at a younger age to save costs. Of course, one of the reasons policies are less expensive for younger purchasers is the likelihood that a younger insurance buyer will allow the policy to lapse before claims are made. Younger buyers should consider the likelihood that the policy might be allowed to lapse in deciding whether to wait before the initial purchase of long-term care insurance.

Most commentators agree that the best age for purchase of long-term care insurance is somewhere in the mid-50s for most people. Younger prospective buyers might still consider buying a policy in particular circumstances (family history of illness or strong risk aversion, for example). Older buyers should not continue to delay purchasing just because the optimum age has passed; costs continue to escalate quickly in the mid-60s and later. Many policies are simply unavailable to prospective buyers after age 80.

Q 12:13 What is the "asset protection" feature available in some states?

Section 6021 of the Deficit Reduction Act will greatly expand the availability of "asset protection" long-term care insurance policies, known as "partnership" policies. Prior to 1993, a few states had experimented with offering long-term care insurance that provided an "asset protection" feature. This meant that the insured could apply for and receive Medicaid while retaining assets equivalent to what the policy had paid out. These states are Arkansas, California, Colorado, Connecticut, Florida, Georgia, Hawaii, Idaho, New York, Indiana, Illinois, and Washington state. In Connecticut, this type of insurance is the "partnership" program.

When OBRA '93 was enacted, with its enhanced requirements for states to seek recovery and tighten eligibility rules, this asset protection feature was grandfathered and the states that had offered asset protection long-term care insurance prior to 1993 were permitted to continue to authorize it, but no more states were permitted to approve such policies. Section 6021 of the Deficit Reduction Act lifts that prohibition and expressly authorizes states to offer this type of policy; moreover, section (c) provides that no later than January 1, 2007, the Secretary of Health and Human Services must develop "standards for uniform reciprocal recognition of such policies among States with qualified State long-term care insurance partnerships under which—(1) benefits paid under such policies will be treated the same by all such States; and (2) States with such partnerships shall be subject to such standards unless the State notifies the Secretary in writing of the State's election to be exempt from such standards." As of March 2006, an AARP study reported that 21 states had adopted enabling legislation to permit the establishment of partnership policies in their states. States that have adopted "partnership" policies since 2006 and in which policies are offered for sale include Arkansas, California, Florida, Idaho, Indiana, Minnesota, Nebraska, Ohio, Oregon, Pennsylvania, South Dakota, Vermont, and Virginia; you can track new policies as they are adopted on the Department of Health and Human Services website, *http://www.dehpg.net/LTCPartnership*. In addition to asset protection, these policies generally offer clear descriptions of coverage, a cost of living rider, and other consumer protections. Although historically the consumer protection features had driven up the cost of the policy as compared to non-partnership policies, in recent years the price gap has narrowed. The other distinguishing feature is a "case management" benefit that was of limited utility for consumers migrating from state to state, but which may now be enhanced if uniform standards and reciprocity rules are adopted under the DRA.

Q 12:13.1 How does the "Partnership Policy" asset protection feature coordinate with Medicaid eligibility?

OBRA '93 includes an express exemption from repayments and liens for assets retained that are equivalent to the benefits paid out under such policies. [42 U.S.C. § 1396p(b)(i)(C)(ii)] Those purchasing partnership policies should choose the highest possible daily benefit, even if the total period of coverage is shorter. This is because the sooner the benefits pay out, the sooner the asset protection is provided. If the daily benefit is too low, the person might be forced to seek Medicaid (and spend assets that might otherwise be protected) before the policy had paid out to its limit. Because such policies anticipate that the purchaser may ultimately require Medicaid, often they do not offer lifetime coverage, but a term of years.

Q 12:14 What should a client expect to pay for long-term care insurance?

Costs for long-term care insurance vary tremendously. The most important determinants of price for most policies include:

1. *Age at policy inception.* A 45-year-old is likely to pay about half the premium of a 60-year-old for comparable coverage, and the premium cost is likely to double again by age 70.

2. *Daily benefit.* It should be obvious that a $100/day benefit will cost more than a $50/day benefit. It will not, however, cost twice as much.

3. *Elimination period, inflation provision, and benefit period.* All of these contribute to the cost of the policy, although none of them will have as large an effect as the other factors.

Given the high degree of variability in policy terms and the different pricing structures of insurance companies, generalization is both difficult and dangerous. The America's Health Insurance Plans study described above (see SQ 12:11) shows an average annual premium (in 2005) of $1,918, with 22% of policyholders paying more than $2,500/year. Both of those numbers reflect increases in the cost of policies over the fifteen years covered by the study, though much of that increase is attributable to relatively more generous policies rather than increasing costs. For example, compare the 2005 average of 5.2 years in home care benefits with the 3.4 year average of 1995— and the "not available" home care benefit of 1990. Similarly, 76% of policyholders elected inflation protection in 2005, while only 40% made that choice in 1990.

Long-Term Insurance Policy Provisions

Q 12:17 What policy terms should a client consider when buying long-term care insurance?

There are a number of fairly standard policy provisions that should be considered when purchasing long-term care insurance. These include:

- Daily benefit rate
- Elimination period
- Benefit period
- Eligibility to receive benefits
- Inflation protection
- Pre-existing condition provisions
- Home health coverage (including "informal" care)
- Nonforfeiture
- Restoration of benefit

The National Association of Insurance Commissioners publishes a guide to help evaluate and compare policies, which can be ordered on-line for free at *https://external-apps.naic.org/insprod/Consumer_info.jsp*. Washington State also has a useful Policy Comparison Worksheet available at *http://www.insurance.wa.gov/publications/long_term_care/ltc_policy_comparsion_worksheet.pdf*.

Q 12:18　What is the daily benefit rate?

The daily benefit rate is the amount available for each covered day of long-term care. Most policies provide care in $10/day increments Private room nursing home care averaged $213 per day in 2007, and a steady increase in rates should be anticipated (long-term care costs increase at a much greater rate than can be accounted for by ordinary inflation). The average 2005 policy provided a $142 daily benefit, according to the America's Health Insurance Plans study described in SQ 12:14. Most modern long-term care policies also include at least some home care coverage, with the average benefit amounting to $135, slightly less than the daily rate for nursing home care.

Q 12:22　What benefit period should a long-term care insurance buyer select?

Once again, the answer will depend on the purposes for which the policy was purchased. There are, however, three typical approaches to determining the appropriate benefit period:

1. *Playing the averages*. The average length of institutionalization is about a year and a half. Most seniors will never enter a nursing home at all. Given those two risk factors, a policy covering two years of institutionalization should cover most people. Of course, the purpose of insurance is to spread the risk of loss; this strategy shifts the risk of loss somewhat, but does not cover the possibility that the buyer will fall outside the "typical" range of experience.

2. *Planning for Medicaid coverage*. As explained previously, prior to the Deficit Reduction Act, eligibility for Medicaid coverage could be obtained after waiting 36 months from the date of substantial transfers of assets. Some individuals purchased long-term care insurance for the purpose of covering that 36-month period of ineligibility, intending to transfer all assets immediately upon

institutionalization, only to have the DRA extend the waiting period to 60 months. Of course, this strategy assumed that eligibility rules would remain static, that the patient would retain the capacity to make transfers upon institutionalization, and that the transfers would actually be made immediately upon institutionalization (rather than deciding to wait for a period of months to see how things work out). To hedge against all those potential problems, an alternate approach would have been to purchase a four-year or five-year policy. Since the DRA, a five-year policy would be the necessary minimum.

3. *Full coverage.* Rather than trying to predict either of the preceding scenarios, a long-term care insurance buyer might choose to insure fully against the risk of loss. This would require purchasing a lifetime policy. Of course, the cost of such a policy will be significantly higher than for a policy with a limited benefit period, and the risk of requiring such coverage is slight (although, if it is required, the benefit is tremendous).

Q 12:30 How should someone select a policy?

Long-term care insurance is now so widely sold that the first step in buying good insurance—an honest and reliable agent—is easier to find. In those states offering "partnership" policies (see Q 12:13), the agent's certification to sell partnership policies may be some indication of competence.

Long Term Care Partners, LLC, the company administering the Federal Long Term Care Insurance Program sponsored by the U.S. Office of Personnel Management, offers a checklist, "Benefits and Features Worksheet," available on the web at *http://www.ltcfeds.com/*.

Tax Issues

Q 12:31 Are long-term care insurance premiums deductible?

Federal tax law finally recognized concerns about the taxability of long-term care insurance benefits and the deductibility of premiums beginning in 1997. Under the Health Insurance Portability and Accounting Act of 1996 (HIPAA), long-term care insurance premiums for qualified long-term care policies are deductible as a medical expense. [I.R.C.

§ 213(d)(1)(D)] The amount of the premium that is deductible is indexed for inflation and is dependent on the insured's age:

Table 12.3. Deductibility of Long-Term Care Insurance Premiums

Age by End of Year	Deduction Limit on Premium (Tax Year 2008)	Deduction Limit on Premium (Tax Year 2007)
40 or under	$ 310	$ 290
41–50	$ 580	$ 550
51–60	$1,150	$1,110
61–70	$3,080	$2,950
71 or older	$3,850	$3,680

It is important to remember that the medical expense deduction is subject to the 7.5 percent adjusted gross income floor; medical expenses cannot be deducted unless they exceed 7.5 percent of adjusted gross income. These and other items are described in detail in IRS Publication 502 (available in print or online).

Q 12:33 Are long-term care insurance benefits taxable?

Under HIPAA, if an individual plan is "qualified" (for tax purposes) (see Q 12:32), benefits received under the plan will not be taxable income. [I.R.C. § 7702B(a)(2)] Benefits received that pay or reimburse qualified long-term care expenses under a qualified long-term care policy are tax-free up to $260 per day or $94,900 annually (2007 figure). [I.R.C. § 7702B(a)] Qualified long-term care services includes necessary diagnostic, preventive, therapeutic, curing, treating, mitigating, and rehabilitative services, and maintenance or personal care services. The services must be for a chronically ill individual and provided pursuant to a plan of care prescribed by a licensed health care practitioner. [I.R.C. § 7702B(c)(1)] A chronically ill individual is any individual who has been certified by a licensed health care practitioner as:

1. Being unable to perform at least two activities of daily living (eating, toileting, transferring, bathing, dressing, and continence) for at least 90 days because of loss of functional capacity (ADL trigger); or

2. Requiring substantial supervision to protect the individual from threats to health or safety because of severe cognizant impairment (cognizant impairment trigger). [I.R.C. § 7703B(c)(2)]

A policy will not be a qualified long-term care policy if there is a "medical necessity" trigger for benefit payments.

Q 12:34 Are there state tax incentives for the purchase of long-term care insurance?

Nearly half of the states offer some state income tax incentive for the purchase of long-term care insurance. The incentives range from income tax credits (in Colorado, a 25 percent credit up to $150 for taxpayers earning less than $50,000) to a straightforward deduction for premiums paid (Alabama, Idaho, Indiana, and Kentucky). For state-by-state details, see *http://www.neamb.com/insurance/ltctax.jsp.*

Practice-Related Issues

Q 12:36 How might an elder law attorney counsel a client regarding long-term care insurance?

1. *Determining the need for insurance coverage.* Mr. and Mrs. Summers (aged 68 and 64, respectively) are concerned about paying for nursing home care in the event either should need to be institutionalized at some future time. Both are in good health today, but Mrs. Summers' mother recently passed away after a long nursing home stay and they watched her assets being consumed by the cost of care. The Summers own their home, two automobiles, household effects, and bank and brokerage account assets of about $400,000. Their annual income from Social Security, pensions, and investments totals about $50,000. They wonder whether they should make gifts to qualify for Medicaid, establish an irrevocable trust, or simply ignore the potential cost of long-term care.

   While long-term care insurance is not for every client, consideration of the appropriateness of purchasing insurance should be undertaken in almost every case. Mr. and Mrs. Summers may indeed be excellent candidates for such insurance. They are relatively young, currently healthy, and have significant assets and income to protect. Because their assets and income are significant, either of them will have a difficult time qualifying for Medicaid eligibility for long-term care subsidies. Because their assets are limited, however, they will also have difficulty paying privately for any needed nursing home care without seriously depleting their assets.

In many, perhaps most, states, Mr. and Mrs. Summers' income would be sufficient to pay the costs of nursing home care. Even so, the non-institutionalized spouse would have difficulty making ends meet in the community without spending down the couple's assets. In general terms, long-term care insurance is a product for the middle class, and Mr. and Mrs. Summers are solidly in that category by most standards. If their assets were twice what they actually have, they might be comfortable self-insuring, since the cost of nursing home care would probably be less than their annual income. If their assets were significantly lower they would be able to qualify for Medicaid easily, and insurance would not be such a compelling option.

Because they are young, Mr. and Mrs. Summers should have an easier time qualifying for long-term care insurance, and the premiums should be markedly lower. Precisely because of their age they are even better candidates for insurance, since any institutionalization in the near future could drain the community spouse's assets for an extended period of time.

Mr. and Mrs. Summers should be advised to look into the availability and cost of long-term care insurance. Assuming that they do not have any medical conditions that make insurance unavailable or expensive, they will be excellent candidates for purchase of a policy.

2. *Evaluating the insurance policy.* Mrs. Rigby is considering purchasing long-term care insurance, and asks for assistance in reviewing the policy terms and prices.

   Most elder law attorneys are poorly equipped to evaluate the pricing of insurance policies, but it may still be possible to help Mrs. Rigby decide on the best course of action. It will be essential to collect information about Mrs. Rigby's financial situation and her reasons for seeking insurance, and to review the policy itself. The financial evaluation will be necessary in order to give advice about the utility of any long-term care insurance policy, and the latter will assist Mrs. Rigby to avoid dangerous limitations in the particular policy.

   In addition to a lawyer's evaluation of the policy, Mrs. Rigby would probably benefit from a second analysis by an insurance salesperson or consultant. When an elder law attorney evaluates an individual long-term care insurance policy, he or she might look for:

   Tax qualification. If Mrs. Rigby's plan is not tax qualified, she will not be able to deduct the premiums for federal income tax purposes. This is not likely to be a major issue, since the income tax deduction is limited to the amount by which total medical expenses exceed 7.5 percent of her adjusted gross income; few individuals will receive any income tax benefit from deductibility of the insurance premiums. The other benefit to tax qualification is more important; if the plan is qualified, any payments made to nursing homes will not be treated as income. Even if later nursing home payments are deductible (and they may not be, under one analysis of federal tax laws), the deduction will be limited by the same 7.5 percent threshold requirement, so at least some of the insurance benefits would likely be taxable.

Daily benefit levels. In order to economize, Mrs. Rigby might make the mistake of purchasing too little insurance. This can result in making her ineligible for future Medicaid eligibility, or in simply reducing the amount of Medicaid coverage she might qualify for.

Definition of ADLs. How does the plan define activities of daily living, and how many of those ADLs must Mrs. Rigby need assistance with before qualifying for benefits?

Home care, assisted living, and other non-nursing home settings. Does the plan provide benefits for in-home care, or for care in other settings outside nursing homes? Most plans either provide such benefits up to the full daily benefit rate for nursing home care or, in some cases, up to one-half the daily benefit rate. If home care is important to Mrs. Rigby, the plan should cover the full daily benefit rate—especially since the cost of home care can easily exceed nursing home costs.

Inflation protection. What mechanism does the plan provide for future increases in nursing home costs? Can Mrs. Rigby purchase additional insurance at the then-current rates in the future? Such "guaranteed insurability" may be an effective inflation protection, though increased costs in the future can be considerable. If the plan provides for automatic cost-of-living increases, that coverage will likely be expensive.

Waiver of premium. Will the policy premiums be waived during any period of institutionalization? How about periods when Mrs. Rigby receives home health care services?

Restoration of benefit. Should Mrs. Rigby cease to pay premiums due to the onset of dementia, will her family be able to restore her benefits by paying a penalty, paying outstanding premiums, etc., and what will be required to claim this benefit from the company?

Benefit periods. Mrs. Rigby might want to purchase lifetime insurance coverage, though such policies can be quite expensive. Alternatively, she might prefer to purchase coverage for, say, a four-year period, anticipating that her children will help her transfer all her assets upon institutionalization and that she will then qualify for Medicaid once the policy benefit period has run. Of course, any such plan must include an appropriate trust or power of attorney to permit the gifting, in case Mrs. Rigby is not then able to direct the handling of her own finances.

Respite care, payments to family caregivers, payments for ambulance transport and durable medical equipment, and other miscellaneous provisions. In Mrs. Rigby's case, any or all of these provisions may be important. She should understand what benefits are available from this and competing plans.

3. *When the need for long-term care arises, evaluating the scope of coverage, assisting clients or their families in making claims, and appealing terminations for nonpayment or denials of claim. Assisting clients in pursuing claims or appealing denials.* Mr. Hubbell's nephew comes to see you after protective services contacted him following several episodes in which his uncle was found wandering around town, unaware of his surroundings. The medical recommendation is that his uncle receive 24-hour care, and aides have been hired to work double shifts. The nephew has been through the papers in his uncle's study and found an old insurance policy that seems to say it covers long-term care, but when he called to file a claim, the company told him the policy was canceled for nonpayment. What should you do?

Policy coverage. First you would review the policy to see whether it truly ever did provide the coverage being sought. If coverage is reinstated, what benefit will it provide? Will the nephew have to fire the aides and go through a licensed agency to obtain coverage? Will the daily benefit make this worthwhile?

Waiver of premium. You would evaluate the provision, if any, waiving payment of premium in the event of incapacity and/or providing reinstatement rights upon payment of unpaid premiums in that event. If no provision is included, you might check with the insurance department to determine whether any such provision is mandatory in your state. You may have to contact the company to advocate for the uncle, obtain health records or letters from medical personnel to substantiate his condition, and possibly threaten suit under unfair insurance practice statutes if reinstatement is unreasonably denied.

Submit claims. You may need to advise the nephew on submission of claims for services and/or direct him to an appropriate medical claims professional to assist him in presenting claims appropriately. Geriatric care managers should have experience in ascertaining what providers can be paid through what insurance.

Advocate for claims or appeal denials. Some coverage makes reference to Medicare laws in defining the scope of care provided, for example, extending the Medicare-covered 100 days of skilled nursing care to 365 days. You may have to argue Medicare law when presenting claims or challenging denials. Ultimately, you may have to appeal denials or seek the advice of a litigator who can assist in that process.

Incorporate coverage into planning. The nephew has reviewed Mr. Hubbell's checkbook and is concerned about several large checks written in March 2006 that he doesn't think can be documented. They were apparently written to relatives on the other side of the family. Assuming there will be no proof of consideration and difficulty in proving that he lacked capacity at that point in time, there is a risk of a penalty period. Is his insurance coverage sufficiently slight that a coverage gap exists and it will be possible to file for Medicaid despite the insurance, in order to start the penalty period?

Advise third parties concerning scope of coverage/method of payment. If the uncle ultimately enters a nursing home, you may be in the position of explaining the coverage to admissions personnel and/or state Medicaid agencies. Some coverage pays the facility directly. Some coverage reimburses after payment is made. Large monthly reimbursements will have to be documented and explained. In an "income-cap" state, receipt of reimbursements may have to be explained to prevent loss of Medicaid coverage.

Chapter 13

Medicare Benefits

The Medicare program provides most of the medical care for Americans over the age of 65. As a consequence, eligibility for benefits and the administration of the program are a central concern for most elderly clients. Although few elder law attorneys regularly practice in the Medicare arena, a passing familiarity with program benefits and limitations is critical to providing adequate legal advice to elders confronting medical problems or the prospect of future medical needs.

Although the extent of Medicare coverage varies, it generally covers hospitalization, home care, durable medical equipment, hospice, and doctor's visits. Some of those benefits are optional, requiring the senior to sign up and pay an extra premium. The enactment of the Medicare Prescription Drug, Improvement and Modernization Act of 2003 has added prescription drug coverage to the Medicare program. This new benefit, along with other recent changes in the structure of the program have made it more critical to understand the extent and limitations of coverage. This chapter discusses eligibility and enrollment requirements; benefits available under Part A, Part B, the new Part D program and Medicare Advantage; Medicare HMOs; and Medigap Insurance.

The first stop for answers about Medicare coverage may be not only the Centers for Medicare and Medicaid Services website, *http://www.medicare.gov*, but also sites maintained by the nonprofit Center for

Medicare Advocacy, *http://www.medicareadvocacy. org*, and the Medicare Rights Center in New York, *http://www.medicarerights.org*.

For elderly clients not yet eligible for Medicare, including those ceasing employment on account of a disability, options may be limited. For most disabled, Medicare coverage is not available until 24 months have passed. To bridge the gap in health coverage, individuals can use (1) rights to continue employer-sponsored health insurance; (2) retiree health benefit programs (discussed in Chapter 20); or (3) private health insurance.

Overview

Q 13:1   What is the purpose of the Medicare program?

Medicare is a federal insurance program that was established to provide medical care for the elderly and the disabled. The Medicare laws are found at 42 United States Code (U.S.C.) Sections 1395 through 1395ccc and the regulations are found at 42 Code of Federal Regulations (C.F.R.) Parts 405 through 489. Medicare is divided into four parts which correspond to benefits roughly as follows: Part A (institutional care), Part B (physician's fees), Part C (Medicare Advantage options), and Part D (prescription drugs).

Q 13:6 What is Medicare Part B?

Medicare Part B primarily provides coverage for physician's services. It also covers diagnostic tests, medical equipment, ambulance services, outpatient physical and speech therapy, certain home care, prostheses, and prescription drugs. [41 U.S.C. § 1395k(a)] Part B is optional. Unlike Part A, Part B requires the payment of a premium for all beneficiaries. Low-income beneficiaries may qualify for government payment of this premium under the "Medicare Savings Programs" known as QMB, SLIMB, and additional programs (see Q 13:14).

Q 13:7 What benefits are excluded from Medicare Parts A and B?

Medicare provides coverage for services that are medically "reasonable and necessary for the diagnosis or treatment of illness or injury or to improve the functioning of a malformed body member." [42 U.S.C. § 1395y(a)(1)(A)] The care received must be skilled. Although most seniors receive substantially all of their medical care through the Medicare program, there are major items not covered by Medicare. For most seniors, the most notable exclusion from coverage is long-term custodial care. Although Congress attempted to add a more extended long-term care benefit in the 1987 Medicare Catastrophic Coverage Act, the overwhelming negative reaction from seniors (who would have been charged a separate tax to pay for the benefit) led to the repeal of the benefit in the next legislative session.

Other uncovered medical care includes eyeglasses, dental care, and annual preventive checkups, although Medicare beneficiaries who elect to receive care through an HMO may have some of these benefits provided, perhaps with a copayment requirement. Recent additions to Medicare Part A have included some routine screenings such as mammograms and a "welcome to Medicare" physical examination.

Q 13:8 What is Medicare Advantage?

The Balanced Budget Act of 1997 (BBA '97) added Medicare + Choice, now known as "Medicare Advantage." Although the Medicare Advantage program is sometimes referred to as "Part C," it is really a collection of alternative means of financing or receiving individual

Medicare coverage. Medicare Advantage does not provide additional benefits or coverage, although it may make Medicare more financially attractive for some beneficiaries or may permit providers to provide additional benefits as an inducement to attract participants. [41 U.S.C. § 1395d] Medicare Advantage also has a slightly different system for processing grievances and appeals.

Q 13:8.0 What is a Medicare Savings Account?

Among the Medicare Advantage Plans are some with a "high-deductible" option. Those who select a high-deductible plan are also eligible to establish a "Medicare Savings Account" or "MSA," where tax-deductible contributions can be placed that may later be used to cover for the plan's deductible. MSA funds may also be used to pay the plan premiums or for other health expenses not covered by the plan. Whether an MSA makes sense will depend upon the relationship between the premium, the deductible, and the amount that may be sheltered in the MSA.

Q 13:8.1 What is the Medicare Prescription Drug, Improvement and Modernization Act of 2003?

Signed into law in December of 2003 by President George Bush, the Medicare Prescription Drug, Improvement and Modernization Act made a number of changes to Medicare. Most notably, the Act provides prescription drug coverage. There has been much political controversy surrounding the act, including whether Republicans or Democrats won or lost, whether drug and insurance companies benefited at the expense of seniors, and whether senior advocacy groups sold out their members for temporary political gain. For some information about the political issues involved from AARP, which supported the act, see *http://www.aarp.org/research/medicare/drugs*. Regulations are included at 42 C.F.R. Part 423.

The Medicare Prescription Drug, Improvement and Modernization Act provides for prescription coverage under what is now being referred to as Medicare "Part D." Participation in Medicare Part D is purely voluntary and it is necessary to enroll to receive benefits. Coverage can be purchased as part of a Medicare Advantage plan, or as separate insurance.

Q 13:8.2 Do Medicare beneficiaries automatically receive drug benefits when they become eligible?

No. Medicare Part D requires enrollment and a monthly premium which varies from plan to plan—some as low as $20, others as high as $75. This payment will be in addition to the Part B premium ($96.40 to $308.30 per month in 2009, depending on the beneficiary's income). In general, individuals becoming eligible for Medicare must enroll during an initial enrollment period that extends from the three months before Medicare eligibility through the three months after the date of Medicare eligibility. A beneficiary who does not enroll during the initial enroll-ment period may be subject to a premium penalty that will be payable monthly for the entire time the beneficiary remains enrolled in Medicare Part D. The amount of the penalty in 2009 is 1% per month of late enrollment; in future years, it may well be higher. (Individuals entitled to the low-income subsidy do not pay a penalty. [Medicare Improve-ments for Patients and Providers Act of 2008 sec. 114, amending 42 U.S.C. § 1395w-112(b)]) Individuals may enroll outside the initial enrollment period during the annual coordinated election period that runs from November 15 through December 31 each year, with coverage to begin on the 1st of the following year. Low-income subsidies are available to reduce or eliminate out-of-pocket expenses associated with the drug benefit including premiums, deductibles, co-payments and costs in the coverage gap (beneficiaries pay 100% of the costs of prescription drugs between the time plan payments plus deductibles reach $2,700 and the time the beneficiary has paid a total of $4,350 [2009 figures]—a phenomenon usually referred to as the "doughnut hole"). Medicare recipients who qualify under one of the "Medicare Savings Plans" (see Q 13:14) or otherwise with incomes below 150% of the Federal Poverty Guidelines (in 2008, 150% of the Guidelines amounts to $15,600 for a one-person household, and $21,000 for a mar-ried couple with no other household members—the numbers are higher for Alaska and Hawai'i residents) and 2008 assets under $11,990 ($23,970 for couples) pay no premium or deductible for Part D and have no gap in coverage, or may receive subsidies for lower rates and a lower penalty for late enrollment. (See SQ 13:8.5) Legislation has been proposed to reduce or eliminate the penalties in order to increase enrollment.

Q 13:8.3 What drug savings are to be expected under Part D?

Part D plans must offer at least a statutorily-defined (or actuarially equivalent) benefit. For 2009, the standard plan provides for a $295 deductible, with coinsurance payments of 25% of the drug costs up to $2,700 in total drug costs. The beneficiary then pays 100% of the drug costs until the beneficiary has paid $4,350 in out-of-pocket costs, what is known as catastrophic coverage kicks in, and the beneficiary pays 5% of drug costs. Low-income Medicare participants will pay less for their drugs. Monthly premium amounts and the benefits received vary widely, affected at a minimum by the type of plan chosen The Kaiser Family Foundation has developed an internet web page to assist in calculating prescription drug savings under the Part D coverage, and Medicare's own website at www.medicare.gov provides a detailed exploration of costs under differing plans, including such detail as which plans have dosage limits or require "step therapy" before higher priced drugs will be covered. To use these tools it is generally necessary to know: (1) precise names of current medications; (2) dosage and frequency; (3) locality requirements (i.e., what pharmacy); (4) whether or not the client qualifies for a low-income subsidy. If an attorney is helping the client make this decision—not a legal task by any means but sometimes requested—it is advisable to ask the client to obtain a printout of yearly prescription purchases from his or her pharmacy.

Q 13:8.4   What is the "Low-Income Subsidy" for low-income Medicare beneficiaries subscribing to Medicare Part D?

Those who qualify for one of four "low-income subsidies" receive a number of benefits. Those eligible include: (1) dual eligibles (those receiving Medicaid); (2) recipients of "Medicare Savings Plan" benefits (see 13:14); (3) those with income not exceeding 135% of poverty and 2008 assets not exceeding $6,290/individual, $9,440/couple; (4) those with income not exceeding 150% of poverty and assets not exceeding $11,990/individual, $23,970/couple (fewer benefits accrue to this fourth category). Common to all groups is a waiver of the premium and the elimination of the "doughnut hole" or lack of coverage once $2,000 has been paid out in benefits and before $4,050 of expenses (small costsharing co-pays will apply). Low income participants also have reduced co-payments for lower-income participants. They will pay $1.05 to $2.25 (depending on income level) for generic and $3.10 to $5.60 for brand name and "non-preferred" drugs. The highest group of subsidy recipients, those with income over 135% of poverty or whose assets exceed the lower limit, will pay a percentage of their premiums (between 25% and 75%) on a sliding scale, a $56 deductible and 15 percent of drug costs in the "doughnut hole." Some states have enacted "wrap-around" legislation to cover the reduced copays that would now be payable by dual eligibles who formerly had no copays for the drugs under Medicaid.

Q 13:8.5   Who provides the Part D coverage—Medicare or private insurers?

Coverage is provided by private insurance companies approved by the government but without direct government management. In areas where no insurance programs are offered, however, Medicare will provide better subsidies to what the new law calls "fallback" insurance plans. The goal is to make sure that every Medicare beneficiary has at least two choices of drug coverage available. Incidentally, no "fallback" plan is permitted to offer drug coverage for the entire country.

Q 13:8.6   Does Part D cover all types of drugs?

No. Certain classes of drugs are not covered at all under Part D and payments for those drugs do not count towards the out-of-pocket "doughnut hole." These are the drugs for which Medicaid coverage is "optional," including drugs for weight gain (which may be used to treat weight loss due to cancer or HIV/AIDS), barbiturates, benzodiazepines (for anxiety drugs like Xanax used to treat acute anxiety, panic attacks, seizure disorders, and muscle spasms in those with cerebral palsy), and over-the-counter medications. By contrast, the program will provide coverage for insulin. Most plans have formularies that limit enrollees to using particular drugs, often generics, rather than any drug available to treat the condition. Also, plans have the right to impose "dosage limits," standard doses so that deviation will be refused without a physician requesting the change and to require "step therapy," whereby patients must first try cheaper, usually older drugs before they can obtain coverage for newer patent medicines.

Q 13:8.7   Are there any exceptions to these drug exclusions?

Yes. Plans must have a process to permit enrollees to ask the plan to cover a non-formulary drug or reduce cost-sharing. If the request is denied, the enrollee is entitled to an appeal. The enrollee must be able to get the doctor to certify that no other drug on the formulary would be as effective as the drug in question or formulary drugs would cause adverse consequences to the enrollee. The Center for

Medicare Advocacy has developed a form, approved by CMS, that may be used to obtain certification from the doctor or pharmacist. [*http://www.medicareadvocacy.org/PrescDrugs_PartDPharmacyFaxForm.pdf*] The exception process does not permit enrollees to request a drug not covered by Medicare Part D, however.

Q 13:8.8   What effect will the new drug benefit have on state budgets?

Prior to Part D, many states paid a significant portion of drug costs for poorer Medicare beneficiaries who qualified for Medicaid coverage. States will see some savings as those costs are shifted to Medicare, but the law requires the states to pay most of those savings back to Medicare. The problem for states has arisen for those dual eligibles requiring drugs for which Medicare Part D does *not* provide coverage. Reimbursement to the states by Medicare and the private insurers has been proposed at the federal level.

Eligibility and Enrollment

Q 13:9   Who is eligible for Medicare?

Medicare is available to the elderly, the disabled, and those with permanent kidney failure requiring kidney dialysis or kidney transplant. [42 U.S.C. § 1395c]

For purposes of Medicare eligibility, "elderly" is defined as someone age 65 or older. Whether one is entitled to receive Social Security or Railroad Retirement benefits will affect whether or not the benefit is provided with no additional charge. For purposes of Medicare eligibility, "disabled" means a person who has received Social Security disability insurance benefits for 24 months. [42 U.S.C. § 1395c] (The 24-month period begins on the date the person is determined to be eligible; for example, someone awarded a lump sum in October to cover benefits for which he or she was eligible starting in April can start the 24-month clock running in April, not October.) The waiting period is also waived for individuals with amyotrophic lateral sclerosis or "ALS" (also known as Lou Gehrig's disease) [42 U.S.C. § 426(h)][SQ 13:10].

Medicare eligibility has never been means tested. With the enactment of prescription drug coverage, costs of Part D coverage will depend on income and, in some instances, assets.

Q 13:9.1   Can an alien or those who have worked overseas qualify for Medicare?

An alien may be eligible for Medicare on the same basis that a citizen may be eligible for Medicare, through receipt of Social Security payments when over 65, for example. However, in most cases Medicare will not pay for services rendered overseas. (See also SQ 14:16.)

Q 13:10   What qualifies a disabled person to receive Part A coverage?

For purposes of Medicare coverage, disability is defined as eligibility to receive Social Security disability insurance for a 24-month period. In other words, any person who receives SSDI will qualify for Medicare after two years of receiving benefits. [42 U.S.C. § 1395c] Note that benefits actually have to have been paid for two years; a disabled person who does not apply for and actually receive benefits will not qualify for Medicare coverage. [42 U.S.C. § 426(b)(2)] Persons with end-stage renal disease qualify for Medicare three months after beginning renal dialysis. [42 U.S.C. § 1395c]; the waiting period is also waived for individuals with amyotrophic lateral sclerosis or "ALS" (also known as Lou Gehrig's disease) [42 U.S.C. § 426(h)]

A person may be disabled but not receiving Social Security disability insurance. Those who receive SSI are not entitled to Medicare by virtue of their SSI eligibility (though of course a SSI recipient may also receive Social Security disability insurance benefits if he or she qualifies). A typical example will be an individual disabled from mental illness that began when he or she was young, or from a catastrophic injury (e.g., an automobile accident). Such persons may not have earned enough "quarters of coverage" to be entitled to Social Security benefits on their own account, and were not disabled early enough (before age 22) to be entitled to benefits on the account of a retired or deceased parent (see chapter 15).

Q 13:11   In general, is any payment required for Medicare coverage?

For the elderly, Medicare Part A benefits are available at no charge for those persons age 65 and older who are entitled to receive Social Security or Railroad Retirement benefits as retirees, dependents, survivors, or on any other basis [42 U.S.C. § 426] (See SQ 13:12.) A Social

Security retirement beneficiary under the age of 65 (e.g., a retiree who took early retirement at age 62) will not qualify for Medicare. By the same token, a 65-year-old who could choose to accept Social Security retirement will qualify for Medicare even though he or she chooses to delay retirement to a later age. Those not receiving Social Security but who have reached age 65 may "buy in" by paying a premium (see SQ 13:12). Special rules apply to government employees. Those who were (1) working on April 1, 1986, or (2) working after June 30, 1991 but covered by a pension, annuity, retirement, or similar fund or system established by a state or by a political subdivision of a state, and (3) not otherwise entitled to Social Security on the account of a spouse, etc., may *not* be entitled to Medicare benefits.

For the disabled person who is eligible for Medicare, Medicare Part A benefits are also available at no charge.

Medicare Part B coverage is available (subject to payment of a premium) for any person who receives Medicare Part A. In addition, any person over age 65 who does not qualify for Part A coverage can nonetheless purchase Part B coverage. [42 C.F.R. § 407.10] In 2008, the Part B premium costs $96.40 per month for lower-income individuals. Those with adjusted gross taxable income of $82,000 ($164,000 for a couple) must pay higher premiums, to be phased in over three years. Beneficiaries will be able to appeal their premiums and may also demand that Social Security adjust income information on file for prior years based on "major life-changing events."

Q 13:12 When must an elderly Medicare beneficiary pay a premium for Part A coverage?

Any person over age 65 who receives either Social Security retirement or Railroad Retirement benefits, or who is eligible to receive either kind of benefit, or in many cases, is a government employee (unless meeting exceptions some of which are described in SQ 13:11) will automatically qualify for Medicare Part A without a premium.

The vast majority of seniors do receive Social Security, so this means that few will have to pay any Medicare Part A premium. Those who have 30 "quarters of coverage" (QCs) under Social Security rules (but not the 40 quarters required for retirement eligibility) may elect to purchase Medicare Part A at the 2009 rate of $244 per month. For those age 65 but with less than 30 quarters of coverage, Medicare Part A can be purchased at $443 per month for 2009. Because coverage for this group is not automatic seniors who do not qualify for Social

Security Retirement or Railroad Retirement may elect not to purchase coverage immediately upon qualifying; for those who delay buying into the Medicare plan, the premiums will ordinarily increase by 10 percent, regardless of how long the beneficiary delays enrollment. This increase in premiums will be waived for a late enrollee who has been covered by an employer-provided medical program since reaching age 65.

A typical non-recipient of Social Security would be an elderly woman who never worked, who is unmarried (or married to a similarly situated person), and who was not married to someone else who worked in a marriage that either lasted ten years or ended in the worker's death. Quite often a wealthy person who has simply clipped coupons or lived off a trust fund her whole life, will decide to buy in to Medicare at age 65.

Q 13:13 Must an elderly Medicare beneficiary pay a premium for Part B coverage?

Yes. Unlike Part A, Part B requires the payment of a premium for all beneficiaries. In 2009, that premium is $96.40 per month (or more, for higher-income beneficiaries) and is ordinarily paid by automatic deduction from Social Security benefits. For those beneficiaries who elect not to enroll in Part B at age 65, premiums are increased (unless they have been covered by an employer-provided health benefit for the interim period). The lowest Part B premiums are presently fixed at 25 percent of the actual cost of the program to the federal government; in other words, Part B coverage is exceptionally inexpensive to the recipients. Accordingly, there are few (if any) Part B eligible beneficiaries who would be well-advised to forego the coverage. Beginning in 2008, the Medicare Part B premium began to be determined based on a sliding scale for higher-income beneficiaries. In 2009, a single Medicare recipient earning over $85,000 or a married recipient earning more than $170,000 will pay $134.90 per month. For those earning over $107,000 (or $214,000 for a married recipient), premiums climb to $192.70 per month. If earnings exceed $160,000 ($320,000 for a married recipient), premiums climb to $250.50/month. Finally, those earning over $213,000 ($426,000 for married couples) will pay $308.30. All earnings figures, incidentally, will be based (in 2009) on 2007 tax return information.

Q 13:14 What if an individual cannot afford to pay the premium?

If a Medicare Part A recipient's income is limited and financial resources (such as bank accounts, stocks, and bonds) are not more than $4,000 (for an individual) or $6,000 (for a couple), the Medicare beneficiary may qualify for assistance under one of several so-called "Medicare Savings Programs" or "MSPs." These are actually paid through Medicaid, and are not part of Medicare at all. Some beneficiaries may qualify for assistance as a Qualified Medicare Beneficiary (QMB) or Specified Low Income Medicare Beneficiary (SLMB) or other "qualified individual." The QMB plan pays the Medicare Part B monthly premium, all deductibles, and coinsurance. QMB income limits are set at 100% of the federal poverty level, which for 2008 means $887 for an individual ($867 plus $20 unearned income disregard) and $1,187 for a couple (the same). The SLMB plan is available to individuals with income not exceeding 120 percent of poverty, which in 2008 is $1,040, $1,400 for a couple. In each case, $20 of unearned and $65 of earned income is "disregarded," and states may increase income disregards to effectively increase the income limits; many states have substantial disregards. SLMB pays the Medicare monthly Part B premium for qualified Medicare beneficiaries. QMB and SLMB are financed through Medicaid, i.e., with a federal match, but no limitation on enrollment. There is another program that pays the Part B premium only for those with income between 120% and 135% of poverty, known as "qualified individuals" or in some states "additional low income Medicare beneficiaries." This "QI" program is paid entirely from federal grants to the states so that enrollment is limited by the dollars awarded. Income limits are set every April by annual adjustment to the federal poverty level. The states can decide whether or not to set asset limits for these programs, and four states (Alabama, Arizona, Delaware and Missouri) have eliminated asset limits entirely. The QI program was at risk for termination as of June 30, 2008, but funding was restored through December 31, 2009 (H.R. 6331, now PL 110-275).

Applications for MSPs are generally filed with the agency that administers Medicaid, not with the Centers for Medicare and Medicaid. Beneficiaries under the "MSPs" or "Medicare Savings Programs" automatically qualify for the low-income subsidy under Medicare Part D.

Q 13:15 When does an individual have to enroll in Medicare?

Individuals who are under age 65 and are receiving Social Security or Railroad Retirement benefits are automatically enrolled in Medicare Part A and Part B. [42 U.S.C. § 1395p(f)] Disabled individuals are automatically enrolled at the beginning of the 25th month of their disability.

Individuals who are not receiving Social Security or Railroad Retirement benefits three months before they turn age 65 and individuals requiring regular dialysis or kidney transplant must apply for Medicare. The initial seven-month enrollment period begins in the third month before the person turns age 65. [42 U.S.C. § 1395i-2(a)] The individual can contact any Social Security Administration office to enroll. An individual who does not enroll during the seven-month initial enrollment period must wait until the general enrollment period (which is held January 1 to March 31 of each year) to enroll. Part B coverage begins the following July.

Individuals who will have to pay a premium for Part A benefits, and government employees eligible for Medicare on the basis of their "Medicare qualified government employment," do not receive Medicare automatically and must enroll. [42 C.F.R. § 406.15] Keep in mind that individuals may become Medicare Part A beneficiaries without realizing in certain situations, for example, as the 65 + spouse of a Social Security recipient who was a state employee and thus receives no Social Security himself/herself.

Q 13:16 Is there a penalty for late enrollment?

Yes. Part A premiums (if a premium is required) go up 10 percent if an individual waits 12 or more months to enroll. [42 U.S.C. § 1395i-2(c)(6)] Part B premiums go up 10 percent for each 12 months that the individual could have enrolled but did not (unless the individual had equivalent employer coverage). The additional premium cost remains for the life of the beneficiary. [42 U.S.C. § 1395r(b)] Certain exceptions to the penalty apply (13:17).

Q 13:17.1 When do Medicare benefits stop?

Medicare Part A benefits not based on disability continue as long as the person is entitled to Social Security or Railroad Retirement benefits, except that for those who cease receiving benefits because of death, Medicare coverage continues through the date of death. Because Social Security is paid "in arrears," if a person receives Social Security benefits in October, Medicare will only continue through September 30th. Medicare Part B benefits may also terminate if the beneficiary (a) elects to have them stop, or (b) if paying a premium (e.g., those who "buy in"), fails to pay the premium.

Medicare benefits based on the beneficiary's disability may continue for up to 7 years and 9 months under various work incentive programs. (See SQ 15:32.1.)

Q 13:18   How can an individual cancel enrollment in a Medicare Advantage Plan?

The Balanced Budget Act of 1997 included "lock-in" rules that would have limited Medicare Advantage beneficiaries to disenrollment only once, from January 1 through March 31 of each year, beginning in 2002. [42 U.S.C. § 1395w-21(e)(2)] However, these new "lock-in" rules were delayed by the enactment of Pub. L. No. 107–108. Through 2005, beneficiaries could still enroll and disenroll whenever they wanted; since 2006, there is a six-month lock-in period. Beneficiaries must call the plan they wish to leave and ask for a disenrollment form; or call 1-800-MEDICARE (1-800-633-4227) to request that disenrollment be processed over the phone; or call the Social Security Administration (or visit the Social Security office) to file a disenrollment request. In most cases disenrollment is concluded the month after a request if it was filed before the 10th day of the month. If the request was made after the 10th of the month, disenrollment will be on the first day of the second calendar month after the request was made. If the beneficiary joins another managed care plan he or she will be automatically disenrolled from the old plan when the new plan enrollment becomes effective. [See *http://www.medicare.gov/*]

There are various exceptions to the "lock in" that can be sought in situations involving mistake, hardship, etc.; see *http://www.medicareadvocacy.org/MA_07_06.14.Disenrollment.htm.*

Part A Benefits

Q 13:20   What are the copayments and deductibles under Medicare Part A?

Medicare has many copayment requirements for care and deductibles from covered care. The deductibles and copayments (all are 2009 numbers and will change each year unless indicated) include:

1. *Part A hospitalization.* During the first 60 days of care, the patient will pay the first $1,068 of care. For days 61 through 90 (the last day of the basic hospitalization benefit), the patient will pay $267 per day.

2. *Part A lifetime reserve days.* After 90 days of hospitalization, the patient will begin to use the 60 lifetime reserve days. Each lifetime reserve day will require a $534 copayment. The combination of

these two hospitalization benefits mean that a Medicare beneficiary who spends 150 days in the hospital in 2007 will be liable for a total of at least $41,118.

3. *Part A skilled nursing facility.* The first 20 days of covered SNF care will not require any copayment or deductible, but the next 80 days (until the patient uses the total maximum of 100 days) will require a $133.50 daily copayment (2009 figures). The total cost to the beneficiary for 100 days of SNF placement (assuming Medicare covers the entire period, which is uncommon) will therefore be $10,680 in 2009.

4. *Part A hospice benefits.* Although hospice-related prescription drugs are covered, there will be a $5 or 5 percent copayment per prescription.

Inpatient Hospital Care

Q 13:22   Is continued Medicare coverage available for care in a hospital when no nursing home bed is available?

Yes. There is a "no appropriate facility" exception to the requirement that hospital coverage be provided only if the care is such that it can only be provided in a hospital. Even if the patient only requires services that could be provided in a skilled nursing facility, "extended coverage" (the nursing home benefit) will be made available while the patient is still in the hospital, if the patient requires skilled care but no appropriate skilled nursing facility placement is available. [42 U.S.C. § 1395x(v)(1)(G)(i); 42 C.F.R. § 424.13(b)]

The two criteria for extended care coverage in a hospital are (1) need for skilled care (which may include skilled assessment and observation), and (2) lack of a nursing home placement that is not the fault of the patient. For example, if the patient requires the use of a ventilator, and no nursing facility placements for "vent beds" are available, the hospital coverage should continue.

The key is the requirement of a skilled level of care, not where the care was provided. [Monmouth Medical Center v. Harris, 646 F.2d 74, 80 (3d Cir. 1981)] If, on the other hand, the patient requires purely custodial care, Medicare coverage under this exception will not be provided, even if a discharge to the home would be medically contraindicated [Gonzalez v. Secretary of HHS, 644 F. Supp. 1086 (E.D.N.Y. 1986) (unsanitary and unsafe home)], or there is no mechanism at home to provide the needed custodial care [Friedman v. Secretary of HHS, 819 F.2d 42 (2d Cir. 1987)].

Once the need for skilled care is clear, the burden is on the provider to show that placement is available and was refused. [Hurley v. Bowen, 857 F.2d 907 (2d Cir. 1988); Friedman v. Secretary of HHS, 819 F.2d 42, 44 (2d Cir. 1987)] The primary burden of locating an appropriate SNF bed is on the discharge planner [42 C.F.R. § 482.43], who must prepare a discharge plan at the physician's request [42 U.S.C. § 1395x(ee)(2)(G)]. While the SNF must be in the "area," there is no clear definition of this term. The CMS Hospital Manual requirements for utilization review committees state that "as a general rule, a community or local geographic area should not be defined in such a way as to require a patient to be taken away from his family and transported over great distances." [CMS Hospital Manual § 290.3.C (Rev. 394); see also CMS Hospital Manual § 275.C, requiring certifying physicians to meet the same standards imposed on utilization review committees including 290.3]"Geographic area" is defined for similar purposes in CMS Hospital Manual Section 275.C as locations within 50 miles unless shown to be "inaccessible" to patients. (The Hospital Manual is online at *http://www.cms.hhs.gov/Manuals/PBM/list.asp#TopOfPage.*)

If, however, placement is available but the family refuses on the grounds that the facility is out of town (even though not far away), or that another facility is preferred, there will be no coverage. [Melson v. Secretary of Health and Human Services, 702 F. Supp. 997 (W.D.N.Y. 1988); Lerum v. Heckler, 774 F.2d 210 (7th Cir. 1985)] (Note that the regulation referred to in case law, 42 CFR Section 405.1627(b) is no longer in effect, apparently having been removed following the switch to a DRG payment system for hospitals.)

Q 13:23   What hospital coverage is provided under Medicare Part A?

Once the preceding requirements are met (see Q 13:21), Medicare Part A covers up to 90 days of hospitalization for a single benefit period (usually a single hospitalization or a series of hospitalizations for the same illness). [42 U.S.C. § 1395d] In addition, the beneficiary has a total of 60 "lifetime reserve" days, which, as the name indicates, can be used only once in the lifetime of the beneficiary. [42 C.F.R. § 409.61(a)(2)] If a patient does not want to use the lifetime reserve days the hospital must be notified in writing either upon admission or at any time within 90 days after discharge. [42 C.F.R. § 409.65(d)] A patient who uses reserve days may request approval from the hospital to have them restored.

During the first 60 days of care, the patient will pay a $1,068 deductible (2009 figure). For days 61 through 90 (the last day of the basic hospitalization benefit), the patient will pay $267 per day (2009 figure). For Part A lifetime reserve days, after 90 days of hospitalization the patient will begin to use the 60 lifetime reserve days. Each lifetime reserve day will require a $534 copayment (2009 figure). The combination of these two hospitalization benefits mean that a Medicare beneficiary who spends 150 days in the hospital in 2008 will be liable for a total of $41,118. (Fortunately, many patients have Medigap policies that typically cover these deductibles and copayments. [Q 13:70–13:73])

Q 13:23.1 What is the scope of Medicare coverage for inpatient psychiatric care?

There is a special limit on inpatient psychiatric care under Medicare: a lifetime maximum of 190 days. [42 U.S.C. § 1395d(c); 42 C.F.R. §§ 409.62 et seq.] Psychiatric coverage is limited to "active treatment" for a psychiatric condition with services provided under an individualized treatment or diagnostic plan, reasonably expected to improve the patient's condition or for the purpose of diagnosis, and supervised and evaluated by a physician. Coverage may be denied if the beneficiary could be safely and effectively treated on an outpatient basis or a lesser care institution, such as a skilled nursing facility. Pre-authorization is required prior to the admission except in case of emergency, or where Medicare had previously approved the care. [32 C.F.R. § 199.4—dealing with coordination between Medicare and "Tri-CARE," the health program for military personnel]

Skilled Nursing Facility Care

Q 13:28 What are the limitations on the skilled nursing care benefit through Medicare?

In order to qualify for the skilled nursing care benefit, the patient must (1) require "skilled services" on a daily basis, "of a kind that as a practical matter can only be provided in a skilled nursing facility, and (2) have been admitted to a Medicare-certified skilled nursing facility within 30 days of a three-day admission to a hospital. (Problems can arise when coverage is denied on the basis that it is only necessary to treat a pre-existing condition unrelated to the hospital stay.)

Services are "skilled" when they "require the skills of or must be performed under the supervision of technical or professional personnel," either because of the services' inherent complexity [42 C.F.R. § 409.32(a)], or because of risks posed by the claimant's special medical complications [42 C.F.R. § 409.32(b)], unstable condition [42 C.F.R. § 409.33(a)(2)], or overall condition [42 C.F.R. § 409.33(a)(1)]. "Skilled nursing services" expressly include "management and evaluation of a patient's care plan, observation and assessment of the patient's changing condition, and patient education services." [42 C.F.R. §§ 409.33(a)(1)–(3)]

"Daily basis" means skilled nursing care seven days a week or therapy five days per week. (Short lapses, such as those caused by another condition that requires a halt to therapy, should not justify a denial.)

Q 13:29 Does Medicare coverage for therapy cease if the patient has "plateaued"?

Services of a therapist are considered and billed as "skilled services." It is common for patients and their families to hear that rehabilitation will be discontinued because the patient has "plateaued," has made as much rehabilitative progress as possible. Without therapy, the care provided in the nursing home may not be "skilled care," and therefore, Medicare coverage will end.

However, the nursing home benefit for "skilled services" does not in and of itself require that the patient have "restoration potential." Federal regulations plainly state that "restoration potential of a patient is not the deciding factor in determining whether skilled services are needed. Even if full recovery or medical improvement is not possible, a patient may need skilled services to prevent further deterioration or preserve current capabilities." [42 C.F.R. § 409.32(c); see also 42 U.S.C. § 1395y(a) (services must be "reasonable and necessary for the diagnosis or treatment of illness or injury or to improve the functioning of a malformed body member")] Indeed, even the Medicare Intermediary Manual chapter on nursing home services states:

> The repetitive services required to maintain function sometimes involve the use of complex and sophisticated therapy procedures and, consequently, the judgment and skill of a physical therapist might be required for the safe and effective

rendition of such services. (See § 3132.1.B.) The specialized knowledge and judgment of a qualified physical therapist may be required to establish a maintenance program intended to prevent or minimize deterioration caused by a medical condition, if the program is to be safely carried out and the treatment aims of the physician achieved. Establishing such a program is a skilled service.

[Medicare Intermediary Manual § 3132.3.A.1.e] Similarly, the Manual gives as an example at § 3132.1.B:

Example. Even where a patient's full or partial recovery is not possible, a skilled service still could be needed to prevent deterioration or to maintain current capabilities. A cancer patient, for instance, whose prognosis is terminal may require skilled services at various stages of his illness in connection with periodic "tapping" to relieve fluid accumulation and nursing assessment and intervention to alleviate pain or prevent deterioration. The fact that there is no potential for such a patient's recovery does not alter the character of the services and skills required for their performance.

Unfortunately, many other portions of the Medicare Intermediary Manual apply a circular reasoning that leads inexorably back to the termination of Medicare coverage for therapy once "restoration potential" has been maximized. Medicare reasons that in most cases, "maintenance therapy" need not be performed by skilled personnel. Once the person has reached his or her maximum "restoration potential" the only apparent alternative purpose for therapy is "maintenance." Therefore, by definition the need for a skilled therapist is no longer "reasonable and necessary." For example, the same section states as a criterion for Medicare coverage for therapy: "The services must be provided with the expectation, based on the assessment made by the physician of the patient's restoration potential, that the condition of the patient will improve materially in a reasonable and generally predictable period of time, or the services must be necessary for the establishment of a safe and effective maintenance program." The examples then go on to give a clear indication that the only purposes for which a skilled therapist might provide services are (1) restorative therapy or (2) maintenance therapy with the ultimate objective of establishing a maintenance program that will not require skilled care. Many providers are more familiar with this guidance than with the presumably overriding provisions of the C.F.R. In a hearing before an administrative law judge, it may be effective to make that argument—that the Medicare Intermediary Manual is not enacted pursuant to the provisions of the Administrative Procedures Act and is not binding—but practically speaking, in many cases the family will be unwilling to incur the risks of liability for payment should the judge rule against them.

In short, practically speaking, Medicare coverage for therapy will probably be terminated (or notice of non-coverage given) whenever the person no longer has "restoration potential." There is still grounds for appeal, however, if it can be shown that the services of skilled personnel were required to maintain condition or prevent deterioration, such as the example shown. What is important is not the patient's potential, but the level of skill required. If the patient's physician agrees that skilled personnel are essential to the patient's care, Medicare ought to cover the therapy. The patient in the nursing home may demand that the claim be submitted to Medicare and then appeal, continuing therapy all the while. However, the patient will risk having to pay for care out-of-pocket if the claim is eventually denied. This is a judgment call for the family, and it may well be that in most cases the family will succumb to fear of financial exposure. The point is, however, that provided the physician will support the claim and provide detailed explanations to back up the support, the appeal should ultimately be successful (see also SQ 13:83).

Interestingly, the Intermediary Manual provisions governing the mental health benefit do recognize the need for maintenance and the prevention of deterioration. Moreover, they also make clear that "restoration" means any improvement whatsoever, rather than restoration to the original functioning level. [Medicare Intermediary Manual § 3112.7]

Centers for Medicare and Medicaid manuals are finally taking note of the issue, however. The Skilled Nursing Facility Manual specifically warns institutions against using "rules of thumb" in making determinations, and chides that facilities "must not notify patients that services are not covered by Medicare because of 'rules of thumb' such as lack of restoration potential, ability to walk a certain number of feet, degree of stability, or because of general inferences about patients with similar diagnosis or general data related to utilization." [Medicare Skilled Nursing Facility Manual § 214.7] Similarly, the fact that a patient can leave the facility for a brief visit such as a wedding does not in and of itself mean that the patient does not require Medicare-covered services. [*Id.*]

Of course, the care must also be "reasonable." The fact that a skilled therapist might be more persuasive, gentle, and less clumsy, so that the patient is more motivated with that individual, would not make it reasonable for Medicare to pay that therapist.

Q 13:31   What is the scope of coverage for skilled nursing facility care provided under Medicare Part A?

Skilled nursing facility care is available for up to 100 days per spell of illness if the preceding requirements are met. [42 U.S.C. § 1395d(a)(2)] The first 20 days are paid in full: No copayment or deductible is required. The patient must pay a copayment for days 21 through 100, and Medicare pays the balance. The 2008 copayment, for example, is $128 per day. The total cost to the beneficiary without supplemental insurance for 100 days of SNF placement in year 2007 (assuming Medicare covers the entire period, which is uncommon) will therefore be $10,240. After the 100th day the patient must pay the entire cost. (Fortunately, many patients have Medigap policies, some of which may cover these copayments. [Q 13:70–13:73])

If Part A payments are exhausted, or expenses are not reimbursable under Part A, the expenses may be reimbursable under Part B if there are medical and other health services and the patient is entitled to Part B benefits. Some supplemental policies or Medicare Advantage plans, as well as TRICARE for military employees, may provide an extended skilled nursing facility care benefit for patients who might otherwise have Medicare coverage were it not for the 100-day limitation.

Home Health Care Services

Q 13:34   For purposes of Medicare home health services coverage, what does homebound mean?

Although a Medicare beneficiary must be "homebound" before qualifying for home health care visits, the beneficiary need not be completely confined to the home. Medicare considers the beneficiary homebound if leaving the home requires considerable effort or is medically contraindicated. If the beneficiary is unable to leave home without the assistance of another person (or the use of a supportive device like a cane, crutches, walker, or wheelchair), he or she may qualify as homebound. Similarly, if the person has dementia and would be a danger to himself or herself or others if leaving home, so that leaving is medically contraindicated, the person is homebound. Homebound status should not be affected by infrequent and short-term absences, such as visits to the doctor, to church, to get a haircut, etc. Absences for other "unique or infrequent" events, such as weddings, funerals, and the like, will not affect homebound status. [Medicare Home Health Agency Manual § 204.1 (Transmittal 302)] The physician is required to certify to the patient's homebound status.

Q 13:39　Who determines whether home care services are covered?

The nursing or home health agency providing services submits the claim to the Medicare intermediary, which then approves or denies coverage. If the agency believes coverage will be denied (and therefore plans to deny, stop, or reduce services) it must provide an advance written notice, known as a Home Health Advance Beneficiary Notice or HHABN. As a result of a nationwide class action lawsuit, specific requirements for HHABNs became effective on March 1, 2001. Unfortunately, home health agencies will often simply inform the beneficiary that he or she no longer qualifies and the bill will not be submitted, for example, because the beneficiary has "plateaued" or "isn't improving," based on a mistaken belief that "restoration potential" is required (see SQ 13:29). The physician should be contacted and asked to determine whether the particular services are still required. If they are, the physician (or other caregivers) should instruct the agency to resubmit and demand a written notice of termination.

The agency must submit to Medicare if the patient requests (although the patient is then liable for the charge if Medicare denies). [See Centers for Medicare and Medicaid Services Medicare Intermediary Manual § 3638.30 (available online at *http://www.cms.hhs.gov/Manuals/ PBM/list.asp#TopOfPage*—click for the Intermediary Manual.)] A pre-termination hearing is not required, however. [Lutwin v. Thompson, 361 F.3d 146 (2d Cir. 2004, *reversing in part* Healey v. Thompson, 186 F. Supp. 2d 105 (D. Conn. 2001)] The court in *Lutwin* did affirm the lower court's ruling that pre-termination notices were required no matter the reason for the termination, and remanded. Upon remand, the court declined to issue an injunction to this effect but did issue a nationwide declaratory judgment that patients "have a legal right to a written ... [p]re-deprivation statement before an HHA reduces or terminates its services (except de minimis alterations in services); ... [e]xplanation of the circumstances in which a beneficiary has the right to have a demand bill submitted; and ... [d]isclosure of information regarding a patient's right to appeal." [Lutwin v. Thompson, No. 3:98CV00418(DJS) (D. Conn. Dec. 6, 2004)]

Hospice Care

Q 13:40 What is hospice care?

Hospice care, a relatively recent development in American health care, focuses on palliative rather than curative treatment. It is a style of medical care provided to the terminally ill and consists of active pain management, counseling, respite care, and concern for the entire family (including caregivers), and excludes care intended to cure or treat disease. Pain management may include dosages that could lead to addiction or even to suppression of the ability to breathe and other autonomic functions; hospice philosophy first addresses comfort of the patient before addressing those concerns.

Q 13:41 What are the eligibility requirements for hospice care?

One of the most extensive benefits provided through Medicare is the hospice benefit. In order to qualify for benefits, the patient must be eligible for Part A benefits and must have been certified as terminally ill. Per 42 C.F.R. § 418.22 of regulations newly issued in November, 2005, Medicare coverage will only be granted if the hospice certification conforms to the following requirements: (1) the certification specifies that the individual's prognosis is for a life expectancy of six months or less if the terminal illness runs its normal course and (2) Clinical information and other documentation that support the medical prognosis accompanies the written certification. In other words, the physician's statement alone will not suffice.

In addition, the patient must affirmatively elect hospice, must choose the particular hospice program (to the exclusion of other hospice programs), the hospice organization must participate in Medicare, and the patient must decide to forgo curative treatment for the terminal condition. Hospice benefit regulations may be found at 42 CFR Part 418.

Part B Benefits

Q 13:46 What benefits are included in Medicare Part B?

Part B primarily provides coverage for physician's services. Specific services covered include:

- Doctor's visits
- Outpatient and partial hospitalization services

- Ambulatory surgical services
- Diagnostic tests
- Ambulance services
- Durable medical equipment
- Home health services
- Prosthetic devices
- Braces, trusses, artificial limbs, and eyes
- X-ray, radium, and radioactive isotope therapy
- Prosthetic devices and orthotics
- Physical, occupational, and speech therapy
- Blood, blood components, and the cost of blood processing and administration
- Blood clotting factors
- Comprehensive outpatient rehabilitation services
- Limited preventative medicine

[42 U.S.C. §§ 1395k, 1395x(s); 42 C.F.R. §§ 410.20–410.73]

Q 13:47　What medical supplies and equipment does Medicare Part B cover?

Medicare Part B helps pay for durable medical equipment such as oxygen equipment, wheelchairs, and other medically necessary equipment prescribed by a physician for use in the beneficiary's home. (A skilled nursing facility is not considered a "home." This can be a problem when these supplies are needed in a SNF, which is expected to provide them as part of the rate, but may insist that these are non-covered extras.) Medicare coverage is available for, among other items, arm, leg, back, and neck braces; medical supplies such as ostomy pouches, surgical dressings, splints, and casts; breast prostheses following a mastectomy; and one pair of eyeglasses with an intraocular lens after cataract surgery. Medicare pays for different kinds of durable medical equipment in different ways. Some equipment must be rented; other equipment must be purchased. [See *http://www.medicare.gov/*] Medicare will not pay for equipment that is NOT primarily and customarily used only for medical purposes, such as air conditioning, and will not pay for equipment used primarily for convenience, such as stair lifts.

Medicare will also not pay for equipment that is mainly for use outside the home.

The Centers for Medicare and Medicaid Services contracts with four companies, known as Durable Medical Equipment regional Carriers, to process claims for durable medical equipment in their respective regions. Medicare will require a prescription from a physician and, usually, a "certificate of medical necessity."

As with other goods and services, a patient has a right to demand that the provider submit a request to Medicare for payment under Part B, even if the provider is virtually certain that the claim will be denied. However, the patient will be liable for the charge, provided the patient has been given proper notice of that initial determination, as demonstrated by the patient having signed an "ABN" or "advance billing notice." If the provider submits, but the patient has not signed the ABN, the provider may have to pick up the cost. [See, e.g., Centers for Medicare and Medicaid Services Program Memorandum Intermediaries/Carriers Transmittal AB-02-119, § 1.1.D. (July 31, 2002)]

Q 13:47.1 When does Medicare not cover ambulance services?

In many communities, volunteer ambulance companies provide ambulance transportation and the emergency response company provides the paramedic. In these circumstances, the emergency response company can only bill Medicare if the service is performed in a rural area under a contract with a volunteer ambulance company that is prohibited by state law from billing for services. Assuming state law permits the volunteer ambulance company to bill for services, Medicare will likely cover the ambulance charges, but the emergency response company can't bill Medicare for the paramedic and will bill the patient directly. Thus, the paramedic charge portion will have to be paid by the patient and will not be covered by Medicare.

Q 13:48 What preventative care is available through Medicare?

Although the Medicare program has historically limited the preventative care provided as part of its benefits, the recent trend has been to increase the availability of preventative care. In addition to an increased emphasis on Medicare HMOs (which usually include preventative care as part of the philosophical approach to care by the HMO), Congress has added coverage for a number of specific screening and preventative care procedures, including:

1. 80% of the cost of annual mammogram (for female patients over age 40, and a baseline for Medicare recipient women age 35–39), beginning January 1, 1998 [42 U.S.C. §§ 1395l, 1395m];

2. Annual pap smears and pelvic exams (for women at high risk or of childbearing age—other women are covered for pap smears and pelvic exams every three years), since January 1, 1998 [42 U.S.C. §§ 1395l, 1395x]; and

3. Prostate cancer screening (for male patients over age 50), since January 1, 2000 [42 U.S.C. §§ 1395x, 1395y]. Currently, Medicare provides coverage for preventative services such as screening mammography, pap smears, bone density tests, colorectal screenings, prostate screenings, glaucoma screenings, and flu vaccinations.

4. Cardiovascular screenings for early detection of cardiovascular disease every two years (blood tests including those for cholesterol levels, lipid levels and triglyceride levels). No deductible or copay applies.

5. Diabetes screening tests consisting of tests for fasting blood glucose levels, no more than once every six months, for individuals at "high risk" for developing diabetes (those with any combination of the following health conditions: hypertension, dyslipidemia, obesity, a previous history of an elevated fasting blood glucose level or previously identified impaired glucose intolerance). No deductible or copay applies.

6. Initial "welcome to Medicare" physical exam, to include both an electrocardiogram and end-of-life counseling, within six months of Part B enrollment (beginning January 1, 2009, within 12 months of Part B enrollment). Lab tests are not covered. There is a 20% copay after meeting the Part B deductible; starting January 1, 2009, the deductible does not apply to this benefit.

7. Glaucoma screenings for those at "high risk."

8. Annual flu shot (fall or winter).

9. Additional preventative benefits as may be authorized by the Secretary of Health and Human Services that "identify medical conditions or risk factors and that the Secretary determines are reasonable and necessary for the prevention or early detection of an illness or disability."

Q 13:49   What services are not covered under Medicare Part B?

Not all outpatient medical care is covered under the Medicare Part B program. [Specific exclusions from coverage are listed at 42 U.S.C. § 1396y(a)] Principal exceptions to the otherwise broad coverage include:

1. Prescription medications (now covered under Part D), other than medication that must be administered by a physician;

2. Dental care (except for dental surgery);

3. Eyeglasses, contact lenses, and eye examinations (unless they are related to eye surgery, such as cataract surgery);

4. Hearing aids or the examinations necessary to fit the hearing aids;

5. Routine physical examinations and immunizations (except, again, that the beneficiary may elect a Medicare HMO that provides such care);

6. Routine podiatric care or orthopedic shoes or supportive devices;

7. Personal comfort items (e.g., television or telephone in the beneficiary's hospital room); and

8. Custodial care.

Q 13:49.1   Are there any limits on the therapy benefit under Medicare Part B?

Yes. Effective January 1, 2007, outpatient rehabilitation services are capped at $1,810 (2008 figure) for any combination of outpatient Part B physical and speech-language therapy services as well as a separate cap of $1,810 for occupational therapy. This limitation was first imposed by the Balanced Budget Act of 1997 but various delays prevented implementation until 2007. An exception applies to outpatient therapy received in a hospital's outpatient rehabilitation department. An "exception process" was also adopted as part of the Deficit Reduction Act signed into law February 8, 2006, and recently extended through December 31, 2009 by H.R. 6331, the Medicare Improvements for Patients and Providers Act of 2008. Some exemptions apply automatically, such as when therapy is sought for a condition or situation on an approved list. In other cases, a request must be made in writing, and in those situations, the claim is deemed approved unless CMS denies the claim within ten days.

Q 13:50 What are the copayments and deductibles under Medicare Part B?

Medicare has many copayment requirements for care and deductibles from covered care. The structure of Medicare's reimbursement formulae can be thoroughly confusing to clients. In addition, many (but not all) of the numbers are indexed for inflation and the annual changes add to the confusion.

Part B requires that the beneficiary pay the first $135 (in 2009) of covered services each year. [42 U.S.C. § 1395l(b)] This deductible is waived when the patient is under continuous treatment that spans the new year.

More importantly, Part B usually pays for only 80 percent of covered services, requiring the patient to pay the remaining 20 percent. Furthermore, Medicare's 80 percent share is calculated based on the "reasonable charges" for those services. [42 U.S.C. § 1395l(a)(1)] This means that the beneficiary's share of medical costs is almost always greater than 20 percent, because the "reasonable charges" are nearly universally lower than the actual costs of services.

Even physicians who do not participate in Medicare are constrained by a "limiting charge" when dealing with Medicare beneficiaries. (They are relieved from the limitation only if they make a written commitment that they will not provide services to any Medicare beneficiaries for two years [42 C.F.R. §§ 405.410 et seq.].) Although such doctors are permitted to charge more than the "reasonable charges" for their services, they may not charge more than 115 percent of those reasonable charges. [42 U.S.C. § 1395w-4(g); Garelick v. Sullivan, 987 F.2d 913 (2d Cir. 1993), *cert. denied*, 510 U.S. 821] This combination of provisions can hopelessly complicate the calculation of the amount a Medicare beneficiary must pay toward doctor bills. A few examples may help to clarify the methodology:

> **Example 13-1.** Doctor A charges $100 for a procedure and Medicare allows $100 for that service. Doctor A's patients must pay the $20 not paid by Medicare and Medicare will pay $80.

> **Example 13-2.** Doctor B charges $110 for the same procedure and Medicare still allows $100. Doctor B's patients must pay $30 and Medicare will pay $80.

> **Example 13-3.** Doctor C charges $120 for the same procedure. Doctor C's patients must pay $35, Medicare will pay $80, and Doctor C

must "write off" $5. (Doctor C's charges may not exceed $115, so the patient need not pay the additional $5.)

Medicare Advantage Program

Q 13:53 What is the Medicare Advantage Program?

The Medicare Advantage program, originally referred to as Medicare + Choice program or Medicare Part C, is a collection of alternative means of financing or receiving individual Medicare coverage (see Q 13:8). Foremost among these is the use of an HMO to manage benefits, and more is often heard about "Medicare HMOs" than "Medicare Advantage." Medicare Advantage does not provide additional benefits or coverage, although it may make Medicare more attractive for some beneficiaries or may provide additional benefits as an inducement to attract participants. [42 U.S.C. § 1395w-21; 42 C.F.R. § 422.101] The Medicare Advantage plan must provide the same services available under Parts A and B and must pass on any cost savings to the beneficiaries. Medicare Advantage is also sometimes used to describe proposed additional benefits, such as (before Medicare Part D came in) prescription drug coverage or long-term nursing care. [41 U.S.C. § 1395d] If supplemental benefits are offered under a Medicare Advantage plan, a separate premium is permitted, but the premium cannot vary among individuals within the plan and must not exceed certain actuarial and community ratings requirements. [42 U.S.C. § 1395-22; 42 C.F.R. § 422.102]

Q 13:54 What are the Medicare Advantage options?

As part of its continuing review of Medicare, Congress in 1997 created several new options for individual Medicare beneficiaries. It is important to realize that the Medicare Advantage Choice program only permits private providers and insurance companies to offer alternative plans; the federal government does not directly provide any of the alternative plans. Consequently, the actual availability of Medicare Advantage benefits will depend on the decisions of local providers to offer alternative plans. Medicare Advantage plans, depending on local availability, may include:

1. *Health maintenance organizations.* Actually, beneficiaries were permitted to select HMO providers for Medicare even before

Medicare Advantage was established. In some areas, HMOs are already providing care for a third or more of Medicare beneficiaries. In other areas, the penetration of HMOs is slight. Furthermore, in some areas where HMOs once had a strong presence, there has been almost a mass exodus, with HMOs leaving the region entirely and participants scrambling to obtain (or re-obtain) Medigap insurance (see Qs 13:70–13:73).

2. *Provider-sponsored organizations (PSOs).* Local hospitals, clinics, or other health care providers may elect to establish qualified Medicare provider organizations. PSOs may resemble HMOs, but will be operated by existing health care providers.

3. *Preferred provider organizations (PPOs).* Insurance plans that permit beneficiaries to select their own health care providers, but that provide lower deductibles and copayments for health care received from an approved list of providers. By contracting with those preferred providers, the plan is expected to reduce costs.

4. *HMO/POS—The point of service option.* Essentially, this permits HMOs to operate captive clinics or other providers.

5. *Provider fee for service (PFFS) option.* Allows beneficiaries to select certain private providers. For those providers who agree to accept the plan's payment terms and conditions, this option does not place the providers at risk, nor vary payment rates based upon utilization. The provider is reimbursed at a rate determined by the plan on a fee-for-service basis. Medicare makes capitated payments to the private pay fee-for-service plan as it would to an HMO or PSO.

6. *Religious fraternal benefit society plan.* A "religious fraternal benefit society" may offer a Medicare Advantage plan to members of its church, or to members of a group of affiliated churches. [42 C.F.R. § 422.57] This type of Medicare Advantage plan is not really a separate category, because the plan must fall under one of the other categories of Medicare Advantage.

7. *Medical savings accounts (MSAs).* When a beneficiary elects this option, Medicare pays for a two-part approach to covering medical costs. First, the beneficiary selects (and Medicare pays for) a high-deductible traditional insurance policy. The unused dollar amount of the beneficiary's benefit is then deposited into a savings account, which can be used for medical care until the high deductible is met. If the beneficiary does not use the medical

savings account, it ultimately passes to the beneficiary's heirs, unless specifically bequeathed by will.

Q 13:55 How can a Medicare beneficiary evaluate the new options available through Medicare Advantage?

The variety of options and the similar-sounding acronyms make the choices more confusing. Area Agencies on Aging typically offer Medicare counseling services and may even offer informative seminars for seniors. National Medicare advocacy agencies have prepared and distribute explanatory literature, most of which is available on the Internet. Providers themselves may offer plan explanations, but beneficiaries should realize that they are promotional efforts. The CMS provides a Medicare Personal Plan Finder that compares plans based on personal circumstances at *www.medicare.gov/Choices/Overview.asp.*

In addition, the federal government funds "state health insurance assistance programs" or "SHIPs" in each state, which can provide counseling for those choosing plans, deciding whether to switch or disenroll, and even in dealing with coverage issues. In many cases, the state agency on aging will be the designated "SHIP," and at no cost, the client can obtain help from experienced counselors in navigating the complex network of choices that are now present in the Medicare coverage system. Individuals may call 1-800-MEDICARE to find the phone number for the SHIP in their state.

Q 13:56 Who is eligible to enroll in Medicare Advantage?

Any Medicare beneficiary who does not have end-stage renal disease at the time of enrollment is permitted to enroll in a Medicare Advantage program, provided only that the program serves the beneficiary's geographic area and the beneficiary agrees to abide by the requirements of the chosen program. [42 C.F.R. § 422.50] Enrollment in the Medicare Advantage plan is accomplished simply by completing the enrollment form.

Q 13:57 When may the Medicare Advantage election be made?

Enrollment in Medicare Advantage must take place in one of these available enrollment periods:

1. In the first six months after the beneficiary becomes eligible for Medicare enrollment [42 C.F.R. § 422.62(a)(4)(ii)];

2. In the period from three months before Medicare eligibility until the last day of the month before eligibility (the "initial coverage election period") [42 C.F.R. § 422.62(a)(1)];

3. During November 15 to December 31 of each year (the "annual election period") [42 C.F.R. § 422.62(a)(2)]; or

4. During the first three months of each year (except that only one election can be made during each annual period) [42 C.F.R. § 422.62(a)(5)]; or

5. For those enrolled in original Medicare wishing to switch to a Medicare Advantage plan *without* drug coverage, any time during 2007 or 2008 [Tax Relief and Health Care Act of 2006].

Q 13:59 What if you move out of a Medicare Advantage plan's service area?

If the particular Medicare Advantage plan provides coverage in the new area, no change in Medicare benefits is required (though the plan itself will require updated address information and may require a change of primary care physician). If the same plan is not available in the new area, the participant must either disenroll (and thereby return to regular Medicare coverage) or enroll in a new plan offered in the new geographic area. Because of the geographic limitations on individual plans, Medicare managed care plans are usually less attractive to Medicare beneficiaries who travel extensively or move frequently.

Q 13:60 Can an individual's enrollment in a Medicare Advantage plan be terminated?

The Medicare beneficiary may choose to disenroll from a Medicare Advantage program at any time by simply filing the disenrollment election form with the program. Unless the beneficiary is eligible to elect another Medicare Advantage program and has actually made an election, disenrollment will return the beneficiary to regular Medicare coverage.

The Medicare Advantage program is permitted to terminate the beneficiary involuntarily only in one of three situations:

1. Failure to make timely premium payments;

2. Disruptive behavior by the beneficiary; or

3. Termination of the Medicare Advantage program for all beneficiaries in the geographic area.

In the last of these situations, the beneficiary is given a special enrollment period to choose another Medicare Advantage plan. If the beneficiary does not make a selection, or if the termination is for nonpayment or disruptive behavior, the beneficiary is returned to regular Medicare coverage. [42 U.S.C. § 1395w-21]

Q 13:61 How long are Medicare managed care plans and private fee-for-service plans required to stay in Medicare?

Medicare Advantage plans are required to continue to operate for a full calendar year. If a plan decides to terminate coverage (or eliminate a particular geographic area), it is required to notify all affected plan participants. Participants are then required to select a replacement plan or return to regular Medicare coverage.

Q 13:62 What premiums does an enrollee in Medicare Advantage have to pay?

Premiums for Medicare Advantage programs must be annually filed with and approved by the federal Department of Health and Human Services. Premiums must be uniform among beneficiaries enrolled in the Medicare Advantage program, and may not exceed set maximum amounts. [42 C.F.R. §§ 422.300–422.308] In addition to premiums specific to the Medicare Advantage plan, participants must also continue to pay the Medicare Part B premium required of all Part B enrollees.

Q 13:63 Can (or should) Medicare Advantage participants maintain their existing Medigap insurance coverage?

For most Medicare Advantage participants Medigap coverage will be duplicative, and the insured will consequently receive little benefit from the Medigap policy. Medigap insureds are permitted, however, to retain their policies, and they may choose to do so for at least a period of time after enrollment in a Medicare Advantage plan. In the event that a Medicare managed care plan terminates coverage in a participant's area, for example, Medigap carriers are required to permit the participant to re-enroll in a Medigap plan, but the costs may be significantly higher than if the original policy had continued.

Q 13:64   What is a Medicare HMO?

For several years, Medicare has permitted health maintenance organizations to provide Medicare services. Under the Medicare HMO arrangement, beneficiaries who choose to join the plan will receive all services from the HMO, and Medicare pays 95 percent of the average cost (to Medicare) of patients in that community. This may mean that the HMO receives a capitated rate of $400 to $500 per month for most areas of the country, and must provide all covered services for its Medicare beneficiaries. In addition, the HMO may (but is not required to) elect to provide additional benefits; frequently, HMOs provide limited eyeglass and eye examination coverage, transportation, periodic checkups, and—very important before the adoption of Medicare Part D—sometimes even a limited prescription drug benefit. The federal government's decision to fix the capitation rate at 95 percent has come under considerable fire. Originally calculated to encourage managed care cost savings, the 5 percent discount has been criticized as instead encouraging HMOs to seek out only relatively healthy Medicare beneficiaries, and systematically to encourage plan participants to transfer back into "traditional" Medicare once they become ill. Medicare HMO operators insist that they do not do this, and point to surveys indicating that their members consistently rate their care as excellent.

Q 13:65   Who may enroll in a Medicare HMO?

As with the other Medicare Advantage plans, Medicare HMOs must accept any Medicare beneficiary who lives in the HMO's geographic service area, agrees to the HMO's regulations, and does not have end-stage renal disease. [42 C.F.R. § 422.50] Medicare HMOs may terminate the beneficiary from coverage only for nontimely payment of any premiums due, disruptive behavior, or termination of the HMO benefit for all beneficiaries living in the geographic area. [42 U.S.C. § 1395w-21]

Medigap Insurance

Q 13:70   What is a Medigap insurance policy?

Although Medicare coverage is quite extensive, there are a number of items not covered by Medicare. Uncovered items include prescription drugs (now handled by Part D coverage), substantial deductibles, and copayments. In order to provide coverage for those items and others, the insurance industry has extensively marketed so-called Medicare supplemental insurance products. [42 U.S.C. § 1395ss] More commonly, Medicare supplement policies are referred to as "Medigap" policies. With the exception of certain additional benefits, in general Medigap simply covers the portion of Medicare-covered items not paid by Medicare. In other words, in most cases if Medicare would not pay, neither will Medigap. Shortly after the institution of Medicare in the mid-1960s, the supplemental insurance industry was rife with abuses (including over-billing, sale of duplicate policies, sale of special-purpose policies with extremely limited coverage, and similar practices). In response, Congress adopted a uniform set of Medigap policy terms: All Medigap policies must offer one of ten pre-defined sets of benefits identified as standardized Plans A through J. In theory, at least, the plans must now offer competitive pricing, security of the insurance company, claims experience, and other, more easily quantified, variables, and avoid confusing and misleading plan provisions. State insurance department websites may offer a quick price-comparison of policies by plan number.

Q 13:71 What benefits are provided in every Medigap policy?

Every Medigap policy must include certain core benefits:

1. The deductible for hospitalization days 61 through 90;
2. The deductible for the "lifetime reserve" hospitalization days 91 through 150;
3. An additional 365 lifetime reserve days with no deductible;
4. The first three pints of blood not covered by Medicare; and
5. The Part B coinsurance (e.g., the 20 percent of allowable charges for outpatient services).

Those benefits are contained in the simplest of the Medigap plans, Plan A. Each succeeding plan builds on those benefits. Plans B and C provide additional benefits that are included in every succeeding plan. Plans D through J mix and match a collection of additional benefits. The standardized Medigap plans are as set out in Table 13-1:

Table 13-1. Standardized Medigap Plans

Plan	Includes All Provisions of Plan	Additional Features
A	Basic provisions only	
B	Plan A	—Coverage for the hospitalization deductible for the first 60 days
C	Plan B	—Daily deductible for SNF days 21-100—Emergency care in a foreign country—$100 annual deductible
D	Plan C (but not the $100 deductible coverage)	—At-home recovery care up to $1,600 per year
E	Plan C (but not the $100 deductible coverage)	—Preventive examinations, flu shots, etc., up to $120 per year
F	Plan C	—"Balance billing" benefits for the portion of out-patient visits not covered under Part B

(Plan F is also available in a "high-deductible" version, under which benefits are not paid until the beneficiary has incurred a total of $1,900 (year 2008 figure)—this deductible does not apply to the foreign emergency care benefit.)

G	Plan D (but not the $100 deductible coverage)	—"Balance billing" benefits, but only at 80% of the non-covered charges
H	Plan C	—50% of prescription drugs after $250 deductible and with an annual limit of $1,250
I	Plan F (but not the $100 deductible coverage)	—50% of prescription drugs after $250 deductible and with an annual limit of $1,250
J	Plan F	—At-home recovery care up to $1,600 per year—50% of prescription drugs after $250 deductible and with an annual limit of $3,000—Preventive examinations, flu shots, etc., up to $120 per year

(Like Plan F, Plan J is also available in a "high-deductible" version, under which benefits are not paid until the beneficiary has incurred a total of $1,900 (year 2008 figure)—this deductible does not apply to foreign emergency care or prescription drug benefits.)

Table 13-1. (Cont'd)

Plan	Includes All Provisions of Plan	Additional Features
K		Begins with only 50% coverage of the blood deductible, the Part B 20% coinsurance, the nursing home co-insurance and the Part A hospital deductible, but then covers 100% of cost sharing for Medicare Part B preventive services and 100% of all cost sharing under Medicare Parts A and B for the balance of the calendar year once an individual has reached the out-of-pocket limit on annual expenditures of $4,620 in 2009.
L		Same as Plan K except 75% coverage where K has 50%; also the 100% cost sharing kicks in after an out-of-pocket limit on annual expenditures of $2,310 in 2009.

[42 U.S.C. § 1395ss]

The site *www.medicare.gov* now offers detailed Medigap plan information through a "Medicare Personal Plan Finder;" another useful resources is the Center for Medicare Advocacy website.

Q 13:71.1   Will Medigap plans pay for the uncovered portion of Medicare Part D drug costs?

Anyone who already has a Medigap policy that provides a drug benefit can continue to receive that benefit, provided that they choose to opt out of the new Medicare drug benefit program. No new Medigap policies with drug coverage can be sold, and no other private insurers will be permitted to sell policies that cover the deductibles and copayments in the Medicare drug program.

Q 13:73   When should one purchase a Medigap policy?

It is usually of prime importance to purchase a Medigap policy during the initial enrollment period, during the first six months beginning the month after a retiree (a) is 65 or older and (b) is eligible for Medicare Part B (usually (s)he enrolls in Part B upon attaining age 65; the common exception is the working person over age 65, who will not purchase Part B until no longer receiving employee coverage; COBRA coverage may be insufficient to delay the initial enrollment period). This is because Medigap insurers may not refuse coverage on any of the policies based on the health of the beneficiary; in other words, the policies must be offered on an "unrated" basis. Thereafter, policies are underwritten, that is, eligibility may vary based on health. This six-month "window" does not open for the person receiving Social Security disability insurance until the month in which he or she reaches age 65 (for those whose birthdays fall on the 1st of the month, the prior month is included as the month in which the person reaches age 65). [Centers for Medicare and Medicaid Program Memorandum Transmittal 02–03 dated December 2002] Prior to that time, he or she is limited to Medicare HMO coverage (if available), or Plans A through C. The disabled beneficiary is not notified about this new six-month window and his or her attorney should be alert to the trigger of the 65th birthday so that the opportunity is not lost.

Example 13-4. John receives SSDI on his 50th birthday (with no retroactivity). He can receive Medicare and purchase a Plan C Medigap policy when he is age 52. Once he turns age 65, however, he will have a six-month window within which to purchase Plans D through J if he so desires. In addition, "open enrollment," on an unrated basis, is available to:

1. Medicare Advantage participants who lose coverage because the plan was terminated, or because the participant moved out of the coverage area or terminated the Medicare Advantage plan for cause.

2. Beneficiaries who were covered by regular Medicare supplemented by a Medigap policy, then changed to a Medicare + Choice program but changed back within 12 months and apply for the Medigap policy within 63 days.

3. Medigap policyholders who are terminated from their prior Medigap plan for one of several reasons.

Although these beneficiaries do have a right to enroll in a new Medigap program, they may in some cases be limited to Plans A, B, C, or F, or to the same plan type they held previously. [42 U.S.C. § 1395ss]

Once the plan is selected, Medigap insurers may set policy premiums on the basis of "age rating." An age-rated premium will increase as the beneficiary ages; while premium costs will likely be lower in early years, they will increase substantially over time. If the insurer does not use an age-rating method (instead charging the same premium for all beneficiaries regardless of age), initial costs may be higher but the beneficiary may save costs over time.

Q 13:73.1   If a retiree has health insurance through an employer, is it Medigap insurance?

Not necessarily. Many employer health plans include a "retiree health insurance plan" that effectively allows the retiree to continue with almost identical insurance to the kind he or she had in place during working life. The difference is that for groups with 20 or more retirees, Medicare will be the primary payer, as it is with a Medigap policy, rather than a secondary payer, as it is with employee health insurance. Medicare cautions that: (1) employers have no obligation to maintain such plans throughout the retiree's lifetime; (2) failing to elect to take Medicare Part B results in a 10% premium increase for each year prior to switching to Medicare Part B; and (3) it may not be possible to get ideal Medigap coverage later on if the employer fails to carry through. On the other hand, the coverage may be far more comprehensive than anything Medicare and a supplemental policy can offer—typically because of better drug coverage.

Note that there will be no late-enrollment penalty for failure to enroll in Medicare Part D if the retiree plan provides equivalent or better drug coverage than Part D offers.

Retiree insurance coverage can prove a trap for the unwary. Many retiree plans do not cover 100% of the Medicare copays and deductibles, but only a percentage, perhaps 80% or 90%. In many cases, this does not seem particularly onerous for the patient. But when the patient is a nursing home resident for more than 20 days, this can add up to $1,000 to $2,000 over the remaining 80 days before the patient has "maxed out" of the Medicare benefit. This is important to consider when counseling someone "spending down" to become eligible for Medicaid. Conversely, when planning a "reverse half-a-loaf" gifting strategy, that retiree coverage permits an individual to become "otherwise eligible" for Medicaid sooner, as the insurance does not cover all of the cost of the nursing home stay. Clients do not always understand the difference between their health insurance coverage and typical "Medigap" coverage. One way to spot retiree coverage is to ask whether the client has any copays. Another is to find out if the coverage is "free."

Medicare Appeals Process

Q 13:74 What are the appeal rights for Medicare beneficiaries?

Appeal processes and rights differ depending on the particular decision, denial, or benefit under attack. Different appeals provisions apply to each of the following:

1. Appeals of determination of eligibility for Part A or Part B, or election of Medicare Advantage (Part C);
2. Appeals of payment denial for Part A benefits;
3. Appeals of payment denial for Part B benefits (including appeals from managed care plan benefit determinations); and
4. Appeals of service denials or charges for Medicare Advantage benefits.
5. Appeals of denials under Medicare Part D (drug benefits).

In addition, any appeal raising questions about whether particular types of services or items are covered by Medicare is further limited. Such appeals may not be entertained by an administrative law judge (ALJ), may not be based on alleged failure to publish the appropriate notice in the Federal Register, and may not be granted on the basis of an inadequate administrative record. [42 U.S.C. § 1395ff(b)(2)]

New appeals procedures were enacted as part of the Beneficiaries Improvement and Protection Act of 2000 (BIPA). [Pub. L. No. 106-554 (2000)]. These were to take effect October 1, 2002. [67 Fed. Reg. 62,478 (Oct. 7, 2002)] While some have been implemented, others have not. New regulations were issued March 8, 2005. [70 Fed. Reg. 11,420] and changes to the Medicare Provider Manual were issued in 2006. See *http://new.cms.hhs.gov/transmittals/downloads/R862CP.pdf (also see http://www.sharinglaw.net/elder/Transmittal862.pdf)*.

In the past, there was a high success rate for appeals to an administrative law judge within the Social Security Administration. Unfortunately, the Centers for Medicare and Medicaid have transferred responsibility for Medicare Appeals from the Social Security Administration to the Department of Health and Human Services, and Part B denials have been switched from hearings to a "reconsideration" process. A recent study by the General Accounting Office, entitled "Incomplete Plan to Transfer Appeals Workload from SSA to HHS Threatens Service to Appellants" stresses the need for contingency plans for anticipated problems with the transition.

In short, the information in this chapter may no longer be current, and the elder law attorney is well-advised to review internet resources such as the Center for Medicare Advocacy website (*http://www.medicareadvocacy.org*) in order to remain current.

Q 13:74.1 How long does it take for Medicare to reach a decision on whether or not a claim is covered?

Technically, the carrier is required to reach a decision within 45 days and the decision is supposed to be mailed within that 45-day period. [42 U.S.C § 1395ff(a)(2)] The initial determination, a "Medicare Summary Notice," goes only to the beneficiary.

Q 13:75 How does a beneficiary appeal a denial of eligibility?

A denial of eligibility for Medicare Part A, Part B, or Part C (Medicare Advantage) coverage is an "initial determination" and subject to appeal. [42 U.S.C. § 1395ff] That process includes these steps:

1. The beneficiary receives the Medicare Summary Notice denying the benefit as an initial determination.

2. The beneficiary must then submit a written, signed appeal of the initial determination, filed within 120 days of receipt of the intermediary's decision with the intermediary office specified on the notice. Under the new regulations, providers and durable equipment suppliers may also appeal the initial determination.

3. The intermediary issues a "redetermination" within 60 days from the last person's appeal. This will be sent to the beneficiary's representative if the beneficiary is represented.

4. If the redetermination confirms the initial denial, the beneficiary may then request a reconsideration within 180 days by filing a request at the location indicated on the redetermination notice. This is in effect a second level of review by the intermediary. It is a "paper review"—new evidence may be submitted on paper, but there is no hearing. "Reconsiderations" are conducted by private contractors called Qualified Independent Contractors (QICs). The Reconsideration process began phase-in starting May 1, 2005 with

appeals relating to hospital, skilled nursing facility, home health, outpatient hospital services, and hospice claims. Prior to 2006, Part B appeals of redeterminations did not go to a "Reconsideration" by a QIC but was handled as previously by a fair hearing with a Social Security Administration administrative law judge.

5. The QIC issues a decision on the Reconsideration within 60 days from the last person's appeal. If it fails to do so, the beneficiary can request to "escalate" the appeal. At that point, the QIC has 5 days either to decide, or allow the appeal to be escalated. Escalated appeals must be heard by the ALJ within 180 days. For Part A appeals, no administrative hearing is available unless the amount in question is at least $100 [42 U.S.C. § 1395ff(b)(2)], doubled for appeals of a determination by a Quality Improvement Organization (QIO). [42 U.S.C. § 1320c-4][SQ 13:77]

6. A decision on reconsideration may then be appealed to federal court within 60 days of the decision. No appeal may be made to federal court unless the amount in question is at least $1,000 for skilled nursing facility, home health and hospice appeals, and at least $2,000 for hospital appeals (doubled for appeals of a determination by a QIO [SQ 13:77]).

Q 13:75.1 What notice must a beneficiary receive concerning appeal rights?

Hospital patients must be given an "Important Message from Medicare" or "IM" within the first two days of admission, and again up to two days before, but no later than four hours before discharge. The IM sets forth the appeals process, explains the right to remain in the hospital without charge if an expedited decision is requested, and the right to receive a detailed notice of the reasons for discharge. Regulations require the patient to sign and date the first IM, but *not* the second.

Q 13:76 What must be included in the denial notice for coverage of hospital benefits?

Because of court action, hospitals and skilled nursing facilities are required to provide particular information and procedures when Medicare benefits are denied:

1. The notice must state that the patient must pay the hospital's charges for hospital care beyond the second day following the date of the notice.

2. Denial notices must include information about the beneficiary's right to demand that the hospital or SNF bill Medicare for the questioned service.

3. On request of the beneficiary, the provider must submit the bill to the fiscal intermediary (so-called "demand billing").

4. No bill may be submitted to the beneficiary until the Medicare intermediary has ruled on the demand bill.

[Sarrassat v. Sullivan, 1989 WL 208444 (N.D. Cal. May 17, 1989) (settlement order)]

Notices are considered to be "delivered" when signed by the patient. However, under new rules, if the patient refuses to sign, the provider may note the refusal in the records and that will be the date of the receipt. As discussed in SQs 13:77 and 13:78, timing is very important, and it is not clear what happens when a beneficiary lacks capacity to sign a receipt, or fails to advise the person responsible for his or her medical decisions that he or she has refused to sign.

Q 13:77 What are the special rules for "expedited review" for denials of continued hospital inpatient coverage?

Hospital inpatients told that Medicare is terminating and that they will be discharged have a special right to request immediate review by a quality improvement organization (QIO), formerly known as "peer review organization." The patient or representative must contact the QIO by phone or in writing before the end of the day of requested discharge. If the QIO agrees with the decision, by noon of the day following the request the hospital or Medicare Advantage plan must give the patient a "Detailed Notice of Denial" advising the patient of the specific facts of his or her condition, as well as the legal basis for the determination that services would no longer be covered by Medicare. Under regulations issued in July 2007, the patient may remain in the hospital at least until noon of the day after the QIO expedited review decision without charge for the stay pending appeal. If the QIO finds that the discharge decision was wrong, the patient can continue to receive covered care in the hospital until another discharge decision is made and a new notice is given. [42 C.F.R. § 405.1206; 42 C.F.R. § 422.62] Reconsideration of a QIO denial is made by the QIC as explained in SQ 13:78.

Q 13:78   What are the special rules for "expedited appeals"?

Starting in July 2005, beneficiaries in the traditional Medicare program have been able to seek expedited review of a skilled nursing facility, home health, hospice, or comprehensive outpatient rehabilitation facility (CORF) services discharge or termination. [69 Fed. Reg. 69252 (Nov. 26, 2004)] The process is similar to the HMO expedited review process (with somewhat stricter standards) and more or less incorporates the special hospital review process. [SQ 13:77] The provider must give the beneficiary a general notice at least 2 days in advance of the proposed end of service. If the service is for less than 2 days, or if the time in between services is more than 2 days, notice must be given by the next to last service (e.g., next to last therapy visit, in the case of home health therapy). The notice must describe the service, the date coverage ends, the beneficiary's financial liability for continued services, and how to file an appeal.

Upon receiving the notice, the beneficiary has until noon of the next calendar day to request expedited review, orally or in writing. Expedited review is permitted only in cases involving discharge (including a cessation of services by a residential provider or a hospice) or from a termination of services where "a physician certifies that failure to continue the provision of such services is likely to place the individual's health at significant risk." [42 U.S.C. § 1395ff(b)(1)(F)] Services furnished by a "non-residential provider," such as home health services, are treated as a termination of services for which a doctor's certificate must be provided. [42 C.F.R. § 405.1202(a)]

The review is performed by the Quality Improvement Organization (QIO) and a decision must be issued within 72 hours. The beneficiary may request a copy of materials submitted to the QIO by the provider, and may submit additional information. The QIO is required to "solicit the views" of the beneficiary, and must evaluate whether the notice is deficient. The QIO's decision must provide a detailed explanation, description of any applicable rules and regulations, and other specific facts. The beneficiary is not financially liable for the continued services until the later of 2 days after receiving the notice or the termination date specified on the notice.

The beneficiary has until noon of the next day to request expedited reconsideration of the notice. Reconsideration is handled by the Qualified Independent Contractor (QIC), although until the QICs are fully operational, the reconsideration may also be done by the QIO. The QIC has 72 hours to issue its new decision.

If the reconsideration also results in denial, the beneficiary may then appeal to an administrative law judge. [See SQ 13:75]

Q 13:79 What appeal rights exist for Part B benefit determinations?

NOTE: This question is deleted.

Q 13:80 How do appeal rights differ for managed care beneficiaries?

Managed care program participants do not have fiscal intermediaries or carriers to appeal to, and so CMS has adapted the appeal procedures for HMO and other managed care plans. The principal provisions of those procedures include:

1. A requirement that the HMO respond to a request for redetermination within 60 days unless there is good cause for further delay, and that the HMO respond to a request for determination on an expedited basis in 72 hours if you claim that your health could be seriously harmed by waiting for a decision about a service.

2. Pursuant to the Medicare Prescription Drug, Improvement, and Modernization Act of 2003, amending section 1869(a)(3)(C)(ii) of BIPA, the requirement that there be a written notice responding to the redetermination request (a "MRN") including the specific reasons for the decision, a summary of relevant clinical or scientific evidence used in making the redetermination, a description of how to obtain additional information concerning the decision, and notification of the right to appeal and instructions on how to appeal the decision to the next level. In addition, a contractor must, upon request, provide the party information on the policy, manual, or regulation used in making the decision. [See CMS Publication 97]

3. If the decision on redetermination is not fully favorable to the beneficiary, the decision must be submitted to CMS for review.

4. For immediate appeal of denial of inpatient hospital coverage, the HMO participant has a right to request an immediate review by a quality improvement organization ("QIO") (formerly referred to as a peer review organization; see 42 C.F.R. Part 475). As with Medicare Part A, the request must be made by noon of the business day following the initial decision, and the QIO must respond within 24 hours. Also as with Medicare Part A, the hospital may not bill the patient until final resolution of the QIO review, at least if the beneficiary did not know or have reason to know that the beneficiary would be liable for payment if there was a denial.

5. Sanctions may be imposed on the HMO for failure to follow the regulations. [42 C.F.R. Part 417]

Q 13:81 What appeal rights are available for Medicare Advantage (Part C) determinations?

In addition to the special appeal rights relating to continued inpatient care coverage, Medicare Advantage beneficiaries may request reconsideration of other denials of benefits and the program must complete its reconsideration within 60 days. If the denial is based on a lack of medical necessity, the review must be by a physician other than the physician making the initial determination, and the second physician must have an appropriate level of expertise in the involved medical area. The Department of Health and Human Services is required to enter into a contract with a separate (outside) agency to conduct administrative reviews, and appeals of those reviews may be made to the Secretary of HHS if the amount in controversy is at least $100. [42 C.F.R. Part 422 Subpart M (42 C.F.R. §§ 422.619 et seq.)]

Q 13:82 What is "expedited review" for Medicare Advantage beneficiaries?

Medicare Advantage beneficiaries have an additional right to request an "expedited" (within 72 hours) decision when asking for reconsideration. In order for a beneficiary to request an expedited review, the beneficiary must have received notice that: (1) a provider intends to terminate services and a physician must certify that termination of services is likely to place the beneficiary's health at significant risk; or (2) the provider intends to discharge the beneficiary from an inpatient provider setting. If the response is unfavorable, the beneficiary can still pursue review applying the traditional claims periods.

Q 13:83 What general principles should be applied when evaluating a possible Medicare appeal?

In deciding whether a Medicare appeal makes sense, the practitioner will of course consider whether there is a legal basis for the appeal, carefully applying the regulations and being conscious that they are frequently misapplied by providers and intermediaries. Assuming a good claim, however, the usual anxiety about cost should be offset by the high success rate for appeals that has historically resulted from the following general principles the administrative judge will apply:

1. As with other Social Security Act cases, Medicare law views the patient's treating physician as the person best able to determine what care the patient needs. The rule that has been adopted by one circuit court, the Second Circuit Court of Appeals, is that "dual certification" as to the need for treatment, by the treating physician and the utilization review committee (a/k/a peer review organization) can only be challenged by CMS if there is "substantial evidence" to the contrary. [State of New York o/b/o Bodnar v. Secretary of Health and Human Services, 903 F.2d 122 (2d Cir. 1990); Schisler v. Heckler, 787 F.2d 76, 81 (2d Cir. 1986)] "The opinion of a non-examining doctor by itself cannot constitute the contrary substantial evidence required to override the treating physician's diagnosis." [Hidalgo v. Bowen, 822 F.2d 294, 296-297 (2d Cir. 1987) (SSI eligibility); see also, e.g., State of New York o/b/o Holland v. Secretary of Health and Human Services, 927 F.2d 57 (2d Cir. 1991); State of New York o/b/o Stein v. Secretary of Health and Human Services, 924 F.2d 431 (2d Cir. 1991); Friedman v. Secretary of HHS, 819 F.2d 42 (2d Cir. 1987)]

2. Whenever there is some doubt as to whether coverage should be extended, the patient should always get the benefit of the doubt. The courts have consistently ruled that the coverage standards set by Congress are to be liberally construed and broadly applied to ensure that the elderly and disabled receive the health care services they need. [See, e.g., Rosenberg v. Richardson, 538 F.2d 487, 490 (2d Cir. 1976); Herbst v. Finch, 473 F.2d 771, 775 (2d Cir. 1972); Haberman v. Finch, 473 F.2d 664, 666 (2d Cir. 1969)] The Courts have also stated that the policy underlying the Act requires a liberal interpretation, and that any doubts should be resolved in favor of coverage. [See, e.g., Herbst v. Finch, 473 F.2d 771, 775 (2d Cir. 1972)] Exclusions from coverage should be narrowly construed lest they inadvertently encompass the qualifications for benefits. [Coe v. Secretary of HEW, 502 F.2d 1337, 1340 (4th Cir. 1974)]

3. Administrative Law Judges are supposedly not affected by political shifts and pressures. They look exclusively to the law and the regulations in deciding cases.

The unknown factor is the switch from Social Security Administration administrative law judges to Department of Health and Human

Services administrative law judges. Certainly, one reason for the switch was the Administration's concern that too many appeals were being granted. The switch is being phased in, and it remains to be seen whether the change will make a difference in outcomes. It has already created a completely different forum for appeals: these are now heard by video teleconferences in which the appellant sits in a Kinko's Copy Center (really) and the judge is located in one of four centralized Health and Human Services hearing offices. Attorneys have already reported poor technology quality and a complete lack of the face-to-face advocacy that historically had resulted in many successful appeals.

Health Insurance Other than Medicare

Q 13:83.1 For aging clients not yet eligible for Medicare, what options are available to meet health care expenses?

The elderly client under age 65 may find himself or herself a victim of the marketplace: ineligible for state-sponsored medical insurance, and unable to pay the high premiums of private health insurance. There are essentially three options available: (1) employer-provided benefits for retirees and their dependents; (2) rights to continue health coverage maintained during employment, under COBRA; and (3) private insurance that may be available, albeit at high cost, under state-run insurance programs known as "health reinsurance" plans for the uninsurable.

Q 13:83.2 Are employers required to provide health insurance to retirees?

No. That is, nothing in federal law requires such coverage. Unionized employees may be entitled to coverage pursuant to a collective bargaining agreement, and state laws may require continued coverage for state employees who retire.

Q 13:83.3 If employers do provide health insurance to retirees, may they deny or limit coverage to older retirees?

Yes and no. They cannot discriminate solely on the basis of age; however, the EEOC currently takes the position that they may decline to offer retirees eligible for Medicare the same benefits offered to non-eligible retirees. That is, they may essentially "wrap around" Medicare with a supplemental policy only, if they so choose. [See further discussion in chapter 20, at SQ 20:28.2]

Q 13:83.4   What are a retiree's rights to maintain health insurance under COBRA?

COBRA, shorthand for the Consolidated Omnibus Budget Reconciliation Act of 1985, allows eligible workers, their spouses, and their dependents to maintain previously existing health coverage for a period of time following certain "triggering events," provided, however, they pay all of the premium. They cannot "pick and choose" benefits, opting for hospitalization only and declining to pay for the broader coverage an employer may have been paying for directly. (However, employers can—but are not required to—give individuals the option of dropping "noncore" benefits, such as dental insurance, or coverage for vision care.) Thus, this possibility may be of limited utility for the disabled or retired worker, not yet eligible for Medicare, with limited funds to pay the high premiums. On the other hand, with limited options available, it can be an important tool and elder law attorneys should be familiar both with the essential components of COBRA, with the local state's parallel "mini-COBRA" provisions—and with the provisions of the Health Insurance Portability and Accountability Act of 1986 that relate to insurance portability. These rules can allow a disabled older person to bridge the gap between employer-sponsored insurance and eventual Medicare coverage.

COBRA rights arise ONLY with respect to group coverage. Continuation rights are available for employees or former employees (retirees) in private business, their spouses (or former spouse), and dependent children. Each eligible person can independently elect to continue under COBRA: even if the worker chooses not to continue (perhaps due to eligibility under Medicare or Medicaid), his or her dependents, spouse, and former spouse can make a COBRA election to continue.

Depending upon who is electing continuation under COBRA, the period of time health insurance may be maintained will vary.

Qualifying Event	Eligible person electing coverage	Maximum period of time to continue coverage
Termination of job or resignation, reduced hours	Employee, Spouse, and Dependent Child	18 months (up to 29 months if eligible for Social Security Disability on account of disability that began within 60 days of termination and provide letter to employer)
Employee entitled to Medicare: Divorce or legal separation, death of employee	Spouse (or ex-spouse), Dependent Child	36 months
Loss of "dependent child" (e.g., marriage; age)	Dependent Child (formerly)	36 months status

Typically, the "event" is computed not as of the date of the event itself but as of the date that coverage would otherwise cease. In other words, for the employee who separates from service on January 16, 2007, if through payroll deduction he or she has paid in for health insurance through January 31, 2007, the start of the 18 months will be February 1st, not January 16th. How to know for sure? Employees or others losing coverage *must* retain the certificate of insurance issued to those whose coverage terminates, and the date on that form will be the "event" date.

Coverage under COBRA terminates when a person who does not yet receive Medicare becomes eligible for Medicare coverage. Thus, a spouse of a person eligible for Medicare may be the true beneficiary of COBRA's continuation features. However, a disabled person who receives Medicare prior to commencement of COBRA does not forfeit COBRA, and may retain both.

The employee, spouse, and children will have 60 days to decide whether to buy COBRA coverage. When an employee terminates employment, it is the employer's "plan administrator" who must inform the employee of this right; for other triggering events, the affected person will have the responsibility of contacting the plan himself or herself. COBRA coverage, even if elected on the 59th day, will be retroactive to the date benefits otherwise terminated. Note that if COBRA benefits are waived, and within 60 days the decision is changed, medical expenses incurred in the interim will NOT be covered. Thus, as a practical matter, if one considers not electing to continue COBRA coverage, it makes sense to defer notifying the plan administrator of that decision until the last possible moment.

COBRA is a federal law that applies only to employers with 20 or more employees. Fortunately, many states have "mini-COBRA" plans that apply COBRA requirements to smaller companies. As of October, 2002, at least 38 states applied such rules to companies with two or more employees, for continuation periods varying from one month to the full COBRA period of coverage.

As the next question explains, it may be important to exercise COBRA rights in order to maintain the HIPAA portability prohibitions on noncoverage for pre-existing conditions.

Q 13:83.5 How does HIPAA combine with COBRA to provide coverage for pre-existing conditions?

HIPAA, the Health Insurance Portability and Accountability Act of 1996. is now best known for its privacy provisions, but one of its most important features is the rule limiting the extent to which group insurance plans can refuse to cover participants with respect to expenses caused by "pre-existing conditions." Since COBRA allows a terminated employee— or spouse or dependent—to continue group coverage, COBRA can keep coverage going until new group coverage can be accessed, including a state-sponsored plan for the uninsurable.

If an individual has had "creditable" health insurance for 12 straight months, with no lapse in coverage of 63 days or more, and then obtains new group insurance, the new group health plan cannot invoke the pre-existing condition exclusion at all. "Creditable" coverage includes coverage under, among others: (1) a group policy; (2) Medicare; (3) Medicaid; (4) military health insurance, Indian Health Service coverage, federal employees coverage, etc.; and (5) state high-risk pools. With less creditable coverage, the new plan can restrict coverage related to pre-existing conditions, but in most cases, only up to 12 months, with credit for "time served"—for months of creditable coverage in the prior plan. Participants leaving a plan must obtain a written "certificate of creditable coverage" as proof of prior coverage, in order to protect their rights.

HIPAA applies to every employer group health plan that has at least two participants who are current employees—even self-insured plans. Like COBRA, some states have gone so far as to extend HIPAA's rules to even single-participant plans. HIPAA also applies for those switching to individual coverage who have 18 months of prior creditable coverage— but a future switch to another policy will not carry with it HIPAA rights, which apply only when leaving a group policy. For individuals to qualify, they must not be eligible for group coverage, Medicare or Medicaid, and must have used and exhausted any prior COBRA rights.

Q 13:83.6   How do employee coverage, COBRA, and Medicare relate to each other when a person retires due to disability?

Suppose an individual is injured and goes "on disability" under an employer's disability insurance plan. (S)he will typically remain insured under the employer's employee insurance plan. If the plan will apply to the individual indefinitely, without any cutoff point, it may be preferable not to qualify for Medicare if the plan converts to a supplement for Medicare-eligible employees or dependents. (This isn't usually an option, as the employer will likely require the employee to apply for Social Security so that it can offset any disability benefit being paid out.) If, however, the individual will lose eligibility as an "employee" after a certain point in time—if (s)he will be "terminated" as an employee for reasons of disability—it will be advantageous to apply for Social Security as early as possible so that Medicare coverage starts before termination. Why? Termination will trigger the employee's COBRA rights to continue coverage ... except that the COBRA right will terminate if the employee subsequently qualifies for Medicare. If, on the other hand, the employee has already qualified for Medicare (after 24 months of eligibility for Social Security Disability), (s)he may keep COBRA and Medicare, with Medicare as primary payor. Depending on the situation and the cost of the employer coverage, it may be preferable to continue COBRA as long as possible and thus, important to qualify for Medicare as early as possible.

Q 13:83.7   Aside from group health plans, how can an older, unhealthy individual obtain health insurance?

Many states have created "high-risk" pools for the otherwise "uninsurable," including those with pre-existing conditions for which HIPAA provides no relief. Pools have no underwriting—they have to accept anyone who applies—but they also have high cost, sometimes up to

200 percent of private pay rates otherwise available to those less hard to insure. Individuals eligible for assistance from other programs like COBRA, Medicaid or Medicare generally cannot access high-risk pools. Some states, such as Vermont, Massachusetts, Maine, and now California, are now developing Medicaid "buy-ins" or other state-sponsored "universal coverage" plans that may provide further relief. Contact the state insurance department for information about that state's high-risk pool. Also, veterans and military retirees may have their own health coverage through CHAMPVA or TRICARE (see chapter 16).

Practice-Related Issues

Q 13:85   What kinds of Medicare and health insurance problems might an elder law attorney encounter?

Following are situations an attorney might typically encounter in an elder law practice: (1) conflicting information about the availability of Medicare coverage, (2) questions about the sufficiency of Medicare long-term care benefits, (3) determining whether Medigap coverage or a Medicare HMO is more appropriate for an elderly client, and (4) advising a client on maintaining health insurance prior to Medicare eligibility.

1. *Transfer of Medicare patient.* Mrs. Jones's daughter complains of the treatment her mother has received since her hospitalization for a fractured hip. First, she says, the hospital insisted on discharging Mrs. Jones to a nursing home before her condition was stabilized, telling her that Mrs. Jones would qualify for 100 days of Medicare coverage in the nursing home. Today (10 days after she was placed at the facility) the nursing home has informed her that her mother no longer qualifies for Medicare coverage and that she will have to begin paying $200 per day as a private patient or move out of the SNF. She wants to know what she can do about the treatment her mother has received.

   Medicare's 100-day SNF benefit is not limited to patients who will "improve," but is available whenever they can benefit from skilled therapy—which includes services to "prevent further deterioration or preserve current capabilities." Apparently the therapist has decided that Mrs. Jones is not "improving," and has overlooked this basis for continuing therapy. One immediate step the daughter can take is to ask the physician to renew the request for therapy.

The nursing home's determination can only be guessed at, however, because no formal notice has been provided and Mrs. Jones's daughter may not have complete or accurate information. The first step should be to demand a written determination of Mrs. Jones's eligibility for Medicare coverage. Because facilities frequently do not provide written notices, the mere request may buy some time for Mrs. Jones, even if only another day of coverage. Once written notice has been received (and reviewed for compliance with the statutory requirements), the denial of coverage can be appealed: Nursing notes, family information, and second medical opinions could be sought to buttress the argument that Mrs. Jones continues to improve or will deteriorate if therapy is not continued. Even if the appeal is unsuccessful Mrs. Jones will probably have gained another day or two of Medicare coverage while the reconsideration is completed.

An important practical problem at this juncture may be the difficulties for Mrs. Jones's daughter to obtain medical records. The law restricts access to medical records to the patient and certain designated individuals. If Mrs. Jones's daughter is not authorized by an advance directive or durable power of attorney to obtain the records, she may have to be appointed conservator or guardian in order to get the facility to release the records. Moreover, even with appropriate authorization, release of the records may take time, often 30 days or more.

Meanwhile, Mrs. Jones's daughter may want to look into suitable placement in an adult care facility or other appropriate institution. Costs should be lower and Mrs. Jones may be able to get by with the lower level of care. Alternatively, Mrs. Jones's assets could be used for continued private care at the SNF, or she may qualify for Medicaid long-term care coverage.

2. *Advising clients on long-term care needs and alternatives.* A married couple consults the attorney about the possibility that one or both might require expensive medical care in the future. Both are in their mid-60s, and they understand that they have both hospitalization and long-term care benefits available through Medicare. They wonder if they need to do anything else.

Although Medicare's hospitalization benefit is significant, the long-term care benefit is woefully inadequate. If this couple has any assets to protect, or any desire to remain out of the welfare-oriented Medicaid program, they should seriously consider long-term care insurance. Such insurance is likely to be both available and reasonably priced at their current (relatively young) age, but will become increasingly expensive if they wait to secure their initial coverage.

In addition, they almost certainly will want to look into purchasing a Medigap policy if they have not already done so. If either is within six months of his or her 65th birthday, or if the first Medicare Part B application has been made within the last six months, the Medigap insurer must accept that spouse regardless of medical condition. They need good advice to help select from the various plan options, competing policies from different insurers, and to decide whether to choose an age-rated premium structure.

3. *Advising about Medicare Advantage.* A client wonders whether to switch from traditional Medicare (plus the Medigap policy he or she currently holds, which costs nearly $200 per month) to a Medicare HMO.

The client should expect several benefits from a switch, including simplicity (no more forms to understand, file, and monitor), better coverage for preventive care, and additional benefits. The HMO might, for example, offer a partial prescription program, or a program that resembles the client's prior Medigap policy but with much lower premium costs. In addition, the cost of the coverage will likely be reduced, especially in light of the expensive Medigap policy held by the client.

On the other hand, several cautions must be voiced. Recently there has been outcry by HMO patients complaining of pressures brought to bear by the HMOs to reduce benefits, by forcing patients to accept discharge or by providing insufficient care. After the initial enthusiasm for Medicare HMOs in some areas (and particularly in rural areas), many plans have left the field; if the Medicare beneficiary gives up Medigap coverage and stays on the Medicare HMO for more than 12 months, it may be expensive to secure replacement Medigap coverage if he or she later decides voluntarily to leave the HMO. The likely use of the other benefits offered by the HMO, such as transportation (it may be a critical issue, or it may be relatively unimportant) and prescription drug coverage (although it sounds good, it may be a limited benefit) should be evaluated realistically. The client should consider that such benefits have been reduced or eliminated in many

Medicare HMOs after enrolling new patients. Perhaps most importantly, the client must recognize that he or she will forgo the freedom to choose his or her own physician if he or she joins the HMO plan and accepts its list of primary care physicians.

4. *Advising about health insurance and maintaining coverage.* Mr. Smith, age sixty, has a stroke and is no longer able to work. His employer provides some disability benefits, and Mr. Smith has private disability insurance coverage, but his employer does not offer health insurance coverage for retirees, including those on disability. What should he do?

Mr. Smith should apply for Social Security Disability benefits, even if his disability insurance payments will be offset by Social Security payments. This is so that he will be eligible for Medicare coverage after 24 months of eligibility for coverage (and Social Security Disability benefits themselves will have a waiting period—see chapter 15). In the meantime, Mr. Smith can elect to continue his existing coverage under COBRA, although he will have to pay a high premium. Since COBRA coverage will only last 18 months, Mr. Smith may need to obtain coverage from the state high-risk pool until his Medicare eligibility begins. HIPAA will ensure that his stroke-related expenses will be covered despite the fact that he has a pre-existing condition. If, however, Mr. Smith declines to elect to continue coverage under COBRA, he will be effectively unable to obtain coverage for his stroke-related expenses probably until he becomes eligible for Medicare.

Q 13:85.1   What should the practitioner do to ensure that his or her advice to the client sufficiently addresses Medicare and insurance issues?

With the wide variety of coverages for medical services, nursing home care and the like, many clients do not understand the scope and extent of their Medicare, supplemental, and Part D coverage. With medical insurance, unlike long-term health insurance, many clients do not have or cannot locate copies of their policies. Given that choices made in disregard of medical insurance coverage may have serious financial repercussions, the careful practitioner may wish to verify coverage in order to give accurate advice. For example, Medicare Advantage coverage may indicate a more limited choice of nursing homes to those on the company's preferred list, while Medicare A or B supplemental insurance may indicate financial exposure from day 21 of a nursing home stay onwards (pro: penalty period may begin to run; con: up to $9,950 in copayments for 100-day stay, which must be paid for in a timely fashion). Since the enactment of the health privacy laws commonly known as HIPAA, insurers will generally refuse to provide information without a signed authorization or release form on file, so it would be prudent for the elder law practitioner to obtain a HIPAA release from the client at the earliest opportunity. Ideally, the release will specifically identify by name the client's insurance carriers and health care providers; provide the client's name, date of birth, and Social Security number; and will be signed by the client (or agent) with a witness. The form should specify a termination date for the authorization. In addition, a special authorization form may be obtained from the Centers for Medicare and Medicaid so that the attorney can communicate with CMS concerning Medicare coverage issues.

Chapter 14

Medicaid Benefits

The federal-state partnership program known as Medicaid pays for about half of formal long-term care costs in America—though most calculations indicate that informal, unpaid family caretakers provide far more care. Seniors receive most of their general medical care through the similarly named (but quite different) Medicare program, but Medicaid is a critical part of the safety net for seniors who confront the possibility of long-term nursing care.

Because Medicaid eligibility is based on both medical and financial need, qualifying for the program's benefits can be difficult. In fact, the rules and regulations governing Medicaid eligibility are bewilderingly complicated, and far beyond the ability of most seniors to navigate unaided. Medicaid eligibility planning is a core element of many elder law practices. This chapter discusses Medicaid eligibility requirements including income and resource eligibility, the minimum monthly maintenance needs allowance, the community spouse resource allowance, spending down assets, the look-back period for the transfer of assets, asset transfer strategies, Medicaid trusts, and estate recovery.

The 2006 adoption of the Deficit Reduction Act of 2005 dramatically altered the landscape for families and individuals trying to plan for long-term care needs [see SQ 14:10.3]. Many of the principles and planning options available before the new law remain viable, however; others have become less attractive but still appropriate in some circumstances, and a handful may have become more attractive with the adoption of the new law.

Overview

Q 14:1   What is the Medicaid program?

Medicaid is a federal-state partnership welfare program, begun in 1965, to provide medical care to the elderly, blind, and disabled poor. Medicaid benefits include acute medical care, outpatient treatment, medications, and long-term skilled nursing care. Increasingly, state programs are also incorporating long-term custodial care in adult care homes, assisted living facilities, and other venues outside the traditional nursing home setting.

Because most elderly citizens are covered by Medicare for inpatient and outpatient care, the Medicaid program's importance for the elderly lies primarily in the two benefits it provides that are not fully covered by Medicare: long-term care and (even after the adoption of a prescription drug benefit as part of Medicare) medications. Unlike Medicare, which operates as an insurance program, Medicaid is designed as a welfare program with eligibility based on financial need, so that not all elderly, blind, or disabled citizens qualify for Medicaid benefits.

Q 14:2 Where is Medicaid law found?

Federal law establishes the Medicaid program and dictates what provisions must be included in state Medicaid programs. Most of the federal statutes are found at 42 United States Code (U.S.C.) Sections 1396 et seq., also known as Title XIX of the Social Security Act. The Supplemental Security Income (SSI) program eligibility rules, on which Medicaid eligibility rules are based, are found at 42 U.S.C. § 1382. In February 2006, major changes were made to the Medicaid laws in the Deficit Reduction Act of 2005. Some key provisions:

- 42 U.S.C. § 1382b (Assets; part of SSI law)
- 42 U.S.C. § 1396 (Nursing homes)
- 42 U.S.C. § 1396p (Liens and transfers) (and particularly 42 U.S.C. § 1396p(c)(1), the new language of the Deficit Reduction Act of 2005 which modifies the lookback period and methods of calculating disqualification periods for transfers)
- 42 U.S.C. § 1396k (Assignment of rights)
- 42 U.S.C. § 1396r (MCCA, including spousal impoverishment rules for income and assets)

The Centers for Medicare and Medicaid also issue regulations implementing these statutes, although as of this writing, regulations to implement the changes in the Deficit Reduction Act have not yet been drafted, and some published regulations may now have been rendered obsolete. Nevertheless, it is important to know where regulations may be found, as much is still unchanged. These include:

- 42 C.F.R. Part 431 (Fair hearings)
- 42 C.F.R. Part 435 (Medicaid eligibility)
- 42 C.F.R. Part 483 (Nursing home requirements)

The Centers for Medicare and Medicaid interpretations of this law as in effect prior to February 2006 can be found in the "State Medicaid Manual," a paper-based manual which is nonetheless available online (navigate to *http://www.cms.hhs.gov/Manuals/PBM/list.asp* and look for Publication #45). This manual, intended to provide a source of interpretive guidance to state Medicaid agencies, can be very helpful, particularly sections 3257 through 3259, also known as "Transmittal 64," which address the transfer and trust provisions of the Omnibus Budget Reduction Act of 1993 (OBRA '93). (These provisions can also be viewed online at *http://www.sharinglaw.net/elder/Transmittal64.htm.*) However, not all states, particularly 209(b) states, follow the CMS interpretations, and at best these can only provide general guidance and perhaps a useful reference in a lawsuit; moreover, major changes enacted by the Deficit Reduction Act may be inconsistent with the manual in some instances, particularly with regard to transfers of assets.

In addition, in July 2006 CMS issued "Guidance Letters to State Medicaid Directors," which may be found on the CMS website at *http://www.cms.hhs.gov/SMDL/SMD/list.asp*, concerning implementation of the Deficit Reduction Act. Of particular interest to elder law practitioners is SMDL 06-018, dated July 27, 2006, and titled "Transfers of assets," and its Enclosures (online at *http://www.cms.hhs.gov/smdl/downloads/SMD072706b.pdf*).

Finally, of great importance in "SSI states" (see SQ 14:19) is the Social Security Administration Program Operations Manual System, or POMS. Formerly available only at Social Security Administration offices or, later on, by purchased computer disk, the POMS is now easily available and searchable online at *https://secure.ssa.gov/apps10/poms.nsf/partlist*.

As a practical, day-to-day matter, most essential for an elder law practice is an understanding of the particular state's own Medicaid program as the state itself interprets it; even with the enactment of the Deficit Reduction Act, state implementation will be critically important in light of the Act's ambiguities. The true working of the state program can only be understood through review of state regulations. The beginning elder law practitioner can expect to spend months if not years in becoming familiar with these provisions. In this area above all others it can be important to find a local mentor to provide quick answers and guidance, or to participate in a discussion group. It is also particularly important to stay abreast of current developments, as the enactment of the Deficit Reduction Act points out.

Q 14:3   Who operates the Medicaid program?

Medicaid is a federal-state cooperative program. Funding for Medicaid benefits comes from both federal and state governments (and, in at least some states, from local government as well). Each state's share of the Medicaid cost varies; in 2007, for example, Mississippi paid just 24.11% of the total Medicaid cost, while twelve states split the cost equally with the federal government. By law, the federal contribution to Medicaid in each state may not be less than 50% nor more than 83% (see *Brief Summaries of Medicare and Medicaid as of November 1, 2007*, prepared by the Office of the Actuary at CMS and online at *http://www.cms.hhs.gov/MedicareProgramRatesStats/downloads/Medicare-MedicaidSummaries2007.pdf*). Eligibility and administration of each state's Medicaid program, however, are handled by the state government, subject to the oversight of the federal Centers for Medicare and Medicaid Services (CMS) (formerly the Health Care Financing Administration, or HCFA; references to "Transmittals" may be given as HCFA Transmittals if issued while the agency was named HCFA). Each state is required to adopt a plan for the administration of Medicaid benefits; the plan must comply with federal minimum requirements. Each state:

1. Establishes its own eligibility standards;
2. Determines the type, amount, duration, and scope of services;
3. Sets the rate of payment for services; and
4. Administers its own program.

To the confusion of consumers, several states have adopted plans that rename Medicaid. Consequently, for example, California residents may erroneously believe that "Medi-Cal" is fundamentally different from Medicaid. Similarly, Tennessee recipients may be more familiar with "TennCare" and Arizona residents with "AHCCCS" (pronounced "access," and standing for the Arizona Health Care Cost Containment System).

Q 14:4 What agencies administer the Medicaid program on the state level?

Each state designates an agency to administer the Medicaid program. In most states, the same agency establishes eligibility rules, administers eligibility determinations, and directs the provision of services. The state agency is often the "Department of Health and Human Services," "Department of Social Services," or some variant; in some states, the state agency includes "Medicaid" in its name.

Q 14:5 What is the difference between Medicaid and Medicare?

Medicaid is a medical welfare benefit. Consequently, participants must be able to show that they qualify for the program financially (as well as meeting other eligibility criteria). Once established, financial eligibility for Medicaid benefits must be reviewed periodically (normally on an annual review cycle). Unlike Medicare, Medicaid generally does not require copayments or deductibles, although some states have begun to include drug copayments and other cost-saving measures as a response to budgetary constraints. [42 U.S.C. § 1396o] Medicaid coverage is also broader, for the most part. Coverage for long-term care is not limited to a number of days, as it is for Medicare, but is provided indefinitely. Medicaid also provides full coverage for medical supplies, vision correction, dental surgery, and other items not covered by Medicare, and for some beneficiaries also pays premiums, copayments, and deductibles for Medicare Part D drug coverage.

Medicare, on the other hand, is a medical insurance program provided for the blind, disabled, and aged, with no financial eligibility requirements whatsoever, although the prescription drug benefit has some differences of application depending upon the income and assets of the member, and beginning in 2007, participants' premiums may differ to some degree based on need. Medicare eligibility is automatically extended to those over age 65 who are eligible to receive Social Security retirement benefits (even though the beneficiary may elect to defer retirement and the right to receive benefits), as well as to those who have received Social Security Disability Insurance (SSDI) benefits for at least 24 months. Even though a Social Security beneficiary may choose to retire earlier than age 65 (and accept a reduced benefit), he or she will not qualify for Medicare coverage until age 65. (See chapter 13 for a detailed discussion of Medicare.) Unlike Medicaid, Medicare does not provide coverage for "custodial" care or other long-term care benefits for an indefinite period. Instead, Medicare provides only a limited benefit for skilled nursing care for a limited period of time. [42 U.S.C. § 1395d]

Q 14:6 What is the difference between long-term care and general medical care under Medicaid?

Medicaid eligibility may cover acute (inpatient) care, regular doctor and clinic visits (outpatient), long-term nursing care, mental health services, and care and treatment of the developmentally disabled. While many elder law practitioners also assist those with disabilities and may have to become familiar with the mental health and developmental disability care systems, the most important distinction, from a strictly elder law perspective, is usually between general Medicaid coverage and Medicaid subsidies of long-term care.

Long-term care may be provided in a wide variety of settings. (See chapter 11 for a discussion of long-term care options.) Patients may require institutionalization in a nursing home, or may be able to stay in an adult care facility (such as a boarding home, adult foster home, or adult care home), a congregate living arrangement (such as assisted living, supportive living, or communal apartments), or even at home. Medicaid coverage may provide assistance in any of these settings, depending upon a state's particular medical assistance plan.

In the vast majority of Medicaid cases in most jurisdictions, however, care is still provided in a nursing home setting. Most of the rules of eligibility and care are predicated on nursing home placement, and the eligibility workers, social workers, and medical providers in the state's Medicaid program will usually be focused on institutional placement. It is important to remember (and to remind clients) that home-based and community-based alternatives are available, and to explore appropriate placements even in the Medicaid long-term care arena. Increasingly, Medicaid agencies are recognizing that it may be possible to cut state costs by better arrangements for providing care at home or in an assisted living environment, and in some cases are being forced to do so in order to comply with the "least restrictive alternative" requirement of the *Olmstead* decision. [Olmstead v. Zimring, 527 U.S. 581 (1999)]

Q 14:7   What care is covered by Medicaid's long-term care benefit?

Federal law requires the states to provide certain minimum benefits. [42 U.S.C. §§ 1396a(a)(10)(A), 1396d(1)(a)] The states can, however, provide additional coverage. While eligibility and the scope of coverage are determined by the states, subject to federal parameters, nursing home care for individuals over age 21 is a mandatory Medicaid benefit. States may extend long-term coverage to other individuals (see Qs 14:17, 14:18). Long-term care may include nursing home care, assisted living, or even in-home care

Q 14:8   Are there any gaps in Medicaid coverage for seniors?

Yes, and these are growing as budget cutting fervor increases. A survey by the Kaiser Family Foundation, "State Budgets Under Stress: How are States Planning to Reduce the Growth in Medicaid Costs?," reports that 41 states have plans to reduce Medicaid spending, including through benefit reduction. Major drawbacks to Medicaid include:

- In general, Medicaid beneficiaries may be required to transfer out of a private room unless medically contraindicated.

- In many states, a skilled nursing facility that participates in the Medicaid program and has met a specific quota of beds occupied by Medicaid recipients is permitted to pass over Medicaid-eligible applicants in favor of private pay applicants.
- Regular Medicaid now largely requires the use of managed care plans; 58 percent of Medicaid recipients now receive managed care and are limited in choices. Moreover, even for those not in managed care, many physicians may not participate in the Medicaid program.
- Services for dental, eye, ear, and foot care are limited (as discussed below); Medical devices, prostheses, and equipment such as wheelchairs and hearing aides, are generally inexpensive and not "top of the line."
- Medicaid does not cover over-the-counter items that may be essential to a client's well-being, such as incontinence products.

Certain "options" not required to be included in state medical assistance plans, such as dental coverage, are either being cut back or eliminated. Idaho and Missouri are two states that have dropped dental care from its Medicaid program for beneficiaries over age 21, except for emergencies (such as potentially life-threatening infections.) Instead of providing dentures, nursing homes will simply grind the food. Even if dental care is included in the Medicaid plan, few dentists may participate. Nursing homes required to provide dental care may be unable to find Medicaid-participating dentists willing to make "house calls" to the nursing home or otherwise accept Medicaid for a private visit by the patient.

Adequate eye care, hearing care, and access to speech technology are also weak in many areas. For example, Missouri has stopped providing glasses to adult Medicaid beneficiaries. There may be reductions in other areas as well. In Arkansas, physical therapy is not provided to those over age 18. In 2004, 21 states either reduced or restricted Medicaid, and 14 more states were slated to make further restrictions in 2005.

Q 14:9 What is a Medicaid "waiver"?

States may apply to the Centers for Medicare and Medicaid for a "waiver" from the requirements of certain provisions of the Medicaid program. In some instances these waivers have permitted states to expand benefits under Medicaid and close some of the aforementioned "gaps." In other instances, the reverse is true.

While there are various waiver provisions in the Social Security Act, including the waiver authorizing home and community-based services, under 42 U.S.C. § 1396n, the provision with the broadest possibilities is Section 1115 (42 U.S.C. § 1315). This section permits waivers from Medicaid rules in order to carry out "demonstration projects" or "experimental, pilot, or demonstration project(s) which, in the judgment of the Secretary, (are) likely to assist in promoting the objectives of (the Medicaid statute)"; in other words, to act as a laboratory. The provision was really intended to provide a means by which states might expand coverage if they could show that a change would be cost-effective; the Center for Medicare and Medicaid website states that "the authority provides flexibility, under the Secretary's discretion, for the provision of services which are not otherwise matchable, allows for the expansion of eligibility for those who would otherwise not be eligible for the Medicaid program." Most waiver programs follow this approach, and can be reviewed on the Centers for Medicare and Medicaid website at *http://www.cms.gov/medicaid/waivers/*. Home care and other programs are often approved through the waiver process. More recently, however, states have been seeking waivers to the spousal protection or other eligibility rules. In 2002–2006, many states filed waiver requests designed to tighten eligibility requirements enormously. Although some were withdrawn by the states or denied, the federal response was to include similar provisions in the Deficit Reduction Act of 2005, signed into law February 8, 2006.

Q 14:10.1 What is MCCA?

"MCCA" (pronounced "mecca") means the Medicare Catastrophic Coverage Act of 1988 (MCCA), which enacted 42 U.S.C. § 1396r-5, containing the "spousal impoverishment" provisions of Medicaid law intended to protect spouses from "impoverishment" by entitling them to a minimum monthly needs allowance and a community spouse resource allowance, as well as their own income.

Q 14:10.2 What does OBRA '93 mean?

"OBRA '93" means the Omnibus Budget Reconciliation Act of 1993, which extended the "look-back period" during which transfers of assets may affect eligibility for benefits and removed the cap on the resulting "penalty period," tightened the rules applicable to trusts established by applicants and their spouses, and also created categories of "payback" trusts for disabled individuals permitting assets to be set aside without counting for Medicaid eligibility purposes; these provisions are primarily included in 42 U.S.C. § 1396p.

Q 14:10.3 What effect does the Deficit Reduction Act of 2005 have on Medicaid and planning for long-term care?

The "Deficit Reduction Act of 2005" (sometimes simply "DRA" or "DRA 2005"), signed into law February 8, 2006, contained sweeping changes to the way Medicaid law deals with transfers made by applicants for benefits or their spouses, treatment of homes, annuities, and other techniques, and which mandated how a spouse's "minimum monthly needs allowance" may be satisfied. The effects of the DRA are widespread, and more fully described in context elsewhere in this Chapter. In general terms, however, the DRA made changes in the following areas:

1. The "look-back" period for transfers by a Medicaid applicant, or the applicant's spouse on or after February 8, 2006, was extended from 36 months (in most cases) to 5 years in every instance.

2. The starting date for penalty periods imposed by transfers was moved from the date of the transfer to the later date on which the Medicaid applicant would have been eligible but for the transfer penalty—in other words, to a date when the applicant is medically needy and has depleted assets to below the resource limits.

3. States must now impose partial-month periods of ineligibility for transfers without consideration (whereas under prior law states were permitted to round the penalty period down the nearest smaller whole-month period, and most states did adopt that methodology).

4. Transfers made during multiple months may now be treated as a single transfer, with the effect of the transfer being calculated on the date of the first transfer.

5. With certain exceptions, including annuitization of retirement assets, an annuity purchase will be treated as an uncompensated transfer unless the State is named as a remainder beneficiary at least to the extent of medical services provided to the institutionalized person; even if not named, pursuant to the DRA the State

will become a remainder beneficiary and will so notify the company. So-called "balloon annuities"—those providing for small payments for a period of years followed by a large payment just before the likely death of the annuitant—are disallowed, as all annuities must be actuarially sound and pay out in equal installments during the term of the annuity. As was the case in most states before the DRA, annuities must also be irrevocable and non-assignable. These changes will apply not only to existing annuities, but to those "annuity contracts" to which certain actions are taken after February 8, 2006, including particularly annuitization. [CMS Letter of Instruction SMDL 06-018]

6. Similarly, loans and mortgages must be actuarially sound (that is, have periodic payments designed to repay the loan over the actuarial life expectancy of the lender) and may not have any provision for cancellation of the debt on death of the lender.

7. Purchase of a life estate in another person's home will be treated as a transfer unless the purchaser lives in the home for at least one year after purchase—even if the purchase price was the full value of the life estate.

8. States must adopt an "income first" approach to calculating the community spouse's entitlement to additional income. In other words, the institutionalized spouse's retirement or annuity income must first be assigned to the community spouse before any effort can be made to increase the value of resources which may be retained by the community spouse.

9. Home equity is limited to $500,000 (or, at the election of the state, $750,000), so that any home with a higher equity will not be treated as an exempt resource (though this section will not apply if the applicant has a spouse or minor, blind, or disabled child living in the home). (The $500,000/$750,000 limits will increase annually, according to the Consumer Price Index, beginning in 2011.)

10. Continuing Care Retirement Communities (CCRCs) and "life care communities" may now require new residents to commit to use of disclosed assets for their future care (subject to spousal impoverishment protections for a CSRA). Initial payments to buy in to such facilities will now be considered available resources for Medicaid eligibility purposes to the extent that such payments are reimbursable on death or departure of the resident, unless the buy-in conveys an equity interest in the facility.

11. The four-state Long Term Care Partnership program has now been expanded to permit any state to offer the same types of policies that were previously available only in California, Connecticut, Indiana, and New York.

12. Existing mechanisms for establishing citizenship and identity have been restricted; generally speaking, an affidavit signed by a person claiming to know the citizenship status and identity of an applicant will no longer be sufficient. As rules have been circulated implementing this provision, the notion of an affidavit of some type has crept back into the mix, so it is not yet clear whether significant problems will arise. Note that this provision applies even to existing Medicaid recipients, who will be required to produce clear evidence of citizenship and identity at their next annual redetermination.

Q 14:10.4　Has the Deficit Reduction Act been amended since its enactment?

Yes. Section 405 of the Tax Relief and Health Care Act of 2006 amended the annuity provisions of the DRA [42 U.S.C. § 1396p(c)(1)(F)(i)] by substituting "institutionalized person" for "individual" with respect to whose expenses must be recoverable from an annuity in order for purchase of the annuity, during the look-back period, not to be considered a transfer. The change was made effective retroactively. In addition, CMS issued Letter of Instruction SMDL 06-018 "clarifying" some of the more obscure provisions of the DRA.

Q 14:10.5　Is the Deficit Reduction Act constitutional?

Yes. Subsequent to passage, the Act was challenged by various individuals and groups on the basis that the written versions of the legislation passed by House and Senate were not identical, due to a clerk's error, and that this was unconstitutional. The four challenges, all now defeated, are the following: (1) *Zeigler v. Gonzales* (S.D. Ala., Civ. Act. No. 06-0080-CG-M, June 28, 2007), brought by an individual attorney in Arizona; (2) *Public Citizen v. United States District Court for the District of Columbia*, _____ F.3d _____ (4th Cir. 2007), brought by the nonprofit group Public Citizen; (3) *One Simple Loan v. U.S. Secy. of Educ.* (S.D.N.Y., 06 Civ. 2979, June 9, 2006), brought by certain student loan funds affected by unrelated portions of the DRA; and (4) *Hon. John Conyers, Jr., et al. v. George W. Bush, et al.*, _____ F. Supp. _____

(E.D. Mich. 2006), brought by members of Congress. In general, the courts applied the "enrolled bill" doctrine to uphold the statute, basically saying that once the President had signed the bill, the fact that the two versions were not identical no longer mattered. Attorney Zeigler's case could theoretically be appealed further, but he is without resources to continue to pursue the case.

Q 14:11   Can anything be done when the state agency does not follow the federal rules for Medicaid?

As with other benefits programs, those denied benefits are entitled to an administrative hearing, which can then be appealed. [42 C.F.R. §§ 431.220 et seq.] In addition, the community spouse may request a hearing to argue the amount of his or her CSRA allocation. This takes time. For major systemic problems, federal court is often the answer. Practitioners may become frustrated when state agencies fail to issue regulations they are required to issue, apply standards that seem to violate the federal rules, or suddenly cut benefits without justification. Elder law attorneys have been forced to take a more active role in challenging these attempts in court. The consensus seems to be that action in federal court is the most likely to succeed; the trouble for clients is that the Eleventh Amendment precludes federal courts from awarding retroactive relief against a state (i.e., it isn't possible to get Medicaid granted retroactively). Nonetheless, injunctive relief may be available, and practices may be changed prospectively. Recently, the First Circuit Court of Appeals put its imprimatur on the proposition that a suit under 42 U.S.C. Section 1983 (for which attorneys' fees may be awarded) was available to compel compliance with Medicaid rules. [Rosie D. ex rel. John D. v. Swift, 310 F.3d 230 (1st Cir. 2002); another such case is Westside Mothers v. Haveman, 289 F.3d 852 (6th Cir. 2002)] In some instances, state court has provided injunctive relief, compelling the award of benefits [Blue v. Bonta, 121 Cal. Rptr. 2d 483 (Cal. App. 2002) (stairway lifts were covered as durable medical equipment)]; more recently, the Second Circuit approved Medicaid retroactive to date of application in the case of Morenz v. Wilson Coker. [see SQ 14:53.1]

Q 14:12   What Medicaid benefits are available to the working disabled?

As part of the Ticket to Work and Work Incentives Improvement Act of 1999, the federal government authorized states to establish plans that would allow those disabled individuals who had been receiving Medicaid to continue to receive Medicaid once they returned to work. This is accomplished by substantially raising the earned income and asset limits for such individuals. For example, Connecticut's program of "Medicaid for the Working Disabled" has an annual earned income limit of $75,000 and asset limit of $10,000, but with significant premium cost-sharing when income exceeds 200 percent of the federal poverty level.

Q 14:12.1   What is a "PCA waiver"?

Some states have applied for waivers to provide care to the disabled by way of "personal care assistants," individuals privately hired and supervised but paid through the Medicaid program, and who provide assistance with activities of daily living to disabled individuals.

Q 14:13   How does one apply for Medicaid?

Applications for Medicaid coverage are made to the appropriate state agency, and follow that state's procedures. It is vital for the elder law practitioner to become familiar with his or her state's own special procedures and policies; generalizations can be fatal. This is particularly difficult pending full implementation of the Deficit Reduction Act of 2005, as states scramble to adapt their own regulations and requirements to meet the eligibility restrictions in the Act. Generally, however, the applicant will be required to show (or have someone demonstrate on his or her behalf) citizenship and residence status, together with all of the financial information necessary to determine eligibility. In practice this means that the applicant or designee must produce a birth certificate, marriage license, spouse's death certificate, naturalization papers, military service records, utility bills, voter registration, and innumerable other documents before even getting to the financial information. Financial information may include current bank statements plus five years' worth of statements and check registers; copies of insurance policies including statements of value; copies of funeral contracts; real estate deeds; etc. Transactions that are questioned must be documented as well as simply explained, as transfers of assets will affect eligibility. Locating financial information can be difficult, particularly if statements have been lost or the applicant formerly lived in another state. Under the provisions of the Deficit Reduction Act of 2005, citizenship or residency must also be shown by specific documents; prior state practices of permitting an affidavit of citizenship will no longer suffice.

The entire process is usually daunting, particularly for the applicant (who is, remember, a candidate for nursing home assistance). The elderly spouse or distant children of the applicant may be only marginally better equipped to provide the details and follow-up required by the Medicaid agency.

Medicaid coverage can be retroactive to any or all of the three months prior to application, assuming that financial eligibility criteria were met at that time. [42 C.F.R. § 435.914] Although a decision regarding Medicaid eligibility must be made within 45 days of an application for the aged, applications are rarely processed this quickly. [42 C.F.R. § 435.911]

Timing can be very important. In some states, if the applicant meets the income and resource criteria by the last day of the month, Medicaid eligibility will be available for the entire month. This requires a rush to the agency office on the last day of the month to get the application in on time. This also means that assuming the applicant has in fact been financially eligible for not only that month, but the three prior months as well, and the nursing home is clamoring for payment, it may be critical to get the application in by the end of the fourth month in order that all four months, the application month and the prior three, be covered by Medicaid. If a family member has inadvisably agreed to pay for care, it will be a better use of time to get the application timely filed than to argue in court later about whether that agreement can stand.

Q 14:13.1   What does a resident (or family) have to pay while Medicaid is pending?

In general, a nursing home resident will have to pay the bulk of his or her income to the nursing home while Medicaid is pending. Called "applied income" in some states, it usually is computed as income minus "personal needs allowance" minus any medical insurance premiums. As to any balance for the private pay charges: there is still some uncertainty about whether or not a nursing home has the right to bill the resident (at private pay rates) while a Medicaid application is pending. A recent CMS transmittal seems to allow this practice. (See further SQ 11:36.2.) The common advice is that payment is not required, but that if the resident or family pays, and Medicaid is granted retroactively, the facility will be required to refund the entire amount paid, on the basis that Medicaid is the "sole source" of payment. (See SQ 11:36.3.) However, one state has taken the baffling view that this is not required.

[Keup v. Wisconsin Dep't of Health & Family Servs., 675 N.W.2d 755 (Wis. 2004)] If so, clients may be in a Catch-22. In a California case dragging on for over three years, that state's Court of Appeals took the state Medicaid agency to task for its failure to implement a system for repayment of Medicaid beneficiaries' expenditures during the eligibility application period, though it did observe that the reimbursement system, when adopted, might choose to reimburse patients for the Medicaid payment amount rather than the private-pay amount they actually expended. *Conlan v. Shewry*, 32 Cal. Rptr.3d 667 (Cal. App. 2005)

Q 14:14 Once Medicaid long-term care eligibility is established, does Medicaid pay for all the costs of long-term care?

While Medicaid pays for all of the costs of care, the patient is required to contribute some portion of that cost, sometimes referred to as "applied income" or the patient's "share of cost." For an unmarried patient, in fact, that contribution will be fixed at nearly all of the patient's income. Medicaid allows the patient to pay Medicare premiums from income (and in some states, supplemental or other health insurance premiums as well), to set aside income for a spouse if needed for that spouse to meet minimal income needs; and to retain a small "personal needs allowance" (the maximum amount of which varies from state to state, but which is usually less than $100), but requires that the balance be paid to the nursing home. Medicaid then pays the balance of the care costs that are not otherwise covered by Medicare—although Medicare is usually a "secondary payor," it pays before Medicaid benefits. A number of states fix the personal needs allowance at 15 percent of the maximum SSI benefit (in other words, $101.10 in 2009), while other states utilize a flat (and usually lower) amount—sometimes as low as $30 per month (the minimum level permitted by federal regulations). [42 C.F.R. § 435.725(c)(1)(i)] The personal needs allowance will be all that the resident retains to meet charges such as haircuts, incontinence supplies, telephone, and television. If the resident retains his or her home, the personal needs allowance will also be the only money available to pay upkeep, taxes, and utilities—unless the home is rented out, in which case any net rental income will be counted as income to the nursing home resident. More importantly, the personal needs allowance and the remaining small amount of resources will be all the resident retains in order to fill the "gaps" in Medicaid such as dental care, eyeglasses, decent hearing aids, and the like.

In general, Medicaid disregards any other obligations that the patient may have. Historically, this has also applied to alimony payments. While a court order of support for a spouse is apparently recognized by MCCA, the law is silent on support of an ex-spouse. In a potentially far-reaching decision, one state has declared that it would be arbitrary and capricious for a state to disregard the alimony obligation when computing applied income. [Mulder v. South Dakota Dep't of Social Servs., 2004 S.D. 10, 675 N.W.2d 212 (S.D. 2004)]

General Eligibility Requirements

Q 14:15 Who is covered by Medicaid?

Medicaid generally covers persons 65 and older, disabled persons, and blind persons whose income and available resources do not exceed a certain amount as set by federal law. [42 U.S.C. § 1396] All Medicaid programs (other than those in so-called 209(b) states, which apply similar but not identical criteria) must cover individuals receiving SSI (Supplemental Security Income) or TANF (Temporary Aid to Needy Families). This group of individuals is referred to as the "mandatory categorically needy." (Legislation known as the "Pickle amendment" permits those disabled persons who lose SSI because a SSD cost of living increase puts them over the SSI limit, will continue to keep Medicaid benefits; similar legislation permits those adult disabled children who lose SSI when a parent dies or retires and they become eligible for SSD, to keep Medicaid. [42 U.S.C. § 1364(c). See generally, POMS § SI 01715.015, "Special Groups of Former SSI Recipients"] In addition, the states also have the option of providing Medicaid coverage for other "categorically needy" groups (see SQ 14:17) and the medically needy (see SQ 14:18). Finally, a new program providing Medicaid to the Working Disabled allows disabled individuals to accumulate assets well above the usual limits and yet retain Medicaid benefits, subject to a buy-in. (see SQ 14:2)

Q 14:15.1 Does a person under 65 have to be found "disabled" by the Social Security Administration in order to qualify for Medicaid?

No. Under 42 C.F.R. § 435.541(d)(2), a state Medicaid agency "must make a determination of disability ... [i]n accordance with the requirements for evaluating that evidence under the SSI program specified in 20 C.F.R. 416.901 through 416.998." Many courts have held that the determination also must be made using the Social Security Administration's five-step criteria. [Sutherland v. North Dakota Dep't of Human Services, 2004 N.D. 212 (2004)]

Q 14:16 When are non-citizens eligible for Medicaid?

Full Medicaid coverage is available only to citizens and to "qualified aliens." Other aliens, who are not "qualified," are only eligible for emergency services. [Personal Responsibility and Work Opportunity Reconciliation Act of 1996; Pub. L. No. 104-193] However, some states have elected to provide comparable benefits to residents who do not meet the test for a "qualified alien," based in some cases on state constitutional law concerning equal treatment of residents. [See, e.g., Aliessa v. Novello, 712 N.Y.S.2d 96 (App. Div. 2000) (denial of benefits to lawful immigrants violates the New York State Constitution)] Where state constitutional law does not require equal treatment, however, denials of Medicaid to aliens who are not "qualified" has been upheld. [Soskin v. Reinertson, 353 F.3d 1242 (10th Cir. 2004)]

A U.S. citizen is:

- any person born in one of the 50 states, the District of Columbia, Puerto Rico, Guam, Virgin Islands, Northern Mariana Islands, American Samoa, Swain's Islands;
- any person born outside the United States but to a U.S. citizen (shown by an INS Certificate of Citizenship); or
- a person born outside the United States who has been approved by INS as a naturalized citizen.

A "qualified alien" (eligible for full Medicaid) is a

- "lawful permanent resident" ("resident alien," who holds a "green card"), admitted prior to August 1, 1996;
- lawful permanent resident admitted August 1, 1996 or subsequently, but only once a five-year ineligibility period has expired;
- lawful permanent resident admitted August 1, 1996 or subsequently who: (a) is a honorably discharged veteran or on active duty in the military with a spouse and dependent child under age 21; or (b) was originally admitted by INS to the United States under a political designation but who has adjusted to lawful permanent resident status within five years; or (c) is an American Indian

born in Canada to whom the provisions of section 289 of the INA apply, or who is a member of an Indian tribe as defined in section 4(e) of the Indian Self-Determination and Education Assistance Act; or

- an alien admitted under a "political designation" (as follows) but only for seven years unless the person is also an honorably discharged veteran, or on active duty in the military with a spouse or dependent child under age 21;
- a refugee admitted under section 207 of the Immigration and Nationality Act (INA);
- a person who sought political asylum and was admitted under section 208 of the INA;
- a refugee whose deportation is withheld under section 243(h) of the INA;
- an alien paroled under section 212(d)(5) of the INA for at least one year;
- an alien granted conditional entry under section 203(a)(7) of the INA in effect prior to April 1, 1980; or
- an alien granted status as a Cuban/Haitian entrant as defined in section 501(e) of the Refugee Education Assistance Act of 1980;
- an Amerasian immigrant admitted pursuant to Section 584 of the Foreign Operations, Export Financing, and Related Programs Appropriations Act, 1988.

Possibly of greater relevance are the "deeming" rules. When an alien is admitted in part due to a sponsorship, the sponsor's income and resources (and those of the sponsor's living-with spouse) are considered when determining an alien's SSI eligibility and payment amount, with certain exceptions. [Social Security Act §§ 1614(f)(3), 1621; 20 C.F.R. § 416.1160(a)(3), (d), 416.1166a; POMS § SI 01320.900] If one member of a couple sponsored the other, and they then separate, the sponsoring citizen's assets and income are then deemed to the alien spouse, unless of course MCCA applies because one is institutionalized.

Some states have begun enacting legislation that denies Medicaid coverage even to "qualified" legal aliens.

Income and resources of a sponsor continue to be "deemed" to the alien until the alien becomes naturalized or has 40 "quarters of coverage" with Social Security. [See SQ 15:6] Exceptions apply, for example those dealing with abuse. [8 U.S.C. § 1631]

Q 14:16.1   What proof of citizenship or residency status is required from a Medicaid applicant or beneficiary?

The Deficit Reduction Act of 2005 imposed new requirements of proof of citizenship or qualified alien status. The new requirements apply to all new Medicaid applications, and to the first annual renewal application for existing Medicaid beneficiaries. While states were previously permitted to accept affidavits from someone familiar with the applicant's citizenship status, the new law requires documents from a specified list to show both identity and citizenship status. In most cases and most states, that means that applicants will be required to produce:

1. A passport, Certificate of Naturalization (Form N-550 or N-570) or Certificate of Citizenship (Form N-560 or N-561) OR

2. A birth certificate, adoption decree, or other official record showing place of birth AND a driver's license or other government photo identification.

The list of acceptable documents is lengthy and difficult to comprehend, but the requirement is clear: the applicant must show both citizenship/nationality and identity, and only passports and certificates of naturalization/citizenship accomplish both purposes simultaneously. As implemented in most states, the requirement of showing place of birth may be satisfied by an affidavit of a person personally familiar with the circumstances of birth. See, for example, the California Department of Health Services All County Welfare Directors Letter available online at http://www.dhs.ca.gov/mcs/dra/.

Q 14:17   Who are the optionally categorically needy?

States have the option of providing Medicaid coverage to the "optionally categorically needy." Optional categorically needy groups include:

1. Infants up to age one and pregnant women not covered under the mandatory rules whose family income is below 185 percent of the federal poverty level (a different percentage may be set by each state);

2. Optional targeted low income children;

3. Certain aged, blind, or disabled adults who have incomes above those requiring mandatory coverage, but below the federal poverty level;

4. Children under age 21 who meet income and resources requirements for AFDC, but who otherwise are not eligible for AFDC;

5. Institutionalized individuals with income and resources below specified limits; persons who would be eligible if institutionalized but are receiving care under home and community-based service waivers;

6. Recipients of state supplementary payments; and

7. Tuberculosis (TB)-infected persons who would be financially eligible for Medicaid at the SSI level (only for TB-related ambulatory services and TB drugs). [42 U.S.C. § 1396a(10); 42 C.F.R. § 435.210-231]

These groups share characteristics of the mandatory groups, but the eligibility criteria are more liberally defined.

With budget constraints looming ever larger, more and more states are cutting or reducing benefits to their optional categorically needy. For example, effective September 1, 2004, Mississippi terminated benefits for 65,000 "Poverty-Level Aged and Disabled" beneficiaries (then obtaining a waiver in order to provide some, but not all, benefits to those cut off).

Q 14:18   Who are the medically needy?

As previously discussed, Medicaid regulations require that all states provide a certain level of services to the "mandatory categorically needy" (i.e., those individuals whose income and assets meet eligibility requirements). The states also have the option to have a medically needy program that allows them to extend Medicaid eligibility to additional qualified persons who may have too much income and resources to qualify under the mandatory or optional categorically needy groups. [42 U.S.C. § 1396a(a)(10)(A)(ii)] The medically needy are those individuals who do not qualify as categorically needy because their income and resources are too high, but whose income and resources are insufficient to meet the costs of necessary medical care. [42 U.S.C. § 1396a(f)] The income and asset requirements may be recalculated when an individual is deemed medically needy or whose medical bills are consistently high enough to merit special treatment.

Not all states recognize the medically needy category, and in fact, states are divided between the "medically needy" states and the "income cap" states. An applicant in an "income cap" state can deal with the "cap" by diverting income to a so-called Miller Trust (see SQ 14:30), which is correspondingly unavailable in a "medically needy" state. Those states that are "medically needy" typically allow medical expenses and/or remedial care expenses to be deducted from the individual's income and/or assets so that the latter fall below the maximum limit allowed. This allows them to "spend down" to Medicaid eligibility, thereby reducing it to a level below the maximum allowed by that state's Medicaid plan. Different procedures will apply in different states. For example, the individual may have to "spend down" on medical expenses the difference between income and the categorically needy limits aggregated over a period of months, rather than on a monthly basis.

Q 14:21   Are the eligibility rules for married couples the same as those for single individuals?

No. The Medicare Catastrophic Care Act of 1988 (MCCA—usually pronounced "Mecca") not only enacted a prescription drug benefit later repealed by Congress, but also included the important provisions of 42 USC Section 1396r-5, intended to prevent "spousal impoverishment" (see also Q 14:47). Stories of the elderly living on pet food because all funds were being used for the spouse in the nursing home led to a series of "spousal protections." These protections apply only to "MCCA couples," that is, couples in which only one spouse is an "institutionalized spouse" and the other is a "community spouse" (see Qs 14:22, 14:23). Primary protections for the community spouse are as follows: (1) the community spouse is entitled to a "minimum monthly needs maintenance allowance" that can be met from the income or other resources of either member of the couple before contributing to costs of the institutionalized spouse's care; (2) the community spouse is entitled to a minimum Community Spouse Resource Allowance, or if the couple's assets exceed that amount, one-half of the total up to a maximum unless greater need is shown; (3) the community spouse is entitled to keep all his or her own income (although if support is sought, it may be obtained only up to 25 percent of the excess of income over the minimum monthly needs maintenance allowance); and (4) there is no recovery from the estate (or lien upon the home) until the spouse is no longer living. Conversely, these protections are offset by the "spousal unity" approach to a couple's assets: the assets of either count towards eligibility and the transfer by either spouse count also towards ineligibility that results from transfers. MCCA is therefore a double-edged sword. In some instances it may even be "better," depending upon the family goals, for one spouse *not* to qualify as a community spouse, where the cure of MCCA is worse than the disease. Another wrinkle: in most states, you are a "spouse," or not, with no halfway measures: no special exceptions from MCCA for estranged or separate couples; no special protections for unmarried couples, no matter how long the duration of their relationship. Needless to say, MCCA is of no use whatsoever for gay couples; even a registered "domestic partner" or member of a "civil union" will not qualify as a spouse under federal law.

Income Eligibility

Q 14:25 What income is counted in determining income eligibility?

Under Medicaid rules in SSI states and many 209(b) states, just as with Supplemental Security Income rules, income is defined broadly to mean any cash or in-kind benefit that could conceivably enable the recipient to obtain food or shelter. [42 C.F.R. § 435.601] Income can be earned or unearned. Income amounts are calculated on a monthly basis. In SSI states, earned income deemed to be countable (or available) includes wages, commissions, and bonuses, whether paid in cash or "in kind" (i.e., payment in the form of food, shelter, or other kinds of barter, in return for services rendered). Even income earned at sheltered workshops is includible for Medicaid purposes. Usually, however, earned income has a slightly preferred status over unearned income; while it still "counts," a portion ($65/month or so) may be "disregarded" for computational purposes. Some 209(b) states may disregard some or all in-kind earned income as counted income, but cash is universally considered to be income. Of course, nursing home patients are unlikely to have earned income, so this "category of income" concern is not so important for most elder law attorneys.

All other receipts are categorized as "unearned income," including gifts from any source, interest on investments, alimony, insurance proceeds, Social Security, workers' compensation, unemployment benefits, annuity, and pension income. While all income must be disclosed, only "countable income"—in SSI states income not excluded by SSI rules and regulations—will be considered in the eligibility determination. Not counted are medical care, food stamps, other types of need-based assistance, or income received by other members of the family that is not otherwise "deemed" available to the individual. [See 42 U.S.C. § 1382a,

20 C.F.R. § 416.1103] Remember, however, that § 209(b) states may set different (more or less restrictive) income requirements. In at least some states, unearned income received in-kind has often remained uncounted, either tacitly or explicitly. States following SSI rules have an exception for payments received pursuant to a reverse annuity mortgage, depending on state policy. Such payments are in effect restoration of principal to the homeowner. Finally, as with SSI, bona fide loans are not income—but they are apt to be re-characterized as gifts. [Faber v. Merrifield, 783 N.Y.S.2d 495 (Sup. Ct. 2004), holding that children's contributions to pay applicant's medical expenses were gifts in the months received, rather than loans.]

Q 14:28 What is an "income cap"?

Some states that provide optional Medicaid coverage to institutionalized individuals impose a cap on income for eligibility purposes. Individuals who meet the other eligibility requirements but whose income exceeds the cap will not be eligible for Medicaid. The "income cap" states currently include Alabama, Alaska, Arizona, Arkansas, Colorado, Delaware, Florida, Idaho, Iowa, Kentucky, Louisiana, Oklahoma, Mississippi, Nevada, New Mexico, Oregon, South Carolina, South Dakota, Tennessee, Texas, and Wyoming. The actual income cap varies from state to state. Most states fix income eligibility at 300 percent of the maximum federal benefit rate—the then-current Supplemental Security Income benefit for an individual. [42 U.S.C. § 1396a(a)(10)(A)] Thus, with SSI capped at $674 (year 2009 figure), most income cap states will limit Medicaid long-term care benefits to individuals with less than three times that amount, or $1,911.

One state, Delaware, calculates the maximum income amount differently. In Delaware, a long-term care Medicaid applicant may have income no greater than 250 percent of the maximum SSI amount plus a $20 "disregard." In other words, the year 2008 maximum income in Delaware is $1,612.50.

Technically, Arizona, Arkansas, Florida, Iowa, Louisiana, Oklahoma, Oregon, and Texas are not income cap states; however, the income cap rules effectively govern those states, because they either do not cover the aged in their "medically needy" programs (Texas) or they do not permit the use of nursing home expenses in calculating the "spend down" for their "medically needy" programs (the other listed states). In other words, although these states offer coverage to those persons who are unable to "afford" their medical care, they do not permit the use of nursing home costs in calculating their ability to pay for that care, even though those nursing home costs are the principal reason the applicant requires Medicaid assistance. In addition, Connecticut's Medicaid-funded program for home care subsidization (as distinguished from its wholly state funded program), which operates by virtue of a waiver from the federal government (see SQ 14:9), operates under an income cap, even though its general nursing care (institutional) program is not governed by an income cap.

Q 14:29 How does an income cap apply to married couples?

Most commonly, income eligibility is an issue when one spouse is facing institutionalization and the other spouse (the "community spouse") is able to remain at home or in some other noninstitutional setting. A married applicant's income eligibility is usually determined by applying the "name on the check" rule (see Q 14:27). Under this methodology, one spouse may qualify for Medicaid assistance, although the other spouse does not.

In the handful of income cap states that are also community property states (Arizona, Idaho, Louisiana, Nevada, New Mexico, and Texas), the rules may be less clear. In some (New Mexico), the total income of the couple (regardless of the name on the check) is combined; if the total income is less than twice the single-person income eligibility level, either spouse qualifies under the income rules. In at least Texas, community property rules affirmatively do not apply; each spouse must qualify under his or her own income eligibility determinations. In Arizona, either approach is permissible; thus, a married applicant may qualify either under the "name on the check" rule or by having total community income less than twice the eligibility limit.

Q 14:30 What can be done to secure Medicaid eligibility for patients whose income exceeds the income cap even though they do not have sufficient income to pay for long-term care?

As a result of changes in federal law implemented in the Omnibus Budget and Reconciliation Act of 1993 (OBRA '93), every income cap state is required to recognize the validity of an assignment of income to an irrevocable trust that meets the requirements of 42 U.S.C.

§ 1396p-(d)(4)(B). The effect of the assignment to a qualified trust is to have the income not counted as available to the applicant for eligibility purposes, although the income remains countable for purposes of calculating the amount the applicant must pay toward the cost of his or her care. These trusts are sometimes called qualified income assignment trusts or qualified income trusts, but are more frequently referred to as "Miller" trusts in honor of the Colorado case that first officially recognized the technique. [Miller v. Ibarra, 746 F. Supp. 19 (D. Colo. 1990)] Miller trusts permit most Medicaid applicants to qualify even in income cap states. (See Q 14:91 for a discussion of Miller trusts.)

In some of the income cap states, state Medicaid agencies have adopted the view that the assignment of income to the "Miller" trust amounts to a monthly uncompensated transfer. Under this analysis the effective maximum income that can be assigned to the "Miller" trust will be equal to the "average cost of care in the community," which varies by state (and sometimes by county or region). The "average cost of care" is usually and more prosaically referred to as the state's "divisor," and is the same figure utilized to calculate the period of ineligibility for gifts as described more fully at SQ 14:58 and set out in the table at the end of this chapter. In states adopting that approach, the effective "income cap" becomes the average cost of care, or divisor, figure.

Where a pension is involved, one available choice for married couples may be to secure a qualified domestic relations order (QDRO) to divide pension income between spouses. In most states a property division can be obtained in a separation (as opposed to a divorce) proceeding. In either case, a QDRO effectively divides pension income between spouses, and may in some cases reduce the income of the institutionalized spouse to below the income cap level.

Resource Eligibility

Q 14:34　Is income also considered a resource?

In general, no. Something will not be considered both as income and as a "resource." The usual rule is that property received is income in the month of receipt and a resource or asset the following month unless it has been disposed of or converted into a non-countable resource. This may give the recipient time to spend or otherwise dispose of the property. Certain exceptions are discussed in chapter 16.

With respect to annuities, however, states have tried to claim that a non-assignable annuity or stream of income should be treated as a resource if it can be sold see Connecticut Department of Social Services Uniform Policy Manual Transmittal UP-07-02. But see also *Ross v. Department of Public Welfare*, 936 A.2d 552 (Pa. Comm. 2007), which expressly rejects the Medicaid agency's attempt to treat the stream of income as an available resource.

Q 14:35 How are inheritances and other unexpected sums treated for income eligibility purposes?

Because income is not a resource, under SSI rules, the individual can spend or otherwise consume unexpected large amounts (or transfer, if in the community and not receiving benefits from a program that applies transfer penalties to any transfer). Possible exceptions: some medically needy states apply a "lump-sum income rule" for unusual amounts of income, so that disposing of the property received will still not work (unless the beneficiary first leaves the Medicaid program prior to receipt). That is, the "lump sum" is recharacterized as if it had been spread out over a period of months.

Example 14-1. John is in a medically needy state. The categorically needy income limit ("CNIL") is hypothetically $500. He receives $750 per month in Social Security Disability, of which the state will hypothetically "disregard" $150 based on his living situation. That leaves $600, leaving him over income by $100 per month. The state will multiply $100 by six months to reach a "spend down" amount of $600.

Once he has spent (or incurred debt for) $600 on qualified expenses (such as his very expensive prescription medicine), he will then be covered by Medicaid for any further medical expenditures during the balance of the six months. However, one December an aunt dies and he receives a check for $3,000. Technically, that $3,000 will be added to his spend down amount, i.e., instead of receiving $600 ($750–$150) multiplied by 6 months, or $3,600 as compared with the limit of $3,000, he will now be considered to have received $6,600 for the same period, giving him an enhanced spend down of $3,600. In effect he will have to spend the ENTIRE inheritance on medical expenses before Medicaid will pay $1. Even if he gives or gambles the money away, or spends it on rent, he would not get the Medicaid until he has spent the $3,600. Of course, if he keeps the money he will be "over-asset" the month after. The only solution may be to have him send a letter declining Medicaid coverage in December before he cashes (or better yet, receives) the check, spend it, and then reapply in January. This is a sufficiently drastic administrative hurdle that the agency may agree to simply ignore the check entirely. Alternatively, if John doesn't expect to have major medical expenses during the six months in which the income is considered available, he could spend it over the six months, and provided it was gone by month seven, he would be eligible again. Similarly, if he does not have to worry about transfer penalties applicable to those receiving SSI, long-term care benefits under Medicaid, or certain other state programs, he could hypothetically keep the lump sum and gift it away in month six, regaining eligibility in month seven.

Q 14:36 How are the resource eligibility rules applied to married couples?

The resources of both spouses, whether owned separately or jointly, are scrutinized when one is applying for Medicaid benefits. If neither spouse is institutionalized, then the assets of both are considered available to both; however, when one spouse enters a facility (or applies for comparable care), an assessment of the couple's assets (sometimes referred to as a "snapshot") is taken. The "snapshot date" is the first day of a continuous thirty-day period of institutionalization, and therefore may be the date of admission to a hospital if subsequently discharged to a skilled nursing facilty. If long-term care benefits are available to those in the community under a home care "waiver," the "snapshot date" is the first date services are provided pursuant to such a waiver. It is important to understand that the "snapshot" may not actually be calculated until months, or years, after the snapshot date, but that the ultimate calculation of available resources will be made as of that date. Treatment of the couple's assets after the snapshot is taken differs from state to state. The "snapshot" may or may not be important, depending upon the amount of the couple's assets and the state. In those states which permit a community spouse to retain one-half of the couple's combined assets, subject to certain maximums and minimums, and the one-half is probably between the maximum and minimum, it is important to determine what the total assets are in order to determine the one-half that may be retained.

Q 14:39 How are jointly owned accounts treated for asset eligibility purposes?

There is a presumption that all bank accounts and similar assets owned jointly belong entirely to the applicant. This might be thought of as the "name on the account rule"—if the applicant's name is on the account, the asset belongs to the applicant, because the applicant would have the right to withdraw all of the funds on deposit. The other joint owner can, however, rebut that presumption, for example, by documenting his or her deposits to the account. This can be a real problem for those who are not careful recordkeepers.

Brokerage accounts in two names typically cannot be disposed of without both parties' signatures. If the other owner refuses to cooperate, the assets should be treated as inaccessible unless there is a way to sever the account, although the Medicaid agency may not always agree with this interpretation. The same should apply to jointly held real estate (see Q 14:45), but it is important to remember that the agency may still lien the applicant's share in the real estate and demand that (s)he ask to sell.

Because assets owned by either spouse are counted for eligibility purposes this rule is not especially relevant for spouses where one is an applicant. It can be problematic, however, when both owners (e.g., siblings) are applicants. The entire value of the asset may be deemed available to each of the owners unless the Medicaid agency can be induced to apply a rule of reason.

Q 14:42 What assets are noncountable exempt resources?

The following assets may not be counted as "available resources" under federal rules:

1. *The applicant's home*, subject to certain equity limits described below, provided either that he or she "intends to return home" or his or her spouse or minor or disabled child or "caregiver child" (See Q 14:62) continues to reside there. The proceeds from the sale of the home continue to be exempt for three months after the sale, to permit the applicant to purchase a replacement home. [Social Security Administration Program Operations Manual System § SI 01130.110] The home is exempt regardless of value, and the exclusion includes "the land that appertains thereto." In most states, the exclusion includes adjacent property regardless of

property tax designations, so that the home and, say, an adjacent vacant lot or adjacent residence, may be exempt. An important variation among states is the "intent to return home" standard. Federal SSI rules apply a subjective intent standard set forth in 20 CFR Section 416.1212(c), which is controlling in "SSI" states where the state must apply rules that are "no more restrictive" than the income and resource standards of the SSI program. [42 U.S.C. § 1396a(r)(2)(A)(i)][Anna W. v. Bane, 863 F. Supp. 125 (W.D.N.Y. 1993)] By contrast, 209(b) states may be able to apply a "reasonableness" test with a requirement that the individual have a reasonable (physician-approved) expectation of returning home in six months or less. [See, e.g., Connecticut Department of Social Services Uniform Policy Manual § 7510.15 *(http:// www.sharinglaw.net/elder/liens.pdf)*]. The Deficit Reduction Act of 2005 applied an "equity limit" to the homes of those without a spouse or minor or disabled child living in the home, $500,000 or at a state's option, $750,000 in equity [42 U.S.C. § 1396p(f)]. This limit will primarily affect individuals living at home and receiving home care services pursuant to a waiver, or individuals in states that had applied a subjective standard for "intent to return." The new limitation does not apply if the applicant's spouse, or minor, blind, or disabled child, lives in the home.

2. *A vehicle.* One automobile per household is excluded regardless of the value if it is used for transportation of the eligible individual/couple or a member of the eligible individual's/ couple's household; following Social Security policy, the assumption is that the automobile is used for transportation, absent evidence to the contrary. [42 U.S.C. § 1396r-5(c)(5)(B); POMS § SI 01130.200]

3. *The entire value of household goods, furniture, furnishings, and personal effects,* unless there are items of unusual value. If there is a "community spouse," these items are exempt whatever their value. [42 U.S.C. § 1396r-5(c)(5)(B)] If there is no community spouse, federal rules set the maximum excluded value at $2,000, but the actual method of determination of higher value varies widely by state. In any event, medical equipment and wedding and engagement rings are exempt regardless of value. As a practical matter, many states have opted to simply ignore such items except in very unusual cases, recognizing the difficulty (and probably low price) of most personal items sold in what would likely be a tag sale.

4. *Property used in the applicant's or spouse's trade or business, and necessary for support.*

5. *Tools of the applicant's or spouse's trade.*

6. *Life insurance policies* with up to $1,500 face value. If the total face value of life insurance policies exceeds $1,500, the cash surrender value will be counted as an available resource. If the total face value does not exceed $1,500, the entire cash surrender value will be exempt—even if it exceeds $1,500, as is often the case with "whole life" policies purchased in childhood for elders now in their 70s or 80s. Term life insurance, though it may trigger the requirement to calculate value (if the face amount exceeds $1,500), will not be an available resource because by definition it has no cash value; some states therefore simply exempt it altogether. The existence of life insurance may make the next two categories of exemptions—burial plots and prepaid funeral arrangements—unavailable to the applicant.

7. *Burial plots* for the applicant and family, plus prepaid costs of burial (as distinguished from funeral) expenses: casket, headstone, and costs associated with opening, closing, and lining the grave are permitted. Furthermore, "irrevocable prepaid burial arrangements" are excluded; funding of these may be restricted by state consumer protection laws and may be required to be held by licensed funeral directors.

8. *Up to $1,500 in "revocable" funeral arrangements,* including an account designated as for funeral arrangements. Such an account may accumulate interest without exceeding the eligibility limits. If life insurance policies have been excluded from assets as having a face value of less than $1,500, this exemption is not available in addition to such excluded policies. This will also be offset by any irrevocable prepaid burial arrangement.

[42 U.S.C. §§ 1382b(a)(1)–1382b(a)(3)]

In addition to those comparatively common excluded assets, a number of additional exemptions with less-frequent applicability include:

1. Resources of a blind or disabled person that are necessary to achieve a plan of self-support;

2. Some stock held by Alaskan natives and allotted land held by enrolled members of Indian tribes;

3. Retroactive Social Security and SSI benefits, for up to six months after receipt;

4. Payments received from the Agent Orange litigation settlement;

5. Reparations received by Holocaust or internment victims;

6. Some funds received from state crime victims' funds, for up to nine months from receipt;

7. State or local government relocation assistance funds, for up to nine months from receipt;

8. Federal or state disaster relief funds and the income on those funds;

9. Earned income tax credit receipts, for one month from receipt; and

10. SSI received on behalf of a minor and deposited into a separate dedicated account in some circumstances.

[42 U.S.C. §§ 1382b(a)(4)–1382b(a)(12)]

Note that federal law does permit inclusion of IRAs and retirement savings as "available" resources when these may be liquidated, even subject to a penalty. [See, e.g., Houghton v. Reinertson, 382 F.2d 1162 (10th Cir. 2004)]

Q 14:43   Is an applicant's home considered an available resource?

Generally an applicant's home, even if it is located out of state, is deemed exempt as long as the applicant, his or her spouse, and/or a minor or disabled child lives there, except that if there is no spouse or minor or disabled child living in the home, only homes with $500,000 of equity (or in states which adopt regulations to such effect, $750,000) are exempt. If an applicant has multiple homes, only one will be excluded. The primary place of residence may be determined by looking at indicia such as where the applicant votes, where he or she receives income payments, or where he or she spends the majority of time.

An unmarried applicant-recipient living in a long-term care facility risks losing the home if he or she does not affirmatively declare on the application his or her intent to return home even if the possibility of returning home is remote; such a declaration will be ineffective in non-SSI states that apply an objective standard to the "intent," unless a physician will confirm that the applicant can reasonably be expected to return home.

In some (but not all) states, homes whose legal titles have been transferred to a revocable trust may be deemed an available resource, because the Medicaid exemption applies only when the individual owns the property in his or her own name. The applicant may then have to transfer legal title back to himself or herself to regain the exemption. Attorneys should keep this in mind when advising their clients on the advantages and disadvantages of living trusts, particularly when the trustors' residence is their primary asset. There are circumstances when a house can be left in a revocable trust, for example, when the value of the house does not exceed the amount the community spouse is allowed to keep ($109,560 in 2009) and the couple chooses to use liquid assets for spend-down purposes (see Q 14:54). Some practitioners report that on some occasions, where there are assets low enough that one-half is below $100,000, it makes sense to put the house in the trust so that the "snapshot" will include more assets for the community spouse; when the house leaves the trust, it becomes exempt and the spouse gets to keep all the liquid assets, depending upon the amounts involved. The efficacy of this approach may be challenged in states applying the logic of *Timm v. Montana Department of Public Health*, 2008 Mont. 126 (2008). In that case the Medicaid agency treated a truck used by the community spouse in his business as an available resource because it was titled to a closely-held corporation. The Montana Supreme Court held that the disparate treatment of property held in what amounted to a wholly-owned legal entity violated the Medicaid applicant's equal protection rights.

Q 14:44   What limits are placed on the value of an exempt home?

Pursuant to the Deficit Reduction Act of 2005, effective 1/1/2006, unless a spouse or disabled or minor child is living in the home, the value of the applicant's equity in the home may not exceed $500,000 ($750,000 in states which opt for the higher figure) for eligibility to be granted. (For applications filed prior to 1/1/2006, no such limit applies.)

Q 14:45   What assets, although not exempt, may not be counted as available for purposes of asset eligibility determinations?

In addition to the exempt property items previously listed, two other categories of assets may be ignored in making the eligibility calculation, depending on the state's precise implementation of federal rules.

First, jointly held real estate may well be treated as being "inaccessible." If the other (nonspouse) owners refuse to sell their shares, and also refuse to buy out the applicant's share, *and* it can be shown that there is no market for the applicant's share, then the applicant's share will not be considered available even if it is a nonexempt asset. Evidence to back this up includes the written opinion of a local real estate agent and a written refusal by the co-owners. Generally, states have not taken the step of requiring an applicant to bring a partition action to access interests in real estate, although this is theoretically possible. In some states, it may also be necessary to claim that selling the asset would be considered a hardship to the co-owner (e.g., he or she would have to move if jointly held real property were sold) in order for the asset to be considered unavailable. Similarly, a "life use" in real estate may also be treated as inaccessible/not considered a "resource," if the other owners refuse to "buy out" the applicant's life estate. However, the agency may require the property to be rented and the income paid to the nursing home.

One major caveat: In some states, the existence of unmarketable or jointly owned property may lead to "conditional" eligibility, requiring continuing efforts to liquidate the interest. If the property actually is sold, the terms of the conditional eligibility may require that the proceeds be applied toward the accumulated cost of care paid by the Medicaid program. Although the family will be careful not to sell, the problem is that this conditional eligibility may result in a lien being placed on the property to secure the applicant's (and agency's) interest in the event of sale, and this may be hard to discharge on the applicant's death. Even if the property passes outside probate, the lien may remain.

The second category of non-counted assets is residential property in which a relative owns an interest where the sale of the property would cause the relative to lose his or her residence. In other words, a home jointly owned with a child, who lives in the home, need not be sold before eligibility can be obtained. This exception, which applies only in "SSI" states, is grounded in Section SI 01130.130 of the Social Security Program Operations Manual System or "POMS" dealing with SSI eligibility.

Overall, the category of "unavailable" or "inaccessible" assets is one that can be explored. If the practitioner finds that the applicant is inadvertently over-asset—for example, finds out that there is an insurance policy previously unknown—it may work to argue that the asset is then "inaccessible" and should not be counted until cashed—at which point it will be treated as income in the month in which the proceeds are received under SSI rules (see Q 14:46). This has also been applied to interests in limited partnerships, restricted stock, non-assignable annuities, and promissory "balloon" notes with non-acceleration provisions. To the extent that the inaccessibility is the result of the applicant's (or spouse's) own legal planning, however, these arrangements may be found to be transfers of assets.

Rules That May be Used to Protect Spouses

Q 14:47.0 In general, what techniques can a practitioner use to protect the income and resources of the community spouse?

The practitioner has available an ever-shrinking toolkit of ways to protect the community spouse, which are discussed in more detail throughout this section. These include:

- Applying existing federal rules that set a minimum monthly maintenance needs allowance for a community spouse, to be met first by allocating income of the institutionalized spouse to the community spouse and second by allocating additional assets to generate investment income;
- Applying existing federal rules to maximize the community spouse resource allowance that may be kept by the community spouse, by an administrative "fair hearing" if necessary;
- Possibly obtaining a court order (in some states, a decree of separate support and maintenance) to determine the community spouse resource allowance after determining the support needs of the community spouse;
- In situations where assets are held primarily by the community spouse or can be transferred to him/her, and the institutionalized spouse or a legally empowered surrogate can assign to the State the rights of support against the community spouse, assisting the community spouse to exercise the right of "spousal refusal" and decline to provide assets to pay for the institutionalized spouse's care;
- Converting excess assets owned by or transferred to the community spouse to a stream of non-counted income through purchase of an annuity, annuitization of a retirement account, loan of funds

to third parties and taking back a note, or other ways that may pass muster under the Deficit Reduction Act rules;

- Converting counted assets to exempt assets (for example, a home) that may later be sold and converted to cash available to meet the community spouse's needs, or to income-producing property, such as a two-family home with rental income;

- Maintaining life insurance on the institutionalized spouse's life, either by allocating the cash value to the community spouse's share, or transferring the insurance to family members in a way that will not otherwise jeopardize benefits;

- Advising the community spouse about the risks and benefits of exempt transfers to disabled children or others who can be trusted (but not required) to assist the community spouse once the institutionalized spouse has been found eligible, or even planning transfers of assets that will incur appropriately managed penalties if necessary; and

- Advising the community spouse about legal separation and divorce

Q 14:47　What provisions in Medicaid law are intended to protect the income and resources of the community spouse?

In general, certain "anti-spousal impoverishment" provisions included in 42 U.S.C. § 1396r-5 provide minimum standards of income and assets for a "community spouse"; in recent years, the utility of these protections have eroded, and practitioners have had to resort to other means to protect a spouse from impoverishment. The history: Prior to the adoption of the Medicare Catastrophic Coverage Act of 1988 (MCCA), all assets and income of either spouse were considered available to an institutionalized spouse, and the eligibility limits were only slightly higher for an institutionalized married person whose spouse remained in the community. The consequence of this policy approach was to encourage divorce (the only means by which a spouse in the community could retain any significant portion of the couple's combined assets). This approach also resulted in substantial hardship occasioned by the requirement that both spouses be impoverished before one spouse could be eligible for care. In addition, because community spouses were (and are) vulnerable to the possibility of institutionalization, the then-existing financial eligibility system made it even more likely that a community spouse would soon become a Medicaid-subsidized institutional resident.

MCCA adopted a sweeping new approach to spousal impoverishment. It also adopted a new prescription drug benefit that was promptly repealed by Congress in the face of widespread dissatisfaction among elderly beneficiaries. When those provisions were repealed, the MCCA spousal impoverishment provisions were left intact. As a result, the community resident whose spouse becomes institutionalized is somewhat protected, although the protection is limited.

The resources of both spouses, whether owned separately or jointly, are scrutinized when one spouse is applying for Medicaid benefits. Separately held property is treated as available to the institutionalized spouse, despite prenuptial agreements, state community and separate property laws, and even property of both spouses settlement agreements in marital separation proceedings. On the other hand, the community spouse is entitled to retain some significant amount of assets while the institutionalized spouse qualifies for Medicaid benefits: The community spouse is permitted to retain his or her own income (see Q 14:51) and even (in some cases) some of the income of the institutionalized spouse (see Q 14:49), and in most cases the community spouse's estate is protected against estate recovery claims made by the Medicaid agency (see Q 14:100).

Protection from Spousal Impoverishment

Q 14:48   How does MCCA attempt to protect the community spouse's income needs?

The community spouse whose institutionalized husband or wife has qualified for Medicaid subsidies is permitted to retain all of his or her own income, including Social Security or other pension benefits in the community spouse's name, investment and other income received only in the community spouse's name and, in community property states, one-half of all income received in both spouses' names. In addition, the community spouse may be entitled to receive additional support from the institutionalized spouse in order to ensure that the community spouse receives at least a minimum income level. This minimum level is referred to as the "minimum monthly maintenance needs allowance" (MMMNA), and is set by federal law. It can be increased, however, pursuant to a formula under federal law if the spouse's shelter expenses are high, up to a set maximum (without recourse to a hearing), but may also be increased by court order or administrative hearing. The federal minimum numbers are changed annually and set federally.

If the community spouse's income is less than the MMMNA, then the institutionalized spouse's income can be used by the community spouse to bring the community spouse's income up to MMMNA, and if this is insufficient, additional assets can be set aside to generate investment income for the community spouse to meet income needs.

The MMMNA is composed of a basic allowance and an excess shelter allowance. The basic allowance is equal to 150 percent of the poverty level for a family of two. [42 U.S.C. § 1396r-5(d)(3)] The excess shelter allowance is the amount by which the community spouse's shelter expenses exceed 30 percent of 150% of the poverty level for a family of two. Shelter expenses include rent or mortgage, taxes and insurance, maintenance fees for a cooperative or condominium, and utilities. [42 U.S.C. § 1396r-5(d)(4)] The figure is adjusted annually. If the community spouse's shelter costs are greater than $525 (effective as of July 1, 2008) per month, the community spouse is entitled to an excess shelter allowance to make up the difference.

The MMMNA will also be affected by a heating and utility allowance, set by the state. As of July 2008, the MMMNA threshold is $1,750 (unlike other eligibility figures, this one is updated midyear). After adjustments, the maximum MMMNA (as of January 2009, since the *maximum* figure is adjusted on a calendar year basis) can go as high as $2,739 without need for any hearing; in some states, the maximum is automatically used as the presumptive amount.

The states that only utilize the $2,739 MMMNA amount include: Alaska, California, District of Columbia, Georgia, Hawaii, Illinois, Iowa, Louisiana, Mississippi, New York, North Dakota, Oklahoma, South Carolina, Texas, and Wyoming.

Q 14:49   How is the community spouse's income increased to reach the MMMNA?

For couples where institutionalization began on or after February 8, 2006, income of the institutionalized spouse must be allocated to the community spouse to meet the MMNA, and only if this is insufficient— without regard to whether the income stream will survive the death of the institutionalized spouse—may additional assets be set aside to generate investment income. This approach, known as "income first" was approved by the U.S. Supreme Court in *Wisconsin Department of Health and Family Services v. Blumer* [534 U.S. 473 (2002)], and was made mandatory for all states with the enactment of the Deficit Reduction Act of 2005 [42 U.S.C. § 1396r-5(d)(6)]. For spouses institutionalized prior to February 8, 2006, in states that had been applying an "asset first" approach that permitted allocation of assets for investment income prior to assigning institutionalized spouse income to the community spouse, "asset first" may still be available.

Example 14-2. In July 2007, Mrs. Ballam's husband is a Medicaid patient in a skilled nursing facility. Income in her name totals $1,100; her husband's net pension and Social Security income totals $1,600. Mrs. Ballam is entitled to receive at least $650 from her husband's income (in order to bring her to the $1,750 figure). Her state does not automatically allow her the full MMMNA amount of $2,610.00, but her monthly mortgage and utility expenses total $725, so she will be entitled to an additional $200 (the amount by which those expenses exceed the annually adjusted $525 figure) as part of her MMMNA. In other words, Mrs. Ballam will receive $850 ($650 MMMNA plus $200 excess monthly shelter allowance) from her husband's income. Mr. Ballam is also entitled to receive $101.10 (in 2009) in personal needs allowance because his state utilizes the personal needs calculation of 15 percent of the maximum 2009 SSI benefit of $674 (see SQ 14:14), and his Medicare Part B premium will also continue to be paid. This means that the monthly payment to the skilled nursing facility will be $558.05 (his Social Security income of $1,600, minus his Part B premium of $96.40, minus his personal needs allowance of $95.55, minus Mrs. Ballam's MMMNA payment of $850).

Example 14-3. Same facts as the previous example, except that Mr. Ballam's income is only a $200 pension he receives from the city government, which had operated outside the Social Security system as a state subdivision. The $850.00 to which Mrs. Ballam is entitled to bring her income up to the $1,750 MMNA cannot be met by her husband's $200 income; indeed, only $106.55 can be allotted to her because he is first entitled to his personal needs allowance. Instead, assets in excess of the community spouse resource allowance (see Q 14:51) may be retained to generate the additional $743.45. The prevailing interest rate is 4 percent. In theory, this would mean that to generate $743.45 per month, or $8,921.40 per year, Mrs. Ballam could retain $223,035 in assets. However, since $223,035 exceeds the maximum allowable of $104,400, she will have to go to a "fair hearing"—either administrative or court—to seek the additional assets.

Q 14:50   Is there any income of the institutionalized spouse that cannot be applied to the community spouse first, before protecting assets?

Apparently, no, not even Social Security benefits. Seven years ago, the Second Circuit Court of Appeals held that the anti-assignment provisions of Social Security forbid the state Medicaid agency from requiring assignment by the institutionalized spouse of Social Security benefits to the community spouse. [Robbins v. DeBuono, 218 F.3d 197 (2d Cir. 2000)] Subsequently, however, the United States Supreme Court decided the case of *Keffeler v. Department of Social Services* [123 S. Ct. 1017 (2003)], which has been cited by other courts as undercutting the rationale of the *Robbins* case and invalidating its conclusions. Although the *Keffeler* case dealt with an entirely different situation—whether the State, when acting as "representative payee" for minors, could apply the minors' Social Security benefits to reduce the amount of support provided by State programs—it applied a strict reading of the term "other legal process" (which the Social Security Act declares may not be used to deprive a beneficiary of his or her benefit), which was interpreted expansively in the *Robbins* case. Since *Keffeler,* the Second Circuit Court of Appeals has rejected the holding of the Robbins case. [Wojchowski v. Daines, 2nd Cir., No. 06-3373-cv. Aug. 2, 2007] The benefits of *Robbins* would appear to be dead, although other courts outside the Second Circuit's ambit might theoretically reach a different conclusion.

Note that in determining what institutionalized spouse income is or is not "available" to meet the community spouse MMMNA, the state may *not* make allowance for the institutionalized spouse's Medicare Part B or other health insurance premium. [42 C.F.R. 435.832(c)]

Q 14:50.1   How much of the community spouse's own income may he or she keep?

In determining eligibility for the institutionalized spouse, the income of the community spouse is not considered. [42 U.S.C. § 1396r-5(b)(1)] In most cases, therefore, states ignore the community spouse's income, and practitioners have gotten into the habit of saying that the community spouse is entitled to keep *all* of his or her own income. An argument has been made, however, that States are still free to pursue the community spouses for contribution as "legally liable relatives," provided that the contribution does not reduce the community spouse's income below the MMMNA. This is the common practice in "spousal refusal" jurisdictions. The Illinois Supreme Court has held that MCCA did *not* prevent the state from seeking contribution from a high-income community spouse. [Poindexter v. State, 229 Ill.2d 194, 890 N.E.2d 410, (2008)] Whether federal courts will reach the same conclusion is an open question.

Q 14:51   What portion of the couple's combined assets may the community spouse retain under the spousal impoverishment rules?

The resources of both the husband and the wife are considered in determining whether the institutionalized spouse satisfies the resource limitation; however, the community spouse is allowed to retain a certain amount of resources. The amount of resources that the community spouse is permitted to retain is called the community spouse resource allowance or "CSRA." The CSRA is composed of countable assets only; the community spouse is also permitted to retain the residence, automobile, and other exempt assets (see SQ 14:42). The institutionalized spouse is permitted to retain the same $2,000 (or less in a few states) in available resources allotted to an unmarried Medicaid applicant. Medicaid regulations allow transfers of property between the spouses to change title to the community spouse (see SQ 14:61), although there may be logistical difficulties if the institutionalized spouse is incompetent but has not executed a durable power of attorney.

In some states, the CSRA is set at a fixed amount by reference to federal figures, adjusted annually (in the year 2009, that figure is $109,560), without regard to the assets held by the couple at the time of institutionalization. The states that only utilize the $109,560 CSRA amount include Alaska, California, Colorado, Florida, Georgia, Hawaii, Illinois, Kentucky, Louisiana, Maine, Mississippi, Massachusetts, North Dakota, Vermont, Wyoming and the District of Columbia.

In some other states, the community spouse is allowed to retain (or receive via transfer) half of the combined non-exempt marital assets, with a minimum of $21,912 and a maximum of the same $109,560 (year 2009 figures) in non-exempt assets. (In a community property state, this is expressed by saying that the community spouse is deemed to own one-half of community assets.) These figures are adjusted annually. The states calculating the CSRA as having a minimum and maximum set by federal calculations include Arizona, Arkansas, Connecticut, Idaho, Indiana,

Kansas, Maryland, Michigan, Montana, Nebraska, Nevada, New Jersey, Ohio, Oregon, Pennsylvania, Tennessee, Texas, and Virginia.

The two approaches briefly described here are not the only techniques employed by the states, even though federal law limits the states to those two choices. Some states have simply failed to update the maximum allowable community spouse figure for several years; others have set an arbitrary or differently computed minimum that is considerably higher than the federal minimum.

Q 14:52   How is the CSRA determined?

As of the beginning of the first period of thirty days' continuous institutionalization a "snapshot" is taken of the assets of both spouses. [42 U.S.C. § 1396r-5(c)(1)(B)] This snapshot calculation may actually be made months or years after the institutionalization began, but must be calculated as of the date of institutionalization (or eligibility for institutionalization). The CSRA is based on this assessment of the couple's resources. The CSRA is calculated at the beginning of the period of continuous institutionalization or medical eligibility for institutionalization, even if application is not made for Medicaid at that time. The resource assessment is made by the state Medicaid agency at the request of the community spouse or the institutionalized spouse, whether at the time of institutionalization or at the (later) time of application for Medicaid benefits.

Resources acquired between the date of the first institutionalization and Medicaid eligibility will not increase the CSRA. Because of this, the snapshot amount (and the resultant CSRA) is fixed at the time of institutionalization even though no Medicaid application is made. Resources acquired by the community spouse after Medicaid eligibility is determined do not affect the Medicaid eligibility of the institutionalized spouse.

Q 14:53   How may one increase the community spouse's CSRA?

Medicaid law permits the CSRA to be increased at a "fair hearing," whether through administrative agencies or appropriate courts. For couples where the spouse was institutionalized on or after February 8, 2006, the income of the institutionalized spouse would first have to be allocated to the community spouse before the CSRA might be increased to provide the community spouse with additional investment assets to generate income; for those institutionalized earlier, some states may still permit an increase in CSRA without regard to the institutionalized spouse's income. Examples 14-3 and 14-4 show the benefit for the community spouse in proceeding to a hearing. Administrative hearings may also be used to increase the *maximum* MMMNA for reasons of "exceptional circumstances" or "hardship." States differ in the strictness of their approach to these exceptions. Examples might be the unusual expense of caring for a disabled adult child, inordinately high shelter expenses for a home that was otherwise impossible to sell or where relocation would cause hardship. "Exceptional circumstances" may or may not include high health costs for the community spouse; in Connecticut, these are now treated as the inevitable problems of old age that were considered by Congress in establishing the standard MMMNA figures. [Burinskas v. Dept. of Social Services, 240 Conn. 141 (1997)]

Q 14:53.1 What is "spousal refusal," and how may it be used to protect the community spouse?

Under 42 U.S.C. § 1396r-5(c)(3)(A), Medicaid eligibility cannot be denied to an institutionalized spouse when the community spouse declares that (s)he intends not to support the institutionalized spouse, provided that he or she has first assigned to the State his or her right to seek support against the community spouse. Until recently, this technique was used exclusively in the State of New York. However, in 2005, the Second Circuit Court of Appeals upheld the district court decision in Morenz v. Wilson-Coker, [415 F.3d 230 (2d Cir. 2005)] which held that this is a correct interpretation of the law so long as there is a way to determine the institutionalized spouses's rights of support (and concluding that these rights existed in Connecticut, where Mrs. Morenz resided). The decision immediately made "spousal refusal" a reality throughout the Second Circuit, and the plain language reading of the statute should encourage those in other states to apply the same approach. Moreover, earlier versions of the Deficit Reduction Act apparently sought to limit "spousal refusal" by insisting that the refusing spouse make assets available for support, but these provisions were removed in the final version, giving further support to the approach's validity. Unfortunately, Connecticut's legislature recently (2007) enacted legislation intended to defeat "spousal refusal" as a technique by invalidating assignments of spousal support rights except where the community spouse either cannot be located, or is "unable" to provide information about his or her assets, a more difficult standard than "unwilling," the previous statutory scheme. Connecticut Public Act 07-02, Section 6. As Medicaid eligibility is contingent in a refusal case upon the spouse's assignment of support rights, defeating the assignment, it was thought, could make the MCCA refusal provisions ineffective. It remains to be seen whether this statute will stand up to judicial challenge, if one is brought.

By contrast, New York spouses have used "spousal refusal" as a technique for years. In its long experience with spousal refusal, the State of New York in later years has become more aggressive in seeking orders of support against the community spouse or making claims against the estate of a deceased community spouse; at most, however, these claims usually result in a settlement below the "spend-down" that would otherwise have been required. In short, *provided* assets are owned by or can be conveyed to the community spouse, and *provided* a mechanism exists whereby the institutionalized spouse can assign rights of support to the state (power of attorney, or conservatorship in which the conservator exercises the assignment), "Spousal refusal" may prove an important tool for the practitioner seeking to help the community spouse. The technique will be less valuable if the institutionalized spouse holds significant tax-deferred assets that will incur income tax upon transfer, or where it is important for the community spouse to be able to access the income of the institutionalized spouse, or if the states develop aggressive techniques for obtaining large support orders against community spouses.

Q 14:53.2 How may annuities be used to help a community spouse?

The community spouse's separate income is not deemed available to the institutionalized spouse (except that presumably where spousal refusal has been chosen, the state might obtain an order of support against the community spouse requiring contributions from income). In many states it has long been possible for the community spouse to use assets to purchase immediate, non-assignable, and irrevocable annuities whereby excess assets are converted to a stream of non-counted income. Even prior to the Deficit Reduction Act, states were losing the ability to limit the use of such annuities. For example, the New Jersey Supreme Court has rejected the state's claim that an actuarially sound spousal annuity must be limited to the amount of the CSRA to escape treatment as an available resource (or its purchase treated as a transfer). [Estate of F.K. v. Division of Medical Assistance and Health Services, 374 N.J. Super. 126 (2005); A.B. v. Division of Medical Assistance and Health Services, (N.J. App. Div. 2005)] The basic concept has always been that purchase of an annuity should not be treated as a disqualifying transfer if purchased for fair market value. This principle was recognized in the CMS State Medicaid Manual (a/k/a Transmittal 64), provided the guaranteed term of the annuity did not exceed the "actuarial life expectancy" of the life on which the annuity was based, applying the tables used in the State Medicaid Manual. Provided further that the annuity was irrevocable and non-assignable, it would also not be available as a resource. More recently, states have argued that even "non-assignable" annuities may be a resource if a company such as J.G. Wentworth chooses to pay consideration for the promise to turn over the "stream of income" from the annuity, so the protected status of annuities as non-available resources is somewhat tenuous at this time. The Deficit Reduction Act includes additional detail concerning annuities that would at least on the surface appear to confirm the validity of annuities purchased with assets of an applicant, and by extension, purchased with assets of an applicant's spouse—although the DRA provisions cast new doubts on the value of annuity planning in at least some individual cases. In the wake of the DRA, the Centers for Medicare and Medicaid Services' implementation of the new rules, and state experimentation, a number of principles have emerged as relevant to annuity planning:

1. *Amount of annuity purchase.* Typically, the appropriate value of the annuity will be set after all other planning steps have been undertaken (purchase of new home, investment in home repairs and automobiles, limited gifts to children, etc.). The amount of the annuity will often, but not always, be the difference between remaining resources and the community spouse resource allowance (the amount permitted to the community spouse), plus an appropriate allowance for annuity income in the first month(s), undervalued assets, and similar adjustments. Thus, after all other planning opportunities have been undertaken, the institutionalized spouse can be made eligible almost immediately.

2. *Term of annuity.* At a minimum, the term may not exceed the actuarial life expectancy of the purchaser under tables determined by Social Security Administration actuarial tables available online at http://www.ssa.gov/OACT/STATS/table4c6.html. Aside from this requirement, there are competing considerations in setting the term of the annuity. For some purposes (e.g., minimizing the couple's total income, delaying the growth of the couple's

assets, and providing for an ultimate benefit for children or other beneficiaries), a longer term is desirable. For most purposes, however, (e.g., total investment return and access to cash), shorter terms are better.

3. *Naming beneficiaries.* The Deficit Reduction Act of 2005, as amended by the Tax Relief and Health Care Act of 2006, significantly complicated annuity planning by providing that the State becomes a "preferred remainder beneficiary" for repayment of medical assistance furnished to the institutionalized person. The State need not be named in first position if the annuitant's spouse, or minor or disabled child is named as first remainder beneficiary instead; in most cases, however, naming the institutionalized spouse as first remainder beneficiary will be an inappropriate choice.

4. *Commercial versus private.* In many states, there is no need to purchase annuities through commercial (insurance) companies—they can be established by contract between the community spouse and children or other family members. In some states attention will be paid to whether the annuity is commercially reasonable (e.g., whether it provides an adequate rate of return), but annuity agreements among family members will be permitted. Still other states prohibit private annuities, or treat the transfers into private annuities as uncompensated transfers (gifts) or as transfers to trusts.

5. *Retirement annuities.* The DRA rules that require naming the state as contingent remainder beneficiary, "actuarially sound" terms, etc., apparently do *not* apply to individual retirement annuities or annuities purchased with qualified plan proceeds—a potentially major benefit to the community spouse who might otherwise have to cash in and spend down retirement savings at great income tax cost. Some states have, however, required that the beneficiary be changed to include the State as a condition of continuing Medicaid eligibility. Uncertainty also remains as to whether this applies to community spouse retirement savings to the same extent as to institutionalized spouse savings (in which case all income would be payable toward costs of care during that spouse's lifetime).

6. *State attempts to cast even non-assignable annuities as available "resources."* The DRA provision on annuities were carefully restricted to whether or not the purchase of an annuity would be considered a disqualifying transfer of assets, but left open

whether and when annuities could still be considered resources. Some states have attempted to prove that even "non-assignable" annuities may be "sold" as a stream of income (for example, North Dakota; see *Estate of Gross v. North Dakota Department of Human Services* [687 N.W.2d 460, 466 (N.D. 2004)]) while other such attempts have been judicially overturned; see *Ross v. Department of Public Welfare*, 936 A.2d 552 (Pa. Comm. 2007). The cost of mounting a legal challenge to such a state statute must be taken into account in those jurisdictions where annuities or other "streams of income" are deemed "resources."

Example 14-13. Mr. and Mrs. Rigby (ages 75 and 70, respectively) have $200,000 in available resources. Mr. Rigby has just been admitted to the nursing home, and it is unlikely that he will return home. Mrs. Rigby may retain $109,560 (2009 figure) in available resources, but the remaining assets (except for Mr. Rigby's $2,000 allowance) must be spent (or gifted, if the penalty period is not a concern) before Mr. Rigby will qualify for Medicaid.

One choice for Mrs. Rigby would be to purchase an annuity with as much as $88,440 of the couple's funds. The annuity should name her as annuitant and beneficiary; she may wish to have payments made to the couple's children upon her death before the annuity ends (though in most states the state must be named as beneficiary first). The annuity can be established for her life or for a term of years, provided that the term of years does not exceed her life expectancy. According to CMS tables, her life expectancy is 14.66 years. After checking price figures with several insurance companies, Mrs. Rigby purchases a single-premium immediate annuity for $88,440. Her monthly payments for 176 months will be approximately $550; if she dies before the final payment is received, succeeding payments will be payable to the State in reimbursement for Mr. Rigby's medical expenses, but any remaining balance could be paid to the children. Mr. Rigby is immediately eligible for Medicaid, although the amount of his monthly income that will be given to Mrs. Rigby is reduced because the annuity provides a significant increase in her monthly income and a corresponding decrease in her MMNA amount (see Q14:48).

Mrs. Rigby could conceivably purchase an annuity from her own children, if her state does not prohibit such a transaction. Provided the annuity meets the criteria of the Deficit Reduction Act, the transfer of funds to the children in exchange for the annuity would not be characterized as a disqualifying transfer. While it is true that if

Mrs. Rigby outlives her life expectancy her children may pay her more than they received, arguably they might have done so any way to preserve her quality of life. Further, although the annuity must be in payout status when Mr. Rigby applies for Medicaid, should Mrs. Rigby live past five years and her children no longer have the funds to make payments on the annuity, if they were unable to continue paying after she enters a nursing home and applies for Medicaid, it is questionable whether the State would find it worthwhile to take legal action to collect the remaining payments.

Q 14:53.3   Rather than purchasing an annuity, might assets be loaned to children?

Yes, although the practice may be fraught with difficulty and unanticipated danger. To the extent that a loan is not realistically capable of recovery, the transaction might ultimately be characterized as a gift. To the extent that the loan is enforceable, and even secured, it will remain an asset. In an appropriate case, however, if a loan is made to a child by the community spouse, with regular payments flowing back to the community spouse and adequate security, and with provisions making the note non-assignable, the effect may be similar to the annuity result—that is, conversion of a resource into a stream of income not countable only against the institutionalized spouse unless the state has a policy of counting a "stream of income" as a resource. As with the annuity approach, one effect of such a loan would be to reduce the community spouse's MMNA entitlement. The Deficit Reduction Act of 2005 also limited the use of loans in Medicaid planning by requiring that the repayment terms be actuarially sound and that there be no provision for cancellation of the indebtedness on death of the lender. The applicant may be required to sell the loan on the secondary market for a lump sum, in which case the borrowing child would have to repay the purchaser of the loan.

Q 14:53.4   Can a Medicaid applicant purchase a life estate in another person's home?

One pre-DRA planning option practiced in at least some locales was to suggest that the prospective Medicaid applicant purchase a life estate in, say, a child's home. If the purchase price was for fair market value (as calculated by factoring in the purchaser's life expectancy), the right to reside in the home could make it the applicant's residence and therefore an exempt resource. The effect of the transaction could be to transfer the purchase price to the next generation without subjecting the home itself to the estate recovery proceedings available to the Medicaid agency on the applicant's death. The Deficit Reduction Act of 2005, however, significantly altered this planning option—though it did not eliminate it altogether. The purchaser of such an interest must actually reside in the home for at least one year; if that test is not met, the purchase will be considered a transfer for less than full consideration even if the price is demonstrably the fair market value of the interest. However, in the occasional case where a future Medicaid applicant already lives with family in a home owned by the family, or could realistically move into such a residence, the DRA does clarify that the technique should work in every state provided that the residency requirement can be met and the purchase is fair. [42 U.S.C. § 1396p(c)(1)(J)]

Q 14:53.5   Can the State revisit the community spouse's assets after eligibility has been determined?

No; that is, it should not do so. Under the MCCA rules, once the institutionalized spouse has received eligibility, the assets of the community spouse are no longer subject to review by the State. [Houghton v. Reinertson, 382 F.2d 1162 (10th Cir. 2004) (Colorado could not apply retroactively a new rule lifting the exemption on 401(k) plans held by the community spouse, because after eligibility is determined, the state has no right to examine the assets of the community spouse.)] However, some states penalize a "transfer" of the home post-eligibility by the community spouse.

Spending Down

Q 14:55   What types of expenditures are permissible while spending down the assets of the institutionalized spouse and the community spouse's assets?

The rule has always been that so long as funds are spent for the benefit of the applicant or his or her spouse, and not for the benefit of third parties, such expenditures will not affect eligibility. Even this truism is now in doubt, as the Massachusetts Section 1115 Waiver proposal would place restrictions on how excess assets might be spent down.

(See SQ 14:9.) Assuming that the traditional rules apply, however, even travel and entertainment are allowed to spend down excess assets. The applicant and spouse would, however, be well advised to apply such funds toward exempt assets, such as paying off the mortgage on the home, purchasing a wheelchair-accessible van, remodeling, or paying off debts and other liabilities. If they have not done so already, they can purchase a burial plot and funeral contract (or purchase a small life insurance policy to cover burial costs) and purchase other assets considered exempt under Medicaid laws. (The insurance cash value can always be tapped later as if it were an extra savings account.) Considering looming cuts in Medicaid benefits, it is also highly advisable for any individual expecting a long nursing home stay to spend funds on a thorough dental examination and dental work, procuring glasses and other hardware that may be unavailable through Medicaid, purchasing orthopedic shoes, and generally attending to any health care needs that may be unmet from government benefits. Even though this process will result in expenditures (and loss of financial flexibility and freedom), it may remove substantial burdens from the community spouse, who already faces a loss of income and a reduction of assets because of the institutionalization of the spouse.

For most people, purchase of exempt assets will require the active involvement of an elder law attorney or other adviser familiar with Medicaid eligibility principles. Moreover, clients schooled in scrimping and saving will have trouble coming to grips with the reality of impending poverty and will require encouragement to take these steps. Depending on the generosity of the state's Medicaid program, it may be absolutely critical to attend to the often-ignored health needs of the soon-to-be impoverished institutionalized individual. For example, if dental care in the nursing home is inadequate and there is any already existing decay, this can quickly escalate into a painful condition that causes tooth loss and a system unwilling to pay for dentures or any restorative dental work. The resident is doomed to spend his or her last days eating creamed corn, which might have been prevented by thorough dental care when there were still funds to pay for it. Obviously, this is care that should be provided through the Medicaid system itself, but in the meantime, attention to these needs can prevent future anguish for the family and the resident.

Expenditures need not only be spent on items of "value," moreover, but also for items that will improve the quality of life for resident and spouse. Examples would be purchase of a television, VCR, stereo, computer (assuming appropriate access), books, videos, tapes, subscriptions, toiletries, clothing, and/or snacks. This will be contingent upon the standards the Medicaid agency uses when determining what items are "personal effects" and which may be converted to cash. Televisions are usually disregarded; state-of-the-art laptops possibly may not be. Too often families are encouraged to purchase the most expensive funeral contract available rather than planning for the quality of life of the institutionalized person and spouse.

In appropriate circumstances and subject to careful review of the state agency's approach to such matters, it may be possible to "purchase" in advance a care contract, particularly if the individual(s) providing services are not related to the resident, such as a friend. This will help to defray the cost and burden of attending care conferences and running errands in the future. A similar result might be achieved through placing funds in a pooled trust account for the disabled, described in 42 U.S.C. § 1396p(d)(4)(C), provided that the particular state does not consider such transfers disqualifying when made by individuals over 65. Region 1 of the Centers for Medicare and Medicaid has issued a memorandum that is being interpreted by some states to mean that funding such an account is subject to penalty (even though the counterargument is made that there is no "transfer" where the funds are for the person's own future use) so it remains to be seen whether this approach will continue to be available.

Last but not least, it is critical for the elder law attorney to make sure that legal fees are paid in full, up front and in advance. Better that these are paid from the "spend down" amount than from the community spouse's share. If the elderly client is single, there will be no more source of payment for legal fees once the client qualifies for Medicaid. (Funds put aside in the attorney's "trust account" are likely to be counted as "resources" should the agency become aware that they are there, even if they are said to be non-refundable.)

The timing of the "spend down" may be critical. There is a time for saving and a time for spending. Expenditures made before the first institutionalization will reduce the total available resources as of the date of institutionalization—the "snapshot" amount. That, in turn, will reduce the amount the community spouse is permitted to retain in those states utilizing any number other than the maximum CSRA as the state's minimum CSRA figure.

Example 14-5. Mr. and Mrs. Carlson have $250,000 in available resources (consisting of investment securities, cash, and certificates of deposit). Mr. Carlson has been diagnosed as suffering from early-stage Alzheimer's type dementia, and the couple would like to receive Medicaid coverage for his anticipated long-term care at the earliest possible moment. The Carlsons live in a state that utilizes the federal maximum CSRA as the minimum, so that if Mr. Carlson is admitted to a long-term care facility in 2009, Mrs. Carlson will be permitted to retain $109,560 (regardless of the level of assets at the time of first institutionalization) while still qualifying Mr. Carlson for Medicaid assistance. In order to hasten Medicaid eligibility, the Carlsons might choose to spend money now to visit their children (who live in three different states) while Mr. Carlson will still be able to interact with his grandchildren—but not to pay to have the children make the visits, as such a payment will be viewed as a gift for the benefit of the children. They might also pay off outstanding debts (including their mortgage) because debts are not counted against assets in determining Medicaid eligibility; this has the effect of reducing their available resources without affecting net worth.

If, however, Mr. and Mrs. Carlson live in a state that uses the $21,912 figure (2009) for the minimum CSRA calculation, they should consider delaying at least some expenditures until after Mr. Carlson becomes institutionalized, or at least, until he can be proven to be medically eligible for institutionalization. If the total available resources are less than twice the maximum CSRA figure at the time of institutionalization, early spend-down will have the perverse effect of reducing the amount that Mrs. Carlson can retain. Careful balancing of the amount to be spent, the categories of "spend down" to utilize, and timing are factors to be contemplated by Mr. and Mrs. Carlson and all others considering a similar course of action. (With appropriate timing, they could use credit cards to visit the grandchildren; the CSRA calculation does not factor in liabilities.)

Asset Transfers

Q 14:57 What is the look-back period for gifts by an applicant or spouse?

The "look-back" period describes how far back in time the agency will "look" to find transfers of assets by the applicant or spouse. OBRA '93 [see Q 14:10.2] increased the prior thirty-month look-back period to 36 months, or 60 months for transfers of assets to a trust, or from a trust established by the applicant and/or spouse. The Deficit Reduction Act of 2005 increased the look-back period to 60 months for all transfers made on or after the effective date of the Act, February 8, 2006. If a gift is made within the "look-back" period, there is no cap on the penalty. If the gift is made "outside" the look-back period, for eligibility purposes it simply never happened.

The attorney should pay close attention to the state regulations governing such transfers, as states may vary in their actual implementation of federal transfer penalty rules, particularly the rules of the Deficit Reduction Act; as of this writing, it is not clear which states will view the transfer provisions as self-executing—effective immediately—and which will require implementing legislation or regulatory adoption.

Eligibility workers are entitled to inquire about transfers made within, but not about those made before, the applicable look-back period. In other words, an outright gift of millions of dollars made more than 60 months before the Medicaid application will not prevent eligibility for Medicaid long-term care coverage, even though the ineligibility period (calculated as described in Q 14:58) might be many years beyond the 60 months if it were computed.

Example 14-6. Mrs. White made a $1,010,000 gift to her only son in January 2003, for the purpose of fully utilizing her federal transfer tax exemption equivalent amount. Shortly thereafter she entered a skilled nursing facility, where she has since resided. In February 2006, her assets dropped below $2,000 and she applied for Medicaid assistance; her state "divisor" for calculating ineligibility is $4,000. How far back must she disclose gifts she has made? Only as far back as February, 2003. She cannot be required to disclose any gift made more than 36 months ago (i.e., before February 1, 2003), and so the large gift in January 2003 will have no effect on her current eligibility. However, if Mrs. White had applied for Medicaid assistance in January, the result might have been very different. In that case, she would have been required to disclose any gift made in January, 2003, and as a result, the gift would have generated a penalty period of ineligibility—depending on the state, that period might have been capped at 36 months or might have run for 252 months, or until January 2024. By contrast, if Mrs. White made her gift of $1,010,000 in March, 2006, and applied for benefits at any time prior to April, 2011, her gift would be within the look-back period and would disqualify her from receiving benefits for 252.4 months under the provisions of the DRA.

Note also that if instead of Mrs. White making a $1,010,000 gift to her son, Mr. White had made a $1,010,000 gift to his mistress and then left for South America, in theory Mrs. White would be similarly ineligible. States' hardship provisions, mandated by the Deficit

Reduction Act and already available in at least limited circumstances in some states before the adoption of the DRA, might afford Mrs. White some protection in such a case.

Q 14:57.1   How will the new 5-year look-back period be "phased in" for applications after February 8, 2006?

The five-year look-back period applies only to transfers made "on or after the effective date of the act." In some states, however, the effective date has been set as some later date by which regulations or procedures were established by the state Medicaid agency. Until February 8, 2009, therefore, it will only be necessary to "look back" 3 years; thereafter, the period will increase month by month until it reaches a full 5 years on February 8, 2011.

Q 14:58   For gifts occurring within the look-back period, how is the "penalty period" calculated?

Although state implementation of the transfer penalty calculation varied significantly under prior law, the Deficit Reduction Act of 2005 mandates that some basic principles be adopted by every Medicaid agency. The total amount of disqualifying gifts is calculated by adding together all transfers made within the five-year look-back period, and then dividing by the state's (or in some instances the county's or region's) divisor, which in theory is based on the average monthly cost of care in the community. The resulting number represents the number of months of ineligibility which, pursuant to the Deficit Reduction Act of 2005, will begin to run in the month in which the applicant is otherwise eligible for Medicaid—in other words, both medically eligible and below the resource and income limits.

Example 14-7. Mr. Summers made a gift of $10,000 to his daughter in August 2006, entered the nursing home one month later and applied for Medicaid eligibility when his assets dropped below $2,000 in December, 2009. His state penalty divisor is $4,000. While he would have been eligible for Medicaid assistance at the time of application under old law, he will now remain ineligible for 2.5 months from the date of his application in December—that is, until late in February, 2009—because the penalty period will not begin to run until his assets have dropped below the $2,000 level.

Example 14-8. Mrs. Carlson made a gift of $25,000 in August, 2006; her state's penalty divisor is also $4,000. She has substantial other assets and is healthy, and she does not enter the nursing home until 2008. On January 1, 2010, after having finally exhausted her assets, she applies for Medicaid assistance; because the August, 2006, gift was within 5 years of her application, her ineligibility period will begin to run in January 2010, and will prevent her from qualifying for Medicaid until mid-July 2010. Mrs. Carlson may be able to show that the purpose behind her 2006 gift was not to secure Medicaid eligibility, or she may be able to qualify under her state's hardship waiver provisions, but if not she will have no resources from which to pay for her care and no assistance for 6.25 months.

Q 14:59 How can one find out the "divisor" used to compute the penalty period?

"Average private pay rates" used to determine ineligibility penalties are set by the individual state agencies, and are not required to be adjusted on a fixed schedule, nor are they reliably published in any centralized location. The elder law practitioner will have to contact the state Medicaid agency, state bar association elder law section, National Academy of Elder Law Attorneys chapter, or vendors providing information to elder law attorneys in order to remain up-to-date on the particular state's annual "divisor" for computing penalty periods.

The real question is: how much would the actual (not hypothetical) client have to pay for his or her actual (not hypothetical) costs during the penalty period? This may involve computations that are more complicated than a simple comparison of nursing home cost to assets, and must factor in other sources of income and additional care costs such as home care for those not already in a nursing home. Even then, it is more useful to determine the actual nursing home costs of those facilities in which the client might become interested when nursing home care is imminent, rather than a statewide "average" figure.

Q 14:60 Besides gifts, does anything else constitute a "transfer"?

Yes, under 42 U.S.C. Section 1396p(c)(1)(A), penalties are imposed whenever an applicant or MCCA spouse "disposes of assets for less than fair market value." "Disposes" has been broadly read to include:

1. Purchase of an annuity that does not comply with the requirements of Section 6012 of the Deficit Reduction Act (including the requirement that the annuity name the State as beneficiary

in the second position to the annuitant, spouse, and minor or disabled child, and that the annuity make regular payments, with no "balloon") [42 U.S.C. § 1396p(c)(1)(F) and (G)];

2. Making a loan that does not qualify with the requirements of Section 6016 of the Deficit Reduction Act (including the requirement that the loan *not* include a provision for cancellation at death, and that payments be made on a periodic basis) [42 U.S.C. § 1396p(c)(1)(I)];

3. Purchase of a life estate in which the purchaser does not reside for a year following the purchase [42 U.S.C. § 1396p(c)(1)(J)];

4. Disclaiming an inheritance or other right to property (assuming even that state law does not prohibit disclaimers by benefit recipients or former recipients [see, e.g., Department of Income Maintenance v. Watts, 211 Conn. 323 (1989); Massachusetts Statutes Section 1918.A (insolvency bars disclaimer)]);

5. Failing to make the statutory election "against the will" of a deceased spouse [see, e.g., Perna ex rel. Bekus v. Department of Public Welfare, 807 A.2d 310 (Pa. Cmwlth. 2002); Estate of Dionisio v. Westchester Dep't. of Social Services, 665 N.Y.S.2d 904 (Mem), 244 A.D.2d 483 (1997) (even though required by the prenuptial agreement); Tannler v. Wisconsin Dep't of Health & Social Services, 564 N.W.2d 735 (Wisc. 1997)];

6. Failure to exercise a "Crummey power" withdrawal right in a trust;

7. Sale of an asset below a supposed "market value"; and

8. Withdrawal by another joint owner of jointly held bank accounts.

The concept of uncompensated transfers may be limited only by the creative thinking of state Medicaid agencies.

Q 14:61 Can assets be transferred between spouses without incurring a penalty?

Yes. There is no penalty for transfers between spouses. [42 U.S.C. § 1396p(c)(2)(B)] In fact, after eligibility has been obtained any resources not transferred to the community spouse may be deemed available to the institutionalized spouse and can affect his or her continued eligibility, so that transfer can be vitally important. Medicaid eligibility is calculated based on the assets available to either the institutionalized or the community spouse, so transfers of assets to the community spouse before the eligibility application will not ordinarily make initial eligibility any easier to obtain (see SQ 14:51). However, after eligibility has been obtained for the institutionalized spouse, some states interpret the provisions of MCCA to permit the institutionalized spouse to transfer to the community spouse only what is necessary to meet the CSRA, or in some cases, the home. Usually nothing else is available to be transferred; the issue will be whether the institutionalized spouse could transfer a subsequent windfall to the community spouse without penalty.

One possible exception to this rule is the different treatment states accord to purchases of annuities for the benefit of a community spouse or transfers in trust for the benefit of a community spouse. These are discussed in SQ 14:73.

It is also critical to be sure, here as in all other aspects of eligibility, that the institutionalized spouse is living in a "skilled nursing facility." In those states in which "rest homes" or other "assisted living" facilities are not paid through Medicaid, but some other program, a transfer between spouses could be treated as a disqualifying transfer, depending upon that program's rules.

Q 14:62 Are there some types of assets that may be given away without incurring a penalty?

Yes. Assets that can be transferred without penalty include:

1. Assets transferred to a third party but for the sole benefit of the spouse [42 U.S.C. § 1396p(c)(2)] (see, however, SQ 14:73);
2. Assets transferred to the applicant's blind or disabled child [42 U.S.C. § 1396p(c)(2)];
3. Transfers into a trust for the sole benefit of a spouse, blind or disabled child or individual [42 U.S.C. § 1396p(c)(2)(B)(i)-(iii)];
4. Transfers of assets belonging to a disabled individual into a so-called "payback" or OBRA '93 trust for a disabled individual under age 65 [42 U.S.C. § 1396p(c)(2)(B)(iv)];
5. Asset transfers to a qualified income assignment trust ("Miller trust") for the benefit of an institutionalized spouse [42 U.S.C. § 1396p(d)(4)(B)] (see Q 14:91);
6. A home transferred to a spouse, child under the age of 21, sibling of the applicant who lived in the home for one year prior to the applicant's institutionalization and who had some ownership

interest in the home, or an adult child who lived in the home at least two years before the institutionalization of the applicant and provided sufficient care to that person to allow him or her to remain in the home [42 U.S.C. § 1396p(c)(2)(A)]; and

7. Transfers to third parties of income-producing assets currently used in a trade or business owned by the applicant or his or her family or the liquid assets of such trade or business.

In addition, a transfer of assets technically will not affect Medicaid eligibility if:

1. The individual intended to receive fair market value or some other valuable consideration [42 U.S.C. § 1396p(c)(2)(C)];

2. The asset was disposed of exclusively for a purpose other than obtaining Medicaid eligibility [42 U.S.C. § 1396p(c)(2)(C)]; or

3. Denial of eligibility would work an undue hardship [42 U.S.C. § 1396p(c)(2)(D)].

These "exceptions" are difficult to obtain in many states, while in others transfers "for a purpose other than obtaining Medicaid eligibility" may include transfers of any exempt asset, even the home.

Assets transferred to an OBRA '93 or "payback" special needs trust for a disabled person under 65, or to a Miller trust for the benefit of an institutionalized spouse will also be allowed, although the requirements for these trusts must be strictly observed (see Qs 14:85, 14:91). Whether or not assets may be "transferred" without penalty to a pooled trust account under 42 U.S.C. § 1396p(d)(4)(C) for a person over sixty-five is currently under review (see Q 14:90). Moreover, each state applies these exemptions differently and may or may not have published its approach in a written rule or regulation.

Q 14:63   What is meant by the "half-a-loaf" strategy of Medicaid planning?

Prior to the Deficit Reduction Act of 2005, the applicant could take advantage of the ineligibility rules by transferring approximately half of his or her non-exempt assets to a third party and retaining the other half to support himself or herself during the resulting period of ineligibility. This strategy was commonly referred to as the "half-a-loaf" strategy (and sometimes as "the rule of halves") for the obvious reason: The DRA changed the calculation dramatically, but has not completely eliminated the planning opportunity. Because the ineligibility period now

begins after the applicant would otherwise be eligible, there is no opportunity to make a gift of roughly half of the applicant's assets and wait out
the ineligibility period. It may, however, be possible in some cases to
either:

1. Make a larger gift, retaining sufficient assets to provide 5 years of
   care coverage, or
2. Make a larger gift and use exempt assets (e.g., the applicant's
   home equity, via a reverse mortgage) to pay for care during the
   ineligibility period.

Q 14:63.1 What is the "reverse half-a-loaf" strategy?

One option suggested in the wake of the DRA would be for the prospective Medicaid applicant to make a gift of substantially all of his or
her assets and immediately make a Medicaid application. The gift will,
of course, disqualify the applicant, but the ineligibility period will be
calculated. If the gift recipient then retransfers the monthly amount
required for care, under at least some states' rules that could be treated
as a "partial cure" of the gift ineligibility period and shorten the wait for
Medicaid eligibility each month. Depending on state interpretation and
federal regulation, the effect could even be to accomplish something
very near to the previously-available "half-a-loaf" approach to Medicaid
planning. Extreme caution should be taken in attempting such a technique, however, as it is unlikely to be favorably viewed and, depending
on the size of the initial gift, may even extend the ineligibility period
past the five-year look back period that would have existed if no Medicaid application was made at the beginning of the process. The utility of
the "reverse half-a-loaf" strategy varies significantly by state. Although
the proposed regulations have not (as of July 2008) been finalized, they
are being implemented and have effectively eliminated the possibility of
"reverse half-a-loaf" planning in Connecticut (as one example).

Q 14:64 Are "post-eligibility" transfers treated differently?

In general, yes, if made by the community spouse. Because the
resources of the community spouse are not attributable to the institutionalized spouse after eligibility has been determined, in most states
the community spouse may transfer almost anything without penalty
after the institutionalized spouse has been awarded eligibility. [42
U.S.C. § 1396r-5(c)(4)]. This means that even the home may be sold

and the proceeds transferred. There are exceptions and variations to this conclusion, however. In an informal 2004 poll of 22 states, it appeared that two—Colorado and Minnesota—still penalized the institutionalized spouse if the community spouse makes "post-eligibility" transfers. Oddly, Wisconsin will allow transfers of the CSRA, but penalize all other post-eligibility transfers by the community spouse. Proposed Connecticut regulations penalize the transfer by a community spouse of proceeds of a reverse mortgage, home equity loan, or similar instrument.

Transfers of the home arguably present a different issue. The federal statutes may be construed, in the aggregate to prohibit the post-eligibility transfer of the home, without a penalty. The statutory construction argument is somewhat difficult: MCCA [42 U.S.C. § 1396r-5(c)(5)] defines "resources" (which are deemed from the community spouse to the institutionalized spouse prior to application, but are no longer deemed available to the applicant after eligibility is granted) to exclude for all purposes of this section, "resources excluded under subsection (a) or (d) of section 1613 [42 U.S.C. § 1382b]." 42 U.S.C. § 1382b(a) excludes the home. By contrast, the transfer provisions define "resources" disregarding the "exclusions" under 42 U.S.C. § 1382b. Therefore, the argument is that while for purposes of eligibility, the home is not "deemed" to the institutionalized spouse either before or after eligibility, the transfer rules in 42 U.S.C. § 1396p(c) expressly reject the "1613(a)" exclusion. (This prohibition would seem to apply even if there is no "community spouse," for example, if both were institutionalized at the time of application.) In point of fact, however, few states seem to follow this interpretation of the statute. In the poll referred to above, only four—Colorado, Connecticut, Minnesota, and certain counties in Ohio—apparently claim that they will apply such penalties. It may be that the other states, like California, apply SSI terminology to declare that the home is not a "resource" and that since only transfers of "resources and income" are penalized, the transfer of the home should not result in a penalty.

Of course, a transfer by the community spouse can affect that person's own eligibility for benefits.

Finally, transfers by the beneficiary, the institutionalized spouse himself or herself, will still cause the imposition of a penalty. For example, if the institutionalized beneficiary receives an inheritance and transfers it to another, it will be considered a transfer of assets that causes imposition of a penalty. Although the same exemptions should apply—such as intraspousal transfers—states may have incorporated into their benefit laws a blanket prohibition on all transfers by recipients without state approval, perhaps even making such transfers void. Such laws have been upheld when it comes to a recipient or former recipient seeking to disclaim an asset—the disclaimer does not so much cause a penalty in some states as it is actually ineffective. [Department of Income Maintenance v. Watts, 211 Conn. 323, 555 A.2d 998 (1989)]

Q 14:64.1 How can an applicant make a claim for relief in the event of "undue hardship"?

Even prior to the Deficit Reduction Act, Medicaid law stated that Medicaid eligibility should not be denied on account of an otherwise disqualifying transfer if the denial would result in "undue hardship." The DRA gave substance to the term "undue hardship" and specifically required a process by which undue hardship could be claimed. In the words of CMS:

> Under the DRA, undue hardship exists when application of a transfer of assets penalty would deprive the individual—

- of medical care such that the individual's health or life would be endangered; or
- of food, clothing, shelter, or other necessities of life.

> Further, the statute specifically requires that States provide the following:

- Notice to individuals that an undue hardship exception exists;
- A timely process for determining whether an undue hardship waiver will be granted; and
- A process, which the notice describes, under which an adverse determination can be appealed.

[CMS Letter SMDL 06-018, Attachment]

How these requirements will be implemented will depend upon each individual state's promulgation of hardship provisions. However, it could be argued that if the State fails to promulgate required procedures, denials may be invalid; or it may also be possible to challenge a denial in federal court if the state's promulgated rule does not truly incorporate the requirements of the DRA. Practitioners may wish to prepare for such arguments by ensuring that a client's family does not create the impression of being able to pay for the care of a family member who may subsequently want to claim that without Medicaid, he or she will be deprived of needed medical care, or clothing and shelter.

Section 6011(e)(1) of the DRA also changed the statute to permit the facility to make a claim of "undue hardship" itself, with the applicant's consent. States may also authorize "bed hold" payments to facilities for the days during which a hardship waiver application is pending, but not more than 30 days.

Liability for Eligibility-Related Asset Transfers

Q 14:66 Will the recipient of gifts from a Medicaid applicant be criminally liable for participating in the transfers?

There is no current federal law that penalizes a recipient of gifts from an applicant in any way, although the applicant who makes gifts may thereby become ineligible for benefits. Of course, a recipient who was involved in securing the gift by tortious or criminal means may be either civilly or criminally liable (or both) for those acts. In addition, at least one state, Connecticut, is attempting to impose a lien or debt status on any transferred property of a person who later applies for Medicaid during the look-back period. The analogy may be to the "preference" items under bankruptcy law, whereby payments to a creditor within nine months of declaring bankruptcy may be recoverable by the bankruptcy trustee. In the Medicaid context, however, this seems highly problematic and subject to legal challenge if it is ever effectuated. Nevertheless, other states, looking at ways to trim Medicaid expenditures, may become persuaded that such a law would be an effective deterrent.

Q 14:67 Is there any criminal liability for an attorney or other adviser who is involved in asset transfer planning?

Rather than making the client criminally liable, the Balanced Budget Act of 1997 (BBA '97) targeted advisers (i.e., lawyers and financial planners) counseling applicants about transfers geared toward attaining Medicaid eligibility. [Pub. L. No. 105-35, § 5755, amending 42 U.S.C. § 1320a-7b(a)] Like its predecessor, "Granny Goes to Jail," the new law was immediately criticized as unenforceable and unconstitutional, and was given a catchy nickname: "Granny's Lawyer Goes to Jail." Once again, the law was so badly written that it attempted to apply criminal penalties even to those who did nothing more than discuss the current law with their clients. The Federal District Court for the Northern District of New York enjoined the federal government from enforcing the criminalization provision, despite the protestations of the Attorney General's office that the law was admittedly unconstitutional and no prosecutions were contemplated or anticipated. [New York State Bar Association v. Reno, 999 F. Supp. 710 (N.D.N.Y. 1998)] Attorney General Janet Reno issued a letter in March 1998 stating that in her opinion the law is unconstitutional under the First Amendment and is thus not subject to prosecution.

Asset Transfer Techniques

Q 14:68 How can resources be spent down?

In disposing of resources, one planning device is simply to convert them to "exempt" assets (e.g., home, furnishings, automobiles) that are not considered resources, or in other words, are exempt from being counted as available (see Q 14:38). Transfer available resources into those exempt categories. This might be accomplished, depending on the situation, by one or more of the following:

1. Purchase of a home, or sale of an existing home and purchase of a new, more expensive home (within the $500,000/$750,000 equity limit imposed by the Deficit Reduction Act of 2005).

2. Home improvements, including roof repair, room addition, wheelchair accessibility work, completion of deferred maintenance (once again, taking care not to increase the equity in the home beyond the $500,000 limit imposed by the DRA or, in states electing to adopt the DRA's permissive $750,000 limit, the higher figure). Even if the improvements cannot be completed by the time the couple hopes Medicaid eligibility will be achieved, they can be paid for in advance, with due caution taken about the trustworthiness of the contractor.

3. Purchase of new furniture, appliances, furnishings (floor coverings, window coverings, etc.).

4. Purchase of a new automobile (sometimes coupled with the gift of the previous, exempt, vehicle, as described here).

5. Payment of the existing home mortgage. To maximize the value of this technique in a marital situation, it may even be advantageous to acquire a mortgage or secured line of credit immediately before institutionalization, and to pay off the indebtedness immediately after institutionalization. In many states, this technique has the effect of increasing the community spouse resource allowance, because even secured indebtedness is not used in the calculation. Once the CSRA is fixed (by institutionalization or documented eligibility for institutionalization), the debt can be retired, leaving a larger net amount in the hands of the community spouse.

For other suggestions (and cautions), see Q 14:55.

Q 14:71   Can the residence be transferred into a revocable living trust?

The effect of a retained life estate coupled with a special power of appointment is tantamount to a beneficiary designation as to real property, akin to the pay-on-death provision commonly available for bank and other financial accounts. Of course, it is possible to effect the same result more directly, simply by transferring the property into a revocable trust; however, in many states, the property held by a trust is treated as non-exempt—apparently on the questionable theory that because the "owner" of the property is no longer the individual, then it cannot be a personal residence. Consequently, in those states at least (e.g., Arizona, Ohio, Tennessee, and others), trust ownership is not a reasonable approach to resolving the problem—though it may be an effective way to increase the CSRA for the community spouse, provided that the transfer into trust is accomplished before the institutionalization of the ill spouse. In one state, Connecticut, a special "trust-busting" statute would make any such trust vulnerable to termination if the grantor or spouse applied for benefits within five years. [Conn. Gen. Stat. § 45a-486] This law has not yet been challenged.

Q 14:72   Is it a mistake to transfer the residence into a living trust in those states treating trust assets as non-exempt?

Not necessarily. Precisely because the trust's assets are counted as available, use of a living trust may be a clever and powerful Medicaid planning technique—depending on the state's interpretation of the rules. If the residence is owned by the trust at the time one spouse first becomes medically eligible for Medicaid, the value of the property will be included in the calculation of available resources. Because that calculation is in turn used to determine the community spouse's maximum allowance in many states, trust ownership of the residence effectively inflates the amount that the community spouse is permitted to retain. By the simple expedient of transferring the residence out of the trust and into the spouses' names (or, if permitted by the trust's terms, into the community spouse's name alone), the couple's assets may be reduced below the eligibility level. As a consequence, long-time trust ownership of the family residence is highly beneficial, at least in those states that both treat trust assets as non-exempt and calculate the community spouse resource allowance by dividing the total available resources (rather than adopting a presumptive CSRA for all applicants). This benefit will, of course, be insignificant for the wealthy couple, whose assets easily exceed two times the maximum CSRA without considering the family residence.

As with all planning techniques, it is critical to be current with the particular state's interpretation of these rules. Some states are "wise" to this technique and will fail to recognize the transfer out of the trust as an appropriate "spend-down" or have decided to "look through" the trust to the exempt asset and refuse to count it when determining the CSRA.

Example 14-12. Mrs. and Mrs. Danielson own their home (valued at $150,000), and $100,000 of available resources. Neither is presently institutionalized or even ill. If one of them should enter the nursing home with their current asset situation, the home would be exempt. Because their state implements the Community Spouse Resource Allowance by dividing the total available resources in half and applying the federal minimum and maximum limits, the community spouse would be permitted to retain $50,000 of the remaining assets. Eligibility would therefore be obtained when the total available resources reached $52,000 (allowing for the institutionalized spouse's $2,000). The community spouse will have to spend, gift, or otherwise dispose of $48,000 of cash.

If, however, Mr. and Mrs. Danielson establish a revocable living trust and transfer their home to the trust, their circumstance may change. If Mr. and Mrs. Danielson live in a state which treats a residence owned by a living trust as an available resource, they may accomplish eligibility much more easily if their home had been transferred to such a trust—even though the motivation may not have had anything to do with Medicaid planning. In fact, Mr. and Mrs. Danielson attended an estate planning seminar at a local resort hotel, and ended up creating a living trust and transferring their home and all the other assets into the trust's name. Upon the later institutionalization of one spouse, the other (community) spouse will be permitted to retain the CSRA maximum of $109,560 (in 2009) because the home will have been treated as an available resource. By simply transferring the home from the trust to the name of both spouses (or to the community spouse alone, if the trust permits such a transfer) *after* institutionalization, the institutionalized spouse will immediately qualify for Medicaid assistance. The cost of establishing a trust will have been repaid many times; in the meantime, in spite of their relatively modest estate size and their state's relatively liberal probate rules, Mr. and Mrs. Danielson will also have received protection from the (modest) cost of probate if neither is ever institutionalized. While many elder law practitioners might criticize the estate planning firm conducting the seminars as a "trust mill," the trust mill may—quite unintentionally—have given Mr. and Mrs. Danielson significant value for their initial investment.

Q 14:73　(Reserved)

Q 14:74　(Reserved)

Q 14:75　When is an annuity useful in Medicaid planning for an unmarried person?

Under prior law, an annuity was sometimes an attractive choice for a single applicant with a shortened life expectancy, since the remaining payments after the applicant's death could go to intended beneficiaries. Under the Deficit Reduction Act of 2005, that occasional advantage has largely been eliminated by the requirement that the state be named as remainder beneficiary—though, in an appropriate case, the goal of securing eligibility may still be an attractive option to effectively reduce the cost of long-term care to the state's reimbursement rate for Medicaid patients.

Q 14:76   Are there problems with annuity planning?

Yes. While in some situations annuities may prove useful, they raise innumerable problems:

- Those who buy annuities before needed may incur taxes to liquidate assets with which to purchase the annuity.

- The elderly are often targeted for sales of deferred annuities with high surrender penalties, effectively locking in assets that may be needed for immediate health or long-term care needs or that might otherwise be used for half-a-loaf gifting.

- If the annuity payout is too small, the individual entering the nursing home may wind up on Medicaid with the company paying "applied income" to the facility with no benefit to the individual, who will also lose the modest benefit of having been a "private pay" (and thus "private room") resident for the period of time his or her assets might have procured.

- Techniques such as balloon payment annuities will now (post Deficit Reduction Act) be considered "gifts" subject to penalty if made during the look-back period; even those purchased prior to February 8, 2006 can backfire leaving the purchaser without resources and without Medicaid. [Gillmore v. Illinois Dep't. of Human Services, 354 Ill. App. 3d 497 (2004)].

- States have cited the practice of using spousal annuities to enhance community spouse income as an "abuse"; as the political climate warms to the draconian waivers that have been proposed, the odds of a congressional attack on the practice increases. [Massachusetts Medicaid waiver proposal].

- Annuities are often marketed with disregard of the true effect on Medicaid eligibility and resulting "mistakes" such as: (1) purchase of a deferred annuity rather than immediate annuity, with further surrender or conversion charges should the annuity be converted; (2) naming the wrong spouse as the annuitant; (3) failure to make the annuity non-assignable; (4) failure to disclose the true costs of the annuity.

- If the annuity arrangement is private, consisting of a transfer to children in exchange for a private annuity contract, it is important to remember that there may be income tax consequences for the transferor if the transferred property has unrealized gain. New regulations make it clear that gain is recognized on such transfers and is reportable over the lifetime of the annuitant. [See 71 Fed. Reg. 61441 (October 18, 2006)]

Q 14:77 How can a self-canceling installment note be used to hasten Medicaid eligibility?

The self-canceling installment note (SCIN) was originally used as a tax-minimization device. By loaning money to family members and taking back a SCIN, a parent could effectively transfer assets to the next generation at less than the face value, particularly if the parent did not anticipate living to his or her actuarial life expectancy. Whatever value SCINs might have had in Medicaid planning, however, was largely eliminated by the Deficit Reduction Act of 2005, which requires that any loan which includes a provision canceling the remaining balance at death of the lender will be treated as an uncompensated transfer of assets. [42 U.S.C. § 1396p(c)(2)(1)]

Q 14:78 (Reserved)

Q 14:79 (Reserved)

Q 14:80 How can a long-term care Medicaid applicant use a family limited partnership or limited liability company to hasten Medicaid eligibility?

In estate tax planning, family limited partnerships (FLPs) and limited liability company (LLCs) are often used to reduce the value of a parent's assets, thereby reducing the estate tax liability on the parent's death. This works by virtue of the reduction in value occasioned by the combination of loss of control of the asset and the resultant lack of marketability; although the original asset may have been valued at one price, 90 percent ownership of that asset is not valued at 90 percent of the original price.

The same logic and mechanism works for Medicaid planning as well. In fact, FLPs and LLCs may work even better for Medicaid than estate tax planning purposes precisely because of the loss of control. By establishing an FLP and transferring all or substantially all of his or her assets to it, a potential Medicaid recipient not only reduces the value of the underlying asset but also establishes the possibility of having the FLP interest ignored for eligibility purposes because it is unmarketable.

Keep in mind, however, that in states with aggressive social services agencies, any restriction on control of assets may be deemed a "trust" and therefore treated as an available resource at the full value—resulting in the double problem of lack of availability of an asset which is being counted as a resource preventing eligibility.

Q 14:83 What are some specific Medicaid planning techniques permitted in individual states?

Although the variation from state to state is tremendous, a number of specific practices merit attention. In some cases, local state practice may be based on an interpretation not previously considered in another state; in other cases, it may be important to be able to advise clients who are moving to or arriving from another state, or who have ill parents or other relatives in another state. Of course, the Medicaid rules vary so significantly among states that no elder law practitioner should expect to be able to give specific advice in a state in which he or she has not actually become familiar with local rules and practices. A list of the more common (and interesting) state variations would include:

1. *Transfer of home (California).* California permits the transfer of the (exempt) home to third persons, reasoning that any transfer of an exempt asset must necessarily be motivated by a purpose other than to qualify for benefits. Given the value of California real estate, this opens a tremendous opportunity. As of this writing—2004—California is considering adopting new regulations that would eliminate this technique.

2. *Spousal refusal (New York and parts of the Second Circuit).* The community spouse's assets can be made unavailable by simply declaring an intent not to support the institutionalized spouse. The institutionalized spouse's right to support must then be assigned to the Medicaid agency (unless he or she is unable to make the assignment because of impairment). [42 U.S.C. § 1396r-5(c)(3)(A)] Medicaid law then limits the amount of the community spouse's income that can be required to support the institutionalized spouse. Coupled with the exemption for interspousal transfers, this creates a powerful planning opportunity, though it may still be unique to New York [Shah v. DeBuono, 711 N.Y.S.2d 824 (N.Y. 2000), *aff'g*, 694 N.Y.S.2d 82 (App. Div. 1999)]

(Connecticut, which was responsible for the federal case Morenz v. Wilson-Coker, 415 F.3d 230 (2d Cir. 2005), has made an "end-run" around the logic of the <u>Morenz decision by legislating limits on the ability of the institutionalized spouse to assign support rights to the Medicaid agency</u>. In addition to the possibility that the Morenz v. Wilson-Coker decision may be applied to the remaining state in the Second Circuit, Vermont, a Florida court appears to acknowledge the validity of the concept. [Gorlick v. Florida Dept. of Children & Families, 789 So.2d 1247 (Fla. App. 2001)] New York has, however, become more aggressive in seeking orders of support against the community spouse, and there is also the problem of a claim against the estate of a deceased community spouse. (See Q 14:100.1.)

3. *Annuity analogized to irrevocable trust (Kansas and Alabama).* Kansas treats all annuities as if they were transfers to an irrevocable trust, imposing a transfer penalty and thereby making the annuity an unusable plan in most circumstances. Alabama apparently adds a good-faith test: An annuity purchased during the look-back period is suspect, while an annuitized retirement account is not.

4. *Rental real estate exempt (Indiana).* Apparently on the theory that rental real estate is an illiquid investment and that the income can be used to subsidize nursing care in any case, Indiana simply exempts all rental real estate. Medicaid planning may be as simple as purchasing a family member's home and renting it back to the family member.

5. *Transferee liability (Connecticut).* Non-exempt gifts within the look-back period create a "debt" owed by transferor and transferee in the amount of medical assistance provided or the value of the gift, whichever is less. [Connecticut Public Acts No. 05-209, § 4] It is worth noting that three years later, there are no cases of this law being applied.

Medicaid Trust Planning

Q 14:86   What is the "testamentary trust" exception to the trust rules?

OBRA '93 states at 42 U.S.C. Section 1396p(d)(2)(A) that:

(2)(A) For purposes of this subsection, an individual shall be considered to have established a trust if assets of the individual were used to form all or part of the corpus of the trust and if any of the following individuals established such trust other than by will:

The essential term in this paragraph is "other than by will." The rules that treat as available any discretionary trust established by applicant or spouse do *not* apply to testamentary trusts. This means that one spouse can name the other in his or her will as beneficiary of a discretionary trust that gives the trustee the right to withhold payments, without affecting the surviving spouse's benefits, *and* without the trust being vulnerable to a state lien on the surviving spouse's death. In states where other planning devices to protect a spouse are weak, this can be an important choice for the spouse likely to die first—statistically, the husband. As a planning technique, this requires either a guess as to which spouse may die first versus who may require long-term care first, or a decision to split the odds and have assets evenly divided between the parties. (In community property states, presumably there is no need to make the choice, unless of course it is possible to first convert community property to separate property.) It also requires a deliberate choice to go through probate, depending upon one's state law respecting the establishment of a testamentary trust outside the probate process. For example, in a common law state the home's joint tenancy must be severed so that one-half will pass to the testamentary discretionary trust under the will of the first to die. This step is so counterintuitive to clients schooled in probate avoidance that it may be overlooked. Of course, it is best used where the first spouse's death appears imminent.

The utility of the technique must be tempered by state law governing the surviving spouse's statutory share. Where that share is large, failure to elect against the will that instead sets up a discretionary trust, may well be treated as a disqualifying transfer by the surviving spouse, to the extent of the value of the statutory share at the time. If that were the only issue, and the surviving spouse has no imminent need for long-term care, it might be worthwhile to accept that risk. The problem is that the court may decide that because the trust was funded, at least in part, by the assets that the surviving spouse failed to claim, the trust is no longer a third-party testamentary trust created by the decedent, but a self-funded trust created by the survivor, and as such, is no longer exempt. [Miller v. S.R.S., 64 P.3d 395 (2003)] With that concern, and particularly if the statutory share is more modest, the surviving spouse probably should make the statutory election but leave the balance of the property protected (provided the will preserves that right against a state law that would deprive the party making the election of any other interest under the will). In some states, the presence of a trust in the will that approximates the statutory share, a "statutory share trust," may eliminate the right of election entirely. Finally, it may be possible to argue that the failure to elect was made for consideration, in that the spouse would have had to forego the discretionary trust in order to receive the elective share. If the discretionary trust contains the entire estate, and the statutory share is a more limited portion, this may be an effective approach.

There has been some attempt to argue that although the trust might not be available, the testamentary creation of the trust was still a disqualifying transfer by an applicant's spouse and should cause ineligibility. This reasoning was soundly defeated in *Skindzier v. Com'r of Social Services* [258 Conn. 642 (2001)].

Q 14:91　What is a Miller trust?

In income cap states an applicant may be unable to qualify for Medicaid assistance yet have insufficient income to pay for long-term care (see Q 14:28). The U.S. District Court in Colorado addressed this conundrum in *Miller v. Ibarra* [746 F. Supp. 19 (D. Colo. 1990)], by permitting the establishment of a trust that consisted solely of an "assignment" of the beneficiary's income (Social Security and pension income) and that directed payment from the trust of just less than the maximum income amount. The trust also provided that any accumulated income remaining at the death of the beneficiary would be used to repay the state for Medicaid costs. OBRA '93 codified a variation of the "Miller" trust. [42 U.S.C. § 1396p(d)(4)(B)] Now available in all income cap states, the Miller (or "qualified income") trust must meet two standards:

1. It must consist solely of pension, Social Security, and other income, plus the accumulated income on those trust amounts; and

2. It must provide that any sums remaining in the trust on the death of the beneficiary will first be used to repay the state for Medicaid expenditures.

The rules that ignore income placed in a "Miller" trust have been construed broadly enough to cover income assigned or transferred into a "d4A" or pooled trust as well. This permits individuals in states that are not "income cap" but apply an income limit to eligibility for certain specialized benefits such as Medicaid waiver home care services to qualify for benefits despite higher income than those programs allow. A complication has arisen where the person is over sixty-five, in light of a recent memorandum from the Centers for Medicare and Medicaid suggesting that transfer penalties might apply in all cases of transfers to pooled trust accounts for the benefit of individuals over sixty-five, but the utility of the technique for establishing eligibility for income-cap programs is so great that a work-around may become available.

Q 14:93   What are "sole benefit" trusts?

A transfer "to or for the sole benefit of" a spouse or disabled child may be permissible without invoking a transfer penalty. [42 U.S.C. § 1396p(c)(2)(B)] Unfortunately, the statute does not include a precise description of the meaning of "sole benefit." State interpretations may differ, for example, on whether a trust "for the sole benefit of" an individual must provide for distribution of the trust principal to the estate of the beneficiary upon his or her death. Section 3257.B.6 of the State Medicaid Manual (Transmittal 64) states:

> a trust is considered to be established for the sole benefit of a spouse, blind or disabled child, or disabled individual if the trust benefits no one but that individual, whether at the time the trust is established or any time in the future. . . . In order for a transfer or trust to be considered to be for the sole benefit of one of these individuals, the instrument or document must provide for the spending of the funds involved for the benefit of the individual on a basis that is actuarially sound based on the life expectancy of the individual involved.

When might a "sole benefit" trust be appropriate? In addition to situations in which the couple wishes to raise the community spouse's income by using the technique, there are other times it could be used not so much to enhance income as to prevent its diminution. For example, if the couple's assets are highly appreciated, there might be a significant capital gains tax if they had to be liquidated to purchase an annuity or otherwise spent. Moreover, if those assets could be held in the name of the community spouse until death, they would qualify for the step-up in basis. Nonliquid assets that the agency insists in treating as available might also be included. Finally, even where annuities are permitted, the community spouse might prefer a trustee to invest the funds rather than receive the potentially lower yield (and negative income tax consequences) of a permanent commercial annuity.

As with annuities, however, the utility of this technique varies depending on the state. If the state, applying its own "availability" rules, determines that a "sole benefit" trust for a spouse will nevertheless be included in the couple's "resources," there may be little benefit to making the change. Moreover, while the spouse can transfer resources after the institutionalized spouse's eligibility, he or she will have no such ability to dispose of "sole benefit" trust assets. Only if the sole benefit trust will be treated as the functional equivalent of an annuity (i.e., beyond his or her control and thus not a resource) does this technique seem useful. The technique is apparently routinely used in the state of Washington; on the other hand, the Third Circuit Court of Appeals held that the assets in such trusts should be treated as available. [Johnson v. Guhl, 357 F.3d 403 (3d Cir. 2004)]

Q 14:96   What is an "income only" trust?

Only the amounts that could be paid to an individual are counted as available. If the individual establishes a trust that absolutely prohibits any payments of principal to the individual under any circumstances, the principal is not counted as available, but the income is even if the trustee refuses to pay it out. An individual may still, therefore, transfer assets into a trust, incurring an ineligibility period, but retaining the use of the income only on the trust for lifetime. This is most attractive to those who have much to lose and plenty of time to get past the look-back period. The grantor does not cede the assets to a third party during his or her lifetime, the survivors receive a step-up in basis provided that a special power of appointment is reserved in the instrument, and (similarly) no gift tax is due.

On the other hand, it seems hardly prudent for most people to lock principal away for life where it can benefit neither the grantor, nor any of the grantor's near and dear, receiving only such pathetically low income as is currently available, anywhere from 1 percent to 4 percent. (OBRA '93 precludes any opportunity for the trustee to transfer the principal to third persons without creating a new penalty.) The most likely candidate may be the house; however, it may be necessary for the grantor to "rent" the house through the payment of expenses, as uncompensated use of the house may be treated by a Medicaid agency as use of *principal* causing the trust to be available.

Estate Recovery

Q 14:98   When is estate recovery allowed?

Each state's estate recovery program is required to seek reimbursement from the probate estate of any Medicaid beneficiary; however, the state plan may not seek recovery from the estate of a recipient until after the death of the recipient's spouse. [42 U.S.C. § 1396p(b)(2)] No recovery may be initiated against the estate of a recipient who is survived by a disabled child or a child under age 21. [42 U.S.C. § 1396p(b)(2)(A)] The Medicaid recipient's home is also exempt from estate recovery programs if either (1) a sibling lives in the home, and lived there for one year prior to the recipient's institutionalization, or (2) a child lives in the home, lived there for at least two years prior to the recipient's institutionalization, and provided care that helped keep the recipient out of the institution. [42 U.S.C. § 1396p(b)(2)(B)]

Notice of the estate recovery program must be given both at the time Medicaid is applied for and at the time of estate recovery. [CMS State Medicaid Manual § 3810.G]

"Estate recovery" does *not* include any recovery from the individual during his or her own lifetime (that is, with respect to benefits properly paid), but only upon his or her death. [See, e.g., State v. Murtha, 179 Conn. 463, 427 A.2d 807 (1980)] By contrast, other state programs may permit lifetime recovery.

Q 14:99 How is "estate" defined for purposes of each state's estate recovery program?

Under federal law, all states must recover from the "estate" of the recipient. [42 U.S.C. § 1396p(b)(4)(A)] While federal law specifically permits the states to expand the definition of estate and make claims against joint tenancy interests, life estates, and other interests that automatically lapse at death, it does not provide any new mechanism to do so. [42 U.S.C. § 1396p(b)(4)(B)] Initially, faced with the difficulty of creating, defining, and administering a program that seeks to recover such assets, most states have demurred; nearly all of the states define "estate" to mean the Medicaid recipient's probate estate. Recently, however, many states have begun to implement "expanded" estate recovery. An example may be found in Connecticut's 2003 legislation authorizing recovery against the unpaid amounts of any annuity ever established with the *applicant's* funds. Conn. Public Acts 2003-03. (It may be possible to defeat this for a spousal annuity by the simple expedient of transferring funds to the spouse who then purchases an annuity.) The Deficit Reduction Act of 2005 expressly requires that annuities purchased within the look-back period name the state as remainder beneficiary in the second position after the death of the annuitant and spouse, but this applies only to annuities purchased during the look-back period. These changes aside, few Medicaid recipients have estates that will be subject to the probate process, so the estate recovery program perhaps has a more terrorizing than financial effect, assuming that title to an institutionalized spouse's assets (including the home) are transferred to the community spouse (see, however, Q 14:100).

Q 14:100   Are there limitations on the estate recovery program?

Yes. By federal law, no state estate recovery program can provide for claims against the estate of a Medicaid recipient if a spouse, a child under age 21, or a blind or disabled child survives him or her. [State Medicaid Manual § 3810A4] It is irrelevant whether the recipient actually left anything to the spouse or disabled child, and it should not be asserted after the (later) death of the spouse or disabled child. States have, however, occasionally been aggressive—and successful—against the estate of a surviving spouse, even when this appears to fly in the face of the law. [See Idaho Dep't of Health and Welfare v. Jackman, 132 Idaho 213, 970 P.2d 6 (1998), which permitted recovery after the death of the surviving spouse to the extent of the predeceasing recipient-spouse's community interest acquired after institutionalization; Estate of Bergman, 2004 N.D. 196 (2004), in which the court ordered the Medicaid agency to void a transfer by a surviving community spouse to her children as being a "fraudulent conveyance" to defeat the State's claim.]

Every state is also required to implement a hardship program. [42 U.S.C. § 1396p(b)(3)] Although hardship principles vary tremendously by state, they typically will exempt small estates, or estates consisting only of a home resided in by a family member who is unable to secure alternate housing. Vermont, for example, has requested a specific federal waiver for its version of hardship: It seeks to forgo estate recovery for modest homesteads when family income is below minimum poverty levels. Note, however, that the requirements for a "hardship" finding may be very precise. In *Estate of Nicholson v. South Carolina Department of Health*, 377 S.C. 590, 660 S.E.2d 303, (2008) a son's application for a hardship waiver was denied because he could not meet the requirement that he was "actually residing" in the home, since he was in prison. The Court ruled that "actually residing" required physical presence, not merely domicile.

Recently, some have challenged estate recovery where the deceased was a tobacco smoker, arguing that the proceeds of a settlement reached by many states with the tobacco companies were actually payment to the states to reimburse for the coverage, and that estate recovery would be double-dipping. While such challenges are new, at least one has been successful. [In re Estate of Raduazo, 148 N.H. 687 (N.H. 2002)]

Practically speaking, where the beneficiary's "estate" really consists only of an account with $2,000 or less (depending on the state), recovery can be avoided by making the account joint with a family member. The account then passes automatically to the family member at death, unless of course the state has opted to include jointly held accounts as the recoverable estate. (A 1998 North Carolina Department of Health and Human Services survey indicates that at that time, California, Iowa, Nevada, South Dakota, and Washington recovered against jointly held property.) If, however, the account is held in the nursing home's "residents' trust account," or in a separately titled account at a bank, most likely the state will take the money through estate recovery.

Q 14:100.1 Can a state recover against the estate of a surviving community spouse?

Technically, recovery can only be made against the applicant's estate. This principle was upheld in the Illinois case *Hines v. Department of Public Aid*, slip op. No. 3-04-0162 (Ill. App. 2005). States have the right to expand the definition of "estate" beyond probate estate to include other property in which the Medicaid beneficiary held an interest at the time of his or her death, and it is this power that has emboldened some states to seek recovery from the community spouse's estate following pre-eligibility inter-spousal transfers. How this trend will play out remains uncertain. For example, a Minnesota court upheld a state statute to the extent it permitted recovery against property of a surviving community spouse at the time of that spouse's death, because the Medicaid beneficiary had held a joint interest in a homestead transferred to the community spouse prior to applying for Medicaid, and the court found that under state homestead law, the beneficiary still had "an interest" in the homestead even after conveying it away. [Estate of Barg, 722 N.W.2d 492 Minn. App. 2006] A similar approach was upheld for North Dakota in *In re Wirtz* [607 N.W.2d 882 (N.D. 2000)]. Bucking the trend toward increased access to a surviving spouse's estate even years after the death of the institutionalized Medicaid recipient is the 2008 case of *Estate of Shuh*, 248 S.W.3d 82 (Mo. App. 2008), in which the Medicaid agency's claim for reimbursement, based on a Missouri statute expressly authorizing such claims, was denied by the appellate court on the basis that the state had not taken the steps necessary to adopt an "expanded" definition of probate estate for recovery purposes. Of course, the *Shuh* court also provided the legislature with fairly explicit instructions on how to make their next legislative attempt effective.

Even though recovery against a community spouse's estate may be problematic, the state does have other forms of recourse when the community spouse dies: (1) The state will almost certainly require the institutionalized spouse to take the legal "statutory share" or "elective share" from the community spouse, even if otherwise disinherited; failure to do so should constitute a disqualifying transfer of assets. (2) Some states may require the institutionalized spouse to seek a "family allowance" or "spousal support allowance" during the pendency of the estate. (3) In states that permit "spousal refusal," the state may file a claim against the deceased community spouse, for failure to support the institutionalized spouse. In those states, it may be as important for the surviving community spouse to divest himself or herself of assets to avoid recovery, as it often is for an individual to obtain Medicaid benefits. This can create a terrible conflict of interest between parent and child, even greater than with the usual Medicaid planning dilemma. With typical Medicaid planning, the possibility of long-term care expenses consuming an inheritance is a possibility or a probability, not a certainty. In a spousal refusal state where the State will make a claim against the community spouse, the inheritance is known to be subject to attack. And yet, divestment may subject the community spouse to risk.

Q 14:101   When can a lien be filed against the property of a Medicaid recipient?

States may (but are not required to) adopt a plan for the imposition of liens against the homes of Medicaid recipients, to be foreclosed only upon the death of the recipient or sale of the residence. The state plan may not provide for a lien in any case in which a spouse, a disabled or blind child, or a child under age 21 occupies the home, or by a sibling who lived with the recipient in the home for one year prior to the recipient's institutionalization. The lien must be dissolved if the recipient returns home. Any lien program must include a notice provision, advising Medicaid recipients of the nature and limitations of the lien and reassuring them that the lien will not result in the forced sale of the home during the recipient's life. [42 U.S.C. § 1396p(a)(1)(A) and (B); 42 C.F.R. § 433.36(g)(2)] Such liens are sometimes referred to as "TEFRA" liens, having been included originally in the Tax Equity and Fiscal Responsibility Act (TEFRA) of 1982.

Liens may also be imposed by a state plan on both real and personal property for the recovery of payments improperly made. [42 U.S.C. § 1396p(a)(1)] Such a lien may be imposed only upon an entry of judgment in a court proceeding. [42 C.F.R. § 433.36(g)(1)]

For jointly held property, where the joint owners do not meet the criteria above, the lien means that probate avoidance may be ineffective. Although title may transfer to the joint owners automatically upon the Medicaid recipient's death, the title will be subject to the lien, and the agency will refuse to release the lien unless the lien is paid (to the extent of the value of the proportionate share of the property).

Finally, some states may consider that their subrogation claim for reimbursement from proceeds of litigation for medical expenses arising from the patient's injury is in the nature of a lien, and as such, may hold the litigator liable for disbursing funds before the lien is paid. (See generally, chapter 17, Special Needs Trusts.)

Medicaid Planning-Related Practice Issues

Q 14:104   How might an elder law attorney assist a married couple in Medicaid planning?

Mr. and Mrs. Jones are both in their 70s. Mr. Jones was recently admitted to the hospital for respiratory problems, and his discharge is pending. He will be released to a nursing facility, and Mrs. Jones has been assured that Medicare will pay for up to 100 days of care in that facility. Once his Medicare benefits run out, she fears that he will be unable to return home and his nursing care is likely to cost about $4,000 per month. They have accumulated a small estate, consisting of their home (worth about $150,000, and with a secured line of credit with a balance of about $10,000), their automobile (an older model sedan), household effects, and bank and stock accounts worth about $200,000. In addition, Mr. Jones receives $1,200 per month in Social Security benefits, and Mrs. Jones receives $600. The couple has three children, and Mrs. Jones expresses her wish that there be something to leave those children after she and her husband pass away. She wonders whether there is anything she can do to plan for the likely long-term institutionalization of her husband.

The first question must be whether Medicaid assistance should be sought for Mr. Jones's care at all. If he is able to return home with some assistance, it may be better for his care (and Mrs. Jones's peace of mind) to provide that care in the home rather than keeping him institutionalized. In states with limited community-care alternatives through Medicaid, it may be problematic to secure the appropriate level of assistance even if Mr. Jones can qualify for Medicaid. This can result in the paradox that, because of Medicaid's preferential treatment of nursing home care, the higher level of care is actually less expensive for Mr. and Mrs. Jones. If Mrs. Jones chooses to provide care in the home in such a situation, she will likely exhaust both their financial resources and her personal caregiving ability by providing home care for even a fairly short period of time. Even at low hourly rates full-time nurse's aides will cost $6,000 to $10,000 per month, and additional costs (food, medications, operating the household, etc.) can push those figures substantially higher.

Assuming that Medicaid eligibility is desirable (either because Mr. Jones will require nursing home care anyway, or because their state provides sufficient home care services through Medicaid), Mrs. Jones should consider how to qualify for Medicaid assistance at the earliest possible time. This is particularly important because, despite assurances Mrs. Jones has received, Medicare coverage for the full 100 days of potential eligibility is actually quite unlikely. Once Mr. Jones is determined to need institutional-level care for the rest of his life, Medicare coverage will end quite abruptly.

Whether the Jones's state calculates the CSRA as one-half of available resources at the time of first institutionalization or simply defaults to the maximum CSRA, the result should be the same. Mrs. Jones will be entitled to retain $109,560 (in 2009) of the available resources (in addition to the home, auto, and household effects), and Mr. Jones's "share" of the assets must be reduced to $2,000 (in that state) before he will be eligible for Medicaid assistance. Depending on state practices and Mrs. Jones's shelter expenses or other unusual expenses, it may be possible to increase the figure that Mrs. Jones may retain by use of the so-called fair hearing process, in either a court or an administrative proceeding. Advocacy will almost certainly be required to increase the CSRA figure, as few states make the calculations simple or routine.

Once the maximum CSRA figure has been calculated, Mrs. Jones will probably still need to dispose of assets. She may prefer to make gifts to her children, but even small gifts may result in a period of ineligibility for Mr. Jones that won't begin *until* their assets are spent down to the CSRA. The only possibility may be to hope that the state will permit the penalty period, and the period of Medicare coverage will run concurrently, in effect making it possible to gift assets that will not create a penalty of more than 100 days. This is more likely to work if Mr. Jones's income is below the applicable "income cap" (income cap states) or "categorically needy income limit" (medically needy states), e.g., $2,022 per month (2009 figures), otherwise Medicare coverage may preclude the start of the penalty period. Of course, that level of planning would require being able to predict the length of Medicare coverage, and it is unlikely that it will be predictable.

Mrs. Jones can also hasten eligibility by maximizing the value of her home exemption. In other words, she can pay off the credit line and even improve the house (and/or furnishings and fixtures). The timing of these steps is important; in this scenario, she is free to pursue both payment of the mortgage and home improvements immediately, but if the facts were changed slightly, so that Mr. Jones's institutionalization had not yet occurred, she would be well-advised to delay these steps until after the CSRA has been calculated, at least in those states that do not simply default to the maximum CSRA. In fact, in those states, if Mrs. Jones was seeking assistance before Mr. Jones's hospitalization, it might sometimes be advisable actually to increase the amount of the mortgage (e.g., by borrowing money using the secured line of credit) and incur monthly mortgage payment obligations in order to increase the CSRA calculation just before institutionalization. After Mr. Jones's admission to the hospital or nursing home, the recently borrowed money can be repaid, thereby bringing Mrs. Jones's assets below the (increased) CSRA figure.

In addition to the home mortgage payoff and home repair, Mrs. Jones can purchase a new automobile (provided that it is used for medical purposes, including Mrs. Jones's visits to her own physician, or to pick up medications for either her or her husband) as a way of sheltering some of her liquid assets. She can also use money for travel (her own or, if he is able, her husband's), entertainment, therapy, medical treatment not covered by Medicare, or medical supplies. After all of those expenditures are completed, she may be able to bring the available resources below the CSRA figure. For example, beginning with the Jones's $200,000 of liquid assets, she might make the following expenditures:

$200,000	Available resources
$(10,000)	Payoff of secured credit line

$(15,000)	Roof repair; enlargement and handicapped accessibility of bathroom
$(28,000)	Purchase of new vehicle (after gift of old vehicle to one child)
$(3,000)	Wheelchair and medical supplies for Mr. Jones
$(5,000)	Travel (Mrs. Jones visiting her family)
$(4,000)	New appliances, carpeting
$135,000	Remaining balance
$(50,000)	Purchase of an immediate annuity
$(85,000)	Remaining available resources

If there are assets remaining, Mrs. Jones may choose to convert some of those assets into income by the purchase of an immediate annuity (for these purposes, investment in a family limited partnership or some types of unsecured loans to family members that qualify under the DRA may have a similar effect). If she chooses the annuity route, she will purchase an annuity in her own name, with herself as annuitant, and with payments made to her alone. She can make her children the alternate beneficiaries, but is required to name the State as first beneficiary on her death (to the extent of Medicaid services provided to her or her husband). In most states, she could at least consider purchasing the annuity from family members, but it may be easier to explain and defend the purchase if a commercial annuity is purchased from an insurance company. In some states, this route may not be available, as the state may still elect to treat the annuity as a "resource." In those states, she would have to purchase the annuity from her CSRA.

By some combination of these techniques, Mrs. Jones can probably make her husband eligible for Medicaid assistance without too much difficulty (of course, it becomes more challenging as the size of their joint estate increases); however, his eligibility does not end the discussion, as there are at least two remaining issues with which she must contend. In addition, she must consider any overriding concern she may have about the quality of care provided under the Medicaid system: Nationwide, Medicaid is currently paying approximately 70% of the private-pay rate for nursing care, and so there will be some inevitable pressure on the care provider to minimize the expense of Mr. Jones's care. She may be sure that Mr. Jones will be moved to a semi-private room, if he is in a private room now, once he qualifies. Other shortfalls in the care provided by Medicaid are discussed in SQ 14:8, and Mrs. Jones may try to ensure that certain services are provided to him with some of the "excess" resources before all is gone.

In addition to the quality-of-care issues, Mrs. Jones must be concerned about the potential estate recovery program and the contribution to care required from Mr. Jones's income. As for the estate recovery program, if Mrs. Jones survives her husband there will be no problem (at least in most states—a handful of states have attempted to pursue estate recovery against surviving spouses despite the clear federal prohibition, and some state court opinions are less than clear about whether such efforts might be permitted). If Mrs. Jones passes away after her husband qualifies for Medicaid there may be some difficulty, particularly with a Medicaid claim against the family home. She may be able to forestall this problem by transferring the home into her own name (either before or after Mr. Jones's eligibility) and simply disinherit her husband by will, although most states will create a statutory right to elect against the will (or some substitute mechanism), and treat Mr. Jones's failure to make that election as a gift in his own right, thereby disqualifying him from continued Medicaid coverage for some period of time after her death. She may also choose to protect her husband by including a discretionary supplemental needs trust for him in her will. Other than the family home, most of the remaining assets can be transferred to Mrs. Jones's name and then to the children without invoking any ineligibility period if she should predecease her husband. If she is in California, or otherwise can risk a period of ineligibility for herself and her husband as a result, she can transfer the home first to herself and then to the children or to a trust naming the children as beneficiaries, or add the children's names to the deed to avoid probate. Otherwise, however, she may be "stuck" with the home, unless she sells it after her husband is eligible, as transfers of non-home property by the community spouse, after the institutionalized spouse's eligibility, do not cause the imposition a penalty period.

After Medicaid eligibility has been obtained, Mrs. Jones will still be required to pay some portion of Mr. Jones's income to the nursing home for his care. She should be able to retain all of her own income (including her Social Security, even if paid under his earnings, the proceeds from the annuity she purchased to reduce assets, and the investment income from the remaining assets transferred into her own name). In addition, she will be entitled to retain a sufficient portion of his income to bring her total income to the MMMNA level (between $1,750 and up to $2,739 in 2009). Finally, Mr. Jones himself can retain a personal needs allowance set by the state to offset his minor personal expenses. After those deductions (and payment of the Medicare Part B premium), the remaining income received in Mr. Jones's name must be turned over to the nursing home. Obviously, this makes the annuity choice somewhat less attractive in the Jones's situation: Even though the annuity neatly solves the asset eligibility problem (up to an unlimited amount), it can reduce the total amount available to Mrs. Jones by reduction of the non-annuity income she is permitted to retain. As a consequence, the annuity option is usually most attractive when the lower-earning spouse is institutionalized, although it may still be a workable solution in the Jones's situation after careful consideration of the options, and depending on where the Joneses live.

In the Jones's case, Mrs. Jones has pension income of $600. She also has at least some remaining assets, which will earn additional income. If she has purchased an immediate annuity or increased her CSRA to ensure more income, her income will have risen accordingly. Assuming that her retirement, investment, and annuity income totals $1,100 per month, she will be entitled to receive at least $650 per month from her husband's pension and Social Security income (to bring her level to at least the threshold MMMNA amount of $1,750 for 2009). Depending on her state and her costs of shelter, that figure may actually be higher. In addition, Mr. Jones is entitled to a personal needs allowance of between $35 and $95.55, depending on the state. In other words, Mr. Jones's $1,200 Social Security income will be distributed as follows each month:

$95.55	to Mr. Jones, to his personal needs account, or to Mrs. Jones for his use
$650	to Mr. Jones
$96.40	deducted for Medicare Part B premium (at least until the State picks this up under the QMB program, at which time Mr. Jones's Social Security will no longer have the deduction and his payment obligation will increase accordingly)
$358.05	to the nursing home for Mr. Jones's care

Note that in some states, if Mr. Jones's income were not $1,200 but only $700, Mrs. Jones might be forced to take less than the $650 MMMNA if she wants Mr. Jones to continue to be eligible for Medicare, as federal regulations state that the MMMNA can be used to reduce income *before* paying the Medicare Part B premium.

Q 14:105 How might an elder law attorney assist an unmarried person with a disabled child in Medicaid planning?

Mrs. Smith, age 85 and a widow, has just been admitted to the hospital for treatment of a broken hip sustained in a fall in her home. Her children are concerned about the likelihood that she will remain in the nursing home after discharge from the hospital, and do not want to see her estate depleted by the cost of that care. This is particularly problematic because one of her children, her 55-year-old developmentally disabled son, has lived with her in the home since birth, and the remaining children fear the effect of placing him outside the home if it must be sold. One of the other children is prepared to move into the home and provide care for the disabled son, but the son's only income is SSI of $382 per month and there is concern about whether it can adequately provide for his needs. Mrs. Smith's other assets include bank accounts of $400,000, her automobile, and household effects.

Mrs. Smith can easily obtain Medicaid eligibility by simply gifting her entire estate to her disabled son. Gifts to (or for the sole benefit of) disabled children do not incur a transfer penalty. Unfortunately, there are at least two other problems with this approach: Mrs. Smith's ability to understand or make the gift may be questionable, and the gift may cut off her son's benefits. Even if the loss of benefits would be outweighed by the assets that would now be available to her son, his ability to handle the resultant gift may be problematic

Assuming that Mrs. Smith can and would like to make the gift (or that a power of attorney with appropriate gifting powers was executed before Mrs. Smith's current disability), the transfer to her son may solve her eligibility problems. In some states, a transfer into a trust for his benefit (with one or more of the remaining children as trustees) may have the same result, although some states insist that a transfer into a trust is not "for the sole benefit" of the income beneficiary, at least unless it is a "payback" trust. If the son has the ability subsequently to transfer the received assets into a trust for his own benefit, her eligibility should not be affected (after her transfer to him, she loses the ability to control, or be affected by, his retransfer). If he is unable to make that transfer, it may require a conservatorship (or guardianship of the estate) proceeding to provide effective management of the money and property transferred to him.

Paradoxically, the transfer of the house to the son should result in an increase in his current SSI benefits. Because Mrs. Smith has been providing shelter, his benefits have been reduced (by one-third the benefit he would otherwise be entitled to receive ($674) plus $20, or $244.67 (2009 figures)). If he owns the home in his own name, or in the name of an OBRA '93 trust, that reduction should cease (because no one is now providing in-kind shelter for him). In fact, if the caretaker sibling pays utilities as part of his or her "rent" obligation, it may be possible to maintain the maximum SSI benefit while reducing or eliminating the cost of maintenance of the home.

If the remaining assets are also transferred to Mrs. Smith's disabled son, he may be disqualified from receiving SSI benefits. After December 14, 1999, any transfer by him of the money he receives from his mother will result in a period of ineligibility for continued SSI benefits unless the money is transferred into a "payback" OBRA '93 trust with provisions for repayment of any Medicaid benefits he may have received as of the time of his subsequent death, and keeping in mind that any payments for food and shelter from the trust will be treated as in-kind support and maintenance, thereby reducing his benefits. Assuming that he has modest medical needs, such a trust may still be an excellent choice for his eligibility planning, and so a two-step transfer (Mrs. Smith to disabled son, disabled son to supplemental benefits trust), or even Mrs. Smith direct to "payback" trust, may be a viable planning choice.

Suppose Mrs. Smith's son were not a developmentally disabled individual receiving SSI, but a child who retired early from a lifetime of work, and is now receiving Social Security Disability Income benefits and a pension on account of an injured back. The scenario described above could work just as well even though Mrs. Smith's son was well-provided for and had no need of her resources. Mrs. Smith might fondly hope that her son would make gifts to his non-disabled siblings after she has been found eligible for Medicaid. There is no requirement that her son *keep* the gift. Unfortunately, you must advise Mrs. Smith that she cannot require her son to re-distribute his gift, and in many cases the fortunate recipient of such a gift may decline to do so.

Q 14:106 How might an elder law attorney assist a moderately wealthy unmarried Medicaid applicant in Medicaid planning?

Mr. Johnson, a widower age 75 and in poor health, has been turned down on his application to purchase long-term care insurance. He anticipates that he may soon require nursing home care. He is concerned about maintaining his assets for his own use and also wishes to maximize what he can leave to his children upon death. Like Mrs. Smith, his assets include a home (worth less than $500,000), automobile, personal effects, and $400,000 in bank accounts and stocks (the financial accounts are mostly held in joint names with one or another of his three children). None of his children is disabled, although one daughter has lived with him since her divorce three years ago.

First, of course, Mr. Johnson must consider whether he wishes to adjust his assets and his plans to accommodate Medicaid eligibility. That question will be intensely personal and will depend on the quality of local Medicaid care, Mr. Johnson's desire to maintain control over his assets as long as possible, and his relationship with his children. Assuming that he chooses to plan for Medicaid eligibility, Mr. Johnson's choices are considerably narrower than in either of the preceding examples.

As in the other cases, in most states Mr. Johnson's home will remain an exempt asset as long as he intends to return home (in most states, intent to return home is determined solely by reference to the applicant's answer on the Medicaid application form itself). He may shelter additional assets by investing them in the home: by paying off any mortgage, adding onto or remodeling the home, or replacing furnishings, appliances, and fixtures, provided that this does not raise the value of his home above the limit in his state since the Deficit Reduction Act (either $500,000 or $750,000). Of course, in his situation the state's estate recovery program may make the value of sheltering home assets problematic, because the home may need to be sold upon his death to repay benefits rather than transferred to his children.

Even if the effect of sheltering assets in his home is solely to delay payment of his nursing home costs, Mr. Johnson may consider taking such steps. By doing so, he not only avoids the interest costs on his nursing home care, but also takes advantage of Medicaid's strong purchasing power: The 15 percent (or more) savings his state's Medicaid agency can save in nursing home costs will ultimately be passed on to his estate even if it fully repays the cost of nursing home care.

Furthermore, in many states Mr. Johnson can consider transferring his home to his children while retaining both a life estate and the power to sell the property (and retain the proceeds) during his life. This may avoid the transfer penalty altogether, and prevent his estate from owning any interest in the property at his later death. If the "power of sale" is not recognized in his state, at least he can retain the life estate, incurring a shorter ineligibility period and keeping the home from his estate at death, thereby escaping the state's repayment claim. Finally, even though none of his children is disabled Mr. Johnson may be able to take advantage of another exception to the transfer penalty rules: transfer of a home to a child who resided with the Medicaid applicant for a period of two years and who provided care that prevented the applicant from requiring nursing care will not invoke a transfer penalty. In other words, if Mr. Johnson can show that his daughter provided care that kept him out of the nursing home, he may be able to give the house to her without incurring any period of ineligibility.

Even if Mr. Johnson can transfer his home to his daughter, or to all of his children while retaining a life estate (and the power to sell), problems remain. First, he must also dispose of the remaining (liquid) assets before becoming eligible. Second, once institutionalized he will be unable to afford the cost of maintaining the home (because nearly all of his income must be paid to the nursing home, even after Medicaid eligibility), so any plan must take into consideration the need for other family members to take over (and to be able to bear) the cost of maintenance.

Of course Mr. Johnson can simply give away both his home and his liquid assets, and incur the ineligibility penalty—effectively five years. Assuming that no application is made until expiration of the look-back period, and that family members can pay any actual costs of care incurred, Mr. Johnson may be made eligible a great deal more quickly than he would if he simply paid for his own care until his money was exhausted. As his attorney, however, it will be important to point out that his family members could predecease him leaving "his" assets to others (by choice or by law); that "his" assets could be subject to the claims of creditors or divorcing spouses of his donees, and that it may be far too risky to put his future well being so completely in the hands of others, no matter how well intentioned. The attorney will also want to point out that at least as long as he owns his home he may be able to forestall the moment of relocation to a nursing home by obtaining a reverse mortgage on the home or otherwise extract accumulated equity to increase liquid assets and thereby pay for home care.

Mr. Johnson may also consider an annuity, although it is unlikely to be an attractive option for him. Mr. Johnson might also consider entering into a personal services contract with one or more of his children. Under such an arrangement, he could pay a flat amount now for a promise of services (medical case management, transportation, respite care, etc.) for the rest of his life. Assuming that the purchase price is reasonable (so that no implication of gift is raised), it should not incur a transfer penalty and should permit his children to receive adequate compensation for the care they anticipate providing for their father. Personal service contracts have been easily accepted by some state Medicaid agencies, and resisted by others; proof of the reasonable value of the services may be problematic if the Medicaid agency challenges the arrangement.

Note: The entire chart appearing in the main text at the end of Chapter 14 is deleted.

Chapter 15

Social Security

Social Security refers to a form of social insurance wherein taxes collected from the employed are used to provide benefits to retired and disabled persons and their dependents. Social Security covers retirement, disability, dependents, and survivors' benefits. This chapter discusses the various kinds of benefit programs, the application process, and issues a practitioner may encounter.

Overview

Q 15:1 What is Social Security?

Social Security was created during the post-Depression years in part to bring the income of senior citizens and disabled persons above the poverty line. Through Social Security and the Retirement (Old Age), Survivors, and Disability Insurance (OASDI) programs the federal government provides assistance to retired and disabled workers and their families. Social Security is not need-based, but rather is a benefit directly tied to a citizen's work history. Workers who pay FICA (Federal Insurance Contributions Act) taxes on minimum annual earnings during a minimum number of quarters are entitled to Social Security retirement and disability benefits, and will qualify their dependents for survivor's benefits. Resources for researching Social Security law include:

- Social Security Act: *http://www.ssa.gov/OP_Home/ssact/*
- Social Security Regulations, 20 CFR: *http://www.ssa.gov/OP_Home/cfr20/cfrdoc.htm*
- Social Security Handbook: *http://www.ssa.gov/OP_Home/handbook/ssa-hbk.htm*
- Social Security administrative rulings: *http://www.ssa.gov/OP_Home/rulings/rulings.html*
- Social Security Program Operations Systems Manual or "POMS": *https://s044a90.ssa.gov/apps10/poms.nsf/aboutpoms*
- Social Security Forms: *http://www.ssa.gov/online/forms.html*
- Claimant representatives' page: *http://www.ssa.gov/representation/*

Q 15:4 Can Social Security benefits be executed on, attached, garnished, or assigned?

Generally, no—but there are important exceptions. The Social Security Act specifically provides that "the right of any person to any future payment ... shall not be transferable or assignable ... and none of the moneys paid or payable or rights existing under this statute shall be subject to levy, attachment, garnishment, or other legal process." [42 U.S.C. § 407(a)] Social Security payments held in a segregated account remain inviolate. [See, e.g., NCNB Financial Services v. Shumante, 829 F. Supp. 178 (W.D. Va. 1993)] They may or may not be protected if deposited to a joint account or commingled with other funds. The exceptions to the no-attachment rules: delinquent federal taxes [26 U.S.C. §§ 6331 and 6334], child support [26 U.S.C. § 6305 and 42 U.S.C. § 462] and alimony obligations [42 U.S.C. § 462].

Because of the "non-assignment" provision, it has been successfully argued that a state Medicaid agency cannot require the spouse in an institution to assign income to the community spouse in order for him or her to meet the monthly maintenance needs allowance, or MMNA. [Robbins v. DeBuono, 218 F.3d 197 (2d Cir. 2000)] However, the *Robbins* decision was recently rejected by a decision of the Second Circuit

Court of Appeals [Wojchowski v. Daines, 498 F.3d 99 (2007)], so this argument is unlikely to succeed in the future. The Court in the *Wojchowski* applied the strict interpretation of "other legal process" expounded in the case of [Washington Dep't of Social Services v. Keffeler, 123 S. Ct. 1017 (2003)].

Eligibility

Q 15:6 What is a "quarter of coverage"?

A quarter of coverage (or QC), now technically called a "credit," is a calendar quarter of a year in which a worker received employment (or self-employment) income of a minimum amount, and as to which FICA was paid. [20 C.F.R. § 404.140] For 2009, the minimum quarterly income to qualify for a QC is $1,090, and if you worked all year and earned at least $4,360 you would get 4 credits. [20 C.F.R. § 404.110] For current benefit and qualification levels, including the earnings necessary for crediting a QC, see the Social Security Administration website (*http://www.ssa.gov/cola/colafacts2008.htm* or *http://www. ssa.gov/OACT/COLA/QC.html*—the latter site includes a chart showing the required earnings for each year since 1978, when the inflation-indexed approach was adopted).

Eligibility for benefits depends on the number of credits the worker has accumulated. For those born after 1929, having 40 credits is required for one to be "fully insured." Having 6 credits out of the 13 "quarters" prior to application makes one "currently insured." [20 C.F.R. 404.115] Either way, one can receive retirement benefits. However, for a worker to qualify for Social Security disability benefits on his or her own work record, the worker must be fully insured and if 31 or older, must have worked 20 of the 40 quarters preceding the onset of the disability (see Q 15:17). [20 C.F.R. 406.421] For younger workers, one must have worked half of the time between age 21 and one's age. Using an example offered by the Social Security Administration: if a person became disabled at age 27, (s)he would need credit for 3 years of work (12 credits) out of the past 6 years (between ages 21 and 27) to qualify for Social Security Disability. In other words one must work more to be eligible for Social Security Disability benefits than Social Security Retirement benefits. Farm workers, servicemen, employees of nonprofit organizations, and citizens working abroad are paid according to special regulations.

Provided a worker has the requisite number of quarters and is otherwise eligible, the worker will be entitled to a primary insurance amount (see SQ 15:7), upon which the benefits of others will also be based.

Those who have worked overseas (alien or otherwise) and do not have sufficient quarters, may receive credit for work overseas if there is a "totalization agreement" with the Social Security system of the foreign country. [See Pratt and Hornbeck, Social Security and Medicare Answer Book (Aspen Publishers, Inc. New York) Qs 7:88 et seq.]

Q 15:7 What is the "primary insurance amount"?

The basis for all calculations of Social Security benefits is the worker's primary insurance amount (PIA). The PIA is calculated based on Social Security contributions made by the worker during the entire work history, with more weight given to more recent contributions (so that a retiree's last earnings—presumably higher than earlier earnings—are given extra weight in the calculation). The PIA determines the amount of benefits that will be paid, although in the case of a retiree the PIA may be reduced for early retirement or enhanced for late retirement. In deciding when to say that a "disability" began, if it was progressive, an individual might conceivably opt for a later onset date in order to have the benefit of higher earnings in computing the PIA, especially because retroactivity of benefits is limited (See SQ 15:20.1).

Retirement Benefits

Q 15:11 What is the amount of the Social Security retirement benefit?

Retirement benefits were always intended to provide supplemental income, and not be the sole source of income for retirees. According to the Social Security Administration's figures, the annual benefit payment in 2008 averaged only about $12,948 per year for a single retired person, and $21,132 for couples; the highest benefit for those retiring at "normal retirement age" of 65 years and 6 months in 2008 was $26,220 per year (the maximum figure increases to $27,876 for 2009). Those who earned more during their lifetime will receive a larger check, but because the benefit is designed to offset poverty, low-income workers might get as much as 56 percent of their pre-retirement salary, while high-income workers could get as little as 28 percent (the average is 42 percent).

Approximately 65 percent of those collecting benefits are senior citizens. Benefits are adjusted each year based on inflation.

Q 15:11.1 Are Social Security retirement benefits ever reduced?

Yes. The "windfall elimination provision" affects the formula used to figure the Social Security benefit amount for someone also receiving a government pension, resulting in a reduced benefit. (It does not affect survivor's benefits.) There are limitations—a reduction may not apply if the pensioner has 30 or more years of "substantial" earnings in Social Security employment, and may be modified for those with at least 20 years of substantial earnings. [See Social Security fact sheet "The Windfall Elimination Provision" (Publication No. 05-10045).] Of course, if the pensioner never participated in Social Security, he or she would not have any Social Security benefit on his or her own account. Another provision, the "government pension offset," affects the benefits of a spouse or survivor of a person entitled to Social Security, where the spouse or survivor him or herself receives a government pension. (See SQ 15:41.)

Q 15:12 When can Social Security retirement benefits be collected?

A qualified worker can collect retirement benefits beginning at the age of 62, but he or she will pay a penalty for early participation. As of 2000, the full retirement age began gradually increasing, and will reach age 67 for those born in 1960 or later. For those born in 1941, for example, full retirement age was 65 years and eight months. That is, while the earliest a person can start receiving Social Security retirement benefits remains at age 62, the earliest a person can receive full retirement benefits is age 65 years and eight months. The increasing age rule applies to persons born in or after 1938 (i.e., those who turned 65 in 2002). For every month before the age of full retirement that the retiree begins collecting benefits, the benefits are cut five-ninths of 1 percent, up to a maximum of 20 percent. The longer an individual waits, the higher the income payment (by about 8 percent per year after 2008), until he or she attains age 70. The benefits do not continue increasing after the applicant reaches age 70. [20 C.F.R. 404.313] Although not directly related to Social Security benefits, Medicare eligibility is often confused with Social Security eligibility. It is important to realize that Medicare coverage does not begin until age 65 (Medicare's eligibility ages do not increase with the increase in Social Security's normal retirement age—at least not yet) regardless of retirement status. Conversely, Medicare eligibility is available to 65-year-olds regardless of their "full retirement age" or actual retirement status.

The "Full Retirement Age" ages for prospective retirees by year of birth are:

Year of Birth	Full Retirement Age
1937 or earlier	65
1938	65 and 2 months
1939	65 and 4 months
1940	65 and 6 months
1941	65 and 8 months
1942	65 and 10 months
1943–1954	66
1955	66 and 2 months
1956	66 and 4 months
1957	66 and 6 months
1958	66 and 8 months
1959	66 and 10 months
1960 and later	67

Q 15:13 Can one defer collecting Social Security retirement benefits beyond the normal retirement age?

Yes. Social Security benefits can be delayed until age 70, and the monthly benefit amount will increase by a fraction of 1 percent for each month retirement is delayed (the actual fraction depends on the year of birth). [20 C.F.R. § 404.313] For those born in 1943 or later, the increased benefit will reach two-thirds of 1 percent per month of delayed retirement, or 8 percent per year of delayed retirement. [20 C.F.R. § 404.313] Social Security counselors will often recommend that the retiree not wait to collect, theorizing that the loss of benefits during the years of delay will not be offset by the increased figure unless the retiree lives an unusually long time. It is also important to remember that Medicare eligibility will not be delayed with delayed retirement; at age 65 Medicare coverage can begin for a Social Security beneficiary who is eligible to retire regardless of whether he or she actually retires.

Q 15:14 What Social Security benefits are available to an insured retiree's spouse and children?

Spouses of covered retired workers may be eligible for benefits. See Q 15:35 et seq.

Q 15:15 What is the Senior Citizens' Freedom to Work Act of 2000?

Retirees receiving Social Security income were traditionally discouraged from earning significant outside income. This has generally been considered an anachronistic provision of the program, dating to Depression days when millions were out of work. A healthy economy and low unemployment have spurred federal legislators to eliminate the cap on earnings for persons aged 65 to 69. Confusingly enough, the penalty for work after retirement continues to apply to those who retire (and begin receiving Social Security benefits) before their normal retirement age. For every two dollars earned (in 2009) over $14,160, a Social Security retirement recipient under age 65 will experience a one dollar reduction in Social Security benefits. If the working retiree reaches age 65 in 2009, he or she will experience a one dollar reduction in Social Security benefits for every three dollars earned over $37,680 (2009 figure)—but the reduction in benefits ends in the month in which the beneficiary reaches normal retirement age (age 66 for those born in 1942). In other words, the lower figure applies to earnings for those who have not yet attained their normal retirement age in the current year, and the higher figure for those who will reach their normal retirement age *but only for the months of the current calendar year before they actually reach that age.*

Disability Benefits

Q 15:19 How is the disability evaluated?

Eligibility for Social Security Disability benefits is based on the applicant's inability to perform any "substantial gainful activity," (SGA), a number that changes annually and for 2008 is $940 per month ($1,570 for someone who is blind). The SSA applies a five-step evaluation process in determining disability:

1. If the applicant is working and the work is substantial gainful activity, he or she will not be found to be disabled regardless of medical condition or age, education, and work experience.

2. The applicant must have a severe impairment, one that significantly limits one's physical or mental ability to do basic work activities.

3. The impairment must be listed in the SSA's "Listing of Impairments" (the listing for adult applicants is available online at *http://www.ssa.gov/disability/professionals/bluebook/AdultListings.htm*) or be equal to one listed, and must be expected to last (or have already lasted) for 12 months, or to lead to the applicant's death.

4. The impairment must prevent the applicant from doing past relevant work.

5. The impairment must prevent the applicant from doing any other work. [20 C.F.R. 404.1520] In some cases an individual who is or has had SGA can still qualify if he or she can show that the compensation was more than the value of the work performed, because of a "benevolent employer," such as a sheltered workshop or family member. Moreover, SGA is measured as net income—if the applicant had expenses in getting to or staying at the workplace, for example, those would be deductible from the gross income to reach the true measure of the earnings.

Q 15:20.1   Can benefits be awarded retroactively?

Up to 12 months of benefits are available retroactively to the approved disabled worker, and up to six months for spouses or dependents. [20 C.F.R. 406.421] It is important to note that retroactivity is 12 months prior to the earliest filing. If a person files and gives up (not uncommon) and the case is closed, it can be reopened within one year for any reason, within four years reopened for good cause, and beyond four years, for certain enumerated reasons. [20 C.F.R. 404.987 et seq.]

Q 15:21   What should the applicant do if the application is denied?

Initial applications are frequently denied, and as frequently appeals are successful. Elder law attorneys should encourage clients to take advantage of the appeals process, preferably by consulting an attorney who specializes in such cases. The Social Security Administration limits fee awards available to attorneys, so in most cases the specialist will not bother to become involved until the appeals stage. On the other hand, it is certainly advantageous to receive the advice of an expert even *before* applying if the disability is one that will be made or broken based upon the language used by the physician when providing a medical opinion. Paying for an hour of advice may be worthwhile, especially given the enormous delays inherent in the appeals process.

Applicants should maintain complete records of all communications, oral and written, and send all letters and applications by certified mail. The client will have only 60 days to file an appeal (see Q 15:33).

Q 15:22 What is the amount of the disabled worker's Social Security disability benefit?

The monthly benefit for a disabled worker is equal to the primary insurance amount. Benefits may be reduced if the worker also receives worker's compensation before age 62. Benefits may also be reduced if the applicant is entitled to other retirement-age benefits before age 65 [20 C.F.R. § 404.317] or similar federal, state, or local benefits. [20 C.F.R. § 404.408] However, disability insurance payments do not affect Social Security disability. [SSA Publication 05-10018] More likely, Social Security Disability payments may offset the private insurance amount.

Q 15:26 Will returning to work affect disability benefits?

A Social Security Disability recipient is permitted to earn a nominal amount without affecting eligibility. The disability program is based on total disability: Any ability to engage in substantial gainful activity (SGA) is disqualifying and the amount of earnings is not completely determinative of the status of disability. There are, however, some guidelines in determining how income affects the continued status of disability:

1. Earnings of less than $700 per month (2009 figure) will ordinarily be presumed not to be substantial gainful employment (but note

that the ability to earn more employment income will disqualify the beneficiary).

2. Earnings of over $980 per month (2009 figure) ($1,640 if blind) will ordinarily be presumed to be evidence of substantial gainful employment.

3. Earnings between those two figures will require the Social Security eligibility worker to evaluate all of the circumstances of the disability and employment.

4. Earnings in a "sheltered workshop" environment are treated specially, and will not disqualify the worker from eligibility. (See SQ 15:19 for a discussion on "net" earnings and benevolent employers.)

5. Social Security disability recipients are usually entitled to a single lifetime nine-month trial work period to determine whether they are able to return to work. During the trial work period, income of less than $700 per month (2009 figure) will not count as substantial gainful employment. Income over that amount will not result in ineligibility, but will use up one of the nine months of trial work eligibility. If at the end of the trial work period the individual is still unable to engage in SGA, he or she will continue to receive benefits. If the individual loses benefits because (s)he continues to earn SGA (s)he may keep Medicare for up to 7 years and 9 months longer.

6. Note that a disabled worker whose disability ends will lose Social Security benefits immediately, regardless of the trial work period rules. [20 C.F.R. 404.430]

7. Social Security does not automatically conduct a medical review of beneficiaries who have received disability benefits for at least 24 months solely on the basis of the beneficiary having started work.

"Ticket to Work" Program

Q 15:27   What is the Ticket To Work and Self Sufficiency Program?

The Ticket to Work and Self Sufficiency Program (Pub. L. No. 106-170) became effective January 28, 2002; the final regulations may be found at 66 Fed. Reg. 67,369–67,442 (Dec. 28, 2001), and are codified at

20 C.F.R. 411. The program provides beneficiaries with disabilities expanded options for access to employment services, vocational rehabilitation services, or other support services. The objective is to assist beneficiaries in obtaining, regaining, or maintaining employment in order to reduce dependency on Social Security and Supplemental Security Income benefits. Participation in the program is voluntary.

Q 15:28 Why was the Ticket To Work and Self Sufficiency Program created?

According to the 2004 National Organization on Disability/Harris Survey, only 35 percent of individuals with disabilities were employed in full- or part-time jobs, compared to 78 percent of those without disabilities. From 1986 to 1999, the number of people receiving disability benefits rose by 80 percent (half receiving Social Security, the other half Supplemental Security Income). This increase has been attributed to the aging of the work force as well as the outreach of the Social Security Administration. Furthermore, according to the U.S. General Accounting Office, less than 1 percent of beneficiaries leave the Social Security and Supplemental Security Income rolls each year as a result of employment.

Due to these circumstances resulting in heightened cost to the government, the Ticket to Work and Self Sufficiency Program was created. The goal of the program is to lessen the dependency of beneficiaries on Social Security and Supplemental Income benefits.

Q 15:29 How does the Ticket To Work and Self Sufficiency Program work?

In February of 2002, the Commissioner began issuing tickets to Social Security disability beneficiaries. Each beneficiary has the option of using these tickets to obtain vocational rehabilitation, employment, or other services from providers in the employment network. The ticketholder is to give the ticket to an employment network who will then work with the ticketholder in designing an employment plan outlining services that will be provided to help the beneficiary reach employment goals. Participating employment networks can be found in the online search function located at the Ticket to Work website: *http://www.yourtickettowork.com/program_info*.

Q 15:30 Is the ticketholder required to become employed as a result of the program?

No. The beneficiary/ticketholder is not required to work but may use his or her ticket to attempt to go to work.

Q 15:31 Has the Ticket to Work and Self Sufficiency Program begun operation?

Yes. As of June 2007, the SSA reported that 10,196,477 tickets had been mailed, and over $7,000,000 paid to Employment Networks.

Q 15:32 Where can a beneficiary find out more information about the program?

A beneficiary may call 1-866-968-7842 (1-866-YOUR-TICKET) or for TDD/TTY users the number is 1-866-833-2967 (1-866-TDD-2-WORK). Ticket to Work program information can be found at *http://www.yourtickettowork.com*.

Q 15:32.1 What happens if a beneficiary loses Social Security for working and then is unable to continue to work?

The Social Security Administration has proposed regulations to implement the Reinstatement of Entitlement (Expedited Reinstatement) provision in section 112 of the Ticket to Work and Work Incentives Improvement Act of 1999. This provision allows former Social Security disability and Supplemental Security Income (SSI) beneficiaries, whose entitlement or eligibility had been terminated due to their work activity during the prior five years, to have their entitlement or eligibility reinstated if they are again unable to engage in substantial gainful activity as a result of disability, rather than having to file a new application. A beneficiary can be paid up to six months of provisional benefits, and may be entitled to Medicare benefits and/or Medicaid, pending the reinstatement decision. These benefits will not be considered an overpayment even if the reinstatement is denied. Beneficiaries then have a 24-month reinstatement period after which they are again eligible to participate in work incentive programs. [See 68 Fed. Reg. 61162–61171 (October 27, 2003), proposing amendments to 20 C.F.R. Parts 404 and 416]. In addition, beneficiaries in a trial work period may qualify for 4½ years of Medicare coverage in addition to the 39 months originally permitted. (See SQ 15:26.)

Dependent's Benefits

Q 15:40 Are spouses of disabled and retired workers eligible for Social Security benefits?

Yes. The spouse of a disabled or retired wage earner [42 U.S.C. § 402(e)(2)(A)] or a disabled surviving spouse of a wage earner is eligible for Social Security benefits [42 U.S.C. § 423(d)(2)(B)]. The spouse is entitled to spouse's benefits based on the earnings record of the worker if the claimant:

1. Filed an application for spouse's benefits;
2. Is age 62 or older, or has in his or her care a child entitled to child's benefits [20 C.F.R. § 404.330]; and
3. Is not entitled to retirement or disability benefits or is entitled to retirement or disability benefits based on a PIA that is less than half of the PIA of the worker. [20 C.F.R. § 404.330]

Q 15:41 What benefits will the spouse of a living retired or disabled worker be entitled to receive?

The spouse's benefit is one-half of the worker's PIA. [42 U.S.C. §§ 402(b), 402(c)] The spouse who is entitled to benefits on his or her own account will receive whichever benefit is greater but will not receive both benefits. [42 U.S.C. §§ 402(b) (for wives), 402(c) (for husbands)]

The "government pension offset" reduces (or eliminates) the spouse's benefit where the spouse receives a government pension by two-thirds of the amount of the pension he or she receives, subject to various exceptions. The effect of this is that if two-thirds of the pension is more than the Social Security spouse's benefit, that benefit disappears. [See Social Security factsheet "Government Pension Offset" (Publication No. 05-10007)] The spouse may still be entitled to Medicare, however. (See SQ 15:11.)

Q 15:42 What benefits will the spouse of a deceased worker be entitled to receive?

Upon the death of a retired worker, the eligible surviving spouse (or ex-spouse; see Q 15:43) generally will receive 100 percent of the worker's PIA.

There are several exceptions to this rule. If the surviving spouse's own PIA is greater, he or she will not receive any additional benefit from the deceased worker's account. If the surviving spouse is over 60 years old but has not yet reached full retirement age, his or her survivor's benefit will be reduced. [42 U.S.C. §§ 402(e) (for widows), 402(f) (for widowers)] If the surviving spouse is under age 60 and has the worker's children in his or her care, he or she will be entitled to a "mother's" or "father's" benefit of 75 percent of the worker's PIA. [42 U.S.C. § 402(g)] The "government pension offset" also reduces (or eliminates) the survivor benefit where the survivor receives a government pension by two-thirds of the amount of the pension he or she receives, subject to various exceptions. The effect of this is that if two-thirds of the pension is more than the Social Security survivor's benefit, that benefit disappears. [See Social Security factsheet "Government Pension Offset" (Publication No. 05-10007)]

> **Example.** Mary, who is 70, has a Social Security retirement benefit of $800 per month. John, her husband, who is 75, has a benefit of $1,200 per month. (If Mary's own benefit were only $200, she would instead receive $600, one-half of John's benefit amount.) Together, they have $2,000 per month. When John dies, Mary receives John's $1,200 and no longer receives her own. Her check will have John's Social Security number as the "claim number."

Q 15:45.1 When do spouse's and children's benefits begin?

Spouses and minor children of an early retiree can collect as soon as the retiree begins collecting and thus boost the retiree's monthly family income by as much as 180 percent. If the worker waits until age 70, the spouse who is not covered by his or her own work history and any minor children must wait with the worker.

Q 15:47 What benefits may the child or children of a *living* retired or disabled worker receive?

Children under age 18 (or under age 19 and attending elementary or high school) are entitled to benefits under the retired parent's account. In addition, a child over age 18 who became mentally or physically disabled prior to reaching age 22 may also qualify for children's benefits. Social Security includes adopted children and children born out of wedlock within the definition. The benefit payable to the child of a retired or disabled worker who is still living is generally one-half of the PIA. [42 U.S.C. § 402(d); 20 C.F.R. § 404.350]

Q 15:51 How much must a wage earner pay toward Social Security each year?

Employees and their employers each contribute 6.2 percent of gross salary to the Social Security system, and another 1.45 percent each to Medicare. In other words, FICA contributions will total 15.3 percent of earnings, with half paid by the employer and half paid by the employee. FICA tax is due on the first $106,800 (2009 figure) of an employee's earnings; earnings in excess of that amount are not taxed for Social Security. [42 U.S.C. 409] Current cost-of-living figures are available online at *http://www.ssa.gov/cola/colafacts2008.htm*]-for updated figures as they are released, simply change the year in the URL.

Q 15:52 Do the self-employed pay more in Social Security taxes?

Yes, but only because no employer makes payments on behalf of the self-employed. Those who work for themselves contribute 15.3 percent of earnings, with a $106,800 cap on covered income for 2009.

Q 15:53 Is Social Security income taxed?

Federal income tax is due on up to 50 percent of Social Security benefits when the recipient's adjusted gross income plus one-half of Social Security benefits exceeds $25,000 for a single person or $32,000 for a married couple. [20 C.F.R. § 404.430] If the same calculation yields an amount greater than $34,000 for a single person or $44,000 for a married couple, 85 percent of the Social Security income over those second threshold amounts is subject to income taxation.

Q 15:55 What if the Social Security benefits are not enough to live on?

Social Security recipients who meet Supplemental Security Income eligibility requirements may receive benefits from both programs, although the total received will not exceed the SSI maximum benefit rate ($674/mo in 2009). (See chapter 16 for a discussion of Supplemental Security Income)

Application for Benefits

Q 15:58   Where are Social Security offices located?

The Social Security Administration, which separated from the Department of Health and Human Services in 1995, is divided into 10 regions and has more than 1,300 district offices throughout the country. Social Security office locations can be obtained online at *https:// s044a90.ssa.gov/apps6z/FOLO/fo001.jsp*, or by calling the Administration toll-free number, 1-800-772-1213 (TTY 1-800-325-0778).

Q 15:59   How does one know if he or she is covered by Social Security?

As of October 1999, the Social Security Administration is required to provide all persons age 25 and older with an annual Earnings and Benefit Estimate Statement, which includes their earnings history and the expected rate of payment at retirement. Anyone may request this statement at any time, either by calling (800) 772-1213 (TTY 1-800-325-0778) or going through the SSA web page: *www.ssa.gov*. The site includes a program to help calculate the primary insurance amount (monthly benefit) and other benefits. The website also includes statistical tables and actuarial information and the Social Security Handbook, which provides detailed answers to innumerable questions about Social Security benefits and procedures.

Chapter 16

Other Benefit Programs

Medicaid, Medicare, or Social Security provide at least some benefits for the vast majority of elderly Americans. Although less common, several other government benefits programs touch the lives of at least some elders. This chapter discusses the Supplemental Security Income (SSI) program, veteran's benefits, and the Railroad Retirement program.

Supplemental Security Income

Q 16:5 What is the maximum SSI benefit?

SSI benefits are set at a maximum amount, which increases annually (in January) in concert with the increase in Social Security benefits (based on increases in the cost of living). For 2008, the maximum federal benefit rate is $637 for a single disabled SSI recipient, and $956 for a married couple; in 2009, $674 for a single recipient/$1,011/couple.

In addition, most states pay a supplemental amount, which may be either mandatory supplementation or optional. SSI recipients living in Arkansas, Georgia, Kansas, Mississippi, and Tennessee will receive a mandatory supplement that may take their total benefits higher than the federal maximum. The additional benefit varies widely, from a supplement paid only to couples to California's $233 for an elderly or disabled individual or $568 for married couples (2007 figures in each instance). Sixteen states provide optional state supplementation only. These states are Alabama, Alaska, Connecticut, Florida, Hawaii, Indiana, Kentucky, Minnesota, Nevada, North Dakota, Rhode Island, South Carolina, Texas, Utah, Vermont, Virginia, and Wisconsin. One state, West Virginia, has no supplementation program, mandatory or optional. This information is available at *http://www.ssa.gov/policy/docs/progdesc/ssi_st_asst/ 2007/* (updated January 2008).

Q 16:6   Can SSI benefits be awarded retroactively?

No, benefits date back only to the date of filing. However, "filing" can include an application filed and abandoned, or denied but never appealed, if it is reopened. Prior applications within one year can be reopened for any reason, and can be reopened within two years for good cause. [20 CFR § 416.1488]

Q 16:7   For what other benefits will an SSI recipient qualify?

In addition to the monthly SSI benefit, in most states an SSI beneficiary will automatically qualify for both food stamps and Medicaid coverage. Medicaid, of course, covers both urgent care needs and long-term nursing care; because SSI benefits are suspended during periods of institutionalization at state or federal expense, SSI recipients will not normally automatically receive institutional nursing care services. General medical coverage through Medicaid is often the most important element of the SSI recipient's benefits, because doctor's visits, hospital and outpatient care, prescription medicines, and in-home services may be worth many times the direct SSI benefit amount each month in at least some cases.

Q 16:8   Who is eligible to receive SSI benefits?

SSI is available to applicants who meet two separate sets of eligibility standards. The recipient must be blind, elderly, or disabled *and* must qualify financially. The recipient must also be a citizen of the United States or a qualified alien and resident of the United States. [42 U.S.C.

§ 1382(f)] (See Q 14:15.) Residents of a public institution are not eligible for SSI. [20 C.F.R. § 416.211] A public institution is "an establishment that makes available some treatment or services in addition to food and shelter to four or more persons who are not related to the proprietor." [20 C.F.R. § 416.201]

Q 16:9 Who is not eligible to receive SSI benefits?

Fugitive felons and those housed in public institutions (including prison or jail) will have benefits suspended during their incarceration or fugitive status. A beneficiary who makes gifts may be disqualified from receiving SSI benefits for a period of months calculated by dividing the total amount of gifts by the maximum SSI benefit.

Q 16:10 When may a noncitizen be eligible for SSI?

Beginning August 22, 1996, noncitizens must meet two requirements to be eligible for SSI. The noncitizen must be a "qualified alien" and meet an exception condition that allows qualified aliens to get SSI. There are eight categories of "qualified aliens" (details can be found at *http://www.socialsecurity.gov/ssi/text-understanding-ssi.htm*). (See also Q 14:16 (because Medicaid rules are to a considerable extent dependent on SSI regulations, many questions of SSI eligibility are also treated in any discussion of Medicaid eligibility).)

Q 16:11 What are the categorical requirements for SSI eligibility?

An SSI recipient must fit into one of three categories: blind, elderly, or disabled. [42 U.S.C. § 1382c(a)(1)(A)] For SSI purposes, those categories are defined as follows:

1. *Blind.* Vision must be limited to 20/200 or less in the better eye *after correction* or the field of vision must be less than 20 degrees. Note that a person with poor vision who does not meet these criteria may nonetheless qualify as disabled if the vision impairment is sufficient to prevent any substantial gainful employment.

2. *Elderly.* Age 65 or older.

3. *Disabled.* Physical or mental impairment that prohibits the applicant from performing any substantial work and that is expected to last at least 12 months (or lead to the applicant's death). In the

case of a child, the test requires the applicant to have "marked and severe functional limitations" as a result of a physical or mental impairment.

[42 U.S.C. § 1382c(a)]

Q 16:12   What are the financial requirements for SSI eligibility?

Because SSI is a means-tested program, SSI recipients must meet income and resource requirements. Long-term care Medicaid eligibility rules (discussed at length in chapter 14) are actually based on SSI financial eligibility requirements, and most of the specifics contained in that discussion apply here as well.

Q 16:13   What are the SSI resource eligibility requirements?

SSI resource eligibility requires that a single applicant have no more than $2,000 in countable resources. A married applicant and his or her spouse must have less than $3,000 of countable resources (even if only one spouse is applying for SSI eligibility). [20 C.F.R. § 416.1205(c)] Resources are defined as "cash or other liquid assets or any real or personal property that an individual (or spouse, if any) owns and could convert to cash to be used for his or her support and maintenance." [20 C.F.R. § 426.1201(a)]

Noncountable resources include:

- Applicant's home
- Tools of trade or business
- Automobile used for transportation of the beneficiary or a member of the beneficiary's household (dollar limitation and usage restriction limitation eliminated effective March 9, 2005). [POMS § SI 01130.200] This is a change from an earlier limit of $4,500 in equity for any car [70 Fed. Reg. 6340–6345)]
- Ordinary household furnishings and furniture (dollar limitation eliminated effective March 9, 2005) [70 Fed. Reg. 6340–6345]
- Burial plots for individuals and immediate family (usually interpreted to include grave liners, caskets, and similar grave-"burial space" items)
- Burial funds up to $1,500

- Life insurance with a face value of $1,500 or less
- Wedding and engagement rings

[20 C.F.R. § 416.1210]

Q 16:14 What kind of trusts will not count as a resource for an SSI beneficiary?

Under SSI policy, two types of trusts will not be counted: (1) a so-called "Medicaid" trust (i.e., a trust that meets the qualifications for not being counted for Medicaid) described in 42 U.S.C. Section 1396p(d)(4), and (2) a third-party "discretionary" trust. Specifically, the Social Security Administration Program Operations Manual Systems Section SI 01120.200.D.1.a. states:

If an individual (claimant, recipient, or deemor) has legal authority to revoke the trust and then use the funds to meet his food or shelter needs, or if the individual can direct the use of the trust principal for his/her support and maintenance under the terms of the trust, the trust principal is a resource for SSI purposes.

Additionally, if the trust provides for mandatory disbursements to the beneficiary and the beneficiary is not prohibited from anticipating, assigning or selling the right to future payments, the current value of these payments may be a resource to the beneficiary. For example, if the trust provides for payment of $100 per month to the beneficiary for spending money, absent a prohibition to the contrary, the beneficiary may be able to sell the right to future payments for a lump-sum settlement.

In sum, "If an individual does not have the legal authority to revoke the trust or direct the use of the trust assets for his/her own support and maintenance, the trust principal is not the individual's resource for SSI purposes."[POMS § SI 01120.200.D.2] A discretionary trust with supplemental needs language, established by a third party, should not be considered a resource for SSI purposes, *whether or not* expenditures for food and shelter are explicitly prohibited.

Q 16:15 What are the SSI income eligibility requirements?

Income eligibility is a little easier to calculate for SSI purposes than for Medicaid long-term care purposes. For SSI, the total income from all sources must not exceed the applicable maximum SSI benefit (including state supplements, where appropriate). If the income is lower than that level and the applicant is otherwise eligible, SSI will pay the difference between an individual's income and the SSI maximum benefit level.

Countable income is defined as anything received in-cash or in kind that can be used to meet the need for food and shelter. For "in-kind" income, the value computed by SSA may include more or less than is actually received. In-kind income is food, shelter, or something that can be converted to food or shelter. [20 C.F.R. § 416.1102] Other "in-kind" assistance is not counted. Income can be earned or unearned and there are different rules for counting each type of income. Countable income must be less than $674 a month for a single adult and less than $1,011 a month for married couples (2009 figures). [42 U.S.C. §§ 1382(a)(1), 1382f] As previously mentioned, countable income can be higher in states that pay SSI supplements.

Q 16:17 What is the difference between earned and unearned income?

SSI eligibility depends on the applicant's income level, and counts both "earned" and "unearned" income. Earned income includes wages and self-employment income, whether paid in cash or by in-kind payments of goods or services. For SSI eligibility purposes, some earned income is excluded from consideration:

- The first $20 per month of most income
- $65 per month of wages and one-half of wages over $65
- Food stamps
- Home energy and housing assistance

[20 C.F.R. § 416.1112]

See *http://www.socialsecurity.gov/ssi/text-income-ussi.htm* for more examples of types of payments and services that are not included as countable income.

Unearned income includes interest, dividends, rent receipts (after deduction of expenses), annuity and pension payments, insurance proceeds, and even lottery or prize winnings. Unearned income is calculated at its value as gross income—in other words, Medicare premiums, garnishments, and automatic withholdings are counted as income even though not actually received by the applicant.

Q 16:18   What are the rules for in-kind support and maintenance?

In-kind support and maintenance (ISM) includes any food or shelter that is given to an individual by a third party. [20 C.F.R. § 416.1130, revised by 70 Fed. Reg. 6340] Effective March 9, 2005, gifts of clothing are not included as ISM. In-kind gifts of necessities (food or shelter) are treated as income although the calculation of benefit reductions may be different depending on the recipient's living arrangements. If the "support and maintenance" is received in the context of a beneficiary who lives in the home of someone with whom he or she does not maintain a "business relationship," the reduction is fixed at one-third of the maximum SSI benefit regardless of actual value (the "one-third reduction" rule). In that situation, the reduction is fixed. [20 C.F.R. § 416.1131] Otherwise, contributions in-kind of "support and maintenance," including payments to third parties who provide support and maintenance items, is valued by the "presumed value rule," whereby the support is valued at one-third of the maximum SSI benefit plus $20 unless proven to have a lower fair market value. [20 C.F.R. § 416.1140] Thus, it is possible to show that the fair market value is less than the one-third figure, but the value will never be more than one-third of the maximum benefit plus $20. More-over, since $20 of unearned income is "disregarded," the difference may be minor. Clearly, if the gift is sufficiently valuable, it may be better to receive the gift and reduce the benefit by one-third. Note also that the gifts are in effect aggregated. (See also SQ 17:31.) Note also that for intra-family rentals, the "one-third reduction" rule is pre-sumed to apply unless the rent is at least the "presumed value" amount of one-third maximum benefit plus $20. [Ellis v. Apfel, 147 F.3d 139 (2d Cir. 1998)]

> **Example 16-1.** John receives $674 SSI in 2009. In January, he receives $100 of food from his mother. His benefit should be reduced by $80. (One hundred dollars is less than one-third multi-plied by $674 or $224.67, and $20 is disregarded.) In February, his grandmother says she will pay the landlord if he moves to a better apartment with $800/month rent. His benefit will be reduced by $224.67 every month that she does this. (The usual $20 disregard is offset by the "plus $20" that applies to in-kind support and main-tenance). In March, his mother provides $100 of food and his grandmother also pays the rent; his benefit is reduced by only $224.67. [POMS § SI 00810.0420]

Q 16:18.1 What payments would be treated as giving in-kind "shelter" support?

Besides actually allowing a person to live in one's home, only certain payments by third parties are treated as "shelter" by Social Security: payments of (1) actual purchase of a home; (2) mortgage (and any insurance required by the mortgage); (3) real property taxes; (4) rent; (5) heating fuel; (6) gas; (7) electricity; (8) water; (9) sewer; and (10) garbage removal. Items 2–9, plus purchase of food, are considered counted "household expenses." Condominium or similar fees are only "in-kind support and maintenance" to the extent that the fees incorporate the other items. Since these are the only counted payments, payments for improvements or repairs are not considered in-kind support and maintenance, and certainly payment of telephone or utilities does not count either. Also, allowing use of land itself is not a household expense and does not count. [POMS SI 00835.465d]

Q 16:18.2 How are loans to an SSI recipient treated?

Providing in-kind support and maintenance as a loan, pursuant to a "bona fide loan agreement," which includes "an oral or written agreement as long as it is enforceable under State law," is not income. [POMS SI 00835.482] A bona fide loan of cash is also not income [POMS SI 01120.220]; however, if there is a question as to whether Social Security will find the loan "bona fide," it can be important to distinguish a loan of cash to be used to purchase food or shelter—which is a loan of in-kind support and maintenance—from a straight cash loan. A "bona fide" loan requires an understanding at the time the loaned cash or item is provided that the borrower has an obligation to repay in all events, not just when the borrower has the financial means to do so. A sense of moral obligation to repay does not make something a loan from inception. A loan agreement should include a feasible repayment schedule, although court cases have sometimes gone farther and concluded that a genuine intention to repay was sufficient even when repayment was not actually feasible.

Q 16:19 Can an SSI recipient receive gifts?

Gifts of *cash* to or for the benefit of an SSI recipient or applicant will be counted as income. In other words, while an SSI recipient may receive cash gifts from, for example, a family member, SSI benefits will be reduced accordingly. Once the $20 "disregard" threshold is reached, cash gifts will reduce the SSI benefit dollar-for-dollar.

In-kind gifts of non-necessities are ordinarily not counted as income, and are therefore completely permissible. Gifts of entertainment, travel, education, therapy, or other treatment can be freely given to SSI recipients. One proviso: An in-kind gift that could be converted into food or shelter will be treated as a cash gift. In other words, providing refundable airline tickets may result in a reduction or loss of SSI benefits, but providing nonrefundable tickets will not. Similarly, coupons for movie theaters technically would cause SSI reductions (provided they exceed the $20 threshold), but the direct payment of movie tickets will not.

In-kind gifts of necessities (food and shelter) are treated as income. The benefit reduction is not, however, calculated dollar-for-dollar, but instead, at the lesser of fair market value or one-third of the maximum monthly benefit (see SQ 16:18).

Veterans Benefits

Q 16:22 What kinds of benefits are available for veterans and their families?

Cash, health care, dental care, pharmacy services, life insurance, and burial benefits are available for eligible veterans and their dependents. Those veterans partially or totally disabled through injury or disease incurred during active training or active duty may be entitled to monthly compensation benefits. Pensions are available to veterans who served during wartime, with benefits varying according to need and degree of disability. Medical benefits, including outpatient and home care services, respite and hospice care are provided to veterans, although with significant limitations on eligibility. Finally, the dependents and survivors of veterans may be eligible to receive compensation, pensions, death benefits, and medical care. The federal statutes governing veterans benefits can be found at 38 U.S.C. Sections 101 et seq. It is important to review the government websites for up-to-date information: *www.va.gov* is the Veterans Administration website, and much information is available at the Veterans Benefits Administration website, *www.vba.va.gov*. The VA benefits manual is online at *http:// www.warms.vba.va.gov*. Lexis-Nexis also publishes a comprehensive Veterans Benefits Manual.

Q 16:23   How does the Department of Veteran's Affairs determine eligibility for benefits?

Veterans' benefits are not entitlements, and the availability of benefits depends on the amount of funding allotted by Congress in any given year and the availability of facilities. For this reason, a priority system has been developed for veterans who have performed active service in the military and who were not dishonorably discharged. [38 U.S.C. § 101(2)] A priority list of veterans entitled to benefits ranks them according to disability level, service experience, need, and ability to pay. The list, in priority order, includes:

1. Veterans determined to have service-connected disabilities of 50 percent or greater

2. Veterans with service-connected disabilities between 30 percent and 50 percent

3. Veterans who are Former Prisoners of War (POWs), veterans awarded a Purple Heart medal, veterans whose discharge was for a disability that was incurred or aggravated in the line of duty, veterans with VA-rated service-connected disabilities 10% or 20% disabling, or veterans awarded special eligibility classification under Title 38, U.S.C., Section 1151, "benefits for individuals disabled by treatment or vocational rehabilitation"

4. Veterans receiving aid and attendance benefits, or determined to be catastrophically disabled

5. Veterans meeting income and asset standards, receiving pensions, or eligible for Medicaid

6. All other veterans not required to make any copayments for their care

7. Veterans above income and asset standards, if they agree to make copayments

[38 U.S.C. § 1705 et seq., 1151 for provisions regarding injury by VA negligence]

In each budget year, the Veterans Administration determines how far down the priority list the actual enrollment of veterans will progress. Links to the various income/asset limits are contained in the publication found online at *http://www.va.gov/healtheligibility/ Library/pubs/EnrollmentRestriction/EnrollmentRestriction.pdf.*

Q 16:27 What benefits are available for service-related disability?

A disability is compensable as long as it was service-related. Once the VA has determined that the disability is service-connected, it then sets a disability rating in 10 percent increments based on the effect the disability has on the veteran's earning ability. [38 U.S.C. § 1114] A 100 percent disability rating will be given when an individual is unable to secure or follow a substantially gainful occupation as a result of service-connected disabilities. This is called "individual unemployability" (IU). A veteran who is at least 60 percent disabled may also be considered for individual unemployability status, when there are factors other than the disability itself that may affect the veteran's ability to find work. [38 C.F.R. § 4.16] Level of education and work history are typical IU variables.

Disabilities may be periodically rerated based on changes in the law, increased medical knowledge and technology, and changes in the disability itself. Compensation ranges from approximately $100 per month for a 10 percent disability to over $2,000 per month for a 100 percent disability. [38 U.S.C. § 1114] Compensation is generally not subject to income tax, garnishment, or attachment.

Pension rates are published on the internet and depend upon size of family and type of assistance being received. As of December 1, 2007, the Maximum Annual Pension Rate for an unmarried person without dependents was $931.75/month ($11,181/year), but additional compensation is provided for those veterans who are housebound or need nursing or other regular assistance. [38 U.S.C. § 1114], as high as $1,842.75/month ($22,113/year) for a person with a dependent receiving "aid and assistance" benefits, plus $159/month per additional child. See *http://www.vba.va.gov/bln/21/Rates/pen01.htm.*

Finally, $90 per month of veterans pension benefits are excluded from income when determining the amount of the contribution towards the costs of nursing home care.

Q 16:28 Can veterans with non-service related disabilities receive pension benefits?

Pensions may be available for wartime veterans with non-service-connected disabilities if they are totally and permanently disabled and financially needy. (VA Disability Pension) The VA applies stringent eligibility requirements for pensions. The veteran must:

1. Have served 90 days during a period of war. (The 90-day requirement should not apply to those who served prior to 1980.)
2. Not have been discharged dishonorably. [38 U.S.C. § 5303(a)]
3. Be disabled, but not as a result of either a service-connected injury or the veteran's own willful conduct.
4. Be low income, below the benefit amount.
5. Not have assets so large that it would be "reasonable" that some part of the assets would be consumed by the costs of care. While the level of assets that raise this "reasonableness" test has not been codified, it is usually assumed to be $50,000. [38 C.F.R. §§ 3.274–3.276]

The pension program guarantees a minimum income to the veteran, so that a qualified veteran with no countable income will receive the maximum annual pension amount. Those with income less than the maximum allowable pension rate may still be eligible. [38 C.F.R. §§ 3.271–3.272.] There are three VA pension programs:

1. *Old-Law Pension.* Available to veterans who became eligible prior to July 1, 1960, and does not count spousal income to determine income eligibility;
2. *Section 306 Pension.* Covers veterans eligible between July 1, 1960 and December 31, 1978, and counts the spouse's Social Security income but not spousal income to determine income eligibility; and
3. *Improved Pension.* Covers veterans eligible after January 1, 1979. This is the only pension program open to new enrollees. Current enrollees must be under 55 and totally and permanently disabled. All income—including spousal income—is counted. A home, burial expenses, and certain other assets are exempt from consideration for need-based benefits, and transfers of property will not be acknowledged by the VA as reducing the countable resources of the applicant.

[38 C.F.R. § 3.3]

Both the Old Law Pension and the Section 306 Pension can be converted to the Improved Pension.

Note that a person who might not have been eligible for a non-service connected disability pension in the community might become eligible for a pension when "impoverished" to the point of being eligible for Medicaid coverage in a nursing home, and the state Medicaid agency may require veterans to apply for the pension. There is some slight advantage to be gained for an institutionalized veteran applying for a pension even if the state agency does not require the application, as the individual will have an additional $90 per month to spend in excess of what is otherwise allowed as a personal needs allowance.

Q 16:29 What is "financially needy" for pension qualification?

Any veteran receiving countable income less than the maximum applicable annual pension rate may be deemed needy. Among those sources excluded from consideration as income are welfare payments, other VA pension benefits, profit from sale of property, burial expenses, educational expenses, Department of Defense survivor benefit annuities, and cash surrender values of life insurance. As of December 1, 2007, the threshhold for the Improved Disability Pension is yearly income of $11,181 for a single individual with no dependents and neither housebound nor in need of "aid and attendance" benefits [see SQ 16:38.1], up to $22,183 for a veteran with a dependent who is in need of aid and attendance benefits (plus $1,909/year for each child). [(See SQ 16:38.1.)

Q 16:31 How is eligibility and the amount of the Improved Pension determined?

The Improved Pension Plan, the current pension program now available to all qualified veterans, deems a veteran eligible if he or she was in active military service for 90 days (continuous or interrupted) during a period of war or was discharged because of a service-connected disability sustained while serving during a period of war. The discharge cannot have been dishonorable. Veterans will also be deemed eligible if they are permanently and totally disabled from a non-service-connected disability, the disability did not result from the veteran's own willful misconduct, and the veteran does not have sufficient income or resources to sustain himself or herself. Generally a veteran will be deemed eligible if he or she has less than $50,000 in assets (not counting a home and ordinary personal effects) ($80,000 for a couple) and income less than the maximum applicable annual pension rate.

Q 16:32 Are surviving spouses and children of veterans eligible for compensation benefits?

Eligible family members include spouses who are legally married to the veteran for at least a year, or for any amount of time if married before or during the veteran's service (legally separated but still married spouses are eligible); children who are minors, in school (up to age 23), or dependent; and financially dependent parents, either natural or adoptive. In order to receive benefits, children must be unmarried, and may be natural, adoptive, or illegitimate. Stepchildren may also qualify for benefits. Similar to Social Security "adult disabled child" benefits, veteran's benefits also cover the "helpless child" disabled prior to age 18. Spousal benefits are lost upon remarriage unless the remarriage was (1) when the remarrying spouse was 57 or older and (2) the remarriage occurred on/after December 16, 2003; however, benefits are reinstated if the remarriage terminates.

Spouses, children, and parents may be eligible for monthly dependency and indemnity compensation (DIC) benefits if the veteran died as a result of a service-connected disability incurred while on active duty, or if the death was not service-connected but the veteran was totally and permanently disabled for at least 10 years as a result of a service-connected condition. [38 U.S.C. § 1318] Pension benefits are available but at a much lower rate than for the veterans themselves, and survivors of veterans who died prior to 1957 must file a special election to receive DIC benefits.

For survivors of veterans who died after January 1, 1993, the surviving spouse may be entitled to $1,091 per month in DIC benefits plus $233 per month (rates effective December 1, 2007) if the veteran had a service-connected disability for at least eight years prior to his or her death. An additional $271 per month is provided for each minor child of the veteran, or if there is no surviving spouse, $462 for the first child, $631 for two children, $885 for three children, and so on. Additional amounts are provided for minor or "helpless" children. For these purposes "income" is counted after a substantial exclusion. For veterans who died before January 1, 1993, the Veterans Administration uses a complex formula. [38 C.F.R. § 1311] For more details, see *http://www.vba.va.gov/bln/21/Rates/comp03.htm#BM01.*

Q 16:33   Are veterans entitled to medical care through the VA?

VA benefits are not entitlements, and the VA is required to provide medical care only to veterans with service-connected conditions, former prisoners of war, veterans exposed to radiation or other toxic substances during their service, and World War I veterans. [38 U.S.C. § 1705(a)]

Veterans with non-service-connected disabilities receive medical care only if they fall into "special eligibility" categories (e.g., former POWs; those with purple hearts; "castrophically" disabled, etc. (see 16:23)). If they do not meet these criteria, they must show that they are financially needy, generally applying a geographical means threshold, using the standards applicable to the Housing and Urban Development figures for housing. "Needy" is still a less restrictive standard for veterans benefits than it is for Medicaid, however. For those discharged since 1980, one year's service is also required, but this does not apply to veterans discharged earlier. The VA website provides a list of 8 "priority enrollment groups."

In response to increasing demand, the VA has begun to institute various programs in geriatric assessment and long-term care, including community service programs. Few veterans qualify, however, and the programs are restricted by the availability of facilities.

Under a new rule adopted in 2002, the VA will grant priority to "severely disabled" veterans, even if the immediate health problem needing attention is unrelated to their military service, and to "moderately disabled" veterans who seek care for disabilities stemming from their service. The new policy would not affect emergency treatment. Prior to the rule, services were provided more on a "first-come, first-served" basis. In addition, under a 2004 directive from the Secretary of the Department of Veterans Affairs, all veterans requiring hospital and/or outpatient care for a service-connected disability must be scheduled for a primary care evaluation within 30 days of their request for care, and if the VA facility is unable to meet this schedule, it must arrange for one at another VA facility, at a contract facility or through a sharing agreement. However, veterans needing emergency care will be treated immediately, and for the severely disabled, the priority includes care for non-service-connected medical problems.

[38 U.S.C. § 1705(c)(2)]

Q 16:35   How is financial ability to pay the cost of care determined?

The priority order of veterans awaiting access to Medicare under the VA system is correlated directly with how extreme the respective disability and impoverishment of the veteran is, and the administration is given fairly broad discretion to consider extenuating circumstances in individual cases to qualify or disqualify the veteran for benefits. The statute [38 U.S.C. § 1722] states that a veteran shall be considered to be unable to defray the expenses of necessary care if he or she is eligible to receive medical assistance under a state plan approved under Title XIX of the Social Security Act [42 U.S.C. § 1396 et seq.], the veteran is currently receiving a disability-related pension, or the veteran's attributable income is not greater than $28,429 in the case of a veteran with no dependents; or $34,117 in the case of a veteran with one dependent, plus $1,909 for each additional dependent (2008 figures available at *http://www.va.gov/healtheligibility/Library/pubs/VAIncome Thresholds/VAIncomeThresholds.pdf*—a formula is provided in the statute to adjust these figures proportionately to increases in pensions since 1990).

Q 16:36   How are copayments determined?

Veterans who have sufficient income or resources to disqualify them from hardship eligibility may still receive medical benefits if they agree to pay copayments. Veterans whose income is determined to be above the means test threshold and below VA's geographically-based income threshold are responsible for paying 20 percent of the Medicare deductible for the first 90 days of inpatient hospital care during any 365-day period. For each additional 90 days of hospital care, they are charged 10 percent of the Medicare deductible. In addition, the patient is charged $2 a day for hospital care. Nonservice-connected veterans and noncompensable zero percent service-connected veterans with incomes above the geographic income threshold will be charged the full Medicare deductible for the first 90 days of care during any 365-day period. For each additional 90 days, they are charged one half of the Medicare deductible and $10 per day. Nursing home copayments equal the lesser of the cost of care, or the sum of the Medicare deductible for the first 90 days plus $5 per day of care. Outpatient copayments are $15 for primary care and up to $50 for specialist care, and prescriptions require an $8 copayment for every

30-day supply (2006 figures). Preventative screenings and immunizations are generally free. Certain veterans are not required to pay copayments:

1. Veterans with a service-connected disability pension;

2. Veterans whose annual income (determined under 38 U.S.C. § 150) is less than the amount in effect under 38 U.S.C. § 1521(b);

3. Veterans receiving care for a veteran's noncompensable zero percent service-connected disability;

4. An episode of extended care services that began on or before November 30, 1999;

5. Care for Vietnam-era herbicide-exposed veterans, radiation-exposed veterans, Persian Gulf War veterans, or post-Persian Gulf War combat-exposed veterans;

6. Care for treatment of sexual trauma; or

7. Care or services for certain veterans regarding cancer of the head or neck.

In 2005, the U.S. Department of Veterans Affairs published final rules on copayments including "spousal protection" disregards, including a complete exclusion for the income, assets, expenses, and allowance of legally separated spouses. The definition of "expenses" has been changed to include: (1) insurance premiums of the veteran and the veteran's spouse and dependents, and (2) personal property taxes, not just income taxes. [38 C.F.R. § 17.111]

Q 16:37 Does the VA's medical service benefit include nursing or other long-term care?

The Veterans Administration operates nursing homes in every region of the country, and qualified veterans *may* receive nursing home care in one of these facilities. [38 C.F.R. § 17.47(a)] VA provides nursing home services through three national programs: VA owned and operated nursing homes, state veterans homes owned and operated by the state, and contract community nursing homes. Each program has its own admission and eligibility criteria. Nursing home care in VA homes is currently restricted to those with 70 percent service-connected disabilities or who require nursing home care because of a service-connected disability. Copayments may also be required. The state veterans homes set eligibility criteria for admission. Veterans who may be provided nursing home care without an income eligibility assessment include:

- Veterans with service-connected disabilities
- Veterans exposed to herbicides while serving in Vietnam
- Veterans exposed to radiation
- Veterans with a condition related to an environmental exposure in the Persian gulf
- Former POWs
- Veterans on a VA pension
- Veterans of the Mexican Border period or WWI
- Veterans eligible for Medicaid

[38 U.S.C. § 1710]

In some regions, the VA provides short-term nursing home care by contracts with outside providers. If the patient is being released from a VA hospital to the nursing home, he or she may qualify for such a short-term contract—usually for a total of no more than six months of care for veterans with non-service-related disabilities. The benefit is unlimited if the veteran has a service-related disability. Where VA nursing home contracts are utilized, the patient is usually not required to contribute to the cost of care. [38 C.F.R. § 17.51]

Finally, retired servicemen and women and family members eligible to participate in the military's "TRICARE for Life" medical insurance may receive a substantial benefit for inpatient skilled nursing facility care: after Medicare terminates, then $250 per day or 25 percent of charges, whichever is less, for facilities in the TRICARE network; for out-of-network facilities, $535 per day or 25 percent of billed charges for institutional services, whichever is less, plus 25 percent of allowable professional charges. Both are subject to a $3,000 annual family maximum. Thus, the retired serviceman with TRICARE for Life should pay nothing for days 1–100 and if the facility private rate is $300/day for days 101+, would pay $75/day for days 101+. Information about TRICARE can be found at *http://www. tricare.mil*. It is important to note that coverage is only for *skilled* nursing care, i.e., care that would be covered by Medicare but for the 100-day limitation. It would not cover residence at a skilled nursing facility that derives solely from the need for assistance with activities of daily living.

Q 16:38.1   Does the VA provide home care benefits?

Veterans receiving pensions, and who need care (or whose family members need care) that we customarily consider "home care," may be eligible for an additional "special monthly compensation" amount called "Aid and Attendance" or "Aid, Attendance and Housebound Benefits," which it intended to offset the cost of providing for such care privately. [38 U.S.C. § 1114(4); 38 C.F.R. § 3.350(h), 3.352]. The "special compensation" is an enhancement of the pension; the high expenses for home care offset income to the point that the person becomes financially needy to justify receipt of a pension.

TRICARE for Life, which provides benefits to military retirees and their families, may also provide home care benefits that are not needs-based, but only for skilled nursing care (the type covered by Medicare), not purely assistance with activities of daily living.

For the "aid and attendance" benefit, eligibility is based on need for care and *net* income, that is, amount by which costs of care exceeds income. Specifically, benefits are available to a veteran who served in time of war or the surviving spouse or surviving dependent parent or child of a such a veteran, and who is determined by physician to be permanently and totally disabled and in need of "aid and attendance,"*and* whose income, after deducting for medical expenses, does not exceed $1,554.50 (veteran), $998.75 (survivor), or $1,842.75 (couple) criteria; *and* whose assets do not exceed $50,000 (individual) or $80,000 (couple). Service "in time of war" usually means an honorable discharge after at least 90 days of active duty (which includes training) with at least one day served during wartime. However, the 90-1 day service requirement did not come in until 1980, so veterans from earlier times might meet the test with even fewer days of service. Family members receiving DIC benefits may also qualify. [38 C.F.R. § 3.351] Need for care is based on proof of *one* of the following:

1. upon presentation by a doctor or other corroborative medical evidence that the person is legally blind; or has visual acuity of 5/200 or less in both eyes, or concentric contraction of the visual field to 5° or less;

2. a statement by a doctor and/or other corroborative medical evidence that the person is in a nursing home because of mental or physical incapacity; or

3. medical or other evidence that the person is "so nearly helpless or blind" as to be incompetent or unable to perform Activities of

Daily Living such as dressing, bathing, eating, etc., or unable to protect themself from the hazards of daily life. [38 CFR § 3.352(a)]

Helpful information may be found at a private consumer website, *http://www.veteranaid.org* as well as new pages on the website of the Department of Veterans Affairs *http://www.vba.va.gov*

Keep in mind that aid & attendance is a pension plus enhancement, and may court as income, which can impact both Medicaid eligibility in income-cap states, and potentially, the CSRA.

The "Aid and Attendance" benefit is a maximum of $1,554.50 for a veteran; $998.75 for a survivor. Example: Veteran has monthly assisted living expenses of $3,154.50 per month and income of $1,600 per month. "Net income" is $−1,554.50. Benefit would be $1,554.50.

The VA also provides services described as "Domiciliary Care," defined as "rehabilitative and long-term, health-maintenance care for veterans who require minimal medical care but do not need the skilled nursing services provided in nursing homes." Eligibility is based on financial need "for those whose annual income does not exceed the maximum annual rate of VA pension or to veterans the Secretary of Veterans Affairs determines have no adequate means of support." Copayments for extended care services (nursing home care) also apply to domiciliary care.

Finally, a deceased veteran's family member receiving DIC, but who does not qualify for "Aid and Attendance," may receive an additional "housebound" allowance if "substantially confined" to their home or an institution because of a disability or disabilities that are reasonably certain to continue throughout the person's lifetime. [38 C.F.R. § 3.351 (e)]

Q 16:38.2 Does the VA provide a prescription drug benefit?

Yes. The prescription drug benefit for veterans should not be overlooked. Veterans may be charged $8 for each 30-day supply of medication if procured directly from a VA facility. [38 U.S.C. § 1722A(a)] Veterans requiring medication for the treatment of service-connected conditions and veterans whose income does not exceed the maximum VA pension, are entitled to receive prescriptions free. In addition, the VA may provide items such as eyeglasses, prostheses, wheelchairs, etc.

Q 16:39   What are the eligibility requirements for medical benefits for families of veterans?

The VA Civilian Health and Medical Program (CHAMPVA) provides medical care for dependents and survivors of veterans. The following individuals are eligible for CHAMPVA:

1. Spouses and children of veterans who were permanently and totally disabled through service-connected injury or disease;

2. Spouses and children of veterans who died of service-connected injuries or diseases or who were totally disabled from service-connected condition at the time of death; and

3. Spouses and children of veterans who were killed in the line of duty within 30 days of entry into active service.

[38 U.S.C. § 1713; 38 C.F.R. § 17.84]

Note that spouse and survivor benefits end if the marriage to the veteran is terminated by divorce or annulment, and if widowed, if the surviving spouse remarries prior to age 55. However, survivor benefits may be re-established if the subsequent marriage is terminated due to divorce, annulment, or death. Children's benefits terminate if the child marries or turns 18 (a full-time student has coverage to age 23) or for a stepchild, if the stepchild no longer lives in the veteran's household.

CHAMPVA is the payer of last resort after recourse to insurance, including TRICARE (Department of Defense) benefits, and Medicare but it is primary comparative to Medicaid and State Victims Compensation Programs. Coverage is based on a percentage of a "covered amount" much like the "reasonable and customary" formula used by health insurance plans or the "Medicare-covered" amount in the Medicare context. There is an annual outpatient deductible of $50 per person or $100 per family for CHAMPVA beneficiaries, but no deductible for inpatient services. There is an annual cap on the copays set at $3000 per family effective January 2002.

Practically speaking, CHAMPVA coverage has limitations. Most frequently used is "CITI" or CHAMPVA Inhouse Treatment Initiative, i.e., beneficiaries receive free covered healthcare provided at the VA, but this is not available at all VA facilities. Also, because Medicare will not cover services at VA facilities and because CHAMPVA pays as a last resort, Medicare beneficiaries must first seek treatment elsewhere.

TRICARE (formerly known as "CHAMPUS") provides medical care for dependents of active duty personnel and for retired military personnel and their dependents. For Medicare-eligible retirees, "TRI-CARE for Life" is a Medicare "wrap-around" that either supplements Medicare coverage or in some instances provides benefits that are not available under Medicare. [See Q 16:11] Military retirees and surviving spouses of veterans killed in action do not participate in CHAMPVA but receive benefits under TRICARE.

Q 16:40 What other benefits are available to veterans?

The VA will authorize the burial of veterans in national cemeteries and will provide a headstone or marker. The VA may furnish and appropriate markers for the graves of eligible veterans buried in private cemeteries, whose deaths occurred on or after December 27, 2001, regardless of whether the grave is already marked with a non-government marker.

The VA also may provide a modest "burial allowance." If the veteran died while in active service or as a result of a service-connected disability, the VA may pay up to $2,000 for burial and internment expenses. [38 U.S.C. § 2302, 2303, 2304, 2307] For other honorably discharged veterans who received a VA pension or died in a VA hospital or veterans nursing home, in the case of a non-service related death, the VA will pay up to $300 toward burial and funeral costs, and $150 plot interment allowance. If the veteran died in a VA hospital or in a state or federal veteran's home, or will be buried in a VA national cemetery, the VA may reimburse the cost of moving the remains. Required documentation includes proof of the veteran's military service, a death certificate, and copies of itemized funeral and cemetery bills, showing the amounts paid and due. Application is made by filing VA Form 21–530.

Life insurance is also available to veterans. Servicepersons in active duty receive automatic coverage of $400,000; upon discharge, they are offered various life insurance options. Veterans are expected to pay premiums except if they are totally and permanently disabled, in which case premiums on the first $20,000 of coverage are waived. [38 U.S.C. § 1922A]. Important: these policies are non-transferable, and therefore will have to be surrendered to reduce assets to permitted thresholds for Medicaid eligibility.

Educational assistance also may be available to a veteran's spouse, children (including stepchildren or adopted children), and survivors under the Survivors' and Dependants' Educational Assistance Program (DEA), 38 U.S.C. Chapter 35.

The surviving spouse of a veteran who died as a result of a service-connected disability, or has been officially listed as missing in action or as a Prisoner of War for more than 90 days, may be eligible for a VA loan guaranty for the purchase of a home. As with other benefits, this benefit is lost by remarriage.

Q 16:41   What are the procedural requirements for filing a claim for veteran's benefits?

For veterans not currently receiving a pension, it is necessary first to apply for an eligibility determination. It is often possible to apply online or by fax, but documents and original signatures are also required. An important document is DD-214 (for World War II veterans, form WD), the veteran's discharge papers. If these are not available, it may be necessary to contact the National Personnel Records Center in Missouri. Eighty percent of the discharge papers of those discharged between 1912 and 1960 were lost in a catastrophic fire in 1973, but the Center will provide substitute papers that are accepted in lieu of the DD-214. Form 180 is required to authorize third parties to receive these documents or other information. Information and contact information is available on the Internet at: *http://www.archives.gov/veterans/evetrecs/index.html.*

Payment of claims is retroactive to the filing of the claim, not the incurring of the disability itself or dates of service. [38 C.F.R. § 3.400] All that is required to set the filing date is written notification to a VA regional office, although eventually a formal claim must be submitted. The VA has a duty to assist claimants, such as by providing medical records and medical examinations. An intricate system of appeals has been established for claims disallowed at the regional office level, leading to the Board of Veterans' Appeals (BVA) (independent of the VA) and, in some cases, the U.S. Court of Veterans' Appeals and the federal circuit court system.

Q 16:41.1   Can attorneys charge for assisting with applications for veterans benefits?

"It depends." At one time, attorneys were not permitted to charge more than $10 for assisting with VA matters. More recently, Congress authorized attorneys to charge fees, but *only* for assisting with appeals following a denial by the Board of Veterans Appeals. [38 U.S.C. § 5904(d)(1)] The veteran must have filed form VA 21–22 with the VA to appoint the attorney as a representative. Fee agreements may be reviewed by the BVA and by the Court of Appeals for Veterans' Claims, and either entity may reduce the fees if they are considered unreasonable. [38 U.S.C. § 5904(c)(2)] Fees not exceeding 20% of past-due benefits are presumed reasonable; fees exceeding 331/3% are presumed unreasonable.

In December 2006, Congress enacted the "Veterans Benefits, Health Care, and Information Technology Act of 2006," requiring attorneys to be "accredited" by the VA in order to receive these fees. [P.L. 109-461, adding 38 U.S.C. § 5904(a)(2)] In June 2008, the VA issued final regulations setting forth the procedure by which attorneys may become "accredited." [73 Fed. Reg. 29851, amending 38 CFR § 14.629] The requirements include an application on VA form 21a (requiring three character references) [*http://www.va.gov/vaforms/va/pdf/VA21a.pdf*], three hours of continuing legal education received within twelve months of registration, and certification of one's standing as a member of the bar. Accreditation must be renewed every two years. Only attorneys who have received a certificate of accreditation by the VA may charge fees. While the "accreditation" regulation appears to be written sufficiently broadly to address *all* assistance to veterans with respect to benefits (prohibiting attorneys who are not accredited from "assist[ing] claimants in the preparation, presentation, and prosecution of claims for VA benefits" [38 C.F.R. § 14.629(b)(1)], there do not appear to be any real repercussions for assisting veterans at no charge, as the sole significance of accreditation is to be able to charge fees for assisting with appeals following BVA denials. The regulatory structure is thus very similar to the regulation of fees that may be paid in representing individuals before the Social Security Administration.

How should the attorney cope with the fee restriction when the issue of benefit eligibility arises in the context of an overall representation? Some attorneys take the view that there is no fee being charged for service in VA matters as such. Another approach is to issue-spot and send the client elsewhere, such as the state department of veterans affairs, or a regional Disabled American Veterans office, or direct the applicant to the VA website. The National Association of County Veterans Service Organizations has a state-by-state listing of organizations that assist veterans online at *http://www.nacvso.org/cvso.asp*. In those instances when one is actively assisting with a specific benefit application, it may be appropriate to write off the associated time by specific reference to the tasks being excised in the billing memoranda, in case of a future challenge.

Railroad Retirement Benefits

Q 16:43 Who qualifies to receive Railroad Retirement benefits?

The basic requirement for Railroad Retirement benefits is 120 months of creditable railroad service. [45 U.S.C. § 231a(a)(1)] The 120 months need not be consecutive; in some cases, military service can be credited toward the 120-month requirement. Since 1974, a creditable month has usually meant any month in which the employee receives at least $25 in wages from a covered employer. Covered employers include all railroads engaged in interstate commerce and some subsidiaries), railroad associations, and national railway labor organizations. During fiscal year 2007, nearly $9.88 billion in retirement-survivor benefits were paid to approximately 567,000 beneficiaries. [See *http://www.rrb.gov/pdf/act/ST07parta.pdf.*] Retirees were clustered in California, Illinois, Nebraska, New York, Pennsylvania, and Texas, with over 11,000 covered retirees in each of those states. [See *http://www.rrb.gov/pdf/act/statedataCY2007.pdf.*]

Railroad Retirement will become less important to the aging population over time. As of December 2007, 277,000 retirees currently receive benefits, a decrease of 10% from prior years. Moreover, only 236,000 current employees were still covered by Railroad Retirement in 2007. [See *http://www.rrb.gov/pdf/act/statedataCY2007.pdf.*]

Q 16:44 Who administers the Railroad Retirement program?

The Railroad Retirement Board (RRB), a three-member board of directors, administers the Railroad Retirement program. The President of the United States appoints all three members; one must be recommended by railroad management, one by railroad labor interests, and the third (who always serves as Chair of the Board) represents the public interest. The Railroad Retirement Board has offices at 844 North Rush Street, Chicago, Illinois 60611–2092, phone: (312) 751–7139 (TTY (312) 751–4701. The RRB also operates a toll-free automated answering service at (800) 808–0772. Local field offices are located in 53 cities in 35 states.

Q 16:46 What happens when a Railroad Retirement beneficiary also qualifies to receive Social Security benefits?

Railroad Retirement operates a two-tier benefit structure. "Tier I" benefits are calculated to approximate what the railroad employee would have received had he or she been covered by Social Security, and "Tier II" benefits are the enhanced benefits paid only to Railroad Retirement beneficiaries. [45 U.S.C. § 231b(b)] If a railroad employee has a work history covered by Social Security, and retired after 1974, the Tier I benefits are reduced by the amount of Social Security benefits. Because the Tier I benefit levels are computed using both Railroad Retirement and Social Security work history, the effect is to prevent double benefits from being paid because of coverage in both retirement systems. Tier II benefits, on the other hand, are computed solely on the basis of Railroad Retirement-covered employment.

The same computations are applied to spousal benefits. In other words, a Railroad Retirement beneficiary whose spouse has work history covered by Social Security will not be able to benefit from both programs: His or her spousal Railroad Retirement benefit will be reduced by the amount of Social Security benefit to which he or she is entitled. [45 U.S.C. § 231c(b)]

For some Railroad Retirement beneficiaries who worked in Social Security-covered employment before 1975 (and whose rights vested before that date), an additional retirement benefit may be available. After 1974, congressional changes to the Railroad Retirement program attempted to prevent dual benefit payments. Funding for the pre-1975 dual benefits is based on separate annual appropriations by Congress, and may be reduced proportionally if budget appropriations are insufficient to cover all vested benefits. [45 U.S.C. § 231n(d)]

For most Railroad Retirement beneficiaries (and spouses), the practical result will be that they will receive a single retirement check from the Railroad Retirement Board that will be calculated in concert with the Social Security Administration. In order to facilitate this process, Social Security records are reviewed by Railroad Retirement Board administrators.

The dual benefit system can lead to a few problems. Railroad Retirement may report payments separately and Social Security may then report them in combination. The result can be "double-counting" by the state Medicaid agency, which will require constant reminders and proof that there has been a mistake in computation.

Practice-Related Issues

Q 16:50   How might an elder law attorney encounter issues involving the Veterans Administration, the Railroad Retirement Board, or the Supplemental Security Income program?

It is important for an elder law attorney to be aware of these benefits, in order to spot the instances in which a client has not accessed all available sources of support and health care. With respect to veteran's benefits, it is important to be aware that the client with a service-connected disability may be entitled to care at a VA nursing home or valuable aid and assistance benefits at home (particularly in a condo-minium setting where cash is important), that the resident with a VA pension may keep $90 per month more than his non-veteran neighbor, and that SSI is still available to the aged client without sufficient quarters of coverage to obtain Social Security benefits. Knowledge of SSI is also critical when dealing not with the elderly as such, but with disabled individuals, particularly those with mental illness, since these disorders often manifest themselves later than age 22 (defeating adult disabled child benefits), but before the sufferer has had a significant worklife of his or her own. As the population ages, elder law attorneys will also see more and more aged parents facing the prospect of providing for middle-aged mentally retarded children who have always lived at home. However, restrictions imposed on representation before the Social Security Administration or VA will continue to create problems for attorneys who want to do their best for their clients but who also must earn a living.

Representation of clients in Veterans Administration matters is particularly problematic, and might include:

1. *Representation in VA claims.* A client whom the attorney has represented in other matters contacts the attorney and asks for help in filing a VA disability claim. The attorney is eager to help this client and the client is willing to pay. What should the attorney know about representation of clients in VA matters?

   Unless willing to represent the client *pro bono*, the attorney should encourage the client to go as far as he or she can on his or her own. Attorneys are not permitted to charge fees for service in VA matters prior to the final decision of the Board of Veterans' Appeals, and in fact the VA is obligated to assist claimants. The attorney may, however, be able to direct the client to the correct telephone numbers or local VA office or provide the correct forms. Once the claim has been denied by the BVA, any representative of the claimant may charge fees not exceeding 20 percent of the benefits awarded through the claim for further efforts on his or her behalf. Fee agreements may be reviewed by the BVA and by the Court of Appeals for Veterans' Claims, and either entity may reduce the fees if they are considered unreasonable.

2. *SSI recipient receiving large inheritance or personal injury settlement.* One common scenario encountered in the elder law practice is the SSI recipient who inherits money, or receives a substantial personal injury settlement. In the case of the personal injury settlement, the injury may even be the cause of the disability leading to SSI benefits.

In either case, the SSI recipient must first analyze the importance of continued SSI eligibility. In many states, the real issue will be categorical eligibility for Medicaid care—particularly in the case of personal injury settlements, where the cost of care may be overwhelming and the settlement amount comparatively modest.

Of course, in the case of inheritance the problem is easily solved by planning on the part of the donor. Establishment of a "pure" discretionary trust (one in which the trustee has the discretion to pay no benefits to the SSI recipient, and the authority to provide non-necessities directly) will ordinarily prevent the loss of SSI benefits and Medicaid coverage. Too often, unfortunately, donors fail to make such plans in advance, and the resultant intestate or outright inheritance will require legal repair work.

Even though the SSI recipient's cost of care may be substantial, if the funds to be received can provide for an extended period of care some consideration must be given simply to receiving the funds and ending benefits. If, for example, the recipient's life expectancy is short, or immediate needs are great, it may be advisable to receive the funds and anticipate that there may come a time when SSI and Medicaid benefits will be available once again—after the funds have been exhausted.

Assuming that continued SSI eligibility is important, the beneficiary will have two basic options (although he or she may mix the two options in an appropriate case):

1. spend the proceeds quickly, or
2. establish a special needs trust.

Spending the money can include one or more of the following (this list is not intended to be exhaustive, but to suggest common expenditures):

- Purchase of a residence
- Adaptation of an existing residence (e.g., for wheelchair accessibility, or to permit live-in caretakers)
- Home repairs (e.g., replacement of appliances, carpeting, drapes, whether for medical or cosmetic purposes)
- Purchase of a single vehicle (e.g., wheelchair-equipped van or other special transportation)
- Acquisition of medical equipment (motorized wheelchair, specialized bed, etc.)
- Special therapy or treatment programs (e.g., experimental procedure not covered by Medicaid and requiring travel to another city)

While special needs trusts are discussed more fully in chapter 17, the general concepts are straightforward. If the SSI recipient is under age 65, and the continued receipt of SSI (and Medicaid coverage) is important, a special needs trust should be considered. The recipient, with the lawyer's help, must weigh the administrative costs and the restrictions on use of the money (food, clothing, and shelter cannot be provided without affecting benefits) against the continued SSI eligibility benefits. Frequently, the SSI recipient may elect to take a significant portion of the funds received and, in the same month, purchase food, clothing, and several of the exempt items suggested previously, placing the remaining amounts in a special needs trust immediately upon completion of those steps. Note that the amount received, though treated as income in the month of receipt for SSI purposes and not otherwise treated as an asset until the month after receipt, will probably be treated as an asset if transferred for less than full value during the month of receipt.

Of course, SSI recipients are frequently incapable of handling the funds, regardless of the effect on benefits. Persons acting for the benefit of the SSI recipient may be family members, payees designated by the Social Security Administration, or a duly appointed conservator. Throughout the discussion of alternatives, the attorney must be mindful of the different roles played by the individuals involved, and the inherent conflicts of interest. For example, family members may have been providing room and board, and may now be considering payment for continued services, or purchase of a residence for the SSI recipient (and, perhaps, the family member in question). While family involvement is important and should usually be encouraged, careful consideration (and occasional reconsideration) of those roles and conflicts must be undertaken.

Part V

Health Care Decision-Making and Protection of the Elderly

Chapter 17

Special Needs Trusts

With the rising cost of care (particularly medical care, but also nursing and personal care), the increase of government involvement in that care, and the maturation of government benefits programs, the problem of providing extra benefits for disabled individuals has spawned a whole cottage industry of legal, social, medical and care management experts in the past two decades. The problem of providing for disabled children is not new, but the effect on government benefits is, and can be devastatingly important. Continued eligibility for government benefits is critical to their continued well-being. Most commonly, continued eligibility is important primarily for the medical benefits offered by Medicaid (particularly in long-term care, whether institutional or home-based) or as an adjunct to Supplemental Security Income benefits (SSI recipients usually qualify categorically for Medicaid eligibility, including acute and chronic medical care as often as long-term nursing care).

"Special needs" and "supplemental benefits" trusts provide for the disabled individual's special needs without jeopardizing his or her public benefits. This chapter discusses self-settled and third-party special needs trusts, requirements for establishing them, permissible distributions, and trustee selection.

Overview

Q 17:5　What provisions should be included when drafting a special needs trust for a disabled beneficiary?

The central purpose of an SNT is to permit the use of trust funds for the extra or supplemental needs of a public benefits recipient. Most SNTs will include language explicitly referring to that purpose. The choice of language, and the importance of including such language, will differ depending on whether the trust is established with assets owned by the disabled person or assets from a parent or other source. Because trusts established with the disabled person's own assets (including personal injury settlements and outright inheritances) must comply with the provisions of 42 U.S.C. Section 1396p(d)(4), the language of such "self-settled" trusts must be much more precise and carefully crafted; trusts established by persons other than the beneficiary, using money the beneficiary is not otherwise entitled to receive, may need only to include language making distributions discretionary with the trustee in order to prevent the trust (and its distributions) from being treated as available to the beneficiary—always depending on state law. If state law presumes that a trust for a single beneficiary is intended for "support" unless explicitly stated otherwise, the trust *must* still include some language as to its supplementary intent. It is probably not enough even to explicitly reserve the right in the Trustee to withhold any payments in the Trustee's "absolute" discretion, since that discretion must be exercised reasonably and for the benefit of the beneficiary.

The assets in the trust must not be considered available resources or the beneficiary will be disqualified from means-tested benefits programs. The trust language should state that it is the intent of the grantor to set up a special needs trust that will *not* jeopardize the recipient's government benefits and that the funds must be used solely for the benefit of the recipient-beneficiary. A self-settled trust must include language requiring repayment to the state for Medicaid benefits provided during the recipient's lifetime. Ideally, trust language will allow for some flexibility in case the laws of the jurisdiction or the Medicaid or Social Security rules change. As long as the intent of the settlor *not* to jeopardize benefits is clearly stated, the trust can be modified to conform to those statutes and rules, provided the right to amend for these purposes has been included in the document.

Even though specific language may not be necessary for a third-party trust to qualify as an SNT, it is advisable for the draftsperson to include in all SNTs provisions that:

1. Make distributions of income and principal purely discretionary;
2. Specifically prohibit the trustee from making cash distributions directly to the beneficiary (although in some circumstances it may be advisable to permit occasional cash distributions, resulting in periods of ineligibility managed by the trustee);
3. Direct the trustee to consider the effect of distributions on public benefits eligibility; and
4. Express the settlor's intention that the trust be used for to supplement rather than replace public benefits (preferably including some specific examples of trust uses).

There has been an important shift in one feature of SNTs for beneficiaries receiving SSI. Prior to the promulgation of provisions concerning SNTs in the POMS, it was widely believed that a trust, to avoid being considered a resource, had to expressly forbid expenditures for food and shelter. The POMS, which are the Social Security Administration's manual governing these matters, do *not* require any such language. Instead POMS Section SI 01120.200.D.2 (available online at *https:// s044a90.ssa.gov/apps10/poms.nsf*) provide that "[i]f an individual does not have the legal authority to revoke the trust or direct the use of the trust assets for his/her own support and maintenance, the trust principal **is not** the individual's resource for SSI purposes." (Emphasis in original.) The importance of this distinction can be great. Many SSI beneficiaries can cope with their food expenses out of the tiny SSI stipend. However, shelter is often quite another matter. If the trust forbids use for shelter, the result may be a trust intended to improve the beneficiary's quality of life, with no ability to keep the beneficiary from relying on a homeless shelter for a place to sleep. In many cases a contribution for shelter will be worth more to the beneficiary than the reduction in benefits caused by application of the "in-kind support and maintenance" rules (see SQ 17:31).

Self-Settled Special Needs Trusts

Q 17:8   What is a "(d)(4)(A)" trust?

The first type of self-settled special needs trust [codified at 42 U.S.C. § 396p(d)(4)(A)] exempts transfers made to a trust that:

1. Is established for the benefit of an individual (only one) who is (a) disabled under Social Security standards, and (b) is under age 65 at the time the trust is funded; if the beneficiary later attains age 65, the trust corpus continues to be treated as unavailable);

2. Is established by the parent, grandparent, guardian, or a court for the benefit of the disabled individual; and

3. Provides for repayment to the state of money paid for the benefit of the beneficiary pursuant to the state's Medicaid plan. Repayment must be made from the assets remaining in the trust on the beneficiary's death up to an amount equal to the total medical assistance paid on behalf of the individual. (Moreover, if more than one state has provided assistance, should the trust remainder prove insufficient, repayment must be made *pro rata*. [State Medicaid Manual § 3259.7]).

This type of trust is usually referred to as a "(d)(4)(A)" trust, an "under 65" trust, or "a payback trust." Such trusts are sometimes referred to as "Zebley" trusts after the named plaintiff in *Sullivan v. Zebley* [493 U.S. 521 (1990)], a class action that generated a substantial SSI back payment for a group of developmentally disabled plaintiffs in the mid-1980s. The proceeds from those settlements were placed in an early prototype of the modern special needs trust. Although the term "special needs trust" was first coined to describe third-party trusts, and although 42 U.S.C. Section 1396p(d)(4)(A) does not expressly require "special needs" limitations, both SSI and Medicaid rules will still treat *distributions* from a (d)(4)(A) trust as income to the extent that they comprise or can be converted into food or shelter, and the State Medicaid Manual accordingly uses the term. Common usage of the term "special needs trust" has, as a result, come to include trusts established pursuant to 42 U.S.C. Section 1396p(d)(4)(A). Although 42 U.S.C. Section 1396p(d)(4)(A) provides that the trust must "contain the assets of the individual," the State Medicaid Manual permits contribution of trust assets by third parties. [State Medicaid Manual § 3259.7.A] As a practical matter it is possible to have a third-party funded OBRA '93 Trust unless one feels it necessary to make a gift to the disabled person who can then contribute the asset to the trust; presumably, contributions for the individual's benefit can be considered assets "of the individual" once they enter the trust. Unless the donor will soon require Medicaid, it is difficult to imagine very many circumstances in which a third party's assets should be contributed to a (d)(4)(A) trust; it will usually be far preferable to separately create a third-party SNT with no payback provision and, generally, more lenient treatment by state Medicaid agencies and the Social Security Administration.

Q 17:8.1 How is a (d)(4)(A) trust treated for income tax purposes?

Some practitioners feel that a (d)(4)(A) trust funded with an individual's own assets should include so-called defective grantor trust powers—powers that under section 672 of the Internal Revenue Code will make the disabled grantor continue to be treated as the "owner" of the trust for income tax purposes. In states that do not permit creditor protection for self-settled discretionary trusts, so that one can expect the grantor/beneficiary's creditors to have recourse to the trust to pay their claims, the trust should be treated as a grantor trust in any event, without retaining such provisions. In those states, establishing the trust also should not be treated as a taxable gift.

With the rare (d)(4)(A) trust that is established by a third party, for example, an elderly parent or grandparent about to go on Medicaid who wants to protect his or her disabled child or grandchild by making a gift of assets in a trust, the (d)(4)(A) trust might not qualify as a grantor trust without those retained powers, and would instead be a complex trust, paying tax at the higher tax brackets that apply to trusts.

An exemption of $3,650 is allowed for "qualified disability trusts" with adjusted gross income that is less than or equal to $166,800 (2009 tax year); the exemption is reduced, but not necessarily eliminated, for trusts with greater income. [I.R.C. § 642(b)(2)(C)] A qualified disability trust is "described in 42 U.S.C. § 1396p(c)(2)(B)(iv)" and "established solely for the benefit of an individual under 65 years of age who is disabled" and who has been disabled during some part of the tax year. Reversionary interests for third parties do not disqualify the trust.

Q 17:14 Must existing Medicaid expenditures be reimbursed before funding of a self-settled special needs trust?

Repayment of Medicaid expenses before establishment of an SNT is an issue not of SNT administration *per se* but of Medicaid's lien recovery rights against personal injury settlements or judgments. When Medicaid expenses are incurred by virtue of a compensable injury (as in the case of an automobile accident caused by someone other than the Medicaid patient), Medicaid is subrogated to the individual's rights. Federal regulations require a state Medicaid plan to require "cooperation" by a Title XIX applicant in obtaining payment from third parties, including "paying to the agency any support or medical care fund received that are covered by an assignment of rights." [42 C.F.R. § 433.147] "Third party" coverage has been held to include both insurers and those tortfeasors who are liable for the cost of services under negligence principles. [Gooch v. Edelman, 398 F. Supp. 723 (D. Ill. 1974)] Therefore, if there is a recovery, Medicaid has a lien against the recovery.

In general, this lien must be satisfied before any proceeds are distributed to or for the benefit of the Medicaid recipient. [42 U.S.C. § 1396k(a)(1)(A)] This is true when an SNT is not established, and most courts have held that the rule is the same when an SNT will be set up to receive the settlement (or judgment). [See Criccio v. Pennisi and Link v. Town of Smithtown, 90 N.Y.2d 296, 683 N.E.2d 301, 660 N.Y.S.2d 679 (1997); Waldman v. Candia, 317 N.J. Super. 464, 722 A.2d 581 (1999); S.S. v. State, 972 P.2d 439 (Utah 1998); Cargill v. State Department of Health, Division of Health Care Financing, 967 P.2d 999 (Wyo. 1998); Cuello v. Valley Farm Workers Clinic, Inc., 91 Wash. App. 307, 957 P.2d 1258 (1998); Herstberg Inter Vivos Trust v. Department of Mental Health, 578 N.W.2d 289 (Mich. 1998)]

Although some early decisions held that 42 U.S.C. Section 1396p(d)(4)(A) permitted funding of an SNT without the necessity of paying back the Medicaid lien, more recent decisions are uniform in ordering that lien recovery must precede the settlement. [Criccio v. Pennisi and Link v. Town of Smithtown, 90 N.Y.2d 296, 683 N.E.2d 301, 660 N.Y.S.2d 679 (1997)] A shrinking number of states may still permit the beneficiary to bypass lien recovery. For example, in one case, California allowed postponement of the lien when it would cause "financial hardship" to the plaintiff. [Garcia v. County of Sacramento, 103 Cal. App. 4th 67, 126 Cal. Rptr. 2d 465 (2002)] The vast majority, however, do not, and the trend favors the majority approach.

In cases other than personal injury recoveries (such as inheritance, or lottery winnings, or even personal injury recovery for an injury not requiring medical care covered by the Medicaid program) there is no lien recovery right before the funding of the trust. Moreover, it now appears that even in personal injury cases, Medicaid's lien applies only to that portion of the award allocable to medical expenses.

While some states had required repayment from all proceeds of a personal injury action including those not allocated to the injury itself, [Richards et al. v. Georgia Dep't of Community Health, Dec. No. S04A0866 (Ga. Nov. 8, 2004)] the United States Supreme Court has now laid that claim to rest. In Arkansas Dept. of Health and Human Services v. Ahlborn 547 U.S. 268, 126 S.Ct. 1752 (2006), the Court held that the lien applies *only* to that portion of the recovery that has been "allocated" to medical expenses. This means that an award that encompasses not only medical expenses but lost wages and pain and suffering will not be wiped out simply because the State's Medicaid outlay exceeds the available insurance coverage expected to pay a claim.

It is also important to remember that state Medicaid agencies are required to adopt and implement hardship procedures. As a result, and in practice, there is always room to negotiate with the state Medicaid agency. 42 U.S.C. Section 1396p(d)(4) was enacted in part to cure the disincentive for Medicaid beneficiaries to bring lawsuits if they would lose all use of the funds. Where the lien may exceed the settlement proceeds, it may be possible to negotiate with the agency to postpone repayment of the lien or reduce the amount to be paid currently. Where the outcome of a case is uncertain, it may be possible to negotiate with the state before obtaining a settlement, on the grounds that without state leniency there would be no incentive to settle the case, but that settlement will provide a surer source of funds for the State.

Q 17:16.1 What is required upon the death of the beneficiary of a self-settled special needs trust?

A self-settled special needs trust governed by 42 USC § 1396(d)(4)(A) must include a provision directing repayment of the state Medicaid agency for "all amounts remaining in the trust upon the death of such individual up to an amount equal to the total medical assistance paid on behalf of the individual...." In other words, the payback provision must fully repay the Medicaid agency in order to maintain eligibility during life.

A number of issues remain unresolved by that simple clause in a one-sentence statute, however. In practice, a provision requiring repayment of multiple state Medicaid agencies in proportion to their payments for the benefit of the beneficiary has proven to be acceptable to the Social Security Administration and the Centers for Medicare and Medicaid Services, as well as the Medicaid agencies of those states where the possibility of a mobile beneficiary has been considered. A number of states have imposed an additional requirement of reimbursement upon the termination of a (d)(4)(A) trust before the death of the beneficiary; although the statute does not contemplate such a provision (or even such a possibility), there are not yet appellate decisions determining the validity of such provisions.

One interesting issue was raised in an Indiana case involving the death of the beneficiary of a self-settled SNT. Parents who had been providing full-time care for the beneficiary for a decade after establishment of the trust petitioned the court (on the beneficiary's death) for payment of past care. The effect of their request, granted by the trial court and approved by the state Court of Appeals, was to pay all but $1,360 of a $143,860 trust to themselves, leaving the balance to "satisfy" the State's $355,632.15 claim. [State v. Hammans, 870 N.E.2d 1071 (Ind. App. 2007)]. Note that Indiana's Medicaid agency has amended its regulation to reverse this holding.

In some cases, the trust may be sufficient to completely repay the Medicaid agency and leave a potential distribution. Generally speaking, courts establishing or interpreting special needs trusts have been reluctant to permit distribution terms that vary from the principles of intestate succession unless the beneficiary was a competent adult. [In re Rogiers, 933 A.2d 971 (NJ Super 2007)].

Q 17:18 Who should *not* consider establishing a self-settled special needs trust?

In some cases, continued eligibility for public benefits is not important enough to subject the beneficiary to the limitations of an SNT. In other cases, the public benefits will not be affected by direct receipt of assets or income, so an SNT places an unnecessary limitation on the beneficiary's access to funds. Some public benefits are not "means tested." For example, Social Security Disability beneficiaries will not have their benefits affected by the acquisition of assets or income. After 24 months of SSD coverage such individuals will qualify for Medicare benefits as well, and those benefits will also be unaffected by receipt of assets or income. Of course, Medicare benefits may not be sufficient to cover all medical needs: Medicare fails to cover medications (except for hospice patients) and some other important medical care. If the trust is large, it will be able to afford payments for a quality Medigap policy and otherwise to pay for the "gaps" in Medicare. Thus, for many

SSD/Medicare beneficiaries the value of an SNT will be limited. Those SSD recipients whose benefits are less than the maximum SSI benefit ($674 in 2009) may also qualify for SSI and Medicaid. Although it may not be critical for such an individual to continue to qualify for Medicaid coverage (after all, Medicare will pay for most of the acute medical needs), in some cases dual coverage will be important. It is also important to note that a self-settled special needs trust is for the sole benefit of one beneficiary, and the individual may wish to benefit third parties, such as minor children, if substantial funds have been received from a lawsuit, which will not be possible once a trust has been funded.

Q 17:18.1 Can a self-settled special needs trust be established to receive a personal injury settlement even though it was specifically intended to provide for the individual's medical needs?

Yes. In a Montana case, the trial court refused permission to establish a special needs trust, reasoning that the personal injury settlement was intended to provide for the plaintiffs' medical needs. The state high court, however, reversed and remanded the case, holding that at least in cases of catastrophic injuries with only partial liability or limited insurance coverage, "a special needs trust may be properly used to preserve the victims' eligibility for Medicaid and other governmental programs. These personal injury plaintiffs are not 'double dipping,' but all involved simply recognize that the compensation paid does not fully compensate the injured parties and thus Medicaid can be preserved to meet their future medical needs."[See In re the Estates of Esterbrook, 80 P.3d 419 (Mont. 2003)].

Q 17:19 What alternatives are there to self-settled special needs trusts?

In some cases rather than establish a special needs trust the disabled beneficiary will prefer to adopt one of these alternate approaches:

1. The assets may be used to purchase exempt property (home, handicap-equipped transportation, etc.). If the purchases can be made quickly, the loss of benefits may be short and the beneficiary's quality of life will be enhanced.

2. Assets can be spent quickly on therapy, treatment programs, or food and shelter. The beneficiary might reasonably determine that "pulling out all the stops" for a brief period may result in some

medical or physical improvement; if not, the beneficiary will return to the same circumstance as he or she was in prior to receipt of the assets.

3. The beneficiary might calculate that, with careful management of the money, he or she will be able to enjoy the benefits from the money for an extended period. Particularly where medical needs are modest, simply accepting the money, foregoing the public benefits, and managing the assets for maximum longevity may be the most attractive choice.

Third-Party Special Needs Trusts

Q 17:20   What is a third-party special needs trust?

A third-party special needs trust is a special needs trust established by one person for the benefit of another, and funded exclusively with assets not belonging to the disabled beneficiary. These trusts are usually established by a parent for the benefit of a disabled child (but could also be established by a child for a disabled parent). A properly drafted third-party special needs trusts allows the grantor to provide for the disabled beneficiary without jeopardizing the beneficiary's public benefits. The principal of a third-party SNT is not an available resource to the beneficiary. Distributions from the third-party SNT will not be treated as income unless either (1) the beneficiary is entitled to receive income distributions or (2) distributions are actually made directly to the beneficiary, or are made in a manner that would permit the beneficiary to convert them into food or shelter. As is true with in-kind gifts to a beneficiary receiving SSI, in-kind provision of shelter from a third-party SNT may result in a proportional reduction in benefits without eliminating the benefits altogether.

Q 17:22   What language should be used when drafting a third-party special needs trust?

In theory, a third-party trust should be able to function as an SNT without specific language, provided that the trustee has discretion as to whether to distribute or accumulate income and principal and meets any other state law requirements for a "spendthrift trust" to be immune from claims of the beneficiary's creditors. Because the beneficiary has no right to anticipate benefits from such a purely discretionary trust, it should not be counted as either an available asset or income to the beneficiary *except* to the extent that trust assets or income are actually distributed to the beneficiary (or expended on in-kind distributions that could be converted to necessities). Of course, if the trust requires the distribution of income to the beneficiary, or gives the beneficiary the power to compel distributions of principal, it will be treated as available. [POMS § SI 01120.200.D.2].

However, even though specific special needs language may not technically be necessary for a third-party trust to qualify as an SNT, in the absence of such language state case law may create a presumption that the grantor had intended the trust to provide for the beneficiary's support, particularly where the trust is large and there is only one beneficiary. Therefore, it is always advisable for the draftsperson to include provisions that:

1. Make distributions of income and principal purely discretionary;

2. Specifically prohibit the trustee from making cash distributions directly to the beneficiary (although in some circumstances it may be advisable to permit occasional cash distributions, resulting in periods of ineligibility);

3. Direct the trustee to consider the effect of distributions on public benefits eligibility; and

4. Express the settlor's intention that the trust be used for supplemental benefits (preferably including some specific examples of trust uses) and not for necessities.

More important, perhaps, is what the trust language should *not* include. For example, Connecticut has recently adopted a statute that will treat as "available," for Medicaid purposes, any trust that is established for the beneficiary's "general or medical support."[Public Act No. 01–02, amending Conn. Gen. Stat. § 17b–261] Even if the language described above were included, inclusion of offending language about "support" would cause the entire trust to be available. "Support" language is particularly dangerous, even if the Trustee retains discretion and no distributions are required. [See, e.g., Metz v. Ohio Dep't of Human Services, 145 Ohio App. 3d 304, 762 N.E.2d 1032 (2001); Kryzso v. Ramsey County Social Services, 2000 N.D. 43, 607 N.W.2d 237 (2000)] Similarly, in Ohio a discretionary third-party trust that permits distributions for "welfare" or "general well-being" will still be considered available *even if* it prohibits distributions that would reduce or replace benefits. [Ohio Admin. Code 5101:1-39-271(C)(4)(b), (c)].

Some professionals advocate the use of a two-trust system, in which the trustee of the first trust has discretion to make payments only to the other trust. The second trust's distribution provisions are limited, in turn, to extra or supplemental benefits. This device retains the full discretion of the first trust's trustee, and the limitations against in-kind distributions that could be used for food or shelter are imposed on the second trust's trustee. This approach is also being advocated in Ohio in light of the new restrictions on third-party trusts.

Finally, it will be important to review the particular state's laws even when drafting a third-party SNT. In some states, express prohibition on distributions that might affect benefits may be an essential term to refute any claim that the trust is for "support." In other states, such as Ohio, this language may be considered "against public policy" and explicitly void, unless the trust either requires termination if it is treated as available, or complies with the limits of Ohio Rev. Code Section 5815.28, including a cap on the amount that can fund the trust ($228,000 in 2009, and statutorily set to increase by $2,000 each year). [Ohio Adm. Code 5101:1-39-27.1(A)(2)(e), (C)(4)(b), (c)]. For a discussion of the history of Ohio's unusual and restrictive statutory provisions, see *Pack v. Osborn*, 881 N.E.2d 237 (Ohio 2007). Meanwhile, the Ohio case law is undecided on the public policy issue. [See, e.g., Carnahan v. Ohio Dep't of Human Serv., 139 Ohio App. 3d 214, 743 N.E.2d 473 (2000); Young v. Ohio Dep't of Human Serv., 76 Ohio St.3d 547, 668 N.E.2d 908 (1996)] It cannot be overemphasized that the practitioner *must* review current laws, even those not yet codified, to be sure that any statutory requirements have been met.

Q 17:26.1   Will the funds from an existing trust be considered available to the beneficiary even if they are transferred to a special needs trust?

It depends. Again, it is important to look at whether the grantor intended to create a special needs trust. If not, the assets may be considered to be "available" to the beneficiary and would endanger Medicaid eligibility. For example, in *Linser v. Office of Attorney General* [672 N.W.2d 643 (N.D. 2003)], the grandfather of a disabled individual established a general support trust for the individual. After the grandfather's death, the individual's guardian established a special needs trust for the benefit of the individual and distributed the assets to the trust. After learning of the asset transfer, the state Medicaid agency discontinued the individual's eligibility, claiming that the beneficiary could seek to enforce his right to have the proceeds transferred to the grandfather's support trust instead. The state Supreme Court agreed with the Medicaid agency, stating that "a reasoning mind could reasonably find by a preponderance of the evidence that the [individual] has a legal entitlement" to immediate availability of the assets. Whether the same result would apply if the Trustee had exercised discretion within the scope of the original instrument to transfer the assets to the new trust, is an unanswered question. This technique, "decanting" an existing trust, must be evaluated on a case-by-case, and jurisdiction-by-jurisdiction basis.

In most states and circumstances, it may be preferable to consider reformation of an existing trust into a third-party special needs trust. This may be accomplished by a judicial determination, typically incorporating a finding that the original settler intended to make the trust purely discretionary, or possibly even including special needs provisions. This approach was specifically endorsed in *Riddell Testamentary Trust*, 138 Wash.App. 485 (2007). The availability of reformation of an option will also depend upon the jurisdiction. In some jurisdictions, reformation is rarely available without the consent of all parties, and presumably the beneficiary could not consent to a "third-party" trust without risking that it would be considered "self-settled" by the Medicaid agency.

Distributions from Special Needs Trusts

Q 17:28   What payments may a special needs trust make without interfering with the beneficiary's government benefits?

The central purpose of an SNT is to provide for supplemental needs without disrupting public benefits. In most cases, that means protecting SSI and Medicaid benefits. Because Medicare and Social Security Disability benefits are not means-tested, they are not affected by the expenditures from the SNT.

Both Medicaid and SSI rules are similar: Any "income" received or considered "available" to the beneficiary will reduce or eliminate the benefits received. [42 U.S.C. § 1382(b)] Cash will affect benefits dollar for dollar (after the occasional $20/month gift). Payments not to the beneficiary, but to pay for "food or shelter" will reduce benefits by approximately one-third of the maximum benefit (for 2009, $674, so the reduction will be $244.67), with or without a $20 adjustment depending on living situation. Payments not to the beneficiary, and for something that could not reasonably be converted to food or shelter (a new furnace; a television, computer or furniture, as some simple illustrations), do not count at all. And finally, all other payments not to the beneficiary but that could be readily converted to cash, count as cash, measured by the fair market value of the item.

Q 17:30 How do payments by the special needs trust for (but not to) the beneficiary affect benefits?

Both Medicaid and SSI permit in-kind distributions by third parties (including trusts) to beneficiaries. Only if the distributions or payments are either food or shelter, or convertible into one of those categories of necessities, do they reduce benefits.

In other words, an SNT trustee who purchases clothes for the trust beneficiary will reduce public benefits. So will the trustee who purchases gift certificates and delivers them to the beneficiary, but only if the gift certificates are for a store that sells food or shelter, or if the store permits the gift certificates to be cashed in or transferred. In the last case, the beneficiary could sell the certificates to others, then use the proceeds to purchase necessities; as a consequence, the certificates themselves will be disqualifying (even if the beneficiary actually uses them to purchase non-essentials). Usually, other kinds of in-kind distributions, such as the gift of a television, are not considered convertible to food or shelter, even though presumably the recipient could sell or pawn the television for that purpose.

The SSI program does have one important exception to these rules. Small gifts are ignored; the first $20 received by the beneficiary in any month will not reduce or otherwise affect the SSI benefit. [42 U.S.C. § 1382a(b)(2)(A)].

Q 17:31 Are in-kind distributions of food or shelter treated like distributions of cash?

No. In-kind distributions of food or shelter invoke special rules. In-kind contribution of food or shelter may reduce, but should not usually eliminate, benefits.

The Social Security Administration has different rules for different living arrangements. First, when a beneficiary is living with family, or generally living with others but not in an institution, and is provided with not only shelter but "maintenance," SSI rules reduce benefits by one-third of the maximum SSI benefit, known as the "value of the one-third reduction" (VTR). [POMS § SI 00835.001] This is the rule as set out in 42 U.S.C. § 1382a(a)(2)(A).

When, on the other hand, the beneficiary receives in-kind support and maintenance (food or shelter) but does not receive both food and shelter from the household in which the beneficiary lives, a slightly different rule applies—benefits are reduced by the lesser of the actual value (or if unknown the market value) or the "presumed maximum value," which is the one-third of the maximum SSI benefit plus $20. [POMS § SI 00835.300] The difference is that the reduction will be $20 higher. [See, e.g., § SI 00835.900 Values for In Kind Support and Maintenance]

In either case, the benefit is not reduced by more than one-third of the maximum benefit or at the most, one-third of the maximum plus $20. This is a tremendously important benefit for SSI and Medicaid recipients (SSI beneficiaries categorically qualify to receive Medicaid benefits), both in the realm of SNTs and in general practice. Many SSI beneficiaries live with family members, who provide extensive care in addition to the shelter; those beneficiaries will experience a reduction in their benefits, but the SSI check will not be eliminated. In turn, for SSI states categorical Medicaid eligibility will be extended so that medical care (which may be the most important component of the public benefits scheme) will be provided. Finally, if the beneficiary is living in an apartment for which another family member provides rental assistance paid directly to the landlord, benefits will not be lost. [POMS § SI 00835.350] Note that effective March 9, 2005, the Social Security Administration has adopted new regulations that eliminate clothing from the definition of income and the definition of in-kind support and maintenance. [70 Fed. Reg. 6340–6345]

One caveat: since the ISM value is the lesser of actual value or one-third the *maximum SSI benefit* (plus $20), there may be some individuals who are also receiving Social Security Disability benefits but of a small enough amount to receive SSI as well. If someone in this situation has (for instance) $20 of SSI and $654 Social Security Disability in 2009, and the SSI is reduced by $212, the person will lose SSI, and in an "SSI state" where Medicaid is dependent upon SSI status, this could be a significant problem.

Q 17:32   What kinds of expenses are considered "shelter" and what are not?

The Social Security POMS lists 10 items that constitute "food and shelter" or "household expense" items, and makes clear that the list is exclusive:

1. Food
2. Mortgage (including property insurance required by the mortgage holder)
3. Real property taxes (less any tax rebate/credit)
4. Rent
5. Heating fuel
6. Gas
7. Electricity
8. Water
9. Sewer
10. Garbage removal

Note. Condominium fees in themselves are not household costs. However, condominium fees may include charges which are household costs (e.g., garbage removal, or the unit's share of a common water supply). To the extent that such charges are identifiable, use them in the computation of inside and outside ISM. [POMS § SI 00835.465]

Q 17:33   How can this treatment of "ISM" be used to benefit an SNT beneficiary?

Because in-kind distributions will usually not eliminate the SSI and Medicaid benefits, it may be appropriate in some circumstances to permit the trust to provide food or shelter directly—particularly shelter, which will likely cost more than the "one-third." This can be done by purchasing a residence for the beneficiary (and titling it in his or her name) or by purchasing or renting a residence and providing it to the beneficiary without cost. Depending on individual circumstances, either approach may be appropriate in at least some cases. In preparing the trust's language, the SNT draftsperson should consider the possibility that shelter at least will be provided in the future.

For public benefits purposes, "shelter" includes not only the beneficiary's residence but also those services necessary for the maintenance of the residence. Taxes, repairs, and necessary utilities (water, sewer, electricity, gas) will be included in the definition of shelter. Telephone, cable television, and other non-essential utilities may be provided without being treated as in-kind distributions of shelter.

Q 17:35 What other kinds of distributions might be made from the SNT?

The SNT Trustee might distribute the following to the beneficiary without affecting benefits:

1. *Vehicle.* A single vehicle (quaintly, the list of acceptable vehicles includes cars, trucks, boats, snowmobiles, animal-drawn vehicles, and even animals) is excluded from available resources regardless of its value, provided it is used for transportation. [POMS § SI 01130.200] Modifications for the handicapped owner may cost $30,000 or more; a new handicapped-modified van may be at least $50,000. Since distribution of a vehicle from the SNT to the beneficiary is not a distribution of food or shelter (and therefore not ISM), no income will be attributed to the beneficiary in a month in which a vehicle is purchased by the trust for the beneficiary, nor will income be attributed when the trust pays the auto insurance. On the other hand, if the trust *owns* the vehicle, the trustee puts the trust assets at risk in the event of an accident by the beneficiary as driver.

2. *Burial space, prepaid funeral arrangements and irrevocable burial trusts.* As with purchase of a vehicle, purchase of burial and funeral arrangements in the name of the beneficiary will not be penalized in any way if the resultant asset is not an available resource. In other words, the SNT can purchase a burial plot and casket, prepay the costs of burial, and set aside $1,500 in funeral expenses (or more, if it is possible under state law to create an irrevocable burial trust). For an OBRA '93 "payback" trust, this is particularly important, as the state's claim must be paid *before* any funeral has been paid for.

3. *Personal effects and clothing.* Purchase of personal effects or clothing (but not including food or shelter) will result in no penalty. It is therefore permissible to purchase furniture, furnishings, computers, televisions, stereo equipment, etc.

4. *Travel.* Airline tickets (and other travel tickets) given to an SSI beneficiary are not income if they are for domestic travel (travel

within the 50 states, the District of Columbia and U.S. possessions and protectorates). Tickets for non-domestic travel must be non-refundable—if they are refundable they will be treated as ISM because the recipient could cash them in and purchase food or shelter. This is true even if the tickets are not cashed in but are actually used for the intended travel. [POMS § SI 00830.521]

5. *Loans to the beneficiary.* A loan to an SSI recipient is not treated as income—provided that the transaction is a bona fide loan. [POMS § SI 00815.350] (See SQ 16:18.) If the loan is not bona fide, the proceeds are income in the month received as gifts. [See, e.g., Faber v. Merrifield, 783 N.Y.S.2d 495 (Sup. Ct. 2004) (contributions by children to pay medical expenses were "gifts" and not loans)] Clearly, any loan should be carefully documented and evidenced by a written note signed by the recipient. Whether or not the borrowing beneficiary is credit-worthy does not apparently affect the bona fide status of the loan, but the repayment must be "feasible." Here again, however, it is desirable to include language expressly authorizing such loans which may otherwise violate the trustee's duties towards other beneficiaries.

6. *Medical care.* Payments for medical and dental care and insurance are not income to the beneficiary. [20 C.F.R. § 416.1103(a)] Even if the beneficiary is on Medicaid, dental insurance would be a highly prudent expenditure.

7. *Educational, vocational, social, and personal services.* So long as payments are not for food or shelter, none of the listed distributions will result in ISM treatment [20 C.F.R. § 416.1124] Note, however, that dorm fees (because they are for room and board) will be treated as income to the recipient.

Taxation

Q 17:38 How is a special needs trust treated for income tax purposes?

Trusts (except for "grantor" trusts, as described later) must file federal and state income tax returns. The trust may have available deductions (e.g., for costs of administration) that reduce the taxable income just as for individual taxpayers. In addition to more familiar deductions, the trust will be entitled to deduct distributions made to or for the benefit of the trust's beneficiary. Those deductions will (to the extent of net trust income) result in the reporting of income to the beneficiary, which will result in the tax ultimately being paid by the beneficiary.

If the trust is a grantor trust, no tax return is required. Federal tax law recognizes that trusts created by (or on behalf of) the grantor for the grantor's benefit should not alter the income taxation of income received by the trust, and so it ignores the existence of the trust. Thus, a grantor trust does not file any separate income tax return, and all of the trust's income is taxable directly to the grantor/beneficiary.

This is important for two reasons. First, treatment as a grantor trust saves the administrative expense of preparing a separate trust income tax return. Second, and more importantly, treatment as a grantor trust will almost always result in a lower federal tax liability, because trust income is taxed at the highest marginal rate of 35 percent after taxable income has reached $10,050 (2006 tax year), instead of after $336,550, as it is for most single taxpayers. [I.R.C. § 1] In other words, to the extent that income is not actually distributed to or for the benefit of the beneficiary, grantor trust treatment can save nearly 15 percent in federal taxes for much of the trust's income.

Q 17:41 Won't the treatment of the special needs trust as a grantor trust result in disqualification of the beneficiary from public benefits?

Once the special needs trust has obtained grantor trust status, it need not file income tax returns. The beneficiary, on the other hand, will then be taxed on the trust's entire income, even though the income is not received directly. As a result that income will have to be reported for the beneficiary, ultimately causing that income tax to come to the attention of the public benefit program administration (e.g., SSI or Medicaid).

"Income" for tax purposes is not "income" for public benefit programs purposes. However, this fine distinction may be over the heads of some functionaries. The beneficiary's income tax return will now show all of the trust's income as if it were the beneficiary's own. Because many benefit programs require the beneficiary to produce income tax returns, which in some cases are the basis for an award of benefits, one has to expect at least an initial problem. Anyone who has tried to get an agency to understand that this year's income will not be the same as last year's, and so the income tax return should be disregarded, will understand the bureaucratic problems that may arise. Therefore, the practitioner should be ready to help explain the situation to the agency so that there is no sudden discontinuation of benefits on the theory that the beneficiary is over assets. Assuming adequate records are kept, it should be easy to demonstrate that the taxable income was not in fact received by the beneficiary, and that the trust provided no food or shelter (or, as described previously, that they were provided in-kind, and that the resultant reduction in benefits was calculated at the time). The sooner this can be explained, the better, preferably prior to any need to submit income tax returns.

Q 17:42 What are the estate and gift tax consequences of funding a special needs trust inter vivos?

Once again, the answer will differ for self-settled and third-party special needs trusts. Transferring the beneficiary's interest in trust property into an irrevocable trust in which he or she retains an income interest will not result in removing the asset from his or her estate, and so the entire trust corpus will be taxable upon the death of the grantor/beneficiary. [I.R.C. § 2036(a)]

Gift tax liability is somewhat more complicated, because the special needs trust will be irrevocable. Some practitioners feel that in order to avoid incurring a gift tax, the self-settled special needs trust should include a testamentary power of appointment. [Rev. Rul. 54–342, 1954–2 C.B. 315] There are some alternative theories for avoiding adverse gift tax consequences for a self-funded special needs trust, which include: (a) the payback requirement in effect means that for all intents and purposes the trust is payable to the beneficiary's estate at death, or at any rate, is likely to be wiped out in order to pay the creditors of the beneficiary's estate i.e., the beneficiary/grantor has retained a reversion over more than the greater of $5,000 or 5 percent of the trust; or (b) the gift is incomplete because of the trust's vulnerability to claims of the settlor/beneficiary's creditors generally as a self-settled discretionary trust. [Holtz v. Commissioner, 38 T.C. 37 (1962), acq., 1962–2 C.B. 4; discussed and clarified in Rev. Rul. 77–378, limiting the reach of Rev. Rul. 62–13 and applying Commissioner v. Vander Weele, 254 F.2d 895 (6th Cir. 1958) and Gramm v. Commissioner, 17 T.C. 1063 (1951), acq., 1962–1 C.B. 4]

One interesting approach to dealing with the estate tax liability for a self-settled special needs trust is described in *Estate of Hicks v.*

Commissioner, TCMemo 2007–182 (2007). Because the injured minor's father also had a related claim (for loss of consortium), the structure of the settlement was to fund a special needs trust with a $1 million loan from the father's settlement proceeds. In that manner, the special needs trust was assured of sufficient liquidity to provide for the beneficiary's needs, while retaining the father's interest in the settlement proceeds. The Tax Court ultimately agreed that the loan was a legitimate transaction, and reduced the value of the beneficiary's estate on his death four years later. Key to the Tax Court decision was the fact that the parties treated the transaction as legitimate, including calculating and paying interest on the loan.

A third-party trust, on the other hand, will be taxable in the beneficiary's estate only to the extent that the beneficiary has sufficient incidents of ownership, such as a general power of appointment. [I.R.C. § 2041(a)] Ordinarily, the drafter of a third-party special needs trust will want to avoid inclusion of the trust assets in the beneficiary's estate, and so will choose to limit any power of appointment. There is some worry that the power of appointment will in some way cause the agency to suggest that it must be exercised (notwithstanding its terms) in favor of the agency. Although at least one court has defeated such a claim [Ahern v. Thomas, 248 Conn. 708, 733 A.2d 746 (1999)], the issue is less clear in New York. Inclusion of a power of appointment not limited to issue may also cause problems if the trust is to serve as the beneficiary of an IRA.

Trust Administration

Q 17:44 What are the advantages and disadvantages of selecting each type of trustee for an SNT?

Selecting any of the common choices of trustee for an SNT has both advantages and disadvantages, which are detailed further here. Also provided are some suggestions for selecting specific persons or entities as trustee for an SNT.

1. *Family members.* Although they may seem like the logical choice, family members are seldom equipped to deal with the details of trust accounting (including tax preparation) and the special requirements of distributions inherent in SNT administration, and at the very least will have to farm out these duties to paid

professionals anyway. Most practitioners with substantial SNT experience have also learned that even the best-intentioned family members seem to be unable to resist the temptation of SNT assets, and will frequently misuse trust assets (either for their own benefit or for food or shelter for the beneficiary, leading to suspension of public benefits). On the other hand, family members are more likely to know the immediate needs of the SNT beneficiary, to appreciate the real-world value of proposed expenditures, and to monitor the effectiveness of treatment, equipment, and discretionary spending for the benefit of the beneficiary. Family members are likely to be less expensive trustees; in fact, family members will usually not charge any fee, and may be precluded from charging fees if they are themselves recipients of public benefits.

2. *Corporate trustees.* Few corporate trustees are familiar with SNT requirements or public benefits rules, although a handful of banks have begun to "specialize" in SNT administration. Most SNT beneficiaries require at least some case management or social work from the trustee, which corporate officers are ill-equipped to provide. Banks and other corporate trustees are likely to be the most expensive alternative, as well. Corporate trustees, on the other hand, will be proficient at trust (and tax) accounting techniques, and offer stability, reliability, and continuity. Especially for larger SNTs (which require substantial investment experience and, at the same time, offer the possibility of negotiated trustee's fees), corporate trustees may be the only choice reasonably available in some areas.

3. *Financial advisers.* Accountants, brokers, financial planners, and others may hold themselves out to be SNT trustees. Unless the individual has particular experience with both public benefits and trust administration—and many do—such individuals are usually poor choices to act as trustee, unless they are ready, willing and able from the outset to consult both with family, and with legal professionals. Fees are likely to be lower than corporate trustees, but substantially higher than family members' fees. When considering a non-professional trustee, look for personal experience; often the proposed trustee's exposure to public benefits and special needs comes from caring for a disabled child, parent, or sibling. Alternatively, endeavor to establish a "team" whereby the accountant or other such person at least keeps costs down but is trained to seek legal advice when issues arise.

4. *Case managers.* Professional case management agencies have grown in number and caseload in recent years, and many states have a well-developed case management industry. In some (but not all) of those states, case management agencies may act as trustees of SNTs. When this option is available, it is peculiarly well-suited for many beneficiaries; management of the SNT funds and the social, medical, and personal needs of the beneficiary often go hand in hand. Case managers may charge almost as much as corporate trustees, but the beneficiary may be receiving much more direct benefit for a slightly lower total cost; in fact, a growing number of corporate trustees are turning to the very same case management industry to provide the needed social service component of trust administration (but at an additional cost to the trusts). On the other hand, case managers tend to come from social service backgrounds, and may or may not be equipped to handle financial, investment, and accounting requirements. When considering case managers or professional private fiduciary organizations as trustee, look for continuity, depth of experience, bonding experience, and positive recommendations from prior beneficiaries. In a growing number of states, professional fiduciaries are being subjected to state regulation; make sure the proposed trustee has complied with state registration requirements.

5. *Lawyers.* Lawyers typically enjoy several exemptions from applicable laws governing trustees: They may not be required (by state law) to qualify as trust companies, or to register as private fiduciaries, and they arguably are exempted from federal registration as investment advisers. A growing number of lawyers have begun to act as trustees for SNTs. Usually, the cost to the trust is higher than the fees charged by family members but lower than corporate trustee fees; some lawyers provide case management services akin to those of professional case management agencies, and some may employ professional agencies to perform those functions. Typically, lawyers will find it easier to secure bond (if it is required), and will be subject to state disciplinary proceedings for their actions as trustee. On the other hand, lawyers (and even law firms) may be unable to guarantee longevity and consistency over time. Many lawyers act as trustee in Massachusetts (where a sizeable practice has been under way for over a century) and Arizona (where the practice is much more recent, but growing); other states have followed suit gradually if at all.

6. *A nonprofit trustee.* In some states, the nonprofit organization that manages the local "pooled" trust may also have the power to act as trustee of special needs trusts. This can be particularly useful when the beneficiary has no other family members to watch over him but the trust is not large enough to attract much interest from an institution.

7. *The team approach.* Some attorneys prefer a trust that has an arrangement between different members of a team: the "Trustee," which may be a corporate fiduciary, which invests and manages the funds; and a "committee" of family members, case workers, etc. who can establish guidelines for expenditures, or even a budget, and can resolve discretionary issues. Some will even include a financial advisor, with the "Trustee" acting more as a custodian. Alternative teams might involve a trustee to make discretionary decisions and a different trustee to handle investments.

Practice-Related Issues

Q 17:50 How do special needs trusts issues arise in the elder law practice?

Although 42 U.S.C. Section 1396p(d)(4)(A) trusts (the most common variant of SNTs) are necessarily restricted to beneficiaries under age 65, elder law attorneys frequently become involved in SNT planning because of familiarity with Medicaid, SSI, and public benefit programs. Third-party SNTs may be drafted for elderly clients to protect their younger (but perhaps still elderly) children or other beneficiaries. With formal federal recognition of SNTs in 1993 (in OBRA '93), the SNT planning arena is fairly young and actively growing. Some typical SNT scenarios encountered by elder law attorneys are described here:

1. *Disabled personal injury recipient.* Gilbert is 34 and was injured in a motorcycle accident 18 months ago. He is a quadriplegic, will not recover use of any motor skills and requires total care. He is mentally competent. Since the accident, he has been cared for first in the hospital (most of the costs covered by his private insurance, but totaling around $250,000) and for the past six months in a nursing home. Because Gilbert had limited savings and no long-term care or private disability insurance, the entire nursing home care period has been covered by Medicaid. The current Medicaid contribution totals $75,000. Gilbert does

receive Social Security Disability Insurance payments of $450 per month.

2. At the time of the accident, Gilbert was separated from his wife. The couple's divorce was finalized thereafter, and his wife retains custody of the couple's two minor children. At the time of the accident, Gilbert had substantial child support arrearages, and he has been unable to make payments since that time.

3. Gilbert's medical condition is now stable. He can take food and fluids orally, but must be spoon-fed, turned, and catheterized. He can be moved to a wheelchair, but has been effectively confined to his nursing home bed by a lack of transportation.

4. Gilbert's personal injury lawyer has negotiated a settlement that, after payment of attorney's fees but before satisfaction of any liens, will amount to a net distribution to Gilbert of $3 million. Medicaid and the private insurance company have paid a total of $800,000 for his care.

5. Gilbert's situation is not atypical. Given his high and continuing cost of medical care, he would deplete his remaining settlement proceeds quickly if he were to pay privately for his care. Gilbert may be a good candidate for a special needs trust.

6. First, Medicaid (and private insurance) liens must be handled. Medicaid is required to engage in negotiations for the reduction of its lien, but is not required actually to agree to a reduction.

7. Gilbert's personal injury lawyer or the lawyer preparing the SNT should contact Medicaid and begin the negotiation process.

8. Once the settlement value has been maximized, the benefit to Gilbert (and his family) should be considered. If the original litigation was brought in Gilbert's and his children's names then the proceeds could be attributed partially to the children (for loss of consortium or support, as state law permits). This division is as much art as science, so Gilbert might consent to a larger-than-usual distribution to his children, depending on his continuing relationship with them and their mother. Similarly, he may choose to use a portion of the settlement proceeds to satisfy his child support arrearages.

9. Gilbert may wish to transfer his remaining settlement proceeds into an SNT. But he may choose not to do so. Because he receives some Social Security Disability benefits, he will soon qualify for Medicare coverage (after 24 months of SSDI benefits). While that will provide significant benefits for Gilbert, it will not pay for his

medications or personal care—two of the items most likely to require considerable expenditures over time.

10. The first barrier to an SNT is a technical one: Gilbert cannot establish the trust himself, as 42 USC Section 1396p(d)(4)(A) requires that step to be undertaken by a guardian, the court, or Gilbert's parents or grandparents. If either of Gilbert's parents is available to execute the trust, this problem may be easily overcome (although even that could be problematic if Gilbert were only able to obtain SSI rather than SSDI—the Social Security Administration takes the position that only someone with "authority" to make the transfer of a person's assets can establish the trust). If not, and because Gilbert is mentally competent, it may be difficult to utilize state guardianship law to establish the trust. If the state does permit a "voluntary" conservatorship proceeding, with no finding of incapacity required, that process may be the appropriate solution.

11. Before transferring settlement proceeds into the trust, Gilbert might choose to expend a significant portion on assets that will benefit him immediately. He might, for example, arrange for the purchase of a wheelchair-equipped van, and for personal supplies and food to last for a period of time, plus prepayment of rent or housing costs. Because the personal injury settlement will cause at least one month of ineligibility for SSI anyway, he can receive food and shelter benefits during that month without increasing his penalty. The trust must, however, be fully funded before the end of the month in which it is received, or another month of ineligibility will be incurred; Medicaid benefits might also be suspended and Gilbert might be required to go back through the application process once he requalifies—in most states, Medicaid eligibility applications are a notoriously unpleasant process.

12. Assuming that Gilbert decides to transfer the remaining settlement proceeds into an SNT, it might yield substantial improvement in his quality of life. The SNT can provide aides to care for Gilbert and take him out in his wheelchair-equipped van. It might even provide a suitable handicap-equipped home (plus continuing upkeep, taxes, and utilities). (If Gilbert is receiving SSI rather than SSD, there may be a reduction in his SSI benefit but continued Medicaid eligibility.)

13. *Misbehavior by the SNT trustee.* Some years later, Gilbert's trust is in place and providing benefits. He continues to receive SSDI,

Medicare, and Medicaid benefits (and SSI or the state supplement if receiving them initially); the loss of any of those benefits could be catastrophic for his continued care. Unfortunately, his trustee has made gifts to other family members from trust assets, and has given Gilbert occasional distributions of cash throughout the term of the trust. She (the trustee) has not disclosed those expenditures to Social Security and has not given Gilbert any accounting for the trust's administration. The lawyer who originally drafted the SNT has now learned of these problems because the trustee has consulted the drafter about how to proceed.

Setting aside the problem of conflicting representation, and assuming that the lawyer owes a duty only to Gilbert, it is important that Gilbert be given complete information about the current situation. While the lawyer does not have a similar obligation to inform Social Security of the problematic payments, it is probably in Gilbert's best interest to do so promptly.

It may be possible to argue that the "clothing" provided to Gilbert was actually medically necessary. If Gilbert's physician will prescribe the use of special clothing, its provision will probably be permitted. Otherwise, the improper purchases may result in a determination that benefits were overpaid, and a reduction in SSI benefits to recover that overpayment. Even if the payments are ultimately determined to have been inappropriate, they should not result in the trust corpus being treated as available. Any reduction in benefits might not affect continued eligibility for Medicaid; if it does, the trust should be able to repay the SSI overpayment without affecting current eligibility. It may even be possible to negotiate a schedule for repayment rather than reimbursing Social Security all at once.

The trustee's other improper expenditures may require appropriate court proceedings to enforce Gilbert's rights. If the trustee was not bonded, it may be impossible as a practical matter to recover any of the lost assets. The trustee can, however, be removed, ordered formally to account, and even surcharged in an appropriate trust proceeding; the special nature of the SNT will not affect Gilbert's state-law rights as a beneficiary.

Chapter 18

Patient Autonomy and Self-Determination

In the past half-century medical advancements have made it possible to extend some lives well past the time when the individual is able to communicate or likely to recover any substantial abilities. Particularly in the past quarter-century the conflict between the treatment imperative on the one hand and the patient's right to autonomy and a dignified death on the other has become especially pronounced. Although the law on patient self-determination has mostly developed in recent years it has developed quite rapidly. It is already possible to describe the patient's right to self-determination with some certainty; the statutory development of advance directives and the case law on the right to refuse treatment both proceeded quickly once undertaken by the states. This chapter discusses informed consent, the patient's right to refuse medical treatment, do not resuscitate orders (DNRs), health care powers of attorney, living wills, and physician-assisted suicide.

Right to Refuse Medical Treatment

Q 18:10 Where the patient is no longer competent and does not have an advance directive, is there a mechanism to exercise his or her right to refuse treatment?

In most states, a substituted decision-maker may speak for an incompetent individual who has not executed a living will or health care proxy. The incompetent individual will not lose the right to have unwanted life-sustaining treatment withheld or withdrawn. The individual's competency must first be determined, which may involve consultation with his or her physician and family. Absent a spouse, close family member, or close friends, a substitute decision-maker will be appointed in a guardianship proceeding.

In addition, at least 28 states and the District of Columbia have statutes that authorize surrogate decision-makers in the absence of advance directives: the District of Columbia, Alabama, Arizona, Arkansas, Colorado, Connecticut, Delaware, Florida, Hawaii, Illinois, Indiana, Iowa, Kentucky, Louisiana, Maine, Maryland, Mississippi, Montana, Nevada, New Mexico, North Carolina, Ohio, Oregon, South Carolina, Texas, Utah, Virginia, West Virginia, and Wyoming. Statutory surrogates are categories of persons listed in order of priority who, if available or reasonably available, are to be consulted by health care providers for patients who lack sufficient capacity to provide informed consent.

Regardless of whether the substitute decision-maker is a court-appointed guardian, or a statutory surrogate, he or she is generally required to follow the patient's wishes if they are known. Courts have developed two standards to guide surrogate decision-making: "substituted judgment" and "best interests." Under the more modern substituted judgment standard, the surrogate attempts to reach the decision that the incapacitated person would make if able to choose. [See In re Fiori, 673 A.2d 905 (Pa. 1996); Eichner v. Dillion, 420 N.E.2d 64 (N.Y. 1981)] This can be accomplished only if a patient has articulated intent to refuse or pursue treatment choices in the past while still competent. If there is no reliable evidence of such intent, the surrogate then follows the more traditional best interest standard. [See Ramussen v. Fleming, 741 P.2d 674, 688–89 (Ariz. 1987)] Under the best interest standard, the surrogate decision-maker assesses what medical treatment would be in the patient's best interests as determined by such objective criteria as relief from suffering, preservation or restoration of functioning, and quality and extent of sustained life. An excellent discussion of the dilemmas for courts in reaching such decisions with persons who never possessed competency to make their wishes known is the case of *Woods v. Commonwealth of Kentucky* [142 S.W.3d 24 (Ky. 2004)], with its vehement and lengthy dissent.

In 2005, the issue of surrogate decision-making became headline news with the story of Terri Schiavo, a woman stricken by an apparent heart attack who lapsed into a persistent vegetative state. She had not executed a living will or a written designation of a health care proxy. Ms. Schiavo's husband was her surrogate under Florida law, and asked to have her feeding tube removed, but her parents disagreed violently. The media coverage picked up three themes: (1) would Terri have "wanted to live this way;" (2) was she "permanently unconscious" at all, or rather, in an uncommunicative state; and (3) was refusing the feeding tube, or requiring its removal, the same as refusing medical treatment. The issue of her actual physical state was theoretically relevant to "what she would have wanted," as her wishes would be relative to a particular physical condition or prognosis. The husband's decision to remove the tube, appealed by the parents, was affirmed through the Florida state court system until the Florida legislature, urged by Governor Jeb Bush, adopted "Terri's law," requiring that the tube be reinserted. The law was then overturned by the Florida Supreme Court as an unconstitutional infringement of judicial branch powers, and the tube removed. The next step was the federal system. Congress was persuaded to adopt federal legislation, specific to the case, requiring that a federal judge conduct an independent review. The federal court, too, approved the husband's request, as did the Eleventh Circuit Court of Appeals. The U.S. Supreme Court declined to review the case, the tube was not reinserted, and Ms. Schiavo died 13 days later. The point is that the case gained such national attention that it is a touchstone for discussions about end-of-life and surrogate decision-making when meeting with clients. The majority of polled Americans supported the ultimate outcome, but were uneasy about (1) the husband's status as surrogate as he had subsequently begun co-habiting with another woman by whom he had children, and (2) the technical determination that Ms. Schiavo was, in fact, in a vegetative state. Media coverage showed her apparently smiling in the arms of her parents, and news headlines counted off the days during which "Terri fights for life." Thus, clients should take particular care in selecting surrogates, limiting specifying circumstances in which a surrogate's authority may cease, and specifying whether to err "in favor of life" or not when deciding whether a person is in a vegetative state, or to make a determination based on quality of life or other factors. The late Pope John Paul's published remarks that artificial nutrition and hydration were not medical care but were to be provided at all times, although not an official Papal Edict, troubled many Catholics and caused others to re-examine the views of their religion when executing advance directives.

Q 18:12   Is an advance directive effective in a state other than the state in which it is executed?

State laws in about two-thirds of the states expressly provide for the recognition of both living wills and durable health care powers of attorney even though the documents are prepared in accordance with the law of another state. Arkansas provides for recognition of an out-of-state living will only, while Pennsylvania recognizes out-of-state powers of attorney but not living wills. Connecticut, Georgia, Idaho, Indiana, Michigan, Nevada, North Carolina, and the District of Columbia have no comity provisions at all. Mississippi and New Mexico approve of out-of-state directives, so long as the documents also comply with those states' laws.

Advance Directives

Q 18:22   Can a DNR order be included in an advance directive?

Because in most states the do not resuscitate order is a physician's prerogative, it cannot simply be incorporated into an advance directive document by the patient. The patient can, however, express his or her preference regarding resuscitation in an advance directive. While that is not a DNR order, the patient's surrogate decision-maker should follow it.

In Arizona a patient can personally direct the withholding of resuscitation. By strict compliance with the statutory provisions, the patient can execute a "pre-hospital medical care directive"—a specialized advance directive upon which paramedics and emergency room physicians can rely in withholding resuscitation. The pre-hospital directive is not the same as a DNR order, since the decision remains the patient's and is not made by the physician. Although a physician's signature is required to effectuate the pre-hospital directive, the signing physician need not be a treating physician for the patient, and certifies only that he or she explained the ramifications of signing to the patient. [Ariz. Rev. Stat. § 36–3251]

Q 18:23   Why would a patient direct the withholding of resuscitation, especially in the home or the community?

While most people view cardiopulmonary resuscitation as a benefit, some disagree. Medical studies point to a surprisingly low success rate for resuscitative efforts, particularly among women and the elderly. In fact, the risk of debilitating injuries (such as broken ribs, pierced lungs, and anoxia leading to brain damage) may be higher than the likelihood of successful resuscitation in many patients. Advanced cardiopulmonary resuscitation efforts may make it possible to treat many patients aggressively. Those who worry about the possibility of being resuscitated for a longer life, but with no guarantee of the quality of that life, should address the question in advance to the extent permitted by local law.

Conversely, there is growing concern that advance directives concerning the withholding or removal of life support systems are also a request for a DNR. Some patients have been unwilling to execute living wills, or to distribute them to providers, for fear that the "DNR" notice on their chart, door, or bed will stop care providers from giving them needed assistance in urgent situations. This kind of concern may justify not only appropriate language in an advance directive, but discussion of the appropriate distribution of documents.

Patient's Privacy Rights

Q 18:23.1   What is "HIPAA"?

"HIPAA" stands for the Health Insurance Portability and Accountability Act. The Act established, for the first time, national standards for the protection of health information. Although HIPAA was enacted on August 21, 1996, privacy rules were not promulgated until 2002. The HIPAA of 1996 required that the Secretary of the Department of Health and Human Services (HHS) issue privacy regulations governing individual health information if Congress did not enact privacy legislation by 1999. Congress did not, and therefore, HHS developed a proposed rule in 1999. The rule was released for comment in 1999 and in

2002. The final privacy rule was published in August of 2002. The final rule can be found at 45 C.F.R. Part 160 and Part 164, Subparts A and E on the Office for Civil Rights (OCR) department website at *http://www.hhs.gov/ocr=hipaa*.

Q 18:23.2   What does the HIPAA Privacy Rule require?

A major purpose of the Privacy Rule is to define and limit the circumstances in which an individual's protected health information may be used or disclosed by "covered entities." Therefore, a covered entity may not use or disclose protected health information except when (1) the Privacy Rule permits or requires the release of the information; or (2) the patient (or the personal representative) authorizes the release in writing.

Q 18:23.3   When does the Privacy Rule require disclosure?

The Privacy Rule requires disclosure of health information by a covered entity when (1) a patient (or his or her personal representative—see SQ 18:23.4) requests access to protected health information; or (2) HHS is undertaking a compliance investigation, review or enforcement action.

Q 18:23.4   Who is considered a "personal representative" for HIPAA purposes?

A personal representative under HIPAA privacy rules is a person legally authorized to make health care decisions on the individual's behalf or to act for a deceased individual or the estate. The rule requires a covered entity to treat a personal representative the same as the individual, with respect to uses and disclosures of the individual's protected health information. However, if there is a reasonable belief that the personal representative may be abusing or neglecting the individual, the rule permits a covered entity to refrain from disclosing. In most instances, a parent is considered a personal representative to the parent's minor child. Details in the regulations can be read at *http://www.hhs.gov=ocr/combinedregtext.pdf*.

Q 18:23.5   Who is a "covered entity" under HIPAA?

"Covered entities" include health plans and health care clearinghouses. Also, every health care provider who electronically transmits health information in connection with certain transactions is a covered entity. These transactions include claims, benefit eligibility inquiries, and referral authorization requests. These covered entities are bound by the privacy standards even if they contract with others to perform some of their essential functions. Compliance with the new privacy requirements was required to begin by April 14, 2003.

Q 18:23.6   What is a health plan?

A health plan is an individual and/or group plan that pays for the cost of medical care, such as HMOs, Medicare, Medicaid, Medicare+Choice and Medicare supplement providers. Two kinds of government programs are not considered health plans: (1) government programs whose primary purpose is not to provide health care, such as the food stamps program and (2) those programs whose principal activity is directly providing health care themselves, such as a community health center.

Q 18:23.7   What is a health care clearinghouse?

Health care clearinghouses process nonstandard information they receive from another entity into a standard format, or vice versa. Health care clearinghouses include such entities as: billing services and community health management information systems.

Q 18:23.8   What does the HIPAA Privacy Rule require covered entities to do?

In general, covered entities are to perform certain duties, such as: (1) notifying patients about their privacy rights and how their information can be used; (2) adopting and implementing privacy procedures; (3) training employees so that they understand the privacy procedures; (4) designating an individual to be responsible for making sure that privacy procedures are adopted and complied with; (5) securing patient records containing patient information.

Q 18:23.9   What information is protected under the Privacy Rule?

The Privacy Rule protects all "individually identifiable health information" held or transmitted by a covered entity (or those it contracts with). "Individually identifiable health information" is information, including demographic data, that relates to: (1) the individual's past, present or future physical or mental health condition; (2) the provision of health care to the individual; or (3) the past, present, or future payment for the provision of health care to the individual. The information must also either specifically identify the individual or there must be a reasonable basis for believing that the information can be used to identify the individual.

Q 18:23.10　Are there circumstances in which a covered entity may disclose protected health information?

Yes. Covered entities may disclose information in obvious situations, such as to the patient, for the purposes of treatment, payment and other health care operations. A 2006 transmittal by the Department of Health and Human Services clarifies that benefit plans may share with a plan beneficiary's "family member, relative or close personal friend" protected health information "directly relevant to that person's involvement with the individual's care or payment for care" and that "other people" may receive information "provided the covered entity has reasonable assurance that the person has been identified by the individual as being involved in his or her care or payment." HIPAA also permits disclosure for purposes of public interest. These particular disclosures are permitted and not required. The following disclosures are included under this category:

1. the disclosure is required by another law including statutes, regulations, and court orders

2. to public health authorities for such purposes as preventing and controlling disease

3. in some instances, information regarding victims of abuse or neglect may be provided to appropriate government agencies

4. for the purposes of judicial or administrative procedures, such as in response to a subpoena

5. to funeral directors for the purposes of identifying a deceased person and determine the cause of death

6. for the prevention of a serious threat to health or safety

7. for law enforcement purposes

The Department of Health and Human Services maintains a useful FAQ or "Q and A" on HIPAA at: http://healthprivacy.answers.hhs.gov.

Q 18:23.11   What are the penalties for HIPAA noncompliance?

There are both civil and criminal penalties for noncompliance. The Department of Health and Human Services may impose civil monetary penalties on a covered entity of $100 per each failure to comply. That monetary penalty may not exceed $25,000 per year for multiple violations of the same privacy requirement. HHS is not permitted to impose a civil monetary penalty under some specific circumstances, such as violation due to a reasonable cause. Criminal penalties of up to ten years' imprisonment and a $250,000 fine are possible if the noncompliance involves the intent to sell, transfer, or use health information for commercial advantage, person gain, or malicious harm.

More information on HIPAA can be found on the Health and Human Services website at *http://www.hhs.gov/ocr/hipaa.*

Although health care providers frequently expressed anxiety about the possibility of sanctions for what they might perceive as minor violations of the HIPAA requirements at the time the law was adopted, the enforcement experience has not revealed any government desire to aggressively address providers' failures. As of mid-2006, according to news reports, DHHS had received almost 20,000 grievances, had closed 73% of its investigative cases, had imposed no civil fines and had initiated prosecution in just two cases. Although over 300 cases had been referred to the Justice Department for possible prosecution, no action had been taken on any of those referrals.

Language of Directives

Q 18:25   Are standardized forms for advance directives readily available?

Besides statutory forms provided by individual state statutes, there are many potential sources for form documents. Every state is required by the federal Patient Self-Determination Act to describe the availability and enforceability of advance directives; the result in some states has been the creation of a widely recognized form that accompanies that description. Hospitals, HMOs, physicians, and nursing homes, all of which are required to provide information about advance directives to their patients, frequently give form documents upon request. If those forms are not the statutory forms, they are usually the product of work by a state hospital, medical, or legal association. The Uniform

Health-Care Decisions Act [9 Uniform Laws Annotated, Master ed., pt. I] which has been adopted in whole or in part by eight states (Alabama, Alaska, Delaware, Hawaii, Maine, Mississippi, New Mexico, and Wyoming) also provides a sample form that an individual can use to create an advance health care directive.

Of course, patients can purchase forms for advance directives from almost any book or stationery store. Most Area Agencies on Aging will provide forms at no cost (or for a nominal fee). Caring Connections, a program of the National Hospice and Palliative Care Organization (NHPCO) has prepared a set of forms acceptable in each state. The forms may be downloaded at *http://www.caringinfo.org*. Also available is an Advance Care Planning Checklist and information on preparing and completing the directives. Forms and help may also be obtained by calling the NHPCO HelpLine at (800) 658-8898. The organization is located at 1700 Diagonal Road, Suite 625, Alexandria, VA 22314, (703) 837-1550.

Chapter 19

Elder Abuse, Neglect, and Exploitation

Abuse, neglect, and exploitation of the elderly are all increasing, despite state and federal efforts to combat the problem. In response to federal initiatives, most states have adopted mandatory reporting laws (usually modeled on pre-existing statutes requiring reports of abuse or neglect of children); adult protective services are also widespread. Although specifics of mandatory reporting requirements will vary from state to state, the behaviors of abusers and their victims often follow the same patterns. Elder law attorneys are peculiarly well situated to see, diagnose, prevent, and remedy abuse, neglect, and exploitation. This chapter discusses the types of abuse, recognizing abuse and neglect, reporting abuse and neglect, and the warning signs of abuse and neglect.

Overview

Q 19:1 How are abuse, neglect, and exploitation defined?

The National Center on Elder Abuse in a study prepared for the Administration on Aging (AOA) and the Administration for Children and Families [a full copy of the report is available online at *www.aoa. gov/eldfam/Elder_Rights/Elder_Abuse/ABuseReport_Full.pdf*] identifies the following seven types of abuse of the elderly:

1. *Physical abuse.* The use of physical force that may result in bodily injury, physical pain, or impairment. Physical abuse may include but is not limited to such acts of violence as striking (with or without an object), hitting, beating, pushing, shoving, shaking, slapping, kicking, pinching, and burning. The unwarranted administration of drugs and physical restraints, force-feeding, and physical punishment of any kind also are examples of physical abuse.

2. *Sexual abuse.* Nonconsensual sexual contact of any kind with an elderly person. Sexual contact with any person incapable of giving consent also is considered sexual abuse; it includes but is not limited to unwanted touching, all types of sexual assault or battery such as rape, sodomy, coerced nudity, and sexually explicit photographing.

3. *Emotional or psychological abuse.* The infliction of anguish, emotional pain, or distress through verbal or nonverbal acts. Emotional or psychological abuse includes but is not limited to verbal assaults, insults, threats, intimidation, humiliation, and harassment. In addition, treating an older person like an infant; isolating an elderly person from family, friends, or regular activities; giving an older person a "silent treatment"; and enforced social isolation also are examples of emotional or psychological abuse.

4. *Financial or material exploitation.* The illegal or improper use of an elder's funds, property, or assets. Examples include but are not limited to cashing checks without authorization or permission; forging an older person's signature; misusing or stealing an older person's money or possessions; coercing or deceiving an older person into signing a document (e.g., contracts or a will); and the improper use of conservatorship, guardianship, or power of attorney.

5. *Neglect.* The refusal or failure to fulfill any part of a person's obligations or duties to an elderly person. Neglect may also include a refusal or failure by a person who has fiduciary responsibilities to provide care for an elder (e.g., failure to pay for necessary home care service, or the failure on the part of an in-home service provider to provide necessary care). Neglect typically means the refusal or failure to provide an elderly person with such life necessities as food, water, clothing, shelter, personal hygiene, medicine, comfort, personal safety, and other essentials included as a responsibility or an agreement.

6. *Self-neglect.* The behaviors of an elderly person that threaten his or her health or safety. Self-neglect generally manifests itself in an older person's refusal or failure to provide himself or herself with adequate food, water, clothing, shelter, safety, personal hygiene, and medication (when indicated). The definition of self-neglect excludes a situation in which a mentally competent older person (who understands the consequences of his or her decisions) makes a conscious and voluntary decision to engage in acts that threaten his or her health or safety.

7. *Abandonment.* The desertion of an elderly person by an individual who has physical custody of the elder or by a person who has assumed responsibility for providing care to the elder.

Most state statutes use similar definitions, though they are typically limited to the three broad categories of abuse (physical, sexual, or emotional), neglect (usually by caregivers who are required to provide care), and (financial) exploitation.

The U.S. Senate's Special Committee on Aging [102d Cong., An Advocate's Guide to Laws and Programs Addressing Elder Abuse 3, 4 (1st Sess. 1991)] distinguishes between active neglect ("the intentional failure to fulfill a caretaking obligation necessary to maintain the elder's physical and mental well-being") and passive neglect (the "unintentional failure to fulfill a caretaking obligation").

Q 19:7   Who can a family caregiver contact for information or assistance?

Every area of the country is required by the Older Americans Act to have an Area Agency on Aging, and the local AAA is usually an excellent resource for caregivers and seniors. Local AAAs are generally listed in the city or county government sections of the telephone directory under "Aging" or "Social Services," and can also be located through a "lookup" website at *http://www.aoa.gov/eldfam/How_To_Find/ Agencies/Agencies.asp.* The Administration on Aging also supports a nationwide, toll-free information and assistance directory called the Eldercare Locator, which can be contacted by telephone at (800) 677-1116. The Eldercare Locator can also be accessed online at *http:// www.eldercare.gov/.* The Eldercare Locator will assist a caregiver or senior looking for the appropriate AAA.

Q 19:8   How widespread are problems of abuse, neglect, and exploitation?

It would be extremely difficult to pinpoint the actual number of cases of elder abuse each year, because it is underreported. Estimates range from 700,000 to 2 million victims per year, with neglect being the most common form of abuse. [Tatara, *Understanding the Nature and Scope of Domestic Elder Abuse with the Use of State Aggregate Data: Summaries of the Key Findings of a National Survey of State APS and Aging Agencies,* 5 J. Elder Abuse & Neglect 35, 37 (1993)] The Subcommittee on Health and Long-Term Care of the House of Representatives Select Committee on Aging reported in 1990 that one out of 20 elderly Americans (a total of 1.5 million persons) may be victims of abuse annually. [Subcommittee, Elder Abuse: A Decade of Shame and Inaction, Comm. Pub. No. 752, 101st Cong., 2d Sess. (Apr. 1990)] The Subcommittee found that while one in three cases of child abuse is reported, only one in eight cases of elder abuse is reported. There are multiple reasons why the reporting rate is so low. The victim may feel powerless, fearful of retaliation, unaware of the legal remedies, or may even believe that abusive treatment is a normal part of the aging process. There also may be instances where the victim is protective of the abuser. [Heath R. Oberloh, *A Call to Legislative Action: Protecting our Elders From Abuse,* 45 S.D. L. Rev. 655 (2000)] The growth of the elderly sector in proportion to the rest of the population (and the increase in sheer numbers, as a result of improved medical care and, arguably, greater affluence) has led to the formation of advocacy groups and law enforcement task forces with the specific purpose of targeting elder abuse. Unfortunately, longer-lived individuals are more likely to suffer from dementia—an estimated 50 percent of all individuals over age 80 have Alzheimer's disease—and are thus more vulnerable as targets.

According to a report of the American Bar Association Commission on Legal Problems of the Elderly (since renamed the "Commission on Law and Aging") ["Elder Abuse and Domestic Violence: What Is the Elder Law Attorney's Role in Recognition and Prevention?," National Academy of Elder Law Attorneys 11th Annual Symposium, May 1999], elder abuse experts warn that cut-backs in welfare and social service programs will create a larger population of potential abusers. Adult children who lose welfare benefits, for instance, may be more likely to exploit and abuse their elderly parents.

The National Elder Abuse Incidence study sponsored by the Administration on Aging with the Administration for Children and Families reported approximately 450,000 elderly persons in domestic settings were abused or neglected during 1996. Of this total, 70,942 (16 percent) were reported and the claims substantiated by Adult Protective Services agencies, but the remaining cases represent a serious problem of under-reporting of abuse and neglect. When cases of self-neglect are added, the number increases to approximately 551,000 in 1996. This report can be accessed at *http://www.aoa.gov/edlfam/Elder_Rights/Elder_Abuse/AbuseReport_Full.pdf*. For more statistical information on elder abuse, see *http://www.elderabusecenter.org*.

Reporting Requirements

Q 19:10   What is the Elder Justice Act?

Legislation known as the Elder Justice Act was originally introduced in the Senate in 2003, but it failed to pass. After repeated failed attempts, it was again introduced in March 2007 in both the House and Senate as H.R. 173 and S. 170 (2007 legislative sessions). The aim of the Act is to improve the detection, prevention, and prosecution of elder abuse. Among other provisions, the proposed legislation would create an Office of Elder Justice within the Department of Justice, and authorize grants and appropriations to enhance long-term care staffing, study victims' special needs, develop pilot programs, and support law enforcement and prosecutors at every governmental level.

In addition, as summarized by the Congressional Research Service, the Act would amend the Social Security Act by adding a new title XXII (Elder Justice) that would establish (1) within the Department of Health and Human Services (HHS) an Office of Elder Justice; (2) within the

Office of the Secretary the Elder Justice Coordinating Council to make recommendations for the coordination of federal, state, and local activities; and (3) the Advisory Board on Elder Abuse, Neglect and Exploitation. Links to the legislation are available on the website of the Elder Justice Coalition, *http://www.elderjusticecoalition.com/legislation.htm.*

Q 19:11   What legal requirements exist to report abuse, neglect, and exploitation?

Forty-three states and the District of Columbia have statutes requiring reporting by certain professionals of suspected elder abuse. Reporting is voluntary in the other seven states: Colorado, Illinois, Iowa, Kentucky, North Dakota, South Dakota, and Wisconsin. [ABA Elder Abuse Report]

States vary somewhat regarding the individuals with a statutory duty to report elder abuse, but generally health care practitioners, mental health professionals, clergymen, nursing home administrators and staff, social workers, and law enforcement officers are required to report abuse. Attorneys, accountants, trustees, guardians, and conservators may also be statutorily required to report exploitation or abuse. Sanctions against those who fail to report include fines or even jail time. In some states, such as Iowa, Michigan, and Minnesota, a reporter who is mandated to report but does not do so may be determined to be civilly liable for damages incurred by the victim. California recently passed the Financial Elder Abuse Reporting Act, effective January 1, 2007, requiring banks to report "suspicious activity" on the accounts of senior citizens, while Maine's similar law provides qualified immunity to banks who make such reports.

In recognition of the fact that the social services approach is not an adequate remedy, most states are beefing up laws to provide criminal and civil remedies for victims. Every state in the union has enacted legislation directed toward elder abuse and has established adult protective service (APS) programs that investigate reports of abuse and make the necessary referrals to social services. Adult protective services have been defined as a system of prevention, support, and surrogate services set up to enable the elderly to maintain independent living and avoid abuse and exploitation. Many law enforcement agencies have set up elder abuse hot lines or established special task forces trained to address elder abuse, and usually the identity of the reporter is kept confidential.

State initiatives have been driven to some extent by federal incentives, including federal funding. [42 U.S.C. § 3058b(a)(2)(C)(ii)] The federal Center on Elder Abuse, governed and funded by the Administration on Aging, serves as a clearinghouse for elder abuse research and programming, and works with participating states to compile information and statistics. According to the House Subcommittee on Health and Long-Term Care, only $3.80 is allocated for each elderly victim by the states, compared to $45.03 per child abuse victim.

In most jurisdictions reports of elder abuse are handled on a confidential basis by local adult protective service agencies, which make a preliminary investigation. State statutes generally give APS services total access to bank accounts, medical records, and other confidential sources to help them determine whether elder abuse exists in a specific case. APS then refers the case to the appropriate health or social agency or, if necessary, local law enforcement officials. Many jurisdictions also have public agencies (public guardians or public conservators) that will assume responsibility for an incapacitated elderly person when there are no family members or friends willing to take on that person's care.

Responsibilities in Cases of Abuse, Neglect, or Exploitation

Q 19:20   How are nursing home residents protected from abuse?

States receiving financial assistance under the Older Americans' Act [42 U.S.C. § 3058g] are required to establish long-term care ombudsman programs, administered on the federal level by the Department of Economic Security, Aging and Adult Administration. The focus of the program is to address the needs and rights of residents of long-term care facilities, and to provide a reporting resource for federal programs. The ombudsman is legally entitled to full access to medical records and to the residents themselves, and has the authority to intervene on behalf of a resident, even when the resident is under legal guardianship. Ombudsmen educate residents of long-term care facilities about their rights and help them develop the assertiveness necessary to enforce their rights. Complaints from residents typically include the unjustified or unexpected discharge or eviction from the facility, poor food quality, personal hygiene, loss or theft of personal property, verbal and mental abuse from staff, accidents and falls, mismanagement of personal funds, roommate conflicts, shortage of staff, and unattended symptoms. Ombudsmen are less useful in protecting residents who are incapable, however, as the ombudsman plays a role more of mediation and counseling than of advocacy. The ombudsman does not, for example, file criminal charges or lawsuits on behalf of a resident who has been victimized.

Medicaid Fraud Control Units (MFCUs), established by federal mandate [Omnibus Reconciliation Act of 1993, Pub. L. No. 103-66, 42 U.S.C. § 1396p(d) (Aug. 10, 1993)], are designed to prosecute complaints of abuse and neglect of patients of residential care facilities that receive Medicaid funds. Currently, 47 states and the District of Columbia participate in the Medicaid fraud control grant program through their state MFCU. They are permitted to investigate the care of both Medicaid and non-Medicaid patients at these facilities. [State v. Thomason, 33 P.3d 930 (Okla. App. 2001)] The state MFCU must operate independently of the state Medicaid program and should be housed or otherwise linked with the state attorney general's office. However, prosecutorial discretion by such units, or the attorney general's office, may result in problems being ignored until a tragedy occurs.

At a minimum, the family should if possible choose a facility carefully. The Centers for Medicare and Medicaid Services (CMS) (formerly the Health Care Financing Authority or HCFA), the agency that oversees Medicare and Medicaid, maintains a database that includes, among other things, reports of deficiencies in the quality of care. Such deficiencies are reported in more than a fourth of nursing homes in the country. The most frequent violations reported by CMS include the failure to prevent bed sores and accidents and the failure to assess patients' needs.

CMS has broad authority to penalize nursing homes that are in violation, including imposing $10,000-a-day fines, but in fact it rarely does so. [See the U.S. General Accounting (GAO) Report HEHS-99-46 at *http://www.gao.gov/archive/1999/he99046.pdf*; other reports may be found at *http://www.gao.gov*] This is true on the state level as well; in 1998, a study issued by the General Accounting Office of the U.S. Congress noted that one in three California nursing homes had been cited for severe violations, but were not fined or otherwise sanctioned. One nursing home had been fined $30,000 within a 15-month period, but none of the fines had been collected by the state. [State v. Thomason, 33 P.3d 930 (Okla. App. 2001)]

Unfortunately, as with most things, budgetary constraints can imperil nursing home residents despite the existence of protective laws. Ombudsmen may find their hands tied from lack of funding, or incorporated into state departments that for reasons of funding, staffing, or corruption discourage action. State Health Departments may be unwilling to enforce state regulations that require the imposition of penalties on already financially strapped facilities, for fear of accelerating a closure. Such financial concerns can imperil nursing home residents as surely as abuse. In Connecticut, a 2002 fire at the Greenwood Health Care Center nursing home caused when a mentally ill resident smoked in bed resulted in the death of at least 11 elderly individuals. Had the state required sprinkler systems in place in nursing homes as a licensure requirement, the tragedy might have been avoided. (Legislation to institute such a requirement was adopted following the incident, requiring the installation of sprinkler systems as of July 1, 2005.) [Conn. Pub. Act No. 03-3, Section 92]

A March 6, 2002 report of the General Accounting Office, "Nursing Homes: More Can Be Done to Protect Residents From Abuse" (online at *http://www.gao.gov/new.items/d02312.pdf*) concludes that more needs to be done to ensure quality of care to nursing home residents and to protect them from abuse. Texas passed a law in 2001 allowing cameras, nicknamed "grannycams," to be installed in nursing home rooms. [Tex. Health & Safety Code Ann. § 242.841] In 2003, eight states—Louisiana, Michigan, Mississippi, New Jersey, Oklahoma, South Carolina, Virginia and West Virginia—introduced legislation on the issue, and in 2004, New Mexico adopted its own "grannycam" law. [2004 N.M. Laws Ch. 53 (eff. May, 19, 2004)]

Remedies

Q 19:22 What civil remedies are available to victims of elder abuse, neglect, or exploitation?

Civil remedies have always been available to the victims, although an increase in public awareness about abuse and exploitation of the elderly has given the victims greater credibility. Victims may be awarded compensatory damages, costs, attorney's fees, and even punitive damages in some states. If the abuse takes place in a care facility, and particularly if the abuser is an employee, the facility can be held liable for damages. Many states are putting in place statutes that mandate special penalties for abusers of elderly persons, or as an alternative allow the defendant to make restitution.

Unfortunately, most individual perpetrators are judgment-proof, having long spent their own funds and funds they have illegally or unethically obtained from the exploitation victim. The attorney who decides to go after the perpetrator anyway may be hampered by the incapacity and frailty of the chief witness, the victim.

After the victim's death, the victim's estate may be able to pursue a claim for damages. Of course, if the victim was a Medicaid recipient, such a claim may only inure to the benefit of the State, and family members who do not stand to gain may not be willing to undertake such an enterprise. Relatives have tried to pursue claims on their own behalf for "infliction of emotional distress." However, "bystander" emotional distress claims of this nature may not be available under state law; even if available, they may only be available to a spouse or perhaps a child, not a concerned friend or relative. [See, e.g., Moon v. Guardian Postacute Servs., Inc., 116 Cal. Rptr. 2d 218 (Cal. App. 2002) (claim by son-in-law dismissed)]

An important issue in determining the financial feasibility of such a suit will be the state's punitive damages laws. In some states, there is no cap on punitive damages, and egregious conduct may be "punished" by an award commensurate with the financial resources of the defendant in order to "send a message." For example, in a 2001 case, the jury awarded a verdict of $21 million in a case of nursing home abuse that resulted in death. [Phillip Lavalis, individually and as Representative of the Estate of Rose Bonton v. Copperas Cove LLC, 2001 Tex. App. LEXIS 8626 (Tex. Dist. Apr. 18, 2001) (the case, which is not officially reported, was apparently settled, as the defendant withdrew its appeal in 2002)] In other states, such as Connecticut, there are caps on punitive damages. In addition to the punitive damages availability, recent movements in Congress and around the country to cap "non-economic" damages should also make it harder to enforce anti-abuse laws through civil suits, as by definition an elderly person in his or her last years of life, with no resources or means of income, is unlikely to have any economic damages at all. However, a recent California case suggests that even where state law limits punitive damages in medical malpractice cases, courts may construe the limitation as inapplicable to elder abuse cases against health care facilities. [Covenant Care, Inc. v. Superior Court, 32 Cal. 4th 771, 86 P.3d 290 (Cal. 2004)]

Q 19:23 What can a practitioner do to prevent abuse of a client who is in a nursing home?

The most important factor in ensuring quality of care for a nursing home resident is active involvement and oversight by friends of family.

For this reason, relocation to a facility near the family may be critical. If there are no friends or family in the area, friends or family should be urged to engage a care manager or advocate to visit the resident periodically and attend care conferences, and of course, to report any abuse.

For those involved in such oversight, whether friends, family, or other third parties, the attorney can provide information and guidelines:

1. Provide a checklist to guide the client through the process of selecting a long-term care facility. When long-term care seems likely, such a checklist might be included as part of the client's package. Some checklists are available at the Medicare website, at *http://www.medicare.gov/Nursing/Checklist.asp;* many others are listed on the national Agency on Aging website and/or published by the state ombudsman's office.

2. Explain to the client and family about resident rights, quality of care, and the care planning process, and provide copies of relevant laws to assist the family in enforcing these rights.

3. Explain how the inspection process works and how to find information about the facility's record of care.

4. Provide the client with telephone numbers for licensing agencies, state ombudsman, and others; at least, advise the client to talk to the local agency on aging and direct the client to appropriate websites.

5. Develop brochures or reference materials for clients to take home and consult at later dates.

6. Revise for your state and provide copies of the checklist "Elder Abuse: Prevention" available online at the American Society of Adult Abuse Professionals and Survivors Website *http://www.asaging.org/elderabuse/documents/prevention.pdf.*

7. Loan to clients, or urge them to purchase, the National Coalition for Nursing Home Reform book "Nursing Homes: Getting Good Care There," which may be ordered online at *http://www.nccnhr.org.*

8. Network with geriatric care managers, case managers, and other persons to whom you can refer clients who need help with nursing home or other placements, and who may be hired to act as "watchdogs" on behalf of absent children.

9. Consider adding geriatric social services to services your office will provide, or include a paralegal with some social work training who can be engaged to make periodic checkup visits on clients in institutions.

Chapter 20

Age Discrimination

Age discrimination is frequently encountered by elderly clients, but difficult to prove in most cases. Although the laws prohibiting discrimination on the basis of race, religion, national origin, and disability are well developed and broadly applied, the only national prohibition against discrimination on the basis of age exists in the context of employment rights. This chapter discusses the Age Discrimination in Employment Act, coverage under the act, and its requirements for bringing suit, proving age discrimination, and remedies. This chapter also discusses protection from discrimination based on employee benefit plans under the Older Workers Benefit Protection Act of 1990. While the typical elder law attorney may lack the competence to prosecute a federal discrimination case without assistance from a more experienced litigator, it is important for an elder law attorney to recognize situations that are appropriate for litigation.

Overview

Q 20:1   What is age discrimination?

Age discrimination, at least in the legal sense, is the practice of age-ism in the employment context. During the 1960s, when minorities were finding their voices and the federal government tried to respond, "gray power" advocates pointed out that productive, experienced, well-trained employees were losing promotions and even their jobs solely on the basis of age. The Age Discrimination in Employment Act (ADEA) [29 U.S.C. §§ 621 et seq.], *http://www.eeoc.gov/policy/adea.html,* was passed in 1967 to "promote employment of older persons based on their ability rather than age; to prohibit arbitrary age discrimination in employment; [and] to help employers and workers find ways of meeting problems arising from the impact of age on employment." [29 U.S.C. § 621(b)]

Q 20:2   How do demographics figure into the importance of ageism in the workplace?

One hundred years ago only 4 percent of the population lived past age 65, while 40 percent of the population was under age 18. Between 1993 and 2003, the number of Americans 65 and older increased by 9.5 percent with a net increase of 3.1 million seniors. [See *http://www.aoa. gov/prof/statistics/profile/2004/2004profile.pdf*] In 2004, one in eight Americans was 65 or older, and by the year 2030 at least 22 percent of the population is projected to be 65 or older; only 21 percent will be under 18. [United States Senate Special Commission on Aging, American Association of Retired Persons, Federal Council on the Aging, U.S. Administration on Aging, Aging America—Trends and Projections, 1991 ed., at xix] For comparison purposes, note that just 4.1% of the population was over age 65 in the year 1990. In 1950 there were about 14 percent as many Americans over age 65 as there were working-age Americans (aged 20 to 64); by 2030, the ratio is expected to increase to over 35 percent and by 2080, to 43 percent. [2005 Annual Report of the Board of Trustees of the Federal Old-Age and Survivors Insurance and Disability Insurance Trust Funds, March 23, 2005] In other words, there are strong social incentives to keep older Americans in the workplace, particularly skilled employees.

Coverage

Q 20:7 Does the ADEA cover older employees in the hiring process?

Yes, in fact its initial impetus came from a congressional study that indicated that discrimination in hiring was a significant problem. [29 U.S.C. § 621(a)] In 2002, 25% of complaints reported to the ADEA stemmed from a hiring incident—a vast increase from earlier figures, but still minor. The problem is that the plaintiff cannot bring a complaint based solely on the fact that a younger person was hired; the plaintiff must prove that but for his or her age, he or she would have been hired. The plaintiff must have some way of finding out whether the candidate hired was better qualified, and if there were other, non-age-related factors that caused him or her not to be hired. [See Armbruster v. Unisys Corp., 62 F.E.P. 395 (E.D. Pa. 1993), aff'd in relevant part, 32 F.3d 768 (3d Cir. 1994); Allen v. Park-Ohio Indus., 66 F.E.P. 1153 (N.D. Ohio 1992)] If the plaintiff believes that the employer has a history of ageism in hiring, he or she may be able to interest a public reporting agency, such as the Equal Employment Opportunity Commission (EEOC) or the State Attorney General's Office, in obtaining the necessary documentation to assemble a class action case.

Establishing and Proving an ADEA Claim

Q 20:11 What is the difference between liability based on "disparate treatment" and that based on "disparate impact"?

Age discrimination claims may be based on "disparate treatment" or "disparate impact" theories of liability. The U.S. Supreme Court in *Hazen Paper Company v. Biggens* distinguished these two theories of liability. [507 U.S. 604 (1993)]

To prove disparate treatment, the employee must show that the employer treated the employee differently from other employees based on that employee's protected characteristic. The employee's protected trait must have actually motivated the employer's adverse actions. Disparate treatment cases may involve a single-motive or mixed-motives basis for an employer's discriminatory action. In *Love-lace v. Sherwin-Williams Company* [681 F.2d 230 (4th Cir. 1982)], for instance, the plaintiff, lacking direct evidence, claimed that he was demoted because of his age, thus creating a presumption of discrimination. The defendants were able to produce other reasons for the demotion—for example, that the plaintiff's store lost money. The plaintiff did not effectively refute these arguments and lost the case on appeal.

Disparate impact cases, on the other hand, involve employment practices, including tests or promotion policies, that are neutral on their face but have a discriminatory effect on one protected group where the difference cannot be justified by business necessity. The *McDonnell Douglas* approach (see Q 20:12) does not apply, and in fact courts often rely on statistical evidence to show the impact of the neutral policy on a protected group. [See Griggs v. Duke Power Co., 401 U.S. 424, 431 (1971)] Courts have questioned the validity of this approach, because of the sheer number of policies and tests that affect older workers only because of their seniority or level of experience. [See Larson, 8 Employment Discrimination (2d ed. Lexis Publishing 2000)] In *Hazen Paper Company v. Biggins* [507 U.S. 604 (1993)] the Supreme Court undermined the disparate impact approach in a fact pattern where an older employee was fired just prior to the vesting of his pension benefits. The Court acknowledged that vested or almost-vested employees were likely to be older than other employees of the company, and framed its examination of the issues on "whether an employer violates the ADEA by acting on the basis of a factor, such as an employee's pension status or seniority, that is empirically correlated with age."[Id. at 608] In the wake of *Hazen Paper* some courts have begun to back off from the disparate impact approach.

In March, 2005, The U.S. Supreme Court resolved a split among the lower courts by holding that ADEA authorized recovery in disparate impact cases. An employer can be held liable for age discrimination based on a facially neutral employment policy if it has a disparate impact on older workers. [Smith v. City of Jackson, Mississippi, 544 U.S. 228 (2005)] Accordingly, the EEOC included in its Semiannual Regulatory Agenda published in the Federal Register on April 24, 2006, its intent to revise the regulations on disparate impact codified at 29 C.F.R. 1625.7(d).

Q 20:14 (Reserved)

Q 20:18 What is the first step in making a claim against the employer?

The ADEA requires victims alleging ADEA violations to report them to the appropriate state agency before or at the same time as they report them to the federal Equal Employment Opportunity Commission (EEOC). [29 C.F.R. § 1614.105(d)] The EEOC enforces Title VII of the Civil Rights Act of 1964, the Equal Pay Act, the Americans with Disabilities Act (ADA), and, as of 1980, the ADEA.

Some states have age discrimination laws (these are referred to as deferral jurisdictions) with broader provisions or stronger remedies than those of the ADEA. Other states have no age discrimination laws at all. If the state has no discrimination law, then a report must be made with the EEOC within 180 days of the alleged discriminatory act. [29 U.S.C. § 626(d)(1)] In deferral jurisdictions the employee must file a report with the EEOC within 300 days of filing the report with the state agency; often the state agency can assist with the filing of both reports simultaneously. The claimant must then wait 60 days before filing a private lawsuit, to give the state or EEOC agency sufficient time to make a preliminary investigation. [29 U.S.C. § 626(d)(2)] If the EEOC or (depending on state law) the state agency files a lawsuit against the employer based on the complaint, the claimant cannot file a private lawsuit. A lawsuit must be filed within 90 days after receiving notice that the administrative proceeding has been terminated. [29 U.S.C. § 626(e)]

As shown in Table 20-1, in 2000, the EEOC reported 16,008 age discrimination charges filed, in 2003, 19,124, and in 2005, 16,585.

Table 20-1. Age Discrimination Cases Filed with EEOC (FY 1992–2005)

Year	Receipts
FY 1992	19,573
FY 1993	19,809
FY 1994	19,618
FY 1995	17,416
FY 1996	15,719
FY 1997	15,785
FY 1998	15,191

Table 20-1. (Cont'd)

Year	Receipts
FY 1999	14,141
FY 2000	16,008
FY 2001	17,405
FY 2002	19,921
FY 2003	19,124
FY 2004	17,837
FY 2005	16,585

(Figures from EEOC Office of Research, Information and Planning Charge Data System at *http://www.eeoc.gov/stats/adea.html*) Of these filings, over half are dismissed as being without reasonable cause, and in only about 4% did the EEOC affirmatively find "reasonable cause". Since 2000, the EEOC has filed an average of 43 ADEA lawsuits per year. [EEOC Litigation Statistics, FY 1992 through FY 2005 Summary Report, Apr. 2006, online at *http://www.eeoc.gov/stats/litigation.html*]

Health Care Benefits and Age Discrimination

Q 20:28.1　Do employers have to offer retirees health care benefits?

No. Although an employer cannot discriminate against older workers as such, it is not required to provide health care benefits to retirees. In 2001, only one-third of large business, and 10 percent of small companies offered retirees health care benefits.

Q 20:28.2　If an employer does offer retirees health care benefits, does it have to offer retirees eligible for Medicare exactly the same health care benefits it offers other retirees?

Unfortunately, it appears the answer is (or shortly will be) "no." Even though a provision permitting employers to make the distinction was deleted from the Medicare Reform bill (it was section 631 of the Senate version of this legislation) after strenuous opposition by AARP and other groups, on April 22, 2004, the EEOC approved publication of a proposed final rule that would have almost exactly the same effect. [See Notice of Proposed Rulemaking at 68 Fed. Reg. 41542 (July 14, 2003) also available at *http://www.eeoc.gov/policy/regs/retiree_benefits.html*] The ruling was originally proposed as a response to a circuit court case that had held to the contrary—that employers could not refuse to offer Medicare-eligible retirees the same health benefits they offered to non-eligible retirees. [See Erie County Retirees Ass'n v. County of Erie, 220 F.3d 193 (3d Cir. 2000) (calling into question what had been and probably still is a widespread employer practice)] However, some had hoped that the Congressional refusal to codify such a ruling in the Medicare Reform Act would indicate a Congressional interpretation contrary to such a rule. No such luck—the EEOC rule, if finalized, will mean that retirees may lose the higher quality health care to which they might otherwise have been entitled. (At the time of this writing, May 2006, the approved proposal by the Office of Management and Budget, before being published as a final rule in the Federal Register, has been relegated to "Long-Term Actions" on the EEOC Semiannual Regulatory Agenda published in the *Federal Register* on April 24, 2006.)

Chapter 21

Grandparents' Rights

The concept of nuclear family has undergone significant changes in recent decades. Divorce, separation, children born out of wedlock, and remarriages—all relatively unusual occurrences a century ago—now have dramatic effects on families. As conflicts have arisen and families have become more separated by geography, ideology and circumstance, grandparents, stepparents, and other family members and caretakers increasingly find themselves with no legal rights to see the children in their lives. Legal intervention has increasingly come about when grandparents have been denied visitation and guardianship rights by one or both parents, and state legislatures (and often state courts) have been eager to provide some help to anxious grandparents and other significant adults in the child's life. This chapter discusses the legal response to this conflict.

Grandparent Visitation Rights

Q 21:4   What is the status of state law on grandparent visitation rights?

Virtually all states currently have some form of a "grandparent visitation" statute, though appellate courts have invalidated some. The provisions, definitions and enforcement of state laws vary greatly. The American Bar Association's summary of the current status of state laws for third-party visitation laws can be found at *http://www. abanet.org/family/familylaw/tables.html.* The AARP includes some information on "kinship care" in its state fact sheets found at *http:// www.aarp.org/research/family/grandparenting/aresearch-import-488. html.* Because this information is in rapid flux it is important to check current developments in each state. States in which a court has invalidated all or part of the state's grandparent visitation statutes, either as written or as applied in the facts of an individual case, include California, Colorado, Connecticut, Florida, Hawaii, Idaho, Illinois, Kansas, Maryland, Minnesota, New Jersey, and Ohio.

Q 21:6   Are grandparents' visitation rights Constitutional?

In light of all of the variation among state statutes and the uproar from parents resisting the implementation of them, the Supreme Court granted certiori to review a grandparents' visitation rights statute. In June of 2000, the Supreme Court handed down a decision in the case of *Troxel v. Granville* [530 U.S. 57 (2000)]. In *Troxel,* paternal grandparents sought visitation with their granddaughters, who were born out of wedlock following the death of their son. Granville, the children's mother, permitted a short visit once per month. The grandparents petitioned for more visitation time. Washington State's highest court struck down that state's permissive grandparent visitation statute as unconstitutional. Section 26.10.160(3) of the Revised Code of Washington permits "any person" to petition for visitation rights "at any time" and authorizes state superior courts to grant visitation whenever it is in the "best interests of the child." The Supreme Court affirmed this decision, ruling that the statute violated parents' fundamental right to make decisions concerning the care, custody, and control of their children. The Court stated that the Fourteenth Amendment gave parents this fundamental right, although it is not absolute. The Court took note of the fact that the state may limit these parental rights in certain ways, including prohibiting abuse or neglect of children, regulating child labor, requiring children to be vaccinated, requiring school attendance, and requiring that children be restrained while riding in motor vehicles. [See *Troxel*, 530 U.S. at 66–67]

The Court reasoned, however, that the Washington statute was "breathtakingly broad," and it violated the fundamental rights of parents. [Id. at 66] The statute has the effect of "permit[ing] a court to disregard and overturn any decision by a fit custodial parent concerning visitation whenever a third party affected by the decision files a visitation petition, based solely on the judge's determination of the child's best interests." [Id. at 67] In *Troxel*, this induced a violation of the Due Process Clause for several reasons. First, it was not alleged that the parent was unfit. There is a presumption that fit parents act in the best interests of their children. [Id. at 67, citing Parham v. J.R., 442 U.S. 584 (1979)] The lower court gave no special weight to the parents' determination. The Court noted "The problem here is not that the Washington Superior Court intervened but that when it did so, it gave no special weight at all to Granville's determination of her daughter's best interests. More importantly, it appears that the Superior Court applied exactly the opposite presumption." [See *Troxel*, 530 U.S. at 66–67] Second, the lower court did not give significant weight to the mother's offer of visitation. The court pointed out that this is a significant factor "because many state statues do not even allow a visitation order for a nonparent unless a parent has denied or unreasonably denied visitation." [Id. at 71] These factors combined provided no protection for Granville's fundamental parental rights. Although the Washington Supreme Court held the statute to be unconstitutional, the U.S. Supreme Court narrowed their reasoning and ruled that the Washington statute was unconstitutional as applied to Granville. Furthermore, it is important to note that the *Troxel* decision was decided by a plurality of four Justices, including two (O'Connor and Rehnquist) who have since left the Court. Two other Justices (Souter and Thomas) concurred, and three others (Stevens, Scalia, and Kennedy) dissented.

Q 21:9   What effect does *Troxel* have on specific state statutes?

Many states have had the opportunity to review their nonparental visitation statute following the *Troxel* decision. In light of *Troxel*, state courts have determined the constitutionality of their statutes. As pointed out by the Indiana Court in *Crafton v. Gibson* [752 N.E.2d 78 (Ind. App. 2001)] states have handed down decisions that fall into three categories:

states that found their statute constitutional, states that found their statute unconstitutional as applied, and states that found their statute unconstitutional on its face. States such as Arizona, Maine, Missouri, Texas, and Louisiana have found their statutes to be constitutional, mainly due to the fact that their statutes are narrower than the Washington statute. Those states' statutes, the courts have reasoned, provide for heightened constitutional protection. Other states such as Kansas, Maryland, Michigan, and California have ruled that their statutes as *applied to particular cases* are unconstitutional. These state courts found their lower courts to have improperly applied *Troxel*, or to have misconstrued the significance of the custodial parent's right to make parenting decisions. A handful of states have ruled their grandparent visitation statute to be patently unconstitutional; the Illinois Supreme Court, for example, has held that its state law on grandparent visitation is facially unconstitutional in *Wickham v. Byrne* [199 Ill. 2d 309; 769 N.E.2d 1 (2002)], as has the Florida Fifth District Court of Appeal in *Belair v. Drew* [776 So. 2d 1105 (Fla. Dist. App. 2001)].

Some state legislatures have modified their visitation and custody statutes in light of the Supreme Court's ruling in *Troxel*. For example, Oregon revised its statute to formally recognize a presumption that parents act in their children's best interest, but retaining the court's authority to determine that the children's interests require granting custody or visitation rights to grandparents. In *In the Matter of the Marriage of O'Donnell-Lamont* [337 Or. 86, 91 P.3d 721 (2004)], the Oregon Supreme Court determined that the revised statute was constitutionally sound and that it permitted the trial court to grant custody to grandparents despite finding that the children's father meant well and earnestly attempted to provide for his children. The court specifically rejected the notion that the grandparents would have to prove "unfitness" of the father to overcome the presumption in his favor. In *Koshko v. Haining*, the Maryland appellate court held that, under *Troxel*, there was a presumption that the parents' decisions were in the child's best interest, but that this presumption could be overcome. In that case, despite no showing of harm to the children from loss of visitation, the court found the presumption overcome based on evidence that the children in this case were actively involved in their grandparents' lives before the family breach, and that involvement benefited the children. [897 A.2d 866 (Md. App. 2006)]

There are significant differences in how states have applied *Troxel* to their own statutes. Law in this area is rapidly developing, and it is advisable to check current information on the status of individual state statutes. Sites such as *http://www.grandparenting.org* and *http://www.aarp.org* contain updated case law and statutes.

Q21:12 Are there alternatives to litigation?

Mediation is an alternative to litigation. Litigation differs from mediation, as litigation is an adversarial tool. Mediation is a more peaceful and cooperative means to reaching a solution with which both parties can be pleased. The process of mediation involves bringing in a neutral third party to help resolve disputes. Each side will have the opportunity to explain their points of view. The parties can then create a legally binding agreement through compromise. For more information about mediation and what is available in a particular area, see the American Bar Association website at *www.abanet.org/dispute* and the American Arbitration Association website at *www.adr.org*.

Grandparent Caretakers

Q21:13 How many children live in grandparent-headed households?

In the last 25 years, the number of children living in households headed by grandparents has increased by over 50 percent. According to the U.S. Census 2000, 6.3 percent of children under 18 live in grandparent-headed households. Approximately one-third of these children have no parent present in the grandparent-headed household. There are grandparent-headed households in every ethnic and socioeconomic group. More information can be found at *http://www.aarp.org/research/reference/publicopinions/aresearch-import-484.html*.

Q21:19 Should a grandparent apply to be a foster parent?

Depending upon the financial exigencies, in some cases a grandparent may wish to apply to the state as a foster parent. This will result in more state intervention, as technically the state will have custody of the child, but there may be sufficient financial remuneration to make the arrangement worthwhile. If the grandparent is relatively solitary, and the grandchild has "no one else," it may even be preferable to have state intervention in place in the event of the grandparent's death. However, many states will not provide the same financial subsidy to a relative acting as foster parent as they will to a stranger. This is changing; check local statutes.

Grandparents Raising Grandchildren

Q 21:22 What is TANF?

In 1996, the Personal Responsibility and Work Opportunity Reconciliation Act (PRWORA) created "Temporary Assistance to Needy Families" as a replacement for "Aid to Families with Dependent Children" and related assistance programs as the partially federally funded welfare program for families with children. Unlike AFDC, which shared costs on a basis similar to the Medicaid program, TANF is a block-grant program; some states even use the TANF block grants to finance the earned income credits. TANF is intended to encourage adult members of such families to seek work; therefore, the grandparent who is "on the grant" and receiving benefits to that will pay for childcare or to encourage the grandparent to work, will receive more benefits than if only the child in the family is a beneficiary. The maximum period for which the adult can receive benefits is five years, over his or her entire lifetime; the child can, however, continue to receive benefits for a longer period of time. State programs implementing TANF vary. The names and addresses of the director of each state agency responsible for TANF administration is available online at the U.S. Department of Health and Human Services website (*http://www.acf.hhs.gov/index.html*).

Q 21:23 Can a grandparent claim a grandchild as a dependent for income taxes, or receive other income tax benefits for raising the grandchild?

There are ways in which a grandparent may be eligible to receive tax refunds or credits. First, a grandparent may be eligible for the Earned Income Tax Credit (EITC). The EITC provides a refund to families who do not have to pay federal income tax. In order to qualify, the grandparent must be employed and meet an income requirement. Also, filing a W-5 form may permit the grandparent to receive advance EITC payments throughout the year thereby increasing the amount received per paycheck.

Some states have Earned Income Tax Credits. Of the 44 states that have personal income taxes (including the District of Columbia), 24 (plus the District of Columbia) now have state EITCs, including: Colorado, the District of Columbia, Delaware, Illinois, Indiana, Iowa, Kansas, Louisiana, Maine, Maryland, Massachusetts, Michigan, Minnesota, Nebraska New Jersey, New Mexico, New York, North Carolina, Oklahoma, Oregon, Rhode Island, Vermont, Virginia, and Wisconsin. Some states allow for refundable credits. See the Website of the State EITC Online Resource Center (*http://www.stateeitc.com*) for more information.

A grandparent may also be eligible for the Child and Dependent Care Credit, designed to help families who must pay for childcare in order to work or look for a job. The credit lowers the amount of federal income tax. The credit amount is dependent on the number of children, family income, and the amount paid for care.

In addition, a grandparent raising a grandchild may be eligible to receive a Child Tax Credit. The credit operates like the Child and Dependent Care Credit in that it serves to reduce the federal income tax liability.

Finally, a grandparent may be able to file as head of household and to claim an additional exemption because the grandchild is a "dependent." Before 2005, the definition of a qualifying child or dependent was different for each of these tax benefits. The Working Families Tax Relief Act of 2004 provided a uniform definition of "qualifying child" that applies to all five tax benefits. Generally, the dependent must satisfy a four-part test to be claimed as a "qualifying child":

1. Relationship—the taxpayer's child or stepchild (by blood or adoption), foster child, sibling or stepsibling, or a descendant of one of these (e.g., a grandchild);

2. Residence—lives with the taxpayer for more than half of the tax year;

3. Age—must be under the age of 19 (24 for a full-time student) at the end of the tax year; and

4. Support—did not provide more than one-half of her or his support for the tax year.

There are, naturally, some additional rules. To be claimed as a dependent, the "qualifying child" must also be a U.S. citizen or national or a resident of the U.S., Canada or Mexico, and, if married, must not have filed a joint return. To claim the Credit for Child and Dependent Care Expenses, the "qualifying child" must be under the age of 13, and to claim the Child Tax Credit, under the age of 17 as well as a U.S. citizen, natural or resident. For more detailed information, see the IRS website at *http://www.irs.gov/newsroom/article/0,,id = 133298,00*.html. AARP provides assistance for grandparents in preparing taxes. AARP can be contacted at 1-888-227-7669 (1-888AARPNOW).

Index

[References are to cumulative supplement question numbers.]

F

L